ROMAN REPUBLICAN THEATRE

Theatre flourished in the Roman Republic, dramatic works of the period including the tragedies of Ennius and Pacuvius, the comedies of Plautus and Terence as well as the mimes of Laberius. Yet apart from the surviving plays of Plautus and Terence the sources are fragmentary and difficult to interpret and contextualize. This book provides an up-to-date and comprehensive overview of all aspects of the topic, incorporating recent findings and modern approaches. It discusses the origins of Roman drama and the historical, social and institutional backgrounds of all the dramatic genres to be found during the Republic (tragedy, *praetexta*, comedy, *togata*, *Atellana*, mime and pantomime). Possible general characteristics are identified, and attention is paid to the nature of the various dramatic genres and their development. The clear structure and full bibliography also ensure that the book has value as a source of reference for all upper-level students and scholars of Latin literature and ancient drama.

GESINE MANUWALD is Senior Lecturer in Latin Language and Literature at University College London. Her research interests cover Cicero's orations, Flavian epic and Neo-Latin literature, on which she has published several books and many articles. Her main focus of research is Roman drama. She has written extensively on the subject, including several articles on Roman comedy, a book on *fabulae praetextae*, Roman historical dramas (2001), and, most recently, a reader on Roman drama (2010).

ROMAN REPUBLICAN THEATRE

GESINE MANUWALD

CAMBRIDGE
UNIVERSITY PRESS

CAMBRIDGE UNIVERSITY PRESS
Cambridge, New York, Melbourne, Madrid, Cape Town,
Singapore, São Paulo, Delhi, Mexico City

Cambridge University Press
The Edinburgh Building, Cambridge CB2 8RU, UK

Published in the United States of America by Cambridge University Press, New York

www.cambridge.org
Information on this title: www.cambridge.org/9780521110167

First published 2011

A catalogue record for this publication is available from the British Library

Library of Congress Cataloguing in Publication Data
Manuwald, Gesine.
Roman republican theatre : a history / Gesine Manuwald.
p.   cm.
Includes bibliographical references and index.
ISBN 978-0-521-11016-7 (hardback)
1. Latin drama – History and criticism.   2. Rome – History – Republic, 510–30 B.C.
3. Theater – Rome.   4. Theater – History – To 500.   5. Literature and history – Rome.
6. Rome – Historiography.   7. Rome – In literature.   I. Title.
PA6067.M36   2011
872′.0109 – dc22   2010054277

ISBN 978-0-521-11016-7 Hardback

Contents

v

Preface

'There is more to a beginning than just a start.' This is how Sander M. Goldberg concluded a recent article (2007a: 29) on appreciating 'archaic literature' as both a work of art in its own right and a step within the literary development. He also warned against regarding early literature as primitive and soon to be superseded. This is indeed a perspective often foisted on early writers by later scholars (ancient and modern) and prevents modern recipients from realizing achievements as well as deficiencies in unbiased fashion.

It is in this context that the present work wishes to place itself, by making a contribution to a clearer understanding of the sweeping and imprecise term 'Roman Republican drama'. Although the nature of the limited evidence presents particular methodological difficulties, it is important to make at least an attempt at getting a more precise view of the different stages and varieties of drama in Republican Rome, both for a proper appreciation of this literary genre and also with regard to Roman literature and culture. Though well aware of the various pitfalls and remaining uncertainties, this book therefore sets out to provide a synoptic overview of Roman drama over the course of the Republican period, exploring connections and developments among the various dramatic genres in their contemporary context, and thereby to offer a useful tool both to readers interested in Roman Republican drama and its role in Roman society and to those studying Roman literary history more generally.

Some of the views put forward will inevitably be contested in due course, particularly because the evidence in this field is scarce and often ambiguous; but it is one of the aims of this book to encourage discussion on this fascinating aspect of Roman culture.

Writing a comprehensive book on Roman drama that would allow me to point out connections between the various elements combining to make up 'Roman Republican drama' and the different areas of current research has long been on my mind, and this study continues work presented in previous monographs and a number of articles.

At different points in its development, research for this study has been carried out in Freiburg, Princeton, Oxford and London. I would like to thank warmly all colleagues and hosts for their continuing support and encouragement and the relevant libraries in these places for making all their resources available to me.

Individual parts of the argument were presented at the Villa Vergiliana in Cumae, in Oxford, London and Nottingham; the stimulating questions and helpful comments of the respective audiences have left their mark on the final product.

Thanks are also due to the participants in the one-day colloquium 'Meaningful Remains: Working with Literary Fragments from early Rome', organized by Costas Panayotakis and myself at Corpus Christi College, Oxford, in March 2007, and the presenters at the panel 'Republican Rome – A Cosmopolitan City', which I ran at the Classical Association Conference in Liverpool in March 2008, for their readiness to take part and for presenting exciting observations and ideas on areas of particular interest to me.

When this book was starting to take shape, I was able to profit from productive discussions with Denis Feeney. At later stages I received generous advice from a number of experts in their particular fields, including Stephen Colvin, Bob Kaster, John North and Hector Williams. Larissa Bonfante, Tim Moore, Costas Panayotakis and Jeremy Tanner kindly agreed to look at drafts of individual sections, which hugely profited from their specialist expertise. Tony Boyle generously read the entire typescript; his comments have been most valuable, as have been those of the anonymous readers for Cambridge University Press. Michael Sharp at Cambridge University Press proved a supportive and encouraging editor throughout; and the book has benefited hugely from thorough checks by my copy-editor, Fiona Sewell.

It goes without saying that writing such a book would not have been possible without the support of all these people, even though they might not share all the views eventually put forward.

LONDON, G.M.

Technical notes and abbreviations

TERMINOLOGY

For the dramatic genres that Roman writers called *fabula crepidata/ tragoedia* and *fabula palliata/ comoedia* respectively the terms 'tragedy' and 'comedy', more common in modern languages, have been adopted, except for contexts that demand precise terminology (where crepidata/*fabula crepidata/*Greek-style tragedy and palliata/*fabula palliata/*Greek-style comedy are used). For most other Roman dramatic genres, however, no established modern-language versions of the names exist and therefore the Latin ones must be kept, though they have been treated like English words (e.g. praetexta, togata).

QUOTATIONS OF AND REFERENCES TO LATIN TEXTS

For fragments of Republican drama the numberings of Ribbeck's third edition of his collections of tragic and comic fragments (R.³) and of Warmington's Loeb edition (W.) have been given (where applicable), since these editions are most readily available and these numbers will allow readers to find the texts in more recent editions. Hence, to keep references brief, the numberings of specific editions (Ennius: Jocelyn [J.]; Pacuvius: Schierl [S.]; Accius: Dangel [D.]; Caecilius Statius: Guardì [G.]; Turpilius: Rychlewska [Ry.]; togata: Daviault [Dav.]; Atellana: Frassinetti [F.]; mimus: Bonaria [B.]; Laberius: Panayotakis [P.]) have been omitted, since these works include concordances.

For Terence and Plautus the Oxford Classical Texts (Plautus: Lindsay; Terence: Kauer/Lindsay) have been used. Ennius' *Annales* are quoted from Skutsch's edition (Sk.), with the numbering of Warmington (W.) also given, his minor works from Vahlen's second edition with the numberings of Vahlen (V.²) and of Warmington (W.). References to Livius Andronicus' and Naevius' epics are based on *FPL³* (Blänsdorf), with the numbering of

Warmington (W.) given in addition. Accius' grammatical works (*Gram.*) are quoted from Dangel's edition (D.), with the numbering of Warmington (W.) added. For fragments of Lucilius' satires the numberings of Marx (M.) and Warmington (W.) are given.

Textual questions are highlighted only where the text is controversial and its establishment has a bearing on the argument. Hence minor differences in readings between the various editions consulted will not normally be mentioned; major differences might be indicated without receiving full treatment.

Longer quotations of Latin text have been translated. English translations of dramatic and satirical fragments have sometimes been inspired by E. H. Warmington's version; translations of other ancient works have been used as indicated; otherwise they are the author's own. For full information on editions and translations see the first section of the bibliography (arranged in alphabetical order of editors' names).

While a simple 'fr.' or a basic distinction between '*Trag.*' and '*Com.*' is often used to refer to fragments of Republican playwrights, a study that discusses the full range of serious and light dramatic genres in the Republican period must give more precise references, particularly since editions such as those of Ribbeck or Warmington have separate sections and/or numberings for the various dramatic genres.

The following abbreviations have therefore been used to distinguish between the dramatic genres: crepidata = *Trag.*; praetexta = *Praet.*; palliata = *Pall.*; togata = *Tog.*; Atellana = *Atell.*; mimus = *Mim.*; incer-*tum* = *Inc.* (depending on the context, this refers to a fragment of an unspecified work of a particular poet or to a fragment for which both writer and work are unknown). Names of playwrights have been abbreviated as follows: Livius Andronicus = Liv. Andr.; Naevius = Naev.; Ennius = Enn.; Pacuvius = Pac.; Accius = Acc.; Plautus = Plaut.; Caecilius = Caec.; Terence = Ter.; Turpilius = Turp.; Titinius = Tit.; Afranius = Afr.; Atta = At.; Pomponius = Pomp.; Novius = Nov.; Laberius = Lab. That results in references of the following type: 'Enn. *Trag.* 9 R.[3] = 18 W.'. In the sections on the individual dramatists in Chapter 4 the names of the respective playwrights are usually omitted.

See also 'Abbreviations used for references to fragments' below.

BIBLIOGRAPHY AND REFERENCES

Since the present work touches on a wide range of different issues, the bibliography is rather extensive. Nevertheless, it is not a comprehensive bibliography of works on Roman drama: it is not complete for all questions addressed, and there are particular gaps, for instance, as regards articles on individual fragments or studies and commentaries on individual preserved comedies. However, this bibliography lists the works that have proved useful for the present study and may provide starting points for those who wish to explore further some of the issues discussed (references to bibliographies or works providing overviews with bibliographical information are given at relevant points).

All these works (and some others) have informed the present study throughout, although some effort has been made to keep the notes brief, and therefore obvious references, particularly in cases of general agreement, are not always indicated. Older works are also sometimes left out as the newer ones cited will provide references to those. Neither can there be extensive discussion of all aspects of views in the secondary literature (especially in older works to which reactions are already available); instead there will often be brief references to further reading and/or to alternative views. In order to keep the argument focused, individual plays will be treated more extensively only if this leads to more general insights; points of detail will be relegated to the notes and/or confined to mentions of standard treatments (where those exist) instead of full discussions.

References to further reading or more detailed discussions of individual problems are given where they are most necessary or best fit the context. Numerous cross-references to other chapters (taking the form of, e.g., 'see ch. 4.1'), therefore, not only refer to discussions of the same issue in a different context and/or from another perspective, but might also lead to further bibliographical information.

Names and titles of works of ancient authors other than those mentioned above are abbreviated according to *OCD* (*The Oxford Classical Dictionary*, third edition, eds. S. Hornblower and A. Spawforth. Oxford and New York 1996), as are general reference works and collections (e.g. *TLL, CAH, CIL*).

DATES

Dates without either BCE or CE are BCE.

ABBREVIATIONS USED FOR REFERENCES TO FRAGMENTS

Acc.	Accius
Afr.	Afranius
At.	Atta

Atell.	Atellana
Caec.	Caecilius
D.	Dangel (Accius)
Enn.	Ennius
FPL³	*Fragmenta poetarum Latinorum*, third edition
Gram.	grammatical works
Inc.	*incertum*
Lab.	Laberius
Liv. Andr.	Livius Andronicus
M.	Marx (Lucilius)
Mim.	mimus
Naev.	Naevius
Nov.	Novius
Pac.	Pacuvius
Pall.	palliata
Plaut.	Plautus
Pomp.	Pomponius
Praet.	praetexta
R.³	Ribbeck, third edition (dramatic fragments)
Sk.	Skutsch (Ennius' *Annales*)
Ter.	Terence
Tit.	Titinius
Tog.	togata
Trag.	crepidata
Turp.	Turpilius
V.²	Vahlen, second edition (Ennius)
W.	Warmington (fragments of early playwrights and Lucilius)

Introduction:
previous scholarship and present approach

Roman drama was one of the earliest literary genres to be established in Rome, emerging against the background of Rome's contact with other cultures and its rise to being a major power in the Mediterranean. Thus the history of early Roman drama is not only of literary interest, but also of political, social and cultural relevance: for instance, the introduction of dramatic performances changed the set-up of public festivals with their specific religious rituals and their role within the political community; theatrical events gained relevance as a public institution. Within this framework a variety of dramatic forms were developed over time, which were shaped by individual playwrights according to their different styles and their respective historical situations. From the late Republican period onwards scholars started to discuss questions of dramatic history and terminology as issues in their own right.

Despite the inherent importance of this literary genre and its early reception, modern research into Roman Republican drama is confronted by the difficulty that evidence is scarce, since a large part of Rome's dramatic literature has not survived.[1] Names of playwrights, titles of plays, *testimonia* and fragments from a limited number of pieces are all that remains for some periods and/or dramatic genres. The only dramas preserved in their entirety are the comedies of Plautus and Terence from the Republican period as well as the tragedies of Seneca the Younger (including a possibly spurious one) and the anonymous praetexta *Octavia* (transmitted in the Senecan corpus) from the imperial era.

---

[1] Perhaps an initial word of caution on the term 'Roman' is in order: 'Roman drama' (or even 'Roman literature') might be regarded as a misleading term, since the early poets were not 'Romans' in a strict sense. But as they created works of 'literature' in Rome's language for Roman audiences (originally in the city of Rome), taking account of topics and conventions relevant to these audiences, the use of the established term 'Roman drama' can be justified. For the sake of convenience, the poets themselves will sometimes be referred to as 'Roman', as they were writing for Roman audiences in Rome.

Modern scholarship on Roman Republican drama, therefore, has virtually been split into two different routes: research on completely preserved
dramas, analysed just like any other extant ancient text, and research on
fragments, often concerned mainly with establishing text and meaning of
individual verses or plays. While it is true that different types of evidence
require different kinds of approaches, all this material concerns the same
issue; yet the two methods and subject areas have seldom come together.
Moreover, the (understandable) focus on complete plays, which are derived
from Greek sources, has meant that Roman plays tend to be considered in
comparison with Greek plays. Hence the view that Roman literature is 'secondary' and 'derivative', which had arisen since the period of enthusiasm
for Greek culture from the eighteenth century onwards (yet has changed
over the past few decades), particularly affected the assessment of Roman
dramatic forms.[2]

These presumptions and this history of scholarship have long influenced the kind of resources produced. For instance, books on practical
and archaeological aspects of 'ancient theatre' tend to devote considerably
less space to the Roman than to the Greek side.[3] The only attempt at a
complete and concise overview of Roman Republican theatre (covering
literary and practical aspects) is W. Beare's *The Roman Stage. A Short History of Latin Drama in the Time of the Republic* (1st edn., 1950; 3rd edn.,
1964), which continues to be a widely used handbook, though its revision
has been called for; for comedy there is also G. E. Duckworth's *Nature of
Roman Comedy* (1952).[4] In the 1950s there was apparently a desire to collect
information on Roman drama: E. Paratore's *Storia del teatro latino* dates to
the same period (1957); it was reprinted in the early twenty-first century as
still being sufficiently relevant and up to date (2005).[5] Useful though these

---

[2] On this issue see e.g. Lana 1947: 46; Lefèvre 1978b: 1–4; Goldberg 1981: 84; Forehand 1985: 37; Conte
  1994: 7.
[3] See e.g. Bieber 1961; Blume 1991 (cf. justification on p. 107).
[4] For assessments of the two works see e.g. Segal 1981: 355; Fantham 1989a: 23 n. 1 (p. 31); Petrone
  1992: 669; Anderson 1993: 3; Brown 2002: 237: 'Beare (1964) is still the basic English handbook on
  the history and staging of Republican Roman drama, though this too is out of date in a number of
  respects and could do with thorough revision.'; N. J. Lowe 2008: 95: 'Beare 1964, while outdated on
  Greek New Comedy and indifferent to archaeological evidence, remains unrivalled in English as a
  synthesis of the literary source material, particularly on lost genres, while, for the extant comedies,
  Duckworth 1952 still covers more ground than any other single volume in English.'
[5] See the editors' preface (2005: x–xi); but see also Petrone 1992: 669. The 1970s saw another round
  of surveys, although some of them were rather brief and/or general (Butler 1972; G. Williams 1972;
  Jiménez Gazapo 1978; Lefèvre 1978a). In the 1980s Dupont provided a short introduction, apparently
  intended for beginning students (1988/1999), and a general study of Roman drama in its sociological
  context (1985). In the early 1990s this was followed by a broad survey of the Roman theatre by Petrone
  (1992). Some discussion of Roman theatre can now also be found in Seidensticker (2010: 82–122). An

works continue to be, they are out of date on a number of points due to discoveries of new texts and further research in several areas.

As regards the literary side of Roman drama, playwrights whose plays have survived in their entirety (Plautus, Terence, Seneca) are well served by editions, commentaries and translations into various modern languages.[6] Comprehensive and/or introductory works on aspects of Roman drama have also been devoted mainly to those poets.[7] Since Plautus and Terence were active in the same dramatic genre (what is traditionally called *fabula palliata* or Roman [New] Comedy) and substantial remains of Greek New Comedy were unearthed in the course of the twentieth century, studies going beyond one playwright have often dealt with (Greek and Roman) New Comedy.[8] More recently, studies on Roman comedy have started to look at the plays' relationship to the contemporary historical and social situation.[9]

By contrast, for Roman dramatic genres preserved in fragments very few general accounts exist, besides brief portraits in comprehensive works on Roman literature.[10] The major Republican tragic poets have been given critical editions and commentaries,[11] but hardly ever have they received monographic treatment; overviews of the whole dramatic genre are only a recent development.[12] A similar situation applies to praetexta, the Roman

earlier collection of essays (Dorey and Dudley 1965) discussed selected aspects, but did not present an overview of Roman drama as a whole.

[6] See the standard bibliographies: on Plautus, Hanson 1965/6; Gaiser 1972; Hughes 1975; Fogazza 1976 [1978]; Segal 1981; Bubel 1992; on Terence, Gaiser 1972; Goldberg 1981; Cupaiuolo 1984, 1992; Lentano 1997, 1998; on Roman comedy, also Hunter in Duckworth 1994: 465–71; for the Republican dramatists see also relevant sections in Suerbaum 2002; on Seneca, Hiltbrunner 1985; Seidensticker and Armstrong 1985; Motto and Clark 1989.

[7] On Plautus see e.g. Leo 1912; Fraenkel (1922/1960) 2007; N. W. Slater 1985/2000; Segal 1987; Anderson 1993; Moore 1998a; Franko 2001; on Terence see e.g. Büchner 1974; Forehand 1985; Goldberg 1986; Cupaiuolo 1991; Moore 2001; Kruschwitz 2004; Kruschwitz *et al.* 2007; on Seneca see e.g. Lefèvre 1972; Boyle 1983, 1997; Dingel 1985.

[8] See e.g. Arnott 1975; Sandbach 1977; Konstan 1983; Hunter 1985; Maurach 2005; Sharrock 2009. Other palliata poets of whose work a substantial number of fragments have been preserved have at least received critical editions (Caecilius: Guardì 1974; Turpilius: Rychlewska 1971).

[9] See esp. Leigh 2004a.

[10] For coverage in literary histories see the relevant sections in e.g. Kenney and Clausen 1982; Conte 1994; von Albrecht 1997; Harrison 2005.

[11] Livius Andronicus: Spaltenstein 2008; Naevius: Marmorale 1950; Ennius: Jocelyn 1967; Pacuvius: D'Anna 1967; Schierl 2006; Artigas 2009 (for the fragments transmitted in Cicero: Artigas 1990); Accius: D'Antò 1980; Pociña Pérez 1984; Dangel 1995.

[12] See Erasmo 2004; Boyle 2006 (comments on these books, with references, in Goldberg 2007b: 580–2). Cf. Boyle's introductory assessment of the state of research (2006: ix): 'This book requires little justification. Roman tragedy was at the centre of Rome's performative life, cultural and political, . . . , but until 2004 there was no monograph in English even attempting to address the evolution of Roman tragedy and its literary, theatrical and cultural importance. The standard book on (at least a

form of 'serious' drama.[13] 'Light' dramatic genres[14] other than palliata comedy, such as togata, Atellana and mimus, have been treated even less frequently, perhaps because farce and mime tend to be regarded as sub-literary and coarse, do not have proper counterparts in Greece and are attested solely by fragments and a limited number of *testimonia*.[15] For these dramatic genres there exist at least editions and some overviews.[16]

The texts themselves are available for all dramatic genres. The surviving output of those Republican dramatists whose work has been transmitted in fragments was made accessible by the seminal work of O. Ribbeck in the second half of the nineteenth century: his collections of the comic and the tragic fragments respectively are still the only critical editions that cover all playwrights and dramatic genres; he also gave important information about his view of the plays in the introductions to the second version of his editions and in his book on Roman tragedy (1875).[17] The fragments of the major Republican dramatists became more conveniently approachable

---

substantial part of) the subject was published 130 years ago in Leipzig: Otto Ribbeck's *Die Römische Tragödie im Zeitalter der Republik* (1875). . . . But Roman tragedy, despite its cultural importance and the increasing emphasis in Classical Studies on cultural history and analysis, still awaits a detailed theatrical and cultural account of its history and evolution.' The traditional reference manual for the contents of the tragedies and their relationship to Greek sources is O. Ribbeck's *Die römische Tragödie* (1875). Another early and more discursive attempt, focusing on particular aspects, is G. Coppola's 'Il teatro tragico in Roma repubblicana' (1940). A solid discussion of Republican drama with emphasis on tragedy is found in the introduction to Jocelyn's edition of Ennius' tragic fragments (1967).

[13] For an overview of this dramatic genre see Manuwald 2001a; see also Zorzetti 1980; Zehnacker 1983; Flower 1995; Wiseman, e.g. 1998. The fragments of Republican praetextae are included in Ribbeck's editions of the tragic fragments (see n. 17 below); besides this there are special editions of the remains of this dramatic genre (Pedroli 1954; de Durante 1966; see also Ussani 1967/8: xxxv–lxiii).

[14] The terms 'serious drama' and 'light drama' will be used throughout as descriptions of the two main forms of drama, each comprising various subtypes of elevated, possibly tragic drama and of entertaining, more mundane drama respectively. These terms rather than 'tragic drama/tragedy' and 'comic drama/comedy' have been chosen as the most neutral comprehensive labels, which minimize associations of specific dramatic genres or particular characteristics. Gratwick (1982a: 93, 127) also uses the terms 'serious drama' and 'light drama' to structure his account of early Roman drama (on the terminological problem see Halporn 1993: 197–8).

[15] Denard (2007) makes a strong case for including 'lost theatre and performance traditions' in scholarly activities.

[16] Editions of the togata fragments: Daviault 1981; López 1983; Guardì 1985 (see review by Jocelyn 1986); Atellana fragments: D. Romano 1953; Frassinetti 1967; mimus fragments: Bonaria 1965, Laberius: Panayotakis 2010. For a brief comprehensive treatment of all these genres and bibliography see Panayotakis 2005a.

[17] Editions of tragic fragments: Ribbeck 1871 (2nd edn.)/1897 (3rd edn.); editions of comic fragments: Ribbeck 1873 (2nd edn.)/1898 (3rd edn.); study: Ribbeck 1875. The third edition presents Ribbeck's final view on the text, but its *apparatus criticus* is less detailed. Both editions contain a few inconsistencies in numbering. The more recent edition of the dramatic fragments by Klotz, of which only the first volume covering the tragic theatre has been published (1953), could be regarded as a replacement for the first volume of Ribbeck's edition; yet it is actually not very different from Ribbeck in many respects, while being less accurate and less comprehensive (see reviews: esp. Skutsch 1954).

in E. H. Warmington's independent bilingual edition in *Remains of Old Latin* in the 1930s (Loeb Classical Library), because this multi-volume work includes English translations, provides short introductions to individual authors and plays and also gives indications of the context of each fragment (in the editor's view).[18]

In the realm of Roman dramatic fragments, researchers have traditionally focused on philological problems, such as the difficult establishment of the text of individual fragments or the reconstructions of plots (often in relation to supposedly corresponding Greek plays). Gradually, further issues are winning greater attention among literary scholars, which include the consideration of the background for the production of dramas, the role of performance and the choice of plots and themes as well as a new look at the relationship to Greek models and the 'Romanization' of the plays.

Among scholars who are more interested in cultural, historical and social issues, the Republican period has recently emerged as a vibrant field of research: it is asked, for instance, why the Romans developed a sophisticated literature, when 'Roman literature' started, what can be assumed about 'pre-literary' and 'oral' traditions at Rome, about their influence on subsequent centuries and their relationship to later written literature, what the cultural and political dynamics in Republican Rome were like, what function entertainment, performance, spectacle and theatricality played in Roman society and what the role of literature was within such a framework.[19]

Progress is also being made in the study of the material aspects of Roman theatrical culture. A recent monograph examines the archaeological evidence of Roman theatres, preceded by overviews of theatre buildings in Sicily and southern Italy.[20] Documentation of the physical outlines of Roman theatres all over the Roman Empire allows comparisons between their characteristic features and those of Greek theatres and hence inferences on performance conditions in the Republican period. However, although implications of archaeological findings directly bear on the study of the

---

[18] The Budé collection has published the togata fragments (Daviault 1981) and the works of Accius (Dangel 1995), while both volumes have received criticism from reviewers (see esp. Gratwick 1982b; Jocelyn 1982, on Daviault 1981; Gratwick 2000; Jocelyn 2001, on Dangel 1995). There is also an Italian edition of *Poeti latini arcaici* (Traglia 1986), of which, however, only the first volume, covering Livius Andronicus, Naevius and Ennius, has appeared in print.

[19] For an overview of these issues and some suggestions see Feeney 2005; on the changing approaches to early Roman literature see also Rossi and Breed 2006: 419–20.

[20] See Sear 2006; see also e.g. Mitens 1988, 1993; Courtois 1989, 1992; on the Roman stage on the basis of reconstructionist productions see Beacham 1991. For scholarship on theatre architecture see Frézouls 1982: 343.

literary remains,[21] they still need to be taken fully into account by literary scholars of Roman drama. For matters of Roman comic staging and stagecraft there is now C. W. Marshall's *The Stagecraft and Performance of Roman Comedy* (2006). Yet although there are numerous works dealing with the overall organization and background of theatrical performances in the Greek world, there are no comparable, comprehensive, up-to-date works for the Roman world.

In the area of theoretical approaches to Latin literature and also in theatre studies new concepts and terminology have been developed and defined, which, to a certain extent, can be usefully applied to the study of Roman drama to complement more traditional ways of analysing dramatic texts. For instance, Roman dramas have traditionally been interpreted in relation to Greek 'models', while views on this connection have changed over the centuries. As regards such potential relationships, useful categories and criteria concerning the issue of 'allusion' or 'intertextuality' have been presented by S. Hinds (1998). Hinds warns against one-sided 'philological fundamentalism' as well as 'intertextualist fundamentalism'; instead, he suggests combining both approaches with circumspection. In this context he challenges the complete 'death of the author' and calls for allowing for an intention-bearing authorial voice in constructing the deeper meaning of a poetic text.[22] Also, Hinds is rightly critical of the unidirectional and non-dialogic reading of two related texts, especially when one of them, the incorporating text or the incorporated text, has been preserved in fragments.[23] Taking up this approach, other scholars have emphasized that, as a result of the particular forms of transmission of Latin dramatic fragments, modern readers see these poets through the eyes of other ancient writers; researchers therefore have to avoid adopting uncritically the portrait painted in those sources.[24]

Without specific reference to the classical world, theoreticians of the theatre have applied methodologies such as performance criticism and semiotic terminology to the theatre.[25] Even though not all those approaches

---

[21] Cf. Goldberg 1998: 19: 'More certain is a general fact: the problems of dramaturgy and social history connected with Roman comedy cannot be entirely divorced from questions concerning the physical space in which these plays were performed.'

[22] See Hinds 1998: 17–51, 144; also Conte 1994: 3.   [23] See Hinds 1998: 101–3.

[24] See contributions in Fitzgerald and Gowers 2007 (with particular reference to Ennius' *Annales*), esp. Zetzel 2007; also Goldberg 2007b: 573 and n. 8.

[25] Cf. Bennett 1997: 9–12: 'Since the 1980s, two areas of dramatic theory have given emphasis to the need for a more developed theory of audiences. The first of these to emerge was performance theory. . . . While performance theorists have broadened the scope of what we might consider theatre, a second area of dramatic theory has, in recent years, paid a new attention to the multivalent

and theories can be applied fruitfully to an ancient dramatic literature largely surviving in fragments, some terminological descriptions provide helpful clarifications: these include, for instance, a distinction between 'theatre' and 'drama', the former referring to theatrical performances and the latter denoting the fictional text as a representative of a literary genre, or between what is produced in the theatre and what is written for the theatre, with their mutual interdependence.[26] Besides, concepts of theatre semiotics provide a theoretical model for situating the theatre of a past period as a meaningful system within the conditions and circumstances of its time[27] and performance venue[28] and thus for considering it within its historical setting, in addition to analysing features of the text. The notions of 'cross-cultural conversation' and 'intercultural theatre' help to describe the transfer of theatre and drama from Greece to Rome as one manifestation of processes that also happen elsewhere in theatre culture.[29]

In view of this state of research in a variety of areas it is a necessary and timely step to combine and develop these various insights into an overview of Roman Republican drama. For the emergence of new approaches and methodologies, along with traditional philological criticism, provides an excellent basis for further study that goes beyond individual playwrights or dramatic genres.[30] A synthesis of evidence and approaches has not actually been attempted yet, though the production of up-to-date, comprehensive collections of data on Roman drama is under way, as handbooks, dictionaries and bibliographies demonstrate.[31] For the literary genre of drama, progress in research on non-literary Roman issues is particularly helpful; for drama must be situated within the contemporary context of its

components of theatre. Semiology has considered these components (not simply what takes place on the stage, or even in the auditorium) and their interaction in the signifying process.' See e.g. Honzl (1940) 1976; Elam 1980/2002; Fischer-Lichte 2003; for a brief overview of the development of semiotic studies related to the theatre see Carlson 1989: 2–4.

[26] See Elam 2002: 2, 3, 191; Fischer-Lichte 2003: 3114.   [27] See e.g. Fischer-Lichte 2003: 3116.

[28] See Carlson 1989: 10.   [29] On these terms see G. J. Williams 2010: 551–64.

[30] A similar development and a corresponding outline of contemporary and possible future research have been described by Rossi and Breed (2006: 397–8) in the introduction to a special journal issue on Ennius' *Annales*.

[31] For recent overviews of the lives and works of individual dramatists and full information on *testimonia* and bibliography see Suerbaum 2002; like most literary histories the handbook is divided according to genres and poets and rarely attempts more general conclusions on Roman drama (see reviews: Gildenhard 2003; Feeney 2005); for a 'dictionary' of the Roman theatre see González Vázquez 2004; for a collection of key texts on Roman drama see Manuwald 2010; for bibliography on Roman tragedy see Mette 1964 [1965]; De Rosalia 1989; Manuwald 2001 [2004]; on Naevius' comic output see Suerbaum 2000a; for a brief overview of important aspects of Roman Republican theatre see Boyle 2006: 3–23.

organizational background and of developments in Republican society, since by its very nature drama is a public genre produced in a diverse civic community.

Against this background the present work intends to look at Roman Republican drama and its background from a variety of perspectives both diachronically and synchronically, in order to provide a synoptic discussion of the whole complex of dramatic works in Republican Rome.[32] It will be discussed, for instance, how Roman drama developed and altered over the Republican period in relation to changes in society, what the relationship between the various dramatic genres was like and what the place of drama was in the contemporary political and social context.[33]

It is hoped that such a synoptic method will make it possible to present processes and mutual influences within Republican drama in contextualized form.[34] An awareness of how the various dramatic genres and their respective characteristics evolved, changed and interacted is essential for a proper understanding of the development of Roman drama.[35] This contributes to reconsidering the role of audiences and later recipients, identifying specific features of Roman drama and of each of its playwrights and genres as well as discerning potential cross-fertilization between the individual dramatic poets and different genres.[36]

---

[32] Investigating the origin and development of the major dramatic genres in Republican Rome might also contribute to increasing the number of studies of literary genres, whose lack was signalled by Cairns (2007: 49–50), even though the definition of a 'genre' is fraught with its own problems (see Conte 1994: 5–7).

[33] The present endeavour is thus in line both with Goldberg's (2006: 446) call for sufficient attention to historical change and with Denard's (2007: 139) view that all theatre and performance traditions should be included in one's considerations as they will all have influenced each other.

[34] This study thus follows principles similar to those outlined in the introduction to Boyle's recent book on Roman tragedy (2006: ix), but broadens its scope by encompassing Republican drama as a whole. Although it has rightly been called into question whether 'literary history is possible', an attempt at a comprehensive description of Roman drama has been made in view of the ulterior aim of literary history (as opposed to history), since it 'subserves the appreciation of literature' (see Perkins 1992; for discussion of the problems inherent in any attempt to write literary history see also Conte 1994: 1–10; Feeney 2002). The current approach also takes into account the notion that the inclusion of the perspective of reception, of intertextual aspects and of the historical position of literary works as well as the addition of a synchronic dimension to the traditional diachronic focus of literary history could contribute to meeting the challenge of writing literary history (see Jauß 1967).

[35] On the importance of considering Roman traditions see also Goldberg 1981: 78, 1986: xii; Panayotakis 2005a: 133. An interesting, albeit controversial attempt to construct a tradition for palliata has been made by J. Wright (1974).

[36] Rüpke (2001) and, more forcefully, A. Barchiesi (2002) in his review have already made the obvious point (with reference to epic) that the poets Livius Andronicus, Naevius and Ennius were three individuals and lived in a time of massive social and political change. For Plautus and Terence see Duckworth 1952: 102. More generally, the inclusion of the study of fragmentary Latin texts is vital

In order to establish such an overall picture, it will be necessary to place dramatists and plays in their historical, cultural and physical context and to regard dramatic performances as part of Roman festival culture.[37] For such an approach, ideally, all aspects mentioned should be considered together, but the need for a clear and readable exposition requires them to be divided among several subsections (with numerous cross-references). On their basis a tentative outline of the characteristics and development of Roman Republican drama, along with a brief outlook on subsequent processes in imperial times, will form the conclusion. The approaches, insights and theoretical concepts outlined will inform the presentation throughout, although they cannot be discussed as such.

Naturally, a comprehensive presentation of Roman Republican drama is confronted with the particular problem of scarce, scattered, ambiguous and partly unreliable evidence.[38] As the high number of festival days and the 130 plays later circulating under Plautus' name (Gell. *NA* 3.3.11) show, the period during which proper stage drama flourished at Rome must have seen a huge number of plays of which little has survived. Furthermore, it can be inferred that a great variety of dramatic entertainment on all levels of formality was popular in Graeco-Roman Italy during the Republican period. The surviving dramas have to be seen as one element within this culture even though specific details of influences and developments may be hard to determine.[39]

But rather than despairing of the possibility of finding out anything at all,[40] an attempt to extract as much as possible from the extant sources – with the necessary caution applied – seems a worthwhile and sound approach. If all available information is scrutinized from a variety of angles,[41] there will be a substantial body of material to work from, which will allow some conclusions.

---

for a proper appreciation of the emergence and characteristics of Roman literature (see Goldberg 2005b: 113–14, 2007a: 23–4; also observations in A. Barchiesi 2002 on early Roman epic).

[37] On the necessity to include the context in any consideration of early Roman drama or literature see Cancik 1978: 318; Gildenhard's criticism (2003) of Suerbaum 2002; Conte's (1994: 2–3) point in the introduction to his history of Latin literature that new literary approaches do not free interpreters from reintegrating the works within their historical contexts. More generally, from a theoretical perspective, see Carlson 1989: 2.

[38] On the particular methodological accuracy required by this situation and the need to distinguish between evidence and hypothesis see Gildenhard 2003; Goldberg 2006: 445–6.

[39] See also Hunter 1985: 20; N. J. Lowe 2008: 85.

[40] See Cancik 1978: 321–2; Dupont 1985: 311 (see 'Overview and conclusions').

[41] This study will follow Hinds (1998: 21) in hoping that it will 'be able to do something to explore and to probe anew – through strategically chosen examples – the methodological pluralism which Conte's writing has established as an ideal'.

Yet it has to be borne in mind that only those types of dramatic performances, writers and plays can be discussed of which there is some record[42] and that the uneven evidence may distort the picture. Thus one will have to accept that there are questions to which definite answers cannot be given (e.g. on details of dramatic structure for genres of which no example is extant in its entirety), but defining those issues and distinguishing between facts and assumptions or well-argued hypotheses are means to make progress in those cases.[43] There may also be the danger of generalizing too broadly, giving the surviving evidence undue weight or using arguments from silence for the purposes of a coherent and complete picture.[44] Again, cautious inferences on the basis of the available sources can be a way forward in such areas.

The overview of Roman drama and theatre presented in this book limits itself to the Republican period, covering the time from the first beginnings of theatrical performances in Rome to the deaths of Caesar and Cicero and the emergence of the Principate. Obviously, Roman drama continued into the imperial period in various forms, but the conditions influencing production and reception of dramatic scripts changed so significantly that another exposition of the political and social context would be required in order to outline the characteristics of Roman imperial drama, its position within the contemporary environment, and the similarities and differences in relation to Republican drama.[45] This would go beyond the intention and scope of this work, which is interested in evolution, development and interactions of the various dramatic genres in the Republican period. Also, the presentation focuses on the city of Rome as the place most important for literary drama in Latin and includes Magna Graecia where relevant. A history of theatre in the Roman Empire as a whole would require a separate volume with a slightly different approach.[46]

As regards terminology, the poets and the period under discussion are called 'Republican' in preference to 'archaic'; for 'Republican' can be understood as a neutral, chronological term, whereas 'archaic' implies an evaluation from the perspective of later writers or literary historians, which does not apply to the time of the poets, since their writings were 'new' at the time.[47] Correspondingly, ancient authors commenting on Republican

---

[42] See Dupont 1985: 311.   [43] See also Farrell 2005: 417 (on Roman epic).

[44] See W. Slater 2004: 144.

[45] On aspects of theatre in the imperial period see Bartsch 1994; Beacham 1999; Heldmann 2000; Duncan 2006: 188–217.

[46] Yet an attempt is made to overcome the criticism of Rawson ([1985] 1991: 469) 'that our view of Roman theatrical history itself is still far too Romanocentric'.

[47] See Hinds 1998: 55–6; Goldberg 2007a.

drama after its main productive period, such as Cicero, Horace, Quintilian or Gellius, are denoted by descriptions like 'later writers' (where no further distinction is necessary), which is meant to give a fairly objective, relative indication of their dates. The terms 'nation' and 'national' are avoided as far as possible due to their anachronistic implications;[48] if they are used for want of a better word, they are not meant to imply a 'nationalistic' perspective or to convey a simplified idea of the complex situation in Republican Rome, but are intended to indicate an emerging literature written in the Romans' own language and dealing with notions important to them.

---

[48] For objections to the use of these terms see Rüpke 2001: 60–2 with n. 96; for counter-arguments see A. Barchiesi 2002.

PART I

Cultural and institutional background

CHAPTER I

Evolution of Roman drama

1.1 CULTURAL CONTACTS

When Greek-style drama emerged in Rome in the mid-third century BCE, Romans had been in contact with peoples in Italy and elsewhere in the Mediterranean for several centuries, and they had got to know their political organizations, their ways of life and various aspects of their cultures (e.g. literature, art, sciences).[1] This situation resulted in exchanges, testified to by commercial activities (e.g. Greek vases in Italy) and the adaptation of customs (such as religious cults or the alphabet). The peoples Romans got in touch with included Carthaginians, Etruscans and Oscans, while the encounter with the Greek civilization (in Greece and the Greek colonies) proved to be particularly important for Rome's cultural development.[2]

Greeks had been present in Italy since the colonization of the coastal areas in the south of the country and of the neighbouring islands (Magna Graecia) during the eighth to sixth centuries BCE; Romans had dealt with those Greeks in political and commercial contexts. Greek artefacts found in Italy and Sicily demonstrate the spread of Greek culture and, specifically, of Greek myths:[3] imported Greek vases from the sixth century BCE onwards as well as locally made vases (esp. in Apulia, Lucania, Campania) particularly from the beginning of the fourth century BCE onwards depict well-known Greek heroes and heroines, while south-Italian vase-paintings include

---

[1] For the historical developments from the beginnings of Rome until the late Republican period, discussions of recent trends in historical research and bibliography see e.g. *CAH²* VII.2–IX; Crawford 1993; Cornell 1995. For other overviews of issues characterizing the Roman Republic see e.g. Flower 2004; Rosenstein and Morstein-Marx 2006; for an attempt at a more differentiated portrait of 'the Roman Republic' see Flower 2010.

[2] For discussions of Roman contacts with the Greek world and the consequences, from different perspectives, see Rawson, *CAH²* VIII: 422–76; Wallace-Hadrill 1988; Gruen 1990, 1992; MacMullen 1991; Horsfall 1993; Dench 1995; Vogt-Spira 1996.

[3] On the Romans' early familiarity with Greek myths and the creation of their own stories see Wiseman 2004; on the literary culture of Magna Graecia see La Penna 1979.

pictures that illustrate myths rarely or never found on artefacts elsewhere.[4] After Athens had founded the Hellenic colony of Thurii in Italy in 444/3 BCE (and Tarentum had launched the Hellenic city of Heracleia in 433/2 BCE), cultural links between Athens and the Italian mainland became even closer. In the fifth century BCE Athenian playwrights such as Aeschylus had already come to Sicily and staged dramatic productions there.

By the completion of the wars against Pyrrhus in 272 BCE, most towns in Magna Graecia were under Roman control. An obvious sign of Rome's expansion towards southern Italy and of her interest in this territory was the construction of the Via Appia; its first section, leading from Rome to Capua, was opened in 312 BCE; during the third century the road was extended to Tarentum and Brundisium. The First Punic War (264–241 BCE), a large part of which was fought in Sicily, was another significant stage in gaining experience of areas with Greek culture for a sizeable part of the Roman populace.

From the late third century BCE contacts between Greeks and Romans shifted in new directions and intensified.[5] This was due, firstly, to the emergence of the 'Hellenistic world', which changed Hellenic culture by making it less exclusively 'Greek' and spreading it over large areas, and, secondly, to political developments, particularly Rome's conquest of large areas of the Mediterranean. In this initial period of intensified contacts with Greece, elements of Greek culture seem to have simply been accepted in Rome without this being a big issue, either because there was no major awareness of the fact that foreign practices were adopted or because this showed participation in the prestigious Greek culture,[6] since the Romans apparently wished to assert their position in the Mediterranean.[7] At this point in time the culture might not have been recognized as 'Greek or Hellenistic', but may just have appeared as the 'superior civilization'.

The process of acculturation was based on a specific relationship between the giving Greeks and the receiving Romans, which one could regard as one-sided borrowing. However, the encounter between Greeks and Romans is more adequately described as an interactive, dynamic process within a

---

[4] See e.g. Trendall 1989: 12. Works of art were produced by 'highly sophisticated' artists and display a 'highly "literate" Greekness', while some distinctive Italic and non-Greek elements, such as style of clothing, were added (see Taplin 2007: 21–2; also Trendall 1989: 16; on representation of 'Olympic games' according to Etruscan conventions see Falchetti and Romualdi 2001: 107–8).

[5] For a brief overview of literature and culture in the period of the conquests see Conte 1994: 71–4; for evidence and bibliography on the events that influenced literature and culture in the early Republican period see the relevant entries in Suerbaum 2002.

[6] See e.g. Dench 1995: 61–2.   [7] See Wallace-Hadrill 1988.

contact zone.[8] That the effects of this co-presence and mutual contact are more noticeable in Roman culture is probably the result of what each side had to offer, along with a remarkable openness and flexibility on the part of the Romans, who were said to be ready to adopt and imitate what suited them and they considered useful (cf. Polyb. 6.25.11; also Cic. *Tusc.* 1.1–6; 4.1–7; Sall. *Cat.* 51.37–8), and their consequent ability in active appropriation and reuse.[9] While processes of cultural adaptation are widespread consequences of contacts between different peoples, the fact that the Romans were confronted with a highly sophisticated and literate culture, at a time when they were about to become an imperial power, but did not yet have comparable cultural traditions of their own, turned the process of Rome adapting elements of Greek culture into a special one.[10] Therefore it is perhaps not a coincidence that Greek cultural achievements became a starting point for the Romans to develop their own literature, arts and sciences (in combination with native influences); the Romans were thus the first people in Europe to shape their own culture on the basis of another, fully developed European culture.

The end of the Third Macedonian War (171–168 BCE) brought a new flood of Greek works of art and literature as well as educated Greeks to Rome. An influential event was the visit to Rome of Crates of Malles (Pergamene critic, grammarian and Stoic philosopher) in 168 BCE. He was one of the teachers of the Stoic philosopher Panaetius of Rhodes (*c.* 185– 109 BCE), who spent extended periods of time in Rome and was associated with P. Cornelius Scipio Africanus minor (*c.* 185–129 BCE) and his friends. The same group included the Greek historian Polybius (*c.* 200–120 BCE), who had come to Rome as one of 1,000 Achaean hostages in 167 BCE and became attached to Scipio. Another groundbreaking event was an Athenian delegation of three philosophers to Rome in 155 BCE, consisting of the sceptical Academic Carneades, the Stoic Diogenes of Babylon and the Peripatetic Critolaus.

The appropriation of the Greek world thus developed on several levels and triggered an intensified interest in different cultural models among educated Romans.[11] This cultural transformation led to Rome's emergence as the new intellectual centre of the Mediterranean, coinciding with political and economic movements.[12] For this period, which is the most

---

[8] See Feeney 1998: e.g. 67–8 (referring to myth and using terms borrowed from Pratt 1992: 6–7); also Rossi and Breed 2006: 420; contrast Vogt-Spira 1996: 11–12.

[9] See Gratwick 1982a: 79; Suerbaum 2002: 87.   [10] See also Batstone 2006: 545.

[11] For instance, from the second century BCE onwards the appropriation of Greek architectural ornamentation increased significantly (see von Hesberg 2005: 43–4).

[12] See Wallace-Hadrill 1988: 225.

dynamic in cultural adaptation, it is certain that an awareness of a difference between 'the Greek way of life' and 'the Roman way of life' increased
or was constructed.[13] By the first century BCE Roman intellectuals began
to measure Roman cultural achievements against those of the Greeks and
to reflect on their own traditions.

The importance of this process for Roman self-understanding is demonstrated by the notorious conflict between 'phil-Hellenic Romans' and 'traditional anti-Hellenic Romans' in the mid-Republic. Although this is too
simplistic a contrast, the relationship of Romans to Greek culture was
frequently ambiguous: they admired it as superior and adopted its criteria, while they remained sceptical of some aspects; hence they adapted it
selectively according to their own purposes.

Roman literary drama was at the heart of these developments: the first
playwrights in Rome were Greeks or 'half-Greeks' (cf. Suet. *Gram.* 1.2)
and came from regions in the Mediterranean under Greek influence; the
emergence of Roman drama in the mid-third century BCE occurred in the
middle of a major Hellenizing phase;[14] this public literary genre reflected
the ongoing political and intellectual movements within Rome in the topics
chosen as well as in the portrayal of characters; it introduced a significant
number of Romans to Greek myths along with theological, philosophical
and literary doctrines; it both presupposed and expanded acquaintance
with Greek language and customs, which suggests that this foreign culture
was being assimilated.[15]

At the same time there was an influx of native traditions. In Italy the main
points of influential contact were the Etruscan and Oscan civilizations,
which not only functioned as indirect intermediaries for Greek culture,
but also offered their own customs and dramatic traditions (see ch. 1.3,
1.4). Thus the cultural mix in southern Italy was a significant factor for
the eventual shaping of Roman literary drama. The impact of this cultural
environment is most famously attested for Ennius, who, according to
Gellius, claimed to have three hearts, and, as Gellius explains, that means
that he knew Greek, Oscan and Latin (Gell. *NA* 17.17.1).[16]

---

[13] See Dench 1995: 30; also Farrell 2005: 426.

[14] See Feeney 1998: 52 (on Roman literature); Sciarrino 2006: esp. 451 (on Roman epic); on the impact
of the various phases of Rome's interaction with the Hellenistic world see Flower 2010: esp. 178.

[15] Beacham's view (1991: 7–8) that Romans of the period would have been unable to appreciate more
refined dramatic performances as they were current in other parts of Italy seems unfounded in view
of the immediate popularity of literary drama in Rome.

[16] Since Ennius was a native of Rudiae, a Messapic foundation in Calabria, it is puzzling that he should
be described as a speaker of Oscan rather than of Messapic (on this problem see Adams 2003: 116–17,

Such a cultural mix can indeed be observed on the linguistic level in literary Roman drama: poets may allude to the original meaning of Greek names (e.g. Varro, *Ling.* 7.82; Enn. *Trag.* 208–10 R.³ = 256–8 W.) or juxtapose equivalent Greek and Latin terms (e.g. Pac. *Trag.* 89 R.³ = 110–11 W.; Afr. *Tog.* 298–9 R.³). Later ancient grammarians have identified words of Oscan origin in Pacuvius (Pac. *Trag.* 64; 215 R.³ = 59; 224 W.), and a Roman comedy by Titinius mentions people who speak Oscan and Volscian, but no Latin (Tit. *Tog.* 104 R.³), while characters from rural towns south of Rome feature in other plays, as suggested by their titles (*Psaltria sive Ferentinatis, Setina, Veliterna*). A large number of Republican dramatists seem to have moved to Rome via southern Italy, where Oscan was the dominant and most widespread local language, representing the most advanced culture in the area.

While these cultural experiences will have influenced Rome's first playwrights, there are hardly any traces of their local languages in the remaining texts,[17] even though Latin still had to be turned into a literary language when Roman drama came into being. Nor did the Romans adopt Greek literary traditions, like other peoples in the Mediterranean, by taking over the Greek language for their own literature.[18] Instead, when plays for public performance in Rome were first introduced, Latin was chosen, being the dominant local language.[19] The Romans' own language was thereby developed into a literary idiom against the Greek background;[20] thus a national literature in Latin was established as a counterpart to the Greek one.[21] This process is a major reason for Latin becoming a literary language and for the creation of a Roman literary tradition, which enabled Romans to accept the first playwrights as 'their poets'; the multicultural start of

---

with references to various attempts at explanation). Ennius might have known Messapic as well as Oscan, while Oscan was the more important language.

[17] There are no significant traces of the poets' background either, unless one assumes that their choice of topics was conditioned by their south-Italian origin (so Erskine 1998).

[18] The Greek language and the format of Greek tragedy were used for a dramatic treatment of the biblical story of Exodus, written by a Hellenized Jew between the third and first centuries BCE (Ezechiel, *Exagoge* [*TrGF* 128; vol. I, pp. 288–301]; for an English translation and commentary see Jacobson 1983; for a French translation and commentary see Lanfranchi 2006; for discussion see also Manuwald 2001a: 254–8).

[19] Early Roman historiography, which was developed by Roman senators at about the same time, initially used the Greek language, one reason presumably being the intention of promoting the Romans' view of their history among non-Romans.

[20] On the role of Latin more generally see Adams 2003: 759.

[21] See e.g. Schiesaro 2005: 271. Although Hunter (1985: 14–15) assumes that the Romans adopted Greek drama to ensure their status in the civilized world, he explains performances in Latin by the intention of the ruling classes to ensure that ordinary people could understand them (see also Gilula 1989a: 100) and to limit the impact of foreign influence. However, a foreign element remained even after translation due to dramatic characters and plots, but this had been integrated into a Roman framework, both by the organizational structure of performances and by the poets' adaptations.

Roman literature also prepared the way for its continuation by writers from different backgrounds.

1.2 IMPACT OF GREEK DRAMA

Although Roman contact with the cultures of other peoples included exposure to different theatrical traditions, the most dominant influences came from the Greeks (particularly via Greek colonies in Magna Graecia) as well as from Oscans and Etruscans, who also functioned as indirect transmitters of Greek culture. Owing to the confrontation with sophisticated theatre, the major genres of Roman drama (like other literary genres in Rome) did not undergo a gradual and independent development from small beginnings to more refined forms, but a pre-literary and shadowy phase was immediately followed by a relatively advanced literary stage, which consisted in Roman versions of fully developed models adapted from elsewhere.

When the Romans started to engage with it, Athenian drama had already spread throughout the Greek world and shown its cosmopolitan appeal (on the generality of tragedy cf. also Arist. *Poet.* 9: 1451a36–b10).[22] For Athenian drama, especially tragedy and New Comedy, could be taken over by other communities, since, besides being geared towards Athenian audiences, it had a potential for universality and adaptability as it dealt with general issues of human behaviour and society.[23]

Re-performances of classical Athenian drama elsewhere in the Greek world will have involved modifications; this is indicated even for Athens itself by Lycurgus' efforts to establish an authorized version in the middle of the fourth century BCE by having an official copy of the texts of the three tragic poets made (cf. [Plut.] *x orat.* 841F). Since re-performances of classical Greek drama in the Hellenistic period will have been adapted to contemporary taste, the Greek drama Romans got to know in Hellenized southern Italy might have differed from the classical Athenian version.[24] That alterations were being made may have paved the way for further adaptation.

By transposing Greek plays into Latin, Roman poets introduced the art of literary translation as an artistic process to Europe, i.e. translation not in the sense of word-for-word literal rendering, but of transferring the general meaning and structure of scenes or plays to a different context: they

---

[22] See Xanthakis-Karamanos 1980: 3–6.   [23] See La Penna (1977) 1979: 56–7; Taplin 2007: 6–7.
[24] See also Taplin 2007: 24.

arranged the texts for Roman society with its own traditions and ways of life; thereby they created autonomous works based on models in another language by means of a cultural transfer.[25] In other words, Rome's evolving literature was started by the decision to adopt literary works from another European culture.[26] Accordingly, the first Roman poets were confronted with a wide variety of models; their choices of what to adapt from a range of options and how to reuse this material constitute their first independent artistic decisions.

For these choices to be made, Roman poets must have been familiar with Greek drama. Greek theatre, including performances of contemporary Hellenistic plays and revivals of classical plays, flourished around the Greek colonies in southern Italy and Sicily, as the remains of theatre buildings and vase-paintings found in southern Italy, dating from the fourth and third centuries onwards, demonstrate.[27] Performances were maintained by Greek companies of the Artists of Dionysus, i.e. guilds of actors and supporting staff that had become established since the third century BCE.[28] Additionally, by Hellenistic times written versions of classical and contemporary Greek plays must have existed; and as most Republican dramatists

---

[25] The notion that Roman literature (like subsequent ones) was derived from Greek literature and was thus the first 'secondary literature' goes back to Leo (1913: 3, 59; see A. Barchiesi 2002) and has frequently been repeated in various forms and with several modifications, the Romans having often been called 'the first literary translators' (see e.g. Duckworth 1952: 3–4; Gentili 1979: 89–105; Gratwick 1982a: 80; Fantham 1989c: 220; Gilula 1989a: 100; Conte 1994: 40; Mayer 1995: 300; Vogt-Spira 1996: 11; Feeney 1998: 66–7; Franko 2001: 151; Suerbaum 2002: 6, 27, 97). However, the Romans did not adopt another national literature within Europe unchanged, but adapted it creatively for a new context (see Feeney 1998: 53; A. Barchiesi 2002).

[26] Schiesaro (2005: 269) remarks that this is 'not necessarily an obvious way to "create" a new genre'.

[27] On Greek theatres in southern Italy and Sicily see e.g. Sear 2006: 48–9; on the availability of Greek theatrical performances in southern Italy see e.g. Gentili 1979: 16–32.

[28] For the late Republic, *ludi Graeci* (also *(ludi) Graeci thymelici* and *Graeci astici*) and *ludi Osci* are mentioned for Rome itself as well as performances of *omnium linguarum histriones*; for the early imperial period a Roman and a Greek theatre are attested in Rome (cf. *CIL* VI 32323 = *ILS* 5050; Cic. *Fam.* 7.1.3; *Att.* 16.5.1; Suet. *Iul.* 39.1; *Aug.* 43.1; *Tib.* 6.4; *Cal.* 20; Nic. Dam., *FGrH* 90 F 127.9.19; Plut. *Mar.* 2.2; Strabo 5.3.6 [C 233]). Yet it is not entirely clear what these terms exactly refer to and how common entertainments of this type were. While *omnium linguarum histriones* (spread throughout the city) most probably denotes the presence of (troupes of) actors from different cultural backgrounds, who would be able to perform in a variety of languages, *ludi Graeci* might not refer to dramatic performances in Greek, but rather to athletic contests, as Cicero's comments suggest. Of the special types of *(ludi) Graeci astici* and *(ludi) Graeci thymelici*, *(ludi) Graeci astici* is likely to refer to dramatic performances, being named after the games for Dionysus in the city of Athens (cf. the term for City Dionysia at Thuc. 5.20.1: ἐκ . . . Διονυσίων τῶν ἀστικῶν), and *(ludi) Graeci thymelici* to musical performances, being named after the Greek word for artists performing in the orchestra (cf. Vitr. 5.7.2). *ludi Osci* probably denotes Atellana performances in Oscan dialect (see also ch. 3.5; for some [differing] views on this issue see Mommsen 1889: 629 n.; Wissowa 1912: 463–4; Shackleton Bailey on Cic. *Att.* 16.5.1, on Cic. *Fam.* 7.1.3; Rawson [1985] 1991: 475; Beaujeu 1988; Manuwald 2001a: 106 n. 113; other commentaries ad loc.).

were scholar poets in Hellenistic fashion, they will have been able to find and study texts of the classical exemplars.

Although for some Roman plays in Greek style no known Greek precedent can be found, most of those for which Greek models can be identified are based on a limited 'canon' of writers already established in Greece. Roman tragedies seem to have followed classical fifth-century models with a preference for Euripides, whereas Roman comedies relied almost exclusively on Hellenistic models, particularly Menander. These Greek poets and their works would have been 'theatre classics' of earlier generations by the time of the first Roman dramatists.[29] There are likely to be multiple reasons for the fact that the Romans seem to have broadly accepted the Greek canon, and these cannot be determined with certainty: since Roman writers had a Greek background, they might have followed Greek value judgements; they may have selected pieces with a proven success record; or these plays were most readily available, and the Romans too regarded them as masterpieces.[30]

Roman tragedies composed on the basis of less well-known myths may be regarded either as following 'post-classical', 'post-Euripidean' or 'late Hellenistic' models (which have not survived) or as independent Roman creations developed from mythical narratives on the structural model of Greek plays. Both methods might have been in use, while observations on canon formation and on the originality and creativity of Roman dramatists favour the second alternative (see ch. 3.1, 5.1). At any rate there is no firm basis for the assumption of a significant role of non-classical models; contemporary Greek Hellenistic theatre presumably had more influence on performance style than on the repertoire.

I.3 ETRUSCAN TRADITIONS

Besides indirectly transmitting elements of Greek culture they had adopted, the Etruscans offered their own cultural traditions to the Romans. As the

---

[29] By assuming that the Romans had adopted the dramatic genre of Rhinthonica (see ch. 1.4) prior to Greek-style comedy and tragedy, P. L. Schmidt (1989: 132–3) posited that the adaptation of Hellenistic forms preceded those of classical models. Yet the basis for this theory is questionable; Romans must have been exposed to Hellenistic and classical Greek drama (albeit in contemporary style) at about the same time.

[30] Mayer (1995) puts forward the theory that Romans felt not qualified to assess Greek literature independently, not wishing to disagree with Greek judgements and not being able to make judgements in this emerging phase of their literature. At any rate Romans chose particular plays from the 'canon' and adapted those to a Roman context, while Mayer (1995: 300) thinks that 'the foreign model was in no way reassessed to take account of local taste and interests'.

written sources left by Etruscans are meagre, details have to be inferred from archaeological finds and comments by non-Etruscan writers, who often are not eyewitnesses to the events or practices described.[31] While modern scholars used to neglect the Etruscan contribution, focusing on the Greek influence, they are now realizing that the impact of Etruscan culture on Roman drama is significant, although details remain hard to establish.[32]

As regards narratives current in Etruria, Etruscans had been exposed to Greek cultural influences since the foundation of Greek colonies on the Italian mainland and the establishment of mercantile contacts. Archaeological evidence confirms that Etruscans were familiar with heroes of Greek myths from the eighth century BCE onwards, and that they chose to depict particular myths or sections of myths that could be seen to have a general applicability and also endowed them with special nuances to make them relevant to their own lives.[33] While it is doubtful whether representations of particular myths were influenced by dramatic performances, it is noteworthy that Etruscan depictions of Greek myths preferred subjects and ways of expression that were also common in the dramatic art.[34]

Additionally, Etruscans seem to have depicted important events from their own history on works of art.[35] Paintings in the Tomba François at Vulci (*c.* 330–310 BCE) show a combination of scenes from Greek myth with representations of the Etruscan individual who had the tomb built as well as fighting between representative warriors of several Etruscan cities.[36] These scenes include the characters of Caelius Vivenna and Mastarna. According to an Etruscan tradition mentioned in a speech by the emperor Claudius, Mastarna, the most loyal friend of Caelius Vivenna, is said to have moved to Rome after the latter's death, occupied the Caelian hill (which he named after his companion) and later become a Roman king under the name of Servius Tullius (cf. *CIL* XIII 1668.1.16–24).

The interpretation of these tomb paintings, and their connection with Roman history in particular, is difficult, but it is likely that they include incidents from Etruscan history. Such a pictorial representation therefore indicates that there was a historical tradition among the Etruscans, which might have been represented in other media as well. In Rome the artistic representation of historical events was to become characteristic of visual

---

[31] On the sources see e.g. Harris 1971: 4–31.
[32] On Etruscan influence on Rome and Roman drama see Szilágyi 1981; Thuillier 1992.
[33] See Bonfante and Swaddling 2006: esp. 9, 69; also Lowenstam 2008.
[34] See Steuernagel 1998: esp. 125.   [35] See Wiseman 1994: 74; Steuernagel 1998: 182.
[36] On the paintings in the Tomba François see Moretti Sgubini 2004.

arts and literature (especially drama and epic). The combination of Greek myth, symbolizing current problems, and local heroes as found in Etruria mirrors the set-up of serious drama at Rome, consisting of tragedies and praetextae.

In the area of performance practices, Etruscan paintings indicate that the Etruscans had a developed festival culture from the sixth century BCE onwards, including solemn processions, sports contests, gladiatorial combats, games in the circus, the play of *phersu*, cult dances accompanied by a player on a wind instrument, the figure of Manducus, mime-like performances[37] and mimetic dances by masked players.[38] Archaeological evidence points to the conclusion that there were dramatic performances in Etruria prior to the Hellenistic period, differing from Greek-style performances; they have been described as 'pre-dramatic', consisting of music, dance (e.g. of satyrs) and simple drama, featuring a *carmen* and masked protagonists.[39]

Etruscan spectacles were apparently connected with political and religious life.[40] Frequently they were held as funeral games of important individuals. A notice in Livy says that it was unlawful to interrupt the rites of the *ludi* in Etruria, but that a king once did so for personal reasons and removed the artists (most of whom were his slaves) in the middle of the performance (Liv. 5.1.3–5); this presupposes an institutionalized festival culture, with the performers being of low social status. The Roman ritual procession to the performance site (*pompa circensis*), which opened each festival and brought gods and participants in the games to the centre of action (cf. Dion. Hal. *Ant. Rom.* 2.71.3–4; 7.72.1–3.1; see ch. 2.3), is said to derive ultimately from the Etruscans (cf. also App. *B Pun.* 9.66), though it later developed to incorporate Greek customs.[41]

Since Livy reports that Roman magistrates called in Etruscan dancers in 364 BCE as a means to combat a pestilence (Liv. 7.2.3–4), it seems that according to a standard Roman view the Etruscans of this period had a vibrant culture of performance in contrast to the Romans, to whom such spectacles were unknown. Although Livy does not give an objective report about the emergence of scenic performances in Rome, the core facts need not be doubted (see ch. 1.5). Additionally, linguistic evidence shows that Etruscan influence contributed to shaping the Roman theatre (cf. also Liv. 7.2.6) because essential theatre words in Latin such as *histrio*, *ludius*, *persona*

---

[37] On this aspect see Maxwell 1996. It is, however, questionable whether Etruscan influence on Roman drama can mainly be referred to the development of mime.

[38] On this aspect see Jannot 1993.   [39] See Jolivet 1993; also Szilágyi 1981; Wiseman 1994: 74.

[40] See Paratore 1957/2005: 13; Jolivet 1993: 375.   [41] See Jannot 1993.

and *scaena* (attested from Plautus onwards) are likely to have been adopted into Latin from Etruscan.[42]

Livy makes it clear for the Etruscan performances initially taken over by the Romans that there was no direct connection of the dances with a narrated story or a narrative song (Liv. 7.2.4). Indeed, even though Varro mentions a certain Volnius, who wrote *tragoediae Tuscae* (Varro, *Ling.* 5.55), it is uncertain whether the Etruscans originally had scenic performances of proper plays or narrative poetry.[43] The terms for dramatic genres at any rate are Latin or modified from Greek ones (e.g. *fabula, comoedia, tragoedia*), while the Etruscan words concern practicalities of staging applicable to all kinds of dramatic performances.

Moreover, the Etruscans must have adopted Greek theatrical culture prior to the Romans.[44] Since the Hellenistic period representations of dramatic scenes on artefacts were influenced by Greek dramatic versions and their topics.[45] The high frequency not only of mythical scenes, but also of what seem to be actual theatre set-ups, combined with a tendency to show actions on stage that were narrated in Greek drama, allows the conclusion that there was a distinctive theatre culture in Etruria.[46] Therefore, the Romans are likely to have experienced another adaptation of Greek theatre in Italy before they started to experiment with their own version.

Still, Etruscan influence on specific features of early Roman drama remains hard to identify. It seems to have had an effect on the institution as such and the organization of festivals, as it provided a paradigm. In view of Etruscan musical and theatrical influences, such as Etruscan actors mentioned by Livy or Etruscan words in the Latin vocabulary such as *histrio*, Etruscan traditions are likely to have contributed to the characteristically strong element of music, theatricality and spectacle in Roman plays.

[42] Szemerényi (1975: 300–19) argued that these terms originated in Greek and entered Latin via Etruscan (accepted by Bernstein 1998: 124–6). Breyer (1993: 169–72, 432–4) has defended the traditional view of the Etruscan origin of those terms against Szemerényi's theories, especially those for *ludius* and *histrio* (see Bonfante and Bonfante 1983: 15, 60).

[43] On the extent of Etruscan literature see Harris 1971: 9–11. References in Livy (9.36.3) to an earlier custom of having children educated in *Etruscae litterae* (as opposed to *Graecae litterae* in later periods) most probably refer to Etruscan *disciplina* (cf. Cic. *Div.* 1.92; see Harris 1971: 9). Since Volnius is mentioned nowhere else, it is uncertain whether this remark might refer to genuine 'Etruscan tragedies' at an early stage or rather to a later period when Etruscans or Romans wrote tragedies with Etruscan elements or characteristics. Hence this single reference does not provide sufficient evidence for identifying *tragoediae Tuscae* or 'Etruscan tragedies' as a distinctive dramatic genre.

[44] On the evidence for comedy see Jolivet 1983.

[45] See (on various aspects) Piganiol 1923: 32–43; Jolivet 1993; van der Meer 1993.

[46] See Thuillier 1992; Wiseman 1994: 74.

For instance, the use of pipes to accompany dramatic performances seems to have reached Rome via Etruria; this applies to both the Etruscans' own traditions and features adopted from elsewhere. The latter may include Carthaginian elements if this can be inferred from the term *tibiae Sarranae* ('Sarranian pipes'; cf. Serv. on Verg. *Aen.* 9.615[618]), named after the Phoenician town of Tyre, also called Sarra.[47] It is uncertain to what aspects of the instrument this name refers; i.e. it might derive from the type of wood and its origin or from the fact that this instrument was commonly found in this area, though not necessarily in connection with the theatre. As Romans dealt with Carthaginians not only in well-known wars, but also in peace, there must have been lively trade links, shown by various treaties.[48] The Romans adopted aspects of the Carthaginian pantheon as well as Carthaginian goods, and they must have acquired a sufficient knowledge of Carthaginian customs to understand and enjoy performances of Plautus' *Poenulus* with its Punic elements. The only item, however, that might point to a specific connection in the area of theatre is the term *tibiae Sarranae*.

1.4 DRAMATIC FORMS IN ITALY AND EARLY ROME

Besides Attic Greek and Etruscan theatrical customs, there were various other performance traditions throughout Italy prior to the emergence of literary drama in Latin. Beyond the cultural and linguistic mixture in southern Italy (including Greek, Latin and local elements), the dramatic traditions of this region in particular, consisting of a wide range of simple comic forms with shared features, had an impact on drama in Rome.[49] As details about the chronological relationship and mutual interdependence of these dramatic forms remain uncertain, clear generic distinctions and descriptions are often difficult.[50] Some of the comic types originally came from Greece, but developed into specific varieties in southern Italy or flourished in this region.

The most obvious evidence for theatrical activity in fourth-century southern Italy is that of vase-paintings, especially the extensive series of so-called 'phlyax vases' (named thus by H. Heydemann in 1886). These vases, most of them dating from *c.* 380–340 BCE, have been found in Sicily and southern Italy, particularly in Apulia. They depict a wide range of scenes,

---

[47] Cf. Gell. *NA* 14.6; Prob. on Verg. *Georg.* 2.506, quoting Enn. *Ann.* 472 Sk. = 236 W.
[48] On Rome's contacts with Carthage see Palmer 1997.
[49] On theatrical life in Italy throughout the Republican period see Rawson (1985) 1991.
[50] For overviews (albeit some of them dated or rather brief) see Dieterich 1897; Nicoll 1931; Bieber 1961: 129–46; Gigante 1967/8; Benz 1995; N. J. Lowe 2008: 83–5.

characters and masks related to dramatic performances.[51] The application of the term 'phlyax' to this type of vases and their vase-paintings was based on an assumed connection with the later literary pieces of Rhinthon, who was regarded as a writer of a form of phlyakes, a specific type of light drama (cf. Rhinthon, T 1–2 K.-A.).

Accordingly, these vases were seen as evidence for the existence of popular farce in southern Italy. Yet new research has revealed that they should rather be interpreted as fourth-century representations of Attic (Middle or Old) Comedy, particularly since inscriptions on them (naming the characters or sometimes even possibly quoting from plays) are in Attic (and not in the local Doric) dialect, masks and costumes resemble those used in Athens and some depictions can be identified as representations of scenes in extant Greek comedies.[52] Moreover, vases showing comic scenes or masks seem to have been manufactured primarily in Tarentum, where a particular Tarentine style was developed. Hence there must have been a particular interest in theatre in Tarentum (which was already proverbial in antiquity), but not elsewhere, which tells against a widespread presence and popularity of local rural comedy.

Although these results mean that a large body of evidence for indigenous comic performances in Italy disappears, the vases still testify to the popularity of theatre and performance practices in southern Italy. They might also be indicative of an attitude to the theatre different from that in classical Athens, where vase-paintings tend not to represent particular theatrical performances. In southern Italy, however, dramatic productions had been adopted as an established art and had not been developed as elements of civic and political life as they had been in Athens; dramatic performances rather had the status of enjoyable entertainment, which could also function as decoration of pottery.[53]

After the re-interpretation of the 'phlyax vases', they can no longer provide evidence for phlyakes, forerunners of the literary *fabula Rhinthonica*. Still, such a form of rustic comedy, featuring burlesques, travesties of myths, parodies of tragedies (with gods in various undignified situations) and everyday (comic) scenes, did exist, probably brought to Italy by Doric settlers and sharing features with Greek Middle Comedy.[54] This

---

[51] See Trendall 1967, 1991.
[52] See esp. J. R. Green 1991; Taplin 1993; approved by e.g. Pöhlmann 1997: 5–6; Beacham 2007: 213.
[53] On the differences in the representation of theatrical scenes see Taplin 1997; also Séchan 1926: 534–42.
[54] See also Wiseman 2000: 285. Athenaeus reports that the word 'phlyakes' was the term used in Italy for a type of comic performances that were also common elsewhere under different names (Athen.

type of drama was made literary by Rhinthon, who came from Syracuse and was active in Tarentum around 300 BCE; his plays were a kind of parody of tragedy, called *tragikoi phlyakes, hilarotragoediae* or (later) *fabulae Rhinthonicae* (cf. Rhinthon, T 1–3; 5 K.-A.).[55] Late-antique scholars defined *fabulae Rhinthonicae* as a form of comic and/or Latin drama.[56] The latter description is probably based on the observation that this type of drama was practised in Italy; but there is no clear evidence for the presence of *fabula Rhinthonica* in Rome.[57]

Even without a connection to this type of drama and its forerunners, the 'phlyax vases' continue to provide evidence for the theatrical style of the period: either they point to itinerant players taking their simple stages and properties around with them, or they indicate a common fourth-century culture of mimetic representation that presumably extended beyond the Greek cities of southern Italy into Latium and Etruria.[58] Since other south-Italian vase-paintings represent the essential elements of specific Greek myths as well as impressions of dramatic performances, the widespread knowledge and popularity of Greek tragedy are also proved.[59] Local Doric Greek comedy in Italy was first given literary form in the fifth century BCE by Epicharmus (cf. Epicharmus, T 1; 18 K.-A.); he seems to have written mainly mythical pieces.[60]

Another type of entertaining performance, mime, was introduced to Italy via Greeks in the south and in Sicily: mimes had existed in Greece since the archaic period and covered a wide variety of performances, largely based on improvisation and the virtuosity of performers. Greek mimes used a simple Doric language; they included song, dance, imitations of every-day scenes and pantomimic representations of mythological scenes (cf. e.g. Xen. *Symp.* 9.1–7); the topics tended to be erotic, burlesque or fanciful; the action was often set in the mundane environment of average families and tradesmen. Mime was made literary by the Sicilian Sophron in the fifth

---

Deipn. 14.621e–f). For a discussion of acting styles and stage conventions in phlyakes inferred from vase-paintings (understood as representations of these performances) see Neiiendam 1992: 15–62.

[55] On Rhinthon and his dramatic form see Gigante 1971.

[56] Cf. Donat. *Com.* 6.1; on Ter. *Ad.* 7; Euanth. *Com.* 4.1; Lyd. *Mag.* 1.40; [Caes. Bass.], *Gramm. Lat.* 6, p. 312.7–9 (= Rhinthon, T 5 K.-A.).

[57] P. L. Schmidt (1989: esp. 121–3) suggested that the dramatic *satura* mentioned in Livy (cf. Liv. 7.2.7; see ch. 1.5) should be identified with Rhinthonica (contra Bernstein 1998: 128). Höttemann (1993: esp. 94–6) regards Rhinthonica as a subgenre of Atellana, namely mythical Atellana. Neither theory can be proved.

[58] See Trendall 1991: 169 and Wiseman 2000: 285–7 resp.   [59] See Trendall 1991: 169–80.

[60] On Doric farce, Epicharmus and the relationship to Greek Old Comedy see Kerkhof 2001. Fragments of Epicharmus in *PCG*, vol. 1 K.-A. A possible influence on later Roman comedy may be indicated by Horace's remark that links Plautus with Epicharmus (Hor. *Epist.* 2.1.58).

century BCE, while pre-literary improvised mimes are likely to have continued.[61] Although mime never reached the status and widespread acceptance of Attic tragedy and comedy, it became popular as an independent dramatic genre and survived locally. From the third century BCE onwards mime spread throughout Italy via the Doric settlements in southern Italy and Sicily; subsequently a Roman form (*mimus/planipes*), blending preceding traditions, was developed (see ch. 3.6).

The Oscans too had a version of popular light drama, *fabula Atellana*, named after the Oscan town of Atella in Campania, where it came from, according to later Roman scholars.[62] The Oscan Atellana originally seems to have been a burlesque farce, showing the bizarre experiences of stereotyped comic characters (cf. Tac. *Ann.* 4.14.3). Its origin as well as details of its introduction to Rome are uncertain: it may have been developed under the influence of forms of Greek light drama performed in the area; and it has been suspected that Oscan workmen, particularly fullers, brought the Atellana to Rome in the course of the third century BCE. In Rome Atellana later acquired literary status (see ch. 3.5).

Early Rome had the so-called Fescennine verses,[63] probably named after the Faliscan town of Fescennia. These verse exchanges were improvised and responsive, and they contained jesting and abuse; they were regarded as rustic and were performed particularly at weddings and harvest festivals; originally they seem to have had an apotropaic function.[64]

So, when Greek-style drama was introduced to Rome, a variety of jesting, often responsive verses and of burlesque, comic, improvised performances, including a strong element of music and dance, displaying simple costumes (sometimes highlighting bodily features) and sometimes using a primitive stage, but not following linear plots, was practised in Italy.[65] All these types of performances seem to have influenced literary comedy in Rome. The larger musical element (in comparison with Greek drama) and the predilection for slapstick scenes are most often suggested as reflections of Italian popular drama.

Aristotle had already indicated that the early history of Greek comedy (in contrast to that of Greek tragedy) was obscure since this dramatic genre was

---

[61] On Sophron (with texts of the fragments and English translations) see Hordern 2004; fragments of Sophron in *PCG*, vol. 1 K.-A. For overviews and evidence on the Greek mime see Wiemken 1972, 1979; also Gianotti 1996.

[62] Cf. e.g. Liv. 7.2.11–12; Val. Max. 2.4.4; Diom. *Ars* 3, *Gramm. Lat.* 1, pp. 489.14–90.7; Euanth. *Fab.* 4.1.

[63] See e.g. Duckworth 1952: 4–5, 7–8; Blänsdorf 1978: 95–6.

[64] Cf. Liv. 7.2.7; Hor. *Epist.* 2.1.145–9; Porph. on Hor. *Epist.* 2.1.145; Fest., p. 76 L.; Macrob. *Sat.* 2.4.21; Serv. on Verg. *Aen.* 7.695; Diom. *Ars* 3, *Gramm. Lat.* 1, p. 479.13.

[65] See e.g. Beacham 1991: 12–13.

not taken seriously; he seems to have assumed that different types of loosely structured light drama existed prior to the emergence of the standard form of classical Greek comedy (Arist. *Poet.* 5: 1449a37–b9). Similarly, popular dramatic entertainments in Italy covered a variety of comic subgenres, but there is no evidence for a comparable variety of serious genres.[66] Still, dramatic techniques common in the comic forms may have influenced not only light literary drama, but also its serious counterpart.

1.5 EMERGENCE OF 'ROMAN DRAMATIC LITERATURE'

Against the background of pre-literary dramatic forms throughout Italy and classical Greek drama, 'Roman literary drama' emerged. The most extensive, but also difficult and doubtful sources for 'pre-literary' and early 'literary' drama in Rome are a chapter in the historian Livy (Liv. 7.2) and the parallel, albeit slightly divergent account in Valerius Maximus (Val. Max. 2.4.4), both versions probably going back to the late Republican polymath Varro.[67]

Elements of this narrative agree with information in other literary sources or with what is generally plausible for drama in the early stages of its development: it is not improbable that performances of instrumental music, song and dance precede the production of literary drama or that artists are first summoned from neighbouring, more advanced peoples; amateurs then try to imitate them; and eventually native artists take over and specific dramatic forms develop. Livy might therefore have fused elements that were generally known by his time into a coherent story, aimed at explaining the contemporary state of the dramatic arts, while the evolutionary model could have been influenced by the paradigm of the development of Greek drama. Although one has to bear in mind that details of the scenario are based on a reconstruction of the late Republican/early Augustan period,

---

[66] However, Wiseman (e.g. 1994, 1998: esp. 1–16, 2004) has argued for an extensive and flourishing tradition of historical drama, going back to the pre-literary period, in Rome (see also Beacham 1991: 2–3; see ch. 3.2).

[67] Cf. also e.g. Hor. *Epist.* 2.1.139–67; August. *De civ. D.* 2.8; Oros. 3.4.5; Tert. *De spect.* 5.5; Plut. *Quaest. Rom.* 107 (289D). On the Livy passage (as a whole or on particular aspects) see e.g. Waszink 1948; Duckworth 1952: 4–10; Pighi 1952; Morel 1969; Jory 1981; Szilágyi 1981; P. L. Schmidt 1989; Pociña Pérez 1996a: 15–20; Bernstein 1998: 119–29; Feldherr 1998: 178–87; Oakley 1998: 37–72; Suerbaum 2002: 51–7; N. J. Lowe 2008: 81–3 (most with information on the extensive bibliography). Scholars interested in Roman drama tend to read the passage on its own, thereby neglecting Livy's narrative intentions; analyses by students of Livy such as Feldherr (1998) and Oakley (1998) present a useful corrective and show that this is not an unbiased overview of the development of drama, but that Livy rather uses the section to make a statement about his own time.

such an outline may contain a nucleus of authentic information and is therefore worth examining.[68]

The development described by Livy can be divided into five phases:

1 As the consequence of a severe pestilence in 365/4 BCE, scenic performances (*ludi scaenici*) were introduced as an innovation – in addition to
the already existing spectacle in the circus (*circi spectaculum*) – in order to
appease the gods. These scenic performances initially were a foreign institution; stage-performers (*ludiones*) were summoned from Etruria. They
performed dances in Etruscan style to the accompaniment of music by
a flute player, but there was no *carmen*, i.e. a song telling a story, and
no acting in imitation of the *carmen*, i.e. a pantomimic representation
of the song's contents. The important characteristic of this phase (Liv.
7.2.3–4) is the introduction of scenic performances, although they were
rather different from later performances of scripted dramas.

2 In the next phase amateur Roman youths (*iuventus*) started to imitate the
Etruscan dancers and probably gradually replaced them. They exchanged
jests in uncouth verses among themselves and accompanied them by
movements in line with their utterances. In this phase (Liv. 7.2.5) verses
were added to the performances, and the Romans appropriated these by
a change in personnel.

3 The institution then became established in Rome. Actors were native
professionals, who were called *histriones*, by a term derived from the
Etruscan word *ister* ('actor'). Apparently the Latin language had not had
a word for professional actors; along with the function the term was
taken over.[69] Additionally, performances became more refined, and the
various elements were combined according to a pre-arranged plan: actors
were no longer satisfied with uncouth, alternate verses, but performed
melodious medleys (*satura*), with song and movements following the
fixed music of a flute player. The crucial development in this phase (Liv.
7.2.6–7) is that music, words and movements came together and were
no longer improvised.

4 A number of years later Livius (Andronicus) was the first person to move
forward from *saturae* to composing a play with a plot (*argumento fabulam*

---

[68] Gratwick (1982a: 78), however, regards these accounts as 'entirely worthless with respect to tragedy, and virtually so for comedy'.

[69] Cf. also Tac. *Ann.* 14.21.1: *a Tuscis accitos histriones*. Isidorus gives alternative etymologies (Isid. *Etym.* 18.48): *dicti autem histriones sive quod ab Histria id genus sit adductum, sive quod perplexas historiis fabulas exprimerent, quasi historiones.* ('And they are called *histriones*, either because this type of people has been brought in from Histria, or because they express dramas complex by their *historiae* [plots], as if *historiones* [story-tellers].') On the ancient etymologies see Maltby 1991: 280, s.v.; on modern views see Walde and Hofmann 1982: 653, s.v.

serere). Livy then digresses and adds information on Livius Andronicus' fortune as an actor in his own plays: Livius Andronicus is said to have once lost his voice in a series of encores, to have asked a boy to take over the singing and consequently acted with more vigorous gestures. Livy defines this as the origin of a distinction between singers and actors, as the latter performed the spoken parts only.[70] He thus includes an aetiological explanation for a particular kind of performance, in which the roles of actor and vocalist are distinguished, in his account of the early stages of Roman drama; he might be thinking of the pantomime of his own day (see ch. 3.7). This phase as a whole, i.e. the emergence of drama with a plot (Liv. 7.2.8–10), signals the significant step of the introduction of literary drama. However, Livy does not give information on the exact date, on the structure of the play or on details of the performance except for mentioning Livius (Andronicus).[71]

5 Since the Roman youths, the amateur actors, were dissatisfied with performances moving from jest towards art, they left the acting of plays (*fabellae*) to professional actors (*histriones*) and revived the tradition of voicing alternate joking verses. These performances later developed into 'after-pieces' (*exodium*) and were joined with *fabula Atellana*, acquired from the Oscans. This type of drama remained the domain of Roman amateurs and was not given over to professionals; Atellana actors therefore continued to retain citizen rights. This phase (Liv. 7.2.11–12) explains how different types of drama came to exist side by side and testifies to another cultural influence.[72]

Livy ends his account by asserting that *ludi* belong to those things that have grown from small and sane beginnings to unbearable madness (Liv. 7.2.13).

Scholars have often criticized the fact that Livy presents Roman drama as having been originally imported from the Etruscans and then having developed indigenously, omitting any mention of Greek influence. However, Livy focuses on form and style of performance rather than on content or story lines. Accordingly, there is no reference to Greek influence, but it

---

[70] However, no other ancient evidence (with the possible exception of Isid. *Etym.* 18.44, which might ultimately go back to the same source) confirms this distinction between actor and singer for proper dramatic performances (see Suerbaum 2002: 54).

[71] According to Aristotle the plot is the most important element of tragedy and inexperienced poets may have difficulties with constructing it (Arist. *Poet.* 6: 1450a15–38). The introduction of plot is a significant development in his brief account of the history of comedy (Arist. *Poet.* 5: 1449b5–9).

[72] Valerius Maximus (2.4.4) indicates that the appropriation of Oscan practices was a planned act, like the calling in of Etruscan actors earlier, whereas in Livy it seems to have been a free decision of the Roman youths and a more general influence. On the text of this section in Livy see ch. 3.5, n. 130.

is not thereby denied altogether. What Livy seems mainly to be interested in is the depiction of a coherent development from small and promising beginnings to something pompous and degenerate; mention of a Greek element in the middle of this process would affect this evolutionary model. That progress made by Livius Andronicus is played down is obvious from the fact that the major change inaugurated by him is reported in a relative clause while the main narrative focuses on his impact on performance style. Livy's highlighting of the Etruscan influence is one-sided, but not completely wrong: that there is an Etruscan element in Roman performances is corroborated by linguistic evidence on the origin of theatre words (see ch. 1.3). Since loanwords tend to be adopted together with the item they denote, it is plausible that actors initially hailed from Etruria and a corresponding designation was adopted.

Scholars have also remarked that, in contrast to Greek drama, remains of cult practices such as dance are not found in Roman drama, as would be expected on the basis of Livy's narrative. However, Livy distinguishes between earlier forms of performance and Livius Andronicus' dramas with a plot, and from this point onwards he differentiates between different types of dramatic forms. Therefore, even according to Livy's model, remains of local traditions are rather to be expected in types of dramatic performances other than the Greek-style ones.

Livy's mention of a 'dramatic *satura*' (Liv. 7.2.7) raises difficult questions, i.e. of whether its existence can be accepted, what it might refer to and what its relationship to the later literary *satura*/satire is.[73] The 'dramatic satire' is certainly distinct from the literary satire as practised by Ennius and later Lucilius and his followers; here the term must have been used in the original sense of 'mixture/medley', denoting a performance consisting of various musical pieces, accompanied by song and dance. However, all attempts to identify this '*satura*' with known dramatic forms are doubtful. It is perhaps best regarded as Livy's description of varied pre-literary performances without a plot.

Details of the development as described by Livy must remain uncertain and cannot be verified. Nevertheless, the year 364 BCE can be seen as marking a significant stage in the history of Roman *ludi*.[74] There is no

---

[73] For an overview of the scholarly discussion and an attempt at explaining Livy's use of the term see Oakley 1998: 55–8; see also ch. 1.4, n. 57. Szilágyi (1981) has argued that Livy's dramatic *satura* might be connected with dances of Etruscan satyrs known from vase-paintings (approved by Wiseman 1994: 74).

[74] Szilágyi (1981) regards it as possible that dramatic representations from Etruria were introduced in Rome prior to 364 BCE, but only became institutionalized and official in that year. Livy's text does not support this view.

obvious motive for the invention of the date 364 BCE by Livy or his sources; events such as a plague and a subsequent appeal to Etruria would have been recorded in official records available to Roman historians. A specific date or reason for the next major step, Livius Andronicus' innovation, are not given by Livy; yet the traditional date (240 BCE) can be inferred from other sources.[75] Livy too has drama start in Rome as a result of a political decision in a critical situation of the community; it is only that his starting point is 364 rather than 240 BCE, which marks a step within an ongoing development.

Since Gellius identifies the date of 240 BCE not only by the consuls of that year (like Cicero), but also by its distance from the deaths of Sophocles, Euripides and Menander, he is likely to be referring to Greek-style drama, and it is plausible that this innovation refers to both tragedies and comedies as stated by Cassiodorus. Surviving fragments show that Livius Andronicus wrote both tragedies and comedies of Greek type; it is uncertain only whether both types were performed on the first occasion as the sources vary between singular (Cicero: *fabula*) and plural (Gellius: *fabulae*; Cassiodorus: *tragoedia et comoedia*).[76] At any rate Livius Andronicus introduced dramas with a plot (*argumentum*) in contrast to earlier improvised performances.

Greek-style drama developed in Rome after Livius Andronicus produced a play or plays at the *ludi* of 240 BCE. No dramatic texts (or fragments of dramatic texts) predating the dramas of Livius Andronicus survive. If Livius Andronicus was not the originator of this kind of drama, he must at least have produced it more memorably or at a more favourable point in time (thereby suppressing any possible predecessors or memory of them), because he later came to be regarded as Rome's first dramatist. It is true that Livius Andronicus' dates were disputed in late Republican times, yet Cicero's arguments against alternative scenarios indicate that the tradition of Livius Andronicus being 'the first' was already firmly established in the late Republic (Cic. *Brut.* 72–3), and this is the only version that

---

[75] Cf. Cic. *Brut.* 72; Gell. *NA* 17.21.42; Cass. *Chron.*, p. 128 *MGH* AA 11.2 (on 239 BCE). There is no contradiction between Livy's account and other sources that focus on a specific date for the introduction of Greek-style drama (as apparently implied in N. J. Lowe 2008: 81); these are just different perspectives.

[76] See also Pociña Pérez 1996a: 2 and n. 2, 13–14. The title(s) of the drama(s) performed are unknown. Scholars have suggested Livius Andronicus' *Equos Troianus* as the first tragedy to be produced in Rome on this occasion (see e.g. Grimal 1975: 270). Erasmo (2004: 10 and n. 1 [p. 155]) and Boyle (2006: 28 and n. 7 [p. 246]) believe that Cicero's use of the word *fabula* on its own in the singular is more appropriate to a tragedy and that this *fabula* therefore was most probably a tragedy (see also Gratwick 1982a: 128).

was passed on. The key fact that Livius Andronicus' plays were adapted from Greek models is not mentioned in any of the ancient sources, but references to *fabula*, *tragoedia* or *comoedia* and to plots in this context imply this essential quality. From this point onwards dramatic performances in Rome consisted of full-scale plays adopted from the Greeks as well as various types of indigenous performances, some of which later turned literary.[77]

Livius Andronicus' Greek-style dramas and their successors (in the same and related dramatic genres) form what is called 'Roman literary drama' or 'Rome's dramatic literature'.[78] These terms are obvious and uncontroversial when they distinguish dramas performed according to written scripts from unscripted, often improvised performances ('literary' not implying a distinction from 'stage drama').[79] Beyond this simple definition, however, the term 'literary drama' raises the questions of whether there are other features that make this kind of drama distinctive and 'literary' and whether the application of this label implies a complete breach with preceding traditions, and also why this kind of drama was adopted in Rome in the middle of the third century BCE rather than at any other time.

An answer to this last question[80] has to take note of the fact that Roman 'literary' drama emerged at a specific point in time,[81] which saw a unique combination of factors: Roman openness and willingness to adopt Greek culture (after prolonged and intense contact with the Greeks), a sufficient sophistication of indigenous traditions to provide trained actors, influences from other Italic peoples, the geopolitical situation after the end of the First Punic War, an urge for Roman self-promotion directed towards both the

---

[77] Cf. N. J. Lowe 2008: 85: 'Broadly speaking, the story of Roman drama is of two intertwined traditions that have quite different kinds of developmental story. On the one hand stands the tradition of literary adaptations of Athenian tragedy and comedy; on the other, the more elusive history of the various performance genres that seem to have established themselves as independent traditions in the Roman world, whatever their roots in popular west Greek and Italic performance' (cf. also p. 86).

[78] Instead of saying that it was Latin literature that began with Livius Andronicus, it would be more adequate, according to Pighi (1952: 275), to talk of 'Greek literature in Latin'. There is some truth in this observation; however, as Latin literature in Rome, though based on Greek models, developed particular characteristics that are the result of an adaptation to a different context and are not found in Greek literature, retaining the traditional terminology seems justified.

[79] Goldhill (1999) warns against literary histories only focusing on 'literature'. Indeed, with respect to Roman drama, the performance as a whole and the context have to be borne in mind, avoiding an exclusive concentration on the text. Still, 'literary' as indicating a certain level of sophistication remains a valid criterion.

[80] This question has often been asked, though never answered conclusively (see e.g. Gentili 1979: 93–4; Vogt-Spira 1996: 15). An answer that is 'correct' beyond doubt cannot be given; yet plausible hypotheses may be put forward (see Feeney 1998: 52; Farrell 2005: esp. 426–7).

[81] See Batstone 2006: 545.

Greek cities of Italy and the Hellenistic world as a whole,[82] a desire in
Rome to catch up with the level of culture and theatre of conquered areas,
the intentions of the Roman nobility, the presence of a poet well versed in
Greek literature and culture, yet able to write proper Latin and to apply
his knowledge of the Greek world so as to produce adaptations interesting
to Roman audiences.[83]

More particularly, this point in time falls a few decades after the onset
of a phase that came to be called the 'Hellenistic period': cultural shifts
required ambitious expanding cities such as Rome to claim a place on an
'international' level and to participate in the then dominant Greek culture;
a new way of dealing with the 'classics' of Greek literature emerged, which
facilitated a more professional engagement with Greek culture as an object
of study or imitation. In this situation Roman magistrates took the decision
to introduce Greek-style drama in Rome on an institutional basis.[84] That
such a performance did not remain a single incident must have been
encouraged by the policy of the nobility and supported by the play's success
with the audience. The movement towards public presentation of stories
and ideas that were pertinent to the audience's concerns and experiences
accorded with a boom in communication and display in the late third
century BCE, as indicated by developments in other literary genres (such as
oratory and historiography) and in architecture.

Although the first Roman playwrights are thought to have been familiar
with theatrical conventions via their contacts with southern Italy, there is
no record (with the possible exception of Plautus) of their being involved
in theatre business in Magna Graecia and having gained experience in
producing plays. It rather seems as if they started writing plays for the
stage after they had come to Rome and had been commissioned. That
means that, although the availability of a qualified poet such as Livius
Andronicus probably contributed to the introduction of proper drama to
Rome, the transplantation was presumably the result of a decision by the
authorities rather than an organic process carried out by actors and/or
writers who sought new areas for activity. Consequently, the early phases

---

[82] See e.g. Gruen 1990: 82, 84; Dench 1995: 68–70.

[83] Livius Andronicus had probably shown his credentials as a poet by composing the epic *Odusia*
before beginning to write dramas. This means that formal 'literature' did not start in Rome in the
'epoch-making year' of 240 BCE, but slightly earlier (on this issue see Suerbaum 2002: 83–7, 97; for
240 BCE as the beginning of 'formal Latin literature' see e.g. Duckworth 1952: 3–4; for a discussion
of the problem see Feeney 2005: 232–3).

[84] See Dupont 1985: 142.

of Roman 'literary' drama were not a mere literary continuation of contemporary Greek drama; instead, a political decision led to a new situation for poets, who had to find their own style for Roman drama, in constant dialogue with Greek models from various periods and with indigenous traditions.[85]

The permanent introduction of Greek-style drama was a significant move in cultural politics and in Rome's literary history, but, as surviving dramatic scripts and fragments indicate, it does not constitute a complete breach with preceding Italic traditions and does not mean that subsequent dramatic forms are based exclusively on Greek models.[86] Roman poets took over the subject matter and the plot-based structure of Greek drama and amalgamated these elements with Italic traditions, adapting them to Roman thinking and formal conventions. At the same time this process implied that Italic traditions became 'literary' to a certain extent.[87]

In around 240 BCE Roman dramatic performances entered a 'literary' stage, as they started to have stories following a plot, to discuss general questions, to develop more sophisticated forms and to follow scripts. Even if this decisive step can be described fairly clearly in hindsight, it raises the questions of whether the first poets themselves were aware of its significance and of whether this change by itself is the reason why Roman drama from this point onwards has come to be regarded as 'literature' in contrast to earlier types of performances in Rome.

The first playwrights may well have been aware that they were doing something new; yet at the time they can hardly have foreseen the far-reaching consequences of their activities. Those gradually became obvious in late Republican/early Augustan times. Therefore the fact that the literary creations of the early poets came to be seen as 'literature' (as opposed to parts of 'events' with a wide-ranging programme) is not only the result of the period during the third and second centuries BCE when the dramatic scripts were produced, but also the consequence of reflections by late Republican/early Augustan scholars and their predecessors in the second century BCE.[88] These people began to regard the first playwrights as part of

---

[85] See also Aricò 1997: 62–3; Suerbaum 2002: 97. For further thoughts on forms of cultural transposition from Greece to Rome see Gilula 1989a.

[86] So e.g. Blänsdorf 1978: 100; Blume 1991: 114.

[87] The practice of combining Greek models and indigenous traditions can also be observed in the architecture of the period (see von Hesberg 2005: 44–7).

[88] See Goldberg 2005b (but see review by Feeney 2006); also 2005a, 2007a; already, Jocelyn 1967: 5.

their culture and to investigate chronological and biographical questions connected with these texts; the dramatic scripts thereby acquired the status of 'literature'.

Writers of the late Republican and early Augustan periods such as Cicero, Varro and Horace were obviously also familiar with the history of Greek literature and looked to it as a paradigm. Some of these men, focusing on literary drama in Greek style, saw Roman theatre as an imported product, highlighting the Greek and/or the Etruscan element.[89] Therefore they came to the conclusion that Rome had adopted literature rather late (long after the corresponding stages in Greek literature and after the foundation of Rome), since they largely disregarded forms of 'pre-literary drama' and indigenous traditions. They even thought that it took a while for scripted drama to reach an acceptable level (since they only counted refined poetry of Greek standard).[90]

Besides the widespread chronology, which had Roman drama start with Livius Andronicus in 240 BCE (and was not actually challenged by the different dating proposed by Accius; see ch. 4.1), there was the view that 'the Muse' 'arrived' in Rome during the Second Punic War (cf. Porcius Licinus, ap. Gell. *NA* 17.21.45), and another one according to which it was only after the Second Punic War that Romans turned to tragedy and managed to produce more refined poetry (cf. Hor. *Epist.* 2.1.156–67). These statements seem to date the beginning of literature in Rome to Naevius or even to Ennius. This does not necessarily imply a contradiction: it may simply indicate that the products of the pioneers were not regarded as proper literature and therefore Ennius (who had self-confidently promoted his standing) was seen as the true founder of Roman literature. Horace, for instance, has Roman literature begin in the time of Livius Andronicus and thus seems to subscribe to the prevailing scenario; at the same time he calls Livius Andronicus *scriptor* ('writer') in contrast to *poetae* ('poets') who followed him later in the Republican period (Hor. *Epist.*

---

[89] Wiseman (2000: 287–9) states a contrast between the 'actual development of dramatic performances in Rome' and the literary accounts by scholars such as Varro, Cicero and Horace (for comments on accounts in Augustan poets see also e.g. Oakley 1998: 47–9).

[90] For the lateness of Roman adaptation of Greek culture cf. Hor. *Epist.* 2.1.156–67; Cic. *Tusc.* 1.3; for the transfer of Greek learning to Rome cf. Cicero's prefaces to his philosophical writings (e.g. Cic. *Tusc.* 1.1; *Fin.* 1.1–10) and the claims of several Roman authors to be the first to transform Greek ideas and literature into Latin (Cic. e.g. *Fin.* 1.1; *Tusc.* 1.1; Lucr. e.g. 1.921–34); for the difficulty involved in this process cf. the complaints, especially by Lucretius, about the poverty of the Latin language (*patrii sermonis egestas*), which makes it difficult to express Greek concepts in Latin (Lucr. 1.136–9; 1.830–3; 3.258–61; Cic. *Fin.* 3.5).

2.1.61b–2); that he does not regard Livius Andronicus' poetry as sufficiently cultivated can explain the different perspective applied in another context.[91] Cicero too does not think very highly of Livius Andronicus' works (Cic. *Brut.* 71).[92]

In combination with the particularly bad state of preservation of the works of many Republican dramatists (for which the early unfavourable assessments might be one reason), such views have continued to determine the opinion on early Roman dramatic literature in the modern period.[93] Although these ancient scholars have transmitted a lot of information about the beginnings of Roman drama to later generations, their accounts are coloured by their own opinions. For instance, they compiled 'canons' of the best writers and established an evolutionary model, in which pioneers were judged according to their literary sophistication in comparison with their successors rather than according to the relevance of their innovative deeds.

The prejudiced perspective may still exert an influence on the assessment of the innovative progress made by the pioneers. Thus the opinions of these ancient writers seem to be a major reason for the 'Enniocentric' view found in some modern literary histories. Such a focus tends to undervalue the achievements of the pioneers, who were not 'archaic' or 'unsophisticated' in their time; instead, they performed independent and innovative acts by transposing Greek texts into a Roman language not yet literate and thus launching literary drama in Rome. Comparing their achievements with attempts by subsequent Roman writers at both Hellenizing and Romanizing an emerging Roman literature is problematic due to the differences in circumstances.[94]

Comments by ancient scholars indicate that a canon of poets was being established: dramatists discussed in these accounts tend to be a limited group of playwrights, and precisely those that are still known and read

---

[91] For satire too Horace distinguishes between an *auctor* and a later, more refined *inventor* (Hor. *Sat.* 1.10.47–9; 1.10.64–7). See also Traglia 1986: 11–12; Stärk in Suerbaum 2002: 151–2; on Horace's attitude to literary history see Feeney 2002; for Horace's views on Plautus see Jocelyn 1995. Hupperth (1961) refers *Graecia capta* to Magna Graecia and *post Punica bella* to the First Punic War and therefore sees no contradiction of other accounts even in chronological terms; yet the context makes this interpretation rather unlikely.

[92] Similarly Quintilian describes Aeschylus, whom he introduces as the first tragic poet in Greece, as *rudis* and *incompositus* (Quint. *Inst.* 10.1.66).

[93] For instance, on Cicero's tendentious account in *Brutus* see Hinds 1998: 66–8.

[94] On these issues see Hinds 1998: esp. 55–6, 62–3; also Goldberg 2007a; on the influence that the selection and views of transmitting writers may have on modern views of early Roman poets see also the contributions in Fitzgerald and Gowers 2007.

today.[95] Apparently there was a feeling that these men, though belonging to a bygone age, were important for Rome's literature and that their writings were relevant. This notion then gave rise to the view that some of the faults later scholars identified in the works of the early poets were due to the times rather than to the poets themselves (cf. Quint. *Inst.* 10.1.97).

---

[95] Cf. e.g. Cic. *De or.* 3.27; *Orat.* 36; *Fin.* 1.4; *Acad.* 1.10; *Opt. gen.* 18; Hor. *Epist.* 2.1.50–62. *De optimo genere oratorum* is of disputed authenticity (see e.g. Dihle 1955), but modern scholarly consensus tends to follow the transmission and attribute it to Cicero (see e.g. Berry 1996: 61–70 [with bibliography in p. 61, n. 32, on p. 72]).

CHAPTER 2

Production and reception

2.1 FESTIVALS AND DRAMATIC PERFORMANCES

In Republican Rome dramatic performances constituted *ludi scaenici*, which were one element of officially organized festivals.[1] Consequently, opportunities for dramatic performances were closely linked to the development of Roman festival culture. This connection affected the status and the perception of drama: on the one hand there was the chance to reach a broad audience, on the other hand plays had to find their place in relation to other entertainments.[2]

Festivals at Rome can be divided into regular games, typically in honour of a particular god and held at specific times throughout the year, and occasional spectacles due to extraordinary events. *Ludi sollemnes* were held regularly by the civic authorities, whereas *munera* were essentially donated spectacles by wealthy families, given, for instance, as fulfilments of vows after military victories (*ludi magni/votivi*), at dedications of temples (*ludi ob dedicationem aedis*) or at funerals in honour of the dead (*ludi funebres*).

All types of festivals could consist of various elements, including 'scenic/stage/dramatic games' (*ludi scaenici*) as well as 'circus games' (*ludi circenses*), such as chariot races, boxing, wrestling, foot-races and wild-beast hunts in the Circus Maximus (cf. e.g. Cic. *Leg.* 2.38; Liv. 33.25.1; 40.52.3; 42.10.5). The entire event started with a procession of the organizing magistrates, priests, contestants, actors, dancers, musicians, religious equipment and statues of the gods to the festival ground (*pompa circensis*) and with sacrifices performed by priests and magistrates (cf. Dion. Hal. *Ant. Rom.* 7.72; Tert. *De spect.* 7.2).

---

[1] On public festivals in Rome see esp. Bernstein 1998; also e.g. Wissowa 1912: 449–67; Piganiol 1923: 75–91; Duckworth 1952: 76–9; Balsdon 1969: 244–52; Blänsdorf 1978: 112–16; Scullard 1981; on festivals as opportunities for dramatic performances see Taylor 1937; Petrone 1992: 426–9; Marshall 2006: 16–20; on the various shows as public entertainment and element of Roman life see Balsdon 1969: 244–339; Nicolet 1980: 361–73; Clavel-Lévêque 1984, 1986; Flower 2004.

[2] See also Dupont 1985: 43; Lada-Richards 2004: 55, 66–73.

According to Roman tradition, official festivals with particular rites had existed since the regal period, a custom adopted from the Etruscans (cf. Liv. 1.35.7–9; Cic. *Rep.* 2.20.36; Dion. Hal. *Ant. Rom.* 3.68.1). In early Republican times there was initially just one regular festival, *Ludi maximi* or *Romani* in honour of Iuppiter Optimus Maximus (cf. Cic. *Rep.* 2.20.36; Liv. 1.35.9; 8.40.2; 10.47.3).

Since the dedication of the Temple of Jupiter (or rather: the Capitoline Triad) on the Capitoline Hill on 13 September 509 BCE (cf. Liv. 2.8.6; 7.3.8; Polyb. 3.22.1) *Ludi Romani* seem to have been celebrated each year on the day of dedication. The number of festival days increased gradually till the games lasted from 5 to 19 September in the late Republic (*ludi scaenici*: 5–12 September). *Ludi Romani* were presided over by superior magistrates (*praesidium ludorum*); their practical organization was transferred to aediles in the fourth century BCE (*cura ludorum*). These games took place in the Circus Maximus at the foot of the Palatine Hill; they originally consisted of sacrifices (*sacrificia*), a ritual procession of cult statues and all participants to the centre of action (*pompa circensis*) and games in the circus (*ludi circenses*).

Besides *Ludi Romani* there were irregular *ludi magni* or *votivi*, also in honour of Jupiter, which were celebrated in fulfilment of a vow by the Senate or a superior magistrate (*votum solvere*) after the successful completion of significant campaigns, such as a battle or the conquest of a town. This type of festival is attested from the early fifth century BCE and was probably similar in outline to *Ludi Romani*.[3]

Major changes to this set-up occurred in the middle of the fourth century BCE, in the course of the restructuring of public offices and the admission of the *plebs* to curule magistrates in 367/6 BCE: the organization of festivals (*cura ludorum*) passed to the new office of two curule aediles, which was restricted to patricians at first, but was soon opened to plebeians in alternate years, while the consuls continued to preside over the games (*praesidium ludorum*).

In 364 BCE, when the curule aedile M. Popilius Laenas was in office, scenic performances (*ludi scaenici*) are said to have been added to the festival (held in the Circus Maximus: cf. Liv. 7.3.1–2), which thereby probably extended in length from four to five days: according to Roman tradition, a pestilence in 365/4 BCE prompted officials to introduce this new kind of performance (dancing accompanied by music), taken over from Etruria

---

[3] Cf. Cic. *Div.* 1.55; Liv. 2.36.1–8; Dion. Hal. *Ant. Rom.* 6.10.1; 7.68–73.

(cf. Liv. 7.2.1–4).[4] None of the ancient sources connects this development with *Ludi Romani*; but this was the only regular festival at the time. The introduction of scenic games significantly altered the character of festivals and paved the way for further developments: from 240 BCE, when magistrates commissioned the poet Livius Andronicus, Roman *ludi scaenici* saw performances of Greek-style drama.[5] The first performances were most probably also given at *Ludi Romani*, still the only regular festival.[6]

The new format of the games did not remain a single event, but soon developed into a regular feature. It is possible that these events quickly acquired prominence, since Hiero II of Syracuse is said by Eutropius to have visited Rome in 237 BCE 'to watch the games' (Eutr. 3.1–2: *ad ludos spectandos*). The number of days reserved for *ludi scaenici* was raised to four in 214 BCE (cf. Liv. 24.43.7); this probably brought the *Ludi Romani* to a total of eight days, whereby *ludi scaenici* and *ludi circenses* obtained equal shares of the festival. In the same period, between the eve of the Second Punic War and the successful completion of this war and of those against eastern kingdoms (*c.* 220–170 BCE), five further regular festivals were added to the calendar.[7]

At the beginning of the Second Punic War another festival for Jupiter was introduced: *Ludi plebeii*, dedicated to Iuppiter Optimus Maximus, were held (probably) from 220 BCE (cf. Liv. 23.30.17, on 216 BCE) and were organized by the plebeian aediles. They took place in the Circus Flaminius (cf. Val. Max. 1.7.4) in the Campus Martius, which was built in *c.* 220 BCE (cf. Liv. *Epit.* 20.17), and happened around the Ides of November (*feriae Iovis* on 13 November), extending from 4 to 17 November in early imperial times (*ludi scaenici*: 4–12 November). This festival included dramatic performances: in 200 BCE it saw the performance of Plautus' *Stichus* (cf. Did. on Plaut. *Stich.*; Liv. 31.50.3).

At about the same time the ancient festival of *Cerialia*, celebrated on 19 April (cf. Ov. *Fast.* 4.393–620), developed into *Ludi Ceriales*. These are attested for 202/201 BCE (cf. Liv. 30.39.8), but were probably introduced shortly before the outbreak of the Second Punic War, in around 220/19

---

[4] Cf. Liv. 7.2.1–3; Val. Max. 2.4.4; Fest., p. 436 L.; August. *De civ. D.* 2.8; Oros. 3.4.1; 3.4.5.

[5] Cf. Cic. *Brut.* 72; *Tusc.* 1.3; *Sen.* 50; Liv. 7.2.8; Val. Max. 2.4.4; Gell. *NA* 17.21.42; Cass. *Chron.*, p. 128 *MGH* AA 11.2 (on 239 BCE). See also ch. 1.5, 4.1.

[6] On the dubious evidence for the *Ludi Tarentini* in 249 BCE and these games as the origin for later secular games see Bernstein 1998: 129–42; Suerbaum 2002: 96.

[7] The period of the mid- to late third century BCE probably also saw the introduction of regular gladiatorial combat at Rome. The earliest gladiatorial show (*munus gladiatorium*) is attested for 264 BCE (cf. Liv. *Epit.* 16.6; Val. Max. 2.4.7), and these events originally were typically part of funeral games (see Welch 2007: 18–22).

BCE, in order to appease the tutelary divinity of the *plebs* and to prepare for potential shortages in the provision of food during the war (cf. Liv. 30.39.8; Ps.-Cypr. *Spect.* 4.4). This specific situation may explain why other gods besides Jupiter were now honoured by *ludi*; in addition to Ceres, the new festival was dedicated to Liber and Libera, all of whom shared a temple.[8] The games were held at this temple close to the Circus Maximus and organized by the plebeian aediles. From the start these *ludi* focused on scenic games;[9] in imperial times they lasted from 12 to 19 April (*ludi scaenici*: 12–18 April), with performances in the circus on the last day.

In the middle of the Second Punic War, in 212 BCE, *Ludi Apollinares* were held for the first time (cf. Liv. 25.12.2–15; Macrob. *Sat.* 1.17.27–30). Initially, they were vowed from year to year; in 208 BCE the reaction to a pestilence caused them to be turned into *ludi annui*, taking place on 13 July (cf. Liv. 27.23.6–7); in imperial times they lasted from 6 to 13 July (*ludi scaenici*: 6–12 July). They were organized by the praetor urbanus and held close to the Temple of Apollo and/or in the Circus Maximus (cf. Liv. 25.12.14; 30.38.10–12). They were adapted from the Greek format and had scenic performances from the outset (cf. Fest., pp. 436/8 L.).

When the cult of Magna Mater (Cybele) was introduced in Rome, a festival was held in conjunction with her entry to Rome in 204 BCE (cf. Liv. 29.10.4; 29.14.14), called *Megalesia* after her Greek designation Μεγάλη Μήτηρ (cf. Cic. *Har. resp.* 24). From 194 BCE the festival included scenic games (cf. Liv. 34.54.3). Annual *ludi* were established in 191 BCE on the occasion of the dedication of the Temple of Magna Mater on the Palatine Hill (cf. Liv. 34.54; 36.36.3–4), when Plautus' *Pseudolus* was performed (cf. Did. on Plaut. *Pseud.*; also Cic. *Sen.* 50); this became the festival of *Ludi Megalenses*.[10] The games were organized by the curule aediles and were held 'on the Palatine Hill . . . in front of the temple in the very sight of the Great Mother'.[11] They took place from 4 to 10 April in imperial times (*ludi scaenici*: 4–9 April).

The last regular festival to be established in the middle Republic was *Ludi Florales*.[12] In 238 BCE, probably as a result of a shortage in food supply,

[8] Cf. Cic. *Verr.* 2.5.14.36; Ps.-Cypr. *Spect.* 4.4; Serv. on Verg. *Georg.* 1.7.
[9] Cf. Ps.-Cypr. *Spect.* 4.4; Ov. *Fast.* 4.393; Tac. *Hist.* 2.55.1; Juv. 5.14.262–4.
[10] *Testimonia* on the date of the introduction of scenic performances at this festival and its establishment as a regular institution are contradictory (194 or 191 BCE); upon close inspection 191 BCE turns out to be the more plausible date (see von Ungern-Sternberg 1975; Bernstein 1998: 193–5).
[11] Cf. Cic. *Har. resp.* 24: *in Palatio . . . ante templum in ipso Matris Magnae conspectu*; also Arn. *Adv. nat.* 7.33.3; August. *De civ. D.* 2.4.
[12] The sources on the date of the introduction of this festival are confusing and alternate between 241 and 238 BCE; the combined evidence makes 238 BCE the more likely date (for the evidence and discussion see Bernstein 1998: 206–23).

the brothers and plebeian aediles L. and M. Publicii Malleoli dedicated a
temple to Flora and held games (*Floralia*).[13] The position of the temple on
the Aventine Hill close to the Circus Maximus (cf. Tac. *Ann.* 2.49.1), the
ritual and the reason for the establishment of the cult are similar to those
for Ceres. Probably on account of a pestilence in 174 BCE, annual *Ludi
Florales*, organized by the plebeian aediles, were vowed and first held in 173
BCE (cf. Ov. *Fast.* 5.295–330; Liv. 41.21.5–9). These first games lasted for two
days, presumably 28 and 29 April (cf. Liv. 41.21.11); the festival extended
from 28 April to 3 May in Augustan times (*ludi scaenici*: 28 April – 2 May).

Like other games introduced in this period, *Ludi Florales* were based on
the Greek format and had scenic performances from the beginning. These
seem to have been held originally in the Circus Maximus, which was close
to the Temple of Flora (cf. Tac. *Ann.* 2.49.1; Ps.-Acro on Hor. *Sat.* 2.3.182),
just as performances at *Ludi Megalenses* took place in front of the Temple of
Magna Mater. Scenic performances at *Ludi Florales* were regarded as especially licentious, even obscene, and characteristically presented mimes.[14]

In addition to these regular public festivals, there were occasional festivals. From the middle Republic increasingly, these were not only set up on
behalf of the whole community, but individual commanders and noblemen
could also celebrate games for particular reasons. As attendance at these
festivals was open to everybody, and as they were often subsidized by the
Senate and frequently occurred in connection with military victories or
dedication of temples, they retained an official and public element, though
they were more difficult for the authorities to control.

Indeed, *ludi votivi* vowed by successful commanders are known for
cases of disagreement between the Senate and the individuals who had
vowed them, either on the question of whether these men were qualified
to celebrate *ludi* or, more often, on financial matters (cf. e.g. Liv. 36.36.1–2;
39.5.7–10). This suggests that these games especially were not only religious
affairs, but also liable to be exploited for personal self-display. This coincides
with attempts by the Senate to limit the sumptuousness of these games and
the amount of money spent.

---

[13] Cf. Vell. Pat. 1.14.8; Plin. *HN* 18.286; Tac. *Ann.* 2.49.1; Varro, *Ling.* 5.158; Ov. *Fast.* 5.279–94.
[14] Cf. Ov. *Fast.* 4.946; 5.183; 5.347–8; Val. Max. 2.10.8; Sen. *Ep.* 97.8; Mart. 1, pr.; Auson. *Ecl.* 16.25–6;
August. *De civ. D.* 2.27; *Cons. ev.* 1.33.51; *Ep.* 91.5; Arn. *Adv. nat.* 3.23.3; Lactant. *Div. inst.* 1.20.10;
Schol. on Juv. 6.250; Tert. *De spect.* 17.3. Wiseman (1999: 200) emphasizes 'that Flora's games were
like the other dramatic festivals in providing an opportunity for the creation and re-creation of the
Romans' concepts of their gods, their city, and their past' through the performances of mimes; this
is a development from his belief that most Roman drama (scripted and unscripted) refers to the
Romans' own mythology and history (see ch. 3.2 and n. 44). However, there is no clear evidence for
this particular characteristic of mimes.

In the late Republic two further regular public festivals were added: *Ludi Victoriae (Sullanae)* and *Ludi Victoriae Caesaris*. Sulla's games were to celebrate his victory over the Samnites, won on 1 November 82 BCE near Porta Collina, and to commit it to public memory (cf. Vell. Pat. 2.27.6; Ps.-Asc. on Cic. *Verr.* 1.10.31 [p. 217 St.]). This festival became regular in 81 BCE, and it lasted from 26 October to 1 November in imperial times (with games in the circus on the last day). It saw performances not only of tragedies and comedies, but also of Atellanae and mimes. This event commemorated both the military achievement of the Roman people and Sulla's leading role. Thus, for the first time a regular festival also celebrated an individual and was dedicated not to one of the major divinities, but to a personified entity. The games were probably called *Ludi Victoriae* initially, and the epithet *Sullanae* was added later to distinguish them from Caesar's games.

Caesar celebrated occasional *Ludi Veneris Genetricis* in 46 BCE, when he dedicated a temple to Venus (cf. Serv. on Verg. *Aen.* 1.720; App. *B Civ.* 2.102.424; 3.28.107; Cass. Dio 43.22.2–23.5); he thereby probably vied with the games given at the opening of Pompey's 'theatre temple' (see ch. 2.4). Besides, Caesar introduced *Ludi Victoriae Caesaris* in 45 BCE, rivalling Sulla in this case; they ran from 20 to 30 July, thus immediately preceding regular festivities at Victoria's Temple on 1 August.[15]

These festivals combined to form an increasingly extended 'social season' running (theoretically) from spring to autumn.[16] The gradual expansion of the festival season over the centuries meant that dramatic performances started from small beginnings at *Ludi Romani*, but soon gained ground: three further festivals, *Ludi plebeii*, *Ludi Ceriales* and *Ludi Apollinares*, came into being and the number of days for scenic performances at *Ludi Romani* had already increased during the active period of the first playwrights, Livius Andronicus and Naevius. The occasions for dramatic performances thereby multiplied and amounted to at least eight days annually in 208 BCE. When Plautus, Ennius, Caecilius and Pacuvius began their careers, there were already four regular festivals; during their lifetimes two further festivals, *Ludi Megalenses* and *Ludi Florales*, were added. Terence, Afranius, Accius and subsequent writers found a fully established structure of six

---

[15] Cf. Vell. Pat. 2.56.1; Suet. *Iul.* 39.1–4; App. *B Civ.* 2.102.423; Cass. Dio 43.22.3; 43.23.1; 43.23.3–4; 43.23.6; Plut. *Caes.* 55.4; Cic. *Fam.* 12.18.2; Sen. *Controv.* 7.3.9; Gell. *NA* 17.14.1–2; Macrob. *Sat.* 2.7.2–8; 3.15.10.

[16] However, due to an irregular and confused system of intercalations until the introduction of the Julian calendar, the calendar year was out of step with the seasons in the second and early first centuries BCE (see Michels 1967: 101–3, 168–72; Gratwick 1982a: 81).

regular festivals. Besides, festivals introduced at later stages included scenic performances from the outset and favoured scenic over circus games; also, the number of days for each festival continued to increase.[17] Moreover, opportunities for dramatic performances could grow further by occasional events and the custom of *instauratio*, i.e. the repetition of a festival as a whole or in part when a religious mistake had occurred (or had been noted deliberately for a particular reason).

Although dramatic performances were part of festivals with a religious background and originally a specific purpose, this apparently did not have immediate consequences for the selection of content or the dramatic genre of plays performed.[18] In principle all types of drama (as well as a variety of different kinds of performances) could be shown at all public festivals. Only for *Ludi Florales* is it attested that performances of mimes were a characteristic feature of this festival; mimes were also shown at *Ludi Victoriae (Sullanae)*. Praetextae dramatizing recent victories are likely to have been performed at festivals connected with their celebration (e.g. vowed by the commander for successful completion), in connection with the dedication of a temple promised during a campaign or at the funeral of the victorious commander.[19]

As for the performance schedule, it is not known how many plays were performed at each festival or on one day reserved for *ludi scaenici*, what the respective proportions for the different dramatic genres were or even whether there were any rules for the distribution of dramatic genres.[20] The fact that in 44 BCE a planned performance of Accius' *Brutus* was replaced by a performance of Accius' *Tereus* at short notice (cf. Cic. *Att.* 16.2.3; 16.5.1; *Phil.* 1.36) indicates (if one can draw conclusions from a single event at a late date in turbulent times) that tragedies and praetextae could be performed in the same slot. When Accius is reported to have said (cf. Cic. *Brut.* 229) that he and Pacuvius each produced a play *isdem aedilibus* ('under the same aediles'), it is not clear whether this implies that tragedies by different dramatists would be shown at the same festival or whether it refers to different festivals organized by the aediles in the same year.

For a few specific plays or works of particular dramatic genres the occasions for their performances are known: at *Ludi plebeii* of 200 BCE the

---

[17] There were about forty-three days of scenic performances per year by the time of Augustus: nine days each at *Ludi Romani* and *Ludi Plebeii*, seven each at *Ludi Apollinares* and *Ludi Ceriales*, six at *Ludi Megalenses*, five at *Ludi Florales*.

[18] See e.g. Blänsdorf 1987: 91; Beacham 1991: 21.   [19] See Flower 1995; Manuwald 2001a: 110–19.

[20] See Flower 1995: 172–3. Some Plautine prologues (esp. Plaut. *Amph.* 50–63; *Capt.* 60–2) indicate that there was a certain expectation as to the dramatic genre of the play at least by the time the performance was about to start (see also ch. 5.3).

plebeian aediles Cn. Baebius Tamphilus and L. Terentius Massiliota had Plautus' *Stichus* performed (cf. Did. on Plaut. *Stich.*; Liv. 31.50.3). Ennius is reported to have died just after a performance of his *Thyestes* at *Ludi Apollinares* of 169 BCE, organized by the praetor urbanus C. Sulpicius Gallus (cf. Cic. *Brut.* 78; *MRR* 1.424); another performance of a tragedy at *Ludi Apollinares* is attested by Cicero for 59 BCE (cf. Cic. *Att.* 2.19.3). Varro talks of a praetexta performed at *Ludi Apollinares* (cf. Varro, *Ling.* 6.18). In 44 BCE Accius' praetexta *Brutus* was replaced by his tragedy *Tereus* at the same festival (cf. Cic. *Phil.* 1.36; *Att.* 16.2.3; 16.5.1). Plautus' *Pseudolus* was presented at *Ludi Megalenses* of 191 BCE (cf. Did. on Plaut. *Pseud.*). Four comedies of Terence (*An.*, *Haut.*, *Eun.*, *Hec. I*) were also originally given at *Ludi Megalenses* (cf. Did. on Ter. *An.*, *Haut.*, *Eun.*, *Hec.*; Donat. on Ter. *An.*, *praef.* 1.6; on *Eun.*, *praef.* 1.6; on *Hec.*, *praef.* 1.6); his *Phormio* was shown at *Ludi Romani* (cf. Did. on Ter. *Phorm.*).[21] Two further comedies of Terence (*Ad.*, *Hec. II*) were performed at the funeral games for L. Aemilius Paul(l)us in 160 BCE (cf. Did. on Ter. *Ad.*, *Hec.*; Donat. on Ter. *Ad.*, *praef.* 1.6; Liv. 31.50.4; 41.28.11; Suet. *Iul.* 84). The tragedy *Thyestes* by L. Varius Rufus was produced as part of the celebrations in 29 BCE after the victory at Actium (cf. Did. in Cod. Paris. 7530 et Casin. 1086 [p. 309 Klotz]). The data proves that tragedies, praetextae and comedies could be shown at various festivals, but does not allow further conclusions on connections between certain plays or dramatic genres and individual festivals.

The significant multiplying of public festivals and their increase in length coincided with developments in the political and social organization, especially Rome's ascent to hegemony in the Mediterranean. The greater number of festivals and the extended length of existing ones may also have had religious aspects; this might have been intended to augment the honour awarded to the gods.[22] In any case the games had political, religious and cultural dimensions.[23] In times of changes and crises, festivals were a convenient means for the political elite to have Rome's position presented both to the Romans themselves and to other peoples; these occasions could demonstrate their attitudes and ideals, thus confirming Rome's national identity as well as its cultural competence and political unity. At the same time, festivals were liable to be exploited as a forum for the nobility, at

---

[21] On the problem of contradictory details in the *didascaliae*, in Donatus (*Ludi Megalenses*: on Ter. *Phorm.*, *praef.* 1.6) and in the manuscript tradition see the overview by Lefèvre in Suerbaum 2002: 236–7.

[22] See Morgan 1990: 26–35.   [23] See Bernstein 1998: 228–9, 248–51; Leigh 2004a: 3.

which they got in contact with the populace and could display themselves in rivalry with their peers (see ch. 2.2).

2.2 ROLE OF MAGISTRATES

The introduction of Greek-style drama at *Ludi Romani* in 240 BCE was a political decision, and festivals continued to constitute public events in the responsibility of the authorities; consequently, there was a close institutional link between politics and poetry from the beginning.[24] Magistrates, who functioned as overseers and coordinators,[25] organized all public festivals. Most were arranged by the curule aediles (*Ludi Romani, Ludi Megalenses*) or the plebeian aediles (*Ludi plebeii, Ludi Ceriales, Ludi Florales*); the urban praetor was responsible for *Ludi Apollinares*.[26] Since all magistracies in Republican Rome were annual, each year saw different officials setting up festivals. This organizational structure exercised a significant influence on the quantity and quality of shows offered. Besides, occasional festivals, such as games at funerals of distinguished citizens or at the dedications of temples vowed by individuals, were run by the respective noblemen.

The organizing magistrates and their colleagues could be present at dramatic performances (cf. Cic. *Sest.* 117). More importantly, they provided venues and commissioned performances of plays.[27] In the middle to late Republic festivals were allocated public funds (*lucar*; cf. Plut. *Quaest. Rom.* 88 [285D]). At least in the late Republic these were typically supplemented from the magistrates' own resources and from those of their political backers and of people under their control. Therefore many scholars believe that

---

[24] See Gold 1987: 41; Gruen 1990: 122–3.

[25] The term *curatores ludorum* for those responsible for organizing the games is attested in Plautus' *Poenulus* (Plaut. *Poen.* 36). The word *conductor* (Plaut. *Asin.* 3; *Trin.* 855; 866) seems to have been used for people who hire others, including actors, to carry out certain tasks; it apparently is not a technical term in the strict sense and not necessarily connected with an official function. Additionally, there is an inscription that defines a person as a *loc(ator) scaenicorum* (*CIL* 6.5819); this term must describe a more permanent job; perhaps it refers to a minor official who was responsible for making arrangements for *ludi scaenici*. On all those terms see González Vázquez 2001a, though neat distinctions are problematic in view of the meagre evidence.

[26] While in the beginning a king or a consul seems to have presided over the public festivals, the organization was passed on to junior magistrates in the fourth century BCE (see also ch. 2.1). This structure must have been adapted in the mid-third century when performances of Greek-style drama were added to the festivals (see Bernstein 1998: e.g. 73, 117, 119). According to Donatus, however, the curule aediles were in charge of *Ludi Megalenses, ludi funebres, Ludi plebeii* and *Ludi Apollinares* (Donat. *Com.* 8.2). For *curatores ludorum* of the individual festivals see the discussion in Bernstein 1998 (with the evidence and further references); on the aediles' *cura ludorum* in the Republican period see Kunkel and Wittmann 1995: 504–9.

[27] On the role of magistrates, their duties and aims see e.g. Bernstein 1998: 142–7, 268–71, 281–2, 298–308; Leach 2004: 101–2.

mass entertainment sponsored by aspiring young politicians became an important political factor as these men hoped to ensure their future careers and to win votes by expenditure on games.[28] However, this view has been challenged on several grounds: the known careers of Republican magistrates provide no evidence for a connection between magnificent games and smooth careers; the influential members of the voting assemblies were not identical with audiences in the theatre; it is questionable whether specific games given earlier would be remembered at the time of voting; annual magistrates would not be interested in acquiring dramatic scripts for future use; the aediles' involvement showed public interest in the encouragement and subsidy of dramatic performances; and it was the poets who hoped to profit from a favourable reception by audiences.[29]

Although not all of these points are unequivocal, and it is idealistic to portray magistrates as entirely disinterested in the impact of games given by them, it is plausible that in the middle Republic expenditure on games was not such an essential factor for the standing of public figures as often assumed. It had, however, become an important event in the late Republic, which is indicated by more and more ornate theatre buildings as well as by remarks in Cicero. Even if still not directly relevant to a political career, lavish and magnificent games seem to have been a significant element in ensuring a nobleman's standing and to have been expected from magistrates;[30] this agrees with the increase in individual self-presentation from the early second century BCE. This development reaches its climax with the dedication of the first permanent theatre in Rome in 55 BCE, which inscribes the memory of a politician in the minds of the populace.

Thus, in the first century BCE festivals were apparently one area in which magistrates could try to outdo predecessors, colleagues and rivals and thereby reinforce their own positions. In the last decades of the Republic, in anticipation of the Principate with its predominance of single men, extravagant festivals focusing on one magistrate, such as *Ludi Victoriae (Sullanae)*, *Ludi Victoriae Caesaris* and the sumptuous spectacles at the inauguration of Pompey's stone theatre (see ch. 2.4), are obvious acts of self-display and attempts at cementing an individual's extraordinary position.

---

[28] See e.g. Balsdon 1969: 262; Nicolet 1980: 363; G. Williams 1982: 5–6; Gold 1987: 41; Gilula 1989a: 101; Beacham 1999: 3–4, 2007: 217; Bell 2004: 190–1; Flower 2004: 324; Leach 2004: 101.

[29] See esp. Gruen 1992: 188–95.

[30] Cf. e.g. Cic. *Q. Fr.* 1.1.26; 3.6.6; *Off.* 2.55–60; *Dom.* 111–12; Asc. on Cic. *Scaur.* [p. 18 C.]; Liv. 25.2.8; Suet. *Iul.* 10; Plut. *Sull.* 5.2; Cass. Dio 37.8.

However, since magistrates financed an event open to the whole populace and contributed to pleasing the gods, holding games was not necessarily regarded as a negative form of ambition and influence; this was probably the reason why the system had the potential to run out of control and could not simply be abolished.[31] As the games became more and more extravagant and consequently required larger and larger funds over the course of the Republic, magistrates and commanders might put pressure on conquered peoples, provinces and allies to meet the costs.[32] They also demanded additional revenues from the Senate; but the Senate intervened and decreed limits for the total amount to be spent, particularly on occasional games held by individuals (cf. Liv. 39.5.7–10; 40.44.9–12).[33] Eventually, rules were set up to limit excesses and to prevent candidates for political offices from using games to win the people's favour. For instance, Cicero as consul introduced a law (*Lex Tullia de ambitu* of 63 BCE) that prevented people who were standing for offices from giving gladiatorial games within the two years preceding their candidature (cf. Cic. *Vat.* 37; *Sest.* 133; Schol. Bob. ad loc. [p. 140 St.]; Cic. *Har. resp.* 56).

As part of their duties as organizers of the festivals, magistrates bought plays from playwrights (perhaps on the recommendation of impresarios) or from impresarios, who had acquired them from poets (see ch. 2.6). Whether there were 'standard rates' per play is unclear, but apparently magistrates were not tied to fixed sums; otherwise Terence's *Eunuchus* could not have earned the poet an unprecedented high amount (cf. Suet./Donat. *Vita Ter.* 3; Donat. on Ter. *Eun.*, *praef.* 1.6*). At the festivals magistrates could award a palm frond as a prize to successful actors or other artists, whence officials might be liable to corruption according to Plautus (see ch. 2.6).

Since politicians must have aimed at performances that would be well received, they might have looked for plays with a strong impact and uncontroversial content or turned to a poet with a proven success record. Yet it is uncertain whether or to what extent magistrates gained information about plays prior to purchase, as are their criteria for selection. The prologue to Terence's *Eunuchus* (Ter. *Eun.* 19b–22) implies that in this case magistrates were given a preview, which was the only way of getting to know a drama in the absence of multiple copies of scripts. However, this event seems to have taken place after the aediles had purchased the play, and it is unknown

[31] See also Beacham 1999: 35–6.
[32] Tacitus dates the beginning of the custom of making the games more elaborate to the conquest of Achaia and Asia (Tac. *Ann.* 14.21.1).
[33] See Balsdon 1969: 262.

how they reacted and whether their reactions had any influence on the final shape of the play.[34] According to the Vita, Terence was asked to recite his first play before Caecilius when he was about to give it to the aediles (Suet./Donat. *Vita Ter.* 3); if this contains any indication of general practices, one might infer that magistrates drew on the expert advice of senior poets when judging newcomers. According to Terence's prologues, both Caecilius Statius and Terence experienced difficulties with being accepted by audiences and opponents at the start of their careers, but these problems occurred when their plays had already been accepted for performance (Ter. *Hec.* 9–57).

Irrespective of details of the selection process, there may have been some correlation between the shape of a play and the officials in charge of the performances. For instance, Terence's *Hecyra* (second performance) and *Adelphoe* were given at *Ludi funebres* for L. Aemilius Paul(l)us in 160 BCE, organized by his natural sons; the topics of education and of the relationship between generations might be seen as particularly suitable for such an occasion.[35] Ennius' *Thyestes* includes considerations on natural bodies and was first performed in the praetorship of C. Sulpicius Gallus, who had an interest in astronomy (see ch. 5.2). Similar connections can be inferred for some revival performances (see ch. 2.9).

The most remarkable intervention in theatre business on the part of the authorities occurred in 115 BCE: according to a notice in Cassiodorus' chronicle, the censors L. Caecilius Metellus (Diadematus) and Cn. Domitius Ahenobarbus banned 'the performing arts' (*ars ludicra*) from the city of Rome with the exception of 'a Latin piper with a singer' (*Latinus tibicen cum cantore*), and also a performance consisting of music and dance called *ludus talarius*.[36] The censors' motives are disputed, as

---

[34] On this scene and its implications see Gilula 1989b: 96–7; Goldberg 2005b: 48–50. This incident suggests that other professionals could try to sneak into such pre-performances and use them as a forum for comments (Ter. *Eun.* 19–26).

[35] See Leigh 2004a: 158–91.

[36] Cf. Cass. *Chron.*, pp. 131–2 *MGH AA* ii.2: *his conss. L. Metellus et Cn. Domitius censores artem ludicram ex urbe removerunt praeter Latinum tibicinem cum cantore et ludum talarium. Ludum talarium* is an almost certain emendation of the corrupt text in Cassiodorus (cf. Mommsen's apparatus). The construction as a whole can be interpreted in different ways: the accusative *ludum talarium*, added by *et*, is most frequently seen as a continuation of the *praeter*-phrase and hence understood as something that was allowed to remain together with *Latinus tibicen cum cantore*; yet it could also continue the object of the predicate *removerunt* and be another element that was banned, along with *ars ludicra*. Since others of the few references to *ludus talarius* suggest that it was something base and licentious, the second interpretation, grammatically possible in a text in the style of Cassiodorus' chronicle, is perhaps the more likely one (see Leppin 1992: 186–8). Even though the syntactic structure of the clause is not unambiguous, it is clear that *Latinus tibicen cum cantore* refers to two categories of people who are involved in stage performances, whereas *ludus talarius* describes a type

is the question of what forms of performances were covered by this order.[37]

Mere financial reasons (i.e. the intention of abolishing a costly practice) seem unlikely; an attempt at eliminating an institution or elements of an institution causing offence is more plausible. Since at this point in time the dramatic genres of crepidata, praetexta, palliata and togata were gradually falling into decline, shows in the theatre must have consisted mainly of revival performances of plays of those dramatic genres, productions of new Atellanae and mimes as well as (presumably non-dramatic) performances of dances. This set-up suggests that the censors might have objected to events on stage on two grounds.

Firstly, there is an anecdote in Fronto about a censor who forbade *ludus talarius*; and this story is likely to refer to the same incident: this censor banned *ludus talarius* since he found it difficult to maintain his dignity when he walked past a performance and not to start dancing to the music himself (Fronto, *Orat.* 10 [p. 157 v.d.H.]). This suggests, together with other mentions of *ludus talarius* (cf. Cic. *Att.* 1.16.3; *Off.* 1.150; Quint. *Inst.* 11.3.58), that officials and intellectuals regarded it as undignified, licentious dancing. This would entail that the censors banned it on grounds of morality and impropriety.

Secondly, some forms of the performing arts might have been regarded as a threat to social and political stability. Apart from a general tendency towards the inclusion of topical references in drama, the incidents of the poets Accius and Lucilius experiencing 'criticism by name' (*nominatim laedere*) by mime actors on stage are significant: they are likely to have occurred around 115 BCE (generally dated to 136 and before 103 BCE), judging from the coincidence of the lifetimes of Accius (*c.* 170–80 BCE) and Lucilius (*c.* 180–103/2 BCE) with that of the judges P. Mucius Scaevola (cos. 133 BCE) and <C.> Caelius, who presided in the poets' cases against those actors (cf. *Auct. ad Her.* 1.24; 2.19; see ch. 5.2). Such events may be indicative of the situation in the run-up to the censors' intervention. Because of some performances potentially developing elements contradicting Roman morals or including politically critical remarks, the censors may have chosen a drastic and radical remedy.[38]

---

of performance. Suerbaum (2002: 54), however, interprets this remark as indicating the involvement of three kinds of people in stage performances.

[37] For various interpretations of the censor's action see e.g. Frank 1931: 12–13; W. M. Green 1933: 302; Préaux 1963; P. L. Schmidt 1989: 91–2 n. 29, 94–5; Wiseman 1994: 78; Jory 1995.

[38] Frassinetti (1953: 96–7) observes that there were several instances of 'scandal' in the last decades of the second century BCE and mentions the experiences of Accius and Lucilius as well as the intervention of the censors as examples.

Such a reason for the censors' move – the aim of preventing potentially controversial or insulting statements from being made publicly on stage and of eliminating licentious spectacles – would agree with the moral jurisdiction wielded by censors. What was allowed to remain seems to have been sober, Roman performances of music and song, lacking the potential for harmful criticism.[39] However, the censors' intervention did not have a noticeable effect since no radical change in the history of Roman drama is recognizable at around 115 BCE: the dramatist Accius was still present in Rome after this date since Cicero claims to have heard certain details from him (Cic. *Brut.* 107); there is ample evidence for revival performances of serious and light dramas in the Ciceronian period (see ch. 2.9); the dramatic genres of Atellana and mime flourished only after this date; and revival performances of tragedies and comedies as well as mime (and Atellana) performances in the first century BCE are notorious for being exploited in the light of the contemporary political situation. In this instance, therefore, the decisions of the political establishment did not have a lasting impact on the development of theatrical performances in Republican Rome.

2.3 RELIGIOUS ASPECTS

In addition to being cultural and political events, Roman *ludi*, like other elements of Roman public life, had a religious or ritual dimension.[40] Most *ludi* were introduced in religious contexts and were held in honour of a god, to make a god propitious, to fulfil a vow or to offer thanks to a god (cf. e.g. Cic. *Cat.* 3.8.20; Liv. 6.42.12; Lactant. *Div. inst.* 6.20.34–6). Dramatic performances were therefore integrated into a religious context; their geographical and temporal proximity to religious ceremonies (cf. Vitr. 5.3.1) visualized this connection (see ch. 2.4).

Festivals began with a 'festival procession' (*pompa circensis*) and ritual preparations, adopted from the Etruscans and then modified under the influence of Greek customs. According to the description in Dionysius of Halicarnassus, this was a procession from the Capitol to the Circus Maximus, and it included magistrates, contestants at the games, troupes of dancers and musicians, and people carrying incense, perfumes and precious objects from the temple treasuries and statues of gods (Dion. Hal. *Ant. Rom.* 7.72; Tert. *De spect.* 7.2). Ritual seats and statues of gods and goddesses

---

[39] Leppin (1992: 160) explains the fact that certain types of performers were allowed to remain in Rome by religious reasons. These might have played a part, so as to guarantee that performances at religious festivals could continue.

[40] See e.g. Hanson 1959: 1–4.

were brought to the theatre, where they were placed in prestigious positions so that the divinities could 'watch' the performances.[41]

The architectural structure of 'theatre temples', such as Pompey's stone theatre, reinforced the connection: priest and/or officials could offer a sacrifice at the temple above the auditorium and then get down to the orchestra below the temple, watched by the audience (cf. Suet. *Claud.* 21.1). Even prior to the establishment of permanent theatres in Rome, dramatic performances were often closely connected to the temple of the tutelary divinity with the performance area located in front of a temple (see ch. 2.4).

On the other hand a specific connection between gods honoured by particular festivals and the contents of plays seems not to have existed.[42] When the penultimate line of Plautus' *Truculentus* says: 'Applaud for Venus' sake: it is her tutelage that this play enjoys.' (Plaut. *Truc.* 967: *Veneris causa adplaudite: eius haec in tutelast fabula.*), this does not mean that Venus is the tutelary deity of the festival, but rather that she is the goddess relevant to the play's amatory motifs. However, independent of the festival context, plays may discuss religious ideas and have gods take part in the action.

The inherent religious character of performances at Roman festivals might be one of the reasons why the church fathers and other early Christian writers vehemently opposed theatre and spectacles (cf. e.g. Lactant. *Div. inst.* 6.20.32–6; Arn. *Adv. nat.* 7.33; Tert. *De spect.*).[43]

2.4 THEATRE BUILDINGS

While the site of the Circus Maximus, where circus games took place, was improved throughout the second century BCE,[44] there was no comparable building activity as regards venues for scenic performances. In fact, resistance to the erection of permanent theatres in Rome continued for a long time (cf. e.g. Tert. *De spect.* 10.4). Theatres therefore remained temporary structures until almost the end of the Republican period, although the people of Rome must have been familiar with permanent theatres in Greece, Sicily and other parts of Italy.[45]

---

[41] On these rituals see e.g. Taylor 1935; Hanson 1959: 126–46; Bernstein 1998: 254–64; Fless 2004.
[42] See also Franko 2001: 152.
[43] See also Leppin 1992: 160. On the attitudes of Christian writers to the theatre see Dox 2004.
[44] On the Circus Maximus during the Republic see Humphrey 1986: 67–72.
[45] A similar development applies to gladiatorial combats: the first amphitheatre in Rome was built only in 30 BCE and the famous Colosseum not dedicated until 80 CE (on early venues for gladiatorial combats see Staccioli 1961; Jory 1986b; on the evolution of gladiatorial fights in Rome and the development of their venues see Welch 2007).

This results in the paradoxical situation that permanent theatres in Rome started to be erected at a time when scenic games consisted mainly of revivals of 'classic' plays and of new pieces of dramatic genres that included a large amount of spectacle, while during the most creative period of Republican stage drama there was no permanent stone theatre in Rome and plays were acted on temporary wooden stages.[46] However, 'temporary' in this context literally means 'erected for a limited period of time' and is not to be equated with 'simple': the structures evolved over the centuries, and in the late Republic theatre buildings were rather elaborate. For the absence of a permanent theatre in Rome throughout most of the Republican period was not due to an inability on the part of the Romans to build such structures, but rather the consequence of a deliberate decision against them.[47]

Initially, different performance venues throughout Rome were used for the various festivals. All of these were not specifically set up as theatres throughout the year, but were turned into theatrical spaces for a limited period of time (cf. Vitr. 5.5.7).[48] The temporary and changing nature of the theatrical spaces must have influenced the impact of dramatic performances;[49] some references to Roman reality in Republican plays may have been determined by the position of the stage at a drama's first performance.[50] Also, the venues were not reserved for drama only, but various sorts of entertainments could apparently take place in the same performance space (cf. Ter. *Hec.* 39–42).[51]

---

[46] See e.g. Frézouls 1974: 35, 1982: 344–5.

[47] On the location and structure of early stages, the architectural history of the Roman theatre and its eventual developed structure see e.g. Saunders 1913; Fensterbusch 1934: 1410–21; Rumpf 1950; Duckworth 1952: 79–88; Hanson 1959; Bieber 1961: esp. 167–89; Beare 1964: 171–83 and app.; Frézouls 1974, 1982, 1989: 338–41; Lauter 1976; Blänsdorf 1978: 122–5, 1987: 90–8; Brothers 1989: 98–112; Blume 1991: 110–11, 122–5; Gruen 1992: 205–10; Bernstein 1998: 291–8; Beacham 1999: 24–35, 51–74; Dumont 2000; Marshall 2006: 31–48; for a collection of evidence and archaeological descriptions of structures and distribution of Roman theatres see Sear 2006; for overviews of theatre buildings in Sicily, Italy and Rome see Mitens 1988, 1993; Courtois 1989, 1992 (see those works for further references to primary literary and to archaeological sources as well as for additional bibliography).

[48] See Marshall 2006: 36, 47.

[49] On the impact of the physical setting on dramatic performances see Carlson 1989: 2, 204–5; on possible methodologies for analysing the influence of the physical setting see Carlson 1989: 10.

[50] On the basis of an examination of the *choragus* speech in Plautus' *Curculio* (Plaut. *Curc.* 462–86), Moore (1991: 359) concludes that 'there is every indication that he speaks from a stage just south of the *comitium*, facing east', since then 'almost everything on the tour would be visible to the choragus and his audience, and spectators would actually be watching the play from some of the locations cited'.

[51] See Gilula 1989a: 101. Originally, gladiatorial combats at funeral games were typically held in the Forum (cf. e.g. Liv. 23.30.15; 31.50.4; see also n. 45 above); since funeral games could include dramatic performances, these are likely to have taken place in the same venue (see Saunders 1913: 93–4; generally Jory 1986b).

The earliest venues for dramatic performances seem to have been the Circus, the Forum or the space in front of the temple of the god of the festival. The Forum is likely to have been used particularly for funeral games and for *Ludi Romani*. A large number of identifiable temporary (as well as permanent) theatres in Rome have an architectural relation to a temple in that the stage is being erected in front of a temple and the monumental access to the temple, towering over the theatre, functions as auditorium (cf. Tert. *De spect.* 10.5; August. *De civ. D.* 2.26).[52] At the early venues, the flights of steps leading up to a temple or the tiers of the circus could be used as an auditorium providing seats for spectators, while the stage area was put up for each festival (cf. Cic. *Har. resp.* 24; for later stone theatres cf. Gell. *NA* 10.1.7; Suet. *Claud.* 21.1). Stage and auditorium seem to have been regarded as separate structural parts in Italy, and the erection of a formal auditorium was not required in order to create a recognized performance space.[53]

A connection between theatre and temple is clearly attested for *Ludi Megalenses*: Cicero states that performances took place in front of the Temple of Magna Mater on the Palatine (Cic. *Har. resp.* 24), where a simple construction of steps around the altar has been unearthed; Plautus' *Pseudolus* is known to have been performed on the occasion of the dedication of this temple in 191 BCE (cf. Did. on Plaut. *Pseud.*; cf. also Cic. *Sen.* 50).[54] The set-up of a 'theatre temple' defined dramatic presentations as part of a religious ceremony and allowed a direct connection between cult rites and scenic performances. That a close relationship between temple, theatre and games was assumed in late Republican and early Augustan times is proved by the proem to Vergil's *Georgics 3*, since the poet envisages such a combination even for a symbolic structure and fictitious event in honour of Octavian/Augustus (Verg. *Georg.* 3.1–48).

Several attempts to erect permanent theatres in Rome throughout the second century BCE, the most productive period of Republican drama, failed (cf. Tert. *De spect.* 10.4): in 179 BCE the censor M. Aemilius Lepidus commissioned an auditorium and a stage (*theatrum et proscaenium*) close to the Temple of Apollo (cf. Liv. 40.51.3), probably intended as a permanent

---

[52] On 'theatre temples' see Hanson 1959; on connections between the structure of Roman theatres, cult practices and performance conventions see von Hesberg 2005: 150–61.

[53] In late Republican and early imperial times individuals, eager to provide impressive performances, might organize not only a variety of performances, but even multiple events in all areas of the city (cf. Suet. *Iul.* 39.1; *Aug.* 43.1). Special splendour could be achieved by giving spectacles in venues that had never been used for that purpose (cf. Suet. *Claud.* 21.1).

[54] On the archaeological aspects see von Hesberg 2005: 151; on the performative and literary aspects see Goldberg 1998 (both providing further references).

(possibly wooden) building for use at *Ludi Apollinares*. This initiative happened simultaneously with the addition of a porticus to the temple itself by order of the other censor, M. Fulvius Nobilior (cf. Liv. 40.51.6). Therefore the whole complex was presumably designed to be transformed into a 'theatre temple', as they were emerging elsewhere in Italy at the time; this is further suggested by the fact that both censors of 179 BCE took an interest in temples and their surroundings, as shown by their other construction projects (cf. Liv. 40.51.2–9).[55] If so, the first attested attempt at a proper theatre building in Rome would have had the basic structure realized by the first permanent theatre erected by Pompey more than 100 years later.[56]

There is no evidence on what happened to this attempt at theatre building in 179 BCE. But if such a theatre was commenced or erected at all, it must have been pulled down again five years later, when another attempt was made. In 174 BCE, the censors Q. Fulvius Flaccus and A. Postumius Albinus pursued an even more ambitious project: as part of their overall building programme, which also included improvements to the Circus, they commissioned a stage to be provided for aediles and praetors (cf. Liv. 41.27.6); hence it must have been envisaged as a multi-functional structure, whose intended location is not known.[57] As further plans were considered soon, this project again either did not materialize or was demolished during construction or soon after completion. The building would have provided a permanent structure available to all magistrates holding games and apparently at all kinds of festivals; there would not have been a close connection between dramatic performances and the gods honoured by a festival. That such a project could be planned at all suggests that a physical connection between the shrine of a god and the venue for dramatic performances could be disregarded in favour of practical considerations, while at the same time this might be one of the reasons why this project did not come to fruition.

The censors of 154 BCE, M. Valerius Messalla and C. Cassius Longinus, made another attempt at erecting a theatre, probably along the south-western slope of the Palatine (cf. Vell. Pat. 1.15.3: *a Lupercali in Palatium versus theatrum*); yet on the initiative of the ex-consul and ex-censor P. Cornelius Scipio Nasica (Corculum) the Senate decreed shortly afterwards that the theatre or auditorium (*theatrum*), whose building was already well

---

[55] See Goldberg 1998: 10 (with references).   [56] See Stamper 2005: 55–6.

[57] The wording in Livy (*censores... locaverunt... scaenam aedilibus praetoribusque praebendam*, 'the censors contracted for a stage to be provided for aediles and praetors') does not permit the conclusion that the performance area could be used by several troupes of actors during one festival (but so Marshall 2006: 49).

advanced, should be demolished. According to Livy this intervention had the effect that for a while the populace had to watch the games standing (Liv. *Epit.* 48; cf. also App. *B Civ.* 1.28.125).[58] This consequence may be connected with a Senate decree recorded in Valerius Maximus, saying that in the city of Rome and within a radius of one Roman mile no seating structures for games (*subsellia*) were to be erected, so that mental relaxation would go together with the virility of a standing posture appropriate to the Roman people.[59] Such an intention agrees with a critical remark in Cicero that the Greeks conducted all public business through the irresponsibility of a popular assembly seated in the theatre (Cic. *Flacc.* 16).

There may have been a fourth attempt at the erection of a permanent theatre in Rome in 107 BCE by the consul L. Cassius Longinus; the well-advanced construction work was destroyed the following year by his successor Q. Servilius Caepio, as the description in Appian, confused and conflated with accounts of the similar failure in 154 BCE, suggests (App. *B Civ.* 1.28.125; cf. also Vell. Pat. 1.15.3).[60] This development could be explained by the anti-senatorial political atmosphere of 107 BCE and the senatorial reaction in the following year; Appian mentions fear of political conflict and the effects of Greek luxury as reasons for destruction. At any rate such events in 107/6 BCE, a few years after the censorial intervention in 115 BCE (see ch. 2.2), would indicate that resentment against the performing arts as well as political interventions on that account continued.

Reasons for the peculiar attitude of Roman officials towards a permanent theatre can only be inferred on the basis of those incidents and the general role of the theatre in Roman society.[61] At any rate it was not the performances that they opposed, but the permanence of physical structures. Whereas for some of the unsuccessful building projects a stage is at issue, others are concerned with *theatrum* and *subsellia*, i.e. constructions for spectators.

Modern scholars generally regard the latter detail as the crucial one: what the authorities fought against was the erection of a permanent enclosed space providing seats for the populace. The nobility is thought to have

---

[58] For an analysis of the ancient sources referring to this incident see Sordi 1988; also Mitens 1993: 98.

[59] Cf. Val. Max. 2.4.2; also Vell. Pat. 1.15.3; Tac. *Ann.* 14.20; App. *B Civ.* 1.28.125; August. *De civ. D.* 1.31, 2.5; Oros. 4.21.4; Tert. *De spect.* 10.4; *Apol.* 6.2; *MRR* 1.449. On seating in the Roman theatre see ch. 2.8.

[60] Cf. North 1992; Goldberg 1998: 11.

[61] That wooden structures would have been a fire hazard in the densely populated centre of Rome (so Bieber 1961: 168) is unlikely as a major reason for the regular destruction of theatre buildings, since there were other wooden structures in the city of Rome, and the Romans would have been able to build theatres in stone at an earlier date if they had wanted something safe and durable.

feared that such a structure would enable potentially explosive political assemblies and provide a forum for idleness and immorality.[62] Against such a view it can be argued that a stone theatre is not an indispensable requisite for holding assemblies independent of scenic performances and that in the late Republic dramatic performances themselves turned into events with a political dimension (see ch. 2.9). Besides, in Rome the Forum remained the dominant political sphere and other spaces were not used for political assemblies.[63]

Financial reasons or opposition to the influx of Hellenistic culture are not satisfactory explanations either, because a substantial amount of money was spent on temporary stages as well as on other elements of the festivals (cf. e.g. Tac. *Ann.* 14.21.2). Some scholars, therefore, have seen this expenditure as the reason for temporary stages, as it allowed organizers to be appreciated for their generosity towards popular entertainment.[64] At the same time the dismantling prevented the commemoration of any individual at a key site of the political community and ensured that the spaces returned to political or religious business once a festival was over.[65]

Another position is that a permanent theatre would have contradicted the principle of an annually renewed responsibility for scenic games by alternating magistrates, since it would discontinue the giving of 'annual notice that the ruling class held decisive authority in the artistic sphere' and convey the impression that drama was 'an unshakable institution, no longer dependent upon the resolve of magistrates and the verdict of the aristocracy'.[66] Even if political decisions on the festivals were designed also to strengthen the ideals and the standing of the nobility, this theory does not entirely explain the paradox; for the festivals did not consist of scenic performances only, and magistrates had no difficulty with improvements to the site of the Circus Maximus.

Possible political reasons notwithstanding, a more plausible explanation is perhaps the hypothesis that a permanent theatre would have interfered with religious rites: it would have prevented the holding of performances in front of the temples of the gods of the various festivals or in the Forum at the heart of the community (unless permanent theatres were built in every possible location). Resistance to a permanent structure therefore could be

---

[62] See e.g. Rumpf 1950: 41–5; Frézouls 1974: 39–40, 1982: 355–6, 1983; Nicolet 1980: 363; Beacham 1991: 66–7; Mitens 1993: 98; Boyle 2006: 22; Sear 2006: 56; critically Gruen 1992: 208–9; Goldberg 1998: 2.

[63] See Rawson (1985) 1991: 472–3; Hülsemann 1987: 137–40.

[64] See Beacham 1999: 30–1. [65] See Bell 2004: 182.

[66] So Gruen 1992: 209–10; see also Bernstein 1998: 296–7; Feldherr 1998: 177; Boyle 2006: 22; sceptically Goldberg 1998: 2; Bell 2004: 182.

an attempt at preserving traditional civic and religious customs as well as cult rites.[67] A close association of temples and theatres is obvious for stone theatres, and it reappears in several descriptions of (potential) theatre buildings.[68] Even later, when permanent theatres had become a familiar feature of Rome, Quintilian says that the theatre may be called 'some sort of temple of this ritual' (*cum theatrum veluti quoddam illius sacri templum vocabimus*), and that consequently religion and honouring of the gods would play a role in advisory speeches about building theatres or founding games (Quint. *Inst.* 3.8.28–9).[69]

One may object that the Romans could have had permanent stone theatres in front of temples earlier, and this would not have contradicted religious customs. However, the notion of celebrating annual festivals might have been an additional significant motive, even if not in the strict political sense: erecting a stage anew each year for a limited period of time set these days apart as special occasions in honour of the respective god, visible even beyond the actual performances.

Although theatre structures in Rome remained temporary almost till the end of the Republican period, the continuous development towards spectacle affected both the physical appearance of theatre buildings and the preference for spectacular effects within individual plays or for more sensational dramatic genres.[70] The first century BCE saw imposing theatre buildings that displayed the presiding magistrate's power and generosity; they also demonstrated the standing of the Roman people (for a later period cf. Tac. *Ann.* 13.45.3): organizing magistrates had, for instance, columns of marble put up, movable stages built, stages adorned with precious statues or covered with ivory, silver and gold, stage equipment made out of precious metals or the auditorium fitted with awnings against the sun (cf. e.g. Val. Max. 2.4.6). The climax of this development towards theatrical extravaganza for temporary structures was reached in 58 BCE with the gigantic structure of the curule aedile M. Aemilius Scaurus (cf. e.g. Plin. *HN* 34.36; 36.5–6; 36.113–15).[71]

---

[67] See Bernstein 1998: 297–8; Goldberg 1998.

[68] The locations of both the failed attempt at a permanent theatre in 179 BCE (cf. Liv. 40.51.3: *theatrum et proscaenium ad Apollinis*) and the later Theatre of Marcellus (cf. *Mon. Anc.* 21 [4.22–3]: *ad aedem Apollinis*) are defined as close to the Temple of Apollo; vice versa the *Fasti* identify the Temple of Apollo as *ad theatrum Marcelli* (cf. *CIL* 1², pp. 215, 252; see Hanson 1959: 29).

[69] See Balsdon 1969: 254–5.

[70] See Courtois 1989: 98, 304. On the effect of changes in theatre architecture on dramatic works in Greece see N. J. Lowe 2008: 65, 67–9.

[71] For further examples and the evidence see e.g. Fuchs 1987: 3–4; Bernstein 1998: 301–3. The revolving theatre of C. Scribonius Curio (erected in 53 BCE for the funeral games in honour of his father)

In 55 BCE Pompey dedicated the first permanent stone theatre in Rome, a monument that had been built after his triumph in 61 BCE; the erection of this structure meant a major change to Roman customs (cf. Tac. *Ann.* 14.20.2).[72] The Theatre of Pompey was soon followed by the Theatre of Balbus (13 BCE) and the Theatre of Marcellus, begun by Caesar and completed and inaugurated by Augustus (13/11 BCE).[73] Pompey's building was a huge complex, including a full theatre and a Temple of Venus (Victrix) on top of the auditorium, whose central wedge of seats formed a monumental staircase leading up to the temple.[74] Thus the traditional arrangement was transferred into stone, a visible connection between theatre building and religious cults was maintained, and no change of custom was required. If, however, this theatre came to be used for all festivals, there would no longer be a connection between the temples of individual gods and games in their honour. The Theatre of Pompey was seen as enormous in size (cf. Plin. *HN* 34.17.39–40; Amm. Marc. 16.10.14) and allegedly had a seating capacity of 40,000 (cf. Plin. *HN* 36.115), while modern estimates talk of 11,000 to 12,000.[75]

Pompey is said to have stressed during the dedication ceremony that he had not built a theatre, but rather a Temple of Venus, whose steps could be used as seats at performances (cf. Tert. *De spect.* 10.5; cf. also Gell. *NA* 10.1.7). This showed Pompey fulfilling religious duties and observing the

---

could be used as two theatres or one amphitheatre (cf. Plin. *HN* 36.116–20). On the difference between early performance venues and the elaborate constructions of the Augustan age cf. also Ov. *Ars* 1.101–8.

[72] On the building and the inaugural ceremonies cf. e.g. Cic. *Fam.* 7.1–4; *Off.* 2.57; *Pis.* 65; Asc. on Cic. *Pis.*; *Pis.* 65 [p. 1; 15–16 C.]; Tac. *Ann.* 14.20.2; Plin. *HN* 7.158; 8.20; Tert. *De spect.* 10.5; Cass. Dio 39.38.1–3; Plut. *Pomp.* 52.5; on a 'second inauguration', after the theatre had been restored after a fire (cf. Tac. *Ann.* 14.20.2), cf. Suet. *Claud.* 21.1. Cicero is mildly critical of the huge amount of money spent on such a structure instead of something more useful (Cic. *Off.* 2.60), while he highlights the lavish opening ceremonies, describing them with utter contempt when commenting in private (Cic. *Fam.* 7.1.1–4; *Pis.* 65). For the archaeological evidence and an analysis of the whole complex see Hanson 1959: 56–79; Fuchs 1987: 5–11; Richardson 1987; Stamper 2005: 84–90; Gagliardo and Packer 2006; Sear 2006: 57–61, 133–5. On Pompey's triumph and various ways of keeping its memory alive see Beard 2007: 7–41; on the theatre and its inauguration see Erasmo 2004: 83–91; Boyle 2006: 155–7; Beard 2007: 22–9; on Cicero's attitude to the events see Beard 2007: 26–9.

[73] On the archaeological details of the Theatre of Marcellus see Sear 2006: 61–5, 135–6; of the Theatre of Balbus see Sear 2006: 65–7, 136–7.

[74] The opening ceremonies are mostly described as inaugurating the theatre (see n. 72 above), but are sometimes defined as the dedication of the Temple of Venus Victrix (cf. Plin. *HN* 8.20), which indicates the close connection between the two. The double function is brought out in Tiro's words transmitted by Gellius (Gell. *NA* 10.1.7): '*cum Pompeius*', inquit, '*aedem Victoriae dedicaturus foret, cuius gradus vicem theatri essent, . . .*' ('when Pompey, he said, was about to dedicate the Temple of Victoria [sic], whose steps also functioned as a theatre, . . .').

[75] For the modern figures see Stamper 2005: 85; Boyle 2006: 150 (with references); Schiesaro (2005: 271) allows for 17,000.

tradition, even though he had not erected a theatre close to the temple of a festival's divinity, but had built a new temple together with a new theatre, dedicated to Venus, a goddess important for Pompey's victories. By having a 'theatre temple' constructed Pompey followed an Italic custom and continued a movement started by the erection of comparable structures just outside Rome slightly earlier, while he might have adapted those under Hellenistic influence.[76]

Even in the mid-first century BCE building a permanent theatre in Rome seems not to have been entirely uncontroversial, as Pompey met with criticism (cf. Tac. *Ann.* 14.20.2). Yet by this time a permanent theatre was apparently tolerated more easily than it had been in the second century.[77] This might be connected with the emergence of powerful individuals in the first century, which eventually led to the establishment of the Principate; i.e. these individuals were able to overcome any remaining resistance to such building projects and were keen to erect lasting memorials to themselves.[78]

After a permanent stone theatre had been built in Rome, temporary stages still continued to be erected, probably again to ensure topographical proximity between dramatic performances and the relevant temple.[79] Fixed stone structures had apparently not become standard overnight, while distinctions were becoming blurred: the 'temporary' theatre of C. Scribonius Curio, erected in 53 BCE (cf. Plin. *HN* 36.116–20), was still in existence and apparently in use two years after its construction (cf. Cic. *Fam.* 8.2.1 [early June 51 BCE]).

---

[76] Cf. Gagliardo and Packer 2006: 93: 'Combining Hellenistic eastern models with Italic fashions, its vast size awed its contemporaries.' Beard (2007: 24) finds it 'hard to say' whether Italic or Hellenistic influence was dominant, but regards a 'combined inspiration' as most likely (26 n. 46 [p. 341]). For comparison with structures outside Rome (Praeneste, Tibur, Gabii) see Stamper 2005: 85–7. The dating of these buildings varies, but their influence (as of similar theatre complexes further away) on theatre design in Rome is likely (see Sear 2006: 44–5; on these structures see also Coarelli 1987: 11–21 [Gabii], 35–84 [Praeneste], 85–112 [Tibur]; Sear 2006: 123–4 [Gabii], 132–3 [Praeneste], 139–40 [Tibur]; for a distinction between several types of 'theatre temples' see Frézouls 1974: 45). It is an attractive hypothesis that *ludi* at Praeneste mentioned by Cicero may have taken place in the local 'theatre temple' (Cic. *Planc.* 63; *Att.* 12.2.2 [46 BCE]). In Greece theatres might be located close to temples in the same precinct, but nowhere has an attempt been made to join theatre and temple to form a single unit (see Hanson 1959: 36–7). According to Plutarch, Pompey took the layout of the theatre at Mytilene, of which he had sketches and plans made, as the model for his own theatre in Rome (Plut. *Pomp.* 42.8–9); however, archaeologists have not yet found any resemblance between the theatre at Mytilene and Pompey's Theatre. Rumpf (1950: 48–50) thinks that an odeion-type structure in Mytilene could have been the model for Pompey (but see Mitens 1993: 100).

[77] See Goldberg 1998: 12–13.

[78] On the political context of the erection of Pompey's Theatre see also Frézouls 1983; Boyle 2006: 152; also, more generally, Gagliardo and Packer 2006: 95.

[79] Cf. arrangements for the secular games in 17 BCE: *CIL* VI 32323 = *ILS* 5050, ll. 100–1, 108–10, 153–4; generally Vitr. 5.5.7; Jos. *AJ* 19.90.

From the earliest times the stage was the essential feature of a Roman theatre; it is called *scaena* or *proscaenium* in Plautus (Plaut. *Amph.* 91; *Capt.* 60; *Poen.* 17; 20; 57; *Pseud.* 568; *Truc.* 10), and the dramatic festivals, the *ludi scaenici*, are named after it (cf. also Ter. *Hec.* 16; 45).[80] This vocabulary indicates that the Roman theatre developed from the stage as its constituent feature, whereas the Greek term 'theatre' (adopted by the Romans) emphasized the auditorium. This assessment is reflected in early theatre structures in Rome, when a stage was erected for each festival, while the auditorium could be provisional.

The precise appearance of the early stages, however, is hard to determine, since there is no primary evidence, as there are no archaeological remains of theatres in Rome until the mid-first century BCE. Therefore details of the structure of early 'theatres' in Rome must be deduced from references in preserved plays, mentions of theatres in other texts, inferences on the basis of architectural structures from later periods or from places outside Rome as well as vase- and wall-paintings (with the necessary caution applied). Still, it is obvious that simple performance spaces developed into the elaborate structures of the late Republican/early imperial period under the influence mainly of Greek theatre buildings (in Greece and Magna Graecia) and of stages used for indigenous performances in Italy and Sicily.[81]

For Greek theatres there are archaeological remains: in the Greek world the Theatre of Dionysus at Athens seems to have been the first to be built entirely of stone and to have reached this state by the time of Lycurgus (338–326 BCE); this initiated major activities of theatre building in all areas inhabited by Greeks, with the structure adapted to local requirements if necessary.[82] Stone theatres of Greek type are known for Sicily and Magna Graecia at least from the third century BCE onwards. After the Second Punic War, these areas declined in importance, while Campania and central Italy

---

[80] Plautus uses the word *scaena* for the stage on which the actors appear, while later authors seem to apply it to the back wall behind the stage (cf. Flavius Caper, *Gramm. Lat.* 7, p. 104.10; Servius, *Gramm. Lat.* 2, p. 381.2). The stage was also called *pulpitum* from the time of Vitruvius onwards (cf. e.g. Vitr. 5.6.2; Hor. *Epist.* 2.1.174; Flavius Caper, *Gramm. Lat.* 7, p. 104.10; Servius, *Gramm. Lat.* 2, p. 381.2). Isidorus claims that *pulpitus* was called *orchestra* (Isid. *Etym.* 18.43; 18.44), but these terms must refer to different parts of the theatre.

[81] The erection of temporary stages over a long period of time does not mean that the Romans did not have to make immediate choices on the kind of stage to be used and could instead gradually develop a layout congenial to their own theatre (so Beacham 1991: 57). In fact they were faced with a decision each year, although, admittedly, modifications are easier with temporary structures. At the same time the experience of different architectural styles in Greek and Italic theatre design put the Romans into the comfortable position of being able to make informed choices and adaptations (see Beacham 1991: 60).

[82] See Mitens 1988: 12–13, 42; Courtois 1989: 65.

flourished during the second century BCE: stone theatres in this region (exhibiting typical features of later Roman theatres) date to this period.

Further evidence on early stages in Italy has been sought from south-Italian vase-paintings, primarily the so-called 'phlyax vases', and from later Roman wall-paintings with theatrical motifs, mainly from Campania. The pictures on these vases used to be regarded as depicting early Italic performances on simple stages, interpreted as precursors of early Roman stages. More recently these vase-paintings have been re-interpreted as being connected with performances of Greek Middle or Old Comedy.[83] Yet irrespective of the type of shows performed on these stages, their form must have reflected a well-known type in fourth-century Italy, which differs from contemporary theatre structures in mainland Greece.[84] These vase-paintings show a low stage supported by posts or columns, occasionally covered by drapery or tablets; sometimes there are steps leading up to the platform. The back of the stage consists of a wall with openings for doors and windows, which may be covered by a roof.

Early imperial wall-paintings from southern Italy depict a particular type of stage and complex scenic façade, which has been described as the 'missing link' between the early temporary stages and the later permanent theatres in Rome.[85] The theory sounds intriguing, but: 'The combination of imperial wall painting, incorporating features found on temporary South Italian stages, and employing Greek *trompe l'oeil* painting techniques is too complex a combination to posit without corroboration.'[86] It is indeed unlikely that wall-paintings made several centuries after stone theatres had been built in Campania still reflect characteristics of temporary stages and are not rather inspired by contemporary buildings or reflect a fictitious construct.

There has also been the theory that Roman stages developed from street-corner theatres, i.e. that they started from temporary performance spaces that made use of crossroads in cities to create a theatre and that characteristics developed for this specific venue were transferred to permanent settings.[87] This is a possible scenario for any development from itinerant performances on temporary stages to permanent theatres, but at least in

---

[83] See Taplin 1993; Pöhlmann 1997; also Dumont 1984. See ch. 1.4.

[84] One will have to allow for the possibility that Italy might have known other (non-documented) forms of stages besides the one type depicted and that these may also have exerted an influence on the Roman theatre (see Frézouls 1982: 349–53).

[85] See Beacham 1980, 1991: 69–84.

[86] So Marshall 2006: 32. See Marshall's criticism (2006: 32–3) of the use of south-Italian vases as evidence and of Beacham's theory.

[87] So Tanner 1969.

Rome temporary stages had rather been located in front of temples or in the Forum.

Owing to the doubtful and controversial nature of the available evidence, there can be no certainty about the origins of what was later to become the typical layout of the Roman theatre. It seems, however, that in southern and central Italy elements of the Hellenistic Greek theatre (common in the western Greek provinces) and local traditions were fused to create a distinctive performance space, while architectural requirements and options as well as performance conventions mutually influenced each other. As features of early Roman stone theatres agree with the characteristics of earlier stone theatres in other parts of Italy, the people of Rome are likely to have adopted a theatre structure established in southern and central Italy and developed it further.

Third- and second-century stone theatres in southern and central Italy consist of a low and deep stage in front of a multi-storey, decorated stage wall. On both sides the stage is enclosed by high walls, which are joined with the auditorium, so that the auditorium and the stage area, each taking up about a half-circle, are placed exactly opposite each other and constitute one coherent building complex. This structure may be connected with a temple towering above the top of the auditorium to form a 'theatre temple', a variant that appeared in Campania, Samnium and Latium in the second century BCE.[88]

Characteristic features of fully developed Roman theatres (some of which go back to the phase of temporary buildings) are made particularly obvious by comparing typical Roman theatres with typical classical Greek ones (cf. Vitr. 5.6–7; also 5.3; 5.5).[89]

Whereas Greek theatre buildings tended to make use of a natural hill for the rising auditorium and to give audiences a view into the distance, complete Roman ones formed compact, artificial, freestanding blocks on flat surfaces. The Romans created an architectural unit out of a simple stage structure and a rounded auditorium. Thus Roman theatres were self-contained, architecturally coherent structures in which the distinct elements of stage building, stage, 'orchestra' and auditorium were fused to form a single, purpose-built entity. This tendency may have been

[88] On 'theatre temples' in Italy see Hanson 1959: 36–55; Coarelli 1987 passim; Mitens 1993: 99–100; on the architecture of Hellenistic theatre buildings in Latium and Samnite territory see Lauter 1976; Hülsemann 1987: 132–7.

[89] See e.g. Rumpf 1950: 40–1; Bieber 1961: 188–9; Lauter 1976; Mitens 1988: 9–11; Brothers 1989: 102–4; Frézouls 1989: 338–44; Beacham 1991: 83, 2007: 223; Dodge 1999: 212–13.

encouraged by the custom of erecting some early temporary stages in the Forum or the Circus on flat surfaces.[90]

Within the overall arrangement of the Roman theatre the auditorium formed about a half-circle only, the stage was low and deep and was terminated by the imposing vertical façade (*scaenae frons*) of the stage building, directing the audience's view to the inside of the theatre. This front wall was originally unadorned and later painted and decorated (cf. e.g. Plin. *HN* 35.23; Val. Max. 2.4.6); the façade normally had three doors, which could be set back into curved or rectangular niches (*exedrae*) to provide small vestibules (*vestibulum*).[91] The projecting wings of the stage building enclosed the stage at either end. This building was originally of modest height and had an accessible flat roof (cf. Plaut. *Amph.* 1008); its front wall later rose to the same height as the auditorium. This façade formed the permanent background to the stage, but the basic decoration was not related to the setting of particular plays:[92] while the three doors signified particular buildings necessary for the dramatic action of each play, any additional decoration of the façade formed a symbolical level of its own. Façades in late Republican temporary theatres and later permanent buildings tended to be decorated with numerous columns and often included statues of gods, particularly of Apollo and the Muses.

Between the stage, which was lower and deeper than in Greece, and the foremost tier of seats lay a flat space, corresponding roughly to the Greek 'orchestra' (and called *orchestra* in imperial times),[93] but not normally used by Roman performers and housing not a chorus (as in Greece), but (in late Republican times) seats for distinguished spectators (cf. e.g. Vitr. 5.6.2; Suet. *Claud.* 21.1; *CIL* 1.594.4.1.48–2.11).[94] Boxes (*tribunalia*) for the providers of the dramas were placed above vaulted side-entrances (located on either side of the auditorium).

That the auditorium and the stage area in a Roman theatre formed separate units of about a half-circle each allowed for monumental

---

[90] Falchetti and Romualdi (2001: 107–8) observe that spectators at Etruscan games are depicted on tribunes, whereas they would sit on natural elevations in Greece; they suggest that this could be one of the few original ideas of the Etruscans. Then the Romans might have adopted the erection of artificial structures for spectators (where necessary) from the Etruscans.

[91] Cf. Pac. *Trag.* 400 R.[3] = *Trag. inc.* 17 W.; Plaut. *Pseud.* 955; *Mostell.* 817; Varro, *Ling.* 7.81; Gell. *NA* 16.5.3.

[92] On the decoration of the *scaenae frons* and on the use of the same iconography in private homes see Leach 2004: 93–122.

[93] Cf. e.g. Vitr. 5.6–7; Suet. *Iul.* 39.2; Fest., p. 436 L.; Paul. ex Fest., p. 195 L.; already Varro, *Sat. Men.* 561 B.

[94] The redefinition of the orchestra has been connected with developments in the Hellenistic Greek theatre (see Dumont 1997).

side-entrances that enabled large groups of characters to gain direct access
to the stage; this accords with a general tendency of Roman drama to
have greater numbers of (subsidiary) characters on stage.[95] The opportunities offered by such a layout were exploited, for instance, in a temporary
structure for the entry of the young ladies Bacchis and Antiphila and their
sizeable entourage in Terence's *Heautontimorumenos* (Ter. *Haut.* II 3–4).
Similarly, when towards the end of the Republic dramatic performances
developed further towards spectacular and lavish spectacle, huge crowds
of people and objects could be paraded over the stage in the manner of
triumphal processions (cf. Cic. *Fam.* 7.1.2; Hor. *Epist.* 2.1.187–207).

Owing to the specific arrangement of the individual architectural elements in a fully developed Roman theatre, the stage was framed on all sides
and placed opposite the spectators; this contributed to audiences being dis-
engaged from the action and attending as onlookers, watching something
that was set in a world of its own and acted by players who typically
were not Roman citizens (see ch. 2.6).[96] In such a context productions
of Greek-style plays or burlesque farces would be less striking, while they
could still be perceived as representing situations relevant to the spectators'
own lives. At any rate, the development of architectural structures, of performance conventions and of the perception of plays went hand in hand
in Republican Rome.

2.5 STAGING, ACTING, COSTUMES, MASKS

Since the same generic set was used for all dramatic performances (with
slight modifications over the course of time),[97] visual details necessary for
the plot and any spectacular features had to be added by the utterances
and gestures of characters, stage-action and the use of equipment.[98] The
transmitted scripts of Roman plays do not contain explicit stage directions,
but some are included in the texts themselves, for example when characters describe the setting and scenery or announce the appearance of new
characters or their own plans to leave.

[95] See Grimal 1975: 265–6.   [96] See e.g. Cancik 1978: 315; Frézouls 1982: 369; von Hesberg 2005: 152.
[97] On the set in the time of Plautus and Terence see Marshall 2006: 49–56. Vitruvius (5.6.8–9) talks
of machines that have three panels with different representations of scenery, which can be turned
according to the atmosphere of individual scenes, and he mentions three different types of scenery
(referring to tragedy, comedy and satyr-play). This agrees with the introduction of painted scenery
attested for 99 BCE (cf. Val. Max. 2.4.6).
[98] Such a simple and fixed stage area might seem unrealistic and unsophisticated to a modern audience,
but one has to bear in mind that the essential characteristic of a stage is its 'image function', i.e.
that it stands for something else; as long as this convention is maintained, anything can function as
a stage (see Honzl [1940] 1976: 74).

Most of this evidence naturally comes from the surviving texts of palliatae. Yet scattered further information allows the inference that similar conventions applied to other dramatic genres in Rome.[99] For instance, since in the late Republic Atellanae could follow plays of other dramatic genres (see ch. 3.5), the same basic conditions are likely to have been valid. This is confirmed by an Atellana fragment that assigns one of the houses represented on stage to a certain character (Pomp. *Atell.* III R.³).[100]

Dramatists were obviously aware that the unchanged layout of the stage could fulfil different functions in different plays (cf. Plaut. *Men.* 72–6). Sometimes it was even emphasized that the poet 'wished' to identify the stage with a certain town or setting for the purposes of the present play, which might or might not agree with standard conventions (cf. Plaut. *Men.* 7–12; *Rud.* 32–3a; *Truc.* 1–3; 10–11). While such comments increase the fictional aspect of the performance and the demands on the imagination of the spectators, identifying locations only verbally allows for a variety of plays to be shown on the same stage without adaptations being necessary. Vice versa, such stage conventions illuminate characteristics of Roman dramatic texts.

The generic set was variously defined in line with the requirements of a given play, by naming the town (e.g. Plaut. *Mil.* 88a; *Truc.* 1–3; 10–11) as well as the inhabitants or the functions of the respective buildings (e.g. Plaut. *Rud.* 33b–5; 61a; *Truc.* 12; 77; 246). For the three doors in the wall at the back of the stage indicated three buildings, whose significance (along with those of the side-entrances) in a particular play was usually made clear in the prologue and/or by other remarks of the stage characters (e.g. Plaut. *Cas.* 35–6; *Rud.* 33b–5; 61). What the doors/buildings represented could vary from private houses inhabited by citizens, pimps or courtesans to royal palaces, different sections of the same complex, temples (cf. Liv. Andr. *Trag.* 13–14 R.³ = 12–13 W.), stables (cf. Pac. *Trag.* 121 R.³ = 133 W.) or a mixture of these; not every play made use of all three doors (cf. also Poll. 4.124).

Originally, there was no stage curtain; the beginning of a play was announced by the prologue speaker and occasionally by a herald (*praeco*); the end was marked by one or all of the characters asking for applause (cf. Hor. *Ars P.* 154–5; Porph. ad loc.; Quint. *Inst.* 6.1.52). The introduction of a curtain (*aulaeum*) in about 133 BCE, in connection with the inheritance from the Pergamene king Attalus III (cf. Donat. *Com.* 8.8; Serv. on Verg. *Aen.* 1.697), enabled the marking of beginnings and endings of plays (by

---

[99] See Beare 1964: 124–5 (with examples).   [100] See Beare 1964: 147.

lowering it at the start and raising it at the end of a performance in classical times), although the curtain probably did not cover the entire height of the stage wall.[101] Besides, an ancillary curtain (*siparium*) could be used, which the ancient sources associate particularly with mimes; it seems to have consisted of simple drapes that might be put up anywhere on the stage to create special effects, since it made it possible to hide (and rearrange) part of the stage and/or some actors and then suddenly uncover the area.[102]

At either end of the stage there was a side-entrance connected with the projecting wings. The side-entrance on the spectators' right is usually assumed to lead to the near distance, i.e. to the Forum and the town centre in a play set in a town (like most palliatae), the one on the left to the more remote distance, i.e. to the harbour and the country (cf. Vitr. 5.6.8).[103] The two directions of 'harbour' and 'town' (*ab classe ad urbem*) are also mentioned in Accius' *Epinausimache* (Acc. *Trag.* 318 R.³ = 305 W.), and they might equally have been represented by the two side-entrances in this tragedy; however, driving back the Trojans from the Greek fleet towards their city has a specific relevance, which warns against general conclusions. Characters in comedy, typically of a middle-class background, might go to the Forum, the harbour or the country to conduct various kinds of business, which accords with their socio-economic reality. A number of tragedies and praetextae must have taken place in warriors' camps, in the open country or near the seashore, but they will have been performed on the same three-door stage, the words of the actors identifying the location.

Since the stage represented an open space, audiences could assume the role of the general public, watching as unaffected onlookers. Consequently, all stage-action must be envisaged as happening in public, even if people discuss their most intimate concerns; conversely the audience can only experience directly what happens outside. Therefore figures come out of the house when the action has to move on (cf. e.g. Ter. *Eun.* 668) or something important has to be said or they are awaiting essential information, even though they do not always say so explicitly, and poets try to make it appear as if people were coming out by chance.[104]

---

[101] On *aulaeum* cf. Cic. *Cael.* 65; Verg. *Georg.* 3.25; Hor. *Epist.* 2.1.189; *Ars P.* 154.

[102] Cf. Donat. *Com.* 8.8; Cic. *Prov. cons.* 14; Paul. ex Fest., p. 459 L.; Schol. on Juv. 8.186. On the two types of curtain see Beare 1964: 267–74; Sear 2006: 8, 90.

[103] On the side-entrances in Roman comedy see Rambo 1915; Beare 1964: 248–55 (with references). The distribution in Rome probably agreed with Attic conventions, but there is some debate among scholars on whether or not this was the case, as it is difficult to establish precise details.

[104] Cf. e.g. Enn. *Trag.* 214–15; 216–17 R.³ = 262–3; 264–5 W.; Acc. *Trag.* 292 R.³ = 280 W.; Plaut. *Cist.* 543–50; 637b–8; *Mostell.* 1–10.

Actions that cannot be shown on stage because of their time, place and/or character, but are essential to the plot, are represented by the device of 'messenger speeches', i.e. reports by characters who have allegedly witnessed an incident taking place indoors or elsewhere; these may contain vivid and elaborate descriptions of locations, actions and emotions. Horace later admits that things seen are more effective and impressive than things heard; still he warns against presenting cruel actions on stage since this would lead to disbelief and disgust (Hor. *Ars P.* 179–88). Connections between the two spheres of onstage and offstage are established when an entering character is shown finishing a speech addressed to people inside (often consisting of orders) or a character on stage turns to give instructions to those inside, and also when actions not to be represented on stage (such as childbirth) happen inside and are reported by a character peeping into the house or coming out of it immediately after the event.[105] Actual movements between inside and outside are supported by mentions of the sound of a palace door in tragedy as well as the motif of the 'creaking door' and of knocking on doors in comedy.[106]

A sense of 'reality' is retained and the clarity of movements enhanced as characters typically re-enter through the same entrance by which they have left, and they often explain what they have done or where they have been. If a person's reappearance from the same entrance is not feasible for dramatic reasons, playwrights can resort to the device of *angiportum/angiportus*, a backstreet supposed to run behind the 'houses' that are envisaged as facing the stage, connecting them by means of their back doors and gardens with each other and also with the town, the harbour and the country. The fact that characters usually comment on their itinerary in those cases (e.g. Plaut. *Mostell.* 931; 1043–6; Ter. *Eun.* 840–7) indicates that movements not clear from the stage-action have to be explained by characters' utterances.

Additionally, entering figures can be announced and sometimes characterized in various ways: they introduce themselves when they are not immediately noticed or the stage had been empty; people already on stage say that they see or hear them approaching (and sometimes comment on their intentions) or inquire after their identity.[107] Similarly, figures leaving

---

[105] Cf. e.g. Plaut. *Merc.* 562; *Mostell.* 1064–7; *Truc.* 95–8a; 449; 711–18; Ter. *Eun.* 469b–70a; 472a; 504b–6a; 538; cf. e.g. Plaut. *Amph.* 1053–72; *Rud.* 615–55; 906–27; Ter. *Eun.* 615–28.

[106] Cf. Pac. *Trag.* 214 R.³ = 222 W.; Acc. *Trag.* 30/1 R.³ = 244 W.; cf. e.g. Plaut. *Men.* 523; *Mostell.* 1062; *Truc.* 350–1; Ter. *Eun.* 1029a.

[107] Cf. e.g. Enn. *Trag.* 296; 298 R.³ = 354; 355 W.; Acc. *Trag.* 122 R.³ = 82 W.; Plaut. *Merc.* 109–10; 271; 329b–30a; 561b; 598–600; 670–1; 699; *Mostell.* 82b–3; 310–12; 419a; 536–8; 686–7a; 997–8a; 1120–1; *Truc.* 93–4; 770–2; 852; 889b–90a; Ter. *Eun.* 79–80; 642; 738; 754–5; 906b; 918–19a; 967b.

the stage usually announce that they are about to go, take leave of other characters or mention a specific errand they have to run.[108]

Owing to the minimal visual guidance of the set, the imaginative faculty of the spectators was both challenged and nourished by poets. In Ennius' version of the Medea story, for example, Medea seems to have been given a kind of tour of Athens (Enn. *Trag.* 243–4 R.³ = 294–5 W.); the description of Athens must have appealed entirely to the audience's imagination. Also, spectators had to accept that some conventions and illusions operated without scenic support. For instance, in a number of preserved palliatae figures on stage are expected to see and hear only what dramatists want them to, so that they (in contrast to the audience) might not notice other characters standing close to them, that they are themselves noticed by others at a convenient moment only, which allows them to eavesdrop without being concealed (e.g. Plaut. *Merc.* 364–85; 477), and that they can voice asides heard by the whole audience, yet not or only in part by other characters.[109] Only occasionally do characters show an awareness of the possibility that others on stage who are not supposed to might hear them (e.g. Plaut. *Truc.* 575–6). Frequently, people hear someone speaking, but do not understand the words, which eventually leads to recognition and conversation between these characters (e.g. Ter. *Eun.* 83b–7).

A few stage properties assisted the imagination of audiences and ensured the smooth running of the plot.[110] The only object by which the stage was permanently decorated was an altar, often of Apollo, but also of Venus, Diana or Lucina, where characters could sacrifice or take refuge during the play.[111] Money paid and counted on stage could be represented (Plaut. *Poen.* 597–9). The same is obvious for characteristic items that allow the recognition of long-lost relatives, typically tokens that were given to them in childhood. Professionals seem to have been identified by the attributes of their jobs such as the cook's knife or the soldier's sword (e.g. Plaut. *Aul.* 417; *Mil.* 1–8). Cicero mentions burning torches of Furies on the tragic stage (Cic. *Rosc. Am.* 67; *Pis.* 46). Beyond that, however, it is not even certain whether all objects elaborately sketched in the texts were present on stage, apart from those essential to the action. For instance, the description of the first ship *Argo* by a herdsman sitting on a tree in Accius' *Medea*

---

[108] Cf. e.g. Plaut. *Merc.* 218–24; 326; 465–8a; *Mostell.* 82a; *Truc.* 313; 848–9; Ter. *Eun.* 206; 492b–4a; 612–14; 894b–909; 970a.

[109] Cf. e.g. Plaut. *Men.* 250–3; 443–5; 477–8; *Mil.* 21–4; 33–5; *Mostell.* 1 3; 1063–74; Ter. *Eun.* 455b–62; 548b–57; 706–10.

[110] On stage properties see Marshall 2006: 66–72.

[111] Cf. e.g. Plaut. *Bacch.* 172–3; *Curc.* 71–2; *Merc.* 675b–80; *Mil.* 411–14; *Mostell.* 1094–105; *Rud.* 664–76; 688–704; *Truc.* 476. See e.g. Dumont 2000: 103 and n. 2.

(Acc. *Trag.* 391–402 R.³ = 381–92 W.) is likely to have been given by an actor positioned at the edge of the stage, in front of the usual three-door background, looking into the distance and gesturing appropriately.

Towards the late Republic, when dramatic performances were developing into spectacles and settings became more lavish, a large amount of equipment could be used, as noted with disdain by intellectuals (e.g. Cic. *Fam.* 7.1.2; Hor. *Epist.* 1.6.40–1; 2.1.187–207). The most notorious example consists of the performances at the opening of Pompey's Theatre, when, as Cicero claims, 600 mules and 3,000 kraters were paraded across the stage (Cic. *Fam.* 7.1.2), probably by re-using and displaying part of Pompey's booty for his self-aggrandizement. In 99 BCE the curule aedile C. Claudius Pulcher had a machine built that could produce sound effects such as an imitation of the noise of thunder (cf. Fest., p. 50.1–5 L.). The increase in spectacle and display continued into the imperial period.

In earlier periods plays did not ignore spectacular effects – they even built on them to win audience approval – but these were achieved by the capabilities of actors, stunning reversals or near-catastrophes included in the plot and full use of the available properties of the stage. For instance, Medea may enter on a winged chariot (Pac. *Medus*), the shade of a dead person can emerge from the underworld (Pac. *Iliona*), houses might be besieged (Ter. *Eun.*), or plots or discussions may imply use of the upper level of the stage building (Plaut. *Amph.*, *Mil.*). Generally, there seems to have been more busy stage-action than in classical Greek plays. For instance, from the beginning there was a greater readiness in Roman drama to bring numerous characters onto the stage simultaneously, so that there were more complex set-ups and more activity was going on, and to act out conversations and incidents on stage; there could be more than three speaking actors at a time, supplemented by mute characters if necessary.[112]

Actors had to be physically and technically capable of meeting the requirements for impressive acting. They needed to have trained bodies and good voices for both speech and song, since they performed in open-air theatres and without the assistance of technical equipment. To make themselves heard, actors on stage probably did not talk to each other, but rather declaimed to the audience. As a great number of verses were accompanied by music (see ch. 5.6), actors had to be able to deliver lines rhythmically and musically. Beyond that, different dramatic characters apparently required

---

[112] Goldberg (1993: 59–60) argues that for the Romans action was an essential part of a performance, in contrast to theatre in Greece, where characters' utterances are of prime importance.

different abilities of actors: Cicero notes that actors, at least in his time, tended to pick roles that suited their abilities (Cic. *Off.* 1.114).

Besides their voices, actors had to be able to employ gestures, movement and body language effectively.[113] Later comparisons between actors and orators in writers such as Quintilian and their advice that orators should not gesture as extensively as some actors (e.g. Quint. *Inst.* 11.3.88–9; 11.3.181–3)[114] show that expressive gestures, emphasizing or complementing what was being said, were recognized as a significant part of stage acting, which must already have been true for earlier periods.[115] Cicero, for instance, indicates that good actors empathized with the characters and adapted their delivery to the emotional states presented (e.g. Cic. *De or.* 2.193; 3.102). The late Republic, when texts of old plays could be applied to the contemporary situation, saw another type of gestures: actors could indicate the application of lines to a member of the audience or to the audience as a whole by pointing at them (e.g. Cic. *Sest.* 122; Val. Max. 6.2.9; see ch. 2.9). Actors' movements might be used to structure scenes, for instance when characters run in and out of the house, to the Forum and back again, or take refuge at an altar, or running slaves arrive in their typical outfit (e.g. Plaut. *Capt.* 778–9; *Merc.* 111–18; *Poen.* 522–3; Ter. *Haut.* 31–2).

Additionally, many tragedies and some praetextae (as well as a few comedies) had choruses. These choruses did not provide choral interludes, but were rather integrated into the action, which contributed to the level of activity on stage and to the involvement of a greater number of people. At least some of the utterances could be spoken by a chorus leader, who might be one of the trained actors, while the rest of the group could be represented by (hired) extras.[116]

Although no law of unity of time and place is known for the Republican period, the action presented on stage tended to be condensed into one significant day, emphasized by frequent references to the present day and the relevance of this day as an important juncture.[117] As only this single day was typically represented on stage, the action might fill the entire day; at

---

[113] For considerations on gestures in ancient drama see Panayotakis 2005b; on technical aspects of the actors' performance see Petrone 1992: 347–70.

[114] On acting styles and conventions in comparison to oratorical techniques see Fantham 2002.

[115] Cf. e.g. Plaut. *Merc.* 130–2; 149–50a; *Mil.* 200–15a; *Mostell.* 10b; 322–4; 332–3; 419–26a; 444–5; 744b–5a; 898b–904; 936b–9; 988; *Rud.* 627b–8a; *Truc.* 123–9; 272b–9; 370b–4; 603–6; 751–4; 838; 911–14a; 924; Ter. *Eun.* 530b–1a.

[116] See e.g. Cancik 1978: 317. On the chorus in Republican tragedy see Hose 1999; on the role of the chorus cf. Arist. *Poet.* 18: 1456a25–30; Hor. *Ars P.* 193–5. On the 'chorus' in comedy see ch. 3.3.

[117] Cf. e.g. Pac. *Trag.* 115 R.³ = 119 W.; Plaut. *Merc.* 586–7a; *Pers.* 34–4ᵃ; *Pseud.* 58b–60a; 177–9a; 372–5; Ter. *Eun.* 1047.

least there are several references to early morning and late night in extant texts.[118] The whole story as given by a prologue speaker and/or narratives of characters could encompass a much longer period as well as a wider variety of places.[119]

As many of the dramatic genres in Rome are named after terms for clothing, it is often assumed that these names hold a clue to actors' costumes.[120] Certainly, the fact that the Romans derived names for dramatic genres from types of garment and used different kinds of footwear metaphorically to denote forms of drama is indicative of the symbolic role of clothes in the Roman world. Yet, for various reasons, direct inferences about the actual costumes on the basis of the names of dramatic genres are problematic.[121]

First, these names work on different levels: some of them are derived from the general garments worn in Greece or Rome (*palliata*, *togata*), some from special variants (*praetexta*) and some from footwear or lack thereof (*crepidata, planipes*). Second, late-antique grammarians talk of these names reflecting the *habitus* of the Greek or the Roman people, and in some scholarly systems *palliata* and *togata* are general names for all Greek or Roman forms of drama (e.g. Diom. *Ars* 3, *Gramm. Lat.* I, pp. 489.14–90.7). Therefore it is safer to assume that these names denote the character of a type of drama and its protagonists, but do not necessarily describe the attire of all actors in performances of works of a specific dramatic genre, although some are likely to have worn the respective type of garment.

Written sources on actors' attire are preserved only from the late-antique period: Donatus (Donat. *Com.* 8.4–7) and Pollux (Poll. 4.115–20) enumerate a range of different costumes for various types of characters, but their accounts do not yield a coherent picture.[122] Visual evidence, such as Campanian reliefs, wall-paintings and terracottas, are also of doubtful value. So there is only the evidence of the plays themselves and a few references in contemporary or near-contemporary writers. Romans will have been

---

[118] Cf. e.g. Enn. *Trag.* 95–6; 177–80 R.³ = 117–18; 222–5 W.; Pac. *Trag.* 347 R.³ = *Inc.* 55 W.; Acc. *Trag.* 123; 693 R.³ = 82; *Inc.* 40 W.

[119] See Blänsdorf 2000 (with reference to Plautus).

[120] On actors' costumes and masks see e.g. Duckworth 1952: 88–94; Beare 1964: 184–95 (with a survey of evidence from dramatic scripts); Petrone 1992: 371–402; for an overview of costumes used in Roman comedy see Saunders 1909 (partly based on later illustrations of Terentian manuscripts).

[121] For a more detailed discussion of these methodological problems with reference to *fabula praetexta* see Manuwald 2001a: 26–9.

[122] Apuleius gives a list of several specific forms of clothing used in dramatic performances (Apul. *Apol.* 13). Some of the terms, for instance *syrma* ('robe with a long train, worn esp. by tragic actors'), are found in Republican dramatic fragments (Valerius, *Mim.* I R.³; Afr. *Tog.* 64 R.³), while others, such as *centunculus* ('patched garment'), are attested nowhere else in the classical period.

influenced by costumes used in contemporary Greek theatres, but clear evidence on Greek costumes for the relevant periods is equally scarce.[123]

Generally, costume as such seems comparatively unimportant as part of the story in palliata comedy. Clothing is typically mentioned only when reference to it has a function in the plot. Since practical considerations suggest that actors had to be able to change costumes quickly and that costumes, especially elaborate ones, were expensive (cf. Plaut. *Amph.* 85; *Curc.* 464–6a; *Pers.* 157–60; *Pseud.* 1184–6; *Trin.* 857–9), property managers might have tried to make do with a limited number of costumes that represented a few types and were of a practical style. In the late Republican and early imperial periods costumes, just like other stage equipment, could be elaborate (cf. e.g. Hor. *Epist.* 2.1.204b–7; see ch. 2.9).

Characters in palliatae wear (the tunic and) the *pallium*, and are thereby characterized as Greeks (cf. Plaut. *Curc.* 288 vs. *Amph.* 68); there is hardly any evidence on how *pallia* for various characters might have differed. Besides, fairly general words for garments such as *vestis, vestitus, vestimentum, ornamenta* and *ornatus* are common as references to clothing in comedy.[124] The expression *ornamenta* occurs when there is mention of the supplier of props (*choragus*) and seems to be the technical term for the elements of theatrical costume (cf. Plaut. *Curc.* 464; *Pers.* 159; *Trin.* 857–8). The use of special clothing comes to the fore when disguise is at issue: men dressing as women or eunuchs, citizens as foreigners or gods as human beings.[125] In these cases, where it is a functional element of the plot, a change or a special type of dress will be described. This allows the assumption that figures with special roles such as eunuchs or foreigners had characteristic costumes.

That costume is used for dramatic effect instead of being governed by strict conventions is shown by the example of doubles: since the two Menaechmi in Plautus' play of this title must appear alike to enable the complex movements of the plot, the traveller from Syracuse must be dressed like his brother, who appears from his own house; therefore the usual characteristics of travellers have been dispensed with. At the same time Plautus ensures that the spectators are not in doubt about the identity of the characters, even though they have been warned of possible confusion at

---

[123] On costumes used in the Greek theatre see Pickard-Cambridge 1988: 177–231.

[124] Cf. e.g. Plaut. *Amph.* 443; 866; 1007; *Asin.* 92; *Bacch.* 125; 482; *Capt.* 37; *Cist.* 487; *Men.* 804; *Mil.* 981; Ter. *Ad.* 63; *Eun.* 1015; *Haut.* 248; 837; 968; *Hec.* 9.

[125] Cf. e.g. Plaut. *Amph.* 116–17; *Capt.* 37; 541; 647–8; 922; 1012–25; *Cas.* 769–70; 814b–54; *Curc.* 392–5; 461–5; 505; 543–5; *Mil.* 791–2; 872; 1177–81; *Pers.* 155–6; *Pseud.* 735; *Trin.* 771; 851; Ter. *Eun.* 369–71; 572.

the start (Plaut. *Men.* 47–8): the two Menaechmi continue to use different side-entrances throughout the play and to make their identity clear by their words and reactions.

In Plautus' *Amphitruo*, where Jupiter and Mercury dress up as Amphitruo and his slave Sosia, the gods wear distinguishing marks attached to their hats, visible only to the audience (Plaut. *Amph.* 142–7). After the opening scene, however, a visual distinction between the two impersonations of the same character is not actually necessary, since the identity becomes evident by their words. Yet because the doubles are present from the start of the play and there is no chance of experiencing all characters in their proper guise, this device might have been intended to help spectators to get into the play.

Conventions of footwear are also to be inferred from references in extant texts: special sandals are worn as part of a foreign-looking disguise (cf. Plaut. *Pers.* 464); other characters, slaves as well as free men and women, wear sandals or slippers.[126] In extant palliatae no character is said to be barefooted or to wear anything other than sandals or slippers: this may be significant, since various types of footwear became synonyms for specific types of drama, the 'slipper' (*soccus*) representing comedy.[127]

Naturally, there is less evidence for outfit in tragedy. One of Plautus' prologue speakers says that the 'comic apparatus' (*choragium comicum*) would be inappropriate for the performance of a tragedy (Plaut. *Capt.* 61–2); this term probably not only refers to costumes, but covers all kinds of stage properties and machinery. At some point tragic actors must have started to wear the 'buskin/high boot' (*cothurnus*); this term later came to be used to denote tragedy in a metaphorical sense.

Surviving tragic fragments contain no references to costume apart from the fact that a number of characters are described as appearing in reduced circumstances after they have experienced sudden reversals of fortune (cf. Poll. 4.117). To illustrate their situation they are described as squalid, shabby, dishevelled and dirty; therefore they are likely to have come onto the stage in rags (like Euripidean characters).[128] Figures appearing in this fashion became such a distinctive feature that the satirist Lucilius in the second

---

[126] Cf. Plaut. *Bacch.* 332; *Cist.* 697; *Epid.* 725; *Mostell.* 384; *Pers.* 124; *Trin.* 720; *Truc.* 478; 631; Ter. *Haut.* 124.

[127] Cf. e.g. *cot(h)urnus*: Hor. *Ars P.* 80; Tac. *Dial.* 10.4; Juv. 15.29; Mart. 8.18.7; *tragicus cot(h)urnus*: Ov. *Tr.* 2.393; Mart. 8.3.13; Manil. 5.458; *soccus*: Hor. *Ars P.* 80; Mart. 8.3.13; *comicus soccus*: Plin. *HN* 7.111.

[128] Cf. e.g. Enn. *Trag.* 285; 287 R.³ = 341; 339 W.; Pac. *Trag.* 9, 20ᵃ⁻ᵇ; 313–14 R.³ = 24; 13–14; 337–8 W.; Acc. *Trag.* 613–16; 617 R.³ = 629–32 W.; cf. Eur. *El.* 184–9; *Hel.* 420–4a; Ar. *Ach.* 410–34; *Ran.* 842; 1061–6; *Thesm.* 910.

century BCE mocked this as a typical and unrealistic characteristic of contemporary tragedy (e.g. Lucil. 597–8; 599–600 M. = 729–30; 727–8 W.).
Other plays include 'doubles' similar to those in comedy, when two young
men of equal age are exchanged for each other or their respective identity
is unclear (cf. Pac. *Iliona, Medus, Chryses*). But if they were not previously
known to the character to whom they are presented in their wrong identity,
disguise is not necessary.

Figures shown in particular situations may have had the appropriate
attire or at least a few props. For instance, at least in later periods actors
representing shades of characters were marked by a specific dress (cf. Schol.
on Hor. *Sat.* 2.3.60). Just as in comedy, a person's attire is mentioned when
it is unusual and/or characteristic (e.g. Naev. *Trag.* 43; 54 R.³ = 39; 43 W.;
Enn. *Trag.* 345–6 R.³ = 418–19 W.). In several tragedies the appearance of
elderly characters worn away by grief and neglect is described.[129] Accius'
Medea features shepherds (Acc. *Trag.* 391–402; 403–6; 407; 409–10 R.³ =
381–96; 397; 398–9 W.), and in Pacuvius' *Dulorestes* the title character
appeared disguised as a herdsman (Pac. *Trag.* 121 R.³ = 133 W.); these
might have carried props indicating their profession. Bacchic plays feature
groups of Bacchants, who carry Bacchic wands (e.g. Naev. *Trag.* 31–2 R.³ =
33–4 W.). Ennius' *Iphigenia* had a chorus of soldiers (Enn. *Trag.* 183–90
R.³ = 241–48 W.), and soldiers will have featured in other plays as well.
In Pacuvius' *Niptra* Ulixes comes onto the stage wounded and carried
by attendants (Pac. *Trag.* 256–67 R.³ = 280–91 W.); Ennius presents the
wounded Eurypylus (Enn. *Trag.* 314–25 R.³ = 169–81 W.).

In plays set in Roman surroundings actors must have had Roman dress.
In praetextae some characters such as consuls might have worn the *toga
praetexta*. Togata fragments mention togas, tunics and shoes (cf. Tit. *Tog.*
24/5; 44; 116; 138; 167–8 R.³; Afr. *Tog.* 105 R.³), but here too it seems
that dress is mainly referred to when there is something special and it is
exploited to characterize a figure or to enable the plot. Besides, social classes
are distinguished by their dress: differences in garments between matrons
and courtesans are stressed (Afr. *Tog.* 133; 182 R.³; At. *Tog.* 3 R.³); young girls
wear the *supparum*, a long mantle (Afr. *Tog.* 123 R.³; Tit. *Tog.* 351 R.³), and
foreigners their characteristic dress (Afr. *Tog.* 284 R.³). Actors in Atellana
and mime probably also had native dress. A particular characteristic of
mime was the bare feet of performers, as demonstrated by the genre's Latin
name (*planipes*).

---

[129] Cf. e.g. *Trag. inc.* 189–92; Pac. *Trag.* 272–3; 274–5; 276; 301 R.³ = 253–6; 297–300; 301; 328 W.

A further important part of the attire of actors of almost all dramatic genres consists in masks.[130] Unfortunately, the questions of whether in the Republican period Roman actors of the main dramatic genres performed masked or when masks were introduced are vexed and controversial, because the evidence of the sources is contradictory:[131] Diomedes says that masks were introduced only by the actor Roscius in Cicero's time; Donatus mentions Cincius Faliscus and Minucius Prothymus, who performed in the middle of the second century BCE, as the first masked actors. He also records that the first performances of Terence's *Eunuchus* and *Adelphoe* had masked players. A comedy of Naevius is entitled *Personata* (*'The Masked Play'*), and Festus comments that some refer this title to the fact that this was the first play to be performed with masks. But as Festus believes that masks for comedy and tragedy were introduced only much later, he thinks that the title indicates that, due to a shortage of comic actors, the drama was performed by Atellana actors, who were correctly called 'masked' since, in contrast to other actors, they could not be forced to lay down their masks on stage.

There is no evidence to corroborate Diomedes' attribution of the introduction of masks to Roscius (who, according to Cicero, performed masked), while the other sources amount to three records of masked performances in earlier periods. Further, all other regions whose theatre culture the Romans experienced prior to the start of literary drama at Rome used masks, where these had proved to be characteristics of actors and convenient aids in dramatic productions. Hence it would be strange if one had to assume that the Romans had dispensed with this device, yet adopted and adapted all other main elements of theatrical practice.

Moreover, the Latin word for mask (*persona*) has entered Latin from Etruscan, which suggests that the device was taken over along with the term. The later development of the word to mean 'person' points to a preceding phase during which it carried the sense of 'mask'. Moreover, the distinctions between the use of masks in various dramatic genres recorded in later writers show that masks must have become familiar and meaningful objects by late Republican times, which again points to their having been in use for a longer period.

---

[130] On masks in the Roman theatre see e.g. Duckworth 1952: 92–4; Beare 1964: 192–4, 303–9; Dumont 1982; Gratwick 1982a: 83–4; Beacham 1991: 183–5; Wiles 1991: 129–49; Petrone 1992: 371–93; Suerbaum 2002: 54; Boyle 2006: 19, 147; Marshall 2006: 126–58.

[131] Cf. Cic. *De or.* 3.221; Diom. *Ars* 3, *Gramm. Lat.* 1, p. 489.11–13; Donat. *Com.* 6.3; on Ter. *Eun.*, *praef.* 1.6; *Ad.*, *praef.* 1.6; Fest., p. 238 L. In Novius *personae* are mentioned (Nov. *Atell.* 2 R.³).

In view of all this, the existence of masks in the Roman theatre from early times onwards is very likely.[132] Writers of the imperial period presuppose masked performances: Quintilian, for instance, not only gives a list of stock characters and their different emotional states, which have to be distinguished, but also mentions a bipartite mask of the *pater familias*, consisting of an angry and a mild half, which allowed the actor to show the side to the audience that represented his current emotional state (Quint. *Inst.* 11.3.74). Over the course of time the varieties of masks available for individual stock characters increased and became more sophisticated; Pollux later gives a long list of tragic and comic masks (Poll. 4.133–42; 4.142–54). Atellanae at any rate seem to have had masks portraying the stock characters from the beginning, while mimes did not have masks.

Cicero claims that he has often seen how the eyes of an actor seemed to glow through the mask at an utterance full of strong emotion that appeared to be felt by the actor (Cic. *De or.* 2.193). Horace agrees that a person's emotional state, facial expression and the words uttered on stage should go together (Hor. *Ars P.* 105–11). Cicero also maintains that moderation of facial expression, voice and movement is a significant component of the dramatic art (Cic. *De or.* 1.18). And he remarks that the eyes are the most important element in the face and therefore the older generation, who had had full experience of Roscius' dramatic career, generally did not praise even Roscius much when he wore a mask (Cic. *De or.* 3.221). This somewhat incongruous evidence presumably means that Cicero believed that good actors had to make an effort to express emotions by their own faces, so as to represent them convincingly, and that this made sense, since even when masks were worn, faces were not hidden completely.

2.6 IMPRESARIOS, ACTORS, MUSICIANS

In the absence of comprehensive contemporary accounts of the organization of dramatic performances in Rome, details have to be inferred from scattered remarks by later writers and references in dramatic texts. Therefore, there is more information on palliata than on other dramatic

---

[132] The only exception to actors wearing masks in plays such as tragedies and comedies might have been prologue speakers, who do not impersonate particular characters (see also Beare 1964: 194–5). They could have appeared in neutral costumes and without masks (cf. Ter. *Hec.* 9), perhaps even being their own selves or representing the troupe of actors (cf. Terence's prologues; see also Gilula 1989b). If prologues were spoken by actors taking on other functions in the body of the play, these will have changed into their characters after the prologue (cf. Plaut. *Poen.* 123; 126). Characters of the play delivering prologues will already have worn the appropriate costume (cf. Plaut. *Amph.* 116–17; 142–7).

genres, but general procedures were probably fairly similar for all dramatic genres.

The following details emerge (described by means of modern terminology): bringing plays onto the stage was the responsibility of an impresario (also referred to as professional producer or actor-manager), who had a group of theatre people as well as some equipment at his disposal.[133] This person is often called *dominus gregis* in modern literature; yet this term is not attested in this sense in ancient sources; instead this individual is identified by the term *actor*, or his activity is described by the corresponding verb *agere*.[134] A few impresarios are known by name: T. Publilius Pellio was instrumental in performances of Plautus' *Epidicus* and *Stichus*,[135] while L. Ambivius Turpio arranged performances for Caecilius and Terence[136] and also other poets (Ter. *Haut.* 43–5).[137] Both these men have aristocratic names and were in contact with members of the nobility; they are therefore likely to have been respectable men of substance.[138] Since Ambivius Turpio functions as a prologue speaker in some of Terence's plays and there is more evidence on him, he appears to have been an important and influential personality, and he determines the modern view of an impresario's position.

Magistrates in charge of organizing a festival seem to have bought plays from dramatic poets, while impresarios could function as middlemen.[139]

---

[133] On this figure see Duckworth 1952: 73–4; Beare 1964: 164–6; Blänsdorf 1978: 116–17; Brown 2002; also González Vázquez 2001a.

[134] See Jory 1966; Brown 2002: 235–6. Both *dominus* and *grex* are attested in descriptions of people involved in dramatic performances (esp. Plaut. *Asin.* 2–3), but there is no evidence for the combination of the two terms (unless the text in this Plautus passage is changed).

[135] Cf. Plaut. *Bacch.* 213–15 (cf. also ch. 2.9 and n. 236); Did. on Plaut. *Stich.*; Symm. *Ep.* 10.2.1.

[136] Cf. Did. on Ter. *Hec.*; Ter. *Hec.* 9–57; Did. on Ter. *Haut.*; Ter. *Haut.* 1–52; Donat. on Ter. *Eun.*, *praef.* 1.6; on *Phorm.* 315[2]; Cic. *Sen.* 48; Tac. *Dial.* 20.3; Symm. *Ep.* 1.31.3; 10.2.1.

[137] On T. Publilius Pellio see Garton 1972: 260, no. 125; on L. Ambivius Turpio see Garton 1972: 236–7, no. 4. Other impresarios mentioned in *didascaliae* to Terence's comedies, particularly L. Atilius Praenestinus (cf. Did. on Ter. *Haut.*, *Eun.*, *Phorm.*, *Ad.*; Donat. on Ter. *An.*, *praef.* 1.6; see Garton 1972: 245, no. 55), are usually associated with revival performances. This has also been assumed for Pellio (see Deufert 2002: 25, 34–5).

[138] See Gratwick 1982a: 80 and n. 4.

[139] Cf. Ter. *Eun.* 20: *Menandri Eunuchum, postquam aediles emerunt* ('Menander's *Eunuchus*, after the aediles purchased it'); *Hec.* 57: *pretio emptas meo* ('bought at my price'); Donat. on Ter. *Hec.* 57; Hieron. *Ab Abr.* 1817, 200 BCE (p. 135h Helm); 1859, 158 BCE (p. 142a Helm); 1863, 154 BCE (p. 142e Helm). See e.g. Gold 1987: 41–2; Lebek 1996: 33–4; Brown 2002: 229–31. Donatus (ad loc.) interprets *pretio emptas meo* (Ter. *Hec.* 57), spoken by the impresario, as *aestimatione a me facta, quantum aediles darent* ('estimate made by me as to how much the aediles should give'), which gives an attractive sense and removes a possible contradiction between the statements in Terence's prologues (see also Brown 2002: 231). For some considerations concerning the legal issues of authors' rights in ancient Rome in comparison with modern regulations (though not all aspects of the complex system are taken into account) see Schickert 2005: 92–8.

'Buying a play' must mean that magistrates contracted a poet to provide a script for a dramatic production at a particular festival or decided to use a script or draft offered. The transaction does not imply that magistrates physically received scripts, as these could have been given to impresarios straightaway. The criteria for the selection of plays are not known; and it is uncertain how much the magistrates knew about a play in advance of the purchase (see ch. 2.2). The system was apparently still in place in the time of Augustus (cf. Ov. *Tr.* 2.507–10).

The prologue to the second production of Terence's *Hecyra* claims that the drama was not brought onto the stage again (after the disrupted first attempt) in order to enable the poet to sell it a second time as a new play (Ter. *Hec.* 5–7). This confirms that plays were bought and sold individually; here the statement is intended to emphasize that the play was put on again to demonstrate its artistic quality rather than for financial reasons. The actual negotiations leading to the restaging of *Hecyra* are unclear.[140]

Terence's *Eunuchus* was the most successful Republican drama, as it was soon presented in a repeat performance and earned the playwright an unprecedented sum of money (cf. Suet./Donat. *Vita Ter.* 3; on Ter. *Eun.*, *praef.* 1.6*). The ancient sources are not unanimous on whether the play was performed twice, probably due to popular demand, or whether, for this purpose, it was sold another time. The latter version might be an inference by commentators from what Terence says in *Hecyra*, a reflection of the usual way of how plays were accepted for performance or an attempt at explaining the extraordinary payment. The fact that the huge sum became connected with the play's success in the tradition raises another problem: other sources indicate that playwrights sold their plays prior to performances, at a point in the run-up of the festival when the eventual success could hardly be foreseen. Therefore, in the case of Terence's *Eunuchus*, the authorities might have been forced to increase payment after the outstanding success of the first performance, and this was then combined with the second performance as an obvious sign of the play's impact.

In such a business context it is remarkable that Terence's impresario Ambivius Turpio appears as a self-confident personality who is made to claim that he is not only governed by short-term economic considerations (Ter. *Hec.* 49), but also pursues artistic goals: he promoted young writers of whose qualities he was convinced, even if their plays failed to be successes

---

[140] Lebek (1996: 33) has put forward the theory that Terence had the option to sell the same play (perhaps in revised form) again because the first contract had become invalid as no full production of the play during a festival had taken place; too little is known about the precise procedures to confirm this assumption.

at once, and had their plays restaged till they were properly appreciated (Ter. *Hec.* 1–57; Did. on Ter. *Hec.*; Ter. *Phorm.* 30–4). This method might have led to economic prosperity in the long run (Ter. *Hec.* 56–7); for he acts as a kind of talent scout and ensures that he will be able to work with these writers throughout their career. Yet this procedure requires a sense for identifying promising candidates and a willingness to make initial losses.

At any rate these details in Terence's prologues, if they are reliable, point to an important role of impresarios in introducing new dramatic developments and show that the backing of powerful impresarios may have been essential for poets to continue their dramatic careers. Besides, they could apparently influence a drama's success: one of Terence's prologue speakers claims that an opponent's play had been successful because of the skill of the impresario rather than that of the poet (Ter. *Phorm.* 9–10). By contrast one of Plautus' characters remarks that he loves the play *Epidicus*, but watches in displeasure when Pellio produces it (Plaut. *Bacch.* 213–15). Even if such comments fulfil particular functions in their dramatic contexts, they reveal that impresarios were seen as having an impact on a play's performance.

Impresarios are likely to have been provided with scripts by poets. So-called actors' interpolations or adaptations for later revivals show that troupes of actors felt free to deal with the texts as they wished. It is unclear, though, how much freedom they had at first performances and to what extent poets were involved in productions (after the time of Livius Andronicus, who is said to have appeared as an actor in his own plays). Some scholars have compared Republican dramatists to modern stage-directors, assuming that they had some influence on performance decisions.[141] Terence obviously altered the prologue to *Eunuchus* in the run-up to the festival and wrote specific prologues for the second and third performances of *Hecyra* (Ter. *Eun.* 20–6; *Hec.* 1–57), but other poets' involvement can neither be proved nor disproved. The self-confident stance of Ambivius Turpio, and the description of his role in promoting young poets and of being approached by poets that Terence has him convey in the prologues, suggest that it was the business of impresarios to bring dramas onto the stage. At the same time poets are presented as having full control over script and plot; it is they who 'wish' events to take place or not to take place and actors/characters to do things (e.g. Plaut. *Asin.* 12; *Trin.* 8–9; Ter. *Haut.* 1–2; 11).

---

[141] See Gilula 1989b.

It is unclear what happened to a play's script after the first performance. Technically it must have remained the property of the buyers (i.e. magistrates), but it was presumably kept in the possession of the impresario until he sold or gave it to another impresario. Successful plays were restaged later during the Republican period, as can be inferred from new prologues, alternative endings, doublings or actors' interpolations. The *didascaliae* to Terence's comedies (although the interpretation of these texts is difficult) suggest that other impresarios organized those revivals, but any financial arrangements are unknown. Dramatic poets typically seem not to have been in charge of their plays after they left their hands. Thus they received nothing but the original purchase price, even though plays might be produced more than once. On the other hand, when plays met with an unfavourable reception, playwrights suffered no direct financial loss since they had already received payment (cf. Hor. *Epist.* 2.1.175–6).[142]

Impresarios were responsible for dealing with the practicalities of bringing plays onto the stage. Typically, they were heads of companies of actors (*grex*), who competed with other troupes for commissions.[143] Impresarios could play the part of the protagonist or function as prologue speakers (cf. Ter. *Haut.* 1–52; *Hec.* 9–57). A provider of props (*choragus*), contracting with the aediles, supplied costumes and other equipment to the actors.[144] A paid herald (*praeco*) could be used to mark the start of a performance (cf. Plaut. *Asin.* 4–5; *Poen.* 11–15).

According to some ancient sources, Rome's first poet, Livius Andronicus, appeared as an actor in his own plays, as was common in his time.[145] His involvement seems to be a sign of Roman drama still being in its infancy rather than illustrating a general practice. Plautus possibly had some experience as an actor before he became a comic poet (cf. his name

---

[142] In the phrase *omnes qui tunc scripta et operas suas in scaenam locaverant* ('all those who had then entered contractual arrangements to give their scripts and performance activities to the stage') (Macrob. *Sat.* 2.7.7), Lebek (1996: 45) interprets the verb *locare* as meaning 'hire out'; he then infers that the owners of the scripts (i.e. the poets) retained their property rights and that those poets were shrewd businessmen. Apart from the fact that by the middle of the first century BCE, to which Macrobius' statement refers (see ch. 3.6), practices common in the second century BCE might have changed, *locare* does not necessarily have this specific sense, but rather indicates broadly that items or services are offered or asked for according to some contractual arrangement. In any case, inferring precise business models from a single and difficult piece of evidence in a late writer is problematic, particularly since there is no emphasis on negotiation details (on the phrase see also Panayotakis 2010: 52 and n. 89).

[143] Cf. e.g. Ter. *Haut.* 1–52; esp. 43–5; *Phorm.* 31–5; Plaut. *Asin.* 2–3; *Cas.* 21–2; *Pseud.* 1334.

[144] Cf. Plaut. *Curc.* 464–86, esp. 464; *Pers.* 159–60; *Trin.* 857–8; Donat. on Ter. *Eun.* 967(2).

[145] Cf. Liv. 7.2.8–9; Fest., p. 448 L.; Euanth. *Fab.* 4.3; *Lib. gloss.* 1.7; 2.11. On Livius Andronicus see Garton 1972: 255, no. 102.

and Gell. *NA* 3.3.14). For other Republican playwrights appearances as actors are not known.[146]

The status of actors in Rome is characterized by some specific features in comparison with the situation in classical Greece: in Republican Rome actors were mainly professionals,[147] whereas in classical Athens actors were citizens taking on the role for the occasion of a festival. However, by Hellenistic times troupes of Greek actors (οἱ περὶ τὸν Διόνυσον τεχνῖται) had developed, who toured Greece along with the Greek colonies and performed revivals of classical dramas and contemporary Hellenistic plays.[148]

According to Roman tradition, the first actors in Rome had been summoned there from Etruria (cf. Liv. 7.2.4; Tac. *Ann.* 14.21.1; see ch. 1.5). Actors continued to be mostly foreigners; the few Roman actors came from low social classes (cf. also Tac. *Ann.* 14.21.1). A number of actors in Rome were slaves or freedmen (cf. e.g. Plaut. *Asin.* 2–3; Cic. *Q Rosc.* 27–8).[149] Mime actors and actresses were regarded as of particularly low social status; they played without masks, and actresses might be forced to undress at the end of performances. By contrast, according to Livy (cf. 7.2.11–12), Atellanae could be performed by young noblemen, who retained their citizen rights.

There is no clear evidence on the size of actors' troupes in Republican Rome; yet conditions in Rome were different from Greece: in Rome all performers, whether speaking or not, were members of a troupe and had to be remunerated. Therefore large companies are unlikely, even though there was no dramatic limit on the number of speaking actors. Indeed, while the majority of scenes in surviving Roman comedies do not require more than three speaking parts (the maximum number in Greek drama), Roman dramatists sometimes brought more than three speaking actors (four or five) onto the stage (cf. Diom. *Ars* 3, *Gramm. Lat.* 1, pp. 490.27–491.3;

---

[146] This is often assumed for Naevius, Rome's second dramatist; yet there is no evidence (on Naevius see Garton 1972: 257, no. 113). Butler (1972: 112) suggests that from 240 to about 200 BCE playwrights acted in their own plays and recruited additional actors for each play and that acting troupes came into existence only after 200 BCE, but this theory cannot be verified.

[147] On actors in Rome see e.g. Frank 1931; W. M. Green 1933; Beare 1964: 166–8; Spruit 1966; Blänsdorf 1978: 102–4, 117–22; Dupont 1985: 93–110; Ducos 1990; Blume 1991: 118–20; Leppin 1992; Petrone 1992: 408–13; Edwards 1993: 121–6; Csapo and W. J. Slater 1995: 275–85; Lebek 1996: 36–42; Bernstein 1998: 248–9; Brown 2002; contributions in Hugoniot *et al.* 2004; Duncan 2006: 160–87; Marshall 2006: 83–125; for an overview of scholarship see Leppin 1992: 18–23.

[148] On the Artists of Dionysus see e.g. Pickard-Cambridge 1988: 279–321.

[149] Again (see n. 146 above) Butler (1972: 112) assumes an evolutionary model: only after about 50 BCE, when acting in legitimate plays fell off drastically, did slaves take over the profession. There is no evidence to support this theory.

491.20–30; Euanth. *Com.* 2.2).[150] As further characters on stage tend to be mute attendants, companies of about four to six trained actors, who could be supplemented by hired extras, are plausible for Rome.

Two or more roles may have been assigned to one player, and actors might have changed roles during performances.[151] The only explicit reference to such a procedure comes at the end of a prologue, when the prologue speaker announces that he will put on a costume and become another person (Plaut. *Poen.* 123; 126); however, this is a special case and does not allow general conclusions. Nevertheless, it proves that the practice of doubling roles was known. This is the most economical way of staging plays and also allows the creation of 'star parts'. At any rate, over the course of time a class of trained actors emerged, who were organized in companies; they performed in Rome and are likely to have toured Italy.[152]

The professional element and the low social status led to contempt for acting for a living. Romans were aware that actors and the theatrical arts more generally were not valued highly in their society, in contrast to Greece.[153] In Cicero's day acting on the public stage for payment was looked upon with so much disfavour (cf. also *Dig.* 3.2.2.5) that the actor Q. Roscius Gallus, after having been knighted (cf. Macrob. *Sat.* 3.14.13), apparently refused to accept payment for further performances (cf. Cic. *Q Rosc.* 22–4). The brief appearance of the mime writer Decimus Laberius on stage caused a temporary loss of his equestrian status (cf. Macrob. *Sat.* 2.3.10; 2.7.2–9; Sen. *Controv.* 7.3.9; also Quint. *Inst.* 3.6.18).

The social position of the majority of actors is probably the reason why actors were denied the political and civic rights of ordinary citizens (cf. Cic. *Rep.* 4.10 [= August. *De civ. D.* 2.13]; Tert. *De spect.* 22.2): appearing on stage could result in disgrace (*infamia*) (cf. *Dig.* 3.2.1; 3.2.2.5),[154] and magistrates were allowed to flog actors anywhere and at any time, a custom that was abolished only by Augustus and restricted to performances (cf. Suet. *Aug.* 45.3; Tac. *Ann.* 1.77.3; also Plaut. *Amph.* 26–31; *Cist.* 784b–5). In the late Republic there could be legal restrictions that prevented actors (like other disrespected groups) from becoming members of the Senate,

---

[150] Horace's rule that no more than three speaking actors should appear at any one time (Hor. *Ars P.* 192) may have been influenced by Attic conventions and/or practices of his time, which brought numerous characters on stage, but dispensed with meaningful dialogue (see ch. 2.9).

[151] On this issue see Duckworth 1952: 94–8; Marshall 2006: 94–114 (with further references).

[152] See Rawson (1985) 1991: 477–8.

[153] See e.g. Cic. *Rep.* 4.10 (= August. *De civ. D.* 2.13); 4.13 (= August. *De civ. D.* 2.11); Liv. 24.24.4; Nep. *praef.* 5; Tac. *Dial.* 10.5.

[154] The praetorian edict quoted in the *Digest* gives disgrace (*infamia*) as the result of appearing on stage. An interpretation quoted in the same context, however, reduces it to appearances for payment.

holding office or voting (cf. *Lex Iulia Municipalis* 123 = *FIRA* 1.18); vice versa, senators and their descendants were banned from appearing on stage (cf. Cass. Dio 54.2.5). Actors (with the exception of Atellana actors) were exempt from military service (cf. Liv. 7.2.12), which can be seen as a sign of disgrace and disadvantage, since one could not pursue a political career without some military experience;[155] but this was also a means of enabling the continuation of dramatic productions even in times of crisis.[156]

Such official measures against actors, which marked them as a particular class of people, were probably designed to prevent political and social upheaval arising from the theatre and to deter members of higher social classes from appearing on stage. These arrangements served to mark a clear distinction between politics and dramatic performances in terms of personnel and thus gave all political action coming from the stage a less authoritative ring.[157] At the same time there was a sociological split between the majority of people on stage and the majority of the audience: Roman citizens vs. slaves, foreigners and freedmen. So watching 'others' perform might have confirmed Roman national and civic identity by contrast.[158] Yet as performances included plays on Roman history and other dramas addressing themes relevant to Roman society, there cannot have been a complete differentiation: performers must have been regarded as appropriate vehicles for transmitting messages pertinent to Roman audiences.

Besides this general low regard for theatre people, there was a recognition of individual achievements: for instance, slaves appearing on stage might win their freedom if they were successful actors (cf. e.g. Cic. *Att.* 4.15.6; Suet. *Tib.* 47). Actors' accomplishments could be recognized and rewarded (cf. Tert. *De spect.* 22). Cicero implies that actors, towards the end of their careers, might retire from the stage out of respect for themselves; i.e. he seems to assume that actors have a reputation in their field that they may care for (Cic. *Fam.* 7.1.2). In late Republican times actors such as Q. Roscius Gallus and Clodius Aesopus became famous stars and earned a fortune. Clearly, being an actor did not necessarily lead to an unrecognized position across the board; instead this skill could be honoured in its own right. Still, Cicero recognized an incongruity between Roscius' profession and his character despite his outstanding merits in both areas (Cic. *Q Rosc.* 17; *Quinct.* 78).

When revivals of classical pieces became common and stage business more important, it was talented actors who were crucial to impressive

---

[155] See Gilula 1989a: 101.   [156] See Jory 1970: 233.
[157] See Feldherr 1998: 170.   [158] So Flaig 1995: 100–6.

performances. In the first century BCE important public figures such as
Sulla or Mark Antony began to socialize with actors, which was a target
of reproach for their opponents.[159] The increasing prominence of actors in
this period has been connected by modern scholars with 'the century of the
individual', and the performance of actors in different roles and in different
plays has been seen as a first step, via mime contests in Caesar's time,
towards pantomime with dancers performing solos, where the virtuosity
of individual actors tended to dominate over plot structures.[160] While this
might posit too smooth a development, it is clear that the personality
and education of actors became a significant factor; and training or being
known to have trained with an acclaimed master could ensure success (cf.
Cic. *Q Rosc.* 29–30). That the qualities of single actors were appreciated
may be a result of the fact that a palm frond as a sign of recognition seems
to have been awarded to successful actors or other artists by the magistrates
from at least the time of Plautus.[161]

Actors tended to specialize in either serious or light drama, yet were
not confined to one variety exclusively (cf. Cic. *Orat.* 109; Quint. *Inst.*
11.3.111). In Terence's time the actor L. Minucius Prothymus apparently
appeared in tragedies as well as in comedies (cf. Euanth. *Com.* 6.3; Donat.
Eun., praef. 1.6), as later did Q. Roscius Gallus (with an emphasis on
comedy) and perhaps Clodius Aesopus (with an emphasis on tragedy).[162]
Men played both male and female roles in almost all dramatic genres; only
mimes also had female performers, which contributed to the particularly
low reputation of mime actors and actresses (see ch. 3.6).

The most famous and successful actor in late Republican times was Q.
Roscius Gallus (*c.* 134/125–63/62 BCE).[163] Roscius was primarily a comic
actor – one of his well-known comic roles was the pimp Ballio in Plautus'
Pseudolus (cf. Cic. *Q Rosc.* 20) – but he also performed in Ennius' tragedy
Andromacha (cf. Cic. *De or.* 3.102; also Cic. *Orat.* 109). He was besides a
teacher of his art (cf. Cic. *Q Rosc.* 30; *De or.* 1.129) and wrote a handbook
on acting (cf. Macrob. *Sat.* 3.14.12). Because of his standing he seems to
have enjoyed the exceptional freedom to decide whether he was willing

---

[159] Cf. esp. Cicero against Mark Antony: *Phil.* 2.20; 2.58; 2.61–2; 2.67; 2.101; 8.26; 10.22; 13.24.
[160] See Jory 1988.
[161] Cf. Plaut. *Amph.* 64–74; *Poen.* 36–9; *Trin.* 706–7; Ter. *Phorm.* 16–17; Cic. *Att.* 4.15.6; *Verr.*
2.3.184; Varro, *Ling.* 5.178; Plin. *HN* 7.184–5. On some of these passages see Maurach 1975: 135–7;
Christenson 2000: 150–1.
[162] Additionally, the names of a number of actors, their preferred dramatic genres and some of the
roles they performed are known from inscriptional evidence and comments by ancient writers such
as Cicero (for a survey of all known Republican actors see Garton 1972).
[163] Cf. Cic. *Arch.* 17; *De or.* 1.130; *Div.* 1.79; Quint. *Inst.* 11.3.111; Symm. *Ep.* 10.2.1. See e.g. Garton
1972: 260–1, no. 128; Dupont 1985: 102–9; Lebek 1996: 36–41; Duncan 2006: 173–82.

or able to perform, whereas other actors performed even if indisposed and might then be hissed off the stage (cf. Cic. *De or.* 1.124; 1.259). His success allowed Roscius to move in elite social circles: he was a friend of Cicero (cf. Cic. *Quinct.* 77; Macrob. *Sat.* 3.14.11) and connected with high-ranking noblemen such as Q. Lutatius Catulus, L. Licinius Crassus and L. Cornelius Sulla. Sulla made him a knight in the late 80s or early 70s BCE (cf. Macrob. *Sat.* 3.14.13); thereafter Roscius refused to accept money for his appearances on stage, according to Cicero. Previously, Roscius had made a fortune by his acting, earning about half a million sesterces annually (cf. Cic. *Q Rosc.* 22–3).[164]

His contemporary, the tragic actor Clodius Aesopus,[165] was also on good terms with Cicero (cf. Macrob. *Sat.* 3.14.11). He is called 'greatest artist' by Cicero (Cic. *Sest.* 120: *summus artifex*) and 'most famous actor of tragic plays in those times' by the scholiast (Schol. Bob. on Cic. *Sest.* 120: *actor illis temporibus nobilissimus tragicarum fabularum*). Aesopus specialized in tragic drama (cf. Quint. *Inst.* 11.3.111; Val. Max. 9.1.2; Plin. *HN* 9.122; 10.141), but may also have performed in comedy (cf. Cic. *Orat.* 109). One of his final appearances in the theatre was his unsuccessful return to the stage at the opening of Pompey's Theatre in 55 BCE (cf. Cic. *Fam.* 7.1.2). Aesopus too made a lot of money and left a fortune of twenty million sesterces (cf. Macrob. *Sat.* 3.14.14).

The impresario also had to arrange with a musician for musical accompaniment (see ch. 5.6). Roman dramatists did not compose their own music for their plays; instead this was added by professional musicians (cf. Cic. *De or.* 3.102; Donat. *Com.* 8.9). The musical element was essential in Republican drama, since a great number of lines were accompanied by music.[166] Each troupe of actors may have had its own instrumentalist, who was probably the composer as well as the performer of the music and who arranged, presumably in consultation with the impresario and/or the actors, how the set of various metres as prescribed by the dramatic script should be turned into music. Remarks in Cicero suggest that the composer was expected to support and emphasize the different moods and the emotional development of characters' utterances (Cic. *De or.* 3.102) and that

---

[164] A textual difficulty precludes identifying the exact sum: the text says that Roscius could have made 300,000 sesterces and have earned 6,000,000 sesterces in the last ten years. One of the numbers must be wrong; but it is obvious that Roscius' acting was regarded as being able to secure a good income, particularly since Pliny says that he earned 500,000 sesterces annually (Plin. *HN* 7.128).

[165] See e.g. Garton 1972: 247–8, no. 67; Lebek 1996: 41–2; Duncan 2006: 185–7.

[166] On music in the Roman theatre see e.g. Beare 1964: 168–9, 219–32; Wille 1967: 158–87; Dupont 1985: 88–91; Moore 1998b, 1999, 2007; Wilson 2002: 64–7; Marshall 2006: 203–44.

the individual disposition of actors could influence the music (Cic. *Leg.* 1.11).[167]

In some cases the name of the composer has been recorded (cf. Donat. *Com.* 8.10): Marcipor, slave of Oppius, made the music for Plautus' *Stichus* (cf. Did. on Plaut. *Stich.*). Flaccus, belonging to a Claudius, provided the music for all of Terence's plays (cf. Did. on Ter. *Haut.*, *Eun.*, *Phorm.*, *Hec.*, *Ad.*; Donat. on Ter. *An.*, *praef.* 1.6; *Eun.*, *praef.* 1.6). Plautus' *Stichus* illustrates the role and effect of the musician: during a drinking party with dialogues in accompanied verse the musician is given a drink, and the metre changes to the spoken verse of iambic senarius for a few lines while the musician drinks (Plaut. *Stich.* 715–24; 758–68), only to continue in accompanied verse afterwards. Elsewhere in Plautus the musician is asked by characters to play tunes at specific points in the play, in addition to his usual function of accompanying characters' speeches (Plaut. *Cas.* 798–9; *Pseud.* 573a). A comment in Cicero may imply that, at least in his time, the musician might have stepped up to individual actors whenever it was their turn, and played their accompaniment (Cic. *Mur.* 26).[168]

The musician was called *tibicen*, because he played the *tibia*, a woodwind instrument with reeds. This instrument was virtually always played in pairs, one fingered by each hand; the two parts of the pair (right and left) might be either equal or unequal in length. There were various forms of pipes (e.g. *tibiae Serranae*, *tibiae Phrygiae*), varying in size and pitch, conveying, for instance, a more sober or a more light-hearted mood; out of those the musician chose the appropriate one or ones for each play, since the same instrument could be used for an entire play or exchanged for a different one in the course of the play.[169] The distribution and tone of the music (indicated by the metres used by the playwright and realized by the musician) must have influenced the impression of the character of plays, scenes and protagonists.

2.7 SOCIAL STATUS OF DRAMATIC POETS

Remarkably, the Republican poets who established Latin as a literary language and initiated the composition of literary works in Latin did not come from Rome, but rather from other parts of Italy or even other

---

[167] Marshall (2006: 234–44) suggests that *cantica mixtis modis* required intense rehearsal and that there was a greater element of improvisation in other musical parts.

[168] For a cautious interpretation of this passage see Marshall 2006: 235–6.

[169] Cf. Donat. *Com.* 8.11; on Ter. *Ad.*, *praef.* 1.6; Did. on Ter.; Diom. *Ars* 3, *Gramm. Lat.* 1, p. 492.10–14.

countries:[170] Livius Andronicus was probably of Greek origin and came from southern Italy (cf. his name and Suet. *Gram.* 1.2). Naevius was a Campanian, perhaps from Capua (cf. Gell. *NA* 1.24.2). Ennius was born in the Calabrian/Messapian town of Rudiae.[171] His nephew Pacuvius was of Oscan origin and born in Brundisium.[172] Plautus came from Umbrian Sarsina.[173] Caecilius was an Insubrian Gaul;[174] Terence was of African origin (cf. Suet./Donat. *Vita Ter.* 1); and Publilius Syrus came from Syria.[175] These three were slaves and later freed by their masters, as probably was Livius Andronicus.[176] Accius was the son of freedmen.[177] L. Livius Andronicus and Q. Ennius were eventually given Roman citizenship (for Livius Andronicus cf. his *tria nomina*; for Ennius cf. Cic. *Brut.* 79; *Arch.* 22).

All the regions of the Mediterranean where Roman dramatists came from, particularly Campania and the area around Tarentum, were heavily influenced by Greek culture. This means that these poets brought knowledge of their local customs and language, along with familiarity with Greek traditions, to Rome, where they found yet another cultural environment. Despite their diverse origins they all used the Latin language for their literary works produced in Rome, presumably catering for their immediate audiences. Due to their background and education these playwrights were used to a cultural mix and able to transpose and create plays in an idiom congenial to the Romans. Therefore these non-Roman playwrights contributed to shaping Rome's language and national identity; perhaps their position as 'outsiders' even allowed them to observe the situation more clearly and to identify specific needs and characteristics more precisely.

The reason for the Romans' accepting these 'foreigners' was probably that the Roman 'national character' was open and flexible within a process of adopting and adapting in contact with other peoples (see ch. 1.1).[178] Nevertheless, Romans were aware of the 'foreign' origin of their poets and their poetic literature, its late introduction and its initial low esteem (cf. e.g.

---

[170] On the background of the first poets in Rome see e.g. Jocelyn 1972: 991; Blänsdorf 1978: 104–5; Dumont 1983. For more biographical details see ch. 4.

[171] Cf. Cic. *Arch.* 22; Enn. *Inc.* 10 W. = *Ann.* 525 Sk.; Hor. *Carm.* 4.8.20; Serv. on Verg. *Aen.* 7.691.

[172] Cf. Hieron. *Ab Abr.* 1863, 154 BCE (p. 142e Helm).

[173] Cf. Fest., p. 274 L. = Paul. ex Fest., p. 275 L.; Hieron. *Ab Abr.* 1817, 200 BCE (p. 135h Helm); Suet. *Vita Plaut.*

[174] Cf. Hieron. *Ab Abr.* 1838, 179 BCE (p. 138b Helm); Suet. *Vita Caec.*

[175] Cf. Macrob. *Sat.* 2.7.6; Hieron. *Ab Abr.* 1974, 43 BCE (p. 157k Helm).

[176] Cf. Gell. *NA* 4.20.13; Suet./Donat. *Vita Ter.* 1; Macrob. *Sat.* 2.7.6–7; cf. Hieron. *Ab Abr.* 1829/30, 187 BCE (p. 137c Helm); Suet. *Vita Liv. Andr.*

[177] Cf. Hieron. *Ab Abr.* 1878, 139 BCE (p. 144h Helm); Suet. *Vita Acc.*

[178] See also Batstone 2006: 561–2. On the position of the first Republican poets as 'outsiders' see Classen (1992) 1993: esp. 82–3 (on Ennius).

Cic. *Tusc.* 1.3; Hor. *Epist.* 2.1.156–67). At the same time Cicero emphasizes in his defence speech for the poet Archias that such writers made an important contribution to establishing a literature in Latin, to providing narratives of Roman history, to creating a sense of national identity and to disseminating a favourable portrait of Rome.

Moreover, the first Republican dramatists were not only 'outsiders', but also of low social status; in contrast to practitioners of other literary genres, they were slaves, freedmen or free foreigners (*peregrini*). Historiographers, on the other hand, typically were Roman senators, since this literary genre enjoyed a greater reputation owing to its supposed practical relevance. Roman orators, who published their public speeches, were obviously Roman citizens too. The satirist Lucilius in the second century BCE was a Roman citizen and a wealthy equestrian (cf. Vell. Pat. 2.9.4; Hor. *Sat.* 2.1.75; Lucil. 671–2 M. = 650–1 W.). Because of his not being active in a dramatic poetic genre, he did not depend on public commissions, and was not obliged to win success with audiences or bound by particular generic conventions; these aspects combined to give him greater poetic and social freedom.

Obviously, there was a distinction between aristocrats with literary ambitions and professional poets of low social status. Only towards the end of the Republic, when the close connection between composing dramas and having them produced on stage dissolved, did educated noblemen, such as Iulius Caesar Strabo or Cicero's brother Quintus, start writing tragedies (see ch. 4.18).[179]

The mime writer Decimus Laberius (*c.* 106–43 BCE) is the only professional dramatist of higher social status (equestrian) known to have written for the stage in the Republican period.[180] While clear boundaries might have been breaking down at the end of the Republic, Laberius' social status still became an element in a challenge by Caesar, who forced Laberius to appear on stage in his own mimes and to lose his equestrian status temporarily and who favoured the slave rival in the sequel to this incident (cf. Macrob. *Sat.* 2.3.10; 2.7.2–9; Sen. *Controv.* 7.3.9). However, it might have been Laberius' critical attitude that prompted Caesar's action: whether criticism of Caesar and of contemporary politics in Laberius' mimes (see ch. 3.6, 4.16) was facilitated by his status is uncertain. Witty repartee

[179] See e.g. Conte 1994: 108–9.
[180] If a praetexta about Cornelius Balbus (cf. Cic. *Fam.* 10.32.3; 10.32.5) was written by himself (which is uncertain due to the wording of the *testimonium*), this would be another instance of a drama by a nobleman performed on stage in about the same period (43 BCE). However, in any case, Cornelius Balbus was not a professional dramatist, and this performance took place in Gades (for more details see Manuwald 2001a: 54–62).

with potential political ramifications seems not to have been uncommon among the educated classes at the time, as the exchange between Cicero and Laberius in the same context (cf. Macrob. *Sat.* 2.3.10; Sen. *Controv.* 7.3.9) and Laberius' earlier rejection of Clodius Pulcher's request for a mime indicate (cf. Macrob. *Sat.* 2.6.6).

The organization of festivals in Rome allowed or forced dramatists to make contact with influential noblemen. As the magistrates responsible changed annually, playwrights got to know members of various families, while in view of years to come and possible commissions they had to remain flexible. Whereas actors were apparently regarded as inappropriate company for public officials (see ch. 2.6), playwrights could mingle with high-standing public figures. This was criticized only when noblemen were suspected of exploiting poets for their own purposes (cf. Cic. *Tusc.* 1.3) or when poets could be accused of having received literary support from noble friends (cf. Ter. *Haut.* 22–4; *Ad.* 15–21; Cic. *Att.* 7.3.10; Quint. *Inst.* 10.1.99; Suet./Donat. *Vita Ter.* 4).

The precise nature of the contact between poets and politicians is disputed among scholars. Since some playwrights wrote praetextae concerning the military or political achievements of particular noblemen, produced plays for individuals' funeral games or received benefits from members of specific elite families, they are often regarded as being close to those and attached to them as 'client poets' (*poeta cliens*).[181] However, such a specific relationship and the corresponding impact on the poetry cannot be confirmed. Later generations of dramatic poets seem to have had more conspicuous relationships with members of the elite; however, this does not indicate a greater dependence by the poets, but rather points to an increased interest in literature and intellectual pursuits among the Roman nobility over the course of the Republican period.[182]

---

[181] On this question (with different views) see e.g. La Penna (1977) 1979: 50–3; Martina 1979; G. Williams 1982: 4–7; Gold 1987: 42–50; Gruen, esp. 1990: 79–123; Goldberg 1995: 31, 111–34; Manuwald 2001a: 119–21 (with respect to praetextae); Boyle 2006: e.g. 53, 123–4; Rossi and Breed 2006: 402–5 (most providing further references). It is only for Plautus (and other comic poets with shadowy biographies) that patronage has never been discussed; the reason might be that Plautus did not write epics or tragedies, which may convey the impression of the glorification of individuals (so N. J. Lowe 2008: 97). Republican playwrights could only be regarded as clients when one accepts a looser definition of 'patron' in the sense of 'wealthy or influential supporter of . . . (a) writer'. Although in her survey of the patron–client relationship (1987: 40–50) Gold starts from this definition (1987: 40), she later talks of dramatists being attached to particular patrons, whom they sought to gratify by producing *fabulae praetextae*, and even links the introduction of this new dramatic genre with the status of poets (1987: 42–8).

[182] See Gruen 1990: 119.

A number of specific relationships are attested or inferred: a notorious case is Naevius' protection by the Marcelli, assumed on the basis of his praetexta *Clastidium*, and his fight with the Metelli, deduced from an alleged verse exchange (cf. Ps.-Asc. on Cic. *Verr.* 1.29 [p. 215 St.]). Ennius was brought to Rome by Cato (cf. Nep. *Cato* 1.4) and received Roman citizenship from Q. Fulvius Nobilior (cf. Cic. *Brut.* 79; *Arch.* 22), whose father had taken him on a campaign to Ambracia (cf. Cic. *Tusc.* 1.3; *Arch.* 27; [Aur. Vict.] *De vir. ill.* 52.2–3) and had been presented in Ennius' praetexta *Ambracia* and his epic *Annales*. Cicero calls Pacuvius a *hospes* and an *amicus* of C. Laelius (Cic. *Amic.* 24), and the poet composed a praetexta on L. Aemilius Paul(l)us. Accius had friendly relations with D. Iunius Brutus Callaicus (cf. Cic. *Brut.* 107; *Arch.* 27); he wrote inscriptions to be displayed on temples and monuments erected by him (cf. Cic. *Arch.* 27; Val. Max. 8.14.2) as well as a praetexta about L. Brutus, the founder of the Republic. Terence produced plays for the funeral of L. Aemilius Paul(l)us (cf. Did. on Ter. *Hec.*, *Ad.*) and was accused of being supported by noble friends in the composition of his dramas (cf. Ter. *Haut.* 22–4; *Ad.* 15–21; also Cic. *Att.* 7.3.10; Suet./Donat. *Vita Ter.* 4).[183] Manumitted slaves such as Caecilius Statius or Terence are likely to have stayed in touch with their former masters.

Ennius had connections with various aristocrats: Cato criticized M. Fulvius Nobilior for having Ennius accompany him on a military campaign (cf. Cic. *Tusc.* 1.3); this suggests that such an arrangement was not common practice. The same Ennius is said by Cicero to have praised several noblemen (even after their deaths, which made his eulogy less suspicious) and given adornment to the whole Roman people by his presentation of individuals (cf. Cic. *Brut.* 57–9; *Arch.* 22). The portrait of the 'good companion' in Ennius' *Annales*, often identified with the poet on the basis of Aelius Stilo's comments (cf. Gell. *NA* 12.4), presents a person who is familiar with a nobleman and is his social inferior, but not completely dependent on him. A humorous anecdote about Ennius and Scipio Nasica (cf. Cic. *De or.* 2.276) also seems to be based on social equality between poet and nobleman.

Dramatic poets clearly were in touch with the highest ranks of society; and members of the nobility will have commissioned playwrights for special occasions and have entertained good relationships with them. Yet this does

---

[183] On the problematic idea of a 'Scipionic circle', to which Terence, his 'patrons' and other poets are thought to have belonged, see (with a collection of sources and bibliography) Suerbaum 2002: 483–7 (with a mildly sceptical view); also Baldarelli 2004: 22–30 (with broad acceptance of the tradition).

not determine the overall status of the respective poets and the outlook of their poetry: in the Republican period all plays were performed at festivals open to the public, and poets did not write dramas exclusively for specific patrons. Therefore dramatists are more likely not to have been attached to particular families as clients; they rather moved freely among the nobility and worked for various families. Besides, they may have had a general literary, political and educational interest of their own in the topics treated, which would make their statements patriotic rather than partisan.[184]

Roman playwrights did not compete with each other in contests, as Greek dramatists did at festivals in Athens;[185] instead they received payment for the provision of dramatic scripts (see ch. 2.2, 2.6). Although Plautus' prologues use *scribere* only with respect to Greek comic writers (e.g. Plaut. *Asin.* 11; *Trin.* 19), while they identify the title of the Latin play or the names of characters as the 'wish' of the poet (e.g. Plaut. *Asin.* 12; *Trin.* 8–9), Terence's prologues make it clear that the poet has written words that he wants dramatic characters to deliver (Ter. *Haut.* 10–15). Since such a procedure must have been imaginable, it is likely that poets composed plays in writing. The scripts would have been outlines of performances, almost like libretti to modern operas, which had to be turned into full performances by impresarios and troupes of actors.

There is no evidence on how much money a play could typically win and how many plays had to be sold per year to guarantee a playwright's income.[186] At any rate, one of Terence's prologue speakers claims that the poet depended on writing plays for his living (Ter. *Phorm.* 18). In economic terms Terence's *Eunuchus* was the most successful Republican drama: it earned the playwright an unprecedented sum of money (cf. Suet./Donat. *Vita Ter.* 3: *octo milia nummorum*; Donat. on Ter. *Eun., praef.* 1.6*: *octo milibus sestertium*).[187] Early Roman poets are said also to have worked as teachers (cf. Suet. *Gram.* 1.2); Pacuvius was both a poet and a painter (cf. Plin. *HN* 35.19; Hieron. *Ab Abr.* 1863, 154 BCE [p. 142e Helm]).

Because of their low social position, playwrights had to acquire self-confidence and ensure their standing by their poetic art; their funerary

---

[184] See e.g. Jocelyn 1972: 1000; Gruen 1990: 122–3 (who emphasizes, perhaps too strongly, that poets followed their own agenda when writing poetry of national relevance).

[185] See e.g. Jocelyn 1972: 999.   [186] On these issues see Gilula 1985/8; Lebek 1996.

[187] The sum paid for Terence's *Eunuchus* was topped only in early Augustan times: L. Varius Rufus received one million sesterces for his tragedy *Thyestes*, composed for Octavian's games after the battle of Actium (cf. Did. in Cod. Paris. 7530 et Casin. 1086 [p. 309 Klotz]), the highest sum ever paid for a drama in Rome (see Lefèvre 1978b: 16).

inscriptions (even if possibly spurious) can demonstrate that their poetic virtuosity was their significant characteristic (cf. Gell. *NA* 1.24). Individual dramatists may have gained a sound level of self-confidence: the late Republican tragic poet Accius, sure of his poetic accomplishments, had a tall statue of himself erected in the Temple of the Camenae/Muses (cf. Plin. *HN* 34.19) and did not get up to greet a fellow member of the 'college of poets' (*collegium poetarum*), Iulius Caesar Strabo, who was a nobleman, but a literary dilettante in Accius' view (cf. Val. Max. 3.7.11).

Earlier, in honour of Livius Andronicus' achievements, writers and actors were assigned the Temple of Minerva on the Aventine as an official meeting place after 207 BCE (cf. Fest., pp. 446/8 L.).[188] As Dionysus/Bacchus was not the god of theatre in Rome (as in Greece), an attachment to another divinity was apparently sought: Athena/Minerva, the goddess of arts and crafts, was an appropriate choice although there was no particular connection between this patron goddess and a specific festival.[189]

Granting the Temple of Minerva as a meeting place to writers and actors was a religious and political decision of the nobility.[190] It has been assumed that it was designed to demonstrate Rome's equality with the Greek world and give the growing artistic profession a structure that could be controlled more easily. The way, however, in which Festus reports this step and the connection with Livius Andronicus' successful hymn suggest an appreciation of the poet's literary contributions to the *res publica* as the dominant motivation. The decision indicates an increasing recognition of writers and actors as an important group within society and signals public appreciation of the performing arts.[191]

In the sources there is no mention of the formation of a guild at this time, but merely of a group of the populace being given a meeting place and a venue for offerings. Since many early playwrights and actors were

---

[188] On the history and character of the *collegium scribarum histrionumque* and the *collegium poetarum* and on the possible relationship between them (with different solutions) see e.g. Jory 1970; Dolç 1971; Crowther 1973; Grimal 1975: 252–5; Horsfall 1976; Quinn 1982: 173–6; Gruen 1990: 87–91; A. Romano 1990; Brown 2002: 227 (with bibliographies). Some scholars assign particular importance to the *collegium poetarum*, regarded as a major force in shaping Rome's literary history and as a forum for the exchange of poetic ideas. However, the lack of sufficient sources makes it impossible to confirm such wide-ranging conclusions.

[189] There is no evidence to prove the assumption that some early playwrights and actors initially were members of guilds of the Artists of Dionysus in southern Italy, that therefore their guild in Rome began under the patronage of Dionysus and that the change to the patronage of Minerva was made when both magistrates and the guild saw the need for a close connection with a Roman deity (so Jory 1970: 230; Gruen 1990: 88–9).

[190] See e.g. Gruen 1990: 88–9.   [191] See Dolç 1971: 272; Gruen 1990: 105–6, 1992: 197.

foreigners, they may have needed special permission to dedicate offerings to Minerva and to take part in Roman state worship.[192] Due to lack of evidence it must remain uncertain how long this arrangement continued to exist and whether or how it relates to the 'college of poets' (*collegium poetarum*) attested for Accius' time (cf. Val. Max. 3.7.11).

Appreciation of individual poets and/or the financial situation might have provoked rivalries between dramatic poets. In literary terms there is a tendency among later poets in relation to well-known existing dramas to take up the topics of predecessors, while presenting them differently, or to choose plots that are connected to those of earlier plays, but not identical to them. A possible feud between contemporary dramatic poets is prominent in Terence's prologues (see ch. 4.9), when he has prologue speakers defend his dramas against the criticism of opponents (Ter. *An.* 5–23; *Haut.* 10–30; *Eun.* 1–43; *Phorm.* 1–24; *Ad.* 1–25) or talk about the failures of the first performances of *Hecyra*, whose disruptions might have been organized by rival poets (Ter. *Hec.* 1–57; *Phorm.* 30–4).[193] Since Terence's prologues include a reference to the comparable fate of Caecilius Statius (Ter. *Hec.* 10–27), Terence's case might not have been a unique experience.

Republican Rome offered numerous opportunities for dramatic performances, and there was a corresponding demand for plays (see ch. 2.1). Since only few great playwrights are known to have been active in any one dramatic genre simultaneously, poets who had established themselves probably had reasonable chances of having their plays accepted for performance. However, in order to profit from this situation, a dramatist's plays had to appeal to the taste of audiences and meet the expectations of the authorities, although there was no actual censorship in Rome.[194] Apart from the fact that the choice of plots and topics might have been limited by dramatic conventions, poets were potentially free to bring onto the stage whatever they wished as long as it was going to be a success and did not violate Roman customs. At least in the beginning obvious topical references and open criticism of contemporaries by dramatists seem to have been disapproved of and discouraged; they came to be included in the late Republic, and indirect references can be identified earlier. Playwrights always sought to make their pieces relevant to contemporary audiences.

---

[192] See Jory 1970: 229–30.   [193] See Gilula 1981: 30; Parker 1996: 600–1.
[194] For the single instance of Sp. Maecius Tarpa, appointed to select the entertainment for the inauguration of Pompey's Theatre (cf. Cic. *Fam.* 7.1.1), see ch. 5.2 and n. 34.

2.8 THEATRE AUDIENCES

Dramatic performances in Republican Rome, being part of public festivals, could potentially attract a large and diverse crowd of spectators, drawn from all groups of the local populace and visitors from elsewhere.[195] Audiences therefore must have been mixed as to background, social class, age, sex and occupation. Comic prologues (esp. Plaut. *Poen.* 5–35; Ter. *Hec.* 28–48) mention free citizens (*liberi*), slaves (*servi*), married ladies (*matronae*), nurses with infants (*nutrices* and *pueri infantes*), prostitutes (*scorta*), attendants on the magistrates (*lictores*) and ushers (*dissignatores*) as members of the audience, even though, due to their humorous nature, these passages might not give an accurate portrait.[196] It is uncertain how many representatives of the various groups in Roman society typically attended and whether the numbers reflected their relative share of the Roman populace.[197] Presiding magistrates and their colleagues could be present *ex officio* (cf. Cic. *Sest.* 117). In Cicero's time performances were regarded as significant public events at which important figures were expected to make their appearance (see ch. 2.9).

As festivals were funded by public money and the contributions of the presiding magistrates (or wealthy families), there was no entrance fee. This situation will have influenced the spectators' attitude both to the magistrates responsible for the entertainment and to the theatre people providing it:[198] audiences were not determined to get good value for money; nevertheless actors will have aimed at pleasing them, since success will have been essential for securing further contracts (cf. e.g. Ter. *An.* 1–3; 24–7).

---

[195] On audiences and seating arrangements at Roman dramatic performances see e.g. Duckworth 1952: 79–82; Beare 1964: 173–5, 241–7; Handley 1975; Blänsdorf 1978: 104–11; Kindermann 1979: 123–214; Dupont 1985: 111–28; Petrone 1992: 414–20; Moore 1994; Marshall 2006: 73–82.

[196] See N. W. Slater 1992b: 138.

[197] Vanderbroeck (1987: 77–81; approvingly Beacham 1999: 59) has put forward the theory that the composition of theatre audiences was subject to manipulation so as to exclude the *plebs contionalis*, that therefore spectators in the theatre differed from participants in popular assemblies and hence could not be regarded as a fair representation of the Roman citizenry. However, there is no evidence for this, and only on the assumption of general accessibility do Cicero's comments on the behaviour of audiences in the late Republic make sense (see Tatum 1990). The composition of the audience allowed Cicero to uphold the fiction that the people present represented the whole citizen body; the same ideology operated for popular assemblies.

[198] See Marshall 2006: 74. Kindermann (1979: 185–6) assumes that some spectators, apparently those from higher social classes and/or those who wished to reserve seats, paid an entrance fee. Yet it is only for gladiatorial games that an increasing tendency of influential politicians to secure tickets for their clients and members of their tribes and thus to influence their vote and ensure their loyalty is attested (cf. Cic. *Att.* 2.1.5; *Mur.* 67; 72).

Thus the taste of audiences and its changes must still have had a significant influence on the style and content of the plays shown.[199]

The fact that dramas were given as part of festivals might also have affected audience expectations and the impact of performances. Because of the holiday context Roman drama has been described as 'escapist fare', privileging spectacle over more reflective aspects.[200] Although ordinary public business was reduced on holidays, games constituted a public event (where the social structure of society was maintained) and an integral part of civic life for the whole community. Even if dramas occurred in a context separated from official business, the religious and political framework of the games turned it into a community event. Generally, entertainment and pertinent reflective elements are not mutually exclusive.

Still, what spectators expected from the plays presumably differed widely; for the various groups in the audience must have represented a range of varying degrees of education and experience. Yet plays can be enjoyed on several levels if only all spectators grasp the main plot.[201] Surviving palliatae show that steps were taken to ensure that everyone could follow the basic story: essential information tends to be conveyed in spoken verse; for instance, almost all prologues or initial scenes in extant Roman comedy, which outline the basic tenets of the plot, are in iambic senarii. The setting, the identity of characters, the relationships among them and frequently also their intentions are described. What all dramatists seem to have attempted moreover is to present successful drama. A major aim must have been to retain the audience's attention until the end of a performance.[202]

Some of Plautus' prologues indicate that theatre crowds enjoyed the event as a whole: actors therefore had to make an effort to win attention at the start, and prologue speakers ask spectators to follow the play attentively and favourably.[203] Such behaviour is only to be expected from mixed audiences in improvised performance spaces and hence does not mean that Roman audiences were more unruly and less cultured than Greek

---

[199] See e.g. Kindermann 1979: 132.

[200] See e.g. Beacham 1991: 16–17; Dumont 1992: 40; Feldherr 1998: 169–70. This would be a characteristic not specific to performances in Rome, but also valid for other societies where dramatic performances are given as part of festivals.

[201] See also Franko 2001: 155.

[202] Cf. Hor. *Ars P.* 153–5; Porph. ad loc.; Donat. on Ter. *Ad., praef.* 1.4*; 3.7; *Eun., praef.* 1.5*; Euanth. *Fab.* 3.1.

[203] Cf. Plaut. *Amph.* 15–16; *Asin.* 1–5; 14; *Cas.* 21–2; *Men.* 1–4; *Poen.* 1–45; Ter. *An.* 24; cf. also Hor. *Epist.* 2.1.199–207.

ones, who are known to have taken refreshments during performances and occasionally been noisy and emotional.[204]

Generally, starting off with comments on the current situation of the audience (as some of Plautus' prologues do) may be regarded as a clever way of making a transition from the pre-performance noise in an open-air theatre to the actual play. Terence's different type of prologue demonstrates, however, that there was the option of beginning with more serious matter straightaway, although the information given in his prologues is not essential for just following the plot. Yet Plautus opened some of his prologues with immediate information on details of the plot or characteristics of the play or did not include a prologue at all.[205] Both playwrights apparently worked on the basis that the attention of the audience could be won from the start. In any case, prologues fulfil an inductive function, negotiating the conditions for the reception of the ensuing dramas:[206] they help to determine the proper roles for actors and audiences, and they both draw the audiences into the world of the play and set the play's plot in motion.

Since Roman comedies include crude jokes and slapstick effects, scholars have assumed that audiences in Rome were less educated and intellectually interested than those in Greece.[207] The failed first two performances of Terence's *Hecyra* (cf. Ter. *Hec.* 1–57; *Phorm.* 30–4) are often mentioned as evidence for the base interests of Roman audiences. But even if one does not accept the over-sceptical position that the account in the surviving prologues to Terence's *Hecyra* is fictitious and rather a comment on contemporary events,[208] close analysis reveals that, at least according to Terence, the audience prepared to watch Terence's play did not leave on hearing news of other entertainments, but that other spectators who had heard the rumour of an alternative performance to be given in the

---

[204] Cf. e.g. Arist. *Eth. Nic.* 10.5: 1175b12–13; Pl. *Leg.* 3: 700a7–1b3; *Rep.* 6: 492b5–c1; Dem. *Meid.* 226. On the behaviour of Greek audiences see Kindermann 1979: 21–2; Pickard-Cambridge 1988: 272–5; Wallace 1997.

[205] Cf. e.g. Plaut. *Aul.* 1–39; *Capt.* 1–68; *Trin.* 1–2; cf. e.g. Plaut. *Cist., Curc., Epid., Merc., Mil., Mostell., Pers., Pseud., Stich.*

[206] See N. W. Slater 1992b.

[207] Polybius' description of the performances at L. Anicius Gallus' triumphal games in 167 BCE (Polyb. 30.22) illustrates the differences between performances in Greece and in Rome from a Greek point of view rather than the lack of sophistication on the part of Roman audiences. In the Greek context Aristotle distinguishes between two kinds of spectators (with respect to music), the free and educated ones and the crowd of artisans, labourers and other people of this kind, who should be entertained in different ways (Arist. *Pol.* 8: 1342a16–28).

[208] So Gruen 1992: 210–18.

same venue broke in, disrupted the ongoing performance and prevented its completion.[209]

Thus there were groups of Romans who were not interested in a performance of *Hecyra* and keen on other kinds of entertainments, while another group had come to see *Hecyra* and apparently enjoyed the first part of the play (cf. Ter. *Hec.* 39). These circumstances tell against a general lack of interest in proper drama among Roman audiences. Moreover, spectators had quickly become familiar with dramatic conventions after the introduction of literary drama, were obviously able to understand (Greek) mythical or fictional stories and apply those messages to their own situation, appreciated allusions to tragedy in comedy and could be confronted with questions of literary history.[210] When Terence pleads for a hearing at the third attempt at getting *Hecyra* performed, he appeals to the discernment of the audience and insinuates that their appreciation of the play would benefit the dramatic art and the quality of the festival; apparently, referring to people's intellect could work as a *captatio benevolentiae*.[211] Equally, when the prologue to a revival performance of Plautus' *Casina* claims that audiences preferred 'old' plays (particularly those by Plautus) to worthless 'new' ones (Plaut. *Cas.* 5–20), this implies that audiences were able to assess plays for their quality and were aware of differences between the works of individual playwrights (see ch. 2.9).

By the period of the surviving comedies audiences had experience of watching Greek-style plays in Rome; and they seem to have gained expertise over time: later dramatists dealt with Greek models more self-confidently, which became possible with the refinement of literary techniques, but must also have corresponded to the increased receptiveness of audiences.[212] Metaliterary, self-referential comments on dramatic genres (see ch. 5.3) indicate that playwrights assumed audiences to be familiar with the standard set-up and generic conventions.[213] Poets would not have included such remarks if

---

[209] See Gilula 1978, 1981; Sandbach 1982; Parker 1996: esp. 592–601; Lada-Richards 2004: 56–8.

[210] On the 'sophistication' of Roman audiences see e.g. Cèbe 1960; Chalmers 1965; J. Wright 1974: 190–2; Handley 1975; Nicolet 1980: 372–3 (contrast e.g. Benz 1995: 152); see also Taplin 2007: 21–2 (on the addressees of Greek-style vase-paintings in Italy); for a defence of the sophistication of the Roman public in the Republican period see also Guillemin 1934. It is sometimes assumed that proper dramatic performances mainly attracted the higher social classes, while the lower ones preferred other entertainments such as gladiator shows, races or farces, and that comedies were more popular with the populace than tragedies (so e.g. Kindermann 1979: 139, 149, 158). But the prologues to extant Roman comedies and the playwrights' techniques of conveying information indicate that they expected diverse audiences; there is no evidence of a varying social composition of audiences according to dramatic genre.

[211] See also Lada-Richards 2004: 60–3.   [212] See Handley 1975; Rawson, *CAH²* VIII: 444.

[213] See e.g. Dumont 1992: 42–3; Parker 1996: esp. 603.

there had been no feedback from audiences; this poetic technique points to the sophistication of spectators.[214]

Cicero highlights the musical and rhythmical sensibility of average audiences (in his time): he not only says that 'experts' could recognize a particular character or drama by the first few bars of its characteristic music (Cic. *Acad.* 2.20; 2.86; see ch. 5.6), but also stresses that audiences noticed immediately when actors got the rhythm wrong and that they reacted with loud shouting and hissing (Cic. *De or.* 3.196; *Parad.* 26; *Orat.* 173).

That a large number of plays performed in Rome were set in Greece and based on a Greek cultural background led to a variety of consequences for audiences. First, the stage assumed an educational function by disseminating knowledge of Greek myth and culture. Second, there was the simultaneous effect of distance and familiarity: on the one hand the stories were set in a dramatic version of everyday Greece or the world of Greek myth; the people involved were not direct reflections of members of the audience, and poets could present aspects or customs unusual in Roman society. This underscores the make-believe element of the theatrical experience, while Greek characters may also represent a way of life from which the Romans are positively distinguished. On the other hand the stories often touched issues relevant to a Roman public, for instance problems within families, the (right) behaviour of rulers or a variety of ethical and moral questions (see ch. 5.2).[215]

Spectators would have some knowledge of Greek slaves and of the basics of Greek myth from their everyday experiences. An awareness of the plays' Greek background and a broad familiarity with Greek conventions seem to have been presupposed by poets, as extant scripts include references to Greek poets, figures from Greek myth or history and Greek place names as well as metatheatrical remarks. Plautus assumes a basic understanding of the Greek language, for instance when he plays with speaking names in Greek (e.g. Plaut. *Merc.* 516b–17a; *Poen.* 91–2).[216]

Later commentators noted incongruities between the Latin-speaking actors and the Greek environment. For instance, Varro criticized the fact

---

[214] See also N. W. Slater 1992b: 134 n. 6, who points out that 'the Lar's very first line [in *Aulularia*] implies an awareness of audience expectation and the need to shape that expectation which we never see in Greek New Comedy'.

[215] Hence the Greek setting does not invite the assumption that the action on stage was not a reflection of Roman society (so Gilula 1989a: 102) and there was pressure 'to alter their original highly sophisticated cultural performance into an inartistic substitute' (so Gilula 1989a: 107).

[216] The same is true for the Punic language and typical Punic occupations, since the speech in Punic by a character in *Poenulus* and the garbled translations of more utterances as well as references to the alleged cargo will be funnier if people have an idea of what it is supposed to mean (Plaut. *Poen.* 930–49; 982–1031; see Palmer 1997: 39–40).

that Ennius alluded to the etymology of the names of Andromacha and Alexander, since the meaning of these names would be obvious in a Greek context, but not so in a Latin one (Varro, *Ling.* 7.82). Cicero found fault with Pacuvius because he had a character talk about words used by 'the Greeks' although the audience is supposed to hear a Greek speaking (Cic. *Nat. Deor.* 2.91). Such criticism is justified on a formal level, but ignores the cultural and linguistic sophistication of poets and the theatre-going public. In the first example the etymological references refer to the adopted Greek names, and it is assumed that Roman audiences have a basic level of Greek so that they realize the literal meaning. The second example is spoken from the point of view of audiences in a passage where the poet introduces complex philosophical concepts.

In the late Republic audiences were quick to see potential topical references in revival performances (see ch. 2.9). At the same time they were not immune to the presentation of morally impressive behaviour: both Cicero and later Seneca attest to the fact that audiences reacted whenever moving scenes, ethically impressive behaviour or moral truths that had a bearing on their own lives were shown (Cic. *Fin.* 5.63; *Tusc.* 1.106; *Amic.* 24; Sen. *Ep.* 108.8–9). Cicero even assigns to the stage and the poet a position as influential as that of a parent or a teacher (Cic. *Leg.* 1.47; cf. also Ar. *Ran.* 1053–6a) and regards the conduct of characters on stage as paradigmatic for people's own lives (see ch. 2.10).

At a visit to the theatre, ushers (*dissignatores*) might help people to find seats; even after performances had begun, they might escort latecomers to available seats (cf. Plaut. *Poen.* 19–22). Hired claques (*favitores delegati*) could influence the applause and thus the success of performers: in the prologue to Plautus' *Amphitruo* it is requested that 'detectives' (*conquistores*) seek these out and prevent them from giving an unfair advantage to particular actors (Plaut. *Amph.* 64–85).

In the beginning, when there was no stage curtain, the start of the dramatic performance would be indicated by the first words of the actors and especially of the prologue speaker; additionally, there could be a herald (*praeco*) to quieten down the audience (cf. Plaut. *Asin.* 4–5; *Poen.* 11–15). It is uncertain whether audiences coming to the venue knew what was awaiting them, beyond the fact that it was clear from the day of the festival whether performances would be scenic or circensic.[217] Evidence from the surviving plays is ambiguous: even though some comedies do not have prologues, existing Plautine prologues seem to assume that audiences do not know

---

[217] See Beare 1964: 170; Handley 1975: 119; Kindermann 1979: 133.

what drama is about to be performed, since they typically give the title of the play, details of the Greek model and sometimes the Roman poet's name. Some prologues even play with audience expectations by pretending to disappoint them as to the dramatic genre.

Terence's prologues, on the other hand, mention the title of the play or the name of the Greek poet only occasionally, but rather seem to expect audiences to have this information or not to wait for it. The prologue speaker of *Heautontimorumenos* reveals the play's title and the fact that it has been adapted from a fresh Greek drama, and then adds that he would tell the audience the names of the poets of the Latin and the Greek plays if he did not believe that the majority knew them already (Ter. *Haut.* 5–9). Donatus seems to suppose that titles were made available to audiences in advance (Donat. *Com.* 8.11); he obviously thinks that plays were advertised by their titles and the names of the playwrights and that this was a means to attract audiences.

Explanations (especially at the beginning of surviving scripts) of the plot of the play, the inhabitants of the stage-houses and the history of individual characters suggest that there were no programmes or other previous information about details. To understand pieces fully, audiences would have to follow performances attentively and possibly supplement the information given with their imagination.

Audience reception of dramatic performances also depends on the physical shape of performance spaces (see ch. 2.4) and the audience's position therein. In Rome this aspect is determined primarily by the temporary nature of early theatres and by the development of dramatic productions into an established element within a stratified society.

In the early days, when plays were performed in the Circus Maximus, in the Forum or in front of temples, a stage was put up, but there was not necessarily a designated auditorium. Instead, audiences would use the tiers of the Circus or the temple steps, possibly supplemented with temporary wooden structures or portable seating provided by spectators for themselves (cf. Liv. 1.35.7–9). Only from the time when proper theatres were being built was there an actual auditorium.

The layout of early performance spaces suggests that typically an audience of only a few thousand could have attended each performance.[218] Although it is difficult to work out precise numbers due to a range of uncertainties, this is a significantly smaller number of people than would

---

[218] See Goldberg 1998: esp. 13–14; also Balsdon 1969: 268; Marshall 2006: 79–80.

have been able to attend a theatrical performance in Greece or a circus event in Rome.[219] The limited size of performance spaces might be one reason why Terence's *Eunuchus* was repeated or 'repetitions for religious reasons' (*instaurationes*) of entire festivals (including another performance of the plays shown during the festival) were arranged, since thereby the overall number of people who could watch a production of a particular play increased. At the same time these estimates mean that only a proportion of the populace was assembled at a dramatic performance at any one time; therefore such an event could not literally bring urban life to a standstill,[220] while the fact that a (religious) festival of the entire community was taking place would still be recognized.

The physical position of the audience in temporary locations was different from that in full-scale Greek or Roman theatres: spectators were closer and physically lower with respect to the stage-action. A relatively small performance space and lack of an orchestra enabled an easy and informal relationship between players and audiences.[221] Audiences might be involved in the play, for instance, by characters addressing them, appealing to their own experiences or drawing them into confidence (e.g. Plaut. *Merc.* 1–8; *Pseud.* 584–5; *Stich.* 446–9; *Truc.* 482–3); this could give performances an interactive dimension.[222]

The structure of known venues indicates that audiences were seated at dramatic performances in Rome. It would be strange if the Romans had not adapted the custom of their own circus games and of dramatic performances in Greece to their dramatic shows. However, *testimonia* on the question of whether Roman audiences were seated are ambiguous. Another, related issue is the gradual introduction of stratified seating.

From Livy (Liv. *Epit.* 48) and Valerius Maximus (Val. Max. 2.4.2) it appears that in 154 BCE a Senate decree was passed on the initiative of the consular P. Cornelius Scipio Nasica (Corculum), saying that in the city

---

[219] See Kindermann 1979: 18–19; Pickard-Cambridge 1988: 261; Csapo and W. J. Slater 1995: 286. The size of audiences in Greece cannot be determined precisely either, but the Lycurgean Theatre of Dionysus in Athens is thought to have had a capacity of around 15,000 (see e.g. Pickard-Cambridge 1946: 138, 141).

[220] See Balsdon 1969: 268; Goldberg 1998: 15–16. This conclusion might appear to be contradicted by Suetonius' report that on performance days guards were posted throughout the city in order to prevent idlers from doing harm in the empty city (Suet. *Aug.* 43.1). But this is likely to refer to performances in the larger stone theatres of the imperial period. Tacitus seems to imply that Pompey's Theatre could hold a large proportion of the populace (Tac. *Ann.* 13.54.3).

[221] On the influence of the shape of performance spaces on the role of audiences see Goldberg 1998: 16–19; on the relationship of audiences to the action see e.g. Kraus 1934; González Vázquez 2000.

[222] On the simultaneously receptive and productive role of theatre audiences see Bennett 1997; taken up in Marshall 2006: 73–82.

of Rome and within a radius of one Roman mile no 'seating structures' (*subsellia*) should be erected and no one should watch the games seated, in order to display Roman manhood (see ch. 2.4). The summary of Livy mentions as a consequence that people watched the games standing 'for a while' (*aliquamdiu*). Tacitus (Tac. *Ann.* 14.20.2) records that Pompey was censured by some elders for the construction of his theatre; Tacitus explains that games used to be given with temporary stages and tiers of seats, whereas in an even earlier period (*si vetustiora repetas*) people had watched the games standing so as to be prevented from becoming idle.

On this basis it has been inferred that originally audiences remained standing in Rome.[223] However, Tacitus refers this custom to a very early period; the theatre demolished in 154 BCE must have included seats for the reaction of the Senate to make sense. According to the summary of Livy this reinforcement had only a short-lived effect, while the wording suggests that it was a temporary interruption of an otherwise continuous tradition. Tacitus records 'temporary seating structures' (Tac. *Ann.* 14.20.2: *subitarii gradus*) for performances prior to the inauguration of Pompey's Theatre.

Hence one may conclude that in the early days, when dramatic performances were introduced to Rome and were not yet a proper institution with the concomitant structures, for a limited period of time, audiences watched standing. Fairly soon, however, seats were introduced, even if temporary and provisional. When masses assembled in the theatre came to be regarded as politically problematic, the ancient custom was interpreted as a display of Roman virility, and this was used as an excuse for strict measures. Yet in this phase of institutionalized scenic performances the custom that had established itself in the meantime could no longer be changed effectively.

There is sufficient evidence that audiences (or at least the major part of them) were seated in the times of Plautus and Terence, since there are numerous passages that presuppose seated audiences, both in prologues or epilogues (whose dating might be controversial) and in the body of the plays; they cannot be explained in their entirety by inconsiderate translation of Greek models, particularly since Roman dramatists generally adapted such technical aspects to Roman customs.[224] Hence for most of the history of dramatic performances in Rome, theatre structures will have had seats for audiences, with presumably a brief interruption after 154 BCE.

Originally seats seem to have been allocated on a 'first come, first served' basis; from remarks on seated and standing sections of audiences in Plautus

---

[223] Isidorus defines a theatre as a place where people watch standing (Isid. *Etym.* 18.42.1).
[224] Cf. e.g. Plaut. *Amph.* 65–6; *Aul.* 718–19; *Capt.* 11–12; *Epid.* 733; *Mil.* 81–3; *Poen.* 5; 10; 19–20; 1224; *Pseud.* 1–2; *Truc.* 968.

it is likely that in his time some venues did not offer sufficient numbers of seats and that slaves and Romans of lower social status were expected to stand if there was a shortage of seats (Plaut. *Capt.* 11–12; *Poen.* 19–24; also Cic. *Har. resp.* 26).[225] Valerius Maximus claims that because of respect for their elders and awareness of their own position Romans always took their seats according to rank even without formal regulations (Val. Max. 4.5.1). From the second century BCE onwards, at any rate, seating was formally arranged according to social class. That prestigious seats were assigned to members of higher social classes shows that drama was recognized as a significant public institution and that, although performances took place on holidays, the social and political structure of Roman society was not suspended.[226]

In 194 BCE magistrates made the first step towards assigning particular areas to individual social classes: senators were given special seats in the low, semicircular space between the stage and the rising rows of the auditorium, which met with the initial disapproval of the populace.[227] The majority of later theatres have a few broad, low steps at the front of the rising auditorium, on which movable chairs must have been placed, and in many theatres a low wall cuts off the area of the senatorial seats from the rows behind them.[228] The senators had their own separate entrances, two vaulted passages (*aditus maximi*) leading directly to their seating area. Above the side-entrances were the seats of honour (*tribunalia*) for the presiding magistrates. In 67 BCE a *Lex Roscia*, put forward by the tribune of the *plebs* L. Roscius Otho (*MRR* 2.145), assigned special seats to the equestrians (those above the equestrian census), namely the first fourteen rows of the auditorium behind the senatorial seats.[229]

---

[225] See Maurach 1975: 133; Pociña Pérez 1976: 435–6; Kindermann 1979: 185–6; Moore 1994.

[226] See e.g. Nicolet 1980: 364; Gruen 1992: 205; Flower 2004: 326. Parker (1999: 164) distinguishes four bands in the Roman theatre, including the actors, people of even lower status than the crowd. This is a valid description of the social status of the groups of people present at dramatic performances, but it is uncertain in what relation to the three-tiered Roman society in the auditorium the actors on the stage were seen.

[227] Cf. Cic. *Har. resp.* 24; Liv. 34.44.5; 34.54.3–8; Asc. on Cic. *Corn.* [pp. 69–70 C.]; Val. Max. 2.4.3. There are multiple traditions, referring the introduction of this practice to different festivals (*Ludi Megalenses* or *Ludi Romani*) and to various people (the censors Sex. Aelius Paetus and C. Cornelius Cethegus or the consul P. Cornelius Scipio Africanus). In any case senior magistrates of 194 BCE commissioned this new seating arrangement on the occasion of one of the major festivals (on the problems caused by the *testimonia* see von Ungern-Sternberg 1975; Bernstein 1998: 193–5).

[228] Cf. e.g. Vitr. 5.6.2; Suet. *Aug.* 35.2; cf. also Juv. 3.178, who describes the theatre audience as *orchestra et populus*.

[229] Cf. Cic. *Mur.* 40; *Phil.* 2.44; *Att.* 2.19.3; Asc. on Cic. *Corn.* (pp. 78–9 C.); Liv. *Epit.* 99; Hor. *Epod.* 4.15–16; *Epist.* 1.1.62; Vell. Pat. 2.32.3; Tac. *Ann.* 15.32; Juv. 3.159 (and Schol. ad loc.); 14.322–4; Suet. *Aug.* 40.1; Plin. *HN* 7.117; Plut. *Cic.* 13.2–4; Porph. on Hor. *Epod.* 4.15–16; Cass. Dio 36.42.1. It

From that time onwards, although dramatic performances continued to be open to everyone, audiences watched performances in the theatre stratified according to social class, giving a tripartite social image of Rome. The different areas (and thus the different ranks) could be designated by the people sitting there, by their extension (e.g. 'fourteen rows') or by their position (e.g. *prima, media, ultima/summa cavea*).[230] Because of this seating arrangement the audience of a particular performance may be described with reference to the different *ordines* (cf. Cic. *Sest.* 120; Tac. *Ann.* 13.54.3).[231] That members of the different *ordines* were visibly present facilitated the interpretation of the audience as representing the whole Roman people and, in case of similar reactions from all parts of the auditorium, as demonstrating unanimity across classes.

2.9 REVIVAL PERFORMANCES

Originally, in Greece as well as in Rome dramas were typically composed for a single performance at a particular festival. Even if there is no evidence for the early Roman period explicitly confirming this practice, it is generally assumed on the basis of conventions in Greece and of what can be inferred about the ways in which plays were acquired by impresarios and magistrates (see ch. 2.2, 2.6); that dramatic poets started to emphasize in the scripts the distinction between 'old' and 'new' plays is a strong indication in favour of this theory (see below).

Initially, repeat performances occurred only in cases of 'repetitions of festivals for religious reasons' (*instaurationes*), when entire festivals with all their components were repeated (see ch. 2.1); and it has been suggested that such repetitions of festivals might have been initiated for the very reason of creating an opportunity for further performances of popular plays.[232] Other

is uncertain whether Roscius' law was a new measure or reinstated an earlier situation reversed by Sulla (cf. Cic. *Mur.* 40; Asc. on Cic. *Corn.* [pp. 78–9 C.]; Vell. Pat. 2.32.3). At any rate this practice seems to have been firmly instituted only by Roscius' law since it is associated with his name (on this issue see Bollinger 1969: 2–3; Pociña Pérez 1976: 438–9; Nicolet 1980: 365).

[230] The latter set of terms is initially a neutral description of locality and turns into loaded vocabulary only against the background of the areas being assigned to different social classes. If Cicero does not make his character Cato use these terms anachronistically, he employs them as mere indications of distance (Cic. *Sen.* 48). Seneca, however, can describe low mimic jokes as directed towards the 'highest part of the auditorium', i.e. the 'groundlings' in a Shakespearian theatre with a different set-up (Sen. *Dial.* 9.11.8: *verba ad summam caveam spectantia*; see also Petron. *Sat.* 126.7).

[231] See e.g. Flaig 1995: 108–9. On seating arrangements in the Roman theatre (in addition to ch. 2.4, n. 47) see e.g. Bollinger 1969: 2–4; Scamuzzi 1969–70; Wiseman (1973) 1987: 79–80; Pociña Pérez 1976; Kindermann 1979: 131–2, 185; Rawson (1987) 1991; Schnurr 1992; Bernstein 1998: 193–5; Parker 1999; for a hypothesis on the seating of women see Lilja 1985.

[232] See Taylor 1937: 295; Owens 2000: 386 and n. 7. See also ch. 4.6.

recorded exceptions are Terence's *Eunuchus*, which was given a second time because of its great success (cf. Suet./Donat. *Vita Ter.* 3; Donat. on Ter. *Eun., praef.* 1.6*), and his *Hecyra*, which was put on again after it had not been possible to produce it in its entirety straightaway (cf. Did. on Ter. *Hec.*; Ter. *Hec.* 1–57).

There is, however, one item that might imply a different practice for regular *ludi*: in the final lines of Plautus' *Pseudolus* the eponymous slave invites the audience 'for tomorrow' if they are willing to applaud and approve of this troupe of actors and the play.[233] This has been taken to mean that there was one play per troupe per festival, which ran throughout the length of this festival.[234] Pseudolus, however, does not tell the spectators to come back to the theatre tomorrow to see another performance, but rather plays with the notion of inviting triggered by the context: after some reluctance, he ostensibly invites the spectators who enjoyed the play to a drink or to dinner on the following day.[235] These lines seem to be a witty variation and combination of the frequent request for applause and of the banquet at the end of Roman comedies (cf. also Plaut. *Rud.* 1418–23), but do not say anything about whether this troupe will again perform on the following day.

So, the earliest reference to a particular performance distinct from the one currently under way is a remark by Plautus' character Chrysalus in *Bacchides*, saying that he loves *Epidicus*, but watches with great displeasure when Pellio is doing it (Plaut. *Bacch.* 213–15). This statement demonstrates an awareness of the fact that the impact of a play may change depending on the performance and that there can be different productions of *Epidicus* of varying quality in relation to the actors and actor-managers involved.[236] This remark (if genuine) could indicate that in Plautus' time dramas might see several different performances, staged by different people; equally, it might refer to the single (allegedly bad) performance of *Epidicus* for which Pellio was responsible (at which Plautus was disappointed)

---

[233] Cf. Plaut. *Pseud.* 1332–5: *hercle me isti hau solent / vocare, neque ergo ego istos; / verum sei voltis adplaudere atque adprobare hunc gregem / et fabulam in crastinum vos vocabo.* ('By god! Those guys never think of inviting me, so I will not invite those either. Well, if you wish to give this company and play your applause and approval, I will invite you for tomorrow.'). This answers Simo's (1331–2): *quin vocas spectatores simul?* ('Why don't you invite the spectators as well?'). Simo had previously been asked by Pseudolus to have a drink together with him (1327: *simul mecum <i> potatum.*).

[234] See most recently Marshall 2006: 80–1.

[235] See Willcock 1987: 139. For absolute *vocare* in the sense of 'invite to dinner' see *OLD*, s.v. *voco* 3; also Plaut. *Asin.* 768; *Merc.* 949; *Stich.* 182; Ter. *An.* 453; *Phorm.* 702.

[236] See Beare 1964: 164–5. Some scholars have regarded these lines as spurious (see most recently Deufert 2002: 25 and n. 45 [with bibliography]). Mattingly (1957: 83–4), for instance, considered these verses as interpolated and referring to a later period of fairly frequent revivals.

or be a metatheatrical (possibly humorous) comment. Because of these uncertainties revivals in Plautus' time cannot be inferred on this basis.

Clearer evidence for the existence of revivals of plays and an awareness of different types of performances can be seen in the fact that Terence's prologues, in contrast to those of Plautus, stress the novelty of the plays (Ter. *Haut.* 4–7; 28–30; *Phorm.* 24–6; *Hec.* 1–7; 56–7; *Ad.* 12); the characteristic of being 'new' also applies to *Hecyra* as long as it has not been performed in full, since by performance plays become 'old' (cf. Ter. *Hec.* 12: *inveterascerent*). Such comments invite the conclusion that in Terence's time it was no longer obvious that a drama produced at a festival in Rome was 'new' and that there was now a desire to distinguish a 'new' play from reruns and reworkings, as highlighting a play's novelty might increase its value and appeal. Even if it is uncertain for Plautus' time whether basically unaltered re-performances already took place, Gellius records that Plautus revised and refined the plays of earlier poets and gave them his distinctive style, so that they came to be ascribed to him (Gell. *NA* 3.3.13). The prologue to Terence's *Eunuchus* might refer to such an 'old' play by Plautus, i.e. his version of an earlier play by Naevius (Ter. *Eun.* 25; see ch. 5.1).

A first indication that the criterion of 'novelty' was starting to acquire prominence might be a remark in Plautus' *Pseudolus*, one of his later plays, first performed in 191 BCE. The eponymous slave says: 'For a man who appears on stage ought to bring some new idea in a new way. If he cannot do this, he should give place to someone who can.'[237] In the immediate context this statement has a specific meaning as the slave explains that he does not yet have an actual plan of how to deal with the situation, but will devise one; beyond that, this observation might also function as a metaliterary call for poets not to present hackneyed structures, but rather to bring new elements or new stylistic features to standard plots, at a time when conventional comic structures had become so familiar that variation was desirable.

The emphasis on 'novelty' soon after the establishment of Roman literary drama (along with complaints about decline not much later) suggests that, especially in its early phases, Roman drama as well as audience expectations developed quickly. In *Amphitruo* Plautus does not make an explicit claim about the novelty of the play itself, but stresses that it is a new version of an old story and contains the new feature of gods disguised as humans (Plaut. *Amph.* 116–30).

---

[237] Cf. Plaut. *Pseud.* 568–70: *nam qui in scaenam provenit, / novo modo novom aliquid inventum adferre addecet; / si id facere nequeat, det locum illi qui queat.*

Proper distinctions can only be set up once there are 'old' and 'new' plays, i.e. once a Roman comic tradition had been developed and the possibility for revival performances of unchanged or reworked existing plays had been created. From then on, as can be inferred from Terence's prologues, there might have been different rules for 'old' and for 'new' plays, and a play may have needed to fulfil certain conditions to be passed off as 'new' (cf. also Cic. *Amic.* 24). Even though there is no evidence on this issue, there might have been separate spots for 'old' and 'new' plays within the Roman festival schedule, similar to the distinction that had become common in Greece, where 'new' plays are said to have been valued more highly (cf. Phryn., p. 309.8–12 *Anecd. Bekk.*).[238]

Clear proof for revivals follows for the middle of the second century BCE. The extant prologue to Plautus' *Casina* belongs to a revival performance about a generation after the play's first performance (Plaut. *Cas.* 5–20): the company has decided to perform one of the 'old' plays since these find more favour with audiences and are better than the 'new' ones. Neither performance of *Casina* can be securely dated, but a date around the middle of the second century BCE for the revival seems likely.[239] An increasing prominence of revivals around the middle of the second century BCE would accord with the dates for revivals of Terence's comedies, which are inferred from the magistrates mentioned in the *didascaliae* and seem to fall within the period 146–141 BCE or even extend to the early 130s BCE.[240] The texts of these *didascaliae* (as well as mere chronological considerations) make it likely that revivals were organized by other producers than those responsible for the original productions. Presumably scripts remained in the possession of impresarios after the first performances and were handed down or sold to future generations, but nothing is known about potential financial arrangements for revivals.

A tendency to look back to exemplary earlier poets is confirmed by Afranius, a writer of togatae active in the second half of the second century BCE. According to fragments quoted from his *Compitalia*, Afranius

---

[238] Leo (1913: 215–16) suggests that separate performances of old and of new plays at the games got institutionalized in the time between Plautus and Terence.

[239] On revivals of Plautus' plays and possible dates see Buck 1940: 54–61; Duckworth 1952: 65–8; Mattingly 1960; Beare 1964: 85–6; Deufert 2002: 29–31.

[240] On the chronology of Terence's plays and their revivals see the overview by Lefèvre in Suerbaum 2002: 236–7 (with bibliography); for a detailed discussion of prologues and *didascaliae* see Klose 1966 (gathering earlier literature); also Tansey 2001. Tansey (2001) may be right in inferring a revival of Terence's *Phormio* for *Ludi Megalenses* in 106 BCE (on the basis of the *didascalia*); this would provide an important piece of evidence for revivals in an otherwise badly attested period between the middle of the second century BCE and the time of Cicero.

respected Terence as an outstanding and incomparable comic poet and admitted that he borrowed from Menander what suited him, as he did from any Greek or Latin author.[241] This agrees with the alleged reason for the revival of Plautus' *Casina*, given in the contemporary prologue, namely the audience's demand for the 'old' plays of the best poets, particularly Plautine ones, out of dissatisfaction with the worthless 'modern' ones (Plaut. *Cas.* 5–20). As dramas by both Plautus and Terence were apparently revived in this period, the *flos poetarum* (Plaut. *Cas.* 18) presumably includes both playwrights, in addition to older poets such as Ennius or Caecilius. Although there are notable differences between these playwrights, they seem to form one group from the point of view of theatre people of this period. This must tie in with actual audience expectations to some extent if such an argument can be used to advertise a performance of an 'old' play.

A recognition of the first dramatists as 'classics' obviously developed around the middle of the second century BCE. This date coincides with the beginnings of philological, literary-historical and editorial activity at Rome (see ch. 2.10).[242] Even if the interests of average audiences and those of intellectuals need not have been identical, both have in common that they turned to older playwrights, who were appreciated and regarded as part of the Roman tradition. The popularity of Plautus in particular is further indicated by the fact that there were eventually numerous spurious plays circulating under his name (cf. Gell. *NA* 3.3). Unfortunately, there is no evidence on the extension of this phase of revival and only insufficient information on details of the plays that were put on again.

More information on a flourishing culture of revivals is available for the time of Cicero.[243] His references to performances of his own day point to the following revivals (twenty to thirty different plays): a tragedy at *Ludi Apollinares* in 59 BCE (Cic. *Att.* 2.19.3 [July 59 BCE]);[244] Accius' *Eurysaces* and *Brutus* and Afranius' *Simulans* at the games given by consul P. Cornelius Lentulus Spinther in 57 BCE (Cic. *Sest.* 118–23; Schol. Bob. on Cic. *Sest.*

---

[241] Cf. Suet./Donat. *Vita Ter.* 7: Afr. *Tog.* 29 R.³. Cf. Macrob. *Sat.* 6.1.4: Afr. *Tog.* 25–8 R.³; cf. also Cic. *Fin.* 1.7; Hor. *Epist.* 2.1.57.

[242] See Tarrant 1983: 302; generally Goldberg 2005b.

[243] For an overview of the evidence for revivals in Cicero see F. W. Wright 1931: 31–79. For comments on drama in Cicero see esp. Zillinger 1911; F. W. Wright 1931; Laidlaw 1960; for Cicero's reception of Ennius see also Zetzel 2007. Both Zillinger (1911: 63–4) and F. W. Wright (1931: 33) emphasize that references to dramas in Cicero's speeches are most likely to come from plays still performed in Cicero's time, since they expect a large audience to be familiar with them.

[244] Dupont (1985: 120) assumes that this tragedy might have been Accius' *Prometheus*, but this can only be a hypothesis, since Cicero gives neither the name of the poet nor the title of the play, and the verses quoted (*Trag. inc.* 115–17 R.³ = 125–7 W.) are not attested elsewhere and not very specific.

118; 120; 122; 123);[245] Accius' (?) *Clytaemestra* and Livius Andronicus' or Naevius' *Equos Troianus* in 55 BCE at the opening of Pompey's Theatre (Cic. *Fam.* 7.1.2; cf. also Cic. *Off.* 1.114); Ennius' (?) *Andromacha* at *Ludi Apollinares* of 54 BCE (Cic. *Att.* 4.15.6 [27 July 54 BCE]; cf. also Cic. *De or.* 3.102; *Acad.* 2.20; *Sest.* 121); Accius' *Tereus* (substituted for his *Brutus*) at *Ludi Apollinares* of 44 BCE (Cic. *Phil.* 1.36; *Att.* 16.2.3; 16.5.1).

There are further plays for which there is no evidence on particular performances, but the way in which they are referred to in Cicero suggests that his comments are based on stage performances rather than on the reading of scripts: Ennius' *Aiax* (?) (Cic. *Off.* 1.114), *Medea* (Cic. *Rab. Post.* 29), *Melanippa* (Cic. *Off.* 1.114), *Telamo* (Cic. *Div.* 2.104), *Thyestes* (Cic. *Orat.* 184); Pacuvius' *Antiopa* (Cic. *Off.* 1.114; *Acad.* 2.20), *Chryses* (Cic. *Fin.* 5.63; *Amic.* 24);[246] *Iliona* (Cic. *Sest.* 126; *Acad.* 2.88; Hor. *Sat.* 2.3.60–2), *Medus* (Cic. *Off.* 1.114), *Teucer* (Cic. *De or.* 2.193); Accius' *Atreus* (Cic. *Tusc.* 4.55; *Off.* 1.97; *Phil.* 1.34), *Epigoni* (Cic. *Off.* 1.114), *Philocteta* (Cic. *Fin.* 5.32); Plautus' *Pseudolus* (Cic. *Q Rosc.* 20); Caecilius' *Synephebi* (Cic. *Rosc. Am.* 47); Terence's *Adelphoe* (Cic. *Sen.* 65); Turpilius' *Demiurgus* (Cic. *Fam.* 9.22.1). Further references in Cicero and contemporary writers might also be based on recent performances; but the wording does not prove it conclusively, and knowledge of a play's plot and some famous and/or meaningful utterances could have been gained in various ways.

Horace confirms that dramas by early Roman playwrights were not only read, but also still shown on stage in his time (Hor. *Epist.* 2.1.50–62). Other sources mention performances of passages from Pacuvius' *Armorum iudicium* and Atilius' *Electra* at Caesar's funeral games in 44 BCE (Suet. *Iul.* 84.2) and of Afranius' *Incendium* even in the time of Nero (Suet. *Ner.* 11.2). The early Principate saw performances of Atellanae (Suet. *Tib.* 45; *Ner.* 39; *Galb.* 13), which might have been revivals; at any rate famous parts seem to have been known to audiences and were exploited for topical references. In the late Republican and early imperial periods revivals apparently did not necessarily imply the performance of entire dramas.

Cicero's wording in some passages suggests that in his time, at least for famous and successful plays, revival performances could be put on

---

[245] Cicero does not identify the festival, but on the basis of the chronology of events relating to his recall from exile these games are assumed to be *Ludi Apollinares* (see e.g. Goldberg 2005b: 55; Kaster 2006: 10–11 and app. 1), although their being organized by the consul is unusual, which may be one of the reasons why Cicero highlights this aspect (Cic. *Sest.* 117).

[246] Cicero alludes to a scene from a play featuring Orestes and Pylades without naming either poet or title (Cic. *Fin.* 5.63), but it now seems to be generally accepted that these remarks refer to Pacuvius' *Chryses* (see most recently Schierl 2006: 195–6, 218–19).

repeatedly.[247] Still, his remark 'the actor, even though he played it daily' (*histrio, cotidie cum ageret*) with reference to an emotional scene in Pacuvius' *Teucer* (Cic. *De or.* 2.193) is likely to be exaggerated; nonetheless, it may indicate that popular plays could see a number of revival performances acted by particular star players.

With the exception of mime writers, no major dramatic poets were alive in the mid-first century BCE; and the shortage of new plays and/or the audience's dissatisfaction with them could have increased the demand for revivals of 'classics'. Interestingly, those revivals seem to have concentrated on a limited canon of established writers or, in other words, contributed to setting it up; for all identifiable revivals concern plays of those poets who came to be regarded as the great Republican tragic and comic playwrights, and those plays of which revivals are known or inferred are those that are cited or referred to most frequently by Cicero.

Cicero mentions a number of serious dramas that were performed again in his time, but refers to only a few revivals of light drama.[248] It is difficult to tell, though, whether this focus is due to a prejudice or argumentative aim on Cicero's part or whether this reflects the actual distribution, possibly caused by the fact that new works in light dramatic genres (albeit not palliata comedies) were still being produced. Since Cicero quotes from a selection of palliata comedies and considers characters in comedies to be as paradigmatic as those in tragedies, he apparently did not disapprove of comedy in principle, which might add credibility to his testimony.

There is hardly any evidence on venues of revival performances, but Roman theatre architecture changed over the centuries, and the last Republican performances could have been staged in the new stone theatre of Pompey (like those given at its opening), a structure in size and sophistication very different from the early, cramped and temporary spaces (see ch. 2.4). The altered dimensions and the resulting different relationship between actors and audiences must have had an impact on the performance and the effect of the plays, apart from the fact that dramas were susceptible to being interpreted differently by audiences of later periods.

Besides, the presentation of dramas is bound to have developed. The extant prologue to Plautus' *Casina* indicates paradigmatically that revivals were not necessarily unaltered repetitions, but that the original plays could be adapted to contemporary circumstances and conventions, for instance

---

[247] Cf. esp. Cic. *Fin.* 5.63: *quotiens hoc agitur, ecquandone nisi admirationibus maximis?* ('As often as this [i.e. a scene from Pacuvius' *Chryses*] is acted, when does it happen without expressions of the greatest admiration?').

[248] See Goldberg 2005b: 55–6 (with Feeney 2006); also Beacham 1999: 5.

with new prologues. Alternative endings transmitted for some comedies as well as double versions of scenes are also attributed to such processes. The same is true for the so-called actors' interpolations more generally, i.e. changes to the text introduced by actors in connection with later performances. Since in Rome dramatists could not control the fate of their plays once they had sold them (and obviously not decades after their deaths), impresarios and actors could use the scripts as their basis and adapt them as they wished; in transmission the distinction between a poet's original script and later changes could become blurred because dramatic texts were not circulated in stable published form immediately after the first performances.[249]

Moreover, changes in the audience's reception of dramas occurred in two respects: firstly, if one is to believe intellectuals of the middle to late Republic, and also in view of the dramatic genres produced, audiences' tastes changed: they seem increasingly to have preferred impressive staging, stunning effects, violent utterances and actions, magnificent costumes and elaborate stage properties over meaningful dialogue. This tendency is obvious from the sumptuous display in revivals of traditional plays, and was recognized with contempt by Cicero and Horace (Cic. *Fam.* 7.1.2; Hor. *Epist.* 1.6.40–4; 2.1.182–207). Cicero also disapproved of changes in musical performance (Cic. *Leg.* 2.39), and Horace criticized the unruly and inattentive behaviour of audiences (Hor. *Epist.* 2.1.197–207). At the same time Horace says that Romans were eager to see plays of their revered poets in the theatre (Hor *Epist.* 2.1.50–62); yet perhaps only by being restaged in such a way were revivals of 'classic' dramas able to win the continued interest of major sections of the audiences (Hor. *Epist.* 2.1.182–8), which, however, did not exclude other approaches.

For, secondly, even though plays originally tended to be free of direct comments on contemporary events, it seems to have become common practice by Cicero's time to read topical allusions into old plays, on the part of organizing magistrates, actors or audiences, and possibly to exploit the occasion as a whole for political statements.[250] Similarly, new mimes written in this period could include veiled topical references, which might equally be highlighted by actors and taken up by audiences (cf. esp. Macrob. *Sat.* 2.7.2–5; see ch. 3.6).

---

[249] For brief overviews of the transmission of the texts of Plautus and Terence see Tarrant 1983: 302–7 and Reeve 1983: 412–20 respectively.

[250] On this issue see e.g. Abbot 1907; Bollinger 1969: 25–9; Kindermann 1979: 129–31, 134, 150; Nicolet 1980: 363–73; Dupont 1985: 119–23; Flaig 1995: 118–24, 2003: 232–42; Lebek 1996: 41–2; Feldherr 1998: 169–78; Parker 1999.

The most extensive information on the political exploitation of revival performances in the late Republic comes from Cicero, who, however, is not a disinterested and unbiased reporter. Performances in 57 BCE with adapted text, for instance, described at length in *Pro Sestio* (esp. Cic. *Sest.* 106–26), concern the attitude to himself and his recall from exile. Altogether evidence for a limited number of different occasions can be identified, all attested by Cicero and the Ciceronian tradition.[251] Some of the situations refer to disturbances at gladiatorial games or people flocking to the theatre as a public and significant place (e.g. Cic. *Sest.* 124–6; *Att.* 2.24.3; 4.1.6; Cass. Dio 39.9.2). Therefore it is uncertain whether actors' comments and audience reactions actually were as prominent and important as Cicero claims.[252] Yet it is certainly safe to assume that the application of texts to the present was possible and not exceptional in this period; otherwise Cicero could not have used this as an argument in his speeches. Moreover, he also refers to such scenarios in letters, for instance asking his correspondents to mention particular events at performances or informing them about situations he had experienced in Rome. This again suggests that political demonstrations at games were regarded as a common feature and as being of general interest.

The reaction to or exploitation of the dramas was apparently supplemented by audience comments on the arrival or the absence of important political figures; for instance, politicians entering a performance venue could be greeted with applause or complete silence or exclamations of approval or disapproval (e.g. Cic. *Sest.* 105; 115–17; *Pis.* 65; 124–7; *Att.* 2.19.3; *Fam.* 8.2.1). Such political demonstrations in the theatre were particularly meaningful because dramatic performances attracted a diverse crowd due to their public nature as official events organized by magistrates. Owing to the stratified seating it must have been obvious at what social class a particular remark was directed or how a specific social class reacted.[253]

The most effective way of shaping the political impact of a performance on the part of magistrates would be the choice of an appropriate drama, since in the case of revival performances the plot and political potential of plays could be known in advance. At *Ludi Apollinares* in 44 BCE C. Antonius, the acting praetor urbanus, had Accius' praetexta *Brutus*, dealing with the foundation of the Roman Republic and the liberation from kingship,

---

[251] Vanderbroeck (1987: 77 and Appendix B) and Tatum (1990: 105) count eight different occasions, but do not distinguish between different types of political exploitation.

[252] See also Bollinger 1969: 28. Flaig (1995: 121–3) seems to take Cicero's descriptions at face value and to generalize from single instances.

[253] See also Flaig 1995: 108–9.

replaced by a mythical tragedy, Accius' *Tereus*; however, even the performance of this play led to politically motivated reactions from the audience (cf. Cic. *Phil.* 1.36–7; 10.8; *Att.* 16.2.3; 16.5.1; App. *B Civ.* 3.24.90).[254] The dramas mentioned in Cicero's *Pro Sestio* and allegedly provoking allusions to Cicero's fate might have been chosen by the consul P. Cornelius Lentulus Spinther, the organizer of the games, as he was a supporter of Cicero.[255] Pompey had Sp. Maecius Tarpa arrange the programme for the games at the opening of his theatre (cf. Cic. *Fam.* 7.1).

Actors too could play a major role in making the performance of a particular play relevant to contemporary issues: even if it would have been difficult to change the original meaning of a given play completely and contemporary events were therefore not directly represented on stage, actors could emphasize certain aspects of a plot or, more frequently, individual lines, giving them a new and specific meaning in a topical context. Cicero indicates that verses of existing plays could seem as if written for a particular contemporary situation (Cic. *Att.* 2.19.3). To bring out such a special sense actors could, for instance, direct gestures or looks towards individuals or social classes while pronouncing meaningful verses, give lines a particular meaning by an appropriate emphasis or add suitable verses from other plays or even lines composed by themselves (cf. Cic. *Sest.* 118; 120–3; Schol. Bob. on Cic. *Sest.* 120; 122; Val. Max. 6.2.9).[256]

The interpretation suggested by actors might be supported by audiences, who could even attempt topical readings of passages that had not been reapplied by actors: audiences could grant or withhold applause, voice laments or other exclamations or ask for encores of particularly telling lines (cf. Cic. *Sest.* 120; 123; *Att.* 2.19.3; Val. Max. 6.2.9). Some reapplied lines might already have had a general 'political' sense in the original play (cf. e.g. Cic. *Sest.* 123), while others were rather neutral and acquired a deeper meaning only from the new emphasis and context (cf. e.g. Cic. *Sest.* 121), which might even disagree with the original plot (cf. Schol. Bob. on Cic. *Sest.* 122).

From Cicero's comments it seems that in his time political messages extrapolated from dramas could become more important to performers and audiences than were plots. This impression agrees with the fact that dramatic performances developed further towards spectacles in the late

---

[254] See also Nicolet 1980: 371.   [255] See Kaster 2006: 351.

[256] On the difficulties of reconstructing the performances mentioned in *Pro Sestio* see Kaster 2006: 352–3 (with references to earlier discussions). Similar developments have been assumed for fourth-century Athens (see Wallace 1997: 108).

Republic. However, giving individual lines a topical meaning and transferring them to living personalities requires audiences to be familiar with
the original plots and the meaning of single verses within them. Accordingly, some literary interest must underlie the political application, even
though the original plot might become less important and less essential in triggering audience attention. Topical reading of plots and lines
is perhaps a phenomenon of revival performances when audiences are
familiar with plays and long for added excitement, supported by a thorough knowledge of the political situation and the intention to comment
on it.[257]

Exploiting dramatic productions as occasions for topical comment is in
line with the turbulent politics of the late Republic, while nothing can be
extrapolated for the first performances in earlier centuries, for which no
comparable evidence exists.[258] Yet the (direct) political reading of old plays
in the late Republic may be regarded as a natural development of already
existing characteristics, since Roman playwrights seem to have tried to
make the topics of their plays (indirectly) relevant to Roman audiences of
their time from the start: from the beginning Roman drama had described
human behaviour with characteristic terms of Roman ideology, which
could acquire a loaded political meaning (see ch. 5.2); for instance, in
Ennius' tragedy *Medea* the title character uses the expressions *rem publicam
gerere* and *patria* when voicing a general statement about the relationship
between one's physical location and one's support for one's country, which
in the first instance refers to the situation of this mythical heroine (Enn.
Trag. 220–1 R.[3] = 267–8 W.). The dramatic genre of praetexta introduced
plays on specific events from Roman history. In the late Republic this
general political relevance of Roman drama was continued by the concrete
application of dramas or lines of plays of all dramatic genres to specific
contemporary events.

All this information about the first century BCE proves the popularity of
performances of Republican dramas up to the time of Horace (Hor. *Epist.*
2.1.50–62). While the political interpretation of old plays rather looks
like a phenomenon of the late Republic, the movement towards more
and more spectacular presentation seems to have started in the second
century BCE, perhaps about the time of the first attested phase of revival,

---

[257] See also Nicolet 1980: 366–7. Hence the politicization of Roman drama does not imply that
audiences thereby took away the plays' aesthetic value, since the plays' original plots remained as
the underlying basis (but see Flaig 1995: 122–3).
[258] See Gruen 1992: 185; Beacham 1999: 30; Baldarelli 2004: 34–6.

based on the element of pageant inherent in Roman drama: new plays produced in this period, such as the tragedies of Pacuvius and Accius, already incorporate such effects, and the satirist Lucilius criticizes these characteristics of contemporary plays in the late second century BCE (e.g. Lucil. 587; 597–8; 599–600 M. = 723; 729–30; 727–8 W.).

The trend towards impressive staging seems to have become stronger at the end of the Republic, and it is also reflected in more and more elaborate temporary stage buildings (see ch. 2.4); this development may be connected with the fact that theatrical spectacle increasingly became an important factor in Roman society.[259] In such a context organizers of games could exploit performances for political messages: for instance, the sumptuous production of two tragedies with suitable topics at the opening of Pompey's Theatre in 55 BCE might have been intended to recall Pompey's spectacular triumph in 61 BCE (cf. Cic. *Fam.* 7.1.2; *Pis.* 65).[260]

The last (new) Roman drama certainly given a full-scale production on stage (and financially remunerated) was the tragedy *Thyestes* by L. Varius Rufus, produced in 29 BCE for Octavian after the victory at Actium.[261] From the Augustan period onwards there is no clear evidence for drama as a regular, full-scale stage entertainment attracting large numbers of people.[262] Still, scattered revival performances of Republican pieces continued; yet those might be turned into spectacles: for instance, at a revival of Afranius' *togata Incendium* actors were allowed to take furniture and household items from the burning house and keep them (Suet. *Ner.* 11.2). Similarly, Claudius staged the conquest and plunder of a city in warlike manner in the Campus Martius (Suet. *Claud.* 21.6). For new works of imperial poets in the first century CE (e.g. Tac. *Ann.* 11.13.1; Plin. *Ep.* 7.17.11) it is unclear whether there were proper stage-performances besides reading, recitation or production of selected virtuoso pieces in a variety of venues (cf. Sen. *Q Nat.* 7.32.3; Tac. *Dial.* 2–3; Plin. *Ep.* 3.1.9; 7.17.11).

---

[259] See Beacham 1999: 43–4.
[260] See Beacham 1999: 64–5; Boyle 2006: 155–7; Beard 2007: 22, 25, 26/8.
[261] Cf. Did. in Cod. Paris. 7530 et Casin. 1086 (p. 309 Klotz); also Quint. *Inst.* 10.1.98; Tac. *Dial.* 12.6.
[262] See Beare 1964: 233. According to Suetonius, Augustus loved *comoedia vetus* and often had it put on at public spectacles (Suet. *Aug.* 89.1). It is not clear, however, whether *comoedia vetus* is used as a technical term and refers to Greek Old Comedy or whether it denotes older Latin plays. The phrase is normally understood as referring to Greek Old Comedy, since other Roman writers use the term in this sense (e.g. Cic. *Brut.* 224; *Leg.* 2.37; Quint. *Inst.* 10.1.9; 10.1.82), although there is no other evidence for performances of such Greek plays in the Augustan period. Pliny seems to mention a recitation of a comedy of this type written by a poet of his time (Plin. *Ep.* 6.21). For a discussion of dramatic performances and recitations in late Republican/early imperial Rome see e.g. Boyle 2006: 145, 160–88; on the later stages of this development see Heldmann 2000.

2.10 READERS AS RECIPIENTS

Even if theatre scripts must have existed in Rome from the outset, they were initially intended for and used by theatre people for arranging productions, while the general public engaged with plays by watching performances. The original scarcity of written versions of dramas available even to literary people is suggested by details given in comic prologues: when the prologue speaker to a revival performance of Plautus' *Casina* in the mid-second century BCE (see ch. 2.9) claims that those who had not seen the first performance would not know the play (Plaut. *Cas.* 13–16), this indicates that it was difficult to get to know plays other than by performances.[263] In about the same period Terence could apparently claim plausibly not to know of earlier dramas by Naevius and Plautus based on the same Greek model as the one presently adapted by him (*Colax*), and his opponent Luscius Lanuvinus voiced the accusation of plagiarism only once he had obtained the chance of attending a preview of Terence's play (Ter. *Eun.* 19b–34).[264] Terence reveals detailed knowledge of another Plautine play (*Commorientes*) elsewhere (Ter. *Ad.* 6–11). Obviously it was not impossible to become familiar with earlier plays, but awareness of previous dramas seems not to have been a matter of course, which suggests that access to them was restricted.

After the first performances, theatre scripts are thought to have remained in the possession of impresarios and their companies. At some point, however, these texts must have become available not only to later generations of theatre people, but also to members of the general public interested in literature. For when scholars started to approach questions of literary history in the second half of the second century BCE, they obviously had access to written texts. Hence the beginnings of reading dramatic scripts coincided with the first philological work on them, which led to an appreciation of the 'literary' potential of drama (see ch. 1.5). Those scholars gathered texts, prepared editions and commentaries, discussed questions of authorship, assessed the various writers and assembled details of theatre history. The ground had been prepared by Terence, who dealt with questions of 'dramatic theory' in his prologues, 'which offer the first body of systematic dramatic criticism in Latin'.[265]

This early scholarly activity is attested mainly by indirect *testimonia*: L. Aelius Stilo Praeconinus (*c.* 154–90 BCE), a grammarian and a teacher

---

[263] See Leo 1913: 213 and n. 2.
[264] See Jocelyn 1967: 50–1; Goldberg 2005b: 48–50; also Gilula 1989b: 97; Stein 2003: 205–12.
[265] See Fantham 1989c: 224; also Gilula 1989b: 95; N. W. Slater 1992a: 86.

of Varro and Cicero, interpreted Ennius' *Annales* (cf. Gell. *NA* 12.4.5) and worked through the corpus of plays attributed to Plautus (cf. Gell. *NA* 3.3.1; 3.3.11–12). His son-in-law Servius Clodius too tried to separate genuine from spurious Plautine plays (cf. Cic. *Fam.* 9.16.4; Gell. *NA* 3.3.1); other men such as Volcacius Sedigitus, Aurelius Opillus and Manilius also assembled catalogues of Plautus' plays (cf. Gell. *NA* 3.3.1). The tragic poet Accius, who was a scholar as well, compiled a list of Plautus' genuine plays (cf. Gell. *NA* 3.3.1; 3.3.9) and established a chronology of early dramatists (cf. Cic. *Brut.* 72–3). In about the same period Volcacius Sedigitus drew up a canon of the ten best comic writers (cf. Gell. *NA* 15.24).

By Cicero's time reading plays had become an established form of reception besides watching performances; there were now two ways of approaching plays, so that recipients could make choices or the two methods could complement each other:[266] Cicero assumes that people of his background will have read plays as well as seen them on stage (esp. Cic. *Rab. Post.* 29); and he presupposes the familiarity of jurors, dialogue partners and correspondents with at least the main representatives of Republican drama. The availability of early Republican literature as written texts meant that these could become school texts, as is known for Livius Andronicus' *Odusia* (cf. Hor. *Epist.* 2.1.69–71).

That familiarity with early Republican literature was not restricted to Cicero is also shown by his practice of frequently not mentioning the names of poets or the titles of dramas or of only quoting the beginning of a line or passage, explicitly or implicitly assuming that addressees or readers will recognize the quotation and know what follows (e.g. Cic. *Div.* 2.104; *Planc.* 59; *Sest.* 126; *Tusc.* 2.44; 4.77; *Att.* 14.14.1; *Fam.* 9.22.1). Learning Pacuvius' *Teucer* (instead of the texts of laws) by heart, a possibility that Cicero envisages (Cic. *De or.* 1.246), makes sense only if scripts of the play's text were accessible. The Author to Herennius believes that any 'moderately educated' person (*mediocriter litteratus*) could select elements from tragedies of Ennius or Pacuvius (*Auct. ad Her.* 4.7); this seems to imply that scripts were available in writing and that, therefore, such a selection process was not too demanding.

---

[266] The relationship between and the respective importance of the reception of plays by reading or watching is one of the issues discussed by Goldberg (2005b). For Cicero's time he assumes that for comedy reading was privileged over watching (e.g. 113–14), but he allows for the 'dual experience of tragedy' (127) and the 'dual nature of tragedy's reception at Rome' (138). But with a view to Cicero's practice of quotation and his remarks on the reception of plays there is no reason to distinguish between comedy and tragedy (see Feeney 2006).

Cicero's contemporaries Varro and Atticus revised the chronology of early dramatists (cf. Cic. *Brut.* 71–3). Varro wrote several treatises on the theatre (e.g. *De scaenicis originibus, De actionibus scaenicis, De personis, De comoediis Plautinis, Quaestionum Plautinarum libri* v); among other things, they defined a group of twenty-one Plautine plays (*fabulae Varronianae*), whose genuineness was accepted by everyone (cf. Gell. *NA* 3.3.3–4), and settled questions of biography and dating. Varro also quoted or alluded to lines and scenes from tragedies or referred to performance situations in his poetry, the *Menippean Satires*.[267] By this time a tradition of scholarly work on early dramatists already existed; therefore late Republican scholars not only discussed the issues as such, but also reacted to the opinions of earlier scholars.

Cicero went beyond philological questions such as that of chronology (Cic. *Brut.* 71–3; *Tusc.* 1.3; *Sen.* 50); he voiced his assessment of poets and discussed the contents of plays, the ways of presentation and the relevance to present-day audiences: referring to a play by Caecilius, Cicero stated that characters on stage are well known, not different from real individuals and thus prototypical examples or representations of character and ways of behaviour (Cic. *Rosc. Am.* 47). On other occasions he claimed the same exemplarity for tragedy (Cic. *Planc.* 59; *Rab. Post.* 29; *Sest.* 102).[268] Even though Cicero was aware of the fictional character of stage drama (Cic. *De or.* 2.193) and the poetic illusion in comedy (Cic. *Tusc.* 4.68), he believed that poets and actors empathized with their characters; against this background he seems to have expressed the view that comedy was a 'mirror of life' (cf. Donat. *Com.* 5.1; 5.5). Accordingly, Cicero took the opinions and attitudes of dramatic characters seriously, reflected on their considerations and the structure of their argument and engaged with their views on cultural and religious or philosophical issues.[269]

Furthermore, Cicero started a process of reflection on the poetic quality and position of Roman dramatic texts in comparison with their Greek predecessors. Since he came back to this issue several times, discussed

---

[267] Cf. Varro, *Sat. Men.* 156; 189 (cf. Enn. *Trag.* 222–3 R.³ = 269–70 W.; also Varro, *Ling.* 6.81); 254 (cf. Pac. *Trag.* 313–14 R.³ = 337–8 W.); 284 (cf. Pac. *Trag.* 397 R.³ = 242 W.); 365; 486 (cf. Enn. *Trag.* 48 R.³ = 67 W.) B.

[268] See also Leigh 2004a: 6–9, esp. 8. On Cicero's use of drama in his speeches see e.g. Dumont 1975; on the views on comedy in Cicero see Blänsdorf 1974.

[269] Cf. e.g. for Ennius: Cic. *Div.* 1.88; 1.132; 2.104; *Nat. D.* 3.79–80; for Pacuvius: Cic. *De or.* 2.155; *Rep.* 1.30; *Tusc.* 2.48–50; *Div.* 1.131; for Caecilius: Cic. *Nat. D.* 3.72–3; *Tusc.* 3.56; 4.68–9. Hunter (1985: 147) points out that '[a]ncient writers on ethical subjects drew heavily upon New Comedy to illustrate the points they wished to make'. Goldberg (1996: 270), however, argues for Cicero that he 'does not describe tragic action to advance an argument', but rather 'to animate'. Such aims are not mutually exclusive, and they may have changed depending on context and literary genre.

it in the prefaces to his own works and commented on objections he expected to be made by people with different views, it is likely that this question not only affected him with respect to his own literary activity, but was considered among educated people in his time. In comparing Latin dramas with their Greek models Cicero stressed (in line with his own argumentative goal) that Latin versions are literary products equally worth reading for a Roman audience (Cic. *Fin.* 1.4–5; *Acad.* 1.10; *Opt. gen.* 18; see ch. 5.1). According to the progress in literary technique, Cicero regarded Livius Andronicus' plays as uncouth and not deserving a second reading (Cic. *Brut.* 71). Elsewhere Cicero called Pacuvius 'the greatest tragic poet' (Cic. *Opt. gen.* 2) and also praised Ennius (Cic. *Tusc.* 3.45). When he set up a tragic triad of Ennius, Pacuvius and Accius and compared these poets to the Greek group of Aeschylus, Sophocles and Euripides (Cic. *De or.* 3.27), Cicero apparently considered the later Republican playwrights as worthy representatives of the Roman dramatic tradition, while the Greek model functioned as a paradigm. Overall, it seems, Cicero regarded Republican drama in its developed form as not inferior to classical Greek drama.

There are, however, discrepancies within Cicero's assessment of some early playwrights: for instance, he draws on Caecilius' characters as examples (Cic. *Rosc. Am.* 45–7) and calls him perhaps the best comic poet (Cic. *Opt. gen.* 2), but criticizes his language elsewhere (Cic. *Brut.* 258; *Att.* 7.3.10). These inconsistencies can be explained by Cicero's focusing on different aspects, by his reporting the views of others in some instances or by developments and changes of his own views, possibly in line with general movements in taste, at any rate among intellectuals.[270] At least during the early part of his career Cicero combined contact with actors and poets as well as the experience of performances with historical and linguistic study of texts. His later statements, rather based on texts, agree with Horace's scholarly assessment of early poets and contemporary performances.

Generally, the genre of drama remained a relevant entity in literary circles during the late Republic and beyond. In the area of literature, drama (particularly tragedy and comedy) had started to exert an influence on other poetic genres, as the works of Lucretius, Catullus and Vergil, for instance, demonstrate. In Horace's *Ars poetica* drama is the main example used to outline a variety of literary techniques and principles. There is obviously the paradigm of Aristotle's *Poetics*, but Horace's poetic treatise is

---

[270] Harries (2007) argues for changes in Cicero's attitude (contrast Zilllinger 1911: 68), noting (2007: 129) that the 'earlier half of the first century seems to have been more at ease with this robust, fertile language', while 'as the fifties darkened, a refined aesthetic marked the growing isolation of the intellectual'. For other possibilities see Zillinger 1911: 45.

different in outline and intent, and a number of examples are specifically taken from Roman drama. At the end of the first century CE Quintilian includes an assessment of Roman dramatists up to his own time in his overview of literature (Quint. *Inst.* 10.1.97–100) and makes extensive use of comparisons between orators and actors in order to illustrate what is required of orators and what they should avoid (e.g. Quint. *Inst.* 11.3.4–5; 72–4; 90–1; 111–12; 178–83). However, by this time, the works of the early dramatists had come to be regarded as archaic in style, a development that had apparently already started in Cicero's time, as some of his assessments show (cf. also Hor. *Epist.* 2.1.50–62). For most Republican dramatic poets, therefore, high regard in the period of Cicero and Varro was followed by disapproval from the Augustan era up to renewed appreciation by 'archaists' in the second century CE.

From the early Augustan period onwards drama ceased to exist as a regular, full-scale stage performance, even though in the early imperial period numerous theatre buildings were erected and decorations recalling theatrical scenes, actors or masks became popular. Accordingly, reading plays became the dominant way of engaging with Republican dramas, while it was recognized that plays were more effective in performance than in reading (cf. Quint. *Inst.* 11.3.4). Later, scholars such as Gellius and Donatus mainly talk of reading and studying (Republican) plays;[271] nevertheless they discuss problems of performance and recognize that the texts were originally intended for performance.

Yet philological work on Republican plays and their use as school texts continued. This allowed Republican drama to survive beyond the decline of proper stage drama. Interest primarily focused on comic texts, as demonstrated by numerous editions and commentaries. Serious drama from the Republican period appears to have played a lesser role in the educational system and the activities of scholars. Hence at some point no further copies of early tragic texts were produced, and this is probably one reason why so much of Republican drama has been lost.[272] Whereas Ennius' epic could make up for its archaic character by its subject matter to a certain extent and comedy could achieve this by its complex plots, entertaining qualities and intriguing philological questions, tragedy when read without its stunning stage effects could win attention only by its messages, which may have been no longer relevant. The lasting value of praetextae on contemporary

---

[271] Cf. e.g. Gell. *NA* 2.23.1–3; Donat. on Ter. *An.*, *praef.* 2.3; *Eun.*, *praef.* 1.5*; *Ad.*, *praef.* 3.7. On Gellius' knowledge of and interests in early Roman drama see Di Gregorio 1988.

[272] On possible reasons for the decline of tragedy see Goldberg 1996: esp. 272–3.

themes was presumably impeded by their topicality; their political directness and the social values presented might have been no longer acceptable
in a changed political system.[273]

As a result, plays that initially played an important role in Rome's
literary culture and were soon discussed by scholars have been transmitted
in fragments only, most of those surviving in late-antique grammarians,
lexicographers and commentators, along with some excerpts in the literary
tradition, primarily in Cicero. Although a canon of recognized dramatists
had established itself, this did not have the consequence that their dramas
were performed and/or read beyond a certain point in time (it just ensured
that fragments of their texts were preserved). From the fragmentary authors,
there is only one piece of text transmitted directly: a papyrus fragment from
Caecilius' play '*Usurer or Money-lender*' (*Obolostates sive Faenerator*), found
in the Latin library in Herculaneum.[274] This proves that Caecilius' plays
were read in the first century BCE.

[273] On this aspect see Manuwald 2001a: 125–6.
[274] On this papyrus see Kleve 1996, 2001. There are also papyrus fragments of two fourth-century
copies of Terence's *Andria* from Greek towns in Egypt (see Jocelyn 1991: 277 and n. 3).

PART II

Dramatic poetry

CHAPTER 3

Dramatic genres

Dramatic festivals in classical Athens saw productions of tragedies, comedies and satyr-plays; in early Republican Italy there were numerous dramatic forms and performance traditions, with indigenous or Greek background. In such an environment the establishment of 'literary' drama in Republican Rome resulted in the simultaneous presence of a variety of dramatic forms. A basic distinction divides these into 'serious drama' and 'light drama', each of which comprises a number of different subtypes.[1]

As surviving scripts and fragments show, Roman dramatic poets were fully aware of generic distinctions and characteristics of individual dramatic genres as well as of the generic expectations of audiences.[2] That 'dramatic theory' was present from almost the beginning can perhaps be explained by the fact that Roman literary drama did not emerge from unreflective practice, but was started suddenly by a decision of the magistrates and the activities of a single poet, a situation that enabled or required reflections on the emerging form on the part of playwrights.[3] Since Republican dramatists, especially Ennius and Accius, were obviously well read in classical and Hellenistic Greek literature, it is possible that they were familiar with Greek dramatic theories and that this knowledge informed their poetic consciousness and their development of drama in Latin.

Initially, all 'theoretical' endeavours took place within the plays themselves (see ch. 5.3, 5.4). Only Accius, the last major tragic poet in the Republic, active when literary criticism had just established itself in Rome (see ch. 2.10), also wrote treatises on drama, *Didascalica* and *Pragmatica* (only surviving in fragments); these works seem to have dealt with issues such

---

[1] Aristotle differentiates broadly between two different types of poetry with regard to their objects (Arist. *Poet.* 4: 1448b24–9a6), which is in fact a distinction between 'serious' and 'light'.

[2] Cf. Plaut. *Amph.* 50–63; *Capt.* 55–62; 1029–36; Ter. *Haut.* 35–40; *Eun.* 35–41. See Thierfelder 1936; N. W. Slater 1992a.

[3] See N. W. Slater 1992a: 85.

as the chronology of poets, the authenticity of works and the appropriate use of language and structural elements.[4] In *Didascalica* Accius set out to describe 'the various genres of poems', which might have included definitions of dramatic genres (Acc. *Did.* 14–15 W. = *Gram.* 12–13 D.: *varia . . . genera poematorum*). No comments on 'dramatic theory' by poets are attested for the period after Terence and Accius; the productive process of working out the characteristics of Roman dramatic genres and principles for composition was perhaps completed by then.[5] This may have been a precondition for noble dilettante poets to start writing tragedy as a spare-time activity as they did at the end of the Republican period (see ch. 4.18).

In view of the Republican poets' generic awareness it might not be mere coincidence that elements of 'early Roman dramatic theory' bear similarities to views attested in Aristotle's *Poetics* and to definitions by his pupil Theophrastus, partly taken up by late-antique Roman writers. For instance, the difference in social status between characters in tragedy and those in comedy is mentioned as a distinctive feature in Plautus (Plaut. *Amph.* 60–3); this may be related to Aristotle's distinction between the characters of poets and the corresponding ones of the figures they create, which, in his argument in the *Poetics*, leads to a distinction between tragedy and comedy (Arist. *Poet.* 4: 1448b24–7; 5: 1449a30); tragedy is also associated with 'heroic fortune' in Theophrastus (Theophr. T 708 Fortenbaugh). Terence, in writing and assessing drama, identifies the categories of *argumentum*, *oratio*, *stilus*, *scriptura* (esp. Ter. *An.* 11–12; *Haut.* 6; *Phorm.* 5), and it is possible, as has been suggested, that these resemble the criteria of 'plot, character, diction, thought, spectacle, lyric poetry' outlined for tragedy in Aristotle's *Poetics* (Arist. *Poet.* 6: 1450a7–10).[6] The ridicule of 'choice words', of the enormous use of stylistic devices and of the overblown style of drama in Lucilius' satires in the second century BCE confirms that discussions about constituent elements of drama were taking place in this period.[7]

The terms *fabula*, *tragoedia*, *comoedia* (and *tragicomoedia* on one occasion) are the only generic definitions attested for the main creative period of Republican drama, found in the works of the playwrights themselves.[8]

---

[4] See also Degl'Innocenti Pierini 1991: 243.   [5] See N. W. Slater 1992a: 101.

[6] See N. W. Slater 1992a: esp. 86–98; also Boyle 2006: 92.

[7] Cf. e.g. Lucil. 650; 597–8; 599–600; 601, 605; 606; 607; 654 M. = 675; 729–30; 727–8; 731; 732; 733; 734; 666 W.

[8] Cf. *fabula*: e.g. Plaut. *Amph.* 94; *Capt.* 52; 54; *Poen.* 8; 1370; Ter. *An.* 3; 16; *Eun.* 23; 25; 33; *Ad.* 7; 9; 22; *tragoedia*: e.g. Plaut. *Amph.* 41; 51; 52; 54; 93; *Capt.* 62; *Curc.* 591; *Poen.* 2 (cf. also *Poen.* 581); *comoedia*: e.g. Plaut. *Amph.* 55; 60; 88; 96; 868; 987; *Asin.* 13; *Capt.* 1033; *Cas.* 9; 13; 30; 31; 64; 83; *Cist.* 787; *Poen.* 1371; Ter. *Haut.* 4; *Phorm.* 25; *Hec.* 866; *Ad.* 6 (cf. also Plaut. *Capt.* 61; *Poen.* 581); *tragicomoedia*: Plaut. *Amph.* 50–63 (see ch. 5.4, n. 81).

In late Republican and early Augustan times further descriptions such as *praetexta, palliata, togata, mimus* and *Atellana* had emerged; the first attestations of these technical terms tend to be later than the earliest surviving texts assigned to the respective dramatic genres.[9] Fully fledged systems of dramatic genres are presented in late-antique grammarians and commentators; these are reflections of the panorama of dramatic genres as it appeared to systematizing scholars in retrospect.[10] Although these scholarly systems are the result of later, organizing approaches, their characterizations still have value as starting points since they seem to go back to the late Republican scholar Varro, to refer to the flourishing period of Republican drama, and to provide definitions that agree in substance with evidence from the Republican dramatic texts and with information given by earlier writers.[11]

While all ancient scholars seem to have applied similar principles in that there are distinctions between Greek and Roman varieties and between serious and light forms of drama, the terminology is not completely uniform. Extant sources have apparently incorporated two traditions (sometimes with some confusion), characterized by different usages of some terms, in particular the application of the descriptions *palliata* and *togata* either to Greek-style and Roman-style comedy or to Greek and Roman drama in general.[12] A reference to Theophrastus in Diomedes (Diom. *Ars* 3, *Gramm. Lat.* 1, pp. 487.11–8.2) and a further, more unspecific reference to 'the Greeks' in the same context suggest that the basic ideas for defining the Greek genres and dividing the dramatic spectrum into four types (for the Greek side) go back to Greek predecessors, possibly Theophrastus or even Aristotle.[13]

In the most complete versions of the system, dramatic genres are divided into their Greek and their Roman varieties and then into four corresponding types for each side. In Diomedes' words (Diom. *Ars* 3, *Gramm. Lat.*

---

[9] Cf. *praetexta*: Cic. *Fam.* 10.32.3; 10.32.5; Varro, *Ling.* 6.18; Hor. *Ars P.* 288; *palliata*: Varro, fr. 306 Funaioli; *togata*: Hor. *Ars P.* 288; Vell. Pat. 2.9.3; Sen. *Ep.* 8.8; *mimus*: Cic. *Fam.* 9.16.7; *Atellana*: Cic. *Fam.* 9.16.7.

[10] Cf. e.g. Diom. *Ars* 3, *Gramm. Lat.* 1, pp. 482–91; Euanth. *Fab.* 4.1–3; Donat. *Com.* 6.1–2; on Ter. *Ad.* 7; Lyd. *Mag.* 1.40; *Lib. gloss.* 1.2–8; 2.9–11.

[11] Cairns (2007: 70) highlights the fact that contemporary writers and audiences were aware of generic distinctions even without naming each genre because of their cultural background, but that modern scholars may use later categories by accepting 'the useful untruth that some, if not all, genres can be categorized in accordance with rhetorical distinctions'.

[12] To avoid confusion, the traditional terminology, also found in writers such as Cicero or Horace, will be used (unless otherwise indicated): 'palliata' and 'togata' refer to two varieties of light drama ('comedy'). On the history of these systems and the differences in terminology see e.g. Ussani 1967/8: 5–89, 1981; P. L. Schmidt 1989; Häußler 1987/8: 301–6, 1990/2 (including further references).

[13] See also Häußler 1987/8: 305; Pociña Pérez 1996a: 1–2. For a discussion of Diomedes' text and its relationship to Greek sources see Fortenbaugh 2005: 352–64 (with further references).

1, p. 482.27–9) that gives *tragica* (*tragoedia*, also called *crepidata*), *comica* (*comoedia*), *satyrica*, *mimica* for the Greek side and *praetextata* (or *praetexta*), *tabernaria* (called *togata* by other writers), *Atellana*, *planipes* (called *mimus* by other writers) for the Roman side.[14] The Greek and the Roman dramatic genres are distinguished by their setting; the various forms on each side differ from each other by tone (serious or light), the social and ethical level of the protagonists and the character of the plots; as they are similar in these respects, Greek and Roman versions in the same position correspond in type. No distinctions as to formal features such as dramatic structure, metrical form or language are applied.

Terminological difficulties as indicated by the confusion in some late sources may have been caused by the fact that the overall situation was more complex for Rome than for Greece, because in Rome dramatic genres taken over from Greece and genuine Roman/Italic ones existed side by side. Greece only had the forms and terms of tragedy, comedy, satyr-play (and mime); further distinctions were partly unnecessary and partly not attempted. Serious drama included plays on historical topics (albeit few in number) besides those on mythical ones, but there was no generic or terminological distinction. In Rome, however, more specific terms were coined, probably owing to the greater variety of dramatic forms and perhaps also due to a more refined generic awareness.[15] These new terms were often derived from distinctive pieces of clothing, typical of Greeks or Romans or of certain groups.

Only for *fabula crepidata/tragoedia* and *fabula palliata/comoedia* are an individual and a date for their introduction identified in the prevailing Roman tradition: Livius Andronicus from 240 BCE onwards (see ch. 1.5, 4.1). This event was obviously felt to be decisive as it introduced literary drama at Rome. Other dramatic genres were developed on this basis, and their establishment was apparently not regarded as equally significant. Therefore the exact dates for the introduction of other dramatic genres are uncertain and can only be inferred from the dates of the first attested playwrights

[14] The grammarians give Atellana as the Roman equivalent to the Greek satyr-play, but do not indicate the presence of proper satyr-plays in Rome, nor are there other sources clearly implying it. Wiseman (1994: 68–85), however, assumes that Roman satyr-play did exist (see also Boyle 2006: 13). His evidence suggests that satyr-play was known in Rome, but does not prove that it was an actual productive genre. The reference to three types of scenery (*tragicum, comicum, satyricum*) in the Augustan architect Vitruvius (Vitr. 5.6.9) seems to describe different forms of available setting, which need not correspond exactly to specific dramatic genres. On this basis the existence of Roman satyr-play as a distinctive dramatic genre cannot be assumed.

[15] See also Häußler 1987/8: 301, 306. On the various comic types in Rome see Fantham 1989a, 1989b; on the systems distinguishing between various comic types in Rome see also Pociña Pérez 1996a: 10–13.

for specific dramatic genres (which often are only approximate). Dating is almost impossible for dramatic genres that developed from indigenous versions, such as Atellana, with details about the early stages of this process hard to establish.

A classification into different dramatic genres tends to encourage the establishment of hierarchies. While Plautus seems to assume that audiences in his time preferred comedy to tragedy (Plaut. *Amph.* 50–63), later scholars valued the 'serious' dramatic genres more highly than the 'lighter' ones, and they required clear generic distinctions in tone and atmosphere (cf. e.g. Hor. *Ars P.* 89–98). However, palliata and togata were often included among the 'acceptable' dramatic genres (besides the quintessentially serious ones), distinguished from the 'lower' light dramatic forms such as mime and Atellana.[16]

3.1 *FABULA CREPIDATA/TRAGOEDIA*

The most common form of serious drama in Rome was *tragoedia*, also referred to as *fabula crepidata* in technical discourse (after the tragic shoe: Gr. κρηπίς, Lat. *crepida*). This term denotes Roman tragedy in Greek style, i.e. drama on sections of Greek myth in an elevated style (usually called 'tragedy' in modern scholarship).[17]

The framework for plays of this type was taken over from Greece: dramas were based on stories from Greek myth, modelled on the structure of Greek tragedy and often adapted from specific Greek plays. It was obvious to the ancients that Roman tragedies were adaptations of Greek models.[18] However, Roman poets seem not to have translated word for word, but transposed the sense, while arranging the plays in language and meaning for Roman audiences living in a different cultural context. Only if some freedom of translation is assumed does an assessing comparison such as Cicero's 'Pacuvius (did) this better than Sophocles' (Cic. *Tusc.* 2.49: *Pacuvius hoc melius quam Sophocles*) make sense (see ch. 5.1).

Tragedies of the same or a similar title by Aeschylus, Sophocles and Euripides can be identified as the possible basis for a number of Roman tragedies with the help of surviving fragments and titles (indicating the

---

[16] Cf. e.g. Hor. *Epist.* 2.1.173; Sen. *Ep.* 8.8; Gell. *NA* 2.23.12; August. *De civ. D.* 2.8.

[17] On *fabula crepidata/tragoedia* see e.g. Coppola 1940; Beare 1964: 70–84, 119–27; Grimal 1975: 260–74; Cancik 1978; Dupont 1985: 163–211; Aricò 1997; Mazzoli 1998; Stärk in Suerbaum 2002: 150–4; Erasmo 2004; Fantham 2005; Schiesaro 2005; Boyle 2006; Goldberg 2007b; bibliography in De Rosalia 1989; Manuwald 2001 [2004].

[18] Cf. e.g. Cic. *Fin.* 1.4–7; *Acad.* 1.10; *Opt. gen.* 18; *Tusc.* 2.48–50; Gell. *NA* 11.4.

dramatized myth); classical Greek tragedies seem to have been the most common source, even though specific models are securely attested by statements of later writers in a few cases only (e.g. Cic. *Fin.* 1.4–5; *Tusc.* 2.48–50; Gell. *NA* 11.4). For other Roman tragedies assumptions on Greek predecessors must remain uncertain, due to the fragmentary state of both Republican plays and a large number of classical and Hellenistic Greek tragedies. For some Roman tragedies no possible Greek exemplar can be identified, when no Greek play on the same protagonist(s) or the particular section of a myth is known. In those cases plays of less famous classical or of post-classical Greek dramatists could have served as models.[19] Or Roman playwrights may have created 'new' tragedies along the lines of the typical structures of Greek tragedy, by dramatizing material found in epic narratives, mythographers or other sources (cf. e.g. Acc. *Epinausimache*).[20] As regards form, Roman poets will have been influenced by characteristics of Hellenistic tragedy; and they apparently followed its tendency towards variations of well-known myths and exciting, complex plots as well as effective dramaturgy, pathetic presentation and stage effects.[21]

Since Roman tragic playwrights were able to draw on a large repertoire of Greek tragedies and Greek myths, what is significant for their poetic intentions and the interests of contemporary audiences is the selection of myths. Famous mythical figures had become associated with particular characteristics, which, at least later, were almost demanded for any play about them (cf. Hor. *Ars P.* 119–30; Quint. *Inst.* 11.3.74). By their very nature myths do not allow major changes to names of protagonists or well-known typical actions, but there is the option of choosing different versions or sections of myths or narrating them from different perspectives or with different emphases. Some predilections of individual poets can be discerned as regards story types and topics as well as an overall tendency to present issues and concepts relevant to contemporary Roman audiences and to choose stories with a high dramatic potential. It is hard to identify further criteria although various theories have been put forward.

For instance, scholars have assumed that aetiological, political and historical notions were dominant, at least for the first tragic poets: Roman dramatists are thought to have selected myths connected with the Trojan War (with pro-Trojan reading) or heroes who had travelled to Italy in its aftermath because these plots could be linked to Roman history or

---

[19] See e.g. Xanthakis-Karamanos 1980: 26–8. On Greek Hellenistic tragedy see Xanthakis-Karamanos 1980.
[20] See e.g. Fantham 2005: 118.   [21] See also Aricò 1997: 61.

to the ancestry of important Roman families.[22] Yet, while it is obvious
that numerous Republican tragedies dealt with topics connected with the
Trojan War and that a number of dramatized myths may be referred to
Rome in this way, it cannot be proved beyond doubt that this connection
featured in the actual plays on specific sections of the myths concerned.
A 'historical' perspective might have been one aspect, but it is unlikely to
explain the entire range of stories chosen.

Some scholars have interpreted the 'historical-political' perspective in a
more concrete sense and have read Roman tragedies as reacting to contemporary political, social or cultural events.[23] Even though dramatic scripts,
like other works of literature, cannot be separated from the time of composition, Roman tragedies on Greek myths are not able to comment on recent
events or topical issues as directly as praetextae.[24] Statements on historical
reality may be made only indirectly via the structure of the dramatized
myths. Thus it is difficult, especially in the absence of precise dates in most
cases, to identify particular topical references beyond the general treatment
of themes relevant in the respective period.

It is therefore more probably a general 'Roman perspective' that has
determined the choice of particular myths or versions of myths because
they dealt with fundamental moral, social or political issues pertinent to
Roman society rather than because they could provide specific reflections
on current events.[25] Just as in classical Greece,[26] tragedies in Republican
Rome seem to have commented on and thus influenced society indirectly
rather than directly. For instance, tragedies presented stories that paradigmatically showed Roman moral values such as virtue, justice, piety and
gratitude; they discussed the legitimacy of rulers, conflicts between conquerors and conquered, the question of the significance of gods and seers
or philosophical issues; and they included situations such as the aftermath
of a war, confrontation with foreigners or struggles within families.[27] However, when other, specific literary genres were developed for discussions of

---

[22] See (with various nuances) e.g. Jocelyn 1967: 11–12; Cancik 1978: 322–3; Lefèvre, e.g. 1978b: 8–10,
14–15, 1990; Gentili 1979: 48–9; Petrone 1992: 451; Zimmermann 2004; Boyle 2006: 28–9; more
generally, on the use of Greek myth by other peoples see Dench 1995: 61–2. La Penna ([1977] 1979:
58–9) highlights the fact that there is little evidence of 'national' re-elaboration of myths in tragic
fragments and that the choice of plots might therefore rather have been inspired by the precedent
of Homer and Greek tragic poets.
[23] See e.g. (with different approaches and emphases) Biliński 1962; Lefèvre 2000.
[24] See also La Penna (1977) 1979: 63–4. See also Petrone 1996, on how myths presented on stage served
as metaphors for struggles on domestic, civil or political levels.
[25] See also Petrone 1992: 450.
[26] On the function of tragedy in classical Greece see e.g. Cartledge 1997: 18–22.
[27] See also La Penna (1977) 1979: 56.

such problems over the course of the Republican period, drama may have lost its significance as a public 'educational' medium, just as happened in Greece.[28] Still, the focus on topics relevant to Roman society and the Roman terminology used from the beginning enabled pertinent comments in Roman plays to be exploited as references to specific topical events at revival performances in the late Republic (see ch. 2.9). Towards the imperial era new tragedies continued this tradition in their own way and became more openly political and critical.[29]

The choice of myths may also have been determined by a search for stories that could help define and confirm Roman national identity. This may have been achieved by differentiating the Romans favourably from others: the story of the Trojan Horse, for instance, cannot have been a boost for Roman self-confidence when they defined themselves as descendants of the Trojans; hence it seems more likely that this narrative was used for an opposition between honest Romans and sly Greeks.[30] Such an interpretation is perhaps corroborated by Accius' *Deiphobus*: the reference to the inscription on the Trojan Horse in this play might point to the trickery of the Greeks (Acc. *Trag.* 127 R.[3] = 251 W.); and the unfaithfulness and unreliability of Ulixes as well as other negative characteristics are mentioned (Acc. *Trag.* 131–2; 133–4 R.[3] = 252–3; 254–5 W.).

This reading may be confirmed by an allusion to the Wooden Horse in Plautus' comedy *Bacchides*, when the scheming slave compares the current situation with the Trojan War and, in particular, his attack on the old man with the attack on Troy by means of the Wooden Horse (Plaut. *Bacch.* 925–78).[31] The slave highlights the mischievous and deceitful character of the Wooden Horse sent by the Greeks (Plaut. *Bacch.* 935–6), states by implication that Troy is stupid (Plaut. *Bacch.* 945) and compares himself to Ulixes, as they are both bold and bad men who saved themselves by tricks (Plaut. *Bacch.* 949–52). However, this perspective cannot be generalized in the sense that all Greeks on stage were presented as 'bad'. If they were portrayed behaving according to Roman values, they could serve as models, as Cicero's approving comments on the presentation of the wounded Ulixes in Pacuvius' tragedy *Niptra* (in contrast to Sophocles' version) indicate (Cic. *Tusc.* 2.48–50).

---

[28] See Wallace 1997: 110.

[29] See Stärk 2000. For more thoughts on the further development of tragedy see 'Overview and conclusions'.

[30] On the problems of 'historical' and 'aetiological' theories in relation to the Trojan Horse and this alternative theory see Erskine 1998.

[31] The 'sources' of the slave's speech and possible references to known tragedies are much discussed (on this issue see Barsby 1986 ad loc.; Scafoglio 2005).

These observations point to the conclusion that Roman tragic poets chose specific Greek myths and/or reinforced particular aspects in the myths so as to be able to bring issues onto the stage that would strike a chord with Roman audiences. As a result of a growing production of dramas, Roman tragic poets were soon confronted not only with Greek models, but also with versions of Latin predecessors, i.e. with a Roman tradition in both form and content. Tragic poets active after the pioneers increasingly turned to myths or parts and versions of myths that had not been dramatized in Rome before and may have been less common. Still, these myths are typically not completely obscure; frequently, they are less well-known versions of or sequels and prequels to common stories, thereby presenting something new and exciting, while being connected with narratives familiar to audiences. At the same time the poets' choices seem not be governed exclusively by a desire to outdo predecessors and avoid clashes; they also agree with the overall poetic design that can be established for individual playwrights (see ch. 4).

The introduction of Greek-style tragedy to Rome is traditionally connected to 240 BCE, when Livius Andronicus produced a play or plays at a public festival; a tragedy will have been given on this occasion or shortly afterwards (see ch. 1.5, 4.1). The major representatives after him during the Republican period were Naevius, Ennius, Pacuvius and Accius, who all wrote praetextae as well. That means that the pioneers Livius Andronicus and Naevius, active in the second half of the third century BCE, were followed by the tragic triad of Ennius, Pacuvius and Accius, active mainly in the second century BCE (Cic. *De or.* 3.27).[32]

Hence, the major productive period of Republican tragedy extended from about 240 into the early decades of the first century BCE. After the death of the youngest tragic poet, Accius, in about 80 BCE, few new tragedies were produced, while there were revival performances of older plays till the end of the Republic. From the output of the 'big five' and other less famous tragic writers about a hundred tragedies are known by title. No Republican tragedy has been preserved in its entirety; all that remains are *testimonia*, titles and fragments. From the late first century BCE onwards, noblemen turned to composing tragedies as a spare-time activity and intellectual pursuit (see ch. 4.18). Tragedies continued to be written into the early imperial period: Seneca the Younger (*c.* 1 BCE – 65 CE) is the only imperial dramatist and the only Roman tragic poet by whom complete plays survive.

---

[32] See also Stärk in Suerbaum 2002: 151–2.

Ancient scholars did not distinguish between tragedy in Greece and tragedy in Rome in their characterizations.[33] According to their broad descriptions, tragedy (in contrast to comedy) features noble and important heroes and kings, deals with serious and sad situations such as grief, fear, exile or death, and often ends in misfortune; the drama is presented in an appropriately elevated style. The action is not too turbulent, but rather well organized, and its basis is not completely fictitious. Apart from the subject matter, tragedy differs from comedy in the social status of the protagonists and the atmosphere of the action, and from praetexta in setting and *dramatis personae*. Plautus confirms the criterion of high rank for the cast in tragedy, which may include gods (Plaut. *Amph.* 50–63); he also seems to regard battles as more appropriate in tragedy than in comedy, which indicates a realization of differences in style and outlook between the two dramatic genres (Plaut. *Capt.* 55–62; cf. also Hor. *Ars P.* 89–98).

Titles of Roman tragedies typically consist of Greek names or Latin versions of Greek names, which identify a hero or heroine who is the protagonist of the play or refer to groups of people (apart from a few exceptions such as Pacuvius' and Accius' *Armorum iudicium* or Accius' *Epinausimache* or *Nyctegresia*). What ancient accounts single out as the decisive characteristic of Roman dramas of Greek type in comparison to indigenous predecessors is the fact that they had *argumenta*, i.e. presented stories with a plot (cf. Liv. 7.2.8; Val. Max. 2.4.4). The preserved fragments allow the assumption that mythical stories were translated into dramatic narrative by the typical features known from complete dramas, such as monologues, dialogues, messenger speeches or divine prophecies.[34] Some fragments and *testimonia* point to the existence of prologues (cf. Lucil. fr. 875 M. = 879 W.) and the presence of choruses.[35]

The existence of choruses does not imply that Roman tragedies must have been divided into 'acts' or 'scenes', i.e. were characterized by a regular alternation of spoken monologue or dialogue and choral songs. The physical layout of the stage area as well as the remains of choral utterances (e.g. Pac. *Trag.* 256–67 R.[3] = 280–91 W.) indicate that Roman choruses were involved in the plot and dramatic dialogues (on the role of the chorus cf. also Arist. *Poet.* 18: 1456a25–30; Hor. *Ars P.* 193–201). That Accius noted

---

[33] Cf. e.g. Diom. *Ars* 3, *Gramm. Lat.* i, pp. 487.11–8.2, 488.14–23; Euanth. *Fab.* 4.2; Isid. *Etym.* 8.7.6; 18.45; *Lib. gloss.* 2.9.

[34] The evidence of fragments and later *testimonia* does not allow the conclusion that Roman tragedy did not have an organically developing action (so Lefèvre 1978b: 43, 55, 66).

[35] On the chorus in Roman tragedy see Hose 1999; on the chorus in the fourth century BCE see Sifakis 1967: 113–20.

that Euripides used choruses in his plays 'rather thoughtlessly' (Acc. *Did.*
11–12 W. = *Gram.* 9–10 D.: *sed Euripidis qui choros temerius / in fabulis*) further suggests that Accius favoured a method that differed from the
one found in Euripides. Moreover, Republican comic poets can be shown
to have abolished the choral songs inserted as act-dividers in Greek New
Comedy and to have transferred the musical element to actors. Therefore, in view of the formal similarities between tragedy and comedy in
Rome, a continuous action without separating choral interludes is likely
for Republican tragedy too.[36] At the same time music had a significant role
in Republican tragedy: the remaining fragments exhibit a large number of
lyric and accompanied lines; spoken sections in Greek texts have sometimes been transformed into sung parts in Latin versions. Like other types
of Republican drama, tragedy consisted of a mixture of accompanied and
unaccompanied passages.

The reactions of later writers, the selection of myths and some fragments allow the inference that Roman tragedies included more and more
dramatic and vivid actions, spectacular scenes and sensational stage effects,
which may have been influenced by both Hellenistic performance conventions and Italic traditions (see ch. 1.2, 1.4).[37] Additionally, the language in tragedies was full of rhetoric and pathos, rich in sound effects
and high-flown compounds, which was criticized by some later writers
(cf. e.g. Cic. *Brut.* 258; Pers. 1.76–8; Sen. *Ep.* 58.5; Mart. 11.90.5–6). Generally, tragic fragments display a high frequency of stylistic features that are
typical of all early Roman poetry, such as alliteration, assonance, asyndeton,
enumeration or artificial word order.

So Roman tragedy presents itself as an original amalgamation of con-
stituents taken from classical Greek tragedy, Hellenistic Greek tragedy and
Italic performance traditions, adapted to Roman views and conventions.[38]
In myths, plots and basic structure, Republican playwrights tended to look
back to the exemplars of Greek tragedy of the fifth century BCE. In performance conventions and plot effects, they seem to have been influenced by
tendencies found in the late Euripides and continued throughout the Hellenistic period, in that there was a penchant for impressive presentation with

[36] In Roman tragedies from the imperial period, however, choral odes can function as dividers between
'acts' or 'scenes'. But since other formal aspects of Senecan tragedy, such as the metrical structure,
are closer to Greek practice, while differing from Roman Republican conventions, this fact does not
allow unambiguous inferences about practices in the Republican period.

[37] See also La Penna (1977) 1979: 97; Conte 1994: 107–8; Aricò 1997: 74–8.

[38] See Grimal 1975: 267–70.

spectacular effects, melodramatic plots, the presentation of protagonists as ordinarily human and the choice of more recondite versions. Roman tragic playwrights apparently removed act-divisions marked by choral songs while re-introducing the chorus as 'actor' and increased the musical element, distributing it among all actors, which was presumably an Italic component. Although Roman tragedy had to offer good entertainment in order to be able to compete with other spectacles, it did not provide amusement only, but also presented meaningful messages; such a combination turns out to be a characteristic feature of Roman tragedy. Thus tragedy (in the tradition of Greek models) could function as a medium for indirect reflections in public on religious, moral, social and political issues concerning the Roman community.

3.2 FABULA PRAETEXTA(TA)

Fabula praetexta or *praetextata* (in a later variant) is a specific and genuine Roman form of serious drama (cf. Hor. *Ars P.* 285–8).[39] The name is derived from a quintessential Roman garment, the *toga praetexta*, which was worn as a symbol of their position by curule magistrates (as well as by priests and by children before coming of age). Accordingly, Roman magistrates and other public figures are protagonists in these dramas, which dramatize scenes from Rome's early (almost mythical) history as well as significant events from the more recent past or contemporary incidents. Although there are a few Greek tragedies on historical subjects (cf. Aeschylus, *Persai*; Phrynichus, *Miletou Halosis* [cf. Hdt. 6.21]), historical drama was not recognized as a separate dramatic genre in Greece.

In tone and formal structure praetextae are similar to (Roman) tragedies of Greek type, and this is what determines their position in the system of dramatic genres found in late-antique grammarians: by their serious and elevated outlook, praetextae are distinguished from the various forms of light drama and correspond to tragedies on Greek myth, while in contrast to the latter they deal with Roman subject matter. The cast of both serious genres is of equally high rank, but praetextae feature public figures such as kings, generals and magistrates instead of mythical heroes, since they present Latin history and Roman public affairs.[40]

---

[39] On *fabula praetexta* see e.g. Neukirch 1833: 23–34; Grimal 1975: 274–6; Zorzetti 1980; Zehnacker 1983; Dupont 1985: 213–28; Häußler 1987/8; Petrone 1992: 461–7, 2001; Flower 1995; Wiseman 1998 (and elsewhere); Manuwald 2001a; Kragelund 2002; Stärk in Suerbaum 2002: 168–70; Erasmo 2004: 52–80; La Conte 2008; bibliography in Manuwald 2001 [2004]: esp. 75–9.

[40] Cf. Diom. *Ars* 3, *Gramm. Lat.* I, pp. 489.14–90.7, 490.10–14; Euanth. *Fab.* 4.1–3; Donat. *Com.* 6.1–2; on Ter. *Ad.* 7; Lyd. *Mag.* 1.40.

The earliest praetextae are attested for Rome's second dramatist, Naevius, who was active from about 235 BCE. His drama on the victory near the town of Clastidium (modern Casteggio) in 222 BCE can only have been written after that date (*Clastidium*), while his dramatization of the story of Romulus and Remus (*Romulus/Lupus*) cannot be dated and may have been produced earlier.[41] All major Republican tragic poets after Naevius, i.e. Ennius, Pacuvius and Accius, wrote at least one praetexta. Still, the overall number of attested praetextae is far below that of tragedies; altogether, about ten titles are known for the Republican period. No Republican praetexta has been preserved in its entirety; all that remains are titles, meagre fragments and a few *testimonia*. Composition of occasional praetextae and revival performances of old praetextae continued till the end of the Republican period (see ch. 2.9); some further praetextae were composed in the early imperial period.[42]

Scholars have put forward the hypothesis that an equivalent of the Roman praetexta existed in Italy prior to its introduction in Rome, since plays at games organized by local rulers might have presented legends of city founders or historic episodes from the more recent past;[43] the Etruscans at any rate seem to have displayed events from their history (see ch. 1.3). Such a general assumption must remain a hypothesis that can be neither proved nor disproved for lack of evidence. If such plays existed, they will have been of local relevance and not have given rise to a literary tradition in Rome. Presupposing unscripted traditions triggered another hypothesis, namely that far more praetextae existed than those attested; it is thought that besides the known literary versions there was a long and flourishing tradition of Roman historical drama, which was an important means of transmitting and spreading Roman history.[44] Again it is hard to argue for or against the existence of unscripted and hence unpreserved plays, but it would be remarkable for a flourishing tradition to have left no traces at all. One must also bear in mind that the aim of preserved literary praetextae seems not to have been to give a full account of Roman history, but rather to display single events of particular importance for Rome.[45]

---

[41] Marconi (1967) conjectured a *fabula praetexta* entitled *Regulus* for Livius Andronicus (on the basis of Serv. on Verg. *Aen.* 4.37; Hor. *Carm.* 3.5), but this proposal has met with criticism (see e.g. Manuwald 2001a: 101 and n. 103; Suerbaum 2002: 99 [with further references]) and has therefore not altered the view that Naevius is the first attested practitioner of this dramatic genre.

[42] Beacham (1999: 5) seems to assume that there was an uninterrupted tradition of composition and probably also of performances of praetextae into the first century CE, but there is not enough evidence to prove this theory.

[43] See Rawson (1985) 1991: 470–1.

[44] See Wiseman 1994: 1–22, 1998: esp. 1–16 (and elsewhere); see also Schiesaro 2005: 273; sceptically Flower 1995: 173–5; Manuwald 2001a: 91–4; Feeney 2006: 234.

[45] See also Häußler 1987/8: 306–7.

That literary praetextae, characterized by their close connection to concrete historical events and their political directness, developed in Rome testifies to the Romans' interest in their history and in reinforcing their national identity during a period in which the Roman Empire was expanding: praetextae, particularly those on contemporary events, displayed and promoted Roman self-confidence. Accordingly, as regards their overall messages, Republican praetextae were predominantly supportive of the *res publica*. Towards the end of the Republican period and into early imperial times praetextae apparently started to alter their character, so that the presentation of political situations began to include critical aspects (see ch. 2.9 and 'Overview and conclusions').

In principle, praetextae could be performed on all occasions for dramatic performances in Republican Rome. However, it seems, if the limited evidence is representative, that there were favoured contexts: praetextae on topics from the early history of Rome were presented at regular festivals such as *Ludi Apollinares* (cf. Varro, *Ling.* 6.18), while plays on events from contemporary history were more likely to be performed at festivals organized by individuals and possibly in connection with the event, i.e. at games in connection with the dedication of a temple vowed during a campaign or at the funeral of the victorious commander.[46]

Because of the subject matter poets writing praetextae, particularly those on contemporary events, were more obviously engaged with politics than were poets writing tragedies or any form of light drama. Since, however, these poets still were not dependent clients of all magistrates starring in praetextae (see ch. 2.7), it does not follow that the plays were commissioned in praise of the protagonists with no poetic freedom left for playwrights.[47] Outstanding deeds of individuals shown on stage seem to have been connected with incidents that affected the whole Roman populace. Nevertheless, dramas based on contemporary events are more directly related to the actual situation in their time than are works of other dramatic genres. Hence it may be no coincidence that the story of L. Brutus, the founder of the Roman Republic, is the only praetexta plot for which two different dramatic treatments (according to the transmitted texts) and an (attempted) revival performance are attested.

Titles of praetextae mention the name of the protagonist(s) or (more rarely) the location of the dramatic action. Naming plays after places is in line with the Roman tendency to connect significant events with places, and

---

[46] See Flower 1995: 172–83; Manuwald 2001a: 110–16.
[47] For this widespread opinion see e.g. Beacham 1999: 5.

therefore this method could only be productive for titles of praetextae. In addition to magistrates, generals or kings as required by the dramatic genre, further figures, such as women, messengers or other people needed for the dramatic action, belonged to the cast. Praetextae could feature a chorus involved in the action, which seems to have consisted of Roman citizens or specific groups of Roman citizens such as soldiers. Because of the historical subject matter, supernatural influence may have been reduced, and gods and religious elements might rather have been represented according to contemporary practices.

Stylistically, praetextae exhibit elements common in all forms of early Roman drama, such as alliteration or artificial word order. By nature, they have a larger number of words denoting Roman institutions than do other dramatic genres. Besides, as the fragments show, praetextae seem to employ the language typical of Roman tragedy; a number of words occur in both genres (in so far as this can be statistically significant in view of the small body of material). There are even instances where later praetextae might not just have used the established tragic language, but picked up on particular verses of earlier tragedies.[48] Poets who wrote both types of plays apparently did not operate with essential stylistic differences between the two varieties of serious drama.[49]

In metrical structure, praetexta fragments display the range of metres generally found in Republican drama; presumably accompanied and unaccompanied parts alternated and music played an important part. As the metres and the types of utterances to be inferred are broadly the same as in other dramatic genres, it is generally assumed that praetextae used the same dramatic elements and forms of speech as other dramatic genres. Specifically, praetextae, being another variant of serious drama, are thought to have been similar to Greek and Roman tragedy in dramatic structure.[50]

The literary and historical significance of the *fabula praetexta* is based on the fact that at a relatively early stage in their literary activity the Romans developed a genuine dramatic genre, modelled in form on Greek tragedy, but original in subject matter. Processes in other literary genres such as historiography or oratory at the time of the emergence of praetexta show that, in this period, Romans became aware of the importance of their history and its display during a crucial phase in the development of the

---

[48] Cf. e.g. Acc. *Praet.* 2 R.³ = 13 W.: Enn. *Trag.* 163 R.³ = 203 W.; Pac. *Trag.* 223 R.³ = 264 W. – Acc. *Praet.* 34 R.³ = 34 W.: Pac. *Trag.* 55 R.³ = 70 W.

[49] See also La Penna (1977) 1979: 53–4.

[50] Due to lack of evidence it cannot be determined whether praetextae followed Hellenistic rather than classical dramatic structure (but so Grimal 1975: 275).

Roman Empire. Although very little of the Republican *fabulae praetextae* has survived, they must have made an important contribution to shaping a Roman national sense, since they displayed significant events from Roman history in an affirmative interpretation to broad audiences.

3.3 FABULA PALLIATA/COMOEDIA

While *fabula crepidata* referred to serious drama of Greek type, *fabula palliata* designated the corresponding form of light drama.[51] This dramatic type was simply called *comoedia* by Republican playwrights,[52] but later acquired the generic description of *fabula palliata*, presumably as a means of distinguishing it from comedy in Roman setting, called *fabula togata*. The term *palliata* with reference to drama is first attested in Varro in the first century BCE (Varro, fr. 306 Funaioli, ap. Diom. *Ars* 3, *Gramm. Lat.* 1, p. 489.18), where it is used as a description for all kinds of dramas of Greek type; in late-antique grammarians and commentators the expression refers specifically to Greek-style comedy.

According to Roman tradition, literary comedy of Greek type was brought to Rome by her first dramatist, Livius Andronicus.[53] Although it is not certain (due to differing information in the sources) whether the year 240 BCE saw performances of plays of different dramatic genres (see ch. 1.5, 4.1), the first production of a comedy will have occurred on this occasion or shortly after the introduction of plot-based drama. Livius Andronicus was followed by Naevius and Ennius, who, like him, wrote both tragedies and comedies. Subsequent writers of comedy restricted themselves to this dramatic genre: Plautus, Caecilius Statius, Luscius Lanuvinus, Terence and Turpilius (and a few more shadowy writers) composed *fabulae palliatae* only. In contrast to poets of serious drama, who tended to produce both

---

[51] On *fabula palliata* see e.g. Smith 1940; Duckworth 1952; Cèbe 1966: 37–123; Lefèvre 1973; J. Wright 1974; Grimal 1975: 285–9; Bain 1977: 154–84; Konstan 1983; Hunter 1985; Pociña Pérez 1996a, 1998; Blänsdorf in Suerbaum 2002: 170–82; Leigh 2004a; Marshall 2006; N. J. Lowe 2008; Sharrock 2009; for an anthology with a selection of texts from all major palliata poets see Traina (1960) 2000; for bibliographies see Introduction, n. 6. More work has been done on palliata than on the other dramatic genres discussed in this chapter, and it is the only dramatic genre that provides complete texts from the Republican period. Therefore the treatment of palliata is more selective and focuses on issues that are most relevant for contextualizing this genre within Roman Republican drama.

[52] Cf. e.g. Plaut. *Amph.* 55; 60; 88; 96; 868; 987; *Asin.* 13; *Capt.* 1033; *Cas.* 9; 13; 30; 31; 64; 83; Ter. *Haut.* 4; *Phorm.* 25; *Hec.* 866; *Ad.* 6.

[53] Cf. e.g. Cass. *Chron.*, p. 128 *MGH* AA 11.2 (on 239 BCE); *Lib. gloss.* 1.7; 2.11. Boyle (2006: 11 n. 21 [p. 240]) suggests that Livius Andronicus' comedies might not have been fully indebted to Greek comedy, but rather consisted of bawdy, musical farce. Yet in view of how Livius Andronicus handled the newly introduced genres of epic and tragedy, his comedies are likely to have been equally influenced by Greek models.

tragedies and praetextae, comic playwrights concentrated on a single light dramatic genre.[54] The dates of the known palliata poets indicate that the productive period of Republican comedy of Greek type extended from about 240 to the late second century BCE.

Fabula palliata is the only dramatic genre in Rome of which entire scripts survive from the Republican period: there are twenty-one (more or less complete) comedies by Plautus (*Amphitruo, Asinaria, Aulularia, Bacchides, Captivi, Casina, Cistellaria, Curculio, Epidicus, Menaechmi, Mercator, Miles gloriosus, Mostellaria, Persa, Poenulus, Pseudolus, Rudens, Stichus, Trinummus, Truculentus, Vidularia*), besides numerous titles and fragments, and six comedies by Terence (*Andria, Heautontimorumenos, Eunuchus, Phormio, Hecyra, Adelphoe*); substantial fragments survive for Caecilius Statius and to a lesser extent for Turpilius.

Palliata comedy in Rome is based on the adaptation of selected Greek comedies. The concept of a succession of different types of comedy in Greece, namely of the so-called Old, Middle and New Comedy, is probably owed to Hellenistic Greek scholars, who might have imposed a schematic model of a sequence of discrete phases on what was rather a gradual shift in the predominance of certain varieties.[55] Yet later Roman scholars absorbed this model and noted that Roman poets took up the less aggressive, less topical and less farcical form of New Comedy, dealing with family problems of private citizens and avoiding open political criticism.[56]

This 'private type' of comedy, which is represented by Greek playwrights such as Menander, Diphilus, Philemon, Poseidippus, Apollodorus or Alexis, is what late-antique scholars have in mind when they discuss Greek and Roman comedy (e.g. Diom. *Ars* 3, *Gramm. Lat.* 1, p. 489.3–8; Gell. *NA* 2.23.1). Such theorists define 'comedy' mainly by distinguishing it from 'tragedy' in *dramatis personae*, subject matter and tone:[57] comedy

[54] Hunter (1985: 15) finds it surprising that Roman poets did not begin to write Latin comedies of the same style without Greek originals, which he explains mainly by the existence of *fabula togata*, as the presence of this dramatic genre would have checked the demand for a completely original *fabula palliata*. However, this argument overlooks the fact that *fabula togata* is a Roman form of comedy influenced by *fabula palliata*.

[55] For discussion of the ancient evidence and the possible origin of this model see Nesselrath 1990: 65–187; for a tentative definition and dating of 'Middle Comedy' see Nesselrath 1990 passim; for calls for caution as regards the adoption of this ancient model and neat distinctions between 'Old', 'Middle' and 'New Comedy' see Csapo 2000; Sidwell 2000.

[56] Occasionally, Roman playwrights might have used Greek plays now classified as 'Middle Comedy', which particularly favoured travesties of myth; this has, for instance, been considered for Plautus' *Amphitruo* (for discussion of this issue see e.g. Hunter 1987).

[57] Cf. e.g. Diom. *Ars* 3, *Gramm. Lat.* 1, p. 488.3–23; Euanth. *Fab.* 4.2; Isid. *Etym.* 8.7.6; 18.46; *Lib. gloss.* 1.2–8.

features protagonists of lower rank; actions are set in a private environment and closer to real life, although plots are fictitious (cf. also Euanth. *Fab.* 2.6). Protagonists are confronted by minor dangers, and after some turbulences plays close with happy endings, when the traditional order is re-established. Comedy is more light-hearted than tragedy, but retains or should retain some dignity and sobriety in comparison with other forms of comic entertainment.[58] According to Horace, comedy does not require less poetic effort just because it presents everyday events (Hor. *Epist.* 2.1.168–70a).

Greek New Comedy offered itself more readily for transposition to Rome than Old Comedy with its topical jokes and political comments, which would hardly be comprehensible to audiences elsewhere unless heavily adapted.[59] This would have required Roman playwrights to insert corresponding direct comments on contemporary Roman politics, which seems to have been uncommon in the early and middle Republic. Greek New Comedy, however, touched on basic questions of human society that apply to all communities. That the potential for transference was important is confirmed by Aristophanes' last play, *Plutus* (388 BCE), which already shows features that were to become characteristics of New Comedy: in this play there are almost no topical allusions and no parabasis; the issue of wealth and justice is presented as a general problem and on the level of private lives; the chorus is rather insignificant, though present throughout; and a slave plays a major role. Its widely applicable character and entertaining qualities, however, made this drama the most popular of Aristophanes' works in later eras. For the same reason fully developed New Comedy, which also owed much to the late Euripides, was transferable to Rome.

Accordingly, Greek New Comedy constitutes the main model of palliata. Some prologues mention the title of the Greek model and/or the name of its writer;[60] in other cases possible sources can be inferred from plots and titles of Roman plays and extant Greek texts. Out of the Plautine plays for which specific models are known or assumed, three comedies are based on Menander, two on Diphilus, two on Philemon and one on Demophilus. Terence took the plots of *Phormio* and *Hecyra* from Apollodorus and those

---

[58] Cf. e.g. Hor. *Epist.* 2.1.173–4; Apul. *Flor.* 16; Euanth. *Fab.* 3.5. On Roman definitions of comedy see Pociña Pérez 1996a: 1–10.

[59] Cf. also Plutarch's judgement on the suitability of Old and New Comedy as dinner entertainment: Plut. *Mor.* 711F–12C. Interestingly, Horace mentions a connection of Plautus' (Greek-style) comedy with the Sicilian Epicharmus and of Afranius' (Roman) comedy with the Greek Menander (Hor. *Epist.* 2.1.57–8).

[60] Cf. e.g. Plaut. *Asin.* 10–12; *Poen.* 50–5a; *Trin.* 18–21; Ter. *An.* 9–14; *Eun.* 19b–20a; 30–4; *Phorm.* 24–8; *Ad.* 6–11; cf. also Ter. *Eun.* 7–13 on Luscius Lanuvinus.

of the remaining four plays from Menander (Donat. on Ter. *Hec.*, *praef.* 1.1).

Whereas in the case of tragedy Roman playwrights were essentially required to keep the protagonists, their names and the setting if the myth was to remain recognizable, there was, theoretically, more freedom for comedy as these plays were based on the experiences of ordinary individuals. In this context a major issue in modern scholarship on palliata has been to identify characteristics of Roman versions in contrast to the underlying Greek ones or, in other words, to determine in what ways Roman poets adapted Greek plays.[61]

Formal changes due to different requirements and conventions on the Greek and the Roman stages are uncontroversial: adaptations in language or scene structure, the simultaneous presence of more than three speaking actors, the lack of act-divisions, a large number of actors' monodies and allusions to Roman institutions are indications of alterations by Roman playwrights. In the absence of sufficient clear evidence for identifying modifications beyond this level, criteria have been inferred on the basis of assumptions on characteristic features of Greek and Roman plays: a number of scholars believe that Greek plays tend to present a tight, logical and forward-moving action, while elements of farce and slapstick, banter among slaves and verbal play, as well as several deceptions, numerous complex turns of the plot or ridiculous figures, point to additions by Roman poets, who wished to entertain audiences by funny and exciting performances and to increase the effectiveness of individual scenes, but did not care about coherent plots, logical structures, well-organized action or meaningful messages.[62] However, comparisons between Roman comedies and their Greek predecessors have to remain hypothetical in almost all cases; therefore it is more fruitful, as has recently been realized, to study the plays as such in their existing form; for this is how they were presented to audiences in performance (see ch. 5.1).

Palliatae obviously include entertaining elements; yet this does not exclude the possibility of their being clearly structured and conveying

---

[61] For overviews of the history of scholarship on this issue see e.g. Halporn 1993: 191–6; Blänsdorf in Suerbaum 2002: 181–2; Sander-Pieper 2007: 7–32; also Blume 1998: 162–79. This line of research started in the late nineteenth and early twentieth centuries (see esp. Leo 1912; Fraenkel [1922/1960] 2007) and continues until the present day (on methodological difficulties see e.g. Franko 2001: 156). More evidence for Greek comedy has become available and opinions on Latin literature have changed; and so have views on the activity of Roman playwrights. More recently some scholars have moved away from approaching Roman comedy mainly on the basis of analytic criticism, and have rather studied the plays in their present form, looking at literary and dramatic aspects (for notable early examples see N. W. Slater 1985; Goldberg 1986).

[62] See e.g. G. Williams 1968: 288; Lefèvre 1978b: 27–41, 67–83; Moore 2001: 246.

messages. Even actions set in a foreign country or fictional characters can have a bearing on Roman life: Cicero regarded protagonists in comedy, like those in tragedy, as real-life figures and exploited them as paradigms for the behaviour of everyday Romans (e.g. Cic. *Rosc. Am.* 47). Although Cicero pursued specific argumentative goals, he probably would not have applied such a perspective in public speeches if his contemporaries had not shared these views to some extent. Terence's late-antique commentators stress that his comedies are both enjoyable and useful as they show examples of different ways of behaviour and thus demonstrate what has to be imitated and what has to be avoided.[63]

Due to the mixture of features appropriate to Greek and Roman settings, their fictional elaboration and the insertion of metatheatrical remarks, the stage-action in palliata does not present a coherent picture of a single society, but rather creates a fantasy world. Yet this does not affect its relevance for Roman audiences: the problems of figures in the plays are connected with the experiences of spectators even if they might laugh at some reactions and solutions rather than regarding them as models.[64] The combination of elements and the setting in a different world gives playwrights the freedom both to provide parallels and to set off modes of behaviour against the usual customs in Rome.[65] What is important for the acceptance of a plot constructed in this way is that it is probable (cf. Arist. *Poet.* 9: 1451a36–b15). If, in Plautus' homonymous play, the slave Pseudolus' comparison of his activities with those of a poet, who makes something fictitious seem plausible (Plaut. *Pseud.* 401–3), can be applied to comedy or to Plautus himself, there was an awareness that what a poet describes may have no basis in reality, but must make sense.

Plautus has been seen to blur the distinction between the imaginary world on stage and contemporary Roman reality by inserting references to Roman institutions and places, which invite the conclusion that elements of the behaviour of the fictional Greeks on stage also apply to contemporary Romans.[66] This reinforces the relevance of the comedies to Roman audiences despite the foreign setting. The potential for transference works on a general level concerning modes of behaviour,[67] while in most cases

---

[63] Cf. Euanth. *Fab.* 2.6; Donat. on Ter. *Eun.*, *praef.* 1.9; *Ad.*, *praef.* 1.9; for the mixture of the serious and the humorous in Greek New Comedy cf. Plut. *Mor.* 712B.

[64] On this issue see e.g. Cèbe 1966: 59; Blänsdorf 1983, in Suerbaum 2002: 178; Bernstein 1998: 244–5; contrast Goldberg 1993: 62.

[65] See also G. Williams 1968: 288, 294; Fantham 1977: 40.

[66] See Moore 1991 (on the *choragus* speech in Plautus' *Curculio*).

[67] See also Franko 2001: 161–2 ('broad topicality').

possible responses to concrete single incidents (and thus dates) cannot be proved.

The fact that specific conventions (e.g. the exaggerated role of slaves) apply in the comedy world has been connected with the Saturnalia, the Roman annual festival whose main day was 17 December and on which the roles of slaves and masters were reversed (cf. Hor. *Sat.* 2.3).[68] It is true that the topsy-turvy world of comedy is reminiscent of the Saturnalia, but some of its features are also present in Greek comedy, and the notion of remoteness and of possibilities not available in the real world is already achieved by the foreign setting. Since the Saturnalia does not include dramatic performances, it seems difficult to establish such a specific connection.

Poets created the Greek-based fictional world by a number of means: titles of palliatae are typically taken from names or characteristics of one of the protagonists or from items essential to the plot. Whereas Plautus tended to Latinize at least those titles that are not proper names, Caecilius and Terence retained the Greek form of titles. According to Donatus, Greek titles give Roman plays more dignity and make them instantly recognizable as palliatae (Donat. on Ter. *Ad.*, *praef.* 1.1).

As for the set-up, one of Plautus' prologue speakers tells the audience that poets of comedies prefer Athens as the Greek setting, so that the surroundings seem really Greek, and announces that the following play will be set in Sicily, where the events are said to have taken place (Plaut. *Men.* 7–12). Indeed palliata plots are localized in Greece and most frequently in Athens.[69] Besides, the Greek context was sustained as poets kept Greek-sounding names for the characters, though they might alter them for special effects.[70] They even retained specifically Greek terms and used allusions to figures of Greek myth and history as well as Greek poets.[71] However, they did not leave the entire set-up unchanged:[72] they also inserted

---

[68] See e.g. Segal 1987; Lefèvre 1988; also Serbat 1975.

[69] See Duckworth 1952: 82; Dumont 2000: 109.

[70] Characters, particularly the trickster slaves, tend to have speaking names (cf. Donat. on Ter. *An.* 226[4]).

[71] Cf. e.g. *ephebus* (Plaut. *Merc.* 40; Ter. *Eun.* 824); Piraeus (Plaut. *Mostell.* 66b); *eleutheria* (Plaut. *Pers.* 29); Achilles and Hector (Plaut. *Merc.* 488); Alcumena and Juno (Plaut. *Merc.* 689b–90); Alexander Magnus and Agathocles (Plaut. *Mostell.* 775–6a); Titan (Plaut. *Pers.* 1–4; 26–7); Thetis (Plaut. *Truc.* 731); Alcumena (Plaut. *Rud.* 86); Hercules (Ter. *Eun.* 1027).

[72] See e.g. Moore 2001: 245–6; Blänsdorf in Suerbaum 2002: 182. Dupont (1985: 249), however, thinks that there is no 'Romanization' in palliata comedy and that Greek New Comedy is the main reference point for these plays. Dér (1989: 297) infers from Terence's prologues that there were three ways of adapting comedy in this period (exemplified by Plautus and Naevius, Terence, and Luscius Lanuvinus). Yet it is doubtful whether such precise distinctions can be made, even though Terence's prologues reveal that discussions about different ways of composing plays were going on, and individual poets had their own styles.

references to Roman or Italic customs, institutions and places,[73] explained Greek customs or replaced them with corresponding Roman institutions and terminology (cf. e.g. Plaut. *Stich.* 446–8), introduced metatheatrical comments on the Greek setting (cf. e.g. Plaut. *Men.* 7–12; *Truc.* 1–3), had characters talk about 'the Greeks' and their typical behaviour[74] or used Roman political and military language.[75]

Besides such adaptations of detail Roman poets could make changes to plot and characterization. Cicero regards Latin versions of *fabulae palliatae*, like those of *fabulae crepidatae*, as literary products worth reading (Cic. *Fin.* 1.4; *Opt. gen.* 18). The extensive comparison of parts of Caecilius' *Plocium* with its Greek model in Gellius (Gell. *NA* 2.23) shows, even though one need not agree with Gellius' evaluative conclusions, that the presentation of the dramatic characters is different in the two versions (see ch. 4.7, 5.1).

A significant way of adapting Greek plots is the technique known as *contaminatio*, the fusion of elements from two Greek plays into one Latin play. This process is possible due to the essential sameness of plot across New Comedy. Still, additions or replacements of scenes, which may feature further characters or show the protagonists engaged in particular or additional activities, change the overall impact and structure of a play. According to Terence, who was accused of making use of two Greek plays for one Latin play by opponents, his predecessors Naevius, Plautus and Ennius had already used this method.[76] This strategy is perhaps one of the clearest indications of the independence of Roman comic playwrights and their self-confident exploitation of Greek material.

The typical dramatic set-up in *palliatae* favours particular topics to be touched upon: plots tend to feature one or more families, various types of relationships among its members, love affairs involving people outside the family and threats to those by others. Thus the relationship between family members, between different generations or between men and women is addressed; this includes the role of slaves or problems of education. Social issues and political problems can also surface, such as the treatment of conquered peoples and foreigners, the confrontation of different ethnic groups, the position and power of soldiers and, more generally, the consequences of war or questions of agrarian and mercantile economies. Ethical values such as faithfulness, piety or morally upright behaviour may be presented. The traditional order is eventually (re-)established by happy endings, clarifying

---

[73] Cf. e.g. Plaut. *Merc.* 664–5; *Mostell.* 226b; 746; 770; *Truc.* 690b–1a.

[74] Cf. e.g. Plaut. *Asin.* 199; *Cas.* 67–78; *Curc.* 288; *Merc.* 525b; *Mostell.* 22b; 64b; *Truc.* 55b.

[75] Cf. e.g. Plaut. *Mostell.* 1047 (*legiones*); Plaut. *Mostell.* 688; 1049 (*senatus*).

[76] Cf. Ter. *An.* 9–21; *Haut.* 16–21; *Eun.* 25–34; Donat. on Ter. *Eun.*, *praef.* 1.11. On *contaminatio* see e.g. Goldberg 1986: 91–122.

people's identity and often rewarding the innocent and punishing the negative characters.[77] Just as Republican tragedy seems to have consisted of a combination of entertaining spectacle and serious messages, a similar mix applies to contemporary comedy; it is only that its messages are conveyed in a more light-hearted way.[78]

Altogether the procedures of Roman comic poets lead to the conclusion that they created a Roman form of comedy by remodelling Greek versions and adapting them to contemporary Roman taste.[79] On top of their familiarity with Greek literature, Roman playwrights must have been acquainted with the various indigenous comic forms in Italy. Plautus in particular is assumed to have had previous experience with Atellana and to have transferred the improvisational element of early Italic performances to Greek-style comedy; in literary comedy, however, this would be 'artificial improvisation' designed by the poet.[80] The resulting mix that constitutes Roman comedy consists of exuberant stage-action in a Greek-based fictional world and an underlying plot that may convey messages relevant to contemporary Roman audiences.[81]

Although comic plots are fictitious and theoretically a wide range of (family) problems could be dramatized, Greek New Comedy and the corresponding Roman type established generic conventions as well as stock characters with typical characteristics.[82] Roman comic playwrights at least from the time of Plautus onwards alluded to generic conventions; consequently both poets and contemporary audiences must have been familiar with them.[83] According to lists in Terence stock figures in comedy include the 'running slave' (*servus currens*),[84] the 'angry old man' (*iratus senex*), the 'greedy parasite' (*edax parasitus*), the 'shameless trickster' (*sycophanta inpudens*), the 'greedy pimp' (*avarus leno*), the 'good lady' (*bona matrona*), the 'wicked courtesan' (*meretrix mala*) and the 'boastful soldier' (*miles gloriosus*); common actions are 'a boy being substituted' (*puerum supponi*), 'an old man being deceived by his slave' (*falli per servom senem*) and 'loving, hating,

---

[77] On some of these topics and their relevance to contemporary society see Leigh 2004a.

[78] See similarly (within a different framework) McCarthy 2000: 5–6; on New Comedy generally see Hunter 1985: 147.

[79] For a defence of the literary value and interest of Roman comedy see Fantham 1977: esp. 21.

[80] On this issue see e.g. N. W. Slater 1985: passim; Fantham 1989a: 26–7; Barsby 1995.

[81] On the popularity of comedy in Rome during the third and second centuries BCE see Pociña Pérez 1991.

[82] On conventions in New Comedy see Bain 1977: 148–53.

[83] Cf. e.g. Plaut. *Amph.* 50–63; *Capt.* 55–62; 1029–36; Ter. *Haut.* 37–40; *Eun.* 35–41. See e.g. Thierfelder 1936; Dumont 1992.

[84] On this figure and its effects (on the basis of an examination of artefacts) see Csapo 1993.

suspecting' (*amare odisse suspicari*). Later writers refer to further items.[85]
Some of these typical plot elements are already mentioned in Theophrastus (Theophr. T 708 Fortenbaugh); characteristic features of comedies by
himself and by his predecessors are listed in one of Aristophanes' parabaseis
(Ar. *Pax* 729–44).

Despite this widespread agreement on features and characters of a typical
comedy among the playwrights, several plots or individual characters in
Roman palliatae deviate from this standard. This can only be a sign of an
advanced stage in the development of the dramatic genre: both playwrights
and audiences were familiar with the conventional type, and they enjoyed
the tension between the ordinary and the novel. Still, in cases of major
variations from the default model, playwrights such as Plautus apparently
felt the need to explain those: they broke the dramatic illusion and discussed
the character of their dramas in prologues (cf. esp. Plaut. *Amph.*, *Capt.*; see
also ch. 5.3). When changes were less radical, they were simply presented
to the public; if they concerned individual figures, these might be made to
utter self-referential comments.[86]

In addition to such modifications, writers of palliatae could employ
elements from further literary genres and other forms of speech. Hence
there are allusions to typical topics and structural elements of epic, tragedy,
prayer, dream narrative, oath, court case or battle narrative, and references
to other forms of comic drama, other comedies or comedy itself. This
exploitation of additional material is most frequently called 'parody', and
a number of examples fall within this category, when forms of speech or
terminology associated with different contexts are used in an incongruous
set-up. However, there are cases such as Plautus' *Amphitruo* and *Rudens*,
where there is no intention to ridicule, but tragic elements, like speeches of
lament or discussions of divine justice and fate, have genuine significance.
In Terence there is less obvious parody than in Plautus, while the more
serious outlook of his plays and the topics discussed come closer to tragedy.

---

[85] Cf. e.g. Hor. *Epist.* 2.1.170b–3: *amans ephebus, pater attentus, leno insidiosus, edax parasitus* ('loving
young man, attentive father, ambushing pimp, greedy parasite'); Ov. *Am.* 1.15.17–18: *dum fallax
servus, durus pater, inproba lena / vivent et meretrix blanda, Menandros erit* ('as long as the scheming
slave, the harsh father, the ruthless female pimp and the flattering courtesan live, there will be
Menander'); Apul. *Flor.* 16.9: *nec eo minus et leno periurus et amator fervidus et servulus callidus et
amica illudens et uxor inhibens et mater indulgens et patruus obiurgator et sodalis opitulator et miles
proeliator, sed et parasiti edaces et parentes tenaces et meretrices procaces.* ('And nonetheless there is
the perjured pimp, the fiery lover, the scheming slave, the cheating girlfriend, the restraining wife,
the indulgent mother, the rebuking uncle, the helpful friend, the warrior soldier, and also greedy
parasites, persistent parents and frivolous courtesans.'); Donat. on Ter. *An.*, *praef.* 1.3.

[86] Cf. e.g. Plaut. *Pers.* 25b (on *servus* as *amans*); Plaut. *Truc.* 483–96 (on *miles gloriosus*). Later commentators noted some of those deviations (cf. Euanth. *Fab.* 3.4; Donat. on Ter. *Hec.*, *praef.* 1.9).

Plautus already proves himself familiar with characteristic elements of standard comic plots and the practice of basing one's own plays on Greek models. By the time of Terence Roman comic poets had recognized that, besides Greek models, there was also a Roman tradition in their dramatic genre: Terence's prologues refer to Naevius and Plautus as predecessors and precedents, make it clear that Terence's opponent Luscius Lanuvinus is a rival in the same genre and introduce Caecilius Statius as an immediate predecessor of Terence, with whom he shares an impresario.[87] Positioning oneself within the tradition could then be turned into an argument enhancing the playwright's credentials: Terence aligns himself with the 'good' examples of antiquity such as Naevius, Plautus and Caecilius Statius on the one hand and distinguishes himself from his opponents such as Luscius Lanuvinus on the other hand.

Terence's prologues allow the inference that reusing Greek dramas already adapted by other Latin poets was disapproved of in the case of plays advertised as 'new'; therefore, being active at a later stage in the history of Roman comedy meant that the number of Greek plays at one's disposal was reduced unless one went on a journey to Greece to find further ones, as Terence allegedly did just before he died (cf. Suet./Donat. *Vita Ter.* 5). Terence's prologues also indicate that those who did not take such steps fought hard about the use of each individual scene available (cf. Ter. *An.* 9–21; *Eun.* 23–34; *Ad.* 6–11).[88] However, there are a few titles attested for both Naevius and Plautus (*Carbonaria, Colax, Nervolaria* [if the relevant text is thus emended correctly]); and the discussion of the use and reuse of Greek plays in Terence favours the interpretation that there were a *Colax* of Naevius and a *Colax* of Plautus, which featured the same two characters of a soldier and a parasite (Ter. *Eun.* 19b–34; see ch. 5.1). The most likely interpretation of this evidence is that in these cases Plautus did not go back to a Greek source, but rather adapted an existing Roman play, as he is attested to have done (cf. Gell. *NA* 3.3.13), and thus did not produce a 'new' play.

These practices trigger the question of the characteristics of the individual playwrights and their relationship to each other. Indeed, differences between the main representatives, Plautus and Terence, have been

---

[87] Cf. Ter. *An.* 5–7; 18–21; *Haut.* 20–3; 30b–4; *Eun.* 7–34; *Phorm.* 1–23; *Hec.* 10–27; *Ad.* 6–21.

[88] In contrast to comic plots, Greek myths used for tragedies had an independent existence besides drama and were therefore open to adaptation and revisiting in various forms. At the same time, the introduction of a particular mythical character already conveyed an idea of the context, whereas in comedy the entire set-up, the plot and the characters had to be invented and presented to audiences (see also Antiphanes, fr. 189 K.-A.).

recognized:[89] in comparison with those of Plautus, Terence's plays include fewer entertaining scenes of comic banter, have fewer metatheatrical comments and fewer references to Roman institutions; they present subtler character portrayals, increase complexity by double plots, replace expository prologues with discussions on literary questions and thereby heighten suspense and surprise at the expense of dramatic irony, while they retain Greek titles and Greek names of characters; Terence also seems to be concerned more with ethical questions than with issues of the political community.

The existence of differences raises the next question, namely whether Terence is an exception due to his poetic personality or a representative of a continuous development in response to increasing sophistication or changes in taste.[90] The prevailing view among modern scholars posits one broadly stable tradition of palliata, with which Terence broke deliberately in a return to Menandrism.[91] Yet it is methodologically unsound to draw conclusions for a dramatic genre on the basis of the evidence for two representatives, who wrote several decades apart from each other, during which significant changes in Roman cultural and social life took place. So it must be checked whether fragmentary plays of other comic poets or *testimonia* on Roman comedy can confirm or contradict this theory.

It is clear, particularly from the prologue to Plautus' *Casina* (Plaut. *Cas.* 5–20), written for a revival performance around the middle of the second century BCE (see ch. 2.9), that changes in the character of comedies occurred quickly throughout the Republican period and that contemporaries were aware of them. For when an 'old' play of Plautus is about to be performed, which will earn the company a profit, the prologue speaker asserts that

---

[89] See e.g. Leo 1913: 246–8; Duckworth 1952: 384, 393; Gaiser 1972: 1104–9; Moore 2001: 245–8.

[90] Earlier scholars tended to see Caecilius as a representative of a decisive transitional stage in the development of Republican palliata, midway between Plautus and Terence (see e.g. Oppermann 1939a, 1939b). This view of a basically linear development was challenged by J. Wright (1974), who believed that 'stylistically, at any rate, Caecilius stands squarely in the Plautine, and hence the Roman tradition' and that 'he adhered to the standard conventions in comic characterization and staging as well'; he argues that the 'complete break with the traditions of the Roman comic stage was not to come until the time of Terence' (125–6) as there was a coherent tradition with the exception of Terence (see also Grimal 1975: 299; Moore 2001: 246; Marshall 2006: 15; besides the reviews of J. Wright's book see also assessments in overviews of scholarship on Roman comedy: Goldberg 1981: 108; Segal 1981: 356). Recently, J. Wright's (1974) theory has been reinforced from a linguistic/stylistic point of view by Karakasis (2005). According to Kleve (2001), 'the occurrence of cantica and obscenities' in the papyrus fragments of Caecilius' comedy 'brings the comedy closer to Plautus than Terence'; Harries (2007: 129–30) also sees Caecilius closer to Plautus. Dér (1989: 283–4) believes that the controversies reflected in Terence's prologues constitute the first occasion in the history of Roman literature when a generation breaks with the tradition of the predecessors.

[91] Pociña Pérez (1996b: 119–20) seems to posit a more gradual and smooth development towards Menandrism and eventual decline, across both palliata and togata.

audiences prefer 'old' plays to worthless new ones. This indicates that plays written in the 150s or 140s were perceived as different from those composed in the late third and early second centuries BCE. Even though the alleged preferences of mid-second-century audiences are used in a particular argumentative context, the description is likely to contain some truth, since only then does such an argument make sense from the producers' point of view. At the same time there must have been some appreciation of 'new' plays, since otherwise they would not have been offered and there would have been less pressure to argue for the superior value of 'old' plays.

Preserved comic fragments of Naevius and Caecilius Statius indicate that features commonly associated with Plautus, such as colourful language or down-to-earth jokes, can also be found in their plays and that elements known for Terence are already present in his predecessor Caecilius Statius: both Caecilius Statius and Terence had their plays staged by the impresario Ambivius Turpio, both had problems having their plays produced in full at the start of their careers but were successful eventually through persever-ance, both were quoted by Cicero as moral authorities, and both discussed questions such as the relationship between generations or problems of education.

While the process need not have been straightforwardly linear, this evi-dence suggests that palliata evolved gradually during the Republican period; the various stages of this development, during which palliata became more serious, restrained and self-conscious, though it did not lose its comic potential, are represented by the sequence of known comic playwrights. One could even claim that comedy and tragedy in Rome were moving towards each other over the course of the Republican period as tragedy became more spectacular and comedy more serious. These processes prob-ably contributed to the eventual decline of palliata since ultimately there was no room for a distinctive further development.[92] Such a scenario receives further corroboration from what can be inferred for the last repre-sentative of Republican palliata for whom some evidence survives, Turpi-lius: he continued both the serious elements of Terentian comedy and the farcical nature of Plautine comedy, but also included features attested for contemporary tragedy and togata.

Since complete palliatae survive from Republican Rome, in the case of this dramatic genre a description of the dramatic structure can be attempted,

---

[92] On possible reasons for the decline of Roman comedy at the end of the Republican period see e.g. Fantham 1977: 49; Goldberg 1993. On these processes see also 'Overview and conclusions' below.

although it has to be borne in mind that conclusions are still based on the example of only two playwrights.

In modern editions comic scripts are divided into a prologue (with the exception of a few plays that lack one) and several 'acts', consisting of a number of 'scenes'. However, the act-divisions are the work of Renaissance editors, following the classical idea of dramatic structure (cf. e.g. Hor. *Ars P.* 189–90). Scene-divisions (based on the entries of new speaking characters) already appear in the manuscripts, even though it is unlikely that they go back to the dramatic poets. Originally, a drama was one continuous performance (apart from the prologue), structured by characters' entrances and exits (see ch. 5.5).

In the manuscripts all utterances are marked as either 'spoken/ unaccompanied part' (DV: *deverbium*) or 'sung/accompanied part' (C: *canticum*); i.e. there is a distinction between unaccompanied passages in iambic senarii and passages in other metres accompanied by music (see ch. 5.6). Only two Plautine plays have what may be called 'choruses' (*advocati* in *Poenulus*; *piscatores* in *Rudens*), and these consist of groups of people involved in the action and appearing on stage for a single episode (see ch. 4.6). As regards the modes of delivery, their distribution and effect, comedy in Rome seems to have been similar to tragedy.

Generally, compared with tragedy, comedy was regarded as less artificial and closer to everyday speech in metre and language, as befitted a dramatic genre featuring ordinary individuals, though it was not completely inartistic (cf. Cic. *Orat.* 184; Quint. *Inst.* 2.10.13). Language and forms of speech in comedy are characterized by variety: they include a stylized version of what must have been colloquial language at the time, but also new coinages, linguistic jokes and effects, literal interpretation of words, plays on names and words in foreign languages. Language and style of palliatae are intertwined with the metrical structure since verse forms such as polymetric *cantica* offer themselves more readily to a colourful and high-blown style. Significant stylistic features are those typical of all forms of Republican drama, such as alliteration, assonance or formation of new words.

3.4 FABULA TOGATA/TABERNARIA

While *fabula palliata* denotes comedy of Greek type, *fabula togata* is the Roman counterpart,[93] named after the characteristic Roman garment, the

[93] On *fabula togata* see e.g. Neukirch 1833 (who uses *togata* in a broad sense and includes praetexta); Courbaud 1899; Beare 1964: 128–36; Vereecke 1971; Cacciaglia 1972; Dénes 1973; Pociña Pérez 1975a,

toga.[94] Whereas the expression *fabula togata* seems to have been the term commonly used for comedy set in Rome among ancient writers, in some grammatical systems (cf. Diom. *Ars 3*, *Gramm. Lat.* I, pp. 489.14–90.7; Euanth. *Fab.* 4.1) it functioned as the overall description of all Roman types of drama (in accordance with a distinction between Roman *toga* and Greek *pallium*), and comedy set in Rome was called *tabernaria* (derived from *taberna*, 'wooden hut').[95] In all systems of dramatic genres established by later grammarians *fabula tabernaria* or *fabula togata* (in the sense of 'Roman comedy') is the logical complement to establish a fourfold division of major dramatic genres with two different types of pairings.

In those systems (cf. esp. Diom. *Ars 3*, *Gramm. Lat.* I, pp. 489.14–90.7; 490.14–18), the two comic forms correspond to each other in types of plot and rank of characters, while they are distinguished by their respective Greek or Roman settings and personages. At the same time togata can be paired with praetexta (as palliata can with crepidata), these genres being the Roman versions of serious and light drama respectively (cf. Hor. *Ars P.* 285–8). The comic forms are distinguished from the serious ones by the lowliness of the protagonists and the private subject matter. They feature ordinary individuals, but this does not mean that all characters in togata are poor and live in simple huts; plays can include characters from various social classes such as bourgeois, craftsmen or slaves (cf. also Fest., p. 480.15–18 L.).

Such a structure reflects the way in which grammarians and commentators viewed the major dramatic genres in Rome in retrospect. Yet it is uncertain when this full set-up was established, since the date of the introduction of togata is unclear and the term 'togata' is attested only from late

---

1975b; Tabacco 1975; López 1977, 1983: 15–29; Juhnke 1978: 302–4; Daviault 1979; Rawson (1985) 1991: 479–81; Guardì 1991, 1993; Petrone 1992: 473–84; Pociña and López 2001; Stärk in Suerbaum 2002: 259–61; for an overview of research since the nineteenth century see Pasquazi Bagnolini 1974, 1975; for bibliography see López 1982, 1994.

[94] For an analysis of the terms *togatus* and *fabula togata* see López 1977; also Courbaud 1899: 1–16; Ussani 1969.

[95] See e.g. Guardì 1991: 209–11. Tabacco (1975) seems to take togata and tabernaria as referring to two different types of Roman light drama, but there is only a difference in the application of terminology. That *togata* functioned as a general term in some systems is proved by Suetonius' information about C. Melissus: 'he also developed a new form of togatae and called them trabeatae' (Suet. *Gram.* 21.4: *fecit et novum genus togatarum inscripsitque trabeatas*). Like other terms for dramatic genres, the name for this subgenre of togata is derived from a particular piece of clothing, the *trabea* worn by equestrians, especially on ceremonial occasions, and regarded as one of the characteristic features of their class (cf. e.g. Val. Max. 2.2.9; Stat. *Silv.* 4.2.32–3). Therefore modern scholars believe that this type of Roman drama featured equestrians as distinctive characters, perhaps in contrast to magistrates in praetextae and ordinary people in tabernariae/togatae (on trabeata see Neukirch 1833: 34–8; he [e.g. 56–7] infers that there was one Roman dramatic genre for each of the three social classes). Details must remain uncertain as nothing of Melissus' dramas survives.

Republican times onwards (see ch. 3). Donatus mentions Livius Andronicus as also the inventor of togata (Donat. *Com.* 5.4), but this information
is generally regarded as unreliable, for it cannot be corroborated by other
internal or external evidence; it rather seems as if Livius Andronicus transferred Greek literary genres to Rome, but did not yet Romanize them fully,
a step that was inaugurated by Naevius when he wrote praetextae and an
epic on Roman history. Crediting Naevius with the invention of togata[96]
would therefore be in line with his poetic profile, but again there is no
evidence to prove this.

Scholars therefore, disregarding the two earliest Roman dramatists and
starting from the character of togata, used to assume that togata emerged
considerably later than the other three main dramatic genres in Rome and
much later than the Roman form of serious drama (praetexta) – namely
that it came into being only in the middle of the second century BCE. It was
understood as a reaction to the growing Hellenization and eventual decline
of palliatae.[97] Even though it is true that few new palliatae were produced
after Terence's death, revivals of Plautine and Terentian plays flourished
in the middle of the second century BCE and beyond (see ch. 2.9). The
public was apparently not fed up with palliatae; there might just have
been a certain dislike of its 'modern' type, if the argument in a prologue
to a revival performance of a Plautine play is representative (Plaut. *Cas.*
5–20). Hence togata is more likely to be the result of differentiation than of
opposition: as palliata, which had originally combined Greek and Roman
elements, started to become more Hellenic (while it had shown precedents
for plot-based comic dramas in Latin), it was possible and desirable to
create a Roman comic form.

It is therefore more plausible that the earliest securely attested writer
of togatae, Titinius, lived before Terence, because in Varro's statement on
three Roman writers of light drama, Titinius, Terence and Atta, the order
of names is most probably chronological (Varro, fr. 40 Funaioli, ap. Char.,
Gramm. Lat. 1, p. 241.27–8), and Titinius' use of metre and language is
close to that of Plautus without seeming to be archaizing.[98] These facts

---

[96] See e.g. Leo 1913: 92; Daviault 1981: 18–19; contra Beare 1964: 39; Guardì 1985: 15; Traglia 1986: 29;
Suerbaum 2002: 109.

[97] See e.g. Neukirch 1833: e.g. 66; Courbaud 1899: 17–27; Cacciaglia 1972: 207–8; contra Duckworth
1952: 68–9; Beare 1964: 129; Dénes 1973: 187; Daviault 1981: 15 (and references in n. 1); Stärk in
Suerbaum 2002: 260; Boyle 2006: 13.

[98] For studies of Titinius' language and style in comparison with Plautus see Przychocki 1922: 186–8;
Vereecke 1971; Daviault 1981: 35–7; Guardì 1981; Minarini 1997. Petrone (1992: 476 and n. 66)
remains cautious and calls to mind the fact that Titinius could also be later than Plautus and be
among the many poets who were indebted to Plautus; yet this would still assign Titinius to a
relatively early period.

point to a probable origin of togatae in the first half of the second or even in the late third century BCE. This assumption makes togata's creation still somewhat later than that of the other major dramatic genres, but keeps it well within the innovative period of Roman drama.

The beginning of the second century BCE, right after the conclusion of the Second Punic War, saw significant developments in Roman society and culture, concerning a variety of areas.[99] In particular, Romans were confronted with intensified contacts with Greeks and their culture; they got to know an alternative way of life and saw an influx of luxury items. Hence it is not unlikely that the establishment of comedy set in Rome happened in the same period, when Roman society was developing fast and tried to reassert its core values against influences from abroad. On this dating togatae emerged when new palliatae were still being written, so that the creative phases of the two forms of comic drama overlapped.[100]

The only securely known representatives of togata are Titinius, L. Afranius and T. Quinctius Atta, and their output seems to cover the second century until early into the first century BCE.[101] Of the triad, Afranius was the most important according to ancient *testimonia*, and from his plays the greatest number of titles and fragments has been preserved. In total about sixty titles of togatae and almost 650 lines of fragments have survived.[102]

The Roman dramatic genre of praetexta presented genuine Roman stories in the corresponding setting, while apparently following the model of (Greek-style) tragedy in form and structure. Information on togata points to the conclusion that the distinction between Greek and Roman was less clear-cut for the light dramatic genres, even though togata was probably the Roman dramatic form that came closest to being a 'mirror of life' on

---

[99] These include the introduction of a large number of new forms of architectural ornaments (see von Hesberg 2005: 49). Cacciaglia (1972: 211–12) connects the origin of togata with the emergence of a new bourgeois class after the victories in the Punic Wars and the consequent wealth (see also Guardì 1985: 15–16), but this can hardly be the only reason.

[100] See e.g. Przychocki 1922; Duckworth 1952: 68–9; Beare 1964: 129; Vereecke 1971: 184–5; Pociña Pérez 1975a: 81, 1975b: 368; Daviault 1981: 19; Stankiewicz 1984; Guardì 1985: 15–19. On the discussion about togata's date of origin see Guardì 1991, 213–16, 1993: 272–4.

[101] The information in a scholion on Horace on writers of praetextae and togatae (Ps.-Acr. on Hor. *Ars P.* 288: *praetextas et togatas scripserunt Aelius Lamia, Antonius Rufus, Gneus Melissus, Africanus* [leg. *Afranius*], *Pomponius.* – 'Those who wrote praetextae and togatae are Aelius Lamia, Antonius Rufus, Gneus Melissus, Afranius (?) and Pomponius.') is generally regarded as mangled and unreliable, since there is obvious confusion between several dramatic genres and their representatives; it is therefore not clear whether any of the individuals named, apart from what seems to be a reference to Afranius, were indeed writers of togatae. A C. Melissus is attested elsewhere as a writer of trabeatae (cf. Suet. *Gram.* 21.4; see n. 95 above), and he might be referred to here if the scholiast got the first name wrong. Pomponius may be the writer of Atellanae (see ch. 4.14) rather than an imperial composer of tragedies and praetextae (see Manuwald 2001a: 50 and n. 83).

[102] On the transmission of togatae see Jocelyn 1991.

the basis of setting, personages and topics.[103] Horace emphasizes that for both praetextae and togatae Roman poets departed from Greek models and celebrated domestic events (Hor. *Ars P.* 285–8), while in its context this statement seems to refer mainly to subject matter rather than to dramatic form.

Despite the Roman framework, togata poets apparently continued to look to Greek New Comedy and its Roman adaptations as their dramatic models:[104] Afranius refers to Terence in a fragment that is likely to come from a metaliterary prologue in Terentian style (Afr. *Tog.* 29 R.³), and the ancient Vita interprets this as reflecting his esteem for Terence as an outstanding and incomparable comic writer (Suet./Donat. *Vita Ter.* 7). In another fragment Afranius admits that he freely borrowed whatever suited him from Menander or anybody else, even Latin poets (Macrob. *Sat.* 6.1.4: Afr. *Tog.* 25–8 R.³). According to Horace people regarded Afranius as comparable with Menander (Hor. *Epist.* 2.1.57); Cicero confirms that Afranius borrowed from Menander (Cic. *Fin.* 1.7), drawing parallels between Afranius' borrowing and Ennius' borrowing from Homer for his epic on Roman history. The late commentator Euanthius compares Plautus, Terence and Afranius as regards the style of their works and their relationship to tragedy and mime as if they were representatives of a single light dramatic genre (Euanth. *Fab.* 3.5). Since the subject matter and plot outline of palliata and togata (family problems and love affairs) were closer together than those of crepidata and praetexta, the Roman version was apparently able to adopt more than dramatic structures from the corresponding Greek form. This practice also shows that material presented in palliatae was regarded as relevant for dramas set in Rome.

Nevertheless, togata differs from palliata beyond the setting.[105] For instance, Seneca claims that in seriousness togata was midway between tragedy and comedy and that it contained meaningful statements; he implies that it talked about philosophical questions (Sen. *Ep.* 8.8; 89.7).[106]

---

[103] According to Courbaud (1899: 97), spectators of togatae could believe that they were watching 'vitam ipsam' ('life itself') instead of a 'spectaculum' ('show'). Obviously, what was presented on stage was a 'dramatic version of real life'.

[104] See e.g. Pociña Pérez 1975b: 368, 1996b: 130–1. On the relationship between palliata and togata see Daviault 1979.

[105] Zillinger (1911: 41), however, believes that there was no difference between palliata and togata apart from the characters' nationality (see also Guardì 1993: 271) and therefore togata was not regarded highly by Cicero.

[106] Even though Ussani (1969: 410) rightly notes that Seneca will have made this assessment from his personal point of view, fragments and other *testimonia* confirm the character of togata indicated thereby.

In the text of Fronto's letters togatae are mentioned as a source of 'elegant' (*urbanae*) *sententiae*, while other light dramatic genres can provide *sententiae* of different character (Fronto, *Ep. ad Ant.* 4.2, *m² in margine^d*) [p. 106 v.d.H.]). Such descriptions could be given only if togatae did not consist merely of entertainment, but also conveyed messages, apparently to a greater degree than palliatae.[107] This agrees with a more solemn outlook and structure indicated by the Menandrean model at least for Afranius. Donatus says that in togatae (in contrast to palliatae) slaves were commonly not allowed to be cleverer than their masters (Donat. on Ter. *Eun.* 57), which is in line with both a more sober set-up and the depiction of (fictionalized) Roman reality.[108] It also agrees with both these features that, according to Gellius, Afranius discussed the term of *sapientia* and its origin in one of his plays, giving both the Greek and the Latin term and identifying *usus* and *memoria* as its 'parents' (Gell. *NA* 13.8; Afr. *Tog.* 298–9 R.³; cf. Sen. *Ep.* 89.7).

Structural and thematic elements of light drama could apparently be employed irrespective of generic differences, appropriated in different ways according to dramatic genres and the poets' individual agenda. Yet the more sober atmosphere in togata precludes the assumption of too close a similarity with Plautine comedy in all respects.[109] Although Plautus' comedies do contain messages, they have a greater potential for entertaining elements, not least due to the foreign setting, which allowed for the creation of a fictional world on this basis. Togatae were not Roman versions of Plautine comedy; they rather presented less fanciful surroundings and characters closer to real-life individuals. After Greek and Roman poets of Greek-style comedy had provided models of successful pieces of light drama, togata poets applied these structures to create thoroughly Roman plays with the corresponding adjustments.

[107] On the greater seriousness of togata see Courbaud 1899: 97–101. Cacciaglia (1972: 211–12) believes that the tone in togata was lower than in palliata, while being superior to Atellana.

[108] Leigh (2004a: 9) rightly stresses that Donatus makes no absolute statement for togatae, but rather talks of 'commonly' (*fere*). Quintilian criticizes the fact that Afranius defiled his plots with indecent love affairs with boys (Quint. *Inst.* 10.1.100), which might trigger the assumption of a lewd and farcical atmosphere in togata (see e.g. Jocelyn 1991: 281). But since Quintilian adds that Afranius thereby exhibited his own way of life, it is more likely not to be a general characteristic of togata, but something peculiar to the poet Afranius. The fragments do not confirm such an element, and there is no other evidence on Afranius' character. An epigram by Ausonius, introduced as a caption for a picture of an indecent woman, mentions Afranius' plays as examples of obscene love relationships (Auson. *Epigr.* 79); in the context this presumably refers to the common love affairs of *meretrices* rather than to homosexual relationships.

[109] So apparently Pociña Pérez 1975a: 85–6, 87–8. On the different background and more sober setting in togata see also Dénes 1973: 189, 195.

A comparable tension between differences from and similarities to other dramatic genres characterizes individual dramatic features of togata.

In language, metre and style no big differences from other forms of Republican drama can be observed.[110] There are no major distinctions in linguistic levels and stylistic features between Greek and Roman or socially higher and lower characters across the various kinds of light drama, except for the names of characters and locations. As one would expect for a comedy set in Rome, vocabulary and ways of expression are rather straightforward and down to earth, yet embellished with the standard stylistic figures of early Roman poetry such as alliteration, asyndeton or enumeration. There are frequent exclamations and addresses, which must be reflections of lively dialogues between characters on stage.

The known writers of togatae share a few identical or similar titles of plays among each other (cf. Afr. – At.: *Megalensia, Materterae*; Tit. – Afr.: *Privigna/Privignus*), but also with palliata (and Greek) comedies (cf. e.g. Caec. *Asotus, Harpazomene*), literary Atellanae (cf. Pomp. *Augur, Decuma fullonis, Satura*; Nov. *Fullones, Fullones feriati, Fullonicum, Gemini*) and literary mimes (cf. Lab. *Aquae caldae, Augur, Compitalia, Fullo, Gemelli, Sorores, Virgo*). Equally, methods of generating titles are similar to those of other light dramatic genres, for instance naming a play after a girl from a certain town (cf. Naev. *Tarentilla*). Reuse of titles seems not to have been a problem; to what extent plots overlapped, however, is difficult to determine on the basis of the remaining fragments.[111]

Atmosphere and surroundings in togata are entirely Roman: all titles are in Latin. Figures who are named bear Roman everyday names, such as Lucius (Tit. *Tog.* 179 R.³), Quintus (Tit. *Quintus*), Sextus (Afr. *Tog.* 19/20 R.³), Servius (Afr. *Tog.* 95 R.³), Titus (Afr. *Tog.* 304/5 R.³), Manius (Afr. *Tog.* 211 R.³), Tiberius (Tit. *Tog.* 32 R.³) or Paula (Tit. *Tog.* 109/10 R.³), or Oscan and south-Italian ones, such as Numisius (Afr. *Tog.* 294 R.³) or Numerius (Afr. *Tog.* 272 R.³),[112] with the exception of names such as Moschis (Afr. *Tog.* 136 R.³), Thais (Afr. *Thais*) or Nicasio (Afr. *Tog.* 189 R.³), referring to courtesans and slaves, reflecting their sociological and ethnic background. The few places mentioned are located in Rome or Italy or have connections to Rome (Tit. *Setina, Veliterna*; Afr. *Brundisina(e)*; Tit. *Tog.*

---

[110] See e.g. Daviault 1981: 21–2; Guardì 1985: 17. On the language of togata see Minarini 1997.

[111] Daviault (1981: 21–2 and n. 1) assumes that togata poets might have used the long-established practice of *contaminatio*. While it is likely that togata poets (and Afranius in particular) combined material from various sources, the process will have been different for comedy set in Rome as it was not based on the adaptation of one or more Greek models.

[112] See e.g. Guardì 1985: 16. On those names see Rawson (1985) 1991: 481 and n. 61, 485 n. 92.

120 R.³: *Tiberis*; Afr. *Tog.* 136 R.³: *Neapolitis*; 233 R.³: *Gallia*; At. *Aquae Caldae*); terms for institutions are Roman (e.g. Afr. *Augur, Compitalia, Megalensia*; At. *Aedilicia, Megalensia*).

Assumptions on dramatic structure can hardly be made in view of the relatively small number of fragments transmitted for each play, particularly in the absence of guidance by a standard plot or a mythical story. However, togatae probably had a plot and did not consist merely of a series of loosely connected episodes; this is almost certain in view of parallels drawn with palliata and praetexta in ancient sources, with particular mention of plot (cf. e.g. Diom. *Ars* 3, *Gramm. Lat.* I, p. 489.29–30; Euanth. *Fab.* 4.1), and of fragments that indicate dialogues and issues developing over the course of a play.

According to Pseudo-Asconius there were fewer characters/actors in Latin plays such as Atellanae and togatae than in Greek-style comedies (Ps.-Asc. on Cic. *Div. in Caec.* [p. 200.14–15 St.]); the preserved fragments, however, do not allow a verification of this statement. The only structural detail that can be established is that plays opened with prologues and continued with characters' monologues and dialogues; there is no evidence for the presence of a chorus.

Prologues could apparently contain metaliterary discussions, as is inferred for Afranius (Afr. *Tog.* 25–8; 29 R.³); at the same time another piece of evidence attests Priapus as a prologue speaker (Macrob. *Sat.* 6.5.6: Afr. *Tog.* 403–4 R.³). Hence both types of prologues – narrative ones perhaps spoken by a deity as in Plautus and metaliterary ones as in Terence – seem to have been possible in togatae,[113] as in palliatae. In both dramatic genres the metaliterary prologue makes its appearance only with a later representative, both these poets being active at about the same time, which suggests a shift of interest among poets and audiences in this time and a corresponding development of dramatic forms.

While the surviving fragments contain almost no allusions to mythical figures or Greek gods (only Priapus: Afr. *Tog.* 403–4 R.³) and few references to Roman gods such as Diana (Afr. *Tog.* 141; 144 R.³) or Lares (Afr. *Tog.* 277 R.³), the fact that togatae are set in everyday Rome or Italy apparently does not rule out divine influence or omniscient deities. As *Sapientia* is quoted speaking in the first person in one fragment (Afr. *Tog.* 298–9 R.³), she must have appeared on stage in personified form, or a character must have narrated an encounter with her or an appearance of her. Yet deities attested in togata fragments are minor ones or personifications, apart from

---

[113] See Daviault 1981: 22–3.

Diana, who, however, seems not to have influenced the action, but to have been honoured. The same is true for gods in Plautus' comedies except for the special case of *Amphitruo*.

In view of what is known about Roman theatrical conventions, togatae will have been performed on the same stages with the standard set-up as palliatae; the setting will just have been differently defined as Rome or a country town in Italy. Indeed, locations familiar from palliatae, such as 'inside the house', 'outside the house', 'the Forum' or 'the country', are mentioned in togata fragments.[114]

As regards topics and *dramatis personae*, togatae present figures common in palliatae, such as slaves (Afr. *Tog.* 189–91; 313–14 R.[3]), parasites (Tit. *Tog.* 45–6; 47; 99 R.[3]; Afr. *Tog.* 366–8 R.[3]), pimps (Tit. *Tog.* 45 R.[3]), courtesans (Afr. *Thais; Tog.* 133; 136 R.[3]; At. *Tog.* 3 R.[3]), courtesans as musicians (Tit. *Psaltria sive Ferentinatis, Tibicina*), nurses (Afr. *Tog.* 179 R.[3]) or twins (Tit. *Gemina*).[115] But they also feature wives (Tit. *Tog.* 38; 41; 70/2 R.[3]; Afr. *Tog.* 99; 222; 241; 376 R.[3]) and husbands (Tit. *Tog.* 39/40 R.[3]); there is mention of marriage (Afr. *Mariti; Tog.* 82; 354–5 R.[3]) and divorce (Afr. *Divortium*). Besides, there are members of the extended family, such as sisters (Afr. *Sorores*), aunts (Afr. / At. *Materterae*), stepmothers (Afr. *Tog.* 57–8 R.[3]), stepchildren (Afr. *Privignus;* Tit. *Privigna; Tog.* 155 R.[3]), daughters-in-law (At. *Nurus*), mothers-in-law (At. *Socrus*) or sisters-in-law (Afr. *Fratriae*); the exuberance of various terms for family relationships in Afranius was already noted by Nonius Marcellus (Non., p. 894 L.: Afr. *Tog. inc.* XXVI R.[3]).

Hence relationships between men and women seem not to concern mainly potentially illicit and extramarital affairs, but rather to take place within a family community or between families: fragments and titles indicate mention of marriages, discussions of projected matches, preparations and consequences of marriages, including topics such as marital conflicts in connection with dowries or estates, the distribution of power and duties at home or unfaithfulness and divorce. The shift from love affairs between young men and mistresses in palliata to a focus on marriages and their consequences in togata means that the human situations presented are closer to everyday life and observe established moral conventions, resembling the conditions in a Roman *gens* headed by a *pater familias*. Also, plots do not necessarily include additional conflicts between generations; there is less

---

[114] Cf. Tit. *Tog.* 60–1 R.[3]; Afr. *Tog.* 47–9; 107–8; 130; 398 R.[3]; At. *Tog.* 7 R.[3]. See e.g. Beare 1964: 132; Guardì 1985: 17, 1991: 211, 1993: 271.

[115] See e.g. Daviault 1981: 23; Guardì 1985: 17.

need for a clever slave to support the lover; and women can play a more important role.

Another group of characters, distinguishing togata from palliata, consists of representatives of various professions or craftsmen, such as fullers or hairdressers (Tit. *Fullones* or *Fullonia*; Afr. *Cinerarius*), which is reminiscent of Atellana and contributes to locating plots in everyday life.[116] This connection is also maintained, beyond the issue of marriage and its corollaries, by references to ordinary domestic chores, topics such as the contrast between life in the city and in the country, the problem of luxury, decadence and changing traditions, religious customs or differences between Romans and other Italic peoples as well as Greeks. Some of these issues seem to reflect upon the situation in contemporary society, since the conclusion of the wars against foreign enemies had brought unprecedented wealth to Rome and forced Romans to confront other ways of life and to engage with people from different countries, while it removed the defence against external threats as one of the foremost aims of public life.

Indications of the public reaction to changes in the situation at Rome are the fierce discussions about the eventual repeal of the *Lex Oppia* (restricting the luxury of women) in 195 BCE, introduced during the Second Punic War in 215 BCE (cf. Liv. 34.1.1–8.3), or the *Senatus consultum de Bacchanalibus* of 185 BCE. Togatae may have commented on such current issues:[117] for instance, an allusion to female luxury in Titinius' *Barbatus* could be connected with the abrogation of the *Lex Oppia* (Tit. *Tog.* 1; 2; 3 R.³).[118] That the luxury of women is a topic also in Plautus' palliatae (Plaut. *Aul.* 167–9; 475–535) confirms that it was a topical issue at the time. Afranius' *Vopiscus* seems to have included a reference to 'laws on marriage and children' proposed by the censor Q. Caecilius Metellus Macedonicus in 131 BCE (Afr. *Tog.* 360–2 R.³), a move that was attacked by Afranius' contemporary Lucilius in his satires (Lucil. 676–86 M. = 636–46 W).[119] If these snapshots are representative, togatae could comment on specific events or issues that were at the centre of public discussions. Plays featuring

---

[116] Togatae and Atellanae share further themes and characters: for instance, fragments of both dramatic genres refer to marriages, wives with dowries, people from rural Italy, Roman festivals, Roman gods or 'philosophical' discussions. On the ubiquitous presence of fullers in Roman light drama see Guardì 1978.

[117] Horace's 'celebrate domestic deeds' (*celebrare domestica facta*) and his parallel between praetextae and togatae (Hor. *Ars P.* 285–8) do not imply that both dramatic genres were equally topical; this rather highlights the fact that both presented 'domestic' (i.e. Roman/Italic) issues instead of plots set in Greece (but see Daviault 1981: 29–30; Guardì 1985: 17).

[118] See e.g. Przychocki 1922: 180–5; Daviault 1981: 30, 33, 92, 94, 95; Guardì 1985, 17: 103–5, 1993: 272; also Vereecke 1968.

[119] See e.g. Daviault 1981: 30, 39, 234, 236; Guardì 1985: 17, 1993: 272.

music girls (Tit. *Psaltria sive Ferentinatis, Tibicina*) may be conventional, since playing instruments was a traditional accomplishment of courtesans, but this detail might have acquired particular relevance in view of the fact that music girls were admitted at Roman dinner parties in 187 BCE (cf. Liv. 39.6.8).[120]

To describe a debauched way of life togata poets use terms such as *pergraecari* or *res Graecae* (e.g. Tit. *Tog.* 85; 175 R.³); as these also occur in palliatae (e.g. Plaut. *Bacch.* 813; *Mostell.* 22; 64; 960; *Poen.* 603), they might be standard words in this context. Yet in a Roman setting they gain added significance as they mark a distinction between Romans and Greeks. In a Roman environment ways of life that are simply present in palliatae can be defined as 'Greek' and are thus contrasted with Roman customs: according to togata fragments a 'Greek lifestyle' manifests itself, among other things, in interest in music girls, courtesans, dining or perfume and is particularly outrageous in the country. The contrast between Greek and Roman may be part of a broader framework in togata, according to which Romans are distinguished from other peoples.[121] For there is talk about individuals bought in Gaul (Afr. *Tog.* 232–3 R.³) and about a person with Gallic clothing and diet (Afr. *Tog.* 284 R.³). Other figures are characterized by their Oscan and Volscian languages, as they speak no Latin (Tit. *Tog.* 104 R.³).

In a couple of verses by Afranius a person says that they are ashamed of introducing anything Greek when talking to a Numerius, since he will ridicule them (Afr. *Tog.* 272–3 R.³); this indicates a contrast between a character who is open to Greek influences and another character who is ignorant or does not approve of them. Unfortunately, the fragment does not reveal whether it is the phil-Hellene or the other person that the audience is expected to laugh at. That at any rate a topical issue is being discussed is confirmed by comparable evidence: Cato had already commented on the use of Greek by contemporary historians (cf. Gell. *NA* 11.8.1–5), and the aim to become and to be perceived totally Greek is ridiculed by the satirist Lucilius (Lucil. 88–94 M. = 87–93 W.). Since Afranius discusses Greek words and their Roman counterparts (Afr. *Tog.* 298–9 R.³), just as his contemporary the tragic poet Pacuvius does, playwrights obviously addressed such questions and could expect some interest on the part of audiences.

Beyond those broad characteristics shared by the three known togata poets, each of them exhibits distinctive features that seem to correspond to

---

[120] See e.g. Daviault 1981: 34.   [121] See Leigh 2004a: 9–12.

their period or their position within the development of this dramatic genre.[122]

Titinius, the first attested writer of togatae, apparently experimented with the new dramatic form and was in the process of creating something that took its starting point from (non-literary) Atellana (yet more serious and less stereotypical) and palliata (yet more serious and Roman), conformed to Roman customs (presenting love affairs transferred to a Roman marital and family set-up) and was of topical interest (alluding to current discussions and social issues). It is in his plays that Roman colour is most noticeable: at least three of them involve cities in ancient Volscian territory (in southern Latium to the south of Rome); and there is mention of people who speak Oscan and Volscian, but no Latin.

Afranius, the second representative of togata, who was active shortly after Terence, at a time of significant Greek influence, seems to have been more sophisticated and conscious of what he was doing. He apparently enjoyed playing with the entire literary tradition before him: Afranius discussed his own poetic practices, mentioned Terence and Pacuvius, alluded to Cato and Lucilius, talked about 'women on stage' (*scenicae . . . mulieres*) and 'bad poems' (*poematorum non bonorum*) and is said to have aimed at imitating the orator C. Titius (cf. Cic. *Brut.* 167); at any rate he made characters in his plays speak in oratorical fashion.[123]

That Afranius refers not only to previous comic poets, but also to (roughly) contemporary writers in other literary genres corroborates his claim that he takes from any writer, be they Greek or even Latin, whatever suits him (Macrob. *Sat.* 6.1.4: Afr. *Tog.* 25–8 R.³). His references to material outside his own dramatic genre are marked, either by the insertion of the writer's name or by the use of characteristic, almost proverbial expressions. This practice indicates that the poet had no intention of hiding his debts, but rather expected his audiences (or parts of them) to recognize them. That he also discussed literary issues (possibly in prologues) and had to defend himself against criticism of his poetic technique, like his contemporary Terence, indicates that literary discussions were going on at the time and that there was an interest in such questions on the part of both poets and audiences. Afranius' penchant for rhetoric accords with the style of Terence's prologues and with dramatic *agones* in Pacuvius and Accius

---

[122] Obviously, such distinctions have to be made with caution due to the scarcity of the available evidence (see the desperate attitude in Beare 1964: 131; also Guardì 1993: 277).

[123] Cf. Afr. *Tog.* 7 (cf. Pac. *Trag. inc.* LIV R.³ = 35 W.; see Zorzetti 1973); 23–4 (cf. Cato, *Orat.* fr. 71 ORF⁴); 25–8; 29; 91; 92; 100–1; 271; 274–5 R.³ (cf. Lucil. 957–8 M. = 696–7 W.; but see Rawson [1985] 1991: 481).

(on Accius cf. also Quint. *Inst.* 5.13.43). The similarity of Afranius' plays to typical features of Terence's and their differences from characteristic elements of both Titinius' and Plautus' works suggest that there was a simultaneous development from 'Roman to Greek' for both palliata and togata.[124]

For the last representative of Republican togata, Atta, it is even harder to establish an individual profile because of the meagre remains of his dramatic output, but he seems to have used this dramatic genre to react to changes in the running of the games, for in his play *Aedilicia* the organization of the games seems to be referred to (At. *Tog.* 1 R.[3]). Although some aspects of the organization of dramatic performances had already been mentioned in Plautine and Terentian prologues (Plaut. *Poen.* 1–45; Ter. *Haut.* 1–2; *Eun.* 19b–22), an entire play on the subject operates on a different scale, and Atta has another play on a specific festival (At. *Megalensia*).

Such a piece might be symptomatic of an interest in the institution of dramatic performances itself in a period when these developed towards spectacle (cf. already Afr. *Megalensia*). The mention of *planipes* in a fragment from Atta's *Aedilicia*, which might allude to a mime actor, would fit in with such an interest.[125] This need not imply that Atta's *togatae* included mime elements, but it might indicate that in his lifetime, just before the first literary mimes are attested, mime actors were recognized and associated with spectacles organized by aediles. In the same period the tragic poet Accius wrote treatises about dramatic performances (*Didascalica, Pragmatica*), which marks a twofold tendency of drama towards spectacle and erudition. The latter point is exemplified in Atta's discussion on the first month of the year (At. *Tog.* 18; 19–20 R.[3]) or in a play on the custom of *supplicatio* (At. *Supplicatio*).

Although due to the Roman setting togata had a more sober tone than palliata from the start, such a development across the three known representatives would invite the conclusion that togata also changed in accordance with general processes in the character and organization of dramatic performances over the Republican period. Then this dramatic genre would have declined at the end of the Republic not because of its own inherent faults, its Menandrism and an increasing seriousness that was not appreciated by the mass of spectators,[126] but, like other dramatic

---

[124] See also Courbaud 1899: 37; Pociña Pérez 1975b: 375.

[125] Reading and interpretation of the crucial fragment of Atta's *Aedilicia* (*Tog.* 1 R.[3]) are disputed (see e.g. Daviault 1981: 254–5 vs. Guardì 1985: 173).

[126] So e.g. Cacciaglia 1972: 244 (who sees a development in parallel to palliata); Guardì 1985: 17–18, 1993: 272; Pociña Pérez 1996b: 130–1. On the 'death of comedy' see Goldberg 1986: 203–20, 1993.

genres, rather owing to the overall situation of dramatic performances at the time.[127]

There were, however, revivals of Afranius' plays, both in Cicero's time (Cic. *Sest.* 118) and later in Nero's (Suet. *Ner.* 11.2), when the pieces were shown according to the conventions of the respective period: they were used for political statements in Cicero's time (see ch. 2.9) and exploited as extravagant and ridiculous spectacles by Nero.[128] At the end of the first century CE Juvenal mentions recitations of togatae among those of works in other literary genres (Juv. 1.3); yet it is not entirely clear whether he uses the term togatae in the sense of 'Roman comedies' or of 'Roman plays' more generally.

3.5 FABULA ATELLANA

Fabula Atellana is a form of light drama (cf. e.g. Petron. *Sat.* 53.13) named after the Oscan town of Atella in Campania (between Capua and Naples), where, according to ancient tradition, it was first performed (cf. Diom. *Ars* 3, *Gramm. Lat.* 1, pp. 489.14–90.7; Euanth. *Fab.* 4.1).[129] Atellana was apparently a kind of burlesque popular farce, regarded as crude, rustic and old-fashioned and considered to be a short, impromptu performance. It featured 'Oscan characters', simple stock characters with specific characteristics (*Oscae personae*: cf. Diom. *Ars* 3, *Gramm. Lat.* 1, p. 490.18–20).

Details of this dramatic genre's emergence and shape among the Oscans remain unclear. At any rate Atellana is a native Italic form of dramatic entertainment, even though it will have been subject to Greek and Etruscan influences over the course of its development. Therefore, while the dramatic forms of crepidata and palliata were essentially adapted from established Greek dramatic genres, and praetexta and togata were presumably created on this model, the Roman literary Atellana evolved in Italy on the basis of a pre-literary Oscan variety of this dramatic form. Atellana shares this characteristic with the Italic mime, but differs from the latter as it did not

---

Courbaud (1899: 103–18) thinks that the new dramatic genre was not sufficiently distinct from the already existing palliata and did not find favour with the general public due to its greater seriousness. Guardì (1993: 277) suggests that another reason for its disappearance was that togata took on more and more characteristics of Atellana. The surviving evidence does not support these theories.

[127] See also Daviault 1981: 31. [128] See also Beare 1964: 135; Daviault 1981: 52.

[129] On *fabula Atellana* see e.g. Munk 1840; Nicoll 1931: 65–79; Szilágyi 1941; Duckworth 1952: 10–13; Frassinetti 1953; Beare 1964: 137–48; Marzullo 1973: 11–37; Petersmann 1974, 1989; Rieks 1978: esp. 351–61; Raffaelli 1987; Fantham 1989a; Petrone 1992: 485–94; Höttemann 1993; Stärk in Suerbaum 2002: 264–72; Panayotakis 2005a; also Denard 2007.

become associated with a particular festival. Both these dramatic genres came to function as 'after-pieces': Atellanae seem to have been performed as 'after-pieces' (*exodia*, after performances of other plays) from some point in the Republican period onwards.[130]

Information about early Atellana is scarce; almost all evidence relates to its later existence in Rome. Therefore the early stages of its development can only be sketched rather vaguely. Atellana seems to have come to Rome at a relatively early date, probably in the third century BCE. Scholars have assumed that Oscan workmen, fullers in particular, brought it to Rome in connection with the festival of Quinquatrus and the cult of Minerva, since these figures continue to play a major role in literary Atellanae.[131] Plautus uses terms describing stock figures of Atellanae, and at least one passage seems to presuppose familiarity with them and their particular characteristics (Plaut. *Bacch.* 1088).[132] Festus posits Atellana actors in Rome for the time of Naevius (Fest., p. 238.12–20 L.); later writers assume this dramatic genre's presence in Rome for the third century BCE (cf. Liv. 7.2.11–12; Val. Max. 2.4.4).

Livy's text, if thus interpreted correctly, suggests that Atellanae in Rome combined features of Oscan farce with traditional Roman verses of jest (Liv. 7.2.11–12). Yet characteristics of the Oscan Atellana must have remained noticeable since the dramatic genre was named after its origin and regarded as a distinctive type. However, there is nothing in the fragments of literary Atellanae in Latin that would be remarkable in a Roman dramatic genre and might therefore be regarded as particularly 'Oscan'. Naturally, in Rome

---

[130] See Liv. 7.2.11; Cic. *Fam.* 9.16.7; Suet. *Tib.* 45; Juv. 6.71–2; Schol. on Juv. 3.175. Several ancient sources describe Atellanae as *exodia*, while only Cicero and the scholion to Juvenal mention that they followed tragedies. Livy's evidence is more difficult: he talks about Atellana's relationship to other dramatic forms and is usually taken to say that improvised jests of youths merged with Atellanae. Oakley (1998: 67–9), however, interprets the text (as constituted by him) as meaning that those jests became attached to Atellanae, i.e. themselves functioned as 'after-pieces' to Atellanae, leaving him with testimony that he himself calls 'seemingly contradictory', and he regards it as 'perhaps unwise to posit too rigid a separation between Atellans and *exodia*'. Whatever the correct reading of the Livy passage is, the context favours the interpretation that the two kinds of performances eventually became one, while it is unlikely that two similar types were given after each other. Nonetheless, N. J. Lowe (2008: 83) rightly calls for caution, noting that this function of Atellana is 'suspiciously analogous to that of satyr-play in the Athenian tragic competitions at the City Dionysia, so the claim may be founded on inference rather than evidence'. The interpretation of the Juvenal passage is also controversial, but here too the reading that Atellana is an *exodium* is the most likely one (on this issue see Courtney 1980: 271–2, on Juv. 6.71).

[131] Cf. Pomp. *Fullones, Quinquatrus*; *Atell.* 13; 27–8 R.³; Nov. *Fullones, Fullones feriati, Fullonicum*; *Atell.* 95 R.³. See Frassinetti 1953: 39–47, 1967: 3–4; Guardì 1978; Rieks 1978: 355–7; Stärk in Suerbaum 2002: 265.

[132] On Plautus' familiarity with Atellana and further, more doubtful references to its characters see J. C. B. Lowe 1989: 168 and n. 43.

Atellanae came to be performed in Latin; this seems to have caused a linguistic adaptation of the names of at least some of the main figures.[133] At the same time there are references to what seem to be dramatic performances in Oscan at Rome until the late first century BCE.[134] Individual Oscan words are attested in Latin Atellanae (cf. Fest., p. 514.28–30 L.: *Atell. inc.* 6–7 R.[3]), but occur also in other Republican dramatic genres. Hence a Romanized form and an Oscan form of Atellana (possibly developed and influenced by contemporary Latin performances) might have existed side by side.[135]

Later grammarians (presumably on the basis of the Latin literary version) classified Atellana as a Roman form of light drama, corresponding to Greek satyr-play: the two dramatic genres are described as similar in plot, words and jests, but differing in the characters on stage.[136] Apart from the grammarians' intention of construing a regular system, this parallel may be based on both the farcical character of these dramas and their position as 'after-pieces' in performance schedules. In late Republican times mimes apparently became more common in this function (cf. Cic. *Fam.* 9.16.7); yet Atellanae were still being performed (as *exodia*) in the early imperial period (cf. Suet. *Tib.* 45; *Ner.* 39; *Galb.* 13).

This final position of Atellanae perhaps agrees with the fact that they could be rather short pieces, if this is the reason for Fronto's diminutive *Atellaniolae* (Fronto, *Ep. ad M. Caes. et inv.* 2.8.3 [p. 29 v.d.H.]),[137] and featured a limited number of characters (cf. Ps.-Asc. on Cic. *Div. in Caec.* 48 [p. 200.14 St.]). That Atellanae acquired the status of 'after-pieces' implies that they were integrated into the schedule at Roman festivals; this particular position might be reminiscent of their origin as a popular, less formalized dramatic form, performed by less professional actors. According to a scholiast, 'after-pieces' had to provide 'comic relief' for the sad atmosphere caused by preceding tragic pieces (Schol. on Juv. 3.175).

In view of the dates of its representatives, the rise of literary Atellana coincided with the decline of palliata and togata.[138] The development of Atellana, therefore, might be a response to a desire for basic entertainment and for performances set in a 'realistic' Roman environment, after palliata

---

[133] Cf. Varro, *Ling.* 7.29: Osc. *Casnar* = Lat. *Pappus*; Fest. Paul., p. 41.18 L.

[134] Cf. Cic. *Fam.* 7.1.3; Strabo 5.3.6 [C 233]; Suet. *Iul.* 39.1; *Aug.* 43.1.

[135] Frassinetti (1953: 48–64) identifies a variety of subtypes of scripted and non-scripted Atellana in both Oscan and Latin; yet precise distinctions of this kind are difficult.

[136] Cf. Diom. *Ars* 3, *Gramm. Lat.* 1, pp. 489.14–90.7; 490.18–20; Mar. Victor., *Gramm. Lat.* 6, p. 82.10.

[137] On the text: *inibi sunt et Novianae Atellaniolae et Scipionis oratiunculae* see van den Hout's apparatus in the Teubner edition (1988: 29): '*novianae et atellaniolae* A : *et* del. Heindorf : *Novianae et <Pomponianae>* Hertz : *Naevianae et Atellaniolae* Rossi'.

[138] For thoughts on reasons for the rise of Atellana see Frassinetti 1967: 7–8.

and togata no longer sufficiently catered for this. The prominence of every-day characters such as fishermen and tradesmen in both Accius' tragedies and Turpilius' comedies, the last representatives of Republican crepidata and palliata respectively, may indicate an interest on the part of audiences in watching real-life characters rather than more remote figures and sto-ries. Atellana could provide the required fare while reducing elevated and elaborate features (such as those criticized by the satirist Lucilius since the 120s BCE) and even ridiculing traditional plots. The topics, characters and settings of Atellana result in everyday, straightforward, entertaining, yet meaningful stories in a (stylized) Roman or mythical environment.

At the same time there will have been cross-fertilization among Atel-lana and other dramatic performances in Italy:[139] early Atellana may have influenced togata and palliata as regards character types, scene structures or comic elements. Vice versa, Greek titles of literary Atellanae such as *Synephebi* recall palliatae, while titles with a mythical background such as *Armorum iudicium* recall crepidatae. Yet the dramatic genres seem to have retained differences in tone and outlook, or at least literary critics such as Horace regarded the genres as distinct and expected dramatists to observe their specific characteristics (Hor. *Epist.* 2.1.168–76; similarly Gell. *NA* 2.23.12): this is at any rate the most likely explanation for Horace's criticism that Plautus' 'greedy parasite' (*edax parasitus*) was rather like a Dossennus; i.e. Horace seems to have expected a parasite in a palliata to be different from a glutton in an Atellana.[140]

Few literary authors quote verses from literary Atellanae or comment on this dramatic genre, which may have to do with its relatively late establishment in Rome and its low regard among intellectuals (cf. e.g. Tac. *Ann.* 4.14.3). However, the attitude to Atellanae could be ambiguous: Cicero, for example, mentions 'Oscan games' (*Osci ludi*) with disdain on one occasion (Cic. *Fam.* 7.1.3), but refers to Novius' jokes approvingly elsewhere (Cic. *De Or.* 2.255; 2.279; 2.285).

The Atellana writer Pomponius was regarded as the inventor of a new dramatic genre despite a (non-literary) tradition before him (cf. Vell. Pat. 2.9.6). This assessment need not imply a major change; it may simply

---

[139] Such interactions are still a matter of debate: as regards dramatic forms preceding Atellanae, many scholars assume a major influence of phlyakes (see ch. 1.4) upon Atellanae (see e.g. Rieks 1978, 353–4, 368–9); this was denied by Höttemann (1993), following earlier suggestions (approvingly Stärk in Suerbaum 2002: 267). Rieks (1978: 352, 368) highlighted a strong Etruscan element for the early stages. D. Romano (1953: 9–23) argued that Atellana has Roman/Latin roots and later merged with Oscan characteristics.

[140] For views on this difficult Horatian passage see Beare 1964: 139; Brink 1982: 213; J. C. B. Lowe 1989: 169 and n. 47; Jocelyn 1995: esp. 230–9. See also ch. 4.6.

recognize Pomponius' achievement of elevating Atellana to the status of a
literary dramatic genre by producing written scripts and adopting a more
professional approach.[141] Pomponius was a contemporary of Novius, these
two writers representing literary Atellana in the early first century BCE.[142]
According to Macrobius, Mummius revived Atellanae after a long period
of neglect following Pomponius and Novius (Macrob. *Sat.* 1.10.3); three
fragments of his Atellanae (not assigned to specific dramas or with uncertain
titles) remain. If Mummius is indeed a later practitioner of this dramatic
genre, it may be of interest that Macrobius refers to him when quoting
verses on the festival of Saturnalia, along with a line by Novius on the same
issue (Nov. *Atell.* 104 R.[3]; Mummius, *Atell.* 3–5 R.[3]). This could indicate
that writers of this dramatic genre active in different periods touched upon
the same or similar topics.[143]

Protagonists in Atellanae were mainly taken from a fixed repertoire of
stock characters with invariable features, the so-called 'Oscan characters'
(*Oscae personae*: cf. Diom. *Ars* 3, *Gramm. Lat.* 1, p. 490.18–20). Extant
titles and fragments of literary Atellanae as well as some *testimonia* point
to at least four stock figures, who share a degree of gluttony, clownish-
ness and foolishness and who bear simple, speaking names: Maccus, the
fool and stupid clown (cf. Apul. *Apol.* 81.3; Diom. *Ars* 3, *Gramm. Lat.* 1,
p. 490.18–20); Bucco, the foolish braggart (cf. Apul. *Apol.* 81; Plaut. *Bacch.*
1088; Isid. *Etym.* 10.30); Pappus, the foolish old man (cf. Varro, *Ling.* 7.29);
Dossennus, the cunning trickster and/or glutton (cf. Hor. *Epist.* 2.1.173;
Sen. *Ep.* 89.7).[144] These types probably did not always appear together; i.e.
not every play starred all of them.[145]

---

[141] Petersmann (1989: 136) points out that Atellana became literary during the Social War, in a period
in which the national self-consciousness of peoples in Italy increased (see also D. Romano 1953: 43).
This might have encouraged poets to develop an originally Oscan dramatic form. Butler (1972: 119)
believes that Atellana was improvisational at first, later acquired literary form and reverted to the
original state after a short period of time. Yet there is no evidence for such a development. Marzullo
(1956) put forward the theory that Novius was earlier than Pomponius and that Pomponius only
gave the Atellana its fully established literary form, but this hypothesis cannot be proved.

[142] Varro quotes one line by an Aprissius that includes the word *bucco* and could therefore come from
an Atellana (Varro, *Ling.* 6.68; see Ribbeck 1898: 332); but there is no further evidence about this
poet (see Frassinetti 1967: 14, 95, 113; Stärk in Suerbaum 2002: 272).

[143] Raffaelli (1987: esp. 127–8) regards the fact that two extant fragments refer to Saturnalia as a confirmation that Atellana had a 'Saturnalian' or 'carnivalesque' character. However, the preservation of
two fragments on the same topic is due to the interests of the transmitting writer, and they indicate
possible topics rather than the character of this dramatic genre.

[144] But see J. C. B. Lowe 1989: 168 and n. 45, who is sceptical of the common characterization of
Dossennus. For possible explanations of the speaking names of these characters see Bonfante in
Frassinetti 1967: vi–viii; Frassinetti 1967: 2–3; Rieks 1978: 352–3.

[145] Atellanae could also have a Manducus, a large-jawed glutton, but the evidence is too flimsy to
regard him as another stock figure or even possibly to identify him with Dossennus. The figure of
Manducus is not mentioned in any preserved title, in contrast to the others. The argument rests

Festus says that Atellana performers were called *personati* in the true sense of the word, since they could not be forced to lay down their masks on stage, whereas actors of other plays had to suffer this, presumably at the end of performances (Fest., p. 238.17–20 L.). This note corresponds with information in Livy (and Valerius Maximus) that Atellanae were performed not by professional actors, but rather by free young men, and that Atellana actors were allowed to do military service and were not removed from their tribes (Liv. 7.2.11–12; Val. Max. 2.4.4).[146] Even though such a description might be a later construction, it indicates that Atellana built on masked stock characters (presumably with the appropriate stock costumes) and that performers might be of a higher social class than ordinary actors and therefore allowed to remain anonymous. The use of masks and the representation of exaggerated stock figures require meaningful gesticulation; indeed, later writers mention the use of gestures by Atellana actors (cf. Juv. 6.71–2; Tert. *De spect.* 17.2).

Despite their set-up, Atellanae seem to have had coherent plots: 'Atellana intrigues/complications' (*tricae Atellanae*) are referred to (cf. Varro, *Sat. Men.* 198 B.). Even a rather short play with a fixed repertoire of characters may be based on a complex story. Mutual deceptions of the stock figures, trickery, misunderstandings and exposure are likely to have been prominent, their effect being based on the stupidity and foolishness of the characters.

Pomponius and Novius share titles that mention the stock figures or common themes (*Dotata, Fullones, Maccus, Pappus praeteritus*), which is not remarkable in a dramatic genre based on standard characters. Therefore it seems likely that such overlapping would not provoke criticism of the sort that Terence incurred in the case of palliata (Ter. *Eun.* 19b–34), though he points to the continuing recurrence of typical figures even in palliata (Ter. *Eun.* 35–41; see also ch. 3.4).

almost exclusively on a corrupt passage in Varro (Varro, *Ling.* 7.95: *dictum mandier a mandendo, unde manducari et a quo in Atellanis † ad obsenum [Dossennum* Mueller] *vocant manducum.*); a fragment of one of Pomponius' Atellanae is also only a doubtful reference (Pomp. *Atell.* 112 R.[3]: *magnus manduco camellus... cantherius*). These pieces of information just suggest the occasional presence of a Manducus in Atellana (for the text in Varro and the view that it does not refer to an Atellana figure cf. Préaux 1962). Whether a reference to Manducus in Plautus (Plaut. *Rud.* 535–6) proves the poet's familiarity with the Atellana figure or refers to a mask that used to be carried in festival processions (cf. Fest., p. 115.20–5 L.) is uncertain.

[146] If these descriptions are historically correct, the position of Atellana actors seems to have changed by imperial times: Tacitus records that Atellana was seen as in particular need of regulations and restrictions from the Senate, and Atellana players must have been among the actors subsequently removed from Rome under Tiberius (Tac. *Ann.* 4.14.3; also Suet. *Tib.* 37.2; Cass. Dio 57.21.3; for a similar measure under Nero see Tac. *Ann.* 13.25.4).

A fragment that indicates where the figure Pappus lives (Pomp. *Atell.* III R.³) suggests that Atellanae were performed with the same set as other dramatic genres, i.e. on a stage representing houses on a street, and perhaps also that there could be a kind of introduction or prologue in which essential information was given, although, in this example, in a jocular tone. Another fragment (Nov. *Atell.* 84–5 R.³) shows that, just as in other dramatic genres, the arrival of new characters could be announced by figures already on stage.

In line with the stupidity and foolishness of the characters, the language in surviving Atellana fragments is rather unsophisticated: characters talk a simple, sometimes slightly incorrect Latin and behave accordingly; there are vulgar and dialect words.[147] If an imperial source is significant, Atellanae could include Greek verses just as palliatae could (cf. Suet. *Ner.* 39.3); some titles at least are Greek (Pomp. *Adelphi, Synephebi*; Nov. *Hetaera, Paedium*), and there are Greek names (Pomp. *Atell.* 64 R.³: Diomedes). Occasional use of Greek is in line with the colloquial language of the period. As regards poetic form, the same metres seem to have been used as in other dramatic genres (senarii and septenarii). Late-antique writers claim that the iambic septenarius was prominent in Atellanae as appropriate to their jocular tone; yet in the surviving fragments the trochaic septenarius is the most frequent metre.[148]

Corresponding to the variable character of this dramatic genre, preserved titles and fragments of literary Atellanae indicate the existence of different variants that could be called 'subtypes': unsurprisingly, a significant proportion of known plays seems to be based on the 'Oscan characters', featuring the stock figures in prominent roles; they are frequently referred to in titles and fragments. They could apparently appear in various specific guises and situations, whereby their characteristics may be ridiculed; they can be shown foolishly unable to cope with particular circumstances, or a drastic contrast between their characteristics and those actually required might be presented. Plays are set in an everyday environment and feature low-life situations; some represent family affairs, rural life and a primitive rustic atmosphere (inferred from titles derived from professions or names of animals). There are also plays that bear titles reminiscent of tragedy; these could be travesties of mythological stories or parodies of tragedies.

---

[147] For observations on the language of Atellana and mimus cf. Bonfante in Frassinetti 1967: v–xxiv; on the style of Atellana see Raffaelli 1987: esp. 116–27.

[148] Cf. Ter. Maur., *Gramm. Lat.* 6, pp. 396–7.2390–7; Mar. Victor., *Gramm. Lat.* 6, p. 135.25–9 vs. Raffaelli 1987: 117.

As Atellanae came to be performed as 'after-pieces' after other plays, they might have presented a light-hearted version of similar material. A further group of Atellanae is formed by pieces with Greek titles reminiscent of palliatae; these may have been either adaptations or again parodic reactions. Another variety (suggested by surviving fragments) seems to have been concerned with popular philosophy and literary criticism, like Latin satire.

Accordingly, topics and themes that can be identified in the remaining texts range from basic bodily functions, the mundane concerns of farmers, various family relationships and love affairs, via Roman gods, Roman festivals and Roman institutions, to mythical figures parodically portrayed, literary comments and allusions to contemporary affairs. Surviving fragments in the literary category include a comment on slaves in comedy, a remark on the success of a poem with the audience or criticism of a named tragic poet (Pomp. *Atell.* 138; 181 R.³; Nov. *Atell.* 67–8 R.³). There might even be metaliterary self-reflection or self-irony when a fragment requests that Dossennus and the fullers should be given food at public expense (Pomp. *Atell.* 27–8 R.³). That, despite their burlesque character, literary Atellanae presented reflective elements, similar to dramatic genres flourishing earlier, might indicate a continuity of those elements on the Roman stage even though audience tastes were changing.

That Atellana was capable of intellectual and stylistic levels beyond mere farce is also indicated by a comment in the text of Fronto's letters, where 'affable remarks' (*comes sententiae*) in comedies and 'elegant' ones (*urbanae*) in togatae are distinguished from 'charming and clever' ones (*lepidae et facetae*) in Atellanae (Fronto, *Ep. ad Ant.* 4.2, *m² in margine^d*) [p. 106 v.d.H.]). This is presumably the reason why Fronto allowed Atellana to be included in the reading list of the aspiring orator (Fronto, *Ep. ad M. Caes. et inv.* 3.17.3 [pp. 49–50 v.d.H.]; test. et fr. 28 v.d.H.), while Quintilian regarded the kind of jokes in Atellana as inappropriate for orators (Quint. *Inst.* 6.3.46–7).[149] Yet Cicero repeatedly refers to a special type of joke in Novius, which apparently consists of unexpected collocations and continuations, with approval (Cic. *De or.* 2.255; 2.279; 2.285). The stylistic quality of Atellana is shown in the fragments by examples of alliteration, assonance, *figura etymologica*, witty statements, word play and puns.

---

[149] The text (Quint. *Inst.* 6.3.47) as transmitted reads: *illa obscura quae Atellanio more captant*; *obscura* is frequently emended to *obscaena* (Teuffel), which is then taken as evidence for the obscene character of Atellana.

One fragment of Pomponius includes the Roman names Memmius, Cassius and Munatius (Pomp. *Atell.* 14/15 R.³). In the absence of any context it is uncertain who is referred to and what is said about these individuals. At any rate the names do not sound like those of dramatic figures, but rather like those of 'real' Romans, which would demonstrate that references to individuals were possible in Atellana,¹⁵⁰ just as a tragic poet is named in another fragment (Nov. *Atell.* 67–8 R.³). The dramatic genre of praetexta proves that affirmative mention of contemporary individuals was possible on the Roman stage (see ch. 5.2); however, a positive presentation seems unlikely in Atellana and is certainly not valid in the case of the tragic poet. Therefore, the special status of Atellana and the fact that performers were allowed to conceal their identities might have paved the way for greater freedom, and some mocking was perhaps conceded in Atellana. It is noteworthy also that for both Pomponius and Novius a play entitled *Pappus praeteritus* ('*Pappus passed over*') is attested, which, according to the remaining fragments, featured the fickleness of the populace and the issue of placing one's trust and hope of support on the wrong voters (Pomp. *Atell.* 105–6 R.³; Nov. *Atell.* 75–6 R.³). The figure of Pappus as the main character turns these dramas into humorous stories, presumably without direct references to specific individuals; nevertheless, the contemporary problem of voting practices is commented on.¹⁵¹

In the early imperial period Atellanae could voice obvious topical criticism, even attacks on the emperor, which were picked up by audiences (cf. Suet. *Tib.* 45; *Ner.* 39.3; *Galb.* 13); Caligula was unable to bear this and had an Atellana poet publicly executed 'because of a little verse with an ambiguous joke' (cf. Suet. *Calig.* 27.4).¹⁵² Attested examples of Atellana verses charged with political meaning do not express criticism explicitly, but rather by means of a clever interpretation of lines and their application to the current situation on the part of actors and/or audiences. On this basis one may conclude that actors could use existing well-known Atellanae to make political statements and hence that in this time revivals of Atellanae could be exploited in the same way as those of tragedies and comedies were in the first century BCE (see ch. 2.9).

---

¹⁵⁰ See Petersmann 1974: 23–4.
¹⁵¹ Such topical references bring Roman Atellana closer to Euripidean and Hellenistic satyr-plays than to earlier examples of the genre by Aeschylus and Sophocles (on the role of topical allusions in Greek satyr-play see Seidensticker in Krumeich *et al.* 1999: 33–4; on Greek satyr-play see Krumeich *et al.* 1999, with texts and references).
¹⁵² On Atellana in the imperial period see Rieks 1978: 368.

3.6 *MIMUS/PLANIPES*

According to ancient grammarians the equivalent in Rome of the Greek *mimus* was *planipes*, a term derived from the bare feet of the performers (or the humbleness of the plot or the performance in the 'orchestra').[153] However, Latin writers use both words for the Roman version of this dramatic genre; *mimus* seems to be more common and *planipes* chosen mainly in technical contexts. Ancient grammarians describe *planipes/mimus* as a simple and humble form, analogous to Greek mime.[154] In Rome mime is similar to Atellana in that it had gone through a pre-literary phase ('popular mime') in Italy before it became literary.[155]

Mime is the only Roman dramatic genre that came to be associated with a particular festival: it developed into a characteristic element of *Ludi Florales* (see ch. 2.1).[156] For 211 BCE, however, the old mime actor C. Pomponius is recorded as active in Rome: he danced to the music of a flute as part of *Ludi Apollinares* (cf. Fest., pp. 436/8 L.; Serv. on Verg. *Aen.* 8.110). Apparently, mimes were not restricted to *Ludi Florales*; at any rate this was not the case in late Republican times, when mimes replaced Atellanae in their function as 'after-pieces' (cf. Cic. *Fam.* 9.16.7 [46 BCE]).[157] Beyond these *testimonia*, there is no evidence on when mimes became a regular element of festivals at Rome and on when and how a particular connection with *Ludi Florales* emerged.[158] Ovid playfully claims that it had to do with the special character of the goddess honoured (Ov. *Fast.* 5.331–4; 5.347–8), while Lactantius criticizes this version as an unacceptable attempt at ennobling the festival (Lactant. *Div. inst.* 1.20.5–10).

Cicero mentions a mime entitled *Tutor* that was 'old' (*mimus vetus*) in his time (Cic. *De or.* 2.259). The meaning and reference point of this remark are unclear; it just shows that mimes were thought to have existed for some time in this period. Still, mime appears to have been one of the last Republican dramatic genres to become literary: this happened only at the very end of the Republic with the two poets Decimus Laberius and Publilius Syrus,

---

[153] On *mimus* (on mime in Rome and on the development of mime in antiquity and beyond) see e.g. Reich 1903; Nicoll 1931: esp. 80–131; Duckworth 1952: 13–15; Beare 1964: 149–58; Giancotti 1967; Marzullo 1973: 39–82; Rieks 1978: 361–8; Cicu 1988; Jory 1988; Fantham 1989b; Petrone 1992: 495–507; Gianotti 1993: 47–55; Dunbabin 2004; esp. Panayotakis 2010: 1–32; also Gianotti 1996; Denard 2007.

[154] Cf. Diom. *Ars* 3, *Gramm. Lat.* 1, pp. 482.27–9; 490.3–10; 491.13–19; Donat. *Com.* 6.2; Lyd. *Mag.* 1.40. On some of these sources and their restricted focus see Panayotakis 2010: 7–9.

[155] Maxwell (1996) argues for a strong Etruscan influence on Roman mime, which is possible, but difficult to prove.

[156] Cf. Val. Max. 2.10.8; Ov. *Fast.* 5.331–2; 5.347–54; Lactant. *Div. inst.* 1.20.5–10.

[157] See Beacham 1991: 129.   [158] See Fantham 1989b: 155 n. 10.

the representatives of Latin literary mime in the Republican period.[159] The dates of these poets accord with Cicero's remark in a letter of 46 BCE that mimes, in place of Atellanae, were now given as 'after-pieces' (Cic. *Fam.* 9.16.7),[160] which implies their recognition and increasing prominence as a dramatic genre around this time. Yet the fact that the dictator Sulla was fond of mime (cf. e.g. Plut. *Sull.* 36.1–2) indicates that this dramatic genre was established in Rome even prior to this change.

Mime gained a proper position on the Roman stage only when most other dramatic genres were already in decline, even though performances of existing and of occasional new pieces continued. Not only conditions in the contemporary theatre, but also the support received from powerful men such as Sulla and Caesar have been mentioned by modern scholars as explanations for the rise of mime.[161] This is not unlikely and would constitute a prime example of the influence of magistrates on the Roman theatre, noticeable in this period also in Pompey's erection of the first permanent stone theatre in Rome and the lavish opening ceremonies (see ch. 2.4). Performances of mimes continued into the imperial period.

Comments on mime by later ancient writers are mainly critical, since they regarded this dramatic genre as low and vulgar, and looked down upon its crude and frivolous aspects.[162] In particular, performances of mime were considered obscene, since women played the female roles and mime actresses could appear naked or strip nude at the end of performances (cf. e.g. Lactant. *Div. inst.* 1.20.10; 6.20.30; cf. also Ov. *Tr.* 2.503–4). Famously, at *Ludi Florales* in 55 BCE, the audience was embarrassed at demanding that the mime actresses should strip bare because of the presence of Cato (Uticensis); having been informed of the situation, Cato left the theatre so that the people could enjoy the accustomed spectacle (cf. Val. Max. 2.10.8; Sen. *Ep.* 97.8; Mart. 1, *praef.*).

Nevertheless, mime seems to have been a versatile and multi-faceted dramatic form. Literary mimes could have meaningful and well-phrased content. Seneca highlighted the fact that there was much in Publilius Syrus'

---

[159] Other mime writers, such as Catullus, Lentulus, Hostilius or Marullus, of whom little is known, seem to have been active in the imperial period (*testimonia* and/or fragments in Ribbeck 1873: 392–4 / 1898: 370–3 and Bonaria 1965).

[160] On the basis of an ancedcote about Laberius and Clodius (cf. Macrob. *Sat.* 2.6.6), presumably dating to 56 BCE (see ch. 4.16), Till (1975: 262) infers that mimes had already replaced Atellanae as 'after-pieces' in this period, but there is no evidence on the point in the performance schedule at which the requested mime was intended to be performed.

[161] See Bonaria 1965: 5; also Jory 1988: 78.

[162] Cf. e.g. Cic. *Fam.* 7.1.1; *Rab. Post.* 35; Ov. *Tr.* 2.497–500; Gell. *NA* 2.23.12; Macrob. *Sat.* 2.1.9. Mimes (and similar spectacles) were fiercely opposed by Christian writers in late antiquity (e.g. Hieron. *Ep.* 52.2; Tert. *De spect.* 17.2; Lactant. *Div. inst.* 6.20.30; Arn. *Adv. nat.* 7.33.5–7).

mimes that could or should be said in comedies and tragedies or even in philosophical treatises, while he was aware that the same plays included low jokes (Sen. *Ep.* 8.8; *Dial.* 6.9.5; 9.11.8).[163] The preserved *sententiae* of Publilius Syrus confirm the presence of popular-philosophical, sententious elements; the verses spoken at particular performances in Caesar's time (see below) and other fragments show that mime could feature topical political comment. Generalizing somewhat, one may therefore conclude tentatively that mime became prominent when it did because it provided a perfect combination (from the audience's point of view) of the two tendencies observable in the development of drama in Republican Rome: meaningful messages and entertaining elements. Mime provided basic entertainment in an everyday setting as well as straightforward moral rules and comments on topical issues.[164]

The extant titles of literary mimes are partly Greek, but mostly Latin. As there is some overlap in titles with those of other light dramatic genres, mimes could obviously take up titles already employed for plays of other dramatic genres; whether or not there was a special connection to earlier plays of the same title cannot be ascertained.

Distinctions between light dramatic genres were apparently not absolute and mime participated in the common comic tradition in Italy.[165] The remaining titles and fragments of mimes include frequent comic characters and themes, which bear similarities to other light dramatic genres: plots are based on relationships and conflicts within families; they feature wives and courtesans, slaves and masters; issues mentioned comprise marriages and festivals, discussions about inheritance and prodigal sons; there are farm animals, tradesmen (e.g. fullers as in Atellanae), fools and love affairs. This evidence is confirmed by later *testimonia* that give masters, slaves, innkeepers, flatterers, young men in love, angry rivals, adulterers, clever women, stupid fools and impersonations of mythical figures as characters in mimes.[166] A Roman setting is indicated by references to Roman gods and festivals as well as places in Italy. Topical comments, moral edification, literary parody, philosophical burlesque (cf. also Ath. *Deip.* 1: 20c–d) and mythological travesties can be inferred for literary mime.[167]

---

[163] See also Beare 1964: 158; Rieks 1978: 367; Panayotakis 2005a: 142; on the ambiguous character of mime see generally Panayotakis 2010: 14–16.

[164] See also Beare 1964: 154, 158.   [165] See also Rieks 1978: 363.

[166] Cf. e.g. Ov. *Tr.* 2.497–500; Arn. *Adv. nat.* 7.33.5; Choricius, *Apol. Mim.* 110.

[167] Wiseman (1999) assumes that mimes (just like other dramas in his view) told stories connected with Roman history, which are traceable in historiography and aetiological elegy (see ch. 1.4, n. 66;

This mixture is reminiscent of Roman satire and seems peculiar to mime among dramatic genres in Rome.

From this range of topics and the remaining longer fragments it is clear that mimes not only presented erotic farce, but must also have had plots and dialogue. They could apparently open with prologues distinguished from the subsequent action (cf. Macrob. *Sat.* 2.7.2; 2.7.4); when Isidorus claims that the plot (*argumentum*) was announced prior to the actual performance (Isid. *Etym.* 18.49), he may be referring to expository prologues. Cicero seems to presuppose that plots in mime (in contrast to those in *fabulae*) were flimsy and not well constructed, so that, when a proper conclusion could not be found, the play was hastily and arbitrarily brought to an end (Cic. *Cael.* 65). Yet elsewhere he describes a mime with the phrase or title 'beggar just now, suddenly rich' (Cic. *Phil.* 2.65: *modo egens, repente dives*), which points to a basic story line.

Besides, mimes could include references to contemporary circumstances and individuals. This is indicated as early as the second half of the second century BCE by anecdotes about the poets Accius and Lucilius, who were each attacked by name (*nominatim*) by a mime actor from the stage and therefore took them to court (cf. *Auct. ad Her.* 1.24; 2.19). The fact that only one of the poets was successful in having the calumniator condemned might indicate that an attack by name from the stage was not an action of which one would automatically be convicted. Preserved fragments do not feature personal names; yet criticism in veiled form may be obvious enough.

Apart from Cato leaving the theatre at *Ludi Florales* (see above), the most notorious incidents connected with mime are the contests of Decimus Laberius and Publilius Syrus in 47/6 BCE, when Caesar challenged the equestrian Laberius to appear on stage in his own mimes (cf. Sen. *Controv.* 7.3.9; Gell. *NA* 8.15; Macrob. *Sat.* 2.3.10; 2.7.2–5) and Publilius Syrus called on all those who were active for the stage at the time to contend with him in a poetic contest (cf. Macrob. *Sat.* 2.7.7–9; also Cic. *Fam.* 12.18.2; Gell. *NA* 17.14.2).[168]

---

ch. 3.2 and n. 44). Yet the only preserved title that might indicate a historical or aetiological drama is Laberius' *Anna Peranna*, and there are no *testimonia* to confirm this particular characteristic of mime.

[168] Macrobius, who gives the most detailed account of this incident, continues with a similar story for pantomime: Pylades being publicly challenged by his pupil Hylas (Macrob. *Sat.* 2.7.12–19). The first story is also mentioned by other writers, while the second one is much simpler, does not involve the two most famous representatives and has fewer political repercussions. Hence the story for mime sounds more plausible and rather like the original one, to which another one for pantomime has been added.

These incidents confirm that mime was an open and flexible form, which allowed for divergences from a standard dramatic set-up and to which an improvisational element was not foreign. Moreover, Laberius' verses are described as having included direct (albeit not *nominatim*) criticism of Caesar, which was picked up by the audience (cf. Macrob. *Sat.* 2.7.5; Sen. *Dial.* 4.11.3). While such criticism might have accorded with Laberius' overall attitude (cf. Macrob. *Sat.* 2.6.6; 7.3.8), it shows that political comment was apparently possible and tolerated to some extent. The fact that Caesar was the reference point of those comments and at the same time dominated the whole set-up shows his powerful position, as well as the impact of magistrates on dramatic performances towards the end of the Republic and the role of drama in public life.

That the engagement of mime with the political situation was not as singular as the circumstances might suggest is indicated by Cicero's fear for a politically active friend of being singled out by Laberius and other mime writers if he acted wrongly (Cic. *Fam.* 7.11.2 [?January 53 BCE]). Elsewhere Cicero corresponds with Atticus about the audience's reaction to mimes by Publilius, which apparently consisted in an expression of views on the contemporary political situation (Cic. *Att.* 14.2.1 [8 April 44 BCE]). Cicero even seems to expect 'mime actors' utterances' (*mimorum dicta*) and reactions by the people (Cic. *Att.* 14.3.2 [9 April 44 BCE]). Hence using new mimes for political comment on current affairs appears to have been such a common feature that it had to be reckoned with.

Owing to the time in which mime came to the fore, to the support received from powerful men and to the proliferation of inscriptions concerning mimes, there are a number of *testimonia* that provide information on practical details characteristic of mime.

There existed organizational structures specific to mime, perhaps already indicated by the fact that it was only in mime that female roles were played by women. Mime actors were organized in troupes or organizations each called a 'college of mime actors' (*commune* or *collegium mimorum*), headed by a 'chief mime actor' (*archimimus*/*archimima*).[169] This person would also be the main actor in performances (*archimimus*/*mimus*), followed in the hierarchy of the division of parts by 'actors of the second, third, fourth part' (*actores secundarum, tertiarum, quartarum partium*).[170]

---

[169] Cf. Plut. *Sull.* 36.2; *ILS* 5208; 5209; *CIL* VI 10106 = *ILS* 5211; *CIL* VI 10107 = *ILS* 5212; *CIL* XIV 2408 = *ILS* 5196.

[170] Cf. Suet. *Calig.* 57.4; Hor. *Epist.* 1.18.14; *CIL* VI 10103 = *ILS* 5199; *CIL* VI 10118 = *ILS* 5201; *CIL* X 814 = *ILS* 5198; *CIL* XIV 4198 = *ILS* 5200. On troupes of mime actors see e.g. Cicu 1988: 159–75.

As the Latin name of the genre (and its most likely interpretation) as well as references to mimicry with all parts of the body in mimes indicate (cf. e.g. Cic. *De or.* 2.242; 2.251; Quint. *Inst.* 6.3.29), mime actors played barefoot and without masks. Accordingly, facial expression, gesticulation and dancing had an important role (cf. *Anth. Lat.* 487a.13–22; Ath. *Deip.* 10: 452f; Isid. *Etym.* 18.49). Rhetoricians considered excessive imitation as typical of mime, but as inappropriate for orators (cf. Cic. *De or.* 2.242; 2.251–2; Quint. *Inst.* 6.3.29).[171] Modern scholars assume that typically only two or three actors performed in any one piece as one actor could represent several characters.[172]

References to a particular costume of mime actors are uncertain. A comparison in Seneca (Sen. *Ep.* 114.6) suggests that slaves in mime could have a Greek cloak (*pallium*), which they might arrange in various ways. Fools traditionally had shaven heads (cf. e.g. Juv. 5.171–3; Arn. *Adv. nat.* 7.33.5). Part of the performance (if not all), at least originally, seems to have taken place in the 'orchestra', while other dramatic genres were performed on the stage (cf. Fest., p. 436.28–31 L.; Diom. *Ars* 3, *Gramm. Lat.* 1, p. 490.6–7).

Even though all actors in Rome were of low social status, the reputation of mime actors was particularly bad, due to the character of this dramatic genre and the fact that both male and female actors performed. Some names of mime actors are known (often from inscriptions), spread over most of the Republican period. They obviously include Publilius Syrus; among mime actresses Mark Antony's consort Cytheris/Volumnia/Lycoris is perhaps the most notorious.[173] That Antony socialized with mime actors and actresses (and a mime writer) was one of the reproaches Cicero levelled against him in the heated political atmosphere of the late Republic.[174] This is a prime instance of the ambiguous attitude of intellectuals to the theatre and particularly to mime, since at the same time Cicero was aware of the potential political impact of performances (Cic. *Fam.* 7.11.2 [?January 53 BCE]).

---

[171] Isidorus distinguishes between the 'singing' of tragic and comic actors and the 'dancing' of mime actors (Isid. *Etym.* 18.43–4).

[172] The sources on Caesar's challenge to Laberius talk of the poet 'acting his mime' (*suum mimum agere*), and there is no mention of further actors needed for or involved in the performance (cf. Macrob. *Sat.* 2.7.2; Suet. *Iul.* 39.2).

[173] For information on Republican actors see Garton 1972; for Publilius Syrus see Garton 1972: 260, no. 126; for Cytheris see Garton 1972: 248, no. 70.

[174] Cf. Cic. *Phil.* 2.20; 2.58; 2.61–2; 2.67; 2.101; 8.26; 10.22; 11.13; 13.24.

3.7 *PANTOMIMUS*

Pantomime (*pantomimus*) was popular and promoted under emperors from Augustus until late antiquity; thus it might be regarded as a predominantly imperial dramatic form. Yet pantomime emerged in the very first years of the Principate under Augustus and perhaps earlier, and its appearance can be seen as the conclusion to developments concerning the Roman stage during the Republican period.[175] Discussion of its emergence and characteristics therefore completes the overview of Republican dramatic genres.

Although there were Greek forerunners and earlier simple forms in Italy, ancient writers dated the introduction of pantomime in Rome to 22 BCE.[176] This view apparently reflects the traditional date assigned to a change from pantomimic dances, already present in Rome, to pantomime proper. Pylades from Cilicia (who also wrote a treatise on pantomime) and Bathyllus from Alexandria are credited in ancient sources with 'developing the Italian style of dance', the former representing the solemn and serious 'tragic' and the latter the light-hearted 'comic' variety;[177] Lucian notes that the Italiotai called the dancer 'a pantomime' (Lucian, *Salt.* 67). All these pieces of information indicate that pantomime came to be seen as a particular Roman dramatic genre.

Despite the conventional date of 22 BCE given in ancient sources, pantomime was certainly present in Rome prior to this: according to Lucian it reached a more developed stage in approximately the time of Augustus (Lucian, *Salt.* 34). Modern scholarship has inferred that pantomime in Rome might go back to the late 40s BCE: the anecdote in Livy's account of the early theatre, namely that Livius Andronicus acted to the accompaniment of a piper and a singer, which increased the vivacity of his gestures (Liv. 7.2.8–10), disrupts Livy's chronological narrative of the development of early drama and may be a reflection of a preoccupation with pantomime in Livy's time;[178] hence Livy might have wished to provide an aetiological

---

[175] On *pantomimus* see Rotolo 1957; Jory 1981, 1996, also 1988; Petrone 1992: 508–13; Gianotti 1993: 55–69; Hall and Wyles 2008.

[176] Cf. Hieron. *Ab Abr.* 1995, 22 BCE [p. 165c Helm]; Macrob. *Sat.* 2.7.12; 2.7.18; Zos. 1.6.1.

[177] Cf. Ath. *Deip.* 20d–e; on Pylades and Bathyllus cf. also Sen. *Controv.* 3, *praef.* 16; Suet. *Aug.* 45.4.

[178] See Beare 1964: 219–20; Jocelyn 1967: 21; Gianotti 1993: 48. Gratwick (1982a: 78–9) sees an allusion to 'mime' in this passage. Suerbaum (2002: 54) believes that Livy's source, Varro, cannot yet have known pantomime, but one must beware of circular argument. N. J. Lowe (2008: 82–3) thinks that 'Livy's source (perhaps the great Republican scholar Varro, who is, however, usually better than this) is certainly mistaken to trace the miming of sung parts back to Livius' own day'. But Livy's text itself indicates reservations about this story (cf. Liv. 7.2.9: *dicitur*), and its insertion in spite of this may indicate its importance within the overall argument.

explanation for this dramatic genre, and the character of pantomime could be one reason for his condemnation of contemporary theatre (Liv. 7.2.13). As the pantomime Pylades is known to have been in his old age in 2 BCE, while Cicero nowhere refers to pantomime as a major factor on the Roman stage, a date in the late 40s BCE or slightly later for the emergence of pantomime as a dramatic form in Rome is possible.[179] Further refinements and an 'official' recognition may have taken place subsequently, perhaps in around 22 BCE.[180]

Such a dating would bring pantomime close to dramatic performances developing into pageants of the sort condemned by Cicero and Horace (Cic. *Fam.* 7.1.2; Hor. *Epist.* 2.1.187–207) and to the flourishing of mime with its emphasis on individuals, 'realistic' display and derivative relationship to tragedy and comedy. Hence this scenario for pantomime gaining prominence would agree well with the development of stage performances in Rome around the middle of the first century BCE inferred from other sources.

Pantomime then developed into a dominant dramatic form in the imperial period, as it was supported by the emperor Augustus and his successors: they provided training establishments for pantomime performers and organized performances of official troupes in Rome and the provinces; they also favoured and protected particular pantomime actors, a number of whom are known by name. Like mime, which became established slightly earlier, pantomime is a dramatic genre promoted by politicians who used these dramatic forms to entertain the populace and ensure their own standing.

The Roman pantomime is a type of dance by an actor (*pantomimus* or *histrio*), accompanied by music. Dancing, singing and instrumental music were distributed over several performers (cf. Hieron. *Ab Abr.* 1995, 22 BCE [p. 165c Helm]); the dancer concentrated on representing character and emotions. In its eventual form pantomime differed from the Greek precedent and earlier Roman versions, for instance, by an increased musical component and by the replacement of a single accompanist with a choir. As the serious variety seems to have been the more common one, pantomimes included the representation of famous mythical characters and their fates, based on tragedies.[181]

---

[179] See Jory 1981 (slightly differently in Jory 1996).
[180] Jory (1996: 2; see also 1981: 148) suggests 'that the first important occasion that featured the new type of presentation was at the games of Marcellus in 23 B.C., rather than 22 B.C., the date indicated by Jerome'.
[181] Cf. Macrob. *Sat.* 2.7.13–17; Suet. *Calig.* 57.4; Arn. *Adv. nat.* 7.33.3.

The modern view on pantomime can be summarized as follows:

Pantomimes (in literary sources the noun always refers to the performer rather than the genre) were silent solo dancers who interpreted with movement and gesture a libretto sung by a choir to the accompaniment of a variety of musical instruments including flutes, pipes, cymbals, lyres, castanets and even organs. Each production, as in tragedy, was based on a story from mythology or history and, unlike a dramatic performance where the characters appear on stage together and interact, the characters in the pantomime were portrayed successively, as the actor interpreted the rôles in a sequence of interlinked but consecutive solo dances.[182]

Since music, dance and equipment were paramount in pantomime, hardly any knowledge of the language was necessary to understand the story or to enjoy the performance (cf. Lucian, *Salt.* 64). Therefore scholars have seen this type of dramatic entertainment as one of the reasons for the wide spread of theatre throughout all regions of the Roman Empire. Equally, this dramatic genre marks the predominance of entertainment and spectacle over plot and content in the continuing tension between the two main elements of Roman dramatic performances. Still, pantomime is not dance and music only, but based on a story taken, for instance, from myth or history.[183] Hence it is justified to classify pantomime as a 'dramatic genre' rather than as a form of dance.

---

[182] See Jory 1986a: 147.

[183] That the plots of pantomimes were adaptations (rather than replacements) of stories also found in tragedies has been seen as a reason for the disappearance of pantomime libretti (see Jory 2008).

CHAPTER 4

Dramatic poets

Assessments of dramatic poets in later ancient writers, highlighting particular qualities, show that specific characteristics of their output could already be observed in antiquity and that each playwright might be seen as having a distinctive poetic profile.[1] For instance, Cicero says in one of his treatises that the tragic poets Ennius, Pacuvius and Accius differ from each other, each excelling in his different way of writing (Cic. *De or.* 3.27; cf. also Cic. *Orat.* 36). In another context Cicero judges a detail in Accius 'better' than in Ennius (Cic. *Tusc.* 1.105), calls Ennius 'a wonderful poet' (Cic. *Tusc.* 3.45: *o poetam egregium!*) and describes Pacuvius as 'the supreme tragic poet' (Cic. *Opt. gen.* 2: *summum . . . poetam . . . Pacuvium tragicum*). Notwithstanding an element of subjectivity, such comments indicate that both Cicero and his audiences assumed differences between representatives of one dramatic genre. A similar situation holds true for the comic side: according to the prologue to Plautus' *Casina*, audiences in the second century BCE preferred 'old' comedies, Plautine ones in particular, because they did not like the 'modern' ones (Plaut. *Cas.* 5–20); Volcacius Sedigitus drew up an evaluative list of palliata poets (cf. Gell. *NA* 15.24); and Plautus' characteristic style became a criterion for decisions on the genuineness of the numerous plays ascribed to him (cf. Cic. *Fam.* 9.16.4; Gell. *NA* 3.3).

Although the works of many Republican playwrights survive only in fragments, attempts at identifying characteristic tendencies in style, motifs, topics and dramaturgy for individual playwrights as well as their roles in the development of their dramatic genres can therefore be justified if the appropriate caution is applied.[2] One has to accept, for instance, that the nature of the evidence does not enable an entirely uniform treatment of all playwrights, but rather directs the attention to different questions.

---

[1] Lana (1947: 44–80 passim), for instance, rightly warns against measuring Terence against Plautus and advises judging Terence as a poet in his own right instead.

[2] For calls for caution see e.g. Beare 1964: 35; Gruen 1990: 95.

For those poets whose work survives in fragments the varying size of the sample and the transmission have to be taken into account, i.e. whether fragments are quoted for their content by literary people or as illustrations of linguistic features by grammarians. An indication of the possible content of a play is often given only by the title, which turns these into important pieces of evidence in such cases, although identical titles do not necessarily imply that the same story is told or that a story is presented in the same way.

Against this background this chapter discusses the major Republican playwrights (their biographies, output and general characteristics), starting with the pioneers who were active in various dramatic genres and continuing with poets specializing in particular dramatic genres in chronological order, the dramatic genres being arranged in the same sequence as in the previous chapter and thus also roughly chronologically. The chapter concludes with brief notes on further Republican dramatists about whom little evidence survives.[3]

4.1 L. LIVIUS ANDRONICUS

Since antiquity Lucius Livius Andronicus (*c.* 280/270–200 BCE) has generally been regarded as Rome's first poet and a pioneer of Latin literature, as he introduced the literary genres of epic, comedy and tragedy (as transpositions of Greek models) in Rome.[4] The chronology transmitted in Cicero was widespread in antiquity and has been accepted almost unanimously in modern scholarship: in 240 BCE Livius Andronicus was commissioned to arrange for the first production of literary drama with a plot in Rome.[5] However, there was also an alternative chronology put forward by Accius (transmitted in Cicero's *Brutus*): according to this model Livius Andronicus was captured in Tarentum in 209 BCE and, after having been brought to Rome as a slave, taught the children of his master M. Livius Salinator and was later freed by him (cf. Cic. *Brut.* 72–3; Hieron. *Ab Abr.* 1829/30,

---

[3] For *testimonia* on the biographies of the Republican dramatic poets see conveniently Rostagni 1956: 15–57 and the relevant entries in Suerbaum 2002.

[4] On Livius Andronicus see e.g. Ribbeck 1875: 19–43 (on tragedies); Duckworth 1952: 39–40 (on comedies); Beare 1964: 25–32; Suerbaum 1968: 1–12, 297–300; Waszink 1972: 873–902; J. Wright 1974: 15–32 (on comedies); Drury 1982: 799–802; Blänsdorf 1978: 125–7; Traglia 1986: 9–21; Gruen 1990: 80–92; Petrone 1992: 517–22; Conte 1994: 39–42; Dumont 1997: 41–3; Suerbaum 2002: 93–104; Erasmo 2004: 9–14 (on tragedies); Boyle 2006: 27–36 (on tragedies); bibliography in De Rosalia 1989: 77–87 (on tragedies); Suerbaum 2002: 93–104; Manuwald 2001 [2004]: 88–101 (on tragedies).

[5] Cf. Cic. *Brut.* 72; *Tusc.* 1.3; *Sen.* 50; Liv. 7.2.8; Val. Max. 2.4.4; Gell. *NA* 17.21.42; Cass. *Chron.*, p. 128 *MGH* AA 11.2 (on 239 BCE); Diom. *Ars* 3, *Gramm. Lat.* 1, p. 489.7–8; *Lib. gloss.* 1.7; 2.11.

187 BCE [p. 137c Helm]); he was commissioned to compose a play for *Ludi Iuventatis* in 197 BCE, which had been vowed by his patron (cf. Cic. *Brut.* 72–3; in 191 BCE according to Liv. 36.36.5–7). As Cicero comments, this dating would remove Livius Andronicus from his position as Rome's first poet and place him later than poets thought to have written after him (Cic. *Brut.* 72–3).

For the chronology that Cicero follows, he refers to the authority of Accius and ancient commentaries; apparently there were various pieces of evidence supporting the position of Livius Andronicus as the first Roman poet, a view that is also reflected in Horace among others (Hor. *Epist.* 2.1.62). Besides, Accius' arguments for the relative chronology of Homer and Hesiod are peculiar and were regarded as 'flimsy' by later writers (Gell. *NA* 3.11.4–5: Acc. *Did.* 1 W. = *Gram.* 1 D.); hence his dating of Livius Andronicus may have rested on similarly questionable grounds. Rightly, therefore, Accius' scenario is usually rejected in modern scholarship, although details, such as Livius Andronicus' Tarentine origin[6] or his status as a slave, are often accepted.[7]

What can be established is that Livius Andronicus came to Rome from southern Italy, as a free foreigner or a slave (who was freed later), and acquired Roman citizenship in due course (cf. his *tria nomina*; Hieron. *Ab Abr.* 1829/30, 187 BCE [p. 137c Helm]). His name points to a connection with the *gens Livia* and a Greek origin (cf. Suet. *Gram.* 1.2: *semigraecus*). Therefore Livius Andronicus must have had experience of Greek and of Italic indigenous theatrical traditions by the time he started his dramatic career in Rome. His poetic activity in Rome is attested for 240 and again for 207 BCE (cf. Liv. 27.37.7–14),[8] which gives an indication of his dates. Besides, ancient tradition has it that he worked as a teacher of Greek and Latin (cf. Suet. *Gram.* 1.2) and appeared as an actor in his own plays.[9]

---

[6] This sounds like a nice construct since the 'love of the Tarentines for the theatre was proverbial' (Beare 1964: 26). Therefore coming from the Greek theatre city of Tarentum would be fitting for Rome's first dramatist. The connection between Tarentum and the theatre might also be the reason why Jerome gives Ennius' birthplace as Tarentum (Hieron. *Ab Abr.* 1777, 240 BCE [p. 133a Helm]), contrary to all other evidence.

[7] On the ancient sources and the modern discussion on Livius Andronicus' dates see e.g. Suerbaum 1968: 297–9, 2002: 94–6; Oakley 1998: 61–3 (with references); on the difficulties of the *Brutus* passage and Cicero's argument cf. Douglas 1966: 63–4.

[8] It has been suggested that Livius Andronicus also wrote a cult song for *Ludi Tarentini* in 249 BCE, but this is uncertain and rather unlikely (see Suerbaum 2002: 96 [with bibliography]; on the games in 249 BCE see Bernstein 1998: 129–42).

[9] Cf. Liv. 7.2.8–9; Fest., p. 448.3–4 L.; Euanth. *Fab.* 4.3; *Lib. gloss.* 1.7; 2.11. On Livius Andronicus as actor see Garton 1972: 255, no. 102; Leppin 1992: 200–1.

Ancient sources describe Livius Andronicus as the first poet to have composed 'plays/stories' (*fabulae*) with 'plots/story lines' (*argumenta*),[10] while they do not say that these dramas differed from preceding performances in Rome by following Greek models. Yet the remains of Livius Andronicus' works and the overall impact of the Greek model on the developing Roman drama (cf. e.g. Hor. *Epist.* 2.1.156–67) make this connection obvious. Owing to differing information in the sources it is uncertain whether a single play or plays of different dramatic genres were performed in 240 BCE. In any case late-antique grammarians and commentators describe Livius Andronicus as the first writer of both tragedies and comedies in Rome.[11]

Livius Andronicus produced a number of tragedies and comedies of Greek type as well as an epic entitled *Odusia* (a Latin version of Homer's *Odyssey*) and a ritual song for Iuno Regina (in 207 BCE). The extant remains of his poetry are meagre: titles of eight to ten tragedies (and about forty, partly incomplete, verses) and of two comedies (and a few fragments), about forty verses from *Odusia* and *testimonia* on the ritual song. There is no evidence as to which play(s) were performed in 240 BCE or on the absolute or relative chronology of the attested works. Yet it is likely that *Odusia* preceded the dramas and that it was this literary achievement that recommended Livius Andronicus as a suitable candidate for introducing literary drama in Latin to Rome.[12]

Of Livius Andronicus' tragedies eight titles are securely attested: *Achilles*, *Aegisthus*, *Aiax mastigophorus*, *Andromeda*, *Danae*, *Equos Troianus*, *Hermiona*, *Tereus*; besides these there is a *testimonium* suggesting a *Teucer* (cf. Varro, *Ling.* 7.3) as well as mentions of the presumably spurious plays *Ino*[13] and *Antiopa*.[14]

The subjects of each of the securely attested tragedies were taken up by at least one subsequent Roman tragic playwright, under the same or different

---

[10] Cf. Liv. 7.2.8; Val. Max. 2.4.4; cf. also Cic. *Brut.* 71–3; Hor. *Epist.* 2.1.62; Quint. *Inst.* 10.2.7; see ch. 1.5.

[11] Cf. Donat. *Com.* 5.4; Diom. *Ars* 3, *Gramm. Lat.* 1, p. 489.7–8; *Lib. gloss.* 1.7; 2.11; Schol. on Hor. *Epist.* 2.1.62. On Donatus' attribution of the introduction of togata to Livius Andronicus see ch. 3.4; on Marconi's (1967) conjecture of a praetexta for Livius Andronicus see ch. 3.2, n. 41.

[12] See e.g. Waszink 1972: 874; Szemerényi 1975: 300; Blänsdorf 2000: 147–8; Suerbaum 2002: 84; contrast Vogt-Spira 1996: 11.

[13] The only transmitted fragment (Ter. Maur., *Gramm. Lat.* 6, p. 383.1931–8; Mar. Victor., *Gramm. Lat.* 6, p. 67.31) experiments with hexameters, which is unlikely for an early poet. Hence it is often attributed to the pre-neoteric poet Laevius (Laevius, fr. dub. 32 *FPL*³).

[14] Nonius Marcellus (p. 170.12–14 M. = 250 L.) transmits two verses of an *Antiopa* by Livius Andronicus. The text is usually emended to *Pacuvius*, and the verses are attributed to his play of the same title (Pac. *Trag.* 5–6 R.³ = 5–6 W.), where they make sense (see e.g. Ribbeck 1871: 77 app. crit., 1897: 87 app. crit.; Klotz 1953: 113–14; D'Anna 1967: 46, 48 app. crit., 185; Schierl 2006: 107–8; but see Mette 1964 [1965]: 49).

titles.[15] Although it is not certain in all cases whether these dramatists followed the same versions of the myths, the return to the material testifies to the popularity of the stories chosen by Livius Andronicus. In terms of dramatic history, another treatment of those myths may indicate that later dramatists were unaware of Livius Andronicus' plays (cf. Ter. *Eun.* 33–4; see ch. 2.10), that his versions were regarded as ready to be replaced or that later tragic poets wished to compete with him. As for comedy, an author of the *Historia Augusta* records that a phrase in Terence's *Eunuchus* (Ter. *Eun.* 426) was among those that were coined by Livius Andronicus (*Pall.* 8 R.³ = 6 W.) and taken up by playwrights such as Plautus and Caecilius (SHA 30, *Car.* 13.5).

The titles of Livius Andronicus' tragedies give a rough idea of the myths treated. Six tragedies deal with subject matter connected with the Trojan War, particularly with its end and aftermath (*Achilles, Aegisthus, Aiax mastigophorus, Equos Troianus, Hermiona, Teucer*). The Trojan War came to be regarded as a central event in Roman history by the Romans. Moreover, there might be a common denominator that made these stories relevant to Romans in the period of the Punic Wars: several plays seem to address the questions of how one should confront the conclusion of a war and its consequences and of how victors are to behave; values such as justice, fairness, piety or reward for achievements feature in the surviving fragments.

The emphasis on fairness is noteworthy in a fragment from *Aegisthus* on the division of spoils (*Trag.* 2–4 R.³ = 2–4 W.), which has been compared with a passage in Seneca's *Agamemnon* (Sen. *Ag.* 421–2). In contrast to Seneca, Livius Andronicus' version stresses that the booty was divided fairly among all participants (*per participes aequiter*). In line with such an attitude the same play includes concern for the feelings of victims (*Trag.* 8 R.³ = 7 W.). These positive values contrast with ingratitude as felt by Ajax: in the play named after him, he recognizes that virtue is initially rewarded, but that remembrance of such deeds fades away quickly (*Trag.* 15; 16–17 R.³ = 15; 16–17 W.). Similarly, obedience and acknowledgement of power are called for by a figure in *Aegisthus* (*Trag.* 13–14 R.³ = 12–13 W.). The choice of the title '*Aegisthus*' (contrast e.g. Seneca's *Agamemnon*) may indicate that this character was viewed as central, and the fragments point to a contrast between a just and an autocratic ruler as one of the play's themes.

This evidence leads to the question of the overall relationship of Livius Andronicus' plays to possible Greek models. Plays of the same title by one

---

[15] Cf. *Achilles*: Ennius, Accius; *Aegisthus*: Accius, Seneca (*Agamemnon*); *Aiax*: Ennius; *Andromeda*: Ennius, Accius; *Danae*: Naevius; *Equos Troianus*: Naevius; *Hermiona*: Pacuvius; *Tereus*: Accius.

of the three major Greek tragic poets can be identified for the majority
of his tragedies (Aeschylus: *Ino* [?]; Sophocles: *Aiax, Hermiona, Tereus,
Akrisios* [*Danae*]; Euripides: *Andromeda, Danae*). The remaining dramas
(*Achilles, Aegisthus, Equos Troianus*) may go back to further classical or post-
classical tragedies; *Aegisthus*, for instance, covers the same subject matter
as Aeschylus' *Agamemnon*. At the same time, it remains a possibility for
Achilles and *Equos Troianus*, which dramatize incidents from the Trojan
War, that Livius Andronicus turned Greek epic material into drama; that
he was familiar with the Homeric epics is obvious from his *Odusia*.[16] If he
developed a tragedy out of an epic narrative, Livius Andronicus would have
done more than transposing Greek dramas for Roman audiences; he would
have introduced the composition of original dramas about Greek subjects
as well, following a variety of sources and the dramatic model of Greek
plays.

Because of the fragmentary state of Livius Andronicus' tragedies and
also of some of the potential Greek models, few detailed comparisons are
possible. One of the two fragments attributed to *Aiax mastigophorus* can
be compared to Teucer's words in Sophocles' *Ajax*.[17] While the notion is
similar, the Greek text focuses on gratitude, which quickly disappears after
death, and the Latin text concentrates on praise for virtue and the fact that
it quickly fades away, without any reference to death. The terminology
roots Livius Andronicus' phrase in a Roman context (cf. *laus, virtus*), and
the implied view that virtue deserves praise agrees with a standard Roman
perspective. Such changes contribute to making the Greek stories and topics
more accessible for Roman audiences. At the same time Livius Andronicus
seems to have ensured that his plays were dramatically effective and thus
had an entertainment value. It is likely, for instance, that his *Tereus* did not
follow the well-known form of the myth, but rather a version transmitted
in Hyginus (Hyg. *Fab.* 45), which increases the number of characters and
the complexity of the relationships between them.

Livius Andronicus' few comic fragments defy any detailed analysis. Still,
their style and content indicate that a distinction between dramatic genres

---

[16] See Fantham 2005: 118 (with reference to *Equos Troianus*).

[17] Cf. *Trag.* 16–17 R.³ = 16–17 W.: *praestatur laus virtuti, sed multo ocius / verno gelu tabescit* ('To virtue
praise is offered, but quicker far it melts than ice of spring.' [trans. Warmington]); Soph. *Aj.* 1266–7:
φεῦ, τοῦ θανόντος ὡς ταχεῖά τις βροτοῖς / χάρις διαρρεῖ καὶ προδοῦσ' ἁλίσκεται ('Alas, how
quickly slips away men's gratitude to the dead and it proves treacherous,...' [trans. A. F. Garvie]).
See e.g. Ribbeck 1875: 26; Warmington 1936: 8; Waszink 1972: 893; but see Jocelyn 1967: 179–80.
The other fragment (*Trag.* 15 R.³ = 15 W.) has been connected with other verses in Sophocles' *Ajax*
(Soph. *Aj.* 646–7). The idea that the passage of time obscures things is similar, but nuances are
again different.

and their specific characteristics was in place: for instance, a question about fleas, bugs and lice (*Pall.* 1 R.³ = 1 W.) is likely to come from a situation different from a typical set-up for tragedy.

In all his literary genres Livius Andronicus made the first steps towards developing a poetic language in Latin. His tragedies contain alliterations, poetic comparisons, metonymy, poetic descriptions and choral songs. For his dramas (both tragedy and comedy) he employed the iambic senarius, the trochaic septenarius and cretics; he thereby established the basic metres of Roman tragedy and comedy.[18]

Livius Andronicus proved to be the right man at the right point in time: the occasion for him to develop his poetic faculties in the area of drama seems to have arisen from the circumstances and official commissions. In this situation he was apparently not satisfied with the easiest solution of a simple translation of a Greek model. Here his poetic talent comes into play: a basic level of 'Romanization', such as replacing Greek names of gods with the corresponding Roman ones, will have been necessary when adapting literary works for Roman audiences, but he went beyond these requirements, as would his successors.

At least for his tragedies, about which conclusions can be drawn, Livius Andronicus seems to have chosen topics important in Roman society or to have adapted the Greek material so that the works were relevant to Roman audiences, and also to have created a structure that guaranteed entertainment by means of vivid stage-action. Thus he introduced the two characteristic poles of Republican drama, which marked its history throughout. That he was able to produce original poetry is indicated by the composition of a ritual song for an entirely Roman context in 207 BCE.

Livius Andronicus' achievements as a poet were apparently appreciated by his contemporaries, as writers and actors were assigned the Temple of Minerva on the Aventine as an official meeting place after 207 BCE (see ch. 2.7). Later authors, such as Cicero, Horace or Livy, however, talked about his works less respectfully and regarded them as rude, uncouth and archaic (Cic. *Brut.* 71; Hor. *Epist.* 2.1.69–75; Liv. 27.37.13). These assessments reflect the literary taste of the late Republic and the early Principate; yet they do not recognize the specific accomplishment of a founder, even if Cicero acknowledges this position and admits that nothing could be invented and perfect at the same time.

---

[18] See e.g. Waszink 1972: 896; Blänsdorf 1978: 126.

4.2 CN. NAEVIUS

Gnaeus Naevius (*c.* 280/260–200 BCE) was Rome's second dramatist.[19] He started producing dramas slightly later than Livius Andronicus, but was also the latter's first and main rival, since they overlapped for most of their dramatic activity in Rome.[20] Information about Naevius' biography is scarce; but according to what he allegedly said himself, he participated in the First Punic War, described in his *Bellum Poenicum* (cf. Gell. *NA* 17.21.45), which provides an indication of his age, and he probably came from Campania, perhaps from Capua (cf. Gell. *NA* 1.24.2). This region belonged to the Osco-Samnite area in terms of language and cultural framework; like many places in southern Italy, it was host to a vibrant cultural mix.[21] Hence Naevius will have been familiar with local and imported theatrical traditions when he started his career in Rome. In antiquity there was already disagreement over the date of Naevius' death, but the sources agree that he was dead by the end of the century (cf. Cic. *Brut.* 60; Hieron. *Ab Abr.* 1816, 201 BCE [p. 135g Helm]).[22]

From about 235 BCE (cf. Gell. *NA* 17.21.44–5)[23] Naevius was active as a poet in Rome: he not only produced comedies and tragedies by transposing Greek models, but also inaugurated the dramatic genre of praetexta and composed a 'Roman' epic on the First Punic War (*Bellum Poenicum*). This epic might have been a work of his old age (cf. Cic. *Sen.* 49–50), and the praetexta on the victory near Clastidium in 222 BCE must have been written after this event; apart from these indications there is no evidence on the dates of his writings. Naevius' works have been transmitted only in

---

[19] On Naevius see e.g. Ribbeck 1875: 44–76 (on tragedies and praetextae); Duckworth 1952: 40–2 (on comedies); Beare 1964: 33–41; Suerbaum 1968: 13–42; J. Wright 1974: 33–59 (on comedies); Blänsdorf 1978: 127–33; Drury 1982: 802–4; Traglia 1986: 22–46; Gruen 1990: 92–106; Petrone 1992: 523–33; Conte 1994: 43–8; Suerbaum 2000a (on comedies), 2002: 104–19; Manuwald 2001a: 134–61 (on praetextae); Erasmo 2004: 14–18 (on tragedies); Boyle 2006: 36–55 (on tragedies and praetextae); bibliography in De Rosalia 1989: 87–95 (on tragedies); Suerbaum 2000a (on comedies), 2002; Manuwald 2001 [2004]: 101–11 (on tragedies and praetextae).

[20] Cf. Suerbaum 2000a: 304.   [21] See Gruen 1990: 92; Suerbaum 2000a: 302–3.

[22] Cf. Suerbaum 2000a: 304. Different ancient traditions give 204 or 201 BCE as the date for Naevius' death (Cic. *Brut.* 60; Hieron. *Ab Abr.* 1816, 201 BCE [p. 135g Helm]). Perhaps the last attested performance of a play by Naevius occurred in 204 BCE, and Naevius died a few years later (cf. Suerbaum 2002: 106).

[23] Gellius dates both the first divorce at Rome and the beginning of Naevius' dramatic activity to the 519th year after the foundation of Rome (i.e. 235 BCE). But D'Anna (1955), analysing the evidence for the former event, has concluded that its most likely date is 231 BCE; this might imply the same date for the first production of Naevius' dramas (instead of the usually assumed 235 BCE). Yet the extent and nature of the possible confusion in this passage are uncertain. Hence it is probably best not to identify a precise year for the start of Naevius' dramatic career; nevertheless, a date in the 230s BCE can safely be assumed.

fragments: there are titles of about thirty-five comedies and about a hundred and forty (partly incomplete) comic verses, titles of six tragedies and about sixty (partly incomplete) tragic verses, titles of two praetextae with a few lines each[24] and about sixty fragments of the epic *Bellum Poenicum* (for Naevius' works cf. also Varro, *Ling.* 7.107–8).

In antiquity Naevius was mainly regarded as a writer of comedies (cf. Gell. *NA* 15.24; Hieron. *Ab Abr.* 1816, 201 BCE [p. 135g Helm]); this accords with the fact that more titles of comedies than of tragedies have been preserved. There are numerous parallels in diction and motifs between the works of Naevius and those of Plautus, and a few titles are assigned to both poets (*Carbonaria, Colax, Nervolaria* [if the relevant text is thus emended correctly]).[25] Terence referred to Naevius as a paradigmatic predecessor when it suited his argument (Ter. *An.* 18–21).

Both Cicero and, in Cicero's view, Ennius acknowledged Naevius' poetic achievements, although Cicero realized that Naevius' writings were not as refined as those of his successors (Cic. *Brut.* 75–6). Naevius' plays may still have been performed in Cicero's time (Cic. *Fam.* 7.1.2); according to Horace, Naevius continued to be read in this period (Hor. *Epist.* 2.1.53–4). While writers later seem to have lost interest in Naevius, his epitaph (transmitted in Gellius) presents Naevius as a 'poet' (*poeta*) who has close associations with the Muses and has advanced the Latin language towards a more sophisticated level (Gell. *NA* 1.24.2: Naev. *Var.* 3–6 W.).[26] Although it is uncertain whether this text was indeed written by the poet as claimed in Gellius, it may represent a contemporary assessment; Gellius admits that it would be a correct description if Naevius had not written it himself. In view of the fragmentary transmission of Naevius' poems it is difficult to judge the accuracy of such an assessment, but in both tragedy and comedy Naevius seems to have used a sophisticated Latin, including stylistic and compositional features such as alliteration, chiasmus, antithesis, asyndetic enumeration, comparison, metonymy, pun, concise saying, poetic description and narrative. And he showed a greater level of originality and independence than his predecessor Livius Andronicus by applying structures found in Greek epic and drama to Roman subject matter.[27]

---

[24] On the number and titles of Naevius' praetextae cf. Manuwald 2001a: 134–61, esp. 143–6 (with bibliography).

[25] Cf. e.g. Naev. *Pall.* 53 R.³ = 58 W.: Plaut. *Stich.* 118–19 – Naev. *Pall.* 82 R.³ = 84–5 W.: Plaut. *Mostell.* 323–4 – Naev. *Pall.* 95 R.³ = 105 W.: Plaut. *Mostell.* 233–4 (see Duckworth 1952: 41). On the problem of identical titles for several palliata poets see ch. 3.3, 5.1.

[26] On this passage see Suerbaum 1968: 31–41.   [27] See Beare 1964: 33; Suerbaum 2002: 116.

By producing comedies and tragedies in Greek style, introducing the dramatic genre of praetexta and composing an epic on the First Punic War, Naevius continued the tradition inaugurated by Livius Andronicus: producing works in a variety of literary genres, transposing Greek comedies and tragedies into Latin and adapting them to a Roman context. At the same time Naevius created new literary genres and developed existing ones further: after Livius Andronicus had introduced Greek literary forms such as drama and epic to Rome (and written 'Roman' poetry only in the different literary form of ritual song), Naevius increased the Roman content of the adopted literary genres: his epic dealt with an incident from Roman history; equally, the new dramatic genre of praetexta dramatized sections from Roman history (on the formal model of Greek drama).[28]

Naevius shares two titles of tragedies with Livius Andronicus (*Danae, Equos Troianus*). Since the two dramatists overlapped during almost all of their careers and none of their tragedies can be securely dated, the relative chronology is uncertain. If Naevius was the second one to treat these topics, as seems to be usually assumed because of Livius Andronicus being regarded as Rome's first poet, he would have been able to draw upon the version of his predecessor as well as on Greek sources.[29] At any rate, from the second Roman dramatist onwards a Roman dramatic tradition was added to the Greek one, and later poets were confronted with both.

Compared with Livius Andronicus, Naevius introduced new topics to the Roman tragic repertoire (partly taken from the Trojan cycle) and dealt with Rome's origins: he wrote a praetexta about Romulus and included the story of Aeneas in his epic *Bellum Poenicum*. Several of his tragedies bear titles that can also be found in earlier Greek drama (cf. Aeschylus: *Lykurgia*, including *Lykurgos*; Euripides: *Iphigenia in Aulis, Iphigenia in Tauris*; Astydamas II: *Hektor* [60 F 1h–2a *TrGF*]). For *Hesiona*, however, no Greek dramatic predecessor can be identified. As in the case of Livius Andronicus, it is possible that Naevius worked directly from Greek epic, or he might have relied on mythological narratives. Obviously, Naevius also approached topics that seem not to have been treated by the three major Greek dramatists, and no particular preference for one of them is discernible.

---

[28] See Suerbaum 2000a: 316. Traglia (1986: 46) believes that Naevius started a process of Hellenization of Latin culture; this may be true with regard to some of the topics found in his tragedies and the stylistic refinement, but it is not valid without qualification for his epic and praetextae, which present thoroughly Roman subject matter.

[29] See e.g. Beacham 1991: 24.

Little can be said about the probable models of Naevius' comedies beyond a general influence from Greek New Comedy. According to the prologue to Terence's *Eunuchus* (Ter. *Eun.* 23–34), Naevius' *Colax* was based on Menander's play of the same title. And the prologue to Terence's *Andria* claims that Naevius was one of the Roman poets who used *contaminatio*, i.e. combined elements from several Greek models into one Latin play (Ter. *An.* 15–21). Terence's reference to the 'carelessness' (*neglegentia*) of Naevius, Plautus and Ennius, in its context, also suggests a rather free treatment of Greek sources.

Because of the fragmentary transmission, few inferences can be made concerning Naevius' dramatic technique and his choice of characters and themes. The fragments of *Danae* and *Lycurgus* allow the conclusion that the tragic action could include encounters between gods and men, laments, heated dialogues, choruses as well as stunning scenes. Myths indicated by titles such as *Hesiona* or *Equos Troianus* offer the possibility of busy and impressive stage-action.

Naevius' comedies seem to have included typical elements of New Comedy, such as parasites (*Colax* [cf. Ter. *Eun.* 23–34]; *Pall.* 60 R.^{3} = 57 W.), braggart soldiers (*Colax* [cf. Ter. *Eun.* 23–34]), rivals (*Pall.* 41–2 R.^{3} = 42–3 W.), prostitutes (*Pall.* 75–9 R.^{3} = 74–9 W.), opposition between fathers and children on account of love affairs and money (*Pall.* 95; 96–8 R.^{3} = 105; 94–6 W.), twins (*Pall.* 2–3 R.^{3} = 2–3 W.), love affairs (*Pall.* 55; 90–1; 96–8 R.^{3} = 60; 88–9; 94–6 W.), banquets (*Pall.* 81 R.^{3} = 72 W.), an important role for slaves (names of slaves as titles) and the use of standard names for characters (*Lampadio, Stalagmus*: cf. Plaut. *Capt.* 875).[30] There are double plots, i.e. two fathers and two sons with similar problems (*Pall.* 83–4; 86 R.^{3} = 80–1; 82 W.), confusions between characters (*Pall.* 2–3 R.^{3} = 2–3 W.) and a presumable multiplication of the twin theme with quadruplets (*Quadrigemini*); all this indicates exciting and complex dramatic action.

That there are also metatheatrical statements, which seem to come partly from prologues (*Pall.* 1; 17; 72–4 R.^{3} = 1; 15; 69–71 W.), points to prologues detached from the action; thereby Naevius created an opportunity to talk about dramatic technique and issues not immediately related to the plot of the plays. This recalls the procedure in his epic *Bellum Poenicum*, where he allegedly mentioned that he had participated in the war described (cf. Gell. *NA* 17.21.45). In his dramas metatheatrical phrases such as 'on the stage' (*in scena*: *Pall.* 17 R.^{3} = 15 W.) or 'in the theatre' (*in theatro*: *Pall.* 72

---

[30] See Suerbaum 2000a: 318.

R.³ = 69 W.) refer to the performance context, presumably disrupting the dramatic illusion.

The clearest evidence for metaliterary prologues is a fragment that consists in an advertisement of the play (*Pall.* 1 R.³ = 1 W.); at least in this instance it was announced by its untranslated Greek title (*Acontizomenos*).³¹ Generally, despite numerous allusions to Roman institutions in the body of the plays, the majority of Naevius' comic titles are Greek.³² Most of Naevius' Latin titles, such as *Dementes* or *Dolus*, could be translations of corresponding Greek words, the only question being why these titles have been translated while others such as *Agrypnuntes* or *Colax* have not.

Reasons for the choice of either alternative for the creation of titles are not immediately obvious, although there are examples indicating that the distribution of Greek and Latin might carry some meaning: the most remarkable instances are the plays *Clamidaria* and *Tunicularia*, since the first title is derived from the name for a Greek garment (*chlamys*) and the second one from that for a Roman one (*tunicula*). Therefore the second title is unlikely to be a simple adaptation of a corresponding Greek title, but rather an analogous formation with a presumably different sense. Both terms occur elsewhere in Roman comedy, and the mixture of terms for Greek and Roman garments is not unusual.³³ Still, a thoroughly Roman expression used as a title for a comedy supposedly set in Greece is remarkable, particularly since further Roman allusions occur in the preserved fragments of this comedy. To explain this peculiar title, one will have either to revive the theory that Naevius invented the dramatic genre of togata (see ch. 3.4) or to assume that he followed a method of meaningful adaptation to a Roman context and that the choice of Greek or Latin is therefore significant. This could mean, for instance, that in *Clamidaria* a *chlamys* played a central role in the adapted plot and this term was therefore retained, whereas in *Tunicularia* it is only in Naevius' version that a *tunicula* becomes important.

Although Naevius inserted allusions to Roman reality such as Roman religious or political institutions, particularly into comedies,³⁴ he retained Greek settings for his dramas except for praetextae. As the same

---

³¹ The preserved fragment sounds like an advertisement for Naevius' own play rather than praise of the homonymous Greek model (so Dér 1989: 283). Charisius' quotation confirms this to be Naevius' title, unless the title is inferred from the line quoted (*Gramm. Lat.* 1, p. 211.7–8).

³² Similarly, Naevius used Greek terms in his plays, which Varro felt compelled to explain (Varro, *Ling.* 7.108, on Naev. *Pall.* 103–4 R.³ = 101 W.).

³³ Cf. Caec. *Pall.* 99; 269 R.³ = 90; 250 W.; Plaut. *Curc.* 611; *Mil.* 1423; *Rud.* 549–50; Turp. *Pall.* 197 R.³.

³⁴ Cf. e.g. *Praenestini et Lanuini hospites* (*Pall.* 21–4 R.³ = 22–6 W.); *Compitalia* and *Lares* (*Pall.* 99–102 R.³ = 97–100 W.); *dictator* (*Pall.* 107 R.³ = *Inc.* 28–9 W.).

phenomenon can be observed in Plautus' palliatae, such insertions were apparently not regarded as incongruous. However, despite allusions to Roman reality, a Greek point of view as required by the main plot seems to have been retained: a character mentions 'Greeks and barbarians' (*Grai atque barbari*: *Trag.* 61 R.[3] = *Inc.* 33 W.). This technique led to a conflation of Greek and Roman perspectives to form a fictional world that was neither entirely Greek nor Roman and therefore open to being shaped by poets.

A remarkable characteristic of Naevius' poetry has been seen by scholars in the fact that he went beyond inserting single references to Roman elements and also aimed for topical political effects: he is thought to have commented on contemporary issues and politicians, even if implicitly without mentioning people's names (*nominatim laedere*).[35] This outspokenness has been connected with alleged criticism of Scipio Africanus (cf. Gell. *NA* 7.8.5–6, on Naev. *Pall.* 108–10 R.[3] = *Inc.* 1–3 W.) and with doubtful evidence both on a feud with the family of the Metelli expressed by alternate verses[36] and on the poet's imprisonment because of disparagement of Roman politicians.[37] However, it is uncertain whether these pieces of information refer to historical events or rather reflect anecdotes or exaggerations developed on the basis of hints in the plays. Conversely, the same is true for Naevius' alleged protection by the family of the Claudii Marcelli: the composition of a praetexta entitled *Clastidium*, dramatizing the victory of M. Claudius Marcellus near Clastidium in 222 BCE, is not a sufficient indication of a long-term bond (see ch. 2.7).

The notion of a politically outspoken (and hence partisan) Naevius, who enjoyed protection from some families, but opposed others and got into conflict with the authorities, has therefore been challenged more recently.[38]

---

[35] See e.g. Marmorale 1950: 39–53; Suerbaum 2000a: 319–20; Boyle 2006: 53–5; but see Conte 1994: 47.

[36] Cf. Ps.-Asc. on Cic. *Verr.* 1.29 (p. 215 St. = p. 72 *FPL*[3]). These verses are quoted as examples for a particular metrical form in a number of later grammarians (Caesius Bassus, *Gramm. Lat.* 6, p. 266.4–9; Atil. Fortunat., *Gramm. Lat.* 6, p. 294.2–4; Ter. Maur., *Gramm. Lat.* 6, p. 400.2515–9; Mar. Plot., *Gramm. Lat.* 6, p. 531.17). The story is developed in Jerome (Hieron. *Ab Abr.* 1816, 201 BCE [p. 135g Helm]). For sceptical discussions of the sources and the narratives constructed on this basis see Jocelyn 1969; Gruen 1990: 92–106, esp. 96–100.

[37] Plautus' description of a barbarian poet in jail (Plaut. *Mil.* 211–12), in combination with Festus' testimony that the Latin poet Naevius was called a 'barbarian' by Plautus (Paul. Fest., p. 32.14–16 L.), does not prove conclusively that this Plautine passage refers to Naevius, particularly since no reason is given for the imprisonment of the 'barbarian poet'. The view that Naevius' comedies *Hariolus* and *Leon* were written in jail as compensation (cf. Gell. *NA* 3.3.15) might have arisen from their being more in line with traditional Roman concepts than are other works by Naevius.

[38] See e.g. Gruen 1990: 92–106; Goldberg 1995: 32–7, with discussions of the biographical anecdotes and thoughts on the consequences of their interpretation for the portrait of Naevius (bibliography and overview of the main theories and problems arising from the biographical notices also in

Indeed, attacks on specific politicians cannot be identified beyond doubt in the transmitted verses: apart from the problematic case of the Metelli, there is no indication that Naevius mentioned names of well-known Romans in negative contexts. He rather seems to have voiced his views on a more abstract level: several fragments may have had a specific meaning in the particular context of the respective play, but can also be understood as having a broader application in a Roman context without pointing to a particular attachment or opposition to specific influential families.

Nevertheless, it is significant that a relatively large number of Naevius' verses can be interpreted as statements on political, social or moral issues and that this sort of gossip attached itself to Naevius. The introduction of the dramatic genre of praetexta and the composition of an epic on Roman history also indicate a political and historical dimension. As there was a tendency for Naevius to relate literary works to the Roman present, for instance by presenting Roman subject matter and discussing Roman issues, he might have been an attentive citizen, who touched upon topical questions, even if in general terms; and this may have corresponded to interests among audiences.

In this context, an interesting phenomenon is the choice of the story of king Lycurgus, who confronted Dionysus/Bacchus/Liber, as the subject for a tragedy, since this entailed the presentation of a god and attitudes to him on stage. The god is victorious in the end and his power is asserted, but he is not immediately accepted by everyone, and he is even ridiculed. Dionysus, called by the equivalent Roman name Liber, and his throng of Bacchic followers are characterized as effeminate, strange and exotic by their attire and behaviour (*Trag.* 31–2; 41–2; 43 R.³ = 33–4; 41–2; 39 W.), while the god insists on the fact that gods hate unrighteous mortals (*Trag.* 37 R.³ = 50 W.) and should not be provoked and thrown into rage (*Trag.* 35; 36 R.³ = 49; 48 W.): he demonstrates his power to destroy and punish (*Trag.* 45 R.³ = 52–3 W.). By choosing to include Lycurgus' resistance to Liber, Naevius introduced not only gods to the Roman stage,[39] but also criticism of gods and seers as an element of Roman tragedy.

Suerbaum 2002: 106); for the traditional view (with various nuances) see e.g. Traglia 1986: 24–7; Conte 1994: 44; Wiseman 1998: 39; Suerbaum 2000a: 307, 319–20, 2002: 106–7, 116–17.

[39] See Suerbaum 2000b. The *Danae* tragedies of both Livius Andronicus and Naevius might have included an appearance of Jupiter. But the surviving fragments do not reveal whether this was the case, irrespective of the difficult issue of dating the respective plays. Even though Naevius' *Danae* seems to have included criticism of Jupiter's behaviour, particularly its effect on human beings, the play is unlikely to have focused on the confrontation between gods and humans to the same extent as *Lycurgus*.

The presentation of a Dionysian theme has often been interpreted as topical, reflecting the influx of oriental cults in the late third and early second centuries BCE along with the authorities' reaction, culminating in the *Senatus consultum de Bacchanalibus* of 186 BCE.[40] Interestingly, Naevius chose the Lycurgus story (dramatized by Aeschylus among other Greek poets) and not the Pentheus story (famous from Euripides' treatment and apparently followed by Accius in his *Bacchae*). The Lycurgus story seems to put more emphasis on the direct opposition of a god and a human being with dire consequences for the human (cf. Hom. *Il.* 6.130–40). This addresses a question that might make the story applicable to the contemporary situation and hence more relevant to Roman audiences.

That Naevius composed a tragedy that might have asserted the power of Liber agrees with the role of Liber and liberty in his comedies: Liber is obviously seen both as an equivalent of Dionysus and wine and as a symbol of freedom. In the comedy *Agitatoria* a character values liberty highly, even above money (*Pall.* 9–10 R.³ = 5–6 W.). If this fragment does not come from an ironic context, it is remarkable in a comic environment, given the values usually pertaining in this genre. In a fragment from an unidentified comedy someone says that they will speak freely at the festival of Liber (*Pall.* 113 R.³ = *Inc.* 27 W.). This sentence, recalling the typical boastful language of comedy slaves, may well have a specific, unspectacular meaning in its context, while it gains its effectiveness from word play and pun;[41] at the same time it has the potential of being understood metatheatrically and indicates an awareness of the notion of free speech and its possible inhibition.

This would be true particularly if the word choice could be credited with additional significance: the term *Liberalibus* is usually referred to the festival of *Liberalia*, held on 17 March; however, this festival did not have scenic performances in Republican times (though there seem to have been *ludi* in an earlier period: cf. Ov. *Fast.* 3.783–6) or other rites for which stress on free speech would make sense. But as Liber, Libera and Ceres formed a divine triad, sharing a temple and a festival (cf. e.g. Cic. *Verr.* 2.5.36; Serv. on Verg. *Georg.* 1.7), Naevius might allude to performances at *Ludi Ceriales*

---

[40] See e.g. Boyle 2006: 47–9. It has been suggested that the (negative) portrayal of the god may have contributed to the repressive intervention of the Senate (see Suerbaum 2002: 109). However, it is the appearance of the Bacchants that is described as irritating, while the deity of Liber and his divine power are not questioned and are finally asserted (at least in the extant fragments). Hence, it is possible that the strange nature of the foreign cult is described and acknowledged, but that at the same time respect for the gods is demanded, which would turn the play into a more general discussion of gods and cults (see Flower 2000: esp. 28).

[41] See Goldberg's (1995: 37) criticism of the frequent metatheatrical interpretation of the fragment.

(cf. Ps.-Cypr. *Spect.* 4.4),[42] yet use the name *Liberalia* for a pun and an emphasis on liberty.

In a fragment from *Tarentilla* Naevius has a character say that what has been approved by his applause or by applause elicited by him in the theatre, no *rex* will dare to shatter: by so much is this slavery better than this liberty (*Pall.* 72–4 R.³ = 69–71 W.).[43] This utterance again used to be taken as an example of Naevius' outspokenness, but in view of the demonstrative pronouns it is now thought to be more specific and more likely to be an exclamation of a slave (or of an actor conscious of his status as a slave). Perhaps this slave enjoys his power over and success with the audience; therefore he rates his position higher than that of a free citizen: people like him have more freedom and impact since their utterances on stage when appreciated by an applauding audience are not confronted by higher powers. Or he distinguishes his position as a slave from that of free men within the play, while claiming that he is powerful and successful, which is appreciated by the audience; it would then be the boastful exclamation of a clever slave who is aware of his independence and success within the play and with the audience, while free men in the play are fooled. Then this fragment would suggest that slaves (in a double sense) rather than free men are the successful figures on stage, and that this is approved and enjoyed by audiences.

A realization of the different status of people depending on their power and their mutual relationship is also indicated by other fragments: in the comedy *Carbonaria* the addressee, who is waited on by many slaves at the table, is contrasted with someone who waits on himself at his meals (*Pall.* 26 R.³ = 27 W.). This paradigmatic person might be a model of poverty or virtuousness. If the idea is that one should not enjoy unnecessary luxury or abuse one's power, it would agree with a fragment from an unidentified play, in which subservient people are criticized (*Pall.* 111–12 R.³ = *Inc.* 25–6 W.). Evidently, Naevius' dramas presented the complexity of (social) interactions among humans.

Likewise, divine influence recurs in further dramas. The power of gods is an aspect in the comedy *Gymnasticus* (though presumably humorously), where someone laments the might of Cupido despite his small size

---

[42] See Bernstein 1998: 170; differently Marmorale 1950: 44; Blänsdorf 1978: 128; Boyle 2006: 14, 48. For a vindication of a lively theatrical tradition at *Liberalia* and the identification of plays specific to this festival see Wiseman 1998: 35–51; for further thoughts on the role of Liber and his ideological significance in early Rome and in relation to the development of Roman *ludi* see Wiseman 2000.

[43] For various interpretations see Suerbaum 1968: 29–31; J. Wright 1972; Gruen 1990: 94–5; Goldberg 2005b: 169. See bibliography in Suerbaum 2000a: 315.

(*Pall.* 55 R.³ = 60 W.), and in the tragedy *Danae*, where the power of Jupiter is mentioned and the god may have appeared on stage (*Trag.* 2; 10; 12 R.³ = 4; 9; 8 W.). In *Danae*, as in *Lycurgus*, the gods' behaviour is discussed irrespective of their divine power, whereby positive and negative features are combined: the view of others that Danae has a share of responsibility for the intercourse between her and Jupiter (*Trag.* 5 R.³ = 10–11 W.) seems to be contrasted with her own opinion that she is being punished albeit innocent (*Trag.* 9 R.³ = 14 W.). Hence the drama apparently implied that Jupiter's egoistic and lustful conduct brought the victim into an uncomfortable position.

Questions of justice or of how to deal responsibly with other people are relevant on a human level too, and as such they surface in several plays: the unscrupulous king Lycurgus, for instance, is prepared to confront the Bacchants by treachery (*Trag.* 26–8 R.³ = 30–2 W.) and regards catching them as the appropriate reaction (*Trag.* 21–3 R.³ = 27–9 W.); when they are finally caught, he inquires from his men whether this was achieved by fight or trickery (*Trag.* 34 R.³ = 44 W.). This contrasts with a statement in *Hesiona*, where 'word' (*lingua*) and 'sword' (*lingula*) are juxtaposed as alternative means of getting one's will (*Trag.* 1 R.³ = 19 W.).

The idea of justice is taken up in the comedy *Agitatoria*: a character complains that he has been bound too tightly and with his case untried (*Pall.* 13 R.³ = 8 W.). A statement from *Proiectus* that the people suffer and therefore the addressee should suffer also (*Pall.* 67 R.³ = 65 W.) seems to be based on the notion of equal and just punishment. A variation by contrast is the idea expressed in the tragedy *Danae* that everyone should be rewarded in proportion to their deeds (*Trag.* 8 R.³ = 13 W.). As Naevius wrote not only an *Equos Troianus*, but also a *Hesiona*, he composed two plays dealing with betrayal in connection with Troy: in addition to a presumably dramatic action, these mythical stories allow the paradigmatic presentation of the problems of openness and fairness.

Some of the moral issues indicated have a particular Roman touch, linguistically as well as conceptually: in a line from *Tarentilla* the addressees are told to turn to *virtus* again and to honour *domus*, *patres* and *patria* rather than *probra* abroad (*Pall.* 92–3 R.³ = 90–1 W.). In the tragedy named after her, Danae laments being driven out of her *patria* (*Trag.* 9 R.³ = 14 W.). In *Hector proficiscens* the eponymous character Hector rejoices about receiving *laus* from his father, who has received *laus* from others, which points to the theme of virtue, glory and heroic warriors (*Trag.* 15 R.³ = 17 W.). That this kind of joy, which acknowledges worth and comes from a worthy partner, can appeal to Romans is demonstrated by Cicero's appreciation of the scene.[44]

Other Naevian fragments recall principles of popular philosophy more generally, such as the statement that mortals must bear many hardships (*Pall.* 106 R.[3] = *Inc.* 37 W.) or that what is ill gotten is ill spent (*Trag.* 51 R.[3] = *Inc.* 38 W.). Vibrant discussion of various moral options may be inferred from several instances of considerations about what is the right and better alternative of action and on the appropriate behaviour in love affairs (*Pall.* 53–4; 125 R.[3] = 58–9; *Inc.* 9 W.). There are also comments on the proper way of speaking (*Pall.* 15–16 R.[3] = 16–17 W.).

All these aspects point to a rather independent poet taking up issues relevant to contemporary society. Such an engagement results in a Romanization beyond the necessary linguistic and formal adaptation of Greek models. This character of Naevius' works is demonstrated by fragments from a variety of plays and, above all, by his creation of the new literary genres of praetexta and Roman historical epic. Such a focus in Naevius' dramas will have contributed to catching the audience's interest and thus to confirming a sense of Roman national identity. By incorporating such ideas into comedies and tragedies that might have had lively stage-action, Naevius' dramas simultaneously provided entertainment.

4.3 Q. ENNIUS

Quintus Ennius (239–169 BCE) was a prolific poet, active in Rome right after the generation of the pioneers.[45] He came from a noble family in Rudiae in Messapian territory (cf. Serv. on Verg. *Aen.* 7.691); he thus grew up in an area characterized by a mixture of cultures and claimed to know Oscan, Greek and Latin (cf. Gell. *NA* 17.17.1). According to ancient tradition M. Porcius Cato brought Ennius to Rome from Sardinia, where Ennius perhaps did military service, in 204 BCE (cf. Nep. *Cato* 1.4). In 189 BCE Ennius accompanied M. Fulvius Nobilior on a campaign to Aetolia, and in 184 BCE he was given Roman citizenship by the son Quintus (cf.

---

[44] Cf. Cic. *Tusc.* 4.67; *Fam.* 5.12.7; 15.6.1; Sen. *Ep.* 102.16. See also Beare 1964: 35–6.
[45] On Ennius see e.g. Ribbeck 1875: 77–215 (on tragedies and praetextae); Duckworth 1952: 43–4 (on comedies); Beare 1964: 72–8; Suerbaum 1968: 43–295 (emphasis on *Annales*); Cancik 1978: 334–7; Drury 1982: 804–7; Traglia 1986: 46–89; Gruen 1990: 106–22; Petrone 1992: 612–21; Conte 1994: 75–84; Manuwald 2001a: 162–79 (on praetextae); Suerbaum 2002: 119–42; Erasmo 2004: 18–28 (on tragedies); Boyle 2006: 57–87 (on tragedies and praetextae); bibliography in De Rosalia 1989: 95–119 (on tragedies); Suerbaum 2002, 2003; Manuwald 2001 [2004]: 112–58 (on tragedies and praetextae); on the reception of Ennius in antiquity see Prinzen 1998.

Cic. *Brut.* 79; *Arch.* 22). In Rome Ennius allegedly lived modestly on the Aventine Hill (cf. Hieron. *Ab Abr.* 1777, 240 BCE [p. 133a Helm]; Cic. *Sen.* 14) and taught Greek and Latin (cf. Suet. *Gram.* 1.2). He died at the age of 70 in 169 BCE, when he had his *Thyestes* produced at *Ludi Apollinares* (cf. Cic. *Brut.* 78; *Sen.* 14; Hieron. *Ab Abr.* 1849, 168 BCE [p. 140a Helm]). Ancient writers claim that he was buried in the tomb of the Scipiones and honoured with a statue erected there.[46]

The biographical tradition indicates that Ennius had connections to various leading magistrates in Rome, some of whom featured in his literary works. He therefore used to be regarded as a prime example of a 'client poet' (*poeta cliens*), who wrote commissioned works supporting his patron(s) (see ch. 2.7). Yet the mere fact that Ennius was in touch with several different noblemen casts doubt on his portrait as a staunch supporter of a particular family. Besides, Cicero highlights the fact that Ennius praised outstanding individuals even after their death and that praise of such men affected the whole Roman people (Cic. *Brut.* 57–9; *Arch.* 22). And the portrait of the 'good companion' in Ennius' *Annales* (Enn. *Ann.* 210–27 W. = 268–86 Sk.), generally read as an indirect description of Ennius' own position, shows that this companion, albeit socially inferior, retains some independence. So Ennius may have composed individual pieces for the benefit of particular people, but this aspect does not seem to have determined his poetry overall.

Ennius was arguably the most versatile Republican poet and made important contributions to the establishment not only of Roman literature but also of national identity, even though he was not a Roman citizen by birth. His epic *Annales* was the first comprehensive narrative of Roman history in Latin (which also established the hexameter as the epic metre in Rome). The appreciation of him in later periods largely rests on this epic and on his tragedies; his few comedies and praetextae are rarely mentioned. Ennius' versatility and his experimenting with content and form are further demonstrated by his so-called *opera minora*, the other works besides epic and drama, particularly by the new literary genre of *Satura* and philosophical writings. He regarded himself as a 'second Homer, a Homer for Rome', since, according to the opening of his *Annales*, Homer's soul had passed into his own; and he posed as a self-confident Hellenistic poet, presenting himself as the first true 'philo-logist' or 'fan/student of words' (*dicti studiosus*: Enn. *Ann.* 234 W. = 216 Sk.).

---

[46] Cf. Cic. *Arch.* 22; Liv. 38.56.4; Hieron. *Ab Abr.* 1849, 168 BCE (p. 140a Helm). For the evidence and some discussion see Suerbaum 1968: 210–12.

Nevertheless, what remains from Ennius' writings is just fragments and titles: more than four hundred (partly incomplete) verses and about twenty-four titles of dramas, including two praetextae and two comedies, more than six hundred lines from *Annales* and about two hundred verses and passages in prose from the *opera minora* (*Satura, Scipio, Sota, Pro-trepticum sive Praecepta, Hedyphagetica, Epicharmus, Euhemerus sive sacra historia*, epigrams). *Thyestes* seems to have been the last of Ennius' plays performed during his lifetime, and the praetexta *Ambracia* must have been written after this town in Aetolia had been captured by M. Fulvius Nobi-lior in 189 BCE (cf. Liv. 38.3.9–11.9; Polyb. 21.25–30); but there is no further evidence on dates of dramas.

The distribution of literary genres in Ennius' output is significant: he continued the broad coverage of his predecessors, particularly the model of Naevius, in that he composed tragedies and comedies of Greek type, praetextae and an epic on Roman history. At the same time he went beyond his predecessors in a more comprehensive approach: his epic is an overview of Roman history; he covered a wider range of myths in his tragedies; by his *opera minora* he introduced entirely new literary genres and ideas to Rome by creating the hitherto unknown genre of satire, providing a first example of lyric in his epigrams and experimenting with various kinds of philosophical discourse. This contrasts with contemporary playwrights such as Plautus who started to focus on specific dramatic genres.

Within Ennius' preserved dramatic output there is a preponderance of serious drama, which may be connected with the dominant influence of Plautus. Like those of Livius Andronicus, Ennius' comic fragments are too meagre to allow substantial inferences; again one can only note that a basic generic distinction in tone and topics between serious and light drama was observed.

As in the case of Ennius' predecessors, a number of his tragedies refer to the Trojan cycle, yet these do not make up the majority, and other mythical cycles are also well represented. While some titles of Ennius' tragedies are attested in Rome for the first time in his oeuvre, others are identical with or similar to those of Roman predecessors (cf. Liv. Andr.: *Achilles, Aiax mastigophorus, Andromeda*; Naev.: *Andromacha, Hector proficiscens, Iphigenia*). However, in the case of a tragedy on Hector, Ennius chose a section of the myth different from the one presented by Naevius, as the full titles show (Naev. *Hector proficiscens*; Enn. *Hectoris lytra*). On the Greek side the majority of tragic topics dramatized by Ennius have precursors in Euripides, while Aeschylus might have provided a model for *Eumenides* and Aristarchus for *Achilles* (cf. also *Lib. gloss.* 2.11).

Since more titles and lines have been preserved from Ennius' tragedies than from those of Livius Andronicus and Naevius, a clearer idea of favoured topics can be gained while outlines of individual plays remain uncertain. As one might expect from the poet of *Annales*, there are numerous aspects that sound thoroughly Roman.

There is emphasis on the theme of moral and virtuous behaviour:[47] issues mentioned include fighting prowess (*Trag.* 63–4 R.³ = 83–4 W.), virtuous endurance of wounds and pain in battle (*Trag.* 314–25 R.³ = 169–81 W.), a proclamation that justice is better than bravery (*Trag.* 160–1 R.³ = 200–1 W.) and the view that a virtuous man should live with bravery and integrity (*Trag.* 257–60 R.³ = 308–11 W.). Besides, there are statements of almost proverbial character on concepts such as *otium* (*Trag.* 183–90 R.³ = 241–8 W.), *sapientia* (*Trag.* 240 R.³ = 271 W.) or *philosophia* (*Trag.* 340 R.³ = 400 W.).

These notions of desirable features for individuals (though applicable also to a whole people) are supplemented with an emphasis on deeds for the community and the *res publica* even if this involves personal sacrifices.[48] This aspect acquires an almost 'theoretical' dimension when characteristics of right or wrong behaviour by rulers are mentioned[49] or when a plot involves the question of legitimate rule and appropriate ways to obtain power (*Cresphontes*).

The context of isolated statements by dramatic characters is obviously uncertain. Yet the length and character of some fragments show that these notions were discussed more extensively than was demanded by the dramatic situation; thus they might have been intended to gain a significance beyond the immediate constraints of the plot. The topics addressed are sufficiently general and in line with Roman values to allow Roman audiences to relate to them. This indicates that Greek mythical stories narrated in the tragedies had been adapted to (contemporary) Roman society.

Additionally, Ennius' tragedies address theological and philosophical questions, which might be due to the poet's philosophical interests and/or the spirit of his time. This aspect is exemplified by the well-known utterance of Ennius' Neoptolemus: 'I must philosophize, in a few things; for doing so in all ways does not please me' (*Trag.* 340 R.³ = 400 W.: *philosophandum est paucis; nam omnino haud placet*).[50] The statement is often interpreted as

---

[47] See also Boyle 2006: 61–2.

[48] Cf. e.g. *Trag.* 1; 128–9; 141–3; 220–1; 249–50; 282 R.³ = 6; 142–3; 187–8; 267–8; 299–300; 338 W.

[49] Cf. e.g. *Trag.* 197–8; 379; 381–2 R.³ = 235–6; 410; 402–3 W.

[50] The precise reading of the text of this fragment is difficult to establish and has led to several different versions (on these problems cf. Jocelyn 1967: 252–3, whose text is given here). But the general meaning of the line is clear.

a rejection of philosophy, conforming to standard Roman prejudices; yet the speaker does propose a certain amount of philosophizing (see ch. 5.2). Ennius' plays also contained elements of natural philosophy, for instance Jupiter being equated with the sun (*Trag.* 237–9; 302 R.³ = 291–3; 351 W.). Irrespective of what assessment of philosophical views was supported by a play as a whole, such discussions confronted audiences with these notions.

Moreover, the topic of the relationship between gods and humans seems to have had significant dominance and breadth. The complex comes to the fore in *Telamo*: according to Cicero's report (Cic. *Div.* 2.104; *Nat. D.* 3.79–80), Telamo argues that, even though there are gods, they do not care for humans, for if they did, good humans would do well and bad ones badly (*Trag.* 269–71 R.³ = 328–9; 330 W.). Although Telamo's argument arises from his personal fortune, the fact that this leads to reflections on the gods gives the issue a wider application. Cicero claims that these views met with great approval from the populace, which might refer to performances in his time. In the same play Teucer regards his descent from Jupiter as important and has his piety towards the gods guide his actions (*Trag.* 279–80; 282 R.³ = 325–6; 338 W.; also *Trag.* 295 R.³ = 353 W.).

Telamo also includes criticism of soothsayers and seers (*Trag.* 272–6 R.³ = 332–6 W.; cf. also *Trag.* 364 R.³ = 331 W.): these people are accused of focusing only on their personal gain and not caring about giving proper advice, another issue discussed by Cicero (Cic. *Div.* 1.88; 1.132). Similar scepticism features in *Iphigenia*, where Achilles criticizes the fact that people look to the sky to determine their actions instead of at what is before their feet (*Trag.* 199–201 R.³ = 249–51 W.).

By contrast, somewhere Apollo appears and outlines the helpfulness of his advice (*Trag.* 350–3 R.³ = 150–3 W.). The dream of queen Hecuba and Apollo's subsequent oracle as well as his influence on Casssandra seem to be important elements in *Alexander*.[51] Bacchic celebrations are described in *Athamas* (*Trag.* 107–11 R.³ = 128–32 W.). In other fragments the roles of the gods and their descriptions sound more conventional (*Trag.* 375; 380; *Trag. inc.* LVI R.³ = *Trag.* 388; 389; 385 W.). This ambiguous picture suggests a tension between the traditional views and roles of gods in Greek and Roman literature and society on the one hand and philosophical and 'scientific' views of the world on the other hand.

Besides, the fragments of Ennius provide the first clear examples of what was to become a characteristic of later Republican tragedy: noble heroes

---

[51] Cf. *Trag. inc.* 5–16 [plausibly attributed to *Alexander*]; Enn. *Trag.* 39–53; 54–6; 57–9; 60–2 R.³ = 38–49; 57–72; 73–5; 76–9; 80–1 W.

and heroines on stage in reduced circumstances, in rags and dishevelled.[52]
This is probably connected with the fact that characters in several tragedies
experience significant changes of fortune,[53] along with the intention of
presenting these situations vividly.

Although Cicero says that Ennius might be appreciated for using everyday language in his poetry (Cic. *Orat.* 36), his poetic style appears to have
been more sophisticated and refined than that of his predecessors (cf. also
Cic. *Brut.* 76). Ennius employs familiar devices such as alliteration, assonance, emphasis and repetition to great effect; his sentence structures are
more complex and show the influence of contemporary rhetoric.

Following upon the two pioneers Livius Andronicus and Naevius, Ennius
continued their broad and flexible approach and developed it further by
covering even more literary genres and topics. Simultaneously, he refined
dramatic techniques and language; in particular he discussed numerous
issues relevant to (contemporary) Roman society with the appropriate
Roman terminology (cf. also Hor. *Ars P.* 55b–8a). He thus came to be
seen by some ancient authorities as the actual founder of Roman literature; Horace, for instance, calls him 'father Ennius' (Hor. *Epist.* 1.19.7:
Ennius... pater).

4.4 M. PACUVIUS

Marcus Pacuvius (*c.* 220–130 BCE), a younger contemporary of Ennius, is
the first Roman playwright to concentrate on serious drama and the only
Roman dramatist who is known also to have worked as a painter (cf. Plin.
HN 35.19; Hieron. *Ab Abr.* 1863, 154 BCE [p. 142e Helm]).[54] Pacuvius came
from Brundisium and had an Oscan background: the form of his name
is of Oscan origin, and ancient grammarians have identified Oscan words
in his tragedies (cf. Pac. *Trag.* 64; 215 R.[3] = 59; 224 W.). Like Ennius (cf.
Gell. *NA* 17.17.1), he might therefore have been familiar with the Oscan,
Greek and Latin languages and cultures. After having been active in Rome
for many years (cf. Cic. *Brut.* 229), Pacuvius retired to Tarentum in old
age; there he was allegedly visited by the young Accius, who read his

---

[52] Cf. e.g. *Trag.* 20–4; 170–1; 283; 285; 287; 345–6; 391 R.[3] = 25–9; 210–11; 323; 341; 339; 418; 419 W.

[53] Cf. e.g. *Alcmeo, Alexander, Andromacha (aechmalotis), Thyestes.*

[54] On Pacuvius see e.g. Ribbeck 1875: 216–339; Beare 1964: 79–84; Drury 1982: 821–3; Petrone 1992:
622–33; Conte 1994: 104–5; Manuwald 2001a: 180–96 (on praetexta), 2003; Stärk in Suerbaum 2002:
154–8; Fantham 2003; Erasmo 2004: 34–42; Boyle 2006: 87–108; bibliography in De Rosalia 1989:
119–32; Stärk in Suerbaum 2002; Manuwald 2001 [2004]: 158–80; for an overview of the history
of scholarship see Schierl 2006: 66–71; on the reception of Pacuvius in antiquity see Schierl 2006:
52–65.

Atreus to him (cf. Gell. *NA* 13.2; Hieron. *Ab Abr.* 1878, 139 BCE [p. 144h Helm]). A rather formulaic epitaph, said to have been written by himself, is transmitted in Gellius (Gell. *NA* 1.24.4). Pacuvius was a nephew of Ennius (cf. Plin. *HN* 35.19) and possibly also his pupil (cf. Varro, *Sat. Men.* 356 B.). Because of his long lifespan, his dramatic activity first overlapped with Ennius, his predecessor in the serious dramatic genre, and later coincided with his successor Accius. As for other dramatic genres, Pacuvius will have experienced the work of Plautus, Caecilius, Terence, Titinius and Afranius and seen how the light dramatic genres developed.

Besides tragedies, Pacuvius wrote a praetexta about the victory of L. Aemilius Paul(l)us (*c.* 228–160 BCE) at Pydna (168 BCE). Also, Cicero has C. Laelius Sapiens (*c.* 190 to after 129 BCE) call Pacuvius 'companion and friend of mine' (Cic. *Amic.* 24: *hospes et amicus meus*). Therefore a close relationship of Laelius and his friends to the poet is often inferred, but one must bear in mind that Cicero presents an idealized set-up and may exaggerate elements that suit him. That Cicero calls Caecilius and Pacuvius 'contemporaries' (*aequales*) of Laelius and Scipio (Cic. *Brut.* 258) might be a description of a period without indicating a closer connection. Still, it is noteworthy that Laelius' friend P. Cornelius Scipio Aemilianus Africanus (*c.* 185–129 BCE) was the natural son of L. Aemilius Paul(l)us, that Laelius is said also to have been in contact with Terence (cf. Cic. *Amic.* 89; *Att.* 7.3.10; Suet./Donat. *Vita Ter.* 2) and Lucilius (cf. Hor. *Sat.* 2.1.65b–75a; Lucil. 1235–40; 1122–3 M. = 200–7 W.) and that at the funeral games of L. Aemilius Paul(l)us, organized by his natural sons, Terence's *Adelphoe* and *Hecyra II* were shown (cf. Did. on Ter. *Ad., Hec.*; Donat. on Ter. *Ad., praef.* 1.6).[55] This points to contacts between a group of leading men in Roman society, who were culturally open-minded, and a number of contemporary poets. However, this does not imply restrictions on the playwrights' poetic freedom, particularly in view of the number of individuals involved (see ch. 2.7).

Of Pacuvius' dramatic output, about thirteen titles of tragedies (and about four hundred and thirty, partly incomplete, lines) as well as four verses of the praetexta *Paulus* survive.[56] In view of his long lifespan and his concentration

---

[55] On Pacuvius' social contacts see e.g. Schierl 2006: 4–5 (with further references). On the 'Scipionic circle' see ch. 2.7, n. 183.

[56] A couple of ancient sources claim that Pacuvius also wrote satires (Porph. on Hor. *Sat.* 1.10.46; Diom. *Ars* 3, *Gramm. Lat.* I, p. 485.32–4); yet no traces remain (but see Flintoff 1990; contra Suerbaum 2002: 304; Manuwald 2003: 138 n. 18; Schierl 2006: 10–11). Alleged quotations from comedies of Pacuvius in Fulgentius (*Expositio sermonum antiquorum* 12, p. 115 Helm [T 11 S.]; 32, p. 120 Helm [T 12 S.]) are rather uncertain (see Stärk in Suerbaum 2002: 157; Manuwald 2003: 138 n. 18; Schierl 2006: 10).

on serious drama, his oeuvre has often been regarded as rather small. To explain this, modern scholars have mentioned that Pacuvius was also active as a painter, that he worked slowly or that he started writing tragedy rather late in life. Yet a late start to his dramatic career can be disproved (see below), and a mere lack of time is not an entirely convincing explanation.[57] Obviously, different percentages of the total output of each poet may have been lost. Also, too little is known about the number of dramatic performances per year and the selection process: as Pacuvius overlapped with another major tragic playwright for most of his productive period, well-known palliata poets were active at the time and togata was gaining in status, there may have been fewer opportunities for him to have plays performed.

What is certain is that the plays he produced had an immediate and last-ing impact. If in one of Varro's satires a Pompilius calls himself a disciple of Pacuvius and traces back a connection to the Muses via Pacuvius and his teacher Ennius (Varro, *Sat. Men.* 356 B.), this implies (even though the con-text is unclear) that Pacuvius might be referred to as an authority in the com-position of dramatic poetry.[58] Cicero says that Pacuvius could be called 'the greatest tragic poet' (Cic. *Opt. gen.* 2: *summum . . . poetam . . . tragicum*).[59]

Contemporary poets in a variety of literary genres reacted to Pacuvius' plays: in three palliatae, Plautus apparently alludes to a scene from Pacuvius' *Antiopa*, as later does Persius in one of his satires.[60] Elsewhere Plautus seems to refer to lines from *Medus* and *Teucer*; the verse from the latter tragedy is also quoted in Cicero's correspondence.[61] Caecilius alludes to a line from *Periboea*; Terence might take up a verse from an unidentified tragedy; Afra-nius refers to a line from an unidentified tragedy by Pacuvius in one of his togatae; Lucilius parodies a line from *Chryses* in his first collection of satires, probably published in the early 120s BCE.[62] Apart from demonstrating the increasing sophistication of Roman literature and intertextual engagements between poets of different literary genres, these comments show that Pacu-vius' dramas constituted a well-known and possibly controversial point of reference.

---

[57] See also Schierl 2006: 102.   [58] See Schierl 2006: 2.

[59] Prinzen (1998: 36–9), however, believes that Cicero valued Ennius and Accius more highly than Pacu-vius (and quoted them more often) and disapproved of Pacuvius' language; in his view Cicero just reported positive judgements by others. On possible reasons for differences in Cicero's assessments see ch. 2.10 and n. 270.

[60] Cf. esp. Pac. *Trag.* 20$^{a–b}$ R.^{3} = 13–14; W.: Plaut. *Cas.* 759–62; *Pers.* 11–12; 712–13; *Pseud.* 771–2; Pers. 1.77–8.

[61] Cf. Pac. *Trag.* 223; 336 R.^{3} = 264; 365 W.: Plaut. *Amph.* 232–3; 1062; Cic. *Fam.* 8.2.1.

[62] Cf. Pac. *Trag.* 279/80 R.^{3} = 304 W.: Caec. *Pall.* 47–8 R.^{3} = 43–4 W. – Pac. *Trag.* 391 R.^{3} = *Inc.* 10 W.: Ter. *Hec.* 128–9 – Pac. *Trag. inc.* LIV R.^{3} = 35 W.: Afr. *Tog.* 7 R.^{3} – Pac. *Trag.* 112 R.^{3} = 116 W.: Lucil. 653 M. = 665 W.; cf. also 876 M. = 880 W.; generally Gell. *NA* 17.21.49.

While Caecilius and Afranius take up lines that can be read as general statements because of their content, Plautus and Lucilius mock overblown and artificial language as well as exaggerated descriptions of characters in dire plight (Lucil. 597–8; 599–600; 653 M. = 729–30; 727–8; 665 W.). Just like other 'archaic' poets, Pacuvius continued to be criticized for his language and style by later writers (Cic. *Brut.* 258; Pers. 1.76–8; Mart. 11.90; Tac. *Dial.* 20.5; 21.7); they ridiculed, for instance, his long and complex compounds and neologisms. What people did not like about Pacuvius' language was perhaps not simply its 'archaic' flavour, but rather the artificial and intellectual quality of his word-formations. Cicero, aware of the fact that judgements on form can vary with individuals, reports that Pacuvius' verses could be called 'ornate and elaborate' in contrast to Ennius' common use of language (Cic. *Orat.* 36; cf. also Gell. *NA* 6.14.6).

Although in his dates and his experience of social and cultural conditions Pacuvius is closer to Ennius than to Accius, later assessments tend to pair or contrast him with Accius. The reason is probably that these two poets were the last two major tragic playwrights in Republican times and the only ones to write serious drama exclusively, so that they could be regarded as representatives of this dramatic genre and of a late style. There are indeed similarities between Pacuvius and Accius in the use of sophisticated and refined words and phrases, in the tendency to create effective scenes by bringing people in reduced circumstances onto the stage and in a 'scholarly' approach to writing dramatic poetry.

At the same time differences were observed between them: in contrast to Accius, literary critics attributed the positive quality of being 'learned/educated' (*doctus*) to Pacuvius (cf. Hor. *Epist.* 2.1.55–6; Quint. *Inst.* 10.1.97). Although the meaning of the epithet *doctus* is not entirely clear, the prevailing modern interpretation refers it to a profound knowledge of myths. Indeed, a wide-ranging familiarity with Greek literature is rather plausible, since other ancient poets who were given this epithet, such as Catullus and Calvus, probably received it on account of their learning. That it was assigned to Pacuvius (and not to other Republican dramatic poets) might demonstrate that he paid particular attention to the selection of plots and diverged from well-trodden paths thanks to his extensive learning.[63]

Hence it became a common view in modern scholarship that Pacuvius preferred rare and obscure myths for his tragedies. But while it is true

---

[63] On Pacuvius' *doctrina* see D'Anna 1976; Castagna 1990: esp. 35–8; Manuwald 2003: 129–30; Schierl 2006: 64–5 (all with overviews and references to earlier discussions).

that his stories typically differ from those of his predecessors, they are not completely far-fetched, but rather connected with well-known myths: Pacuvius tended to dramatize versions or parts of familiar myths that had been treated less often, for instance sequels to well-known stories such as those of Medea or Orestes and Iphigenia. He could thereby build on the audience's familiarity with the basic story and still present something novel and interesting.

Yet the eventual choice of plots seems not just to have been designed to avoid clashes and overlaps with predecessors or to ensure success with audiences; instead, since certain motifs and elements of plot structure occur in several tragedies, it is plausible that the precise selection of myths was designed to enable the creation of satisfactory plots and the treatment of particular themes (see below), since these very stories allowed their inclusion. Pacuvius may have had prologues that explained the background to the stories presented (cf. Lucil. 875 M. = 879 W.).

The selection of less obvious versions or sections of myths raises the question of sources: some of Pacuvius' titles match those attested for major Greek tragic poets, and Cicero mentions Euripides' homonymous play as a model for Pacuvius' *Antiopa* (Cic. *Fin.* 1.4); other titles have no equivalent among the known Greek tragedies, and in these cases the underlying stories can only be inferred on the basis of mythographical evidence.[64] This points to the use of a wide range of sources and an independent approach in transforming those into plays agreeing with the poet's intentions and attractive to Roman audiences. Indeed, although Cicero records a close similarity between Euripides' and Pacuvius' *Antiopa*, he elsewhere says about Pacuvius' *Niptra*, with reference to the characterization of Ulixes, that Pacuvius' version was 'better' (*melius*) than that of Sophocles (Cic. *Tusc.* 2.48–50). While Cicero's assessment is his subjective view, as he sees the Pacuvian Ulixes behave according to standard Roman values, it implies a difference between the two versions.

This dexterity in choosing and adapting stories seems to have been complemented by dramaturgical virtuosity, while there is a possible connection between dramatic techniques employed and versions of myths chosen that lend themselves to impressive presentation: almost all known dramas are characterized by special scenic effects (such as the appearance of a shade from the underworld in *Iliona* or Medea's winged chariot in

---

[64] This applies, for instance, to *Medus*, a sequel to the Medea story as treated in Euripides and Ennius, even though Diodorus Siculus mentions Attic tragedies dealing with the return of Medea and Medus to Colchis and their killing of Perses (Diod. Sic. 4.56.1–2).

Medus), the presence of strange and exciting figures, particularly noble people in reduced circumstances (as in Ennius or Accius), a sophisticated linguistic shape and/or a vivid, partly complex plot structure.

The specific versions or sections of myths that Pacuvius chose for his plays allowed the discussion of important and relevant issues: Pacuvius' plays often deal with family relationships, friendship, loyalty and care for each other as well as a well-ordered community life, justice, sensible use of political power and a legitimate, 'good' ruler as envisaged goals. Frequently, a satisfying ending is reached when family members are finally reunited, after having recognized each other just in time before a crime is committed, take revenge for injustice they have suffered and help to (re-)establish a well-ordered political system. Hence, there is discussion of social and political as well as of philosophical questions and criticism of gods and seers, but there is no fundamental shaking of beliefs.

Because of the basic thematic and structural consistency as well as slight differences in presentation and complexity across all identifiable tragedies, along with some external evidence, a tentative hypothesis on the chronology of Pacuvius' dramatic output may be attempted.[65] The praetexta *Paulus* was obviously written after the battle of Pydna in 168 BCE, but owing to the limited number of fragments and the generic difference, this information does not contribute to establishing dates for tragedies. Since Plautus seems to allude to a passage from *Antiopa* (a tragedy that features family conflicts, individuals in desperate circumstances and a discussion about the best way of life) in three of his comedies, it must have been written before 184 BCE, the year of Plautus' death or at least of his last documented production, and as one of these comedies, *Pseudolus*, can be dated to 191 BCE, the *terminus ante quem* for *Antiopa* can be brought down to 191 BCE. As Caecilius refers to a line from *Periboea* in one of his palliatae, the tragedy (on a struggle for power and justice, conflict among family members and an exiled person in desperate circumstances) must predate Caecilius' death in 168/7 BCE.

In the discussion of a scene attributed to Pacuvius' *Chryses*, Cicero has Laelius say that a performance of this 'new play' (*nova fabula*) had taken place 'recently' (*nuper*) (Cic. *Amic.* 24). Within the literary fiction this means that the piece is envisaged to have been performed for the first time not long before the date of the dialogue, set a few days after Scipio's death

---

[65] For a more detailed presentation of this theory see Manuwald 2003: 137–43; for other theories on the dates of Pacuvius' tragedies see Schierl 2006: 5 and n. 27, and passim.

in 129 BCE (cf. Cic. *Amic.* 3). If this reference has a basis in historical reality, one might assume that the first performance of *Chryses* happened some time but not too long before 129 BCE, and that this tragedy was therefore among the latest of Pacuvius' plays. Pacuvius is known to have had plays produced in Rome at least as late as 140 BCE (cf. Cic. *Brut.* 229), and the prominence of philosophical issues in *Chryses* would accord with the increased attention to philosophy in Rome, particularly among Scipio and his friends, after the visit of three Greek philosophers in 155 BCE. Lucilius' choice of *Chryses* as a target for parodic references in the first collection of his satires supports the conclusion that *Chryses* was a recent piece and therefore of relevance in around 130 BCE.

These indications of possible dates would give one example each of a tragedy from an early period (*Antiopa*), from an early to middle period (*Periboea*) and from a late period (*Chryses*). All three tragedies bear the structure typical of Pacuvius as regards the construction of a complex plot with positive ending, the topics treated and the use of dramatic effects, but the presentation seems simpler in *Antiopa* and most refined and sophisticated in *Chryses*. Therefore one might venture the hypothesis that what can be regarded as characteristic of Pacuvius was already present when his documented dramatic activity started, but that it developed over the course of his career. The premise of an increasing complexity may allow a cautious relative dating of his other tragedies: *Atalanta*, *Dulorestes*, *Iliona* and *Medus* seem to be as developed as *Chryses* and thus late plays, while *Niptra* and *Teucer* are rather reminiscent of *Antiopa* and *Periboea*. The tragedies *Armorum iudicium*, *Hermiona*, *Orestes* and *Pentheus (vel Bacchae)* can hardly be dated by these means.

Pacuvius was an almost exact contemporary of the palliata poet Caecilius Statius, who, however, died much earlier. And some qualities identified for Pacuvius can be found in Caecilius in a similar way. For instance, both share impressive stage effects combined with pathetic arrangements. While their anomalous language was criticized by later writers, the dramatic effects, the moving and well-constructed plots and the contents of their plays came to be appreciated. Their plots and topics provided Roman audiences with reference points for reflections on moral, social and philosophical questions, a focus continued by Terence, Afranius and Accius. Audiences seem to have enjoyed the impressive spectacular effects, but also responded to the topics discussed and the sentiments expressed, as the later reception of Pacuvius' dramas shows.

4.5 L. ACCIUS

Lucius Accius (170–*c.* 80 BCE), the last major tragic poet in Republican times, wrote serious drama and treatises.[66] He was the son of freedmen (cf. Hieron. *Ab Abr.* 1878, 139 BCE [p. 144h Helm])[67] and spent his adult life in Rome, where he presumably refrained from forensic activity (cf. Quint. *Inst.* 5.13.43) and was active as a learned poet and scholar of the Hellenistic type. As a young man, he is said to have read his tragedy *Atreus* in Tarentum to the elderly Pacuvius, who found what he heard 'sonorous and grand' (*sonora . . . et grandia*), but also 'somewhat too harsh and unrefined' (*duriora paulum et acerbiora*) (cf. Gell. *NA* 13.2; also Hieron. *Ab Abr.* 1878, 139 BCE [p. 144h Helm]).

From 140 BCE at the latest Accius produced dramas in Rome (cf. Cic. *Brut.* 229; also Gell. *NA* 17.21.49); he was still having new works performed at the very end of the century (cf. Cic. *Phil.* 1.36; *Att.* 16.2.3; 16.5.1).[68] During the early part of his career, Accius overlapped with his older contemporary Pacuvius; after Pacuvius' withdrawal to Tarentum, Accius seems to have been the sole tragic poet of note in Rome. Roughly contemporary playwrights of other dramatic genres were the palliata poet Turpilius and the togata poet Atta, while competition from other forms of entertainment and dramatic varieties was starting to increase.

Like other intellectuals of his time, Accius was in touch with leading men in Rome; Cicero claims to have had conversations with him (cf. Cic. *Brut.* 107). In particular, D. Iunius Brutus Callaicus (cos. 138 BCE) is said to have been on friendly terms with Accius (cf. Cic. *Brut.* 107; *Arch.* 27; Val. Max. 8.14.2) and to have had 'poems' (*carmina*) by Accius inscribed 'on the entrances of his temples and monuments', the scholion identifying these verses as Saturnians for the entrance to the Temple of Mars.[69] Hence a

---

[66] On Accius see e.g. Ribbeck 1875: 340–607 (on tragedies and praetextae); Beare 1964: 119–28; Casaceli 1976 (on language and style); Degl'Innocenti Pierini 1980 (on style and grammatical works); Drury 1982: 823–5; Pociña Pérez 1984; Petrone 1992: 634–41; Conte 1994: 105–6; Manuwald 2001a: 196–237 (on praetextae); Stärk in Suerbaum 2002: 158–66; Erasmo 2004: 42–50 (on tragedies); Boyle 2006: 109–42 (on tragedies and praetextae); bibliography in Pociña Pérez 1984; De Rosalia 1989: 132–44 (on tragedies); Stärk in Suerbaum 2002; Manuwald 2001 [2004]: 180–225 (on tragedies and praetextae); on Accius' life in its cultural and social context see Baldarelli 2004: 11–45.

[67] The alleged connection with Pisaurum (cf. Hieron. *Ab Abr.* 1878, 139 BCE [p. 144h Helm]) is doubtful even though Accii are later attested in this area (cf. Cic. *Brut.* 271; Plin. *HN* 7.128).

[68] Cicero says about a performance of Accius' *Tereus* in 44 BCE that it took place 'in the sixtieth year' (*sexagesimo post anno*) after the play was written and/or first performed (Cic. *Phil.* 1.36). This information is often used to infer a date for *Tereus*, but 'sixty' looks like a round figure as Cicero uses them elsewhere (e.g. Cic. *Phil.* 5.19; *Fam.* 12.2.1) and therefore is more likely to indicate an approximate rather than a precise date.

[69] Cf. Cic. *Arch.* 27; Schol. Bob. on Cic. *Arch.* 27 (p. 179.5 St.); also Val. Max. 8.14.2.

close relationship between D. Brutus, Accius and the latter's literary activity has been assumed; Accius' praetexta *Brutus*, dramatizing the story of the founder of the Roman Republic, has often been seen as evidence of the poet writing in the service of D. Brutus. However, there are no indications of a specific patron–client relationship, and the extant fragments of the praetexta do not indicate that it had a 'political' reference beyond the more general impact of its subject matter (see ch. 2.7).[70]

Ancient sources portray Accius as a rather self-confident personality: he was unmoved by the comments of the elderly Pacuvius (cf. Gell. *NA* 13.2; Hieron. *Ab Abr.* 1878, 139 BCE [p. 144h Helm]); he erected a tall statue of himself in the 'Temple of the Muses' (*Aedes Camenarum*) although he was rather small in stature (cf. Plin. *HN* 34.19; Lucil. 794 M. = 844 W.); he showed contempt for a nobleman in the 'college of poets' (*collegium poetarum*) because Accius regarded him as a dilettante writer of tragedies (cf. Val. Max. 3.7.11; see ch. 2.7). A mime actor who criticized Accius by name on the stage was taken to court by him and found guilty by the judge P. Mucius (cf. *Auct. ad Her.* 1.24; 2.19; see ch. 2.2). Further, Accius said in his writings that he and Pacuvius had produced plays in the same year, he being fifty years younger (cf. Cic. *Brut.* 229); this is perhaps a sign not only of Accius' scholarly interests, but also of his intention of connecting his own dramatic activity with that of a famous predecessor and claiming a place for himself in the history of Roman tragedy.

The contemporary satirist Lucilius criticized unrealistic and fanciful elements in Accius' dramas (cf. Gell. *NA* 17.21.49). This is one reason why much has been made of an alleged more wide-ranging opposition between Accius and Lucilius, often connected with Accius' membership in the 'college of poets' and Lucilius' association with the 'Scipionic circle'.[71] But there is no evidence to show that Lucilius' comments concerning Accius went beyond the general mockery of literary genres criticized for their lack of 'realism'.

---

[70] For discussions of the relationship between Accius and D. Brutus and the role of the praetexta *Brutus* see e.g. Manuwald 2001a: 119–21, 223–4; Baldarelli 2004: 15–22 (with differing views and further references).

[71] See e.g. Dangel 1995: 21–2; Baldarelli 2004: 22–34 (with references). The only mention of the *collegium poetarum* in Accius' time is the anecdote in Valerius Maximus (3.7.11), and it does not provide information on whether Accius was the head of this body or on the views it may have promoted (see ch. 2.7). Lucilius mocks the tall statue of the short Accius (Lucil. 794 M. = 844 W.), but this is an ideal target for a satirist; and as Pliny also reports this incident and describes it as 'noted by authors' (Plin. *HN* 34.19), it does not indicate a particular opposition between Accius and Lucilius.

As a dramatist Accius focused on serious genres, like his predecessor Pacuvius; yet for Accius far more dramas are known. Titles of about forty-five tragedies, some of which may be double titles, and of two praetextae survive as well as almost seven hundred (partly incomplete) verses. Moreover, Accius was a literary critic and grammarian influenced by Hellenistic scholarship; he wrote treatises on grammatical, theatrical and literary questions (*Didascalica*, *Pragmatica*), an epic *Annales* and so-called minor works (*Parerga*, *Sotadica*, *Praxidicus*).

Even though Ennius provides a precedent for a versatile poet who went beyond drama and epic and was active in a variety of literary genres, Accius is the only Republican playwright who also wrote separate works on literary questions and theatre history and thereby engaged with the subject in theory and practice. This academic interest agrees with developments in the late second and the first centuries BCE, when scholars who were not dramatic poets themselves started to discuss aspects of literary history (see ch. 2.10).[72]

The reason for Accius' view that Hesiod preceded Homer, namely that Homer withheld information that he had found in Hesiod (Gell. *NA* 3.11.4–5: Acc. *Did.* 1 W. = *Gram.* 1 D.), suggests that Accius presupposed for Homer the literate society that can be inferred for his own day, where one would know works of earlier writers and take them into account. That Accius dealt with Greek tragic poets not only as possible models for his tragedies, but also as objects for scholarly discussion is indicated by his criticism of Euripides' use of choruses (*Did.* 11–12 W. = *Gram.* 9–10 D.). Accius' penchant for word play and etymologies was presumably informed by his academic studies, even though similar tendencies can be observed in the work of the learned Ennius and also in Plautus.[73]

Accius shares a number of titles of dramas with one or two Roman predecessors, particularly with Ennius,[74] and there might be more overlap in the treatment of the same or similar myths under different titles. Irrespective of Accius' enormous output it is natural that this phenomenon is most noticeable in the last Republican representative of this dramatic genre. Beyond titles and myths, there are verbal similarities between lines by Accius and

---

[72] On Accius' literary treatises and his views on drama see N. W. Slater 1992a: esp. 98–101.

[73] Cf. e.g. Acc. *Trag.* 4–9; 82–3; 156; 296 R.³ = 452–7; 45–6; 123; 274 W.; cf. e.g. Enn. *Trag.* 38; 65; 208–10 R.³ = 56; 109; 256–8 W.; Plaut. *Merc.* 516b–17a; *Poen.* 91–2.

[74] Cf. Livius Andronicus: *Achilles, Aegisthus, Andromeda, Tereus*; Ennius: *Achilles, Andromeda, Athamas, Hecuba, Medea, Telephus*; Pacuvius: *Armorum iudicium*.

those by earlier Roman tragic poets.[75] Obviously, it was not a problem to present another tragedy on the same myth; however, there are indications that playwrights opted for sections of myths not yet dramatized, selected alternative versions or placed emphases differently, as, for instance, the different dramatic versions of the Medea story by Ennius (*Medea* [*exul*]), Pacuvius (*Medus*) and Accius (*Medea sive Argonautae*) indicate.

Accius also shares one title with a dramatic predecessor in the comic genre, since he composed an *Amphitruo* as had Plautus, who had classified this drama as a 'tragicomedy' on formal grounds (Plaut. *Amph.* 50–63). As Accius voiced an opinion about the genuineness of plays ascribed to Plautus, presumably in his treatises (Gell. *NA* 3.3.9: Acc. *Did.* 19–22 W. = *Gram.* xv D.), he was obviously familiar with Plautus' works. The fragmentary state of Accius' *Amphitruo* makes it difficult to establish details of his version, but tone and plot seem to have been different from Plautus' play and entirely appropriate to tragedy.

The large number and variety of preserved titles seem to indicate that Accius explored the full range of mythical cycles. Correspondingly, all three major Greek tragic playwrights have plausibly been identified as inspirations for individual tragedies; several sources are likely to have been used in a few cases; some titles are attested only among Hellenistic tragedy or have no equivalent on the Greek side. Other tragedies dramatize scenes from Greek epics and may have been developed from those, possibly under the influence of scholia; at any rate a few titles come from the scholarly and not from the Greek dramatic tradition.[76]

It has even been assumed that Accius worked systematically, aimed at giving a full panorama of myth across all his tragedies and organized his oeuvre in coherent and connected cycles to create a continuous narrative.[77] A scholarly approach to writing tragedies would not be alien to Accius or his time, and he was obviously interested in genealogy and genealogical connections between myths, as the great number of patronymic titles and of sections in his plays, possibly prologues, concerned with family history or prehistory show.[78] Still, this theory has its problems: apart from being,

---

[75] Cf. e.g. Acc. *Trag.* 581–4 R.³ = 585–8 W.: Enn. *Trag.* 234 R.³ = 287 W. – Acc. *Trag.* 56; 470 R.³ = 325; 470 W.: Pac. *Trag.* 340; 214 R.³ = 376; 222 W. On references to earlier Roman tragic poets in Accius see Casaceli 1976: 99–110.

[76] See e.g. D'Antò 1980: 27–8.

[77] See esp. Dangel 1990, 1995: 31–4, 41–5; endorsed apparently by Baldarelli 2004: 38–40; for criticism see e.g. the reviews of Dangel's edition, esp. Gratwick 2000; Jocelyn 2001.

[78] Cf. e.g. *Trag.* 50; 376; 377–9; 609–10 R.³ = 324; 360; 370–2; 614–15 W.; Serv. auct. on Verg. *Aen.* 8.130.

in its most developed form, an overly neat construction, which does not allow for the loss of any title or mistakes in the transmission of titles, it is problematic to infer such wide-ranging intentions in a poet, particularly when dates and contexts for the composition of individual plays are lacking. This theory would also entail that Accius saw his dramas as a coherent whole, in the sense of an 'edition of his complete works', since an overall concept becomes evident from the entire oeuvre rather than from single performances of individual plays; it is implausible that Accius wrote all the tragedies and had them performed in the order in which they are supposed to be connected.

The search for myths effective on the Roman stage or the intention of presenting particular topics might have been more important factors in Accius' decisions on the choice of myths: individual tragedies are characterized by recurring themes. These include topics frequent in Roman tragedy, such as warfare and its consequences, problems within families or the functions of gods and seers, as well as aspects that seem to be especially prominent in Accius' oeuvre, such as an emphasis on genealogy, ancestry and the consequences of deeds done in the past which may affect later generations.[79] This element might be part of the larger complex of relationships within families, particularly between members of different generations (e.g. *Trag.* 58–9; 64–5 R.³ = 21; 28–9 W.). It is connected with the theme of proper rule when someone's descent and membership in a house or family become legitimizing factors (*Trag.* 205; 206–8; 209–13; 231–2 R.³ = 169–77; 194–5 W.). Individuals in power can degenerate into tyrants, hated by their subjects (*Trag.* 203–4; 269–70; 651 R.³ = 168; 256–7; *Inc.* 18 W.).

A frequent (traditional) motif, ridiculed by Lucilius (Lucil. 597–8; 599–600 M. = 729–30; 727–8 W.), is the presentation of formerly respected noble individuals in reduced circumstances,[80] often due to reversals of fortune, in a few cases also to old age. Some of these figures manage to maintain their nobility and are recognized by other characters on the basis of their noble bearing or innate virtues.[81]

That virtue is regarded as a key feature of a noble man's character irrespective of his fortune is apparent from the famous line addressed by

---

[79] Cf. e.g. *Trag.* 42–4; 50; 162–3; 206–8 R.³ = 13–15; 324; 129–30; 170–2 W.; Serv. auct. on Verg. *Aen.* 8.130.

[80] Cf. e.g. *Trag.* 86; 339–40; 349; 350; 374–5; 613–16; 617 R.³ = 50; 333–4; 345; 346; 335–6; 629–32 W.; on the role of fortune cf. *Trag.* 109–10; 179–82 R.³ = 68–9; 139–42 W.; on the role of old age cf. *Trag.* 56; 67–8; 85; 114; 245 R.³ = 325; 30–1; 49; 74; 210 W.

[81] Cf. esp. *Trag.* 88–9; 187–8; 339–40; 613–16; 618; 619–20 R.³ = 51–2; 151–2; 333–4; 629–31; 633; 625–6 W.

Ajax to his son Eurysaces, which is different in Accius from the model in Sophocles (Soph. *Aj.* 550–1: ὦ παῖ, γένοιο πατρὸς εὐτυχέστερος, / τὰ δ' ἄλλ' ὁμοῖος· καὶ γένοι' ἂν οὐ κακός. – 'My son, may you be more fortunate than your father, but in other respects like him; you could not then be bad.' [trans. A. F. Garvie]): Sophocles' 'in other respects' as a contrast to fortune has been replaced by *virtus* (*Trag.* 156 R.³ = 123 W.: *virtuti sis par, dispar fortunis patris.* – 'Be equal to your father in virtue, unequal in fortune.'). This agrees with the significant role of morally upright behaviour in Accius, and moral observations tend to be phrased in sententious style.[82]

The role of gods in Accius' plays is twofold: on the one hand they are regarded as responsible for events and are addressed in prayers (*Trag.* 62–3; 159; 167–8 R.³ = 24–5; 126; 153–4 W.); on the other hand there is doubt as to whether gods care for humans (*Trag.* 142–3 R.³ = 93–4 W.; cf. Soph. *Ant.* 922–4) and criticism of the seer Calchas (*Trag.* 169–70; 171–3 R.³ = 134–5; 136–7 W.). Accius has two plays, *Bacchae* and *Stasiastae vel Tropaeum Liberi*, that dramatize direct confrontations of human beings with a god, to the disadvantage of the humans.

There are almost no discussions that could unreservedly be called 'philosophical', of the type prominent in Pacuvius. This might be coincidence, due to the vicissitudes of transmission. However, Cicero uses quotations from Accius to illustrate ways of drawing character as well as forms and tones of speaking (e.g. Cic. *De or.* 3.217–9; *Off.* 1.97; *Tusc.* 2.19; 2.33; 3.62), but rarely discusses the views, actions and argumentative techniques of Accius' figures – virtually only with reference to Atreus (Cic. *Nat. D.* 3.68; *Planc.* 59; *Sest.* 102) – yet he does so more frequently with regard to characters in Pacuvius, Ennius, Caecilius or Terence.[83] In line with the times, Accius' oeuvre might therefore have shown a distinction between dramas and 'scholarly' discussions.

On the level of presentation, there are elaborate and graphic sketches of dramatic characters (by others), scenery and events, which must have appealed to the audience's imagination and made the plays more vivid; obvious examples are the description of the approach of the *Argo* by a shepherd who has never seen a ship before (*Trag.* 391–402; 403–6 R.³ = 381–96 W.), of (possibly) the discovery of Sinon near Troy by a fisherman (*Trag.* 128–9; 130 R.³ = 248–9; 250 W.) or of Philocteta's abode on Lemnos (*Trag.* 525–36 R.³ = 527–40 W.), the remains of what must have been

---

[82] Cf. Acc. *Trag.* 109–10; 154–4ᵃ; 193; 272; 296 R.³ = 68–9; 120–1; 157; 263; 274 W.

[83] Cf. e.g. Cic. *Div.* 1.131; *De or.* 2.155; *Rep.* 1.30; *Tusc.* 2.48–50; 4.68–9; *Amic.* 24; 64; *Fin.* 2.41; 5.63; *Sen.* 24–6; *Nat. D.* 3.65; 3.72–3; *Rosc. Am.* 46–7; *Cael.* 37–8; *Fam.* 7.6.1.

messenger speeches narrating Atreus' murder of the children (*Trag.* 219; 220–2 R.³ = 186; 187–9 W.) or the behaviour of Bacchants (*Trag.* 256; 257; 258 R.³ = 219; 221; 220 W.), or a report about the storm that scattered the Greeks on their return from Troy (*Trag.* 33; 34 R.³ = 237; 238 W.).

Accius' dramatic corpus is characterized by a sophisticated use of language: he employed rich linguistic ornamentation for colourful and impressive descriptions, to support a flamboyant characterization of the protagonists, to ennoble sentiments of heroism and moral courage and to reinforce the expression of emotions. Later ancient writers recorded the fact that recipients recognized Accius' rhetorical skill, and he was credited with a high, forceful and polished style (cf. Ov. *Am.* 1.15.19; Hor. *Epist.* 2.1.56; Quint. *Inst.* 10.1.97), though others continued Lucilius' criticism of artificial and old-fashioned language (cf. Lucil. 650 M. = 675 W.; Pers. 1.76–8; Mart. 11.90; Tac. *Dial.* 20.5; 21.7). The influence of contemporary rhetoric on Accius' tragedies is obvious, not only in the wording, but also in structural techniques; there are set speeches in dramatic speaking contests, so much so that Accius was allegedly asked why he did not plead in the Forum although this was done so forcefully in his tragedies (cf. Quint. *Inst.* 5.13.43). Further, titles such as *Bacchae* or *Stasiastae* point to the involvement of choruses, which is corroborated by fragments. In these examples the groups that constitute the choruses are integral to the plots, and Accius would therefore not be liable to the criticism that he levelled against Euripides' inorganic use of choruses (*Did.* 11–12 W. = *Gram.* 9–10 D.).

As for meaning and impact, various scholars have put forward the theory that Accius' dramas are 'political' in that they react to significant developments during his lifetime, such as the activities of the Gracchi or the introduction of foreign cults into Rome, and that they exploit myth to make specific statements about Roman history, particularly Rome's early history, and thus help to consolidate the Romans' view of themselves.[84] Both points are valid in a broad sense; it is, however, more difficult and questionable to pin down precise references to individual people or events.[85]

When they were revived in Cicero's time, Accius' plays, like those of other playwrights, were exploited politically (cf. Cic. *Phil.* 1.36; *Att.* 16.2.3; 16.5.1; *Sest.* 120–3). Yet later evidence can give conflicting information

---

[84] See generally Boyle 2006: 123–42.

[85] Santorelli (1980) calls for focusing not only on Accius as the learned philologist, but also on Accius as a poet keenly interested in the society of his time. However, not all theories on areas touched by the poet or on precise connections to particular circumstances that have been put forward by modern scholars can be verified (for possible connections to contemporary issues see e.g. Santorelli 1980; Dangel 1990; Beacham 1991: 124; Baldarelli 2004: 38–40, 305, 314–17; on this see Goldberg 2007b: 579–80).

about the original play: the imperial tragic playwright Seneca quotes a line that has been attributed to Accius' *Atreus* (*Trag.* 203–4 R.³ = 168 W.), the famous dictum 'let them hate as long as they fear' (*oderint dum metuant*), in one of his philosophical treatises (Sen. *Dial.* 3.20.4); he calls this utterance 'dreadful and odious' (*dira et abominanda*) and adds the comment: 'You would know that it was written in the times of Sulla.' (*Sullano scias saeculo scriptam*). If this description were accurate, it would date the tragedy to the early decades of the first century BCE; this would identify it as one of Accius' last plays and also as a new play that presents the audience with a reaction to and comment on contemporary politics.

According to Gellius, however, the young Accius visited the elderly Pacuvius and read his *Atreus* to him (Gell. *NA* 13.2). This description would turn *Atreus* into a rather early play, one of Accius' first attempts, written while Pacuvius was still alive, which would exclude references to Sulla. Unfortunately, it is uncertain how much weight can be attributed to either of the two sources, which focus on different aspects. Seneca might have transferred conditions valid in his own time (and suitable to his argument) back to Accius' time and thus inferred a composition date, while the other story might have used a quintessentially Accian play as a paradigmatic example to illustrate the relationship between two tragic poets.

The facts that even in antiquity there does not seem to have been a unanimous dating of at least this play and that its interpretation might be subject to the recipient's agenda should warn modern scholars against identifying precise references or dates. Nevertheless, it is true that tyrants are ubiquitous in Accius' dramatic output, and this is likely to be a reaction to the political situation in the late second and early first centuries BCE, which saw an increase in powerful individuals. Moreover, scattered fragments show that the dramas addressed various aspects that could be connected to the social and political struggles in Accius' period. These aspects include the legitimization of power and its potential abuse, elements of a Republican constitution, the role of honour in public life, the conditions for the populace and the relationship between influential individuals as well as between ruler and ruled.[86]

Emphasis on dealings with foreign peoples is reduced in comparison with Pacuvius' plays; instead Accius' dramas touch upon problems that might

---

[86] One could even venture to link the importance of genealogy and of the status and the legitimization provided thereby with the increasing influx of 'new men' to Rome and the Roman Senate (on 'new men in the Roman senate' see Wiseman 1971).

occur within a community; this accords with the fact that the focus of
Rome's political activities had shifted from wars against external enemies
to internal struggles within Italy or Rome itself. For instance, the two
Bacchic plays (*Bacchae, Stasiastae vel Tropaeum Liberi*) discuss the impact
of foreign cults, but concentrate on the receiving end. A connection of
these plays with the actual influx of these cults to Rome, which triggered
the *Senatus consultum de Bacchanalibus* in 186 BCE, is unlikely since these
events would no longer be topical. The Bacchic myths can, however, be
seen as a means 'to explore the terrible consequences within a community
which had suffered a deep internal division over the reception of a new
idea or policy'.[87]

Against this background it is noteworthy that Accius composed a play
with the rather unspecific title *Hellenes*; its two remaining fragments indicate that it dealt with warfare. As there is talk of an attack on city walls
(*Trag.* 385 R.³ = 377 W.), it may have focused on the Greeks before Troy (or
another town) and given a portrayal of their ideas and tactics.[88] That the
other fragment talks about people 'who regard all other things as guiltless
apart from disgraceful behaviour' (*Trag.* 384 R.³ = 376 W.: *qui nisi probrum
omnia alia indelicta aestimant*) might suggest that Greeks were presented
as a people with weird views. The drama would then have taken up a
traditional feature of Republican tragedy, reasserting Roman identity and
values against those of other peoples. Such a perspective might also be valid
for *Deiphobus*, in which Greeks and their trickery concerning the Wooden
Horse seem to have been condemned. In an environment of internal strife
the Romans' own values were highlighted.

Accius, the scholar poet, continued developments in Roman tragedy that
can already be seen in Pacuvius, with whom he is sometimes paired by
later writers; they are to be regarded as characteristic of a later stage of
Republican drama. These include the penchant for meaningful and effective sections or versions of myths, often not yet shown on the Roman
stage, the presentation of exaggerated scenes and the use of rhetorical, artificial language. Further, Accius' grammatical interests lead to a 'scholarly'
approach to tragedy, in full awareness of preceding poetry and relevant
scholarly literature. A rather academic approach to writing drama and a

---

[87] See Flower 2000: 30; for other views see e.g. Dangel 1995: 338–9.

[88] Dangel (1995: 289), in developing Ribbeck's considerations (1875: 425–31), assumes that the play
dealt with Peleus, Achilles' father. Yet this view seems largely governed by her intention of turning
the piece into an introduction to the cycle of Achilles (see above and n. 77); moreover, there is not
enough evidence for such a specific attribution.

tendency to use plays to present antiquarian questions are also observable in Atta's contemporary togatae.

Literary discussions in Accius' treatises recall topics mentioned in Terence's and Afranius' prologues. These poets had already practised literary criticism, voicing it in (detached) parts of their plays; Ennius had metaphorically described his relationship to Homer in the first book of his *Annales*. Beyond these forerunners, Accius was the first Roman dramatist to treat questions of literary history and dramatic techniques in separate treatises. Thus, just like Cicero in the field of oratory and rhetoric slightly later, he was active in both theory and practice.

In line with Roman dramatic tradition, Accius' plays were made exciting by colourful descriptions and stunning effects; they were relevant to the time in bringing issues onto the stage that could be applied to the contemporary situation. However, if the statement that poets are beaten more often by the 'excessive gullibility or tastelessness' of audiences than by their own faults (*Pragm.* 5–6 W. = *Gram.* 18–21 D.) reflects Accius' own experiences, it might indicate that he was not entirely happy with audience reactions.

4.6 T. MACCIUS PLAUTUS

Titus Maccius Plautus (*c.* 250–184 BCE) was the first Roman dramatic poet to concentrate on one dramatic genre only. He is also the earliest Roman dramatist from whom complete plays survive and the Roman playwright from whom the greatest number of dramas is extant; therefore he is the earliest representative of palliata for whom characteristics can be identified with a greater degree of certainty.[89]

Plautus came from the Umbrian town of Sarsina.[90] His Roman *tria nomina* are unusual for an Umbrian, and it has therefore been assumed that they are meant to express his Roman aspirations (Roman *praenomen* Titus), his Umbrian origin (*cognomen* Plautus, derived from the Umbrian *plotus*,

[89] On Plautus see e.g. Leo 1912; Fraenkel (1922/1960) 2007; Duckworth 1952: 49–56; Beare 1964: 56–69; Arnott 1975: 28–45, 1977; Sandbach 1977: 118–34; Blänsdorf 1978: 135–222; Chiarini 1979; Zagagi 1980; Drury 1982: 808–12; Konstan 1983: 33–114, 142–64; N. W. Slater 1985/2000; Segal 1987; Gruen 1990: 124–57; Petrone 1992: 534–85; Anderson 1993; Conte 1994: 49–64; Moore 1998a; Franko 2001; Blänsdorf in Suerbaum 2002: 183–228; Maurach 2005: 62–5; N. J. Lowe 2008: 97–114; bibliography in Hanson 1965/6; Gaiser 1972; Hughes 1975; Fogazza 1976 [1978]; Segal 1981; Bubel 1992; Blänsdorf in Suerbaum 2002; for the history of scholarship see introduction to Fraenkel 2007 (see also Wiles 1988); on text and transmission see Tarrant 1983; Zwierlein 1990–92; Deufert 2002 (Zwierlein's and Deufert's theory that a great deal of the present text is the work of a later interpolator has not won general acceptance); on Plautus' contemporary popularity see Parker 1996.
[90] Cf. Fest., p. 274.12–14 L.; Hieron. *Ab Abr.* 1817, 200 BCE (p. 135h Helm); Plaut. *Mostell.* 770.

'flatfoot') and his background as mime and Atellana actor (*nomen gentile* Maccius, recalling Maccus, one of the stock characters of the Atellana).[91] Even though this explanation must remain uncertain, it agrees with the portrait that anecdotal evidence on Plautus' life indicates.

Ancient writers transmit the fact that Plautus made money at the theatre (Gell. *NA* 3.3.14: *in operis artificum scaenicorum*), which most probably refers to a technical or organizational activity rather than to writing poetry. According to those sources he later lost his fortune in trade and then had to earn his living by working in a mill, during which time he still wrote three comedies.[92] Cicero says that Plautus died in 184 BCE (Cic. *Brut.* 60), but this may just have been the last recorded date of a production of one of his plays. Since Cicero elsewhere implies that Plautus was an 'old man' (*senex*) when his *Truculentus* and *Pseudolus* (191 BCE: Did. on Plaut. *Pseud.*) were produced (Cic. *Sen.* 50), he was born probably around 250 BCE.

At the start of his career Plautus will have overlapped with the older Naevius; later on Caecilius Statius will have started to produce palliatae. As for poets of other dramatic genres, Plautus coincided with Ennius, Pacuvius and presumably Titinius. Plautus' main predecessor in the dramatic genre of palliata was Naevius: Plautus seems to have developed and elaborated upon the basis Naevius had provided. It is perhaps a reflection of this connection that the two poets are sometimes mentioned together by later ancient writers (e.g. Cic. *De or.* 3.45; *Rep.* 4.11).

Plautus was also a contemporary of Cato, and his main period of activity falls in the time of and just after the Second Punic War (cf. Gell. *NA* 17.21.46–7). Plautus' earliest extant comedies have tentatively been dated to the last decade of the third century BCE, and Cicero testifies to the fact that Naevius and Plautus had produced numerous comedies before 197 BCE (Cic. *Brut.* 73). The majority of Plautus' preserved comedies seem to belong to the last years of the Second Punic War and subsequent decades, although few can be dated precisely.[93] For some comedies dates have been proposed on the basis of allusions to contemporary individuals and events (though the identification of some of those is doubtful) and of formal characteristics of the plays such as the quantity of song and the metrical structure.

---

[91] See Blänsdorf in Suerbaum 2002: 185. An alternative explanation in N. J. Lowe 2008: 97: '*Plautus* is a variant form of *planipes* ("flatfoot"), attested as a nickname for performers in the barefoot Latin mime; *Maccius* means "son of Maccus", the buffoonish hero of the Oscan *fabula Atellana*; while even the innocuous-looking praenomen Titus was used as a pet name for the male organ of business.'

[92] Cf. Gell. *NA* 3.3.14; Hieron. *Ab Abr.* 1817, 200 BCE (p. 135h Helm).

[93] Cf. *Stichus*: 200 BCE (cf. Did.); *Pseudolus*: 191 BCE (cf. Did.); *Truculentus*, *Pseudolus*: in old age (cf. Cic. *Sen.* 50).

Irrespective of exact chronological details, Plautus seems to have been active in Rome as a successful dramatist for more than two decades around 200 BCE. Modern scholars have seen an indication of his popularity in the fact that all known instances of 'repetitions for religious reasons' (*instaurationes*) of entire festivals (cf. e.g. Liv. 31.50.3) fall within the period of Plautus' career, as excuses for those repetitions may have been sought in order to have further performances of popular dramas.[94] This theory is not invalidated by possible other reasons of a religious or political nature, since those can be backed up by the prospect of the production of popular dramas.

During his creative period Plautus must have been a prolific poet. And in addition to his genuine output, further plays later circulated under his name; Gellius reports a figure of 130 plays (Gell. *NA* 3.3.11). Because of uncertainties over authorship Plautus was one of the earliest Republican playwrights to become the object of scholarly discussion, when ancient critics tried to distinguish the genuine from the spurious plays. Various attempts were made until Varro identified a core of twenty-one comedies that were accepted as genuine by everyone (cf. Gell. *NA* 3.3). These were called *fabulae Varronianae*; and it is virtually certain that the surviving twenty-one (almost complete) comedies are these *fabulae Varronianae*. In addition to the twenty-one comedies transmitted in the manuscripts, thirty-four further titles (including two double titles) with eighty-eight fragments and another eighty-two fragments from unknown comedies survive, some of which may be genuine.

According to Gellius (Gell. *NA* 3.3.1; 3.3.3; cf. also Cic. *Fam.* 9.16.4), criteria for critics to regard comedies attributed to Plautus as genuine were their trust in 'Plautus himself and the characteristics of his mind and diction' (*ipsi Plauto moribusque ingeni atque linguae eius*) or their being influenced 'by the style and wittiness of the language typical of Plautus' (*filo atque facetia sermonis Plauto congruentis*). Obviously ancient scholars believed that they could identify particular qualities in Plautus' genuine plays, which made his dramatic poetry distinctive and thus revealed spurious works. The perception of a special status for Plautus is also indicated by another piece of ancient evidence, the well-known epitaph, allegedly written by himself (cf. Gell. *NA* 1.24.3): it says that 'comedy mourns, the stage is deserted' after Plautus' death. Here Plautus is portrayed as the one

---

[94] See Taylor 1937: 295; Owens 2000: 386 and n. 7. For a list of *instaurationes* of *Ludi Romani* and *Ludi plebeii* (with references) see Taylor 1937: 292; Bernstein 1998: 283–4; for some further considerations on reasons for *instaurationes* see Bernstein 1998: 282–91.

and only comic writer, who represents comedy and cannot be replaced; that laughter, play and wit and also 'countless rhythms' (*numeri innumeri*) wept at his death indicates that mastery of the comic genre and metrical versatility were seen as characteristics of Plautus.

The available evidence supports the notion that certain features, albeit also found in other poets to a lesser extent, were particularly distinctive of Plautus. One such characteristic of Plautus' plays is their metrical variety, displayed particularly by so-called 'songs' (*cantica*). As Roman playwrights turned spoken monologues and dialogues in the Greek models into accompanied utterances and reduced choral parts, there was a need to compose songs for individual actors, and those in Plautus exhibit particular metrical virtuosity, while reinforcing the atmosphere of the respective scenes (see ch. 5.6).

Another, connected element is Plautus' linguistic exuberance and inventiveness, which was already recognized by ancient scholars.[95] His language was admired particularly by the archaist Fronto; and no writer is recorded as having criticized Plautus' word-formations, as is the case with contemporary tragic poets. His style includes hyperbolic comparisons, nonce-formations, bizarre identifications, riddles, military imagery in inappropriate contexts, jokes exploiting formulae and concepts of Roman law as well as comparisons with figures from myth.[96]

As Plautus' metrical and linguistic creativity is consistent across his oeuvre, it must be independent of the possible sources for his comedies. Plautus has some of his prologue speakers identify the title and/or the author of a Greek drama that has served as the basis. This shows that the starting points for his comedies were dramas of Greek New Comedy by a variety of poets such as Menander, Diphilus and Philemon, perhaps occasionally also works of Middle Comedy. Plautus appropriated those into Latin, sometimes changing the title. While some prologues state that he turned the play into 'Latin' (*Cas.* 31–4; *Poen.* 53–4), others say that he turned it 'barbarian' (*Asin.* 11; *Trin.* 19). This does not refer to an inferior form of transposition, but rather adopts a Greek perspective, with the playwright ridiculing his own activity.[97]

---

[95] Cf. Varro, *Sat. Men.* 399 B.; Quint. *Inst.* 10.1.99; Fronto, *Ep. ad M. Caes. et inv.* 4.3.2 (pp. 56–7 v.d.H.).

[96] On Plautus' style and language see e.g. Blänsdorf 1978: 206–14; on forms of expression and argument see Blänsdorf 1967.

[97] For an interpretation of *barbarus* as a term expressing self-confidence and the aim of distinguishing oneself see Petrone 1983: 33–7; on *barbarus* see also Jocelyn 1969: 36.

While it is certain that Plautus worked from Greek models and adapted them for the Roman stage, the extent and effect of these changes have long been one of the major topics in Plautine scholarship, connected with a search for 'lost Greek originals' and the respective image of Plautus as a poet (see also ch. 5.1). Since none of the Greek plays used by Plautus survives intact, there is a limited basis for objective description. This is why comparisons have often been founded on particular concepts of characteristics of Greek and Roman plays: thus, on the assumption of strictly logical plots, a subtle and humane tone and morally edifying results as characteristics of Greek comedies, some critics have thought that Plautus did not care about economical and internally consistent plot-construction and that therefore passages containing farcical humour, bantering slaves or similar characteristics are owed to Plautus, who was interested primarily in the comic impact of individual scenes. Scholars used to see him, like other Republican playwrights, as rather indebted to Greek models, but have now come to regard him as more 'original'.[98] Just what this originality consists in is still a matter of debate; but overall Plautus is credited at least with formal changes, structural modifications, the elaboration of stock characters, the addition of metatheatrical elements and the insertion of Roman touches; and it is becoming more and more accepted that his comedies are poetic creations in their own right.

The best piece of actual evidence is a papyrus fragment discovered and identified in the twentieth century, which must come from Menander's *Dis exapaton* (*P. Oxy.* sine numero [O13]), compared with a section of *Bacchides* (*Bacch.* 494–562), which is Plautus' version of the same sequence. These passages show that easy, clear-cut answers are difficult: in this case Plautus has followed the sense and the main course of action in the Greek play closely, while he has changed the dramatic form, both on the micro-level of language and metre and on the macro-level of the organization of scenes. For instance, the style is more pompous and burlesque; common names have been altered to Greek-speaking names (e.g. the slave's name Syros turned into Chrysalus); act-break and choral interlude have been removed in line with the conventions of Roman drama; some scenes and speeches have been omitted, while others have been enlarged and/or given a new position. Hence suspense is prolonged and dramatic irony further exploited, moral aspects are underlined, and the sequence is more effective

---

[98] For an overview of research into Plautus' 'originality' and criteria see Blänsdorf 1996: 133–6; for a discussion of approaches to Plautus' 'models' see Danese 2002. Arnott (1977) had already called for studying Plautus' plays in their extant form.

theatrically: there is play on dramatic conventions, and a discussion on the character of friendship is added, full of dramatic irony, since one of the young men holds off revealing to the other that the description of a false friend actually applies to him in the speaker's view, which eventually prepares an explanation of the whole situation (misunderstandings due to the existence of two sisters with the same name).[99]

All this happening in just one section indicates that Plautus was capable of various ways of transposing, exhibiting different degrees of independence. The poet himself seems to have regarded his method of composition as creative, occasionally surpassing Greek paradigms, if one is to believe what is put in the mouth of a scheming slave (*Mostell.* 1149–51). Indeed Terence attests to a method of rather free translation for Plautus as well as for Naevius and Ennius (Ter. *An.* 18–21). Plautus is therefore likely to have made choices about how to transform Greek plays on a case-by-case basis, which points to poetic principles for the composition of dramas. In this context it is interesting to note that Cicero characterizes Plautus' kind of wit and joking as 'elegant, polite, intelligent, witty' (*elegans, urbanum, ingeniosum, facetum*), aligns him with Greek Old Comedy and distinguishes this practice from a more base and vulgar kind of joking (Cic. *Off.* 1.104; cf. also August. *De civ. D.* 2.8).[100] In Cicero's view at least, Plautus' comedy is therefore not crude entertainment, but amusing in a more refined way.

That Plautus chose and adapted models thoughtfully is also indicated by his shaping of the standard New Comedy plot (see ch. 3.3). In many cases the poet handles the distribution of information carefully so that individual figures (and the audience) learn everything they need to know to follow the action at the respective places. The final solution is frequently brought about by revelations unforeseen by the protagonists such as the actual identity or the sudden appearance of characters. The plot might receive additional tension when the situation had initially appeared hopeless. The slaves' intrigues do not always continue as planned (or as apparently planned); (seemingly) unexpected turns and additional twists often contribute to their final success.

---

[99] On the comparison between the *Bacchides* passage and the corresponding Menander fragment see e.g. Bain 1979; Barsby 1986 ad loc.; Anderson 1993: 3–29.

[100] Horace admits that earlier Romans praised Plautus' 'rhythms and wit' (Hor. *Ars P.* 270–4), but for him this indicates that both witty style and the composition of verses as well as the taste of earlier generations were not as refined as they were in his time. Zillinger (1911: 25) maintains that Cicero's emphasis is on the presence of refined jokes in more serious books rather than on their occurrence in Plautus. But Cicero asserts a more sophisticated way of joking equally for both Plautus and philosophical writings.

Even though the eventual solution often becomes possible only through unexpected incidents or discoveries, what is carefully organized is how characters react to these turns of events and integrate them into their plans or change those accordingly. Hence activities and intentions of various characters and new circumstances due to the workings of 'chance' combined and exploited by the protagonists lead to success. This is most obvious when intrigues engineered by clever slaves are conceived, developed and adapted in a series of monologues and asides in front of the audience, as in the case of the slaves Tranio in *Mostellaria* and Pseudolus in *Pseudolus* (cf. also *Epid.* 81–101). Both compare what they do to a poet creating a story (*Mostell.* 510; *Pseud.* 401–4a; cf. also *Cas.* 860–1): in arranging the intrigue, appearing to develop it on the spot and assigning certain roles to other characters, the scheming slaves assume a position that is comparable to the role of a poet or impresario.

In *Pseudolus* the poet adds a continuous secondary level to Pseudolus' actions, consisting of comments on the typical characteristics and duties of comedy slaves: in his soliloquies Pseudolus reflects upon what is expected of him, how he will deal with it and how sudden events affect his scheming.[101] The playwright seems almost fed up with producing stock plots and therefore starts playing with conventions. According to Pseudolus (*Pseud.* 401–4a), a poet comes up with something that is, albeit all lie, similar to truth, i.e. probable (cf. Arist. *Poet.* 9). This may be applied to the poet Plautus; for what is presented in his comedies is fictional and sometimes unexpected, but it is not altogether unlikely or impossible; a greater influence of chance is accepted for events leading up to the plot of the play. In some cases Plautus even points out in the prologue that the story is a construct arranged by the poet and demands corresponding imagination on the part of audiences (e.g. *Cas.*, *Merc.*).[102]

This careful plot construction, where the distribution of information is tightly controlled and sudden events happen at the right points in time and are then put to clever use, indicates that Plautus did not transpose any plot according to a standard method, but rather selected models and adapted them according to his own poetic agenda. This implies that he did not create scenes and characters for the benefit of their immediate comic effect without worrying about the coherence of the plot. That Plautus was fully aware of what he was doing is further indicated by so-called

---

[101] On metatheatrical aspects in *Pseudolus* see e.g. N. W. Slater 1985: 118–46.

[102] Sharrock (2009: 131–40) even sees the motif of the 'playwright as slave' as a clever way of presenting comedy as something seemingly assembled at random, but actually subtle and sophisticated.

metatheatrical elements, i.e. interruptions of the dramatic illusion, actors' utterances revealing their awareness of being actors in a drama, playing with or commenting on standard comic conventions or addresses to the audience outside prologues (see ch. 5.3).

The stories constructed for his comedies are used by Plautus to present various types of conflicts that arise from love affairs in relation to the conventions of society. Plots thus comment on different kinds of love, social customs, justice and punishment, morally correct behaviour, faithfulness and loyalty or dealings with foreigners. There are no direct topical statements, and it is hard to determine the playwright's point of view, but issues discussed are relevant to contemporary Roman society: for instance, dealing with foreigners, presenting moral values and doing one's duties accord with a time of war and of expansion of the Roman Empire; the contrast between stern morality and extravagant, debauched living, criticism of luxury, questions of education and 'philosophical' thoughts are appropriate to a period that was also characterized by an influx of Greek culture.[103]

In order to bring such themes and situations onto the stage, Plautus exploited the freedom provided by an imprecise and stylized Greek setting; he thus tackled potentially serious issues in a comic environment. At the same time the poet might incorporate topics, style and conventions of serious drama. On the one hand, there is parody of tragedy and ridicule of tragic conventions when those occur in inappropriate surroundings or when specific scenes and verses are alluded to.[104] On the other hand, Plautus appropriated elements of tragedy, apparently without the intention of an incongruous clash. This is particularly true for plays that do not comply with the standard comedy plot, most notably *Amphitruo*, which Plautus defines as a 'tragicomedy' (*Amph.* 50–63), but also *Captivi* or *Rudens*, which both exhibit features recalling tragedies and where, at least in *Captivi*, Plautus points to deviations from the standard comedy set-up and the similarity to situations in tragedy (*Capt.* 55–62; 1029–36).

As Roman playwrights abolished choral songs as act-divisions and gave musical parts to individual actors, choruses were no longer necessary. No surviving Roman comedy has choruses in the strict sense. In two of Plautus' plays, *Poenulus* and *Rudens*, there are groups of identical characters

---

[103] For considerations on the nature of the relationship between Plautus' dramas and contemporary reality see Gruen 1990: 124–57 passim; for considerations on the topical relevance of *Stichus* (200 BCE) see Owens 2000.

[104] Cf. esp. *Pseud.* 707: *ut paratragoedat carnufex!* ('how the rascal para-tragedizes!'), commenting on an exaggerated speech full of diminutives, alliterations and emphasis on the number three; cf. also *Cas.* 759–62; *Pers.* 11–12; 712–13; *Pseud.* 771–2; *Bacch.* 933. See ch. 5.4.

(advocates and fishermen) who enter and exit together and therefore could be called 'choruses' although they appear only in a single scene each (*Poen.* III; *Rud.* II 1–2). A late grammatical source claims that Plautus had choruses in his comedies (*Lib. gloss.* 1.7); it also says that Plautus did so after the example of the Greeks.[105] Modern scholars have assumed instead that Plautus' 'choruses' were modelled on contemporary Roman tragedy.[106] At any rate Plautus' 'choruses', like those of Republican tragedy, are involved in the action.

Apart from tragedy, Plautus was familiar with Atellana. The uncertain evidence of his personal name aside, he uses terms that describe stock figures of Atellanae, and in some instances he seems to interpret those as prototypes exhibiting particular, low and vulgar characteristics (*Asin.* 11; *Bacch.* 1088; *Merc.* 10; *Rud.* 535–6). Despite problems of interpretation, these passages could indicate that Plautus regarded his characters as different from the stock figures of Atellanae. Indeed, although his characters have recurrent roles and functions, they have some individuality, which is observable even on the level of personal names.

Horace, however, complains that Plautus' parasites are too similar to the Dossennus of Atellanae (Hor. *Epist.* 2.1.170b–6). In his argument this is one example illustrating the widespread, yet incorrect opinion that comedy requires less effort and attention from playwrights than tragedy (Hor. *Epist.* 2.1.168–70a). Thus the passage seems designed to show Plautus' negligence in composition and character-drawing, which does not agree with Horace's standards of polishing. The statement is apparently intended to indicate that Plautus is so careless that he does not present a proper palliata parasite, but rather an Atellana character.[107] Plautus himself seems to have been convinced that his dramatic genre is *comoedia* and is distinguished from *tragoedia*. Some of the elements in his comedies that recall impromptu farce might have been influenced by indigenous dramatic traditions,[108] but this connection is not what he chose to highlight.

Focusing on the functions and achievements of characters of lower social status, some scholars have put forward the theory that the spirit of Plautine comedy is 'Saturnalian', which denotes a temporary abolition or inversion

---

[105] Other ancient sources say that there was no chorus in Roman comedy (Donat. on Ter. *Eun., praef.* 1.5; Euanth. *Fab.* 3.1; Diom. *Ars* 3, *Gramm. Lat.* I, p. 491.20–30).

[106] See J. C. B. Lowe 1990. On the chorus in Greek fourth-century tragedy see Sifakis 1967: 113–20; on the comic chorus in the fourth century BCE see Hunter 1979.

[107] On the interpretation of this difficult passage see also ch. 3.5 and n. 140.

[108] On the possible influence of native Italic comedy on Plautus see e.g. Little 1938; Lefèvre *et al.* 1991.

of conventions.[109] Others have thought that the dramas rather serve to reaffirm the integrity of the citizen group, since rules are not abandoned, but used against outsiders (which does not shatter the moral code) or turned against members such as fathers, who are normally capable of exploiting them in their own interest.[110] Perhaps Plautine comedy is a bit of both, though this may be a somewhat reductive description: it is true that in the world of comedy some rules continue to be valid (e.g. slaves still fear punishment; marriage between free-born citizens is the only acceptable form of a permanent love affair; money has to be paid at a certain time to carry out transactions); at the same time figures such as slaves who are not particularly powerful or adventurous in real life have recourse to unusual means, take risks and are able to realize plans and achieve results. Such a situation is possible because the plays are set in a Greek-based fictional environment rather than in Rome. What is shown is potential dangers and solutions; this eventually reinforces society as established in Rome, particularly as there is a return to social and moral order at the end: correct identities and relationships are discovered, dishonest characters are punished, marriages take place, and slaves lose their prominent position.

Although he was the first Roman dramatic poet to be active in a single dramatic genre only, Plautus demonstrates a remarkable variety in form and meaning of plots within this genre.

4.7 CAECILIUS STATIUS

Caecilius Statius (*c.* 230/20–168/7 BCE) was a palliata poet active between Plautus and Terence.[111] He was an Insubrian Gaul, perhaps from Mediolanum (modern Milan) (cf. Hieron. *Ab Abr.* 1838, 179 BCE [p. 138b Helm]), and probably came to Rome as a slave. According to Gellius, his servile origin explains the name Caecilius Statius (Gell. *NA* 4.20.12–13). Jerome reports that Caecilius flourished in 179 BCE and died in 168 BCE (Hieron. *Ab Abr.* 1838, 179 BCE [p. 138b Helm]).

Caecilius can be regarded as a contemporary of the tragic poet Pacuvius (cf. Cic. *Brut.* 258), since the inferred birthdates of both playwrights fall around 220 BCE, even though Caecilius died much earlier than Pacuvius.

---

[109] See e.g. Segal 1987; Lefèvre 1988. Chiarini (1979 passim) connects Plautine comedy more generally with a festival environment. See also ch. 3.3.

[110] See Konstan 1983: 29–31.

[111] On Caecilius Statius see e.g. Duckworth 1952: 46–9; Beare 1964: 85–90; J. Wright 1974: 87–126; Juhnke 1978: 224–7; Pociña Pérez 1980; Drury 1982: 813–14; Petrone 1992: 586–90; Conte 1994: 65–7; Blänsdorf in Suerbaum 2002: 229–31 (with bibliography).

Additionally, according to ancient sources, Pacuvius was Ennius' nephew and perhaps also his pupil (cf. Plin. *HN* 35.19; Varro, *Sat. Men.* 356 B.), and Caecilius was Ennius' house-mate (cf. Hieron. *Ab Abr.* 1838, 179 BCE [p. 138b Helm]). Thus both poets will have had intimate knowledge of the work of Ennius, who was the last Roman dramatist to write both serious and light dramas. Ennius' two successors each continued one of the two main forms of drama. At the start of his career Caecilius will have overlapped with Plautus, and he probably also experienced the work of Titinius.

Caecilius is typically discussed by modern scholars in comparison with Naevius and Plautus as his immediate predecessors and with Terence as his immediate successor. Caecilius' own palliatae have been transmitted only in fragments, which needs to be taken into account in comparisons. What remains are forty-two titles of comedies, almost three hundred (partly incomplete) lines quoted in later writers and, what is unique for Roman drama, a papyrus fragment (originally containing 550 lines) of the play '*Usurer or Money-lender*' (*Obolostates sive Faenerator*).[112]

Most of the titles of Caecilius' comedies are Greek, like those of Naevius and Terence, but unlike those of Plautus. The papyrus including the record of the drama's title proves that double titles giving both the Greek and the Latin form of the word or phrase could be used. A large number of titles found in Caecilius are also attested in Menander; several recall those of Philemon and some those of other writers of Greek New Comedy; a very few may relate to writers of Middle Comedy; some do not have a known Greek equivalent.[113] If this distribution of titles reflects the selection of models, this may indicate a tendency towards a more Hellenic, Menandrean outlook on comedy; in contrast to Naevius and Plautus, extant fragments exhibit only few Roman allusions.

Beyond the evidence to be inferred from titles, important testimony for Caecilius' relationship to Greek models is provided by later writers: in Cicero's considerations on the relative merits of original Greek texts and their transformations into Latin, Caecilius' *Synephebi* (taken from Menander) is included among the prototypical examples of Roman dramas (Cic. *Fin.* 1.4–5; *Opt. gen.* 18; see ch. 5.1). Cicero apparently thinks that all dramatists mentioned in this context have transformed Greek models into Latin versions that are well worth reading for Romans. Beyond such a broad

---

[112] On the papyrus from Herculaneum see Kleve 1996, 2001.

[113] Depending on how the title *Andria* (attested only at Non., p. 152.18–22 M. = 223 L.) is read, Caecilius might share one title with Terence (see ch. 5.1). This has troubled scholars, who have therefore read *Andrea* in a different interpretation (see documentation in e.g. Ribbeck 1898: 41–2).

assessment, Gellius provides valuable evidence on Caecilius' techniques of transposition, since he transmits extracts from Caecilius' *Plocium*, along with the corresponding verses from Menander's version, and comments on the adaptation (Gell. *NA* 2.23).[114]

Gellius criticizes Caecilius because he has changed and thereby worsened Menander's text. Indeed, Caecilius' 'translation' appears to be a relatively free version, while its assessment is another matter.[115] Naturally, there is the obvious adaptation of metre, word choice, style and similes to a Roman framework. Despite the original Greek plot and the retention of Greek names the setting and the world of ideas are given Roman colour: the Roman institution of 'taking the auspices' (*auspicium*) is referred to (*Pall.* 181–2 R.³ = 134–5 W.), and a public trial before the people in the Forum is envisaged (*Pall.* 184; 185 R.³ = 176; 175 W.).[116]

Further changes contribute to a different portrait of the figures talking and being talked about in these extracts and to a focus on other issues: even if the characters in the Latin version, such as the old man cheated out of a beautiful maidservant by his ugly wife, also describe their situation in general terms, they outline their problems more forcefully, express their feelings in a more personal manner, refer the consequences of actions to themselves and, in particular, are more conscious of their relationship to society as they fear poverty, gossip and disgrace. Caecilius has turned the Greek text into another play with a distinctive focus: his version both provides entertainment by exaggerations in the set-up and presents the characters' problems as relevant to Roman audiences.

Although it is hard to assess the overall dramatic impact of Caecilius' plays, apart from such insights into the composition of individual characters and scenes, he enjoyed high esteem in antiquity: his comedies seem to have had revivals till the end of the Republic; since Cicero quotes lines from Caecilius in his speeches, the audience must have been familiar with Caecilius' plays, his figures and their characteristics (see ch. 2.10). In *De optimo genere oratorum* Cicero says that Ennius might be called the greatest epic writer if one thought so, Pacuvius the greatest tragic poet and Caecilius 'perhaps' (*fortasse*) the greatest comic one (Cic. *Opt. gen.* 2). The high regard

---

[114] On the relationship between Menander's and Caecilius' *Plocium* see esp. Traina 1974: 41–53; Riedweg 1993 (with bibliography). Lennartz (1994: 89–94) thinks that Caecilius (like all Republican dramatists) either translated literally or left out clearly identifiable passages or replaced them with other material (see ch. 5.1). Büchner (1974: 14) assumes that Caecilius, in contrast to Plautus and Terence, translated rather literally.

[115] See Blume 1998: 166–7.

[116] Greek terms are retained in other plays (e.g. *Pall.* 223 R.³ = 214–15 W.: *mysteria*; 253 R.³ = 245 W.: *Attica*; 269 R.³ = 250 W.: *chlamyde*).

for Caecilius is corroborated by Volcacius Sedigitus' canon of the ten best writers of comedy, where Caecilius wins the first place (Gell. *NA* 15.24), by Quintilian's statement that the ancients extolled Caecilius (Quint. *Inst.* 10.1.99) and also by Gellius, who calls Caecilius (in a different context) 'this famous writer of comedies' (Gell. *NA* 4.20.13: *ille comoediarum poeta inclutus*).

However, Caecilius apparently had difficulties in having his plays staged at the start of his career. In the prologue to the third production of Terence's *Hecyra* (see ch. 4.9), the prologue speaker and actor-manager Ambivius Turpio says that what is happening to Terence now occurred to Caecilius before: Caecilius' plays were driven off the stage at their first productions, but Ambivius Turpio encouraged and supported the poet and had his dramas staged again; when the plays were fully performed and recognized, they were enjoyed and became established; the poet, as Ambivius Turpio says, was given back the place from which he had almost been ousted by opponents (Ter. *Hec.* 10–27).[117]

This information triggers the question of whether this controversy has left any traces in the text of Caecilius' plays, in a way similar to what is found in Terence. That Caecilius' palliatae included metatheatrical remarks is clear from the fragments (esp. *Pall.* 243–4 R.^{3} = 236–7 W.; see below); yet the position of such lines in the plays is unknown. However, there is one piece of evidence that might point to literary prologues: according to later critics Caecilius is reported to have said that Menander had appropriated Antiphanes' *Oionistes* from beginning to end for his *Deisidaimon* (cf. Porph. ap. Euseb. *Praep. evang.* 10.3.13 [465d]). This statement might have been not just an element of objective scholarship, but rather an argument in defence against charges of stealing material from earlier poets of the sort Terence was also confronted with, and it is most likely that it was in prologues that Caecilius argued for his position by referring to this precedent, as this would explain most easily how this item entered the secondary tradition.[118]

If, then, Caecilius as well as Terence were confronted by opponents, against whom they had to defend themselves, and were initially driven off the stage, but Ambivius Turpio was interested in both of them, the two poets might have shared particular characteristics, even if other ancient sources testify to differences in specific areas such as language or character

---

[117] Juhnke (1978: 225, 226) attributes Caecilius' failure first to an intrigue of his opponents and later to his poetic intentions disagreeing with public taste. The presentation in *Hecyra* favours the former reason.

[118] See Goldberg 2005b: 49. Leo (1913: 250) states that Caecilius had already had this type of prologue before Terence, but does not cite any evidence.

portrayal. Both poets may have written plays that presented something unusual or unexpected, yet whose potential for success was recognized by Ambivius Turpio (and perhaps rival poets). The story, though chronologically problematic, that Caecilius enjoyed the *Andria* when the young Terence read his play to him (cf. Suet./Donat. *Vita Ter.* 3; Hieron. *Ab Abr.* 1859, 158 BCE [p. 142a Helm]) also indicates that some affinity was perceived between them.

One reason for Caecilius' eventual success might have been sophisticated plot construction; Varro mentions that Caecilius excelled in the dramatic quality of his plots (Varro, *Sat. Men.* 399 B.).[119] Besides, according to another statement by Varro, Caecilius (and Trabea and Atilius) easily moved the emotions (Varro, fr. 40 Funaioli, ap. Char., *Gramm. Lat.* 1, p. 241.27–9).[120]

Caecilius' comic style apparently met with the disapproval of more intellectually minded critics: in his criticism of comedy Lucilius seems to have provided a kind of running commentary on a passage from Caecilius' *Hymnis* that features a desperate lover, overemphasizing and ridiculing his situation.[121] Even if the focus of this criticism is not entirely clear, it is not unlikely that Lucilius basically opposed the same characteristics in comedy as in tragedy; i.e. he criticized comedy for its swollen language and overblown representation, for instance when characters, such as the figure in the passage, declaim excessively about their great and perpetual love or when actions and feelings are described in an exaggerated way.

In the area of language, later authors corroborate Lucilius' criticism of Caecilius (cf. Cic. *Brut.* 258; *Att.* 7.3.10; Gell. *NA* 2.23.21). The fragments show that Caecilius, like all Republican poets, frequently used alliterations and other sound effects, enumerations of synonyms, Greek words, compounds, new coinages and puns;[122] there might also be parody of the epic topos of multiple tongues to praise adequately (*Pall.* 126–8 R.³ = 121–3 W.). In particular, the use of 'songs' (*cantica*) as well as the colourful and expressive language recall Plautus.

---

[119] See Blänsdorf 1974: 151 and n. 35.

[120] There is no clear evidence that Caecilius included elements of mime in his plays (so e.g. Blänsdorf 1978: 99): in Volcacius Sedigitus (cf. Gell. *NA* 15.24) the characterization *mimicus* is not attested; it is rather Gronovius' conjecture for the transmitted *comicus*; and in Gellius (*NA* 2.23.12) *mimica* is Gellius' own assessment of the character of Caecilius' play in comparison with Menander's version.

[121] Cf. e.g. Lucil. 808–9; 810; 815; 817; 818–19; 878; 879–80; 881; 882–3; 884–5; 886; 887; 888–9; 890; 891–3; 894 M. = 963; 964; 965; 897; 890–1; 900; 901–2; 903; 904–5; 906; 907; 908; 887–8; 892; 893–5; 889 W.

[122] Cf. e.g. *Pall.* 62–4; 138; 150; 190; 199–209; 211–14 R.³ = 57–8; 127; 143; 180; 189–99; 201–4 W.

As for the contents of Caecilius' plays, a number of titles and fragments as well as the papyrus fragment point to the standard comic plot of a love affair and its obstacles, including abducted children, prodigal sons, stingy fathers or problems with borrowed money.[123] Plays of recognition, in which free-born children are recognized at the right point in time by means of tokens, are indicated by titles like *Plocium* and *Symbolum*. Figures such as Demea (*Pall.* 216 R.³ = 206 W.), Parmeno (*Pall.* 50 R.³ = 47 W.) or Davus (*Davos*) bear names typical of comic characters.

As is appropriate in the context of comic love plots, a description of love as a powerful god is found among the few references to gods (*Pall.* 259–63 R.³ = 238–42 W.). The power of love is also indicated by a remark implying that being in love prevents people from responsible care for fields and household (*Pall.* 218–19 R.³ = 208 W.). Issues raised in the fragments include the presentation of family relationships, especially between fathers and sons,[124] of people's feelings and of human conditions, such as poverty or old age,[125] of the problem of the education and legitimacy of children, as well as of the questions of how to behave towards others and how one might be regarded in society. In many cases fragments from several plays deal with the same themes, and Cicero refers to some of these topics as characteristic of Caecilius. While a particular interest in social issues seems prominent in Caecilius' fragments, topics such as education or difficult relationships within the immediate family recur in Terence.

At the same time, some titles and fragments indicate differences from the stock comedy plot: they show emphasis on details of action or character traits that are not essential to a typical love story. Even among the standard figures there are variations: although fathers are stock characters in comedy (cf. Hor. *Sat.* 1.4.48b–56a), a specific type of father must have been prominent in Caecilius and almost proverbial.[126] In *Pro Caelio* Cicero addresses Caelius and wants to speak to him with the authority of a father; he deliberates on which kind of father to play (*Cael.* 37–8).[127] Cicero first mentions several examples of remarks by Caecilian fathers (*Pall.* 230–42

---

[123] Cf. *Harpazomene, Meretrix; Pall.* 11–12; 26; 44–5; 62–4; 65; 74; 223; 245–6 R.³ = 12–13; 23; 38–9; 57–8; 59–60; 67; 214–15; 251–3 W.

[124] Cf. e.g. *Hypobolimaeus sive Subditivos, Plocium, Synephebi; Pall.* 42–3; 62–4; 65; 139–40 R.³ = 40–1; 57–8; 59–60; 130–1 W. (on the title and the likely number of plays on '*Hypobolimaeus*' see Ribbeck 1898: 54–6; Guardì 1974: 139–41).

[125] Cf. *Pall.* 28–9; 73; 119/20; 173–5; 210 R.³ = 25–6; 66; 114; 167–9; 200 W.; Cic. *Sen.* 24–6.

[126] On father figures in Republican comedies and their relationship to society see Manuwald 2007 (with references).

[127] On this passage see e.g. Geffcken 1973: 22–3; Blänsdorf 1974: 147–8; on comedy in *Pro Caelio* see Geffcken 1973; Leigh 2004b.

R.³ = 224–35 W.), introduced by the phrase 'some forceful and harsh Caecilian (father figure)' (*Caecilianum... aliquem vehementem atque durum*);
he closes the argument by alluding to a lenient and mild father from Terence's *Adelphoe* (Ter. *Ad.* 120–1). Hence one may infer that, although father
figures occur in almost all Roman palliatae, each of the poets was associated with particular types, probably because the respective characteristics
surfaced most memorably in his plays, which points to their individual
shaping of conventional material. Quintilian corroborates the existence of
characteristic differences between the types of fathers in these two comic
writers (Quint. *Inst.* 11.1.39).

In contrast to the 'typical' Caecilian father, Caecilius' *Synephebi* features
a father who is extremely mild and lenient, so that his son in love complains because the father does not offer him the opportunity of cheating
him out of money (*Pall.* 199–209 R.³ = 189–99 W.).[128] In the same play
the common behaviour of a courtesan (*meretrix*) is reversed, because she
does not want to take money from her lover (*Pall.* 213–14 R.³ = 203–4 W.).
The exaggerated outrage at this situation points to an ironic context, and
the son's complaint about the mild father probably has to be interpreted
similarly. Since Cicero disapproves of the son's reasoning as it goes against
common opinion (Cic. *Nat. D.* 3.72–3), this figure's remark is likely to be a
metatheatrical joke. A similar reference to common patterns of behaviour
in comedies is found in an announcement in *Fallacia*, where a dramatic
character believes that he will be undone if he does not make haste and
squander all his wealth (*Pall.* 46 R.³ = 42 W.); this gives a special twist to
the play, since a harsh education (*Pall.* 42–3 R.³ = 40–1 W.) and spend-
ing paternal wealth (*Pall.* 44–5 R.³ = 38–9 W.) are mentioned in other
fragments.

Obviously, Caecilius not only presented variations of typical comic figures in his plays, but also inserted explicit allusions to the conventions of
comedy. That he made metatheatrical statements about typical comic characters is proved by the phrase 'stupid old men in comedy' (*Pall.* 243–4 R.³ =
236–7 W.: *comicos stultos senes*; cf. Cic. *Sen.* 36; *Amic.* 99–100). Another
fragment expresses an awareness of the fact that the world of the theatre is
different from the real world (*Pall.* 181–2 R.³ = 134–5 W.).

---

[128] A father who does not want to be angry with his son like other fathers, wishes to provide his son
with the money he needs to get his beloved and therefore encourages his slave to cheat him out
of money appears in Plautus' *Asinaria* (esp. Plaut. *Asin.* 49–50a; 64–83). There the contrast with
the standard behaviour of fathers in comedy is also alluded to, but as it is not seen as a negative
element by the characters concerned, the reversal is not pushed to a similar metatheatrical climax.

Caecilius' presentation of common human experiences was supported by forceful proverbial sayings (*sententiae*).[129] Even if they may come from humorous contexts, these *sententiae* concern moral behaviour and orientation in life and society. Such statements reflect humanism in the guise of popular philosophy, for instance 'live as you can when you cannot as you wish' (*Pall.* 177 R.³ = 171 W.: *vivas ut possis quando nec quis ut velis*). In a discussion of poverty Cicero quotes a line from Caecilius and juxtaposes it with references to Socrates and Diogenes (Cic. *Tusc.* 3.56: Caec. *Pall.* 266 R.³ = 255 W.). One of the Caecilian phrases concerns bearing injustice if free from insult, and this occurs in similar form in both Pacuvius' *Periboea* and Caecilius' *Fallacia* (Pac. *Trag.* 279/80 R.³ = 304 W.; Caec. *Pall.* 47–8 R.³ = 43–4 W.). Since the notion is rather a factual description in Pacuvius and an elaborate and pathetic general phrase in Caecilius, the comic poet is likely to be the one who has taken it up. It is possible that the comment might refer to a minor inconvenience, so that the exaggerated descriptions and distinctions seem ridiculous, but a basic moral notion is still being addressed.

Caecilius apparently wrote comedies that included serious thoughts on moral and social issues, but also provided effective drama, a combination that is equally found in his contemporary, the tragic poet Pacuvius. Issues and moral values prominent in Caecilius' plays are mostly related to the immediate family, the corresponding relationships and the impact of one's personal affairs on one's position in society, which looks forward to his successor Terence, just as the apparently more limited range of Greek models and the use of Greek titles do. By contrast, Caecilius' predecessors Naevius and Plautus not only drew on a wider variety of models and plot variations, but also touched on a broader range of socially and politically relevant questions.

So, although Caecilius seems to have followed the Plautine tradition of his predecessors in aspects such as metrical variety, use of colourful language or employment of linguistic effects and puns, in other respects such as choice of themes or engagement with the literary tradition he looks forward to Terence. Nevertheless, Horace records that Caecilius was regarded as pre-eminent in 'dignity' (*gravitas*) and Terence in 'art' (*ars*) (Hor. *Epist.* 2.1.59); obviously, differences between the works of the two poets were perceived, and Terence's dramatic poetry was regarded as more refined (corroborated by Quintilian, *Inst.* 10.1.99). That Caecilius' works

---

[129] Cf. *Pall.* 47–8; 79–80; 85; 135; 169–72; 176; 177; 259–63; 264; 266 R.³ = 43–4; 81–2; 87; 126; 163–6; 170; 171; 238–42; 257; 255 W.

were seen as forceful, but not as artistically sophisticated to the same extent as those of Terence, could confirm Caecilius' position between Plautus and Terence within the development of Roman comedy.[130]

4.8 LUSCIUS LANUVINUS

In the prologues to Terence's comedies his dramatic technique is justified against the accusations of a rival, who is called 'a malicious old playwright' (*malevolus vetus poeta*: Ter. *An.* 6–7; *Haut.* 22; *Phorm.* 1; cf. also *Eun.* 6–26), but never named. According to Terence's commentators (Donat. on Ter. *An.* 7[6], *Eun.* 10[2]; Eugr. on Ter. *An. prol., Phorm. prol., Phorm.* 1, *Haut.* 22; Schol. on Ter. *Eun.* 4 [p. 95 Schlee]) this person is Luscius Lanuvinus, a palliata poet, who is given the ninth place in Volcacius Sedigitus' canon (cf. Gell. *NA* 15.24).[131]

Luscius Lanuvinus (second century BCE) is not known from other ancient sources. His name suggests that he came from Lanuvium, a place in Latium; and he is likely to have been an older contemporary of Terence, producing palliatae for the Roman stage and possibly fearing for his position in view of competition from Terence.[132] The impression of him is one-sided and presumably inaccurate, since information about him comes exclusively from his opponent. Terence's prologues mention two of Luscius Lanuvinus' plays, *Phasma* and *Thesaurus*, at least one of them and probably both modelled on Menander; the plots are summarized in Terence's commentators (Ter. *Eun.* 7–13; Donat. ad loc.). In typical rhetorical fashion, it is claimed that Terence has more accusations against his opponent's poetry to make in case attacks against himself continue (Ter. *An.* 22–3; *Haut.* 34–5; *Eun.* 14–19a); but there is no evidence as to what, if anything, might be alluded to. Generally, it is asserted that the other's poetry is so bad that a recent success was due only to the efforts of the producer (Ter. *Phorm.* 9–11).

---

[130] Beyond allocating an intermediate and transitional position between Plautus and Terence to Caecilius (see Oppermann 1939a, 1939b), scholars are divided: some regard Caecilius as close to Terence and different from Plautus (see e.g. Lana 1947: 155, 157, 159; Conte 1994: 66), while others think that his works were rather traditional and following the Plautine tradition, different from the more 'Hellenized' Terence (see e.g. J. Wright 1974: 87–126; Beacham 1991: 45).

[131] On Luscius Lanuvinus see e.g. Duckworth 1952: 65; Beare 1964: 114–15; Garton 1972: 41–139; Dér 1989 (but see Lentano 1997: 558); Lefèvre in Suerbaum 2002: 254–5 (with bibliography).

[132] Donatus records that Luscius Lanuvinus was an 'old man' (*senex*) when Terence was still a 'young man' (*adulescentulus*) (Donat. on Ter. *Andr.* 7[6]); yet this description might have been developed from remarks in Terence's prologues. While it is obvious from Terence's text that Luscius Lanuvinus produced plays before Terence, Terence's term 'old' (*vetus*) need not refer only to Luscius Lanuvinus' age, but could also imply a description of his poetry as 'old-fashioned', 'hackneyed' or 'having been around for a long time' (cf. *OLD*, s.v.), used almost like a 'terminus technicus' such as *vetus fabula* and *nova fabula* (cf. also Ter. *Phorm.* 13–15, for a contrast between '*vetus poeta*' and '*novus poeta*').

As for dramatic technique, the criticism of Luscius Lanuvinus' poetry as well as the examples mentioned in Terence lead to the conclusion that Luscius Lanuvinus had a conventional approach and was a bad poet and that his plays included exaggerated, unrealistic, almost ridiculous scenes and plots (Ter. *Haut.* 30–2; *Eun.* 7–13 [and Donat. ad loc.]; *Phorm.* 6–8).[133] Terence's intriguing description 'By translating well and at the same time writing badly, he turned good Greek plays into bad Latin ones.'[134] seems to indicate that in his view Luscius Lanuvinus had chosen an appropriate Greek play and turned the Greek into acceptable Latin, but failed to produce good-quality Latin verse and satisfactory dramatic structures.[135] This might imply that Terence perceived a lack of poetic shaping for the new Latin dramas generated from Greek models, perhaps because the writer had not been able to ensure that plays when adapted to the Roman stage (and thus newly 'written') resulted in well-rounded pieces with logical plots. This criticism is usually interpreted as an attack on over-literal translation, yet it need not be restricted to this aspect and, in view of its context, may include faults in structure.

Since elsewhere Terence feels obliged to insert a defence of having combined material from several Greek plays into one Latin play, while in one case one of the Greek plays had allegedly already been used by other Latin poets (Ter. *An.* 15–21; *Eun.* 19b–34), Luscius Lanuvinus must have regarded following untouched Greek plays as the crucial basis for Latin drama. In this context critics like Luscius Lanuvinus are associated with 'obscure pedantry' (Ter. *An.* 21: *obscura diligentia*), in contrast to the 'carelessness' of the older poets Naevius, Plautus and Ennius (Ter. *An.* 20: *neglegentia*), who are presented as Terence's paradigmatic models.

Overall, this conflict reveals at least as much about Terence and the contemporary atmosphere as it does about Luscius Lanuvinus. According to Terence's prologues, Luscius Lanuvinus started the argument, and Terence only reacted and defended himself, willing to end the quarrel as soon as Luscius Lanuvinus stopped; this creates the impression of a stubborn critic (Ter. *An.* 5–7; *Phorm.* 18–23; *Eun.* 4–6; 16–19a). This confrontation shows

---

[133] Terence specifically criticizes the fact that in his *Thesaurus* Luscius Lanuvinus had the defendant make a claim before the plaintiff explained the situation (Ter. *Eun.* 10–13), which goes against normal practice (see also Donat. on Ter. *Eun.* 10[2]; Eugr. on Ter. *Eun.* 10). Modern scholars, however, have tried to vindicate Luscius Lanuvinus, arguing that he followed the rules of dramatic art rather than of real life (see Garton 1972: 73–92, with references). But this is not the point of view that Terence seems to have adopted.

[134] Cf. Ter. *Eun.* 7–8: *qui bene vortendo et easdem scribendo male ex / Graecis bonis Latinas fecit non bonas.*

[135] In such literary contexts *scribere* seems to imply a creative activity on the part of the poet; in Plautus it is regularly used with reference to the author of the Greek model (Plaut. *Asin.* 11; *Trin.* 19).

that an emerging Roman comic tradition did not mean that all representatives of a particular dramatic genre followed the same poetic principles.
Luscius Lanuvinus' views on how to write comic drama differed from Terence's, and this contrast, along with possible rivalry for commissions and
public favour, may explain their opposition.[136] Interestingly, the controversy among poets took place in public, and it contributed to clarifying
the poetic principles of both Terence and his opponent (in their respective
interpretations) to audiences.

4.9 P. TERENTIUS AFER

Publius Terentius Afer (*c.* 195/4–159 BCE) is the second writer of preserved
palliatae after Plautus, and the successor of Caecilius.[137] Terence's *cognomen*
Afer points to a Punic or Libyan origin, and the ancient Vita has him born
in Carthage. After Terence had come to Rome, he is said to have worked as
a slave of the Roman senator Terentius Lucanus. Because of his intelligence
and handsome appearance, his master gave him a sound education and
manumitted him early. Terence allegedly read his first comedy, *Andria*,
to the aged Caecilius, his predecessor in the palliata, and the play won
the latter's enthusiastic approval (cf. Suet./Donat. *Vita Ter.* 3; Hieron. *Ab
Abr.* 1859, 158 BCE [p. 142a Helm]). While the story is chronologically
problematic, since Caecilius died in 168/7 BCE, and Terence's six comedies
were performed between 166 and 160 BCE, it might give an indication of
how the relationship between the two poets was perceived (see ch. 4.7).
After Terence had these six comedies produced, he is said to have travelled
to Greece, but did not return from the trip. Various stories about his death

---

[136] There is no evidence 'that at the bottom of the whole affair was the corporate jealousy of the poets'
guild' (so Duckworth 1952: 65). Some scholars have developed the notion of a continuing argument
between palliata poets promoting different styles of writing: Luscius Lanuvinus subscribing to
Caecilius' principles, which Terence opposed (so e.g. Leo 1913: 255). Yet Terence's prologues rather
suggest an affinity between Caecilius and Terence (cf. Ter. *Hec.* 10–27), while there is no indication
of a connection between Caecilius and Luscius Lanuvinus (see Lana 1947: 158–9). The limited
information on the background of these poets precludes interpreting the conflict within a broader
context: Luscius Lanuvinus, the traditional, conservative poet, against Terence, the modern, phil-
Hellenic one, continuing the practices of Caecilius (so Lana 1947: 159–61).

[137] On Terence see e.g. Duckworth 1952: 56–65; Beare 1964: 91–112; Büchner 1974; J. Wright 1974:
127–51; Arnott 1975: 45–56; Sandbach 1977: 135–47; Juhnke 1978; Drury 1982: 814–20; Konstan
1983: 115–41; Forehand 1985; Goldberg 1986; Cupaiuolo 1991; Petrone 1992: 591–611; Conte 1994:
92–103; Moore 2001; Lefèvre in Suerbaum 2002: 232–54; Kruschwitz 2004; Maurach 2005: 96–130;
Kruschwitz *et al.* 2007; N. J. Lowe 2008: 115–32; bibliography in Gaiser 1972; Goldberg 1981;
Cupaiuolo 1984, 1992; Lentano 1997, 1998; Lefèvre in Suerbaum 2002; on text and transmission see
Reeve 1983; on Terence's contemporary popularity see Parker 1996. For calls to appreciate Terence
as a Roman poet and to look at the impact of his plays in their extant form see Goldberg 1986:
xii–xiii; Panayotakis 2005a: 133; Kruschwitz *et al.* 2007: viii.

at a relatively young age in *c.* 159 BCE appear to have circulated; according to one of them Terence had numerous plays converted from Menander with him when he died.[138]

Terence was reportedly on friendly terms with P. Cornelius Scipio Aemilianus Africanus (*c.* 185–129 BCE) and C. Laelius Sapiens (*c.* 190 to after 129 BCE) (cf. Cic. *Amic.* 89; *Att.* 7.3.10; Suet./Donat. *Vita Ter.* 2). Although the so-called 'Scipionic circle' is a problematic concept (see ch. 2.7), the noblemen and the poet must have been in touch because Terence had to defend himself against the accusation that noble friends had written his plays or at least had aided him in their composition (*Haut.* 22–4; *Ad.* 15–21); these charges are also mentioned by other writers, who specify Scipio and/or Laelius as the alleged authors.[139] Two of Terence's plays (*Hecyra* II, *Adelphoe*) were given at the funeral games for L. Aemilius Paul(l)us, organized by his natural sons P. Cornelius Scipio Aemilianus Africanus and Q. Fabius Maximus Aemilianus. Hence Terence is likely to have been in contact with leading members of contemporary society who had phil-Hellenic interests and also with other poets such as Pacuvius and Lucilius, who shared those acquaintances.

Terence is the only Republican dramatist whose output seems to have been preserved in its entirety and also the only one for whom there survive production notices (*didascaliae*) to the plays, which give information about dates and occasions for the dramas and about the people involved in the productions. On the basis of consuls and aediles mentioned in these texts as being in office when the plays were produced, the following chronology of the first performances of Terence's six comedies has been established (despite problems created by the texts in their transmitted form):[140] *Andria* in 166 (*Ludi Megalenses*); *Hecyra* I in 165 (*Ludi Megalenses*); *Heautontimorumenos* in 163 (*Ludi Megalenses*); *Eunuchus* in 161 (*Ludi Megalenses*); *Phormio* in 161 (probably *Ludi Romani*); *Hecyra* II and *Adelphoe* in 160 (*Ludi funebres* for L. Aemilius Paul(l)us); *Hecyra* III in 160 BCE (*Ludi Romani*). The actor-manager Ambivius Turpio produced all six plays, and Flaccus, belonging to a Claudius, provided the music for them (see ch. 2.6): obviously, Terence collaborated with a stable team of theatre people throughout his career.

---

[138] On Terence's life see Suet./Donat. *Vita Ter.* 1–7; Donat. *Vita Ter.* 8–10; *didascaliae*; Hieron. *Ab Abr.* 1859, 158 BCE (p. 142a Helm). For some discussion see Fantham 2004: 21–5.

[139] Cf. Cic. *Att.* 7.3.10; Quint. *Inst.* 10.1.99; Suet./Donat. *Vita Ter.* 4.

[140] For these problems and bibliography see ch. 2.1, n. 21. Although *Andria* is attested as Terence's first play, it is possible that the extant prologue was added later for another performance, since it seems to presuppose preceding unsuccessful productions and criticism from the poet's opponents (so Leo 1913: 235 n. 1).

Four of the six comedies (*Andria, Heautontimorumenos, Eunuchus, Adelphoe*) are based on Menander, the other two (*Hecyra, Phormio*) on Apollodorus of Carystus.[141] In three plays *contaminatio* has been used, i.e. scenes or characters from a second play have been included: *Andria* additionally contains elements of Menander's *Perinthia*, *Eunuchus* of Menander's *Colax*, and *Adelphoe* of Diphilus' *Synapothneskontes* (*An*. 9–14; *Eun*. 30–3a; *Ad*. 6–11). The choice of a rather uniform body of models may have contributed to the coherent impression of Terence's dramatic output. Terence was viewed in relation to Menander by the ancients, though assessments differ: while Cicero regarded Terence as an apt transposer who was the only one to bring Menander to the Romans, Caesar saw him as a 'halved Menander' (*dimidiatus Menander*), since he was Menander's equal in style, but lacking in force (Suet./Donat. *Vita Ter*. 7: Cic. fr. 2 *FPL³* / Caes. fr. 1 *FPL³*).

Terence's plays remain within the standard set-up of New Comedy. They are all set in a private context; and apart from characters going on business trips and running similar errands, there is little impact from the outside world. Issues raised consist of human problems, presented within a bourgeois environment. The plays cover a limited spectrum of experience; they focus on moral and emotional aspects of human relationships, particularly young people in love and the obstacles they are confronted with, their relationship to their parents and problems of growing up and of education;[142] after some twists and turns a happy ending is reached, often by the recognition of people's true identity or successful negotiations. Since Terence retains a stylized Greek setting, he does not present a mirror of contemporary society; still, he invites audiences to empathize with the characters and engage with their problems, as overtly Greek elements have been removed and well-organized plots focus on the plays' main themes. Correspondingly, there are fewer farcical and potentially distracting elements such as excessive dinner parties and extended scenes of dance and song on stage.

Modern scholars therefore tend to regard Terence as having pursued a more sober, 'Hellenized' style of comedy and having avoided the comic exuberance and fantasy world of Plautus.[143] This is a valid description of

---

[141] Cf. Did. on Ter.; Donat. *Vita Ter*. 10; on Ter. *Hec.*, *praef*. 1.1; *Phorm.*, *praef*. 1.1; Eugr. on Ter. *Haut. prol.*; *Hec. prol.*

[142] The focus on young men emerging into adulthood and on father–son relationships in Terence's plays has been connected with his role as an educator, as he may also have worked as a teacher (see Fantham 2004).

[143] For a convenient overview see N. J. Lowe 2008: 117–21.

their respective poetry, but should not be seen as an assessment of quality. Euanthius praised Terence for having stayed within the realm of comedy and not having transgressed its boundaries by moving into tragedy as other comic writers like Plautus or Afranius had (Euanth. *Fab.* 3.5). Clearly, Terence was seen to have avoided the obvious blurring of the tragic and the comic genres found in Plautus' *Amphitruo* or in parodies of tragedy. Terence rather expressed serious thoughts within a comic framework. This effect was corroborated by the presentation of paradigmatic characters, which might explain why Varro praised Terence for his character-drawing (Varro, *Sat. Men.* 399 B.). Moreover, Terence's plays are made exciting and meaningful by 'double plots' (*Haut.* 6), i.e. by the introduction of two pairs of lovers, two fathers and/or two sons, which allows the construction of contrasts and intertwined actions.[144]

A further element that contributes to coherent and smooth plots is the reduction of overtly 'metatheatrical' elements, which, however, does not mean that there is no metatheatre in Terence. On the contrary, the pro-logues in their entirety discuss literary questions, and Terence frequently plays with comic conventions in the body of the plays; the metatheatrical aspect is just more subdued, and openly breaking the dramatic illusion is avoided.[145] For instance, in *Andria* the story that the lovers invent to cover them is characterized as improbable nonsense by the slave (esp. *An.* 1 3), but it accords with the typical set-up of comedies and turns out to be true. *Phormio* features a parasite with unusual characteristics, as he adopts the part of the main scheming slave. In the same drama an actual slave is told that he is expected to save one of the young men and find the money that is needed; he then claims to have come up with a plan though this remains typically vague (*Phorm.* III 3). The whole scene almost conveys the impression that this slave needs to be informed of the appropriate role and function for figures like him in comedies; yet what he then manages to do is basically to engage Phormio to arrange this matter, as in this play the parasite Phormio has taken the slave's position, as it were (*Phorm.* IV 2).

Terence's figures occasionally mention 'acting' and 'comedies', and these remarks have metatheatrical relevance, while they do not go against character-drawing and context. For instance, in *Andria* the slave suddenly talks to the maid in a way that is incomprehensible to her in view of previous conversations, and he does so because he realizes that they are being overheard by the potential father-in-law, who is to be convinced of a particular state of things; afterwards the slave explains his behaviour,

---

[144] On this technique see Gilula 1991.   [145] On metatheatre in Terence see Knorr 2007.

and the maid then criticizes him for not having warned her. Thereupon he answers: 'Do you think that it makes only a little difference whether you act spontaneously, as nature wants it, or as instructed?'[146] This statement can be referred to the actors on stage: they might be told in advance how to act, but this is not necessarily the best way of staging plays since impromptu acting might be more natural and thus more convincing; yet the 'impromptu acting' in this case is likely to have been studied and thus exemplifies the artificial quality of naturalness in the theatre. At the end of *Hecyra* young Pamphilus says: 'I do not want the same to happen here that happens in comedies, where everybody finds out everything. Here, those for whom it was appropriate to find out know already; those for whom it is not right to know will not find out or ever know.'[147] Indeed his father is never informed of the actual state of affairs.

Terence plays with the stereotypical characterization of fathers in comedies, developed into an opposition of stern and lenient fathers. *Adelphoe* is an entire play devoted to this issue, but it features in other comedies too. For instance, in *Phormio* the father voices his anger by wishing to let his son know 'that by his fault, I, this mild father of his, have become an extremely harsh one'.[148] In *Andria* the father does not want to charge his son unreasonably (*An.* 11), and the son is governed, among other concerns, by 'respect for my father, who, with such a generous mind, has allowed me up to now to do whatever I fancied' and therefore does not want to oppose him.[149] 'Mild' fathers apparently came to be regarded as typical of Terence, in contrast to their characterization in Caecilius (cf. Cic. *Cael.* 37–8; Quint. *Inst.* 11.1.39–40; see ch. 4.7).

The language in Terence's comedies is more restrained than in those of his Roman predecessors: the number of alliterations and assonances, elaborate similes and allusions, digressions, neologisms, Greek expressions, colloquial phrases or comic long words is reduced. Accordingly, Terence was soon praised for his 'pure language'.[150] Equally, the metre and rhythm of his verses are closer to everyday speech, as there are fewer accompanied lines; there is a steady increase in the percentage of unaccompanied iambic senarii from *Andria* to *Adelphoe*, and a steady decrease in the total number

---

[146] Cf. *An.* 794–5: *paullum interesse censes ex animo omnia, / ut fert natura, facias an de industria?*

[147] Cf. *Hec.* 866–8: *placet non fieri hoc itidem ut in comoediis / omnia omnes ubi resciscunt. hic quos par fuerit resciscere / sciunt; quos non autem aequomst scire neque resciscent neque scient.*

[148] Cf. *Phorm.* 261–2: *. . . , nunc sua culpa ut sciat / lenem patrem illum factum me esse acerrimum.*

[149] Cf. *An.* 260–3: *tot me inpediunt curae, quae meum animum divorsae trahunt: / amor, misericordia huiu', nuptiarum sollicitatio, / tum patri' pudor, qui me tam leni passus est animo usque adhuc / quae meo quomque animo lubitumst facere. eine ego ut advorser? ei mihi!*

[150] Cf. Suet./Donat. *Vita Ter.* 7: Cic. fr. 2 *FPL³* / Caes. fr. 1 *FPL³*; also Ter. *Haut.* 46: *in hac est pura oratio.*

of changes in metre. At the same time Terence developed an elaborate musical language with clear musical patterns, i.e. meaningful changes of metre where he had them.[151]

One of the most characteristic features of Terence's dramatic technique is his use of prologues: while prologues in Plautus mainly serve to give basic information about the 'literary-historical' facts of the respective play and particularly to inform audiences of the main elements of the plot, Terence does not have narrative, expository prologues; instead, he discusses questions of literary criticism and dramatic principles. Thus the prologues provide insights into his place in the Roman dramatic tradition as well as into his relationship to audiences (see also ch. 4.8). As the poet has prologue speakers talk about the way of dealing with Greek models and react to charges against the poet, this material cannot have been taken over from Greek plays. This is why these prologues are regarded as representing the earliest extended passages of literary criticism in Latin and of definitely original Latin verse.[152] Terence is the earliest Republican dramatist who certainly employed this type of prologue and who used it exclusively; correspondingly, he has the prologue speaker in *Andria*, his first play, draw attention to the fact that he has been forced to turn his prologues to responding to the reproaches of opponents rather than explaining the plot (*An.* 5–7).

Yet such a focus of prologues is not entirely unprecedented in Rome. Some Plautine prologues already talk about the literary characteristics of the respective plays: on a basic level that involves mentioning the title of the play and its Greek predecessor, but it may include special attributes of a drama: there are comments on the play's generic character in *Amphitruo* (Plaut. *Amph.* 50–63), on elements appropriate for a comedy in *Captivi* (Plaut. *Capt.* 55–62) or on particular, potentially unexpected decisions by the poet in *Casina* (Plaut. *Cas.* 64–6). Caecilius' palliatae included metadramatic remarks, and there is some evidence that he might have justified himself against reusing material from earlier plays in a prologue (cf. Porph. ap. Euseb. *Praep. evang.* 10.3.13 [465d]; see ch. 4.7).

This would imply that Terence was not the first playwright to have meta-literary prologues that defend the poet against accusations of opponents.

---

[151] See Moore 2007.

[152] See e.g. Leo 1913: 251; Fantham 1989c: 224; Gilula 1989b: 95; N. W. Slater 1992a: 86; Moore 2001: 243. On Terence's prologues see Fabia 1888; Goldberg 1986: 31–60; on their performative aspects, different types of prologues and the relationship between poet and prologue speakers/actors see Gilula 1989b; on the 'dramatic theory' implied in these prologues see N. W. Slater 1992a: 86–98.

Still, it may be only in Terence that this type of prologue became a characteristic feature, while it was used occasionally in Caecilius or, as in Plautus,
in addition to an exposition of the plot. Such a situation could explain why
Terence felt obliged to explain his procedure, and ancient commentaries do
not mention precedents. Also, if the type of prologue used by Terence has
forerunners in earlier comic poets, this would be one indication of the fact
that he did not break with the palliata tradition, but developed it further
and gave it an individual form (see below). The practice of talking about
dramatic principles and the relationship to predecessors in what seems to
have been a prologue was taken up by Afranius for his togatae (Afr. *Compitalia*), though he apparently did not use this type of prologue exclusively
(see ch. 4.12).

In Terence's comedies poetic activity and dramatic performance are not
mixed: Terence does not appear or speak in his own person in the prologue,
but has a member of the troupe or the impresario, who assume an individual
personality, deliver the prologue on his behalf.[153] This follows the model of
parabaseis in Aristophanes, where the chorus leader speaks on behalf of the
poet, and of prologues in Plautus; it is only Afranius (slightly later) who
alters this convention and has the poet speak directly in his own person in
what seems to have been a prologue.

Despite their particular focus, Terence's prologues are not completely
detached from their plays, and they continue the conventional function
of prologues, namely to announce the play and to secure a hearing. The
discussion in each prologue takes up issues that are relevant to the particular
play and thereby conveys hints on the playwright's interpretation of the plot
and its aims.[154] Further, it has been suggested that Terence chose 'oratorical
prologues', which amount to defence speeches against accusations (cf.
Haut. 11–15; *Hec.* 9), to win his audience, just as Plautus makes fun of details
of juridical processes throughout his plays.[155] Indeed, Roman audiences
seem to have been interested in oratory and juridical disputes and therefore
might have enjoyed such debates.[156] Besides, Terence was writing just after
the end of the Third Macedonian War (171–168 BCE); as one result a Greek
library came to Rome, the grammarian and philosopher Crates of Malles

---

[153] See Gilula 1989b.

[154] Arguing that there is a connection between plays and prologues, Gowers (2004) interprets metaliterary statements in the prologues as indirect descriptions of characteristics of the plots. While
it is questionable whether in all instances such precise connections can be made, it is clear that
comments on the characteristics of his own or other dramas indicate Terence's views on dramatic
technique that shape the respective drama.

[155] On rhetorical elements in Terence's prologues see esp. Fabia 1888: 283–314; Goldberg 1983.

[156] See Moore 2001: 244–5; but also Conte 1994: 98.

visited, and 1,000 Achaean hostages, including the historian Polybius, arrived in Rome (see ch. 1.1). Since the Roman populace was thus forced to confront an increased influx of elements of Greek intellectual life, plays written against this background and taking up literary questions could have been of increasing interest to audiences (as suggested also by the topics found in contemporary tragedies by Pacuvius and in the slightly later togatae by Afranius); programmatic statements on the character of the dramatic genre could have appealed to them.[157]

As Terence refutes criticism in the prologues by referring to his dramatic principles, these texts reveal aspects of his poetic views (e.g. on contamination, shape of the plot or the constituent elements of comedies). Even though the prologues do not give a coherent exposition, they recall categories found in Aristotle's *Poetics* and thus illustrate a significant awareness of poetic principles (see ch. 3).[158] By using the prologues to provide responses within a controversy with his opponents, Terence manages to include sophisticated discussions in dramas without obviously going beyond the framework of comedy.[159] Terence never names his main opponent; instead, he confronts him as a paradigmatic representative of a particular way of writing, which allows him to attack this style more forcefully. Obviously, the comments on single plays (*Haut.* 30–4; *Eun.* 6–15; *Phorm.* 6–11) or the intervention at a preview (*Eun.* 19b–26) must relate to a single individual, but the views discussed might apply to more representatives.[160]

---

[157] See also Sharrock 2009: 63, 93. Terence has been thought to promote a new, 'Hellenized' attitude, in line with the position of the noblemen of his acquaintance and directed against conservative views supported by other members of the nobility and contemporary playwrights (see e.g. Lana 1947; Perelli 1973). However, open discussions are reduced to the prologues and concern only literary matters. On the changes in society between the time of Plautus and that of Terence and their possible effect on Terence see Cupaiuolo 1991.

[158] See N. W. Slater 1992a: esp. 86–98.

[159] In comparable fashion, Aristophanes refuted objections to and amazement at his poetic career and dramatic principles and discussed his relationship with the audience in parabaseis (e.g. Ar. *Ach.* 626–64; *Eq.* 507–50; *Nub.* 518–62; *Pax* 729–44; *Vesp.* 1015–59).

[160] J. Wright (1974: 183–5) suggests, in taking up older hypotheses, that this 'group' might have been the 'college of poets' (*collegium poetarum*), which was instrumental in ensuring a coherent and fundamentally conservative palliata tradition. But apart from the fact that evidence on this association is shadowy (see ch. 2.7), there is no indication in Terence's prologues that the opponents of Terence (and Caecilius) belong to an organized group. It has also been said that 'it would not be fanciful to read implied criticism of Plautus into the polemical prologues of Terence'; but as Terence could not promote his ideals 'without overt criticism of old favourites like Plautus that would be unacceptable from an upstart foreigner', he 'exploited a man of straw, the obscure Luscius of Lanuvium' (so Fantham 1989c: 224–5). While Terence's rejection of principles defended by Luscius Lanuvinus is likely to cover others with similar views, it is not immediately obvious that Plautus would be a target, as Terence mentions him as a paradigmatic predecessor in his first prologue (*An.* 18).

The charges answered by Terence cover a variety of areas, such as the use of sources, compositional techniques, style, poetic independence and creativity. He highlights and answers different accusations in each prologue even though some dramas could be seen as exhibiting the same 'faults'. If his responses mirror the actual criticism, the points singled out changed: the opponents may have put forward a variety of accusations in order to get rid of Terence and not have fought consistently for or against a certain set of principles. Alternatively, it might be Terence who selected different charges for comment out of those that had been made, so as to be able to discuss a wide range of aspects of dramatic technique in the limited space of prologues. In fact, both tendencies may have been at work, with Terence using the accusations to delineate his own poetic profile.

Although it has rightly been noted that the content of the prologues brings Terence close to roughly contemporary poets such as Ennius, Accius and Lucilius, who also talk about literature,[161] there is a significant difference of literary genres: none of these poets had extended metaliterary discussions as part of dramas. But drama, if it does not include parabaseis (to which prologues are similar to some extent), does not offer opportunities for the treatment of literary questions without disruption of the dramatic illusion. Including such comments in a prologue is the only option available to a poet who wishes to state his views in a drama without affecting the plot; Plautus also comments on the dramatic genre of the subsequent play in the prologue. Accius later seems to have drawn a distinction: he dealt with literary questions in treatises on dramatic issues.

Another aspect on which Terence's prologues contribute information is the dramatic history of some of his plays and his relationship with audiences. At first glance, evidence for Terence's success with audiences is conflicting: on the one hand *Eunuchus* earned its author an unprecedented sum in fees and was soon shown in a repeat performance (cf. Suet./Donat. *Vita Ter.* 3; on Ter. *Eun.*, *praef.* 1.6*).[162] Its success at *Ludi Megalenses* of 161 BCE must have been what prompted the aediles to have another Terentian comedy, *Phormio*, staged at *Ludi Romani* of the same year.[163]

On the other hand it took *Hecyra* three attempts to get a full staging, according to the prologues (as well as *didascaliae* and ancient commentaries).[164] What seems clear from the wording in the prologues

---

[161] See Conte 1994: 98.

[162] On the financial aspects see Gilula 1985/8; more generally Lebek 1996. See also ch. 2.7.

[163] See Gilula 1985/8: 74–5. For the dates cf. Did. on Ter. *Eun.*, *Phorm.*

[164] On the *Hecyra* prologue(s) see esp. Klose 1966: 47–80; Gilula 1978, 1981; Sandbach 1982; Parker 1996: 592–601; Lada-Richards 2004.

is that the first two performances were disrupted not by audiences running away because they had heard of other entertainments going on elsewhere, but rather by new people coming into the venue since they were under the impression that other performances were due to be given there. This story puts the blame for the failure on the circumstances rather than on inherent flaws in the play or on its lack of appeal to contemporary audiences. It implies that there were people who had come to see *Hecyra* (whether they still wanted this after they had watched the beginning or whether they were glad about the interruption is another matter). That there was some interest in the play explains why the producer, Ambivius Turpio, persevered and had the comedy put on again, particularly since between the first and the second productions successful plays of Terence's intervened.

Some scholars have gone further and doubted the reliability of Terence's report or made further inferences from it. One has questioned the story, arguing that there were no failed performances of *Hecyra*, but that the references are fictitious, introduced as allusions to contemporary events and stage practices, meant to condition audiences.[165] However, such a reading seems over-sceptical; the mere fact of a disturbance (not its interpretation) is likely to be historical, particularly since it is referred to in another prologue as well (*Phorm.* 30–4).

Others have thought that the real cause for the play's failure was its 'Hellenized' style, unappealing to Roman audiences; for at the second attempt *Hecyra* was scheduled to be shown together with *Adelphoe* at funeral games, and there is no evidence for troubles concerning the performance of *Adelphoe*, which is seen to be closer to the Roman comic style; gladiators would be adduced as the most remarkable feature of the various spectacles on this occasion.[166] It is true that the apparently different fate of the two dramas is remarkable: either fortune was indeed adverse to *Hecyra*, and there was no clash with other (alleged) performances for *Adelphoe*, while there was for *Hecyra*; or one will have to assume that the interruption of *Hecyra* was not merely due to bad luck. For some scholars have thought that it was not by chance that these events coincided (or allegedly coincided) and prevented the performance of *Hecyra* from going ahead, but that this had been arranged by Terence's opponents.[167]

That there was disruption seems clear from Terence's comments, and it must have been either caused by chance or pre-organized. The possibility

---

[165] See Gruen 1992: 210–18.
[166] See Goldberg 1995: 40–3 (who states [41 n. 24] that 'Gilula,..., and Sandbach,..., interpret the evidence of the prologues correctly but accept it uncritically').
[167] See Gilula 1981: 30; Forehand 1985: 22; Parker 1996: 592–601.

of a play's being driven off the stage without a hearing is already mentioned in Terence's first prologue (*An.* 26–7). As outlined in another prologue, this apparently happened to Terence's predecessor Caecilius as a result of attacks by opponents, even though, according to the impresario, Caecilius' plays were a success once they were known, i.e. performed in full (*Hec.* 14–23). Hence Terence might have wished to indicate that plays can be disrupted by the interventions of opponents and that this can affect a playwright's career. The wish that the comedy may be performed in silence to an open-minded audience without interruption is uttered in some prologues with reference to the failed first performance of *Hecyra* (*Haut.* 35–6; *Phorm.* 30–4). The plea for a fair hearing and a fair judgement, the appeal to the influence of the audience and the request not to let the dramatic art be reduced to a few in the prologue to the third performance of *Hecyra* (*Hec.* 28; 31–2; 46–8) invite the conclusion that at least the impression is to be created that Terence is under threat from rivals (cf. also *Phorm.* 1–3; 18). The impersonal description of the events that ended the performances of *Hecyra* could imply that Terence wished to put the blame on others without naming anyone.

That what happened at the first performance of *Hecyra* is called 'a novel form of inauspicious event and disaster' in the prologue to the second performance (*Hec.* 2: *novom . . . vitium et calamitas*) might indicate that the incident disrupting the performance was not common and therefore was not just due to coincidence.[168] According to this interpretation the dramatic history of *Hecyra* would point not to a particular failure on Terence's part, but rather to the success of his plays as soon as they were produced, since otherwise measures of trying to prevent him from producing plays would have been unnecessary. That Terence made the effort to explain to audiences what had happened and to ask them for proper appreciation of his plays indicates that he cared for a good relationship with the public and did not assume that they were generally averse to his plays.

Although the prologue to *Hecyra* does not explain Terence's poetic principles, it would, then, just as others do, talk about his position in the contemporary dramatic framework. If one is to believe the information in other prologues, rivals tried to prevent the performance of other plays of his too: when 'the old malicious playwright' branded *Eunuchus* as a 'theft' (*furtum*) at a preview, since Terence had allegedly taken over characters

---

[168] If Caecilius was prevented from showing his plays in full straightaway, as Terence claims, being driven off the stage would not be an entirely unprecedented event. Perhaps Terence wishes to indicate that the circumstances in his case were 'novel'.

from earlier Latin plays (*Eun.* 19b–26), this intervention was apparently an (unsuccessful) move to stop its production. The charge that noblemen assisted Terence in writing his plays (*Haut.* 22–4), which implicitly acknowledges their good quality, also seems directed at accusing him of cheating and thus limiting the attractiveness of his dramas.

These glimpses into the opponents' tactics add support to the theory that when Terence's plays were produced they were successes;[169] since other poets could not imitate or equal these, they tried to get rid of the rival. Terence insinuates that his main opponent was not able to win appreciation by his writing, but needed the support of the producer for his few successes (*Phorm.* 9–11). A further hint might be that it is the *Phormio* prologue that includes references to the lack of success of competitors and their attempts to discourage Terence from further poetic activity, as well as an allusion to the failed first performance of *Hecyra*; as *Phormio* was the poet's second production within a year after the success of *Eunuchus*, this might have caused intensified attacks against him and at the same time boosted his self-confidence; the following year saw the second and the third productions of *Hecyra*.

What also tells against a continued lack of success is the fact that Terence's comedies saw revival performances, as can be inferred from the *didascaliae*. These revivals seem to have occurred mainly in the 140s BCE, i.e. at about the time when Plautus' comedies were revived due to popular demand and actors' companies looked back to 'old' plays of the now dead 'garland of poets' (*flos poetarum*; cf. Plaut. *Cas.* 5–20). The argument in the *Casina* prologue, along with the probable date of its revival, points to the conclusion that Terence (just like Plautus) was regarded as belonging to the 'old masters' contrasted with present-day writers. These revivals fall within a time in which the togata poet Afranius admired Terence and imitated some of his characteristic features (Afr. *Compitalia*).

Modern scholars often relate the success of Terence's individual plays to the respective extent of their 'Hellenic' or 'farcical' elements, since more entertaining plays would go down better with audiences. Hence the success of *Eunuchus* is attributed to the fact that it offers good comedy and funny stock characters; the play immediately following upon it, *Phormio*, also has stock characters. But in both cases these figures do not conform to the standard format of their types; they rather appear in unusual roles or display uncommon characteristics. And if the preceding interpretation of time and motivation of the opponents' accusations is correct, these plays

---

[169] See Parker 1996: esp. 591–607; Moore 2001: 245; Lada-Richards 2004: 60.

were written when Terence was already suffering from opposition that wanted to drive him from the stage because of previous successes with other plays. Accordingly, in the prologues to both plays Terence self-confidently refutes criticism and asserts his own way of shaping these figures.

The portrait of Terence's own dramatic principles that emerges from these discussions includes the following elements: he insists that his plays are new plays written independently of other Romans; he employs *contaminatio* and uses Greek models freely in a way that suits him; accordingly he requests more from poets than just translation, but rather the creation of one's own meaningful and logical plots without unrealistic exaggeration, which also implies clear language; he is aware of the significant role of stock figures in comedy and acknowledges their continued use, while he introduces what seem to be stock figures, who are, however, endowed with slightly unusual and particular characteristics.

If the picture of the situation at the theatre in Terence's time is pieced together correctly, it would indicate rivalry between playwrights. While there are no other indications for measures such as those alluded to in Terence's prologues, there is evidence for competition and the desire to assert one's individual profile against predecessors and contemporaries from the time of the emergence of a Roman literary tradition. The earliest sign is perhaps Ennius' disparaging comment about predecessors, called *Fauni* and *vates*, in his *Annales*, alluding to earlier poets including Naevius, and his simultaneous avoidance of another narrative of the First Punic War after Naevius' *Bellum Poenicum* (cf. Cic. *Brut.* 71; 75–6). Further, there is the tendency to pass over topics already treated by predecessors or to present them in different fashion. Also, Afranius (and possibly Caecilius) had to defend themselves against accusations of too much borrowing. Accius asserted his stance against dilettante rivals, critical mime actors and perhaps also his predecessor Pacuvius.

If Terence's prologues are interpreted as pointing to rivalry with other contemporary playwrights, who tried to oust him from the stage because of his achievements, and thus confirming Terence's success beyond the inferences from *Eunuchus*, there will be consequences for the view of his place in the history of palliata. For modern scholars have claimed that Terence was the exception to an otherwise coherent palliata tradition and that later poets preferred to return to the Plautine model, since Terence's 'Hellenized' style had been unsuccessful,[170] or in somewhat modified terms, that Terence diverged from Greek New Comedy as well as from his Roman

---

[170] See J. Wright 1974; also Conte 1994: 98–9.

predecessors by bringing adjustments or innovations to Roman palliata,[171] and also that he triggered the 'death' of comedy, since there were no further ways of development after his experiment.[172]

Yet revivals of Terence's plays a few decades later, Afranius' admiration for him, and Turpilius' continuation of elements of the more refined and sober style of palliata indicate that Terence's precedent was influential.[173] At the same time, Terence placed himself in the tradition of Naevius, Plautus and Ennius; he set himself off against his present-day colleagues, with whom he engaged in controversial debates (*An.* 18–21; *Haut.* 20–1; 28–34; *Eun.* 16–19a); and he had Ambivius Turpio compare his fortune with Caecilius' fate (*Hec.* 14–27). Indeed, Terence preferred Greek models and Greek titles, plot structures, variations of stock motifs and topics such as the relationship between members of different generations that seem to have been present already in Caecilius; he refers to Plautus as a paradigmatic predecessor in the technique of *contaminatio* and used Menander's *Kolax* as a model just as Plautus (*An.* 18–21; *Eun.* 25–34).

Hence Terence is likely not to have attempted to break away from tradition; instead, he developed the palliata further, thereby creating particular elements that are characteristic of all his plays (e.g. logical and complex plot construction, plausible character development beyond the use of mere stock figures, a few basic comic effects), but not as dominant in other Roman comic poets. Therefore it is unlikely that Terence was the exception to a coherent palliata tradition and that the 'death of comedy' was down to his experiments with the form. After his time palliata was continued by Turpilius, and then proper drama on the stage was beginning to decline generally due to the overall cultural and historical situation.

4.10 SEX. TURPILIUS

Sextus Turpilius is the last known writer of palliatae in the Republican period; the only biographical information about him is the notice in Jerome that he died in old age (*senex admodum*) in Sinuessa in 104/3 BCE (Hieron. *Ab Abr.* 1914, 104 BCE [p. 148d Helm]).[174] Thus he must have been a (perhaps slightly older) contemporary of Accius and Atta, have overlapped with Afranius and probably have seen Terence's plays. He is ranked seventh,

---

[171] See e.g. Moore 2001: 246. [172] See e.g. Goldberg 1993.

[173] Donatus implies that Terence was spurred on by success right from the start (Donat. on Ter. *An.*, *praef.* 1.7).

[174] On Turpilius see Beare 1964: 115–16; J. Wright 1974: 153–81 (but see n. 176 below); Blänsdorf in Suerbaum 2002: 258–9 (with bibliography).

right after Terence, in Volcacius Sedigitus' canon of comic writers (cf. Gell. *NA* 15.24).

Thirteen titles and just over two hundred (partly incomplete) lines of Turpilius' plays have been preserved. Like those of Caecilius and Terence, all his titles are Greek; five of them are also attested for Menander, while some might come from Middle Comedy. The fragments indicate the presence of the usual characters (with the typical Greek names) and motifs of the palliata, such as love affairs (*Pall.* 37–9 R.³), marriages (*Pall.* 3; 41; 163; 164; 166 R.³), evil pimps (*Pall.* 133–5 R.³), (greedy) courtesans (*Pall.* 33; 42; 160–2; 185–8 R.³), slaves (*Pall.* 69–70 R.³), strict old men/fathers (*Pall.* 35–6 R.³) and the tricks/intrigues of scheming slaves against old men (*Pall.* 136–8; 205–6 R.³). When a speaker who has cheated his father of money refers to the 'old example/precedent of lovers' (*veteri exemplo amantium*) in describing his behaviour (*Pall.* 36 R.³), this statement might have metatheatrical force and indicate the poet's awareness of the conventions of his dramatic genre. On the formal level too, Turpilius' plays exhibit techniques in adapting Greek plays that are known from Plautus and Terence, for instance when an opening monologue is changed to a dialogue (*Epiclerus*: Turp. *Pall.* 50–3 R.³ vs. Menander, fr. 129 K.-A.).

Turpilius' palliatae, however, also include other aspects: sailors, fishermen and conditions at sea seem to feature frequently (*Pall.* 21–2; 23; 48–9; 139–41; 214–16 R.³; *Leucadia*); this points to an interest in everyday occupations, as perhaps foreshadowed in Naevius' comedies and paralleled by the chorus of fishermen in Plautus' *Rudens* and by the fisherman in Accius' *Medea sive Argonautae*, as well as by the craftsmen in togatae and Atellanae. As regards topics, there might be a contrast between town and country in *Hetaera* (*Pall.* 77–8; 82–3 R.³), the country possibly being a place where one of the characters spends time with women.

Some fragments have the shape of sayings and often also a (popular-) philosophical touch, addressing issues such as wisdom, modesty or frugality and wealth (e.g. *Pall.* 9–10; 28; 40; 142–44; 213 R.³). In the absence of information on speakers and contents, it is uncertain whether these remarks were meant to be serious or mocking, but an expression of general truths is likely to have some force. The combination of comic plot and serious aspects would indicate a similarity to Terence's technique, though encompassing a wider range of topics and situations, and also to tragedy and togata. Another aspect that recalls togatae with their more 'realistic' and 'Roman' depiction of family structures is the fact that at least in one play (*Epiclerus*) there was not just an emotional love affair between two individuals, but the plot rather seems to have involved a whole family, with all members caring for each other and discussing plans.

These facts have given rise to discussions about Turpilius' position in the history of palliata. As for his dates, although his date of birth is not known, it is unlikely that he became so old that he would have produced a number of plays before Terence's career and thus been an influence on Terence;[175] as he died almost forty years after Terence, it is more plausible that he produced the bulk of his plays after Terence's death. This dating of Turpilius' activity implies that he had the entire palliata tradition as represented particularly by Naevius, Plautus, Caecilius and Terence before him.

The evidence of Turpilius' preserved titles points to an avoidance of obvious clashes with predecessors and the choice of new and extravagant titles instead. This does not entail that basic plots would have been essentially different, apart from minor variations. At the same time, though apparently basing himself on Menander for a large part of his output, Turpilius included comic scenes of Plautine type, such as deceptions of old men by scheming slaves or dialogues of bantering slaves. This twofold aspect of his titles and fragments does not permit a clear-cut answer that ignores one half of the evidence.[176]

A more probable description of Turpilius' position will therefore have to take both sides into account, since such a dual nature can be paralleled in predecessors in both the light and the serious dramatic genres: on the one hand Turpilius seems to have continued the tendency towards a more refined and learned style of drama, just as his contemporaries Accius and Atta preferred new, complex and erudite titles; on the other hand he apparently made his plays attractive by including reminiscences of Plautine comedy. Earlier poets such as Pacuvius and Caecilius had attempted to ensure the success of their plays by stunning scenes, and Turpilius, writing in a time in which audiences apparently preferred revivals of Plautine comedy to productions of new plays (Plaut. *Cas.* 5–20; see ch. 2.9), tried to achieve the same effect by different means. His choices, therefore, are not

---

[175] Suggested by J. Wright 1974: 153–4, against the *communis opinio*.

[176] J. Wright (1974: 153–81), arguing against the view that Turpilius followed Terence and pursuing the idea that Terence was the exception to an otherwise coherent palliata tradition (see ch. 3.3 and n. 90), brushes aside the evidence of the titles and the lack of Roman allusions, and focuses on stylistic and structural similarities to Plautus. Goldberg (1986: 203–4) also thinks that Turpilius preferred 'the old formulae to the newer Terentian forms'.

so much indicative of his assessment of predecessors or of the success of their techniques in their time, but rather show that he, like them, adapted standard comic techniques to the requirements of his time.

Additionally, the possible appropriation of Middle Comedy plays and a play entitled *Leucadia*, including the love affair between Sappho and Phaon, allow the conclusion that Turpilius might have continued comedy's development towards the presentation of more serious topics and introduced 'supernatural' or 'mythical' references in comedy, as Plautus had done in *Amphitruo* (with the appropriate caveats) and as was becoming popular in the emerging Atellana. *Leucadia* is likely to have been based on Menander (cf. Serv. on Verg. *Aen.* 3.279), although the title is also attested for a number of other Greek comic poets. While it now seems plausible that Turpilius' play did not tell the story of Sappho and Phaon directly, the setting and the fact that information about Phaon as the founder of the local temple was included suggest that similarities between the situation of a helpless lover described in the play and the mythical characters were hinted at, which might involve a divine element and an aetiological explanation. According to the report of Cicero, who quotes several fragments from the play and comments on them (Cic. *Tusc.* 4.72–3: Turp. *Pall.* 115–20 R.³), the desperate lover appealed to all the gods for help except Venus. Cicero agrees with the characterization of this character, apparently voiced by other figures in the play, as 'insane', and mocks his emotional exclamations and his expectation that the whole divine realm should care for his amatory difficulties. Cicero seems to have regarded the dramatic character's lamentation as an exaggerated emotional scene inappropriate in the context (cf. *at quas tragoedias efficit!*). At any rate such a play might indicate that Turpilius integrated themes and plot structures more characteristic of tragedy into his plays, while maintaining a comic framework.

Whether or not Turpilius' combination of elements from the dramatic tradition was successful is hard to tell. Cicero quotes from his comedies twice and recalls a performance involving the famous actor Roscius (Cic. *Fam.* 9.22.1; *Tusc.* 4.72–3); the comedy that starred Roscius is called a 'well-known/famous comedy' (*comoedia nobilis*) by Diomedes (Diom. *Ars* I, *Gramm. Lat.* I, p. 402.12–13). So Turpilius must have achieved some success, but as he was the last representative of the dramatic genre of palliata, there was no productive reception of his work by subsequent playwrights, and he does not seem to have been of interest to later writers apart from grammarians, who transmit the vast majority of fragments.

4.11 TITINIUS

Titinius is probably the earliest known writer of comedies set in Rome, of *fabulae togatae*.[177] Virtually nothing is known about his biography, and his dates are therefore disputed, a question that is closely connected with views on the time of and the reasons for the origin of his dramatic genre (see ch. 3.4). Modern *communis opinio* favours an early date: i.e. Titinius is placed before Terence and close to Plautus and is thought to have been active in the years just after the Second Punic War. This dating is based on a statement by Varro, consisting of an apparently chronological list of names of dramatic poets (Varro, fr. 40 Funaioli, ap. Char., *Gramm. Lat.* I, p. 241.27–8), on the archaic language of the fragments and on probable allusions to incidents in the early second century BCE.[178]

The evidence from approximately fifteen titles and about a hundred and eighty (partly incomplete) lines indeed points to Titinius' being an early representative of togata: there is a noticeable similarity to elements of both Atellana and Plautine palliata, which might point to a dramatic genre that is evolving and trying to find its own distinctive position within the framework of light dramatic genres. For instance, the title *Fullonia* (or *Fullones*) recalls characters and titles typical of literary Atellana; fullers and their trade are also mentioned in palliatae (Plaut. *Asin.* 907; *Aul.* 508; 515; *Pseud.* 782). Equally, although according to Donatus slaves in togata are usually not allowed to be cleverer than their masters (Donat. on Ter. *Eun.* 57), the announcement to acquaint the addressee with a 'comedy', which might refer metaphorically to an intrigue (*comoedia*: *Tog.* 81/2 R.³),[179] or the mention of an 'architect' (*architecton*: *Tog.* 129 R.³) could indicate scheming slaves, since these words are used in such metaphorical (and metatheatrical) senses in Plautus (Plaut. *Trin.* 706; *Poen.* 1110); references to pimps or parasites also recall palliatae. In formal terms Titinius' fragments display a

---

[177] On Titinius see e.g. Neukirch 1833: esp. 97–101; Courbaud 1899: esp. 29–32; Przychocki 1922; Vereecke 1968, 1971; Cacciaglia 1972: 212–13; Pasquazi Bagnolini 1975: 37–43; Martina 1978; Daviault 1981: 31–7 and passim; Guardì 1981 (on language), 1985: 18–19 and passim; Stärk in Suerbaum 2002: 261–2 (with bibliography).

[178] An emendation in Lydus as adopted by some editors (Lyd. *Mag.* 1.40: τότε Τιτίνιος instead of the transmitted τὸ τετίνιος; others have read τότε Τίνιος or τότε Λίβιος) would place Titinius in the time of the Second Punic War (see Wünsch 1903: XXXV, 41). But the resulting text does not make sense since the passage refers generally to drama in Rome. Martina (1978) argued for a date of 120 to 100 BCE for Titinius and placed him after Afranius, but an early dating remains more plausible.

[179] This seems to be the most likely reading of the transmitted text (so Daviault 1981: 112; Guardì 1985: 54); Ribbeck (1898: 171) emends to *remedium* ('remedy').

wide variety of metres, archaic forms and words as well as stylistic features such as alliteration, enumeration or wordplay.[180]

At the same time Titinius' plays exhibit characteristics that distinguish togatae from palliatae, in particular frequent comments on ordinary relationships within or between families, such as marriage arrangements, or the notable presence of Roman and Italic places and institutions. For instance, Italic (Volscian) towns feature in three titles, referring to people coming from those (*Psaltria sive Ferentinatis, Setina, Veliterna*); one fragment describes people who speak Oscan and Volscian since they do not know Latin (*Tog.* 104 R.³). Because of these references to the region to the south of Rome it has been suggested that Titinius might have come from this area and that togata as a dramatic genre may have connections with it.[181] Although precise assumptions on Titinius' birthplace are problematic in view of the meagre evidence, the lively and varied theatrical tradition in southern Italy may have been familiar to him and contributed to the creation of an indigenous form of comedy.

In terms of dramatic technique Titinius was praised for his character-drawing in antiquity (cf. Varro, fr. 40 Funaioli, ap. Char., *Gramm. Lat.* I, p. 241.27–8). Owing to the fragmentary remains, it is hard to verify this assessment, but the surviving titles show that his plays included individuals with special physical or professional attributes. What can be discerned more clearly are some of the themes in Titinius' plays. For instance, beyond the standard comic plot, there seem to have been comments on topical issues: *Barbatus* has references to female luxury (*Tog.* I; 2; 3 R.³), which may allude to the debate on and the eventual repeal of the *Lex Oppia* in 195 BCE (cf. Liv. 34.1.1–8.3). Two plays about music girls (*Psaltria sive Ferentinatis, Tibicina*) could refer not only to a traditional accomplishment of courtesans, but also more specifically to their admittance to Roman dinner parties in 187 BCE (cf. Liv. 39.6.8; also Plaut. *Mostell.* 959–60; *Stich.* 380–1). This may tie in with contempt for new, lascivious and luxurious Greek ways of life in other fragments (*Tog.* 85; 175 R.³).[182]

---

[180] For studies of Titinius' language and style in comparison with Plautus see Przychocki 1922: 186–8; Vereecke 1971; Daviault 1981: 35–7; Guardì 1981; Minarini 1997.

[181] See Mommsen 1850: 319; taken up by Rawson (1985) 1991: 479–80. By contrast, Daviault (1981: 32 and n. 2) assumes that Titinius was born in Rome, since the majority of known Titinii come from Rome, and there are no ancient comments on Titinius' background.

[182] Martina (1978), who defends a later date for Titinius (see n. 178 above), sees references to other political issues in the fragments. Obviously, allusions to topical events can never be proved for sure in fragmentary texts; but evidence from other writers confirms that the issues identified above were of interest and regarded as worthy of note in their time (see ch. 3.4).

Due to lack of context, it is impossible to ascertain the overall presentation of dramatic characters who voiced such opinions and thus make inferences for the poet's view on these issues; but these themes are likely to have been referred to in the plays because they were of significant public interest at the time. The new dramatic genre of togata, where setting and framework were close to the real-life experiences of Roman audiences, made it possible to address directly actual concerns of the people at the time; simultaneously the dramatic impact was further ensured by basically keeping the form and the topic of love affairs (though in more conventional form) that worked for palliatae.

4.12 L. AFRANIUS

Lucius Afranius was regarded as the most important togata poet by the ancients. The largest number of extant togata fragments comes from his works; still, almost nothing is known about his dates and biography.[183] Statements by ancient writers (e.g. Vell. Pat. 2.9.3) and some internal evidence place his poetic activity in the second half of the second century BCE: he was writing after Terence (see below) and as a contemporary of (or shortly after) the orator C. Titius (cf. Cic. *Brut.* 167); this makes him also overlap with Pacuvius, Accius and Turpilius.

Forty-three titles and about four hundred and thirty lines (partly incomplete) that have been preserved reveal some of Afranius' characteristics and preferred topics. On the basis established by Titinius, Afranius seems to have developed the dramatic genre further and given it a distinctive form: as palliata was becoming more 'Hellenic' by Terence's time, togata underwent a similar development by Afranius' time; there is no longer an obvious similarity to aspects of Plautine comedy, but rather a noticeable influence from Menander and Terence. On a formal level, for instance, in comparison with Titinius, there are fewer rare words and less variety of metres, which points to fewer 'songs' (*cantica*), while there are more succinctly and memorably phrased sententious statements.[184]

The impact of Menander and Terence is proved by the playwright's own statements: Afranius respected Terence as an outstanding and incomparable comic writer (Suet./Donat. *Vita Ter.* 7: *Tog.* 29 R.[3]), and freely admitted that he borrowed from Menander what suited him and he could not do

---

[183] On Afranius see e.g. Neukirch 1833: esp. 165–75; Courbaud 1899: esp. 34–9; Cacciaglia 1972: 215–19; Pasquazi Bagnolini 1975: 44–7, 1977 (on language); Daviault 1981: 37–47 and passim; Drury 1982: 820–1; Stärk in Suerbaum 2002: 263–4 (with bibliography).

[184] On Afranius' language see Pasquazi Bagnolini 1977; Minarini 1997.

better, as he did from any Greek or Latin writer (Macrob. *Sat.* 6.1.4: *Tog.* 25–8 R.³), which Macrobius mentions as a particularly obvious example of this practice (Macrob. *Sat.* 6.1.3). Cicero confirms that Afranius borrowed from Menander (Cic. *Fin.* 1.7), and Horace reports that Afranius was regarded as comparable with Menander (Hor. *Epist.* 2.1.57). Additionally, Cicero says that Afranius aimed at imitating the orator C. Titius (Cic. *Brut.* 167), in whose speeches Cicero found examples of 'pleasantries' and 'stylistic refinement' (*argutiae* and *urbanitas*), while he considered Afranius as 'having a very lively wit' (*perargutus*).

Since Afranius looked to Menander and Terence for his togatae and claimed to borrow from any writer what suited him, he presumably did not follow a particular work by any predecessor for an entire play, but is more likely to have been generally influenced by earlier writers and to have incorporated selected elements into his own works. Cicero at any rate saw a precedent for his own way of using adapted passages from Greek philosophers such as Plato or Aristotle in his treatises in the way in which Ennius made use of Homer for his *Annales* and Afranius of Menander (Cic. *Fin.* 1.7), both poets not transferring entire Greek literary pieces, but rather exploiting Greek models for thoroughly Roman literary works according to their own agenda. Allusions to writers such as Pacuvius, Cato or Lucilius as well as the influence of contemporary oratory have been identified in Afranius' fragments (see ch. 3.4).

Metaliterary statements on Afranius' poetic technique (*Tog.* 25–8; 29 R.³) probably come from a prologue in Terentian fashion, in which the poet responded to criticism by justifying his principles of borrowing from earlier writers. Yet Afranius differs from Terence in having the poet speak in his own person instead of having a prologue speaker talking about him. This change makes such a discussion more detached from the rest of the drama and brings it closer to a proper defence speech.[185] Such a structure is not surprising in a poet of whom Cicero reports that he had an orator among his models and was 'eloquent' (*disertus*) in his plays (Cic. *Brut.* 167). In the area of prologues too Afranius shows versatility rather than adherence to one model, since he also seems to have had prologues spoken by deities, which are likely to have been narrative and expository (*Tog.* 403–4 R.³).

These features of Afranius' poetic technique, in addition to other metaliterary statements (e.g. *Tog.* 100–1; 271 R.³), point to a creative

---

[185] On the *Compitalia* 'prologue' and its relationship to the contemporary literary situation see also Degl'Innocenti Pierini 1991.

independence. The 'literary mode' was probably in line with the times: Afranius' poetic principles seem to have been attacked, and he found it necessary to defend them in his plays, just as Terence (and perhaps Caecilius) did. Reminiscences of oratory in the style and structure of speeches are also found in the plays of his tragic contemporaries Pacuvius and Accius, as well as in Terence's prologues. Literary criticism is exercised by the satirist Lucilius in his satires and by the dramatic poet Accius in his treatises.

Still, Afranius' togatae did not consist entirely of erudite and literary stuff, but had down-to-earth, entertaining plots of the typical comic kind, dealing with human relationships and their problems. In line with the outlook of togata, the main actions affect entire family groups; issues such as marriages, dowries, the relationship between husband and wife in general or arrangements for the future of children and partners play a role. The family community seems to have been a major focus; Afranius enlarged the spectrum of family members and relationships to the extended family: the proliferation of terms for more unusual family relationships in Afranius was already noticed in antiquity (Non., p. 894 L.: *Tog. inc.* xxvi R.³).

Although the family seems to have been prominent, other relationships, typical of light drama, were not lacking: figures such as courtesans and scheming slaves are mentioned (e.g. *Thais*; *Tog.* 133; 136; 189–91 R.³); however, their Greek names and their activities distinguish these dramatic characters from family members. The question of what types of love affairs were covered is intriguing, for Quintilian accuses Afranius of having 'defiled his plots with indecent love affairs with boys, thereby exhibiting his own way of life'.[186] However, there is no evidence in the fragments to support this allegation. Perhaps Quintilian found the introduction of extramarital affairs into common family settings incongruous, and the only explanation he could think of was the poet's character, for which there is no other evidence either. Such criticism may have been provoked particularly since togata plays were set in Roman surroundings and the world depicted was close to everyday reality, so that unorthodox deviations would be noted more easily. What is clear is that there was a distinction between different types of love and desire in Afranius (*Tog.* 23–4; 221 R.³).

Afranius' togatae continued to include comments on Roman and topical issues; here too the spectrum seems to have been enlarged in comparison with Titinius': the craftsmen featured in a title are no longer Atellana fullers, but there is a hairdresser (*Cinerarius*). There is a broader range in

---

[186] Cf. Quint. *Inst.* 10.1.100: *togatis excellit Afranius. utinam non inquinasset argumenta puerorum foedis amoribus, mores suos fassus!*; also Auson. *Epigr.* 69.

geographical terms: Afranius' plays go beyond the area south of Rome and include references to ladies from Brundisium and Neapolis (*Brundisina(e)*; *Tog.* 136 R.³). References to religious affairs (*Augur, Omen*) and Roman games (*Compitalia, Megalensia*) look forward to Atta. Like Titinius, Afranius has probable allusions to current events that generated discussion, in this case the 'marriage and children laws' of the censor Q. Caecilius Metellus Macedonicus in 131 BCE (*Tog.* 360–2 R.³), which are also commented upon by the contemporary satirist Lucilius (Lucil. 676–86 M. = 636–46 W.).[187]

The plays apparently showed a contrast between Romans and Greeks, observing, for instance, sociological and ethnic distinctions in that slaves and courtesans bear Greek names (*Thais*; *Tog.* 136; 189–91 R.³), while other characters have Roman names. Another wave of Greek influence towards the middle of the second century BCE, with Greek libraries and Greek intellectuals coming to Rome, is perhaps reflected when Afranius, like his contemporary Pacuvius (Pac. *Trag.* 89 R.³ = 110–11 W.), distinguishes between Latin and Greek terms for the same concept when talking about *sapientia* (*Tog.* 298–9 R.³).

Overall, surviving fragments and *testimonia* seem to indicate that Afranius was familiar with the available literary tradition and ready to exploit it, and also well aware of issues and interests prevalent in his time. On this basis he apparently developed the dramatic genre of togata further and gave it a distinctive and more sober shape. Plots were set in (stylized) everyday and familiar surroundings, while comprising a variety of elements in form and content; this made it possible to present Roman audiences with humorous situations reminiscent of their everyday lives as well as intellectually stimulating aspects.

4.13 T. QUINCTIUS ATTA

T. Quinctius Atta is the last of the triad of clearly attested togata poets: he died in Rome in 77 BCE (cf. Hieron. *Ab Abr.* 1940, 77 BCE [p. 152e Helm]); he was therefore a contemporary of the tragic poet Accius and of the writers of literary Atellanae Pomponius and Novius.[188] All that survives

---

[187] Some scholars used to assume a particular, long-standing feud between Lucilius and Afranius (on this issue see Daviault 1981: 39–40). But there is no evidence for a general conflict; the fragments just show that the two contemporaries might pick up on the same topical issues and allude to each other's works (*Tog.* 274–5 R.³; Lucil. 957–8 M. = 696–7 W.).

[188] On Atta see e.g. Neukirch 1833: esp. 153–6; Courbaud 1899: esp. 32–4; Cacciaglia 1972: 213–14; Pasquazi Bagnolini 1975: 43–4; Daviault 1981: 47–51 and passim; Guardì 1985: 19–20 and passim; Stärk in Suerbaum 2002: 262 (with bibliography).

of Atta's dramatic output are twelve titles and nearly twenty-five (partly incomplete) verses.[189] However, the best-known actors of his time, his younger contemporaries Aesopus and Roscius (see ch. 2.6), seem to have starred in his plays; and audiences enjoyed the performances (cf. Hor. *Epist.* 2.1.79–82). Horace, however, who transmits this information, seems to be doubtful of the smooth and straight flow of Atta's plays. This may agree with the fact that Atta was praised for his character-drawing by Varro (Varro, fr. 40 Funaioli, ap. Char., *Gramm. Lat.* I, p. 241.27–8), which could attract famous actors to his plays, while there are no comments on topics or plots.

Judging on the basis of the few preserved titles and fragments, Atta seems to have presented family affairs (*Materterae, Nurus, Socrus*) and a variety of topics significant for Roman life; his plays apparently touched upon issues such as Roman games (*Aedilicia, Megalensia*), lascivious life in a spa (*Aquae Caldae*), sacrifices and religious customs (*Gratulatio, Lucubratio, Supplicatio*) or mercenaries (*Tiro proficiscens*); there was also a discussion about the first month of the year (*Tog.* 18; 19–20 R.³). These details confirm the specific Roman outlook of the dramatic genre of togata and may exemplify the general trend towards a form of drama that includes both spectacle and erudition in this period.

4.14 L. POMPONIUS

Lucius Pomponius from Bononia (modern Bologna) was active in 89 BCE (cf. Hieron. *Ab Abr.* 1928, 89 BCE [p. 150d Helm]); i.e. he was a contemporary of the historiographers called younger annalists (Vell. Pat. 2.9.6) and will have overlapped with the tragic poet Accius and the togata poet Atta.[190] Ancient writers who mention Pomponius describe him as a writer of Atellanae (Macrob. *Sat.* 1.10.3; 6.9.4; Sen. *Controv.* 7.3.9), and he was even credited with having invented a new genre (Vell. Pat. 2.9.6). However, Novius seems to have been a contemporary of his, these two being the two main writers of literary Atellanae, and there existed at least a pre-literary Atellana previously. Hence, the description of Pomponius as 'inventor' most probably recognizes that he turned Atellana into a literary dramatic

---

[189] Nonius Marcellus mentions epigrams by Atta (Non., p. 202.26–7 M. = 298 L.), but the text may be corrupt. A reference to a piece called *Satura* (Isid. *Etym.* 6.9.2) gives the title of a togata rather than being an allusion to a work in satiric mode.

[190] On Pomponius see e.g. Frassinetti 1967: 8–11; Raffaelli 1987; Stärk in Suerbaum 2002: 269–71 (with bibliography).

genre. No more details are known about Pomponius' biography or his dramatic production. Of his dramatic output about seventy titles of Atellanae and almost two hundred (partly incomplete) lines remain; in some cases it is uncertain whether two transmitted versions of titles refer to one or two plays or whether fragments attested for a Pomponius are actually his.[191]

Surviving titles and fragments feature the stock characters of Atellanae; they must have played major roles in those plays (e.g. *Bucco adoptatus*, *Bucco auctoratus*; *Maccus*, *Macci gemini*, *Maccus miles*, *Maccus sequester*, *Maccus virgo*). In addition to the characteristics connected with their type, the titles indicate particular circumstances for these characters, which would increase the comic impact of the figures and their stories. Another well-represented area is the world of ordinary craftsmen, such as fullers, and of farmers. Various, sometimes rather mundane, details of rural affairs or of running a farm are present in titles (e.g. *Vacca vel Marsuppium*, *Verres aegrotus*, *Verres salvos*). A contrast between town and country is expressed in some fragments (e.g. *Atell.* 7; 45–6; 102 R.³).

As the core group of Atellana plots focuses on a limited number of stock characters, the titles of plays (by one poet or by different poets) are more likely to be similar or even identical, though this need not imply similar plots. What seems unique in Pomponius, however, among all known titles of Republican drama, is an obvious distinction between earlier and later versions of a play with the same title by the indication of 'earlier/first' or 'later/second' in the title (cf. *Anulus posterior*, *Macci gemini priores*). Either these Pomponian titles are the result of transmission, when, for instance, scholars tried to distinguish between several similar plays, or in Pomponius' time a claim to novelty and creativity by means of a new title for another work by the same playwright was not required, or it was even an advantage to recall a previous performance of a similar play. There are literary precedents for such titles in Euripides and Menander.

Beyond titles that indicate specific Atellana themes, other titles of Pomponius' plays are shared with those of palliatae and togatae; additionally there are mythical titles, some of which are shared with those of crepidatae. This variety of titles indicates a broad range of topics and perhaps styles

---

[191] A scholion on Horace mentions a Pomponius in a list of writers who wrote praetextae and togatae (Ps.-Acr. on Hor. *Ars P.* 288). This text is generally regarded as mangled and unreliable (see ch. 3.4, n. 101), and it is not even clear whether this Pomponius is the writer of Atellanae; therefore this statement cannot prove that he also wrote praetextae and/or togatae (but see Frassinetti 1967: 8). Equally, a *Satura* attested for Pomponius (Non., p. 112.7–8 M. = 160 L.; Prisc., *Gramm. Lat.* 2, p. 200.7–8; 282.16–18) is the title of an Atellana (see e.g. Ribbeck 1898: 301–2; Stärk in Suerbaum 2002: 271) rather than an indication of a work of the *satura* type (so Frassinetti 1967: 108) or a satyr-play (so Wiseman 1994: 65–85; see also ch. 3, n. 14).

in Pomponius' Atellanae, and it suggests that Atellanae plots need not be based on the adventures of the stock characters. There is no evidence on whether or how such pieces might have interacted with tragedies and comedies prior to Atellanae shown as 'after-pieces'. Since tragedies and comedies with the same titles are attested for earlier periods, it would be possible, for instance, that Atellanae commented on those when following upon them at revival performances. It has been assumed that the one extant fragment of *Agamemno suppositus*, which mentions 'thunder', alludes to 'theatre thunder' that occurred in the preceding tragedy (*Atell.* 4–5 R.³);[192] yet the mention of thunder that would wake up anybody who might be asleep could equally be an allusion to a standard feature of tragedies or dramatic productions. It is perhaps more likely that 'after-pieces' commented on general features of tragedies and comedies, such as style or typical dramatic elements, and thus could be shown after any tragedy or comedy.

The setting and topics of discussion in Pomponius' Atellanae appear rather low; some fragments seem almost obscene and preoccupied with bodily functions: plots take place in domestic settings or rural surroundings; there is talk about farm animals, eating and drinking, washing and bathrooms.[193] Dramas apparently included topics frequent in many forms of light drama such as love affairs, marriages and their problems, music girls, various forms of deceiving other people, or mistaken identity and recognition among family members.

As is natural for a dramatic genre originating in Italy, although there are Greek names (*Atell.* 64 R.³: Diomedes), the focus seems to have been a predominantly Roman/Italic and contemporary one: Roman gods or gods with Roman names are referred to (*Atell.* 51; 78; 133; 163 R.³); Roman institutions, places in Italy and beyond or topical affairs are mentioned (e.g. *Campani, Galli Transalpini, Kalendae Martiae, Lar familiaris, Pappus praeteritus*; also *Atell.* 115–16 R.³: *Graeca mercede*). The most intriguing fragment in this context comes from *Auctoratus* and mentions Memmius, Cassius and Munatius (*Atell.* 14/15 R.³). Since these sound like actual names of real Romans, while it is unclear which of the individuals bearing these names might be meant, there might be a direct contemporary reference (see ch. 3.5).

Moreover, there are comments on (meta)literary matters. The line 'if I know what you wish, just like a filthy slave in comedy' contains a metatheatrical comment on slaves in comedy, while the disparaging description of

---

[192] See Stärk in Suerbaum 2002: 269–70.   [193] See also Raffaelli 1987: esp. 127, 130–1.

the slaves gives it a form appropriate to the dramatic genre of Atellana.[194] If another fragment is rightly attributed to Pomponius (*Atell.* 182 R.[3]: *poema placuit populatim omnibus*), he used the literary term *poema*, which Lucilius defined and of which Accius distinguished several types, and there is a discussion about the relationship with audiences, another topic that Accius commented upon in one of his treatises.[195] As metaliterary comments are frequent in other light dramatic genres in Rome, their occurrence in literary Atellanae is not surprising; this indicates that this light genre too included aspects beyond mere entertainment. The play entitled *Philosophia* might be a satiric treatment of this theme, if the one remaining fragment is significant (*Atell.* 109–10 R.[3]).[196]

Almost all fragments of Pomponius have been transmitted by grammarians, commentators and lexicographers; and he is only rarely referred to in other contexts, typically just identified as a writer of Atellanae. The common result of this situation is particularly prominent in what is extant for Pomponius: since the transmitting writers quote fragments because of their unusual words, forms or constructions, his verses seem to be full of those. This data is certainly not entirely representative, even though Atellana might have used a more colloquial and outspoken language than other dramatic genres; yet Novius' language seems to be more refined. At any rate Pomponius also included comments on topical and literary matters in his dramas, which might confirm Velleius Paterculus' description of him as 'famous for his thoughts, unsophisticated in his language' (Vell. Pat. 2.9.6: *sensibus celebrem, verbis rudem*).

4.15 NOVIUS

Like Pomponius, Novius was a writer of Atellanae (cf. Macrob. *Sat.* 1.10.3; Fronto, *Ep. ad M. Caes. et inv.* 2.8.3 [p. 29 v.d.H.]);[197] he was also a contemporary of Pomponius (cf. Macrob. *Sat.* 1.10.3), the two of them representing literary Atellana in the early first century BCE; he will have overlapped with the tragic poet Accius and the togata poet Atta as well.[198] Nothing further

---

[194] See *Atell.* 138 R.[3]: *si sciam quid velis, quasi servi comici conmictilis.*

[195] Cf. Lucil. 338–47 M. = 401–10 W.; Acc. *Did.* 14–15; *Prag.* 3–6 W. = *Gram.* 12–13; 18–21 D.

[196] The attribution to Pomponius of the few verses that sound even more sophisticated and have a philosophical aspect (*Atell.* 191; 192–3 R.[3]) is disputed (see Stärk in Suerbaum 2002: 271) and must remain uncertain.

[197] On the text in the Fronto passage see ch. 3.5, n. 137. Marzullo (1956: 182) infers on this basis (keeping the transmitted text) that Novius was also active in other literary genres besides Atellana, but there is no clear evidence for this.

[198] On Novius see e.g. Frassinetti 1967: 11–13; Stärk in Suerbaum 2002: 271–2 (with bibliography).

is known about Novius' biography or details of his dramatic performances. Since it is Pomponius (*fl.* 89 BCE), rather than Novius, who was credited with having invented the dramatic genre (cf. Vell. Pat. 2.9.6), Novius is generally assumed to have been active slightly later or less prominent.[199] At any rate fewer titles and fragments are known for him; just over forty titles and just over a hundred (partly incomplete) lines have been preserved.

Novius' titles partly cover the same areas as those of Pomponius: the experiences of Atellana stock characters and the world of tradesmen and farmers such as fullers and vintners, as well as mythical topics, although the range is not as wide. Novius shares some titles with known Republican tragedies, and his remakes of mythical stories seem to have been parodic, when in *Phoenissae* a character threatens to kill another with a 'club made from bulrushes' (*Atell.* 79 R.[3]: *clava scirpea*) or *Andromacha* has a comparison with a vintner and his barrel (*Atell.* 4[a–b] R.[3]). In other plays the usual topics of Atellana and other light drama surface, such as the stock characters presented in a variety of situations, love affairs and their difficulties or problems with inheritance and wives with dowries.

Even on the basis of the titles it is remarkable that among the various occupations fullers appear to be prominent, featuring in three titles (*Fullones, Fullones feriati, Fullonicum*; cf. also *Atell.* 94–5 R.[3]). Indeed Novius' fullers later became proverbial; Tertullian remarks about a Greek boxer who is said to have fallen in love with a lover-boy: 'Well, he earns a crown amidst the *Fullers* of Novius and he has rightly been mentioned by the mime-writer Lentulus in his *Catinenses!*'[200] This statement allows the inference that Novius, though basically using the same repertoire as Pomponius, displayed distinctive, recognizable characteristics. Although Atellanae were based on stock characters and a limited range of activities, there was apparently potential for individual emphases and shaping of the material.

In other areas too the focus in Novius seems slightly different from what can be observed in Pomponius. For instance, even though bodily functions and events in the countryside or on a farm continue to play a role, the language and notions are not as crude and down to earth; there is nothing comparable to Pomponius' titles *Verres aegrotus* and *Verres salvos*,

---

[199] That Cicero has interlocutors in *De oratore* (set in 91 BCE) refer to Novius does not imply that Novius was already a well-known dramatist by 91 BCE, since dates given in a literary work written several decades later need not be entirely accurate. These references do confirm, however, that Novius was seen as a poet active in the early first century BCE.

[200] Cf. Tert. *De pall.* 4.4.2: *inter fullones iam Novianos coronandus meritoque mimographo Lentulo in Catinensibus commemoratus* (trans. V. Hunink).

and various aspects of eating are not mentioned as frequently. Generally, a variety of family relationships occur, but there is also an awareness of the contemporary world: there are references to places in Italy (*Atell.* 46; 48; 70 R.[3]) as well as to Roman institutions (e.g. *Quinquatrus*: *Atell.* 95 R.[3]; *Saturnalia*: *Atell.* 104 R.[3]) and topical affairs (esp. *Pappus praeteritus*).

Finally, the fragments include (meta)literary comments: Novius seems to have criticized the tragedies of Titus/Titius, probably the second-century orator and playwright C. Titius, who also made an impression on Afranius (*Atell.* 67–8 R.[3]).[201] Novius' *Exodium*, whatever the precise relevance of this title is, is likely to have commented on pieces in the final position within a performance, either as a self-referential remark on the place of Atellanae or as an allusion to the earlier form of *exodia*, which later combined with Atellanae (cf. Liv. 7.2.11).[202] The title *Mortis et vitae iudicium* recalls a similar scene in Ennius' *Satura* (cf. Quint. *Inst.* 9.2.36).

So Novius' Atellanae seem to reflect both a simple, rural life in Italy and more sophisticated motifs, integrated into a Roman/Italic and contemporary setting. If one accepts that Pomponius was the 'inventor' of this dramatic genre and Novius wrote slightly later, one could venture the hypothesis that Pomponius' Atellanae retained more of the flavour of the original, pre-literary genre, whereas with Novius Atellanae became more refined and moved closer to other Roman forms of light drama. This hypothesis might be corroborated by the fact that Cicero mentions special types of jokes in Novius approvingly in his discussion of wit in *De oratore* (Cic. *De or.* 2.255; 2.279; 2.285), but never refers to Pomponius in the same way. Since, apart from Atta, no major writers of palliatae or togatae were active in the early first century BCE, there was a vacuum into which Atellanae could move. Hence, irrespective of their precise dating, Novius' Atellanae could indicate that Roman audiences still had an interest in dramatic performances with a certain intellectual level; at the same time Atellanae satisfied a desire for basic entertainment, just as the roughly contemporary mime did.

---

[201] Marzullo (1956) argues that Novius might have preceded Pomponius. To support this dating, Marzullo (1956: 177–8) assumes that Novius might allude to Livius Andronicus, whose probable first name was Titus. Apart from the fact that such a comment is more effective with reference to a contemporary or near-contemporary poet, it would be unusual for Livius Andronicus to be referred to as 'Titus'. This first name is given to Livius Andronicus only in Jerome (Hieron. *Ab Abr.* 1829/30, 187 BCE [p. 137c Helm]), where confusion with the historian Livy is generally assumed; Livius Andronicus is thought to have been called 'Lucius' as attested elsewhere.

[202] For the second interpretation see Frassinetti 1967: 12, 109, the former being the more common and more plausible one.

4.16 D. LABERIUS

Decimus Laberius (*c.* 106–43 BCE) was a writer of literary mimes in the late Republic.[203] He composed mimes for the stage,[204] although he came from an equestrian family (cf. Suet. *Iul.* 39.2; Macrob. *Sat.* 2.3.10; 2.7.2; 2.7.8; 7.3.8); this higher social status sets him apart from other Republican dramatists professionally writing for the stage (see ch. 2.7, 4.18). Laberius was probably born in *c.* 106 BCE; at least he is said to have defined himself as being sixty years of age in a piece of poetry performed at an event in 47/6 BCE (Macrob. *Sat.* 2.7.3). Towards the end of his life, Laberius withdrew to Puteoli (modern Pozzuoli), where he is reported to have died in the tenth month after Caesar's assassination, i.e. (most probably) in January 43 BCE (Hieron. *Ab Abr.* 1974, 43 BCE [p. 157i Helm]).

Besides this, only a few, yet significant facts are known about Laberius' biography: Clodius Pulcher requested a mime from Laberius, probably when he was curule aedile in 56 BCE (or in the following years up to his death in 52 BCE); however, the poet declined and explained his refusal with a witty and critical response (cf. Macrob. *Sat.* 2.6.6). That Clodius Pulcher approached Laberius for a mime implies that by this time the latter was already a well-known poet; Laberius' reaction indicates that he appropriated poetic independence for himself and did not feel obliged to comply with all the requests of politicians.

Laberius was later subject to two challenges in 47/46 BCE: according to ancient tradition he was first forced by Caesar to appear on stage in his own mimes and thus to lose his equestrian status temporarily;[205] then Publilius Syrus called on all those who were active for the stage at the time to contend with him in a poetic contest.[206] Because of Laberius' only slightly veiled criticism, Caesar turned his favour to Publilius Syrus and awarded him the palm; yet he returned the equestrian ring to Laberius and thus reinstated him in his equestrian status (presumably on the earlier occasion). These events illustrate the close relationship between politically influential men and dramatic poets in this period, the immediate impact of

---

[203] On Laberius see e.g. Bonaria 1965: 5–9, 103–5; Till 1975; Panayotakis 2005a: 142–4, 2010; and literature on mime (see ch. 3.6, n. 153).

[204] Cf. e.g. Plin. *HN* 9.61; Gell. *NA* 3.12.4; 3.18.9; 16.7.1; 17.14.1; Hieron. *Ab Abr.* 1974, 43 BCE (p. 157i Helm); Macrob. *Sat.* 2.7.1–9; Ps.-Acr. on Hor. *Sat.* 1.10.5.6. For testimonia on Laberius see Panayotakis 2010: 33–6 (and 36–57 for discussion).

[205] Cf. Sen. *Controv.* 7.3.9; Gell. *NA* 8.15; Macrob. *Sat.* 2.3.10; 2.7.2–5; 7.3.8; Suet. *Iul.* 39.2.

[206] Cf. Macrob. *Sat.* 2.7.7–9; also Cic. *Fam.* 12.18.2; Gell. *NA* 17.14.2. The account of the main source (Macrobius) is often seen as referring to a single incident at the games of Caesar in 46 BCE (*Sat.* 2.7.7); however, it seems that Macrobius' narrative is confused and conflates two distinct events, the earlier of which has been dated to 47 BCE (see Panayotakis 2010: esp. 37, 44–7, 54).

politics on dramatic poetry as well as the prominent position of dramatic performances in public life.

What remains of Laberius' mimes is just over forty titles and about a hundred and fifty (partly incomplete) lines; the verses spoken upon Caesar's challenge constitute the longest piece extant from the Roman mime.[207] Later writers acknowledged the wittiness, critical irony and elegant thoughts of Laberius, but disapproved of his diction, which they regarded as crude and unpolished, condemning its colloquialisms and neologisms (Gell. *NA* 3.12.2–4; 10.17; 16.7; Hor. *Sat.* 1.10.5–6).

The titles and a few significant fragments reveal possible characteristics of Laberius' mimes. A small number of titles are Greek, but the vast majority is Latin. There is an overlap with those known from other light dramatic genres, with Atellana, togata and palliata, which indicates that Laberius exploited the shared comic tradition of Italy. Titles and fragments feature common comic characters and motifs: plays show families and their problems; in addition to wives and marriages, there are courtesans, love affairs, slaves and masters; there is mention of inheritance and prodigal sons. The involvement of farm animals and tradesmen indicates rural and simple settings.

Despite this atmosphere, Laberius' mimes were evidently not designed to entertain only: some fragments imply contemporary relevance and/or an allusion beyond the immediate plot. For instance, the statement 'we were concerned about the number of verses, not of rhythms' (*Mim.* 55 R.[3]: *versorum, non numerorum numero studuimus*) sounds like a metaliterary remark even though context and reference point are uncertain.

Several fragments mention Greek philosophers such as Pythagoras, Democritus or the Cynici (*Mim.* 17; 36; 72–9 R.[3]). In *Cancer* the Pythagorean doctrine of metempsychosis is alluded to (*Mim.* 17; *Inc.* XXI R.[3]).[208] Christian writers, opposed to this doctrine, found it more appropriate to mimes than to philosophical schools (Min. Fel. *Oct.* 34.6–7; Lactant. *Div. inst.* 7.12.30–1), while it is uncertain whether they had its use in a particular mime in mind. Irrespective of the assessment of the doctrine, it is likely to have been referred to in Laberius' *Cancer* in a comic way; for instance, the title character may have turned out to have been a human being in an earlier incarnation. When in *Compitalia* one character

---

[207] Panayotakis (2010: 455) notes that this 'prologue' is very different from the other fragments in a number of ways and that this makes its attribution to Laberius suspicious.

[208] The wording of the second passage (*Mim. inc.* XXI R.[3]) can only be inferred (cf. Tert. *Apol.* 48.1), and it is not explicitly attested for Laberius' *Cancer*. Yet owing to the Pythagorean context, its attribution to the same mime is plausible (see Ribbeck 1898: 366; Bonaria 1965: 108).

tells another to follow them to the bathroom (*latrinum*) so that they can get a taste of Cynic doctrine (*Mim.* 36 R.³), the humorous incongruity is obvious, but there might still be a more serious comment on the Cynics' tendency to question everything ordinary and traditional and to live according to nature with the bare necessities of life. The comic application is obvious when a rich and stingy father uses the example of Democritus' blinding himself to describe his situation in dealing with a debauched and prodigal son (*Mim.* 72–9 R.³).

Laberius' mimes also had comments on the contemporary situation. For instance, *Ephebus* includes laments over the degeneration and loss of power of the Roman people (*Mim.* 42–3; 44–5 R.³). A fragment from *Necyomantia* (*Mim.* 63–4 R.³) apparently mocks the facts that Caesar increased the number of aediles to six in early 44 BCE (cf. Suet. *Iul.* 41.1; Cass. Dio 43.51.3; *Dig.* 1.2.32) and that there were rumours about plans of his to allow polygamy so as to legitimize his love affairs (cf. Suet. *Iul.* 52.3). This comment, at least in the extant lines, is indirect and implicit, and above all funny, and therefore it probably does not contain an obvious cause for offence and would not lay the writer open to charges.[209] That Laberius' mimes were known among contemporaries for allusions to the present situation is clear from a remark by Cicero: in fear for the welfare of politically active friends he warns them not to behave so as to provide material for mockery to Laberius (Cic. *Fam.* 7.11.2 [?]January 53 BCE]).[210]

Obviously, Laberius was able to exploit the possibilities offered by his dramatic genre in relation to the circumstances. This also emerges from his behaviour when challenged by Caesar: according to the sources Laberius' enforced performance included a 'prologue', which talked about his life and career and the consequences of this event; the play itself continued with remarks such as 'Now, Quirites, we lose our liberty.' (*porro, Quirites! libertatem perdimus*) or 'He whom many fear must fear many.' (*necesse est multos timeat quem multi timent*), all of which can be read as implying veiled criticism of Caesar, which was recognized by the audience (Macrob. *Sat.* 2.7.2–5: Lab. *Mim.* 98–124; 125; 126 R.³). The distinction between 'prologue' and play proper seems to suggest that topical criticism, albeit specifically

---

[209] It is sometimes thought that this play could have been performed only after Caesar's death (see Bonaria 1965: 116), which would make such criticism less dangerous, though also less topical and relevant. Since Laberius is said to have died in Puteoli in the tenth month after Caesar's assassination (Hieron. *Ab Abr.* 1974, 43 BCE [p. 157i Helm]), he is thought to have withdrawn from Rome previously, but there would have been time for a performance of this mime in the latter part of 44 BCE.

[210] Cf. also Macrob. *Sat.* 2.7.2: *Laberium asperae libertatis equitem Romanum*; Gell. *NA* 17.14.2: *Laberii maledicentia et adrogantia.*

devised for the situation, could be more explicit in the 'prologue' than in the actual play. The 'prologue' is reminiscent of Terence's prologues, which also deal with matters not related to the plot of the play and talk about the poet's experiences as a dramatist. Yet in Terence criticism concerns fellow playwrights, and he takes care to present his rejoinder as a provoked response.

After these public appearances Caesar awarded victory to Publilius Syrus, but allowed Laberius, whom, according to his own words, he generally favoured, to retain (or regain) his equestrian status (cf. Macrob. *Sat.* 2.7.5–8). Perhaps Caesar thought that controlled criticism might support his position, or he regarded this as the safest way to silence Laberius. Interpreting individual lines of plays as references to current political circumstances was a feature of revival performances at the time (see ch. 2.9); these events, along with other comments on the contemporary situation, show that it could also operate in new plays and function as an important political element.

Although the evidence for Publilius Syrus' mimes is of a different kind and comparisons are problematic, those seem to have been more 'moral' and less 'political'. Perhaps political comment came naturally to Laberius or was easier for him because of his social status; the reason given for his refusal to produce a mime for Clodius Pulcher, namely that the latter could do no more than have him go into exile and come back like Cicero (cf. Macrob. *Sat.* 2.6.6), reveals a similar attitude.

4.17 PUBLILIUS SYRUS

Publilius Syrus, an actor and writer of mimes, is probably the latest of the well-known Republican playwrights.[211] His cognomen indicates that he hailed from Syria, and he is likely to have been born at the beginning of the first century BCE.[212] He later came to Italy; there is a tradition that he arrived as a young slave, together with the astronomer Manilius and

---

[211] On Publilius Syrus see Bonaria 1965: 9–10, 130–1; Panayotakis 2005a: 144–5; on topics and transmission of the *sententiae* see Schweitzer 1968.

[212] Cf. Macrob. *Sat.* 2.7.6; Hieron. *Ab Abr.* 1974, 43 BCE (p. 157k Helm). That Publilius Syrus was born in Antioch has been inferred on the basis of alterations to the text in Pliny (Plin. *HN* 35.199), when the transmitted *lochium* in *Publilium lochium mimicae scaenae conditorem* has been changed to *<Anti>ochium* or deleted as being implied in the next item: *consobrinum eius Manilium Antiochum*. Whatever the correct reading is, the term *Antioch(i)us* does not clearly indicate a connection with Antioch anyway. Pliny the Elder also reports that the mime writer Publilius (if the transmitted *Publi mimorum poetae* is correctly emended to *Publi<li>i*) was given the nickname 'sow udder' (*sumen*) because of his luxurious and extravagant eating habits after having been freed (Plin. *HN* 8.209). This name is not attested elsewhere and seems not to have been in common use.

the grammarian Staberius Eros (Plin. *HN* 35.199), but this detail looks like an overly neat construction designed to refer the origin of three different arts back to the passengers of one slave ship.[213] Publilius Syrus gained manumission, allegedly partly by his wit and beauty, and received a careful education (cf. Macrob. *Sat.* 2.7.6–7; cf. also Plin. *HN* 8.209). At some point he started to produce mimes with great success in the towns of Italy. He was therefore brought to Rome for games organized by Caesar in 46 BCE and was presented as the star of the show; his appearance led to the contest between himself and the older equestrian poet Decimus Laberius (cf. Macrob. *Sat.* 2.7.7–9; also Cic. *Fam.* 12.18.2; Gell. *NA* 17.14.2).

Of Publilius Syrus' dramatic output only two titles and a few fragments remain.[214] What he is most famous for, apart from the contest with Laberius, is the so-called 'proverbial sayings' (*sententiae*). Apparently his style was sententious and therefore invited the culling and collecting of one-liners with proverbial meaning from his writings. The reason for their effectiveness and popularity is indicated by Gellius' (and Macrobius') words: 'sayings of Publilius... neat and well adapted to the use of ordinary conversation'.[215] In their preserved form, these *sententiae* are single verses, phrased succinctly and memorably, often with the help of stylistic devices such as alliteration, assonance, antithesis or paronomasia. These features were recognized in the rhetorical tradition, where witty remarks are characterized as 'sayings of Publilius' (*Publilianae sententiae*) (cf. Sen. *Controv.* 7.2.14; 7.3.8; 7.4.8). As for contents, these *sententiae* reflect general human, predominantly moral observations, experiences and pieces of advice: they address fundamental questions such as life and death, justice and injustice, liberty and slavery or changes of fortune; they comment on issues of human behaviour such as love affairs, the treatment of fellow human beings, avarice and liberality, wisdom and foolishness or the effects of passions and emotions. The sententious, almost philosophical tone of Publilius Syrus' mimes, reminiscent of 'higher' genres, was highlighted by Seneca (Sen. *Ep.* 8.8; *Dial.* 6.9.5; 9.11.8).

[213] For the evidence and a sceptical discussion see Kaster 1995: 165–7, on Suet. *Gram.* 13. Publilius is described as 'founder of the mimic scene' (*mimicae scaenae conditor*) in this passage, while it is more likely that Laberius preceded him: Laberius was already an old man at the contest before Caesar in 46 BCE (Macrob. *Sat.* 2.7.3), while Jerome dates Publilius Syrus' dominance on the Roman stage to 43 BCE (Hieron. *Ab Abr.* 1974, 43 BCE [p. 157k Helm]).

[214] Whether or not the sixteen verses given in Petronius' *Satyrica* (Petron. *Sat.* 55.6 = Publ. *Mim.* 3–18 R.³) are genuine is still a controversial question (for doxography see Bonaria 1965: 10); in view of their contents it is perhaps more likely that they are not.

[215] Cf. Gell. *NA* 17.14.3: *Publilii sententiae... lepidae et ad communem sermonum usum commendatissimae* (trans. J. C. Rolfe); Macrob. *Sat.* 2.7.10.

Although, owing to the collection of *sententiae*, Publilius Syrus is one of the more important Republican playwrights from the point of view of reception, the limited number of extant titles and fragments (apart from the *sententiae*) makes it impossible to get an idea of further distinctive characteristics of his mimes. If the story about the contest to which he challenged the other contemporary writers for the stage is indicative of the character and style of his mimes, this would mean that they included an improvisational element and witty repartee. This would be reminiscent of the origin of this dramatic genre and was perhaps facilitated by the fact that Publilius Syrus both wrote mimes and acted in them. A high frequency of rather formulaic *sententiae* would accord with this style of composition. For the dramatic genre of mime, it is also significant that his mimes seem not only to have had a general human and moral aspect, but also, like those of Laberius, to have included comments on the contemporary political situation or at least lines that could be interpreted as such (cf. Cic. *Att.* 14.2.1 [8 April 44 BCE]).

4.18 'MINOR' PLAYWRIGHTS

In addition to the 'major' Republican dramatic poets, there are a few others who are known from scattered *testimonia* or surviving titles or fragments (besides about a hundred and twenty lines from light drama, mostly palliatae, and some two hundred and sixty lines from tragedies transmitted without indication of author or work).[216] In most cases the evidence is not sufficient to establish proper portraits of these playwrights. Yet their mere existence and activity prove that writing plays was a more widespread phenomenon than the usual focus on the 'major' representatives might suggest. Those had already come to be regarded as the more important poets in antiquity, which in turn influenced the attention given to their works and determined the amount of information and number of texts surviving. If the relative proportions of the remains are indicative, Greek-style tragedy and comedy seem to have been the most popular dramatic genres among all playwrights.

In the field of tragedy, there is a Pompilius: in an epigram by Varro he calls himself a pupil of Pacuvius, who, in turn, is called a pupil of Ennius and Ennius a pupil of the Muses (Varro, *Sat. Men.* 356 B.). Since only one verse

---

[216] The remains are included in Ribbeck's editions of the comic and the tragic fragments (1871/3 and 1897/8) respectively.

by Pompilius is extant (Varro, *Ling.* 7.93: *Trag.* 1 [p. 263] R.³), there is no chance of getting an idea of his plays, which, by implication, must have been tragedies. Varro's epigram testifies to a developing Roman tradition, where a succession of poets was acknowledged and an association with established earlier poets could boost one's standing.

The first century BCE saw an emerging class of noblemen who practised dramatic composition, mainly of serious drama, in their spare time (cf. Hor. *Ars P.* 382–4).²¹⁷ They presumably wrote for reading and recitation rather than for full-scale productions on stage; at any rate performances of their plays are not attested. These men, active at the very end of the Republican period, included figures such as C. Asinius Pollio (cf. Verg. *Ecl.* 8.9–10; Hor. *Carm.* 2.1.9–12; Tac. *Dial.* 21.7), Cassius of Parma (cf. Porph. on Hor. *Epist.* 1.4.3; Ps.-Acr. on Hor. *Epist.* 1.4.3), and allegedly even Julius Caesar (cf. Suet. *Iul.* 56.7: *Oedipus*) and Octavian himself (cf. Suet. *Aug.* 85.2: *Aiax*); details of their works are not known in most cases.

One of the first representatives of this group was C. Iulius Caesar Strabo (apparently also called Vopiscus and Sesquiculus) (*c.* 130–87 BCE). He was a contemporary of Accius, though, unlike him, not a professional poet. Accius is said to have looked down upon him, because he regarded Caesar's tragedies as being of low quality, and not to have risen when Caesar entered the 'college of poets' (*collegium poetarum*), even though Caesar was Accius' superior in social terms (cf. Val. Max. 3.7.11). Yet others seem to have valued Caesar's tragedies more highly (cf. Asc. on Cic. *Scaur.* [p. 25 C.]). In addition to writing tragedies, Caesar was an active and successful politician and orator; he is one of the interlocutors in Cicero's *De oratore*.

Three titles of tragedies are known for Caesar: *Adrastus*, *Tecmessa* and *Teuthras*. Such titles are not attested among the oeuvre of any earlier poet in Rome; as well-known and popular myths had already been treated (perhaps too often), he may have looked to new topics, particularly since he was not obliged to please the public or the magistrates or because there was the literary ambition to present something new. Cicero singles out Caesar's mixture and inversion of styles and literary genres (of tragic and comic and of dramatic and forensic) without producing anything incongruous or inappropriate, and his jocularity, lightly flowing, elegant style and gentle, refined expression without total loss of strength (Cic. *De or.* 3.30; *Brut.*

---

²¹⁷ See e.g. Goldberg 1996: 270; Beacham 1999: 4; Boyle 2006: 144–5. The practice of non-professionals writing scripts may have affected further dramatic genres: in the *Philippics* Cicero disparagingly highlights the fact that one of Antony's followers had composed mimes (Cic. *Phil.* 11.13). While the low regard of mimes among intellectuals suits Cicero's argument and he might therefore have exaggerated an involvement with drama, it must have sounded like a plausible allegation.

177). In the area of style, too, Caesar seems to have been innovative. The basis for such experiments was presumably a general tendency towards blurring the characteristics of various literary genres.[218]

Quintus Tullius Cicero (*c.* 102–43 BCE), Cicero's brother, is another example of a gentleman who practised dramatic composition as a leisure activity (cf. Schol. Bob. on Cic. *Arch.* [p. 175 St.]); he is made to express his admiration for and enjoyment of Sophocles in one of Cicero's dialogues (Cic. *Fin.* 5.3). Quintus wrote several tragedies (e.g. *Electra*, *Erigona*), including four composed during a sixteen-day leave during a campaign in 54 BCE; at least some of them were apparently adaptations of Sophocles (cf. Cic. *Q Fr.* 2.16.3; 3.1.13; 3.5.7; 3.7.6–7).[219]

As early as the second century there was the orator C. Titius, who also wrote tragedies and was imitated by the togata poet Afranius (cf. Cic. *Brut.* 167). He is said by Cicero to have been astute and witty in his tragedies, but not really 'tragic'. Since no fragment of his tragedies remains, it is impossible to verify Cicero's description. But if there is some truth in it, it might be another indication that clear distinctions between dramatic genres were beginning to disappear, while scholars such as Cicero did not entirely approve of that.[220]

In the area of comedy, there are the poets mentioned in the ranking by Volcacius Sedigitus (Gell. *NA* 15.24); in addition to Caecilius Statius, Plautus, Naevius, Terence, Turpilius, Luscius Lanuvinus and Ennius, it included Licinius, Atilius and Trabea.

Licinius Imbrex (cf. Paul. Fest., p. 97.4 L.) is called an 'old writer of comedies' (Gell. *NA* 13.23.16) and is clearly a Republican playwright. From his output only the title of a comedy, *Neaera*, and two verses from this comedy have been preserved (cf. Gell. *NA* 13.23.16). He is ranked fourth in Volcacius Sedigitus' canon, just after the winning triad (Gell. *NA* 15.24).[221]

Though Atilius, probably active in the first half of the second century BCE, features in Volcacius Sedigitus' canon of comic poets, he not only wrote comedies, but rather followed the original custom of Livius Andronicus, Naevius and Ennius in composing both comedies and tragedies. He is one of the comic poets who were credited by Varro with easily moving emotions (Varro, fr. 40 Funaioli, ap. Char., *Gramm. Lat.* 1, p. 241.27–9), but soon he fell into disfavour: his style is described as 'iron' and 'very

---

[218] On Caesar Strabo see Ribbeck 1875: 610–12, 614–18; Stärk in Suerbaum 2002: 167–8.
[219] On Quintus Cicero see Ribbeck 1875: 617–25.   [220] On Titius see Ribbeck 1875: 612–14.
[221] On Licinius Imbrex see Blänsdorf in Suerbaum 2002: 257.

harsh' by Porcius Licinus, which is taken up by Cicero (Cic. *Fin.* 1.5; *Att.* 14.20.3). Nevertheless, parts of Atilius' *Electra* were performed at the funeral games of Caesar in 44 BCE (cf. Suet. *Iul.* 84.2). The model for this *Electra* was Sophocles' homonymous play (cf. Cic. *Fin.* 1.5), that for his comedy *Misogynus* perhaps Menander (cf. Cic. *Tusc.* 4.25). Cicero regarded Atilius' Latin version of Sophocles' *Electra* as rather bad (Cic. *Fin.* 1.5). In addition to those two titles, three fragments from Atilius' plays remain.[222]

Trabea was active probably at the beginning of the second century. He belongs to those poets who abundantly express emotions and can easily move them (cf. esp. Varro, fr. 40 Funaioli, ap. Char., *Gramm. Lat.* I, p. 241.27–9), and he is ranked eighth in Volcacius Sedigitus' canon of comic poets (Gell. *NA* 15.24). Two fragments (six verses) of Trabea's dramas remain.[223]

Vatronius, Aquilius and Iuventius are even more shadowy; they seem to have been less successful poets in the time of Plautus; they do not feature in Volcacius Sedigitus' canon.[224]

---

[222] On Atilius see Ribbeck 1875: 608–10; Blänsdorf in Suerbaum 2002: 256.
[223] On Trabea see Blänsdorf in Suerbaum 2002: 255.
[224] On Vatronius see Blänsdorf in Suerbaum 2002: 255; on Aquilius 256–7; on Iuventius 257.

CHAPTER 5

Dramatic themes and techniques

5.1 'TRANSLATION' AND GREEK INTERTEXTS

Roman 'literary' drama came into being through the production of serious and light dramas in Latin based on Greek precursors, while genuine Roman 'literary' dramatic genres were developed later. Hence the question of how Roman dramas relate to Greek predecessors has always been an important issue in discussions of Roman drama.[1] In a narrow sense this problem affects mainly crepidata and palliata, the two dramatic genres that are based on Greek (classical) tragedy and Greek (New) comedy. In a wider sense the relationship to Greek literature is relevant for all varieties of Republican drama, since the other dramatic genres, although presenting Roman subject matter and/or emerging from indigenous forerunners, were established fully only after the appropriation of Greek drama in Rome, so that dramatic structures and/or motifs of Greek drama will have influenced Roman 'literary' drama more generally.

Due to fragmentary transmission or even almost complete lack of evidence for plays of some dramatic genres and periods on both the Greek and the Latin sides, clear-cut answers are not easy, and this is probably one reason why the issue remains a controversial question.[2] Scholars' answers range from the view that Greek-based Roman plays are basically literal translations of Greek models to the opinion that Roman poets used Greek dramas as starting points, but transformed them into plays suitable for

---

[1] On the issue of 'translation' with regard to Roman poets see e.g. Coppola 1940: 11–32; D'Anna 1965; Traina 1974; Petrone 1992: 433–42; Lennartz 1994; Danese 2002. Whereas the majority of modern scholars now seems to regard the practice of Roman poets as 'free translation' or 'adaptation', Lennartz (1994) argues for 'literal translation' in most cases and complete replacement of the Greek text in others, while he denies the possibility of relatively independent transposition along the lines of a corresponding Greek play (for a discussion of Lennartz' theories see Manuwald 2001b).

[2] On the history of scholarship with respect to Roman comedy see Halporn 1993: 191–6; for Plautine comedy see Sander-Pieper 2007: 7–32; for discussions of available evidence and of approaches concerning the relationship of Roman comic poets to Greek plays see Barsby 1995, 2002; for some considerations on method see Danese 2002.

Roman audiences rather freely and might sometimes not even have used a specific Greek dramatic model.[3] Whatever the most likely description is, the fact that the first Roman poets made choices of what and how to 'transfer' and 'adapt' is a significant artistic decision and amounts to the beginnings of literary criticism (see ch. 1.2). Their relationship to Greek predecessors should therefore be studied value-free and rather be seen in literary terms as a connection between intertexts.[4] On this premise attempts may be made to describe the connections between Greek and Roman dramas.[5]

That Roman crepidatae and palliatae are typically based on Greek models is clear from statements in comic prologues (where Plautus and Terence identify the Greek dramas used as a basis or refer to the fact that the present play has been adapted from a Greek one[6]), from Cicero's discussions of the relative merits of Greek texts and their Latin transformations (Cic. *Fin.* 1.4; *Opt. gen.* 18) and from comments in authors such as Cicero, Varro or Gellius, who compare Greek and Latin versions of the same play.[7] These passages show that producing a Latin play by transforming a Greek one was not regarded as something negative or 'unoriginal', but rather accepted as standard practice.[8]

---

[3] In addition to 'Greek model' or 'Greek predecessor', scholars frequently use the phrase 'Greek original'. This is unproblematic when it indicates that the Greek play was the first to present a particular topic or plot. However, it is misleading when it implies that the Greek play is the 'true' and 'real' play and the Latin play is a reproduction at best. In order to avoid evaluative terminology, the more neutral terms 'Greek model' and 'Greek predecessor' or the literary description 'intertext' are preferred here.

[4] See Sharrock 2009: 20 and n. 72.

[5] This is obviously only one aspect of the study of a Roman drama; such an attempt to describe the relationship objectively is in line with a more recent turn in scholarship to interpreting the Roman plays as such rather than studying them analytically with respect to Greek models: Goldberg (1986: xii) had already called for 'a broader base for our opinions' and for analysing the literary and dramatic qualities of Latin plays in their present form without trying to establish the origin of individual elements (also Sharrock 2009: 19–20). Cupaiuolo (1991: esp. 7) focused on existing plays for his analysis of the relationship of Terence's dramas to society, without discussing the question of how they acquired this form. Similarly, Sander-Pieper (2007: 29–31) makes a plea for studying Plautus' comedies as finished products in the contemporary context. Barsby (1995) also questions the attention to the Greek original and the resulting assessment of the Roman version and calls to mind that Roman palliata is a creative fusion of Greek and Italic traditions. Danese (2002) opposes limiting the study of 'models' to Greek comedy and making evaluative comparisons between Greek and Roman versions; instead he argues for accepting Plautine comedy as a form of free rewriting and for taking into account the perspective of original audiences, who enjoyed the finished product and did not worry about the origin of individual elements.

[6] Cf. e.g. Plaut. *Asin.* 10–12; *Merc.* 9–10; *Mil.* 86–7; *Poen.* 50–5a; *Trin.* 18–21; Ter. *An.* 9–14; *Haut.* 4–9; *Eun.* 19b–20a; 30–4; *Phorm.* 24–8; *Ad.* 6–11; also Ter. *Eun.* 7–13.

[7] Cf. e.g. Cic. *Tusc.* 2.48–50 (Sophocles' *Niptra* and Pacuvius' *Niptra*); Suet./Donat. *Vita Ter.* 3 (Menander's *Adelphoi* and Terence's *Adelphoe*); Gell. *NA* 2.23 (Menander's *Plokion* and Caecilius Statius' *Plocium*); 11.4.1 (Euripides' *Hekabe* and Ennius' *Hecuba*).

[8] Seneca considers appropriating and reusing material shaped by earlier poets as an acknowledged and justified method (Sen. *Ep.* 79.5–6).

For determining details of this process, a passage in Gellius, which gives both excerpts from Menander's *Plokion* and the corresponding versions by Caecilius Statius (Gell. *NA* 2.23), as well as a papyrus fragment of Menander's *Dis exapaton* (*P.Oxy.* sine numero [O13]), which matches a section of Plautus' *Bacchides* (Plaut. *Bacch.* 494–562), are the best pieces of evidence. These two cases that allow comparisons (along with individual lines from tragedies) indicate that Roman playwrights kept the main story line of the Greek dramas and the general sense of individual passages; at the same time they adapted wording, metre and music according to Roman conventions and modified the presentation of characters as well as the tone and structure of individual scenes, which could affect the plot as a whole (cf. also Donat. on Ter. *An.* 9[2]). While some of these adjustments were necessary in the adaptation of Greek texts to the Latin language and Roman stage conventions, others went beyond what was required for a mere transformation.

In particular, Roman poets adapted the plays not only to the requirements of the Latin language and Roman dramatic conventions, but also to the interests of contemporary audiences and the contexts of production. In a passage from *Hecuba*, for instance, Ennius basically expresses the same idea as Euripides (Eur. *Hec.* 293–5; Enn. *Trag.* 165–7 R.^{3} = 206–8 W.), but his wording makes the situation clear, and he uses Latin terminology (e.g. *ignobiles*: 'ignoble') and stylistic features of early Roman poetry such as alliteration and assonance. That Roman plays by the same playwright can be seen to exhibit a certain unity in terms of linguistic features and preferred plots and motifs indicates that, to some extent, Roman poets gave transposed plays their distinctive shape.[9]

Defining the methods of Roman playwrights precisely is also difficult because *testimonia* referring to this issue seem to be contradictory. For instance, in his comments on Greek texts and their Latin versions, Cicero talks about 'Latin plays translated word for word from the Greek' on one occasion, but mentions Roman poets 'who have reproduced not the words but the meaning of the Greek poets' elsewhere (Cic. *Fin.* 1.4–7; *Acad.* 1.10).[10] Both statements are probably triggered by the respective

---

[9] See also Conte 1994: 57.

[10] Cf. Cic. *Fin.* 1.4: *fabellas Latinas ad verbum e Graecis expressas*; *Acad.* 1.10: *qui non verba sed vim Graecorum expresserunt poetarum*; also *Opt. gen.* 18; *Fin.* 3.15. A similar phrase (*verbum verbo . . . reddere fidus / interpres*) recurs in Horace (Hor. *Ars P.* 131–5), but the context is not restricted to adaptations into Latin from Greek. Horace argues that it is possible to create a new and original piece of literature on the basis of a well-known story; yet in order to achieve this, one must not proceed as an over-faithful translator or anxious imitator. Jerome later says with regard to his practice of

argument:[11] in the first passage Cicero argues that it is ridiculous not to read philosophical treatises in Latin when one reads Latin dramas without reservation even though these are translations of the Greek. The second passage is also based on the contrast that people read Latin dramas, but not Latin philosophical treatises; yet here it is emphasized that reading philosophical texts in Latin will be much more enjoyable than reading texts by Latin dramatic poets, who transpose the sense of the Greek. In both cases Cicero tries to point out that philosophical works in Latin make good reading for Romans and corroborates this by differently focused comparisons with dramatic literature.

Since Cicero, again in a different context (Cic. *Tusc.* 2.48–50), compares the Latin and the Greek versions of the same play (Soph. / Pac. *Niptra*) and regards the Latin one as 'better' (*melius*), he obviously assumed that there could be differences.[12] As Cicero uses the same term to compare two Roman descriptions of Achilles dragging Hector's body ('Accius is better' – *melius Accius*), he apparently allows for individual shaping on the part of Roman dramatists (Cic. *Tusc.* 1.105). Therefore Cicero is most likely to have thought that Roman adaptations of dramas kept to the Greek model so closely that comparisons could be made, but that at the same time they showed a certain amount of independent composition.

Such comparisons by ancient writers indicate that distinctions between Greek and Latin versions were recognized, though assessments differed: while Cicero preferred the Latin version of *Niptra* because of its presentation of a virtuous character, Gellius condemned the way in which the Greek *Plokion* had suffered from Caecilius' changes (Gell. *NA* 2.23). Gellius admits that Roman comedies sound fine and pleasing if read on their own; but when they are compared with Greek models, he believes that their inferiority becomes obvious (Gell. *NA* 2.23.1–3): he disapproves of changes in style and tone, which have ruined the beautiful Greek version. Gellius does approve, however, of Ennius' adaptation of lines from Euripides' *Hekabe* (Gell. *NA* 11.4.1); the reason is probably that these keep relatively close to the sense and tone of the Greek, although they have been altered to suit Roman style and terminology.

---

transposing Greek (religious) texts into Latin that 'he does not translate word for word, but expresses the meaning on the basis of the original meaning' (Hieron. *Ep.* 57.5.2: *me . . . non verbum de verbo, sed sensum exprimere de sensu*) and refers to Republican playwrights (as well as Cicero) as precedents (Hieron. *Ep.* 57.5.1–6; 106.3.2–3; *Mich.* 2, *praef.*; cf. also Sen. *Ep.* 58.7; Gell. *NA* 11.16).

[11] See also Jocelyn 1967: 23–7.

[12] Similarly, 'Varro prefers the beginning of *Adelphoe* [by Terence] even to the beginning in Menander' (Suet. / Donat. *Vita Ter.* 3).

While it is obvious from their background and references made in their writings that Republican dramatists, particularly Ennius and Accius, were familiar with classical and Hellenistic Greek literature and reflected on the relationship between Greek and Roman literature, they have not left explicit discussions of how Roman poets dealt with Greek plays. Palliata prologues, though they address various aspects of writing dramas, do not reveal general principles either. Plautus, in his longer prologues, frequently has the speaker give the title of the Greek model and the name of its author; as for the adaptation process he typically has the person say that 'Plautus' has transposed the drama into Latin, which is sometimes called '*barbarus*', and mention the new title (Plaut. *Asin.* 10–12; *Merc.* 9–10; *Mil.* 86–7; *Poen.* 50–5a; *Trin.* 18–21). Plautus is obviously aware of his creative role, but he does not reveal anything about his techniques or principles in those contexts. A single passage, put into the mouth of a slave, indicates that he seems to have regarded his compositional activity as so independent that he believed that some of his slave intrigues could surpass those of Greek comic poets (Plaut. *Mostell.* 1149–51).

Terence allows further insights because he sets off his own technique against that of opponents. The very fact that he talks about ways of using Greek plays shows that at least by this time Roman playwrights did not translate mechanically, but were in a position to make individual decisions on the method used.[13] Terence has the prologue speaker in *Eunuchus* say the following about an opponent's writings: 'By translating well (*bene vortendo*) and at the same time writing badly (*scribendo male*), he turned good Greek plays into bad Latin ones.'[14] As *vertere* refers to the process of transposing Greek plays into Latin ones and *scribere* to composing the Latin text, the combination seems to mean that this poet had selected a suitable Greek play for transposition into Latin, but had not managed to produce good Latin verse and dramatic structures, which is confirmed by the examples mentioned in subsequent lines (Ter. *Eun.* 9–13). According to Terence, such a method makes the resulting product in Latin a bad play despite its good Greek basis.[15]

This discussion invites the conclusion that Terence expects a playwright not just to be able to transpose a Greek model, but also to produce a

---

[13] See also Moore 2001: 244.

[14] Cf. Ter. *Eun.* 7–8: *qui bene vortendo et easdem scribendo male ex / Graecis bonis Latinas fecit non bonas.* On this passage see also ch. 4.8.

[15] Cicero confirms that literary works can be transposed badly or even worsened when turned from Greek into Latin (Cic. *Fin.* 1.5: *male conversam Atili* [on a Latin version of Sophocles' *Electra*]; 1.8: *de malis Graecis Latine scripta deterius*).

well-rounded play in Latin. That Terence 'contaminated' scenes from different Greek plays into one play in several instances indicates that he himself followed an approach that exploited Greek models to create what he regarded as 'good' Latin plays.[16] The impression of free treatment of Greek versions by Terence seems to be contradicted by a statement in the prologue of *Adelphoe*, where he has the prologue speaker talk about a single scene from a second Greek play, which has been integrated into *Adelphoe*: 'the poet has appropriated this scene into his *Adelphoe*; he has presented it reproduced word for word'.[17]

The prologue's explicit statement that Terence followed the wording of the Greek model for this scene is made in a specific context, where the poet defends himself against having made use of a play already transposed by Plautus and talks about the method adopted for this single scene (which Plautus had left out). This scene features a young man abducting a girl from a pimp and might therefore have seemed effective and suitable to Terence. The poet perhaps wanted to stress that this scene was based on a section of a Greek model not yet seen in Rome. He may have wished to counter the implied suggestion that he included bits from other parts of the play already adapted by Plautus, which is harder to prove in case of free translations (how 'literal' Terence's translation actually was is another matter), and also to show that Plautus had omitted an excellent scene. In sum Terence seems to have been aware that different ways of transposing Greek plays into Latin were available to Roman poets and to have chosen the method best suited to his purposes in each case.

This is confirmed by Cicero's comments: the passages mentioned show that he posited various ways of transposing Greek literary texts or extracts from them into Latin and allowed for the possibility that Roman dramatic poets adapted Greek plays freely. Roman writers will have produced translations with varying degrees of literalness, according to their

---

[16] Cf. Ter. *An.* 9–21; *Haut.* 16–21; *Eun.* 25–34; Donat. on Ter. *Eun., praef.* 1.11. Terence mentions Naevius, Plautus and Ennius as precedents, presumably thinking of their comedies. Contamination has also been suggested for tragedy (see N. W. Slater 1992a: 90). In view of the similarity of techniques in comedy and tragedy this is a viable possibility (for a discussion see Schierl 2006: 17–20), but in the absence of sufficient material it can be neither proved nor disproved. At any rate contamination in tragedy would work differently, since this dramatic genre does not rely on stereotyped plots and characters to the same extent as comedy.

[17] Cf. Ter. *Ad.* 10–11: *eum hic locum sumpsit sibi / in Adelphos, verbum de verbo expressum extulit.* Starting from the basic literal sense of *exprimere*, McElduff (2004: 122) interprets Terence's expression as meaning more than not translating literally, but also suggesting that Terence was 'milking' the Greek text for what it was worth. While the choice of the verb *exprimere* may trigger such connotations, the particular expression and the argument in this passage as well as the occurrence of similar phrases in other contexts (cf. esp. Cic. *Fin.* 3.15; see n. 10 above) rather suggest that Terence is here said to have translated this particular scene literally (irrespective of what he actually did).

intentions and to the requirements of individual passages. However, the fact that Roman poets made not only word-for-word translations, but also translations according to sense, and might have alternated between the two methods, shows them to be creative individuals[18] rather than 'slavish translators'.[19] In view of such an active engagement with Greek drama, scholars have even argued that Roman poets should be seen as 'readers' or 'interpreters', who pursue their own creative agenda in transforming plays and aim at creating something new.[20] Roman dramatists might have felt free to rework classical Greek plays, since they thereby basically continued what later Greek dramatists had already done (cf. Phryn., p. 39.19–23 *Anecd. Bekk.*). Additionally, they could have been inspired by the way in which Greek troupes of actors were modifying classical scripts for revival performances.[21]

Irrespective of the chosen method of reworking, preferred sources in the realm of tragedy seem to have been the classical Athenian tragic poets of the fifth century BCE (Aeschylus, Sophocles, Euripides), while comedy tended to rely on fourth-century Hellenistic poets such as Menander and Diphilus. Even these Hellenistic plays were 'classics' by the late third and early second centuries BCE; so what tragic and comic poets in Rome had in common was that they apparently turned to established classics rather than to contemporary pieces.[22] Where this cannot be confirmed by *testimonia* or extant lines that allow comparison, hypotheses often rest on titles; however, it has to be borne in mind that the same story can be treated under different titles and that identical titles do not have to refer to the same version of a story. Also, in cases of titles attested for both a well-known Greek dramatist and one or more less famous ones, it is a plausible inference that Roman dramatists followed the prominent versions, but not a necessary conclusion.

For some Roman dramas no Greek model can be identified, since there is no record of a Greek play with the same title or a similar title that would suggest an identical story on the basis of what is known about the respective plots. The traditional response to such a situation has been the assumption of lost Greek dramas from the classical or Hellenistic periods, particularly of lost post-classical, post-Euripidean plays in the case of tragedy.[23] But such

---

[18] See e.g. Conte 1994: 41; Dench 1995: 66.   [19] For this older view see e.g. Beare 1964: 70–1.
[20] See Halporn 1993: esp. 199, 202, 208.   [21] See e.g. Gentili 1979: 30–1; Boyle 2006: 12.
[22] See e.g. Fantham 1977: 32; Xanthakis-Karamanos 1980: 22.
[23] On post-Euripidean tragedy and its relationship to Roman tragedy see also Xanthakis-Karamanos 1980: esp. 26–34.

theories must largely remain hypothetical, and a wider variety of possible starting points for Roman dramatists needs to be considered: for instance, scholars now regard it as possible that Roman poets were able to create plays on the basis of texts in other literary genres and their knowledge of Greek dramatic structures. Nevertheless, because Roman drama developed on the basis of classical Greek dramas and of their revivals in the Hellenistic period as well as of productions and scripts of Hellenistic Greek dramas, the Hellenistic approach to drama will have been a relevant factor for Roman poets. However, Hellenistic drama is more likely to have influenced the form of presentation and the preference for certain topics rather than the choice of particular plays or myths (see ch. 1.2).

The method of dealing with Greek material will also have changed over the course of the Republican period. Just as Livius Andronicus' *Odusia* seems to have been a transposition of the Homeric *Odyssey*, and his successor Naevius created an epic on a Roman topic on the structural paradigm of Greek epic, later Roman playwrights will have composed their plays more independently and with reference to the emerging Roman tradition (as the evolution of praetexta and togata also indicates). This may be shown, for example, by the series of Republican Medea tragedies: Ennius probably started from Euripides' *Medea* and made some changes to this model; Pacuvius either followed a Hellenistic model or composed his own version on the basis of mythographical sources along the lines of Greek tragedy;[24] and Accius created a play from an epic source (Apollonius Rhodius' *Argonautika*).[25]

The mere fact that Roman poets presented dramatic stories that were not covered by the most famous Greek plays shows that Roman playwrights had a substantial knowledge of Greek literature and culture and were able to make use of this for their dramatic creations. Irrespective of whether Roman dramatists transposed hardly known Greek plays or developed plots from narrative sources, they will have offered something novel to audiences. At the same time they ensured that new plays related to the spectators' experiences by choosing stories that were similar to those already shown on stage (and/or generally known); they also kept well-known characters, but chose different aspects of and stages in their lives, varied familiar plot

---

[24] In his discussion of the wide range of Medea stories, Diodorus says (Diod. Sic. 4.56.1 [trans. C. H. Oldfather]) that 'it is because of the desire of the tragic poets for the marvellous that so varied and inconsistent an account of Medea has been given out' and alludes to Athenian tragedies including the return of Medea and Medus to Colchis, which sounds similar to Pacuvius' *Medus*. This might indicate that there was a wider range of versions of this myth available than is identifiable today.

[25] See also Fantham 2005: 118, suggesting such a procedure for even earlier Roman poets.

structures and motifs or provided sufficient information for audiences to situate the plot within the mythical context or a fictional environment. Roman poets thereby made poetic decisions on how to adapt particular Greek stories to a Roman environment and to present meaningful versions to Roman audiences.[26]

In order to make informed choices, Roman playwrights must have had access to a repertoire of plays and stories. Although the works of several Republican poets reveal that they were 'scholar poets' in Hellenistic fashion, well read in classical and Hellenistic literature, including scholiasts, there are no records about their education, apart from that of Terence (cf. Suet./Donat. *Vita Ter.* 1), and Plautus is often regarded rather as a 'man of the theatre'. Yet poets are likely to have read scripts of Greek plays, in particular of the most popular and most widely circulated ones. Greek myths had been known all over Italy for centuries.[27] Besides, Roman poets could have watched performances of Greek dramas in Italy, memorized them or taken notes, received information from actors involved or got theatre scripts from members of actors' troupes.[28]

Accordingly, all Greek plays about which Roman playwrights had managed to get sufficient information were available for reworking in principle; however, poets seem to have been governed in their selection by conventions. Interesting evidence again comes from comedy: in the prologue to *Eunuchus* Terence has the prologue speaker defend the poet against accusations that he had used as a model a Greek play or parts of a Greek play that had already been transposed by earlier Roman poets (Ter. *Eun.* 19b–34). Terence does not deny that some of his characters have been taken from this particular Greek play, but he does deny that the earlier Latin versions based on it were known to him. In another prologue it is stressed that Terence inserted a single scene from a drama already adapted by Plautus as the earlier poet had omitted this scene in his version (Ter. *Ad.* 6–11). Therefore it is plausible that in Terence's time going back to Greek dramas already used by Roman poets (unless signalled) was not regarded as good practice (cf. also Donat. on Ter. *Eun., praef.* 1.11). The pressure to transpose fresh Greek plays agrees with anecdotal evidence for Terence's death during a journey to Greece from which (according to one version) he was

---

[26] See generally Feeney 1998: 50.

[27] On the evidence from vase-paintings see Séchan 1926; Taplin 1993, 2007.

[28] On the wide range of possibilities for Roman playwrights to get acquainted with Greek plays see N. W. Slater 1990: 121–2.

about to bring back a great number of plays converted from Menander (cf. Suet./Donat. *Vita Ter.* 5).

There is, however, one intriguing statement in the argument in the prologue to Terence's *Eunuchus*. The opponent's charge is reported as being based on the following claim: *Colacem esse Naevi et Plauti veterem fabulam* (Ter. *Eun.* 25).[29] As the prologue speaker, referring back to this line (Ter. *Eun.* 33–4), talks of *eae fabulae . . . Latinae* (in the plural) according to the transmitted text, the reference must be to two plays and not to one play produced collaboratively; such a co-production would have been unprecedented anyway. The line can then be translated either as 'there is a *Colax* of Naevius and an old play of Plautus' or as 'there is a *Colax* by Naevius, and another by Plautus, an old play'.

Since there are a few fragments assigned to a *Colax* by Plautus, in addition to fragments from a *Colax* by Naevius, plays entitled *Colax* were obviously ascribed to both poets and, consequently, there were two palliatae by different poets sharing the same title.[30] Yet owing to the fragmentary state of those plays it is uncertain whether they followed the same model or the same plot. Nonetheless, the existence of two plays of the same title by different Roman playwrights looks like a precedent for what Terence is being accused of. Therefore reference to this fact on the part of the opponent seems inappropriate as it might invalidate his reproach or give Terence a starting point for his defence.

The qualification 'old play' (*vetus fabula*), however, must have a particular significance rather than just giving an indication of the dates of these dramas (see ch. 2.9). Indeed, Gellius reports that Plautus used to revise and update plays of 'old poets' (*veteres poetae*), which thereby gained characteristic features of his style and came to be ascribed to him (Gell. *NA* 3.3.13). Hence Terence's opponent might have wanted to point out that Menander's *Colax* had been adapted for the Roman stage by Naevius and that Plautus had produced a reworking of Naevius' version (which was therefore an 'old play' according to the categories of the Roman theatre). When Terence then went back to the same Greek model, this step appears even worse in view of the existence of two previous Roman versions. This line of argument would imply that what Plautus did was not a precedent for Terence's procedure since it would have been obvious that he had worked on the basis of an existing Roman play, while Terence, without laying an explicit

---

[29] On the problems and possible readings of this line (with references to earlier discussions) see Stein 2003: 212–16; also Beare 1964: 37; Blänsdorf in Suerbaum 2002: 217.

[30] The same is true for *Carbonaria* and *Nervolaria* (if the relevant text is thus emended correctly).

claim to 'novelty' for this comedy (as in other prologues), introduced his play as if no previous Latin plays of this type existed (inadvertently, as he claims).[31] It would follow that 'new' Roman palliatae could only be created from hitherto unused Greek comedies.

There is no comparable evidence about the conventions of using Greek models for tragedy; this may be due to the fact that relevant passages have not been preserved or that tragedy could not accommodate metatheatrical discussions as easily as comedy. However, the question might not have been as pressing for tragedy as it was for comedy: for whereas the subject matter for tragedies was provided by a variety of myths and different versions of the same myths, which were in the public domain independent of individual dramatic treatments, the fictitious nature and basic uniformity of New Comedy plots might have encouraged the attribution of specific variations of the standard plot to particular poets and plays. In a number of cases, titles or treatments of myths are attested for several tragic playwrights in Rome, but these dramas do not necessarily present the stories in the same way.[32] Still, Roman tragic poets seem to have tried to avoid covering the same ground as their predecessors, for instance by choosing different sections of well-known myths. Or what must have been essentially the same story is presented under various titles, with presumably different aspects coming to the fore.[33] Thus there seems to have been a similar aim for novelty and individuality among tragic poets to that among comic poets, where procedures are more obvious.

Roman Republican playwrights appear to have been thoroughly familiar with the available Greek intertexts and made deliberate choices on what and how to adapt, so as to present new and distinctive poetic versions, following Roman conventions and being of interest to contemporary audiences.

---

[31] Simon (1961), however, reads the passage as implying a change of attitude: the notion of 'theft of intellectual property' was establishing itself in Terence's time, but had not existed in the period of Plautus.

[32] Fantham (2005: 118) is sceptical of the existence of tragedies with the same title by different poets.

[33] For praetextae on contemporary events the problem of an existing previous version would not have occurred, but it could come up with reference to events from earlier Roman history. Indeed the story of Brutus, the founder of the Roman Republic, is the only one for which two versions might be attested (on this issue see Manuwald 2001a: 238–9, with references). If the extant verses are representative in any way, the focus of the two plays may have been different. Besides, these dramas were written in the late Republic when revivals were already common, an attempt at which is attested for Accius' *Brutus* (cf. Cic. *Att.* 16.5.1), so that the uniqueness of particular versions was gone.

5.2 TOPICS AND THE CONTEMPORARY CONTEXT

The study of techniques of composition and of the dramatic output of individual poets leads to the conclusion that playwrights made informed choices about which stories to dramatize. In addition to preferences that can be observed for each dramatist (see ch. 4), there are the questions of whether any topics might be discovered that could be described as frequent in or characteristic of Republican drama as a whole and whether there is any connection between those and the contemporary context.

As a starting point it has to be established whether Roman poets were subject to any restrictions on their choice of plots and topics. No actual censorship seems to have operated in Rome, in the sense of there being an institution that might ban works from 'distribution'.[34] Nevertheless, since magistrates effectively decided which plays were to be performed at upcoming festivals, the authorities had an impact on the selection and thus the character of plays; however, criteria for their choices are not known (see ch. 2.2, 2.6). On general grounds officials are likely to have wished for their shows to be immediate successes with the populace and to confirm rather than endanger Roman traditions. Hence magistrates will have encouraged affirmative or at least uncontroversial plays that were bound to find favour. For this purpose they might have preferred tried and tested set-ups, dramatic impact and standard messages (and, later, poets with a proven track record) and not have encouraged a great deal of experiment or of potentially subversive social and political comment.

A discussion about the Roman attitude to the presentation of well-known individuals on stage in Cicero's *De re publica* (Cic. *Rep.* 4.11–12 [= August. *De civ. D.* 2.9]) is often adduced as evidence for a ban on presenting living Romans on stage.[35] Yet the remains of Cicero's text do not refer to a law threatening punishment for critical dramas, in

---

[34] Sp. Maecius Tarpa seems to have been appointed to select the entertainment at the opening of Pompey's Theatre (cf. Cic. *Fam.* 7.1.1). Yet this is the only such instance known, and the fact that Cicero mentions it might indicate that it was unusual (see Ribbeck 1875: 656; Balsdon 1969: 264–5). The view that this set-up was exceptional and therefore memorable is corroborated by the fact that Horace twice refers to the same person as an example of a judge of literary works (Hor. *Sat.* 1.10.37b–9; *Ars P.* 386b–8a). The Commentator Cruquianus, however, seems to have generalized from these passages, when he writes 'or to undergo censure by Metius [= Maecius] Tarpa or another critic' (Comm. Cruq. on Hor. *Sat.* 1.10.38 [p. 403]: *vel Metij Tarpæ alteriusve critici subire censuram*).

[35] On this basis it is often stated that it was forbidden to praise or blame any living man on the stage in Rome (see e.g. Beare 1964: 42; Dupont 1985: 219–20; Feldherr 1998: 171). While the extract mentions both praise and blame, it is unclear, as the context is missing, whether the aspect of praise played a particular role in the argument. Since it can be inferred that the discussion in this section was concerned with criticism of actual individuals, which was regarded as inappropriate for the stage (as it was the business of censors or courts of law in Rome), it is not unlikely that in the concluding

contrast to the mention of punishment for mocking songs as outlined by the Law of the Twelve Tables. The phrasing of the passage points to dislike and disapproval among traditional Romans rather than a normative rule. Praise of contemporary individuals was apparently not impossible, as praetextae show; plays of this type even included references to topical events. Perhaps it was just critical references to named individuals on stage that were disapproved of, which prevented 'criticizing by name' (*nominatim laedere*/ὀνομαστὶ κωμῳδεῖν) after the model of Greek Old Comedy as a general practice. The inference, on the basis of an allusive reference in Plautus (Plaut. *Mil.* 211–12), that poets could be imprisoned for unbridled speech rests on shaky grounds (see ch. 4.2).

In the second century BCE two mime actors criticized the poets Lucilius and Accius from the stage; these actors were taken to court by their victims, albeit with contrasting success (cf. *Auct. ad Her.* 1.24; 2.19). The differing results (even though the specific circumstances of each case are unknown) may point to the conclusion that naming someone on stage (even critically) did not inevitably lead to punishment. Terence, in his prologues, refers to poetic predecessors by name, but describes contemporary opponents by their poetry and their opinions; Plautus mentions a contemporary impresario by name (Plaut. *Bacch.* 214–15). Lines that name Roman individuals, including a tragic poet, have been preserved from Atellanae (Pomp. *Atell.* 14/15 R.[3]; Nov. *Atell.* 67–8 R.[3]); as actors in this dramatic genre were allowed to hide their identities and could come from higher social classes, they might have been granted more freedom. Also, greater leniency might have operated in the case of theatre people than in the case of politicians.

This framework did not make Republican drama entirely 'apolitical',[36] although in the beginning it tended to be only indirectly controversial or politically critical. On the contrary, Republican drama engaged with a variety of issues relevant to contemporary society. By its very nature drama deals with human relationships, among family and friends, but also within the community, such as between colleagues, within government or between representatives of different peoples. By their choice of themes and characters Roman plays could demonstrate qualities such as *virtus*, *pietas*, *iustitia*, *modestia* or *integritas*, law and order brought back or punishment for those who deserve it; they could present reversals of fortune, problems solved by human negotiations, respect and esteem for particular individuals, the

---

remark 'praise' was added to 'blame' by the speaker in the dialogue, by Cicero or by Augustine so as to create a common and effective rhetorical combination, while reservations against praise on stage were not the main focus in this passage (for a more detailed discussion see Manuwald 2001a: 121–3).

[36] Thus apparently Beacham 1991: 16–17; Dumont 1992: 40.

best behaviour towards foreign and/or conquered peoples or the relative importance of political or family ties. Such notions were often expressed by terminology specific to Roman ideology (e.g. Enn. *Trag.* 220–1 R.³ = 267–8 W.), which allowed audiences to relate to the issues presented and enabled a potential transfer to specific topical situations (see ch. 2.9). Republican drama seems to have displayed a strong sense of individuals being respected and honoured according to their achievements and a desire to reach a well-organized ending with everyone in place socially and morally, to keep law and order or to acknowledge everyone's social positions.³⁷ This attention to morality may be one reason why stories featuring problematic relationships such as incest are not attested for the Republican stage (e.g. Phaedra, Oedipus).

Relevant issues were exemplified by characters detached from the real lives of audiences and situated in more or less fictitious surroundings, both in plays based on Greek models and in those set in Roman contexts. Owing to the exemplarity of dramatic characters and actions, these were not direct reflections of the audiences' own immediate experiences. The problems presented thereby acquired a certain level of abstraction, and audiences were made to reflect on their attitudes to the examples shown on stage. At the same time, Cicero considered characters in both tragedy and comedy as paradigmatic and as models for real-life individuals (see ch. 2.10). Even Plautus has a character say that comic poets do some teaching, while he is self-consciously uncertain about the lasting effect (Plaut. *Capt.* 1033–4; *Rud.* 1249–53).

Moreover, Roman drama developed throughout the Republican period and responded to issues that were becoming topical. For instance, during the period of expansion of the Roman Empire, the number of dramas that feature members of foreign peoples and deal with conquerors and the conquered increased. Roman plays could even contain positive portrayals of foreigners like Greeks, Persians and Carthaginians (Plaut. *Pers.*, *Poen.*). The question of the appropriate behaviour towards foreign and/or conquered peoples is thereby addressed.

In the period of intensified exchange with Greece, discussions of philosophical and religious questions multiplied in contemporary plays, which

---

³⁷ On connections between the contemporary situation and tragedy see also Boyle 2006: 61, 70, 123; for case studies showing the relevance of comedy to Roman audiences see Leigh 2004a. Earl (1960) argued that Plautus introduced Roman topicality into Greek plots by using contemporary political vocabulary, including terms such as *virtus* and related concepts, which exemplified the Roman aristocratic ideal.

allows the conclusion that these issues had become relevant in Rome.[38] Ennius' Neoptolemus, for instance, proclaims that he must philosophize, but also that a limited amount of philosophizing is sufficient (Enn. *Trag.* 340 R.³ = 400 W.); this statement is frequently referred to by later writers. It is uncertain whether the view attributed to Neoptolemus is based on the character's assessment of philosophy or due to his situation as 'a man of action', for whom 'business' (*negotium*) is more important than 'leisure' (*otium*); at any rate philosophizing is not entirely rejected.[39] Afranius has characters talk about 'wisdom' (*sapientia*: Afr. *Tog.* 298–9 R.³); and Pacuvius' plays include discussions of the structure of the universe (Pac. *Trag.* 86–92; 93 R.³ = 107–8; 109; 110–11; 112–14; 115 W.) and of the role of fortune (Pac. *Trag.* 366–75 R.³ = *Inc.* 37–46 W.), which are taken up by Cicero and the Author to Herennius (Cic. *Div.* 1.131; *Auct. ad Her.* 2.36).

In Plautus and Terence there is rejection and ridicule of philosophy (e.g. Plaut. *Merc.* 147; Ter. *Eun.* 262b–4), while there are also attempts at philosophical considerations. Yet when these get too extended, they are cut off and brushed away; long 'philosophical' discourses were apparently considered as inappropriate (e.g. Plaut. *Pseud.* 687). On the other hand a remark on natural bodies regarded and addressed as gods appears in Ennius' *Thyestes*, which was produced in the praetorship of C. Sulpicius Gallus (169 BCE), who had a scientific interest and expertise in astronomy (cf. Cic. *Sen.* 49; *Rep.* 1.23; Val. Max. 8.11.1; Plin. *HN* 2.53). It is therefore likely that he (and men of his acquaintance) would have been pleased with such elements in drama or might even have encouraged them; Terence's first play, *Andria*, was performed during the same official's consulship (see ch. 2.2).[40]

Discussions on whether gods care for men and whether seers and soothsayers should be believed can be found in the works of several dramatists (e.g. Enn.; Pac.; Acc.); they seem not to have impinged on traditional Roman religion. Statements about gods made on stage were apparently regarded as valid, so that Cicero took issue with them (e.g. Cic. *Div.* 1.88; 1.132; 2.104; *Nat. D.* 3.79–80). He even reports that Ennius had a character say – to the loud acclaim and agreement of the people – that gods existed,

---

[38] See e.g. Garbarino 1973: 1.2; Grimal 1975: 272; Cancik 1978: 332–4; Boyle 2006: 91. For a collection of relevant texts, *testimonia* and brief discussion see Garbarino 1973; on the issues addressed and their relationship to contemporary philosophical schools see Schlesinger 1910.

[39] On the interpretation of this fragment see Garbarino 1973: 2.581–2; on the text see Jocelyn 1967: 252–3.

[40] See also Ribbeck 1875: 203–4.

but were not caring for men (Cic. *Div.* 2.104: Enn. *Trag.* 269–70 R.³ = 328–9 W.). [41]

Some plays featured gods in more prominent roles, such as Naevius' *Lycurgus* or Plautus' *Amphitruo*; obviously it was not impossible to present gods on stage.[42] Nevertheless major deities seem not normally to have been involved in the action; divinities that appear on stage (as prologue speakers) are, for instance, a Lar familiaris and Arcturus in Plautus or Priapus in Afranius.[43] That Mercury and Jupiter take part in the action in Plautus' *Amphitruo* apparently called for some explanation in the play's prologue (Plaut. *Amph.* 86–95a). Gods on stage are all-powerful and can treat humans as they wish; they are shown in particular episodes of their 'lives', but not in their functions as rulers of the world.

There is no evidence for the middle Republic that dramatic performances were political demonstrations. By contrast, revivals in the late Republic might be exploited for topical political comment (see ch. 2.9), and in this period this element could also be included in new plays. At performances in the late Republic the popularity of distinguished politicians might be demonstrated by audience reactions to their arrival; and the people's attitude to particular circumstances and measures could be made clear by the topical interpretation of plays or individual lines by actors and audiences. Late Republican mimes included criticism of contemporary politicians and their measures, but no names or details are mentioned directly in preserved fragments (see ch. 3.6). Praetextae, which could bring events from recent Roman history onto the stage, developed critical aspects in imperial times; during the Republic, their overall messages seem to have been supportive of Roman ideology and of individuals representing it.

The quintessential aim of dramatic performances, to entertain audiences in ways that appeal to them and/or address issues that are relevant to them, was presumably achieved in various ways depending on the plays' setting: Roman varieties of dramatic genres such as praetextae or togatae reproduced a recognizable (stylized) Roman environment, while Roman plays derived from Greek predecessors, such as crepidatae and palliatae, were further

---

[41] Gods as influences on human life had been present in Greek tragedy from the beginning; discussions on their role and functions started to surface in Euripidean tragedy and were prominent throughout fourth-century Greek tragedy.

[42] Wiseman (1998: 17–24) calls to mind that the Romans 'could both laugh at the gods and at the same time take them seriously as benefactors and protectors' (24).

[43] In Plautus' *Aulularia* the prologue speaker is a Lar familiaris, a Roman deity; he starts by introducing himself, since the audience might wonder who he is. This invites the conclusion that his appearance does not conform to standard audience expectations (see also N. W. Slater 1992b: 134 n. 6).

removed from Roman reality. Therefore, they might have been allowed greater freedom in incorporating unusual features; this raises the question of how Greek stories and Greek ways of life might have been comprehensible and attractive to Roman audiences. When presenting Greek material to Roman audiences, Roman poets seem to have found different solutions for this recurrent problem, as these decisions will have been influenced by their poetic personalities and the circumstances of their time. Yet since all these decisions make sense in themselves, they should be seen 'as recurrent yet essentially static renegotiations of the same cultural move' rather than as elements forming 'a progressive series of steps'.[44]

From the surviving dramatic scripts and fragments it is obvious that Roman poets frequently did not keep a purely Greek setting when they transposed Greek models. For instance, in breaking the dramatic illusion, they explained customs common in Greece, but not in Rome (e.g. Plaut. *Cas.* 68–78; *Stich.* 446–8a); they replaced references to Greek customs with those to Roman ones; they included allusions to Roman institutions as well as to Roman or Italian localities and towns (e.g. Plaut. *Capt.* 90; 489; 877b–85a; Ter. *Eun.* 255–9); they imitated Roman conventions such as praetorian edicts (e.g. Plaut. *Curc.* 280–98) or ridiculed certain groups of Greeks (e.g. Plaut. *Curc.* 288), while they could retain the idea that Romans and other peoples in Italy (like almost everyone else) and their traditions were 'barbarians' from a Greek point of view (e.g. Plaut. *Capt.* 884a; *Cas.* 748; *Stich.* 193–4; also *Asin.* 11; *Trin.* 19).

Such tensions and explanations could be put to effect: for instance, in one of his comedies Plautus presents a banquet of slaves, and he has the slave explain that slaves were allowed to do this in Athens (Plaut. *Stich.* 446–8a). Although Plautus seems to expect some familiarity with Greek language and customs, he feels obliged to point out that he follows Greek, not Roman customs, when he brings onto the stage something that contradicts Roman conventions and could be regarded as strange and subversive.

Further, Plautus uses the transition from Greek to Latin for comic effects: he has word plays on the literal meaning of Greek or Greek-inspired names and apparently expects audiences to understand the jokes (just as Ennius expected audiences to understand references to the literal meaning of names of Greek mythical characters). Plautus also assumes familiarity with basic Greek formulae: in *Captivi* he has a character swear the truth of what he is saying by a series of oaths (Plaut. *Capt.* 877b–85a); the person starts with the common Greek oath 'By Apollo!' (Plaut. *Capt.* 880) and then goes on

---

[44] So Hinds 1998: 63, 82.

to develop oaths of his own. Interestingly, he still uses the Greek form of oaths and the Greek language, but changes the entities by which he swears to the names of towns in Italy, given in Greek with their Greek names. This causes amazement on the part of the interlocutor, who reacts by asking why he is swearing by 'barbaric towns' (Plaut. *Capt.* 884: *barbaricas urbes*). The exchange is an intriguing combination of Greek and Latin, in which references to Italic items are included, while the notion of a Greek background is maintained.

Elsewhere in Plautus 'Greek' and 'Greece' are referred to as if these were entities foreign to the characters on stage. In *Stichus*, for instance, a character mentions 'a Greek song' (*cantio Graeca*), which follows in Greek without a translation into Latin (Plaut. *Stich.* 707). Even though understanding the exact meaning of this line is not essential and the content is indicated by the context, inserting a verse of Greek seems not to have been a problem (when the audience had been warned). Several times wild, lascivious and debauched behaviour is described by the term 'behaving like a Greek' (*pergraecari*: e.g. Plaut. *Bacch.* 813; *Mostell.* 22; 64; 960; *Poen.* 603); this word also occurs in togatae, where it is more natural in the mouth of non-Greeks (see ch. 3.4).

These examples suggest that Roman playwrights did not just include explanations of Greek customs or insert some local colour as necessary, but rather made good use of the opportunity of mixing Greek and Latin elements in order to create more attractive dramas. The tension between the two cultures was in place from the start of dramatic performances since extant prologues to comedies make it clear that the plays are Latin adaptations of Greek dramas, while they emphasize that the action is set in Greece. In the course of the action there are switches between Roman and Greek points of view.

The evidence for the effect of this mixture and adaptation is less straightforward, and therefore this issue is controversial in modern scholarship. Some scholars have argued that Roman plays based on Greek predecessors are escapist entertainment set in a fantasy world (particularly with reference to comedy),[45] while others find in them messages for Roman society and adaptations to Roman ways of thinking; they describe the underlying process as 'Romanization' (particularly with reference to tragedy).[46]

---

[45] So e.g. G. Williams 1972: 220; Beacham 1991: 16–17; Dumont 1992: 40.
[46] So e.g. Grimal 1975: 267–70; Faller 2000; Boyle 2006: e.g. 61–2 (with further references). It has even been claimed that statements made on the stage were particularly authoritative in the ancient world, since there was no other medium of comparable prestige (see Dumont 1987: 629).

Obviously, the audience's relationship to the action on stage was different in Rome from what it used to be in Greece since characters and customs on a Roman stage trigger a different set of associations, even though mythical stories and figures shown in tragedy would be removed from 'real life' for Greek audiences as well and dramatic representations always have a fictional component. However, dramatic stories set in Greece can become relevant to Roman audiences when they discuss values and codes of behaviour that are central to society in general or touch upon issues of particular interest to Republican Rome.

That this kind of application was intended is particularly obvious in the selection of plays. In the area of tragedy, Roman poets seem to have chosen myths (or versions or sections of myths) that allowed them to pursue particular topics of social or political relevance. In the area of comedy there was not such a wide range of plots to choose from to facilitate the development of specific topics. Still, Roman comic writers selected some more unusual plot varieties (and even played with transgressing conventions) and also tried out variations of the standard plot, which allowed them to address a range of issues relevant to the Roman people (see ch. 3.3). The majority of these topics might be meaningful to any society and also of special significance to Republican Rome in a period of consolidation and expansion.

Topicality in the sense of references to specific events in Roman history is less likely (other than in praetextae), though a number of political, histor-ical and aetiological reasons for the choice of myths by Roman poets have been envisaged.[47] While tragic plots could include references to places significant in Roman history or to mythical heroes and heroines whose biography includes connections to Rome, it is uncertain whether the dra-mas developing those stories put any emphasis on such relations. Yet this has been assumed by some modern scholars, primarily with reference to the Trojan War.

It is certainly true that a sizeable number of Roman tragedies are based on the Trojan War and its aftermath. However, this is almost natural since this was a prominent mythical story, about which major Greek epics had been written and which had provided the basis for a number of Greek tragedies. Hence the fact that two early Roman tragedies deal with the story of the Wooden Horse, which puts the Trojans, the supposed

---

[47] For instance, scholars have assumed a political and aetiological function for Roman tragedy, as a means to explain and ennoble the origin of the Romans and thereby to assert Rome's position in the contemporary world, or have connected individual tragedies with particular historical events (see e.g. Lefèvre 1990: 9–10, 2000).

ancestors of the Romans, in a bad position since they appear gullible and simple-minded, makes it doubtful whether such stories were designed to glorify Rome's past. The incident of the Wooden Horse is perhaps more likely to have appealed to Romans because it showed devious Greeks, from whom they could favourably distinguish themselves.[48] In Plautus' plays too, Greek ways of life are often presented negatively and as allowing behaviour unthinkable in Roman society, which makes these comedies both enjoyable and edifying. This does not remove the possibility that in plays without a contrast between Greeks and other peoples, Greek heroes could embody paradigmatic ways of positive behaviour.

Roman plays adapted from Greek models and set in Greece do not mirror the 'real-life' conditions of contemporary Roman audiences, but they have a 'real-life' and 'Roman' significance in that issues that were relevant to Romans at the respective points in time are treated on a paradigmatic level. Besides, poets seem to have aimed for some obvious 'Romanness' so that settings were not too foreign and mysterious, in addition to a more oblique 'Romanness' created by the selection of stories. Plays of dramatic genres set in a Roman context are more direct reflections of Roman conditions and allow less freedom for shaping a fictional atmosphere, but they are still not immediate representations of 'reality'; yet they too discuss issues of topical interest in Roman society. In their different ways the various types of drama touch on similar issues, which invites the conclusion that these were indeed those that mattered in Republican Rome.

5.3 METATHEATRE AND PERFORMANCE

Whereas the surviving texts of Roman dramas used to be studied as scripts, scholars have come to acknowledge in recent decades that the texts are just one element of comprehensive spectacles (including e.g. music, delivery, costumes, gestures, interaction with audiences, setting); the scripts themselves might even point to the fact that they were written as a basis for performances. That the characteristics of particular productions can affect the impact of plays was recognized by Republican dramatists (cf. Plaut. *Bacch.* 214–15; Ter. *Phorm.* 9–11) and later explored by Quintilian in comparisons between actors and orators (Quint. *Inst.* 11.3.4).

---

[48] On possible interpretations and relevance of the story of the Wooden/Trojan Horse to Roman audiences see Erskine 1998.

Obviously, it is more difficult today to appreciate plays from the ancient world as 'performances' than as scripts, since there are almost no records of original performances, only limited information about revival performances and few relevant archaeological remains from the Republican period. Still, clues to performance details must be sought and interpreted, and the peculiarities of scripts have to be checked as to whether there might be performance reasons for them.[49] This approach works best for completely preserved plays in analyses of their dramatic structure as it contributes to a better understanding of the composition and theatricality of those dramas.

Obvious examples of performative elements are characters' utterances that function as stage directions, when, for instance, characters on stage describe movements and gestures or announce the arrival of others or their own intention to leave in a certain direction or to conduct specific business. Monologues and dialogues will have been accompanied by gestures, especially when moments of great emotion and passion are presented. Complex scenes may include figures overhearing others and commenting in asides to be heard only by the spectators; generally thoughts and deeds can be shared with audiences as in monologues. The dramatic action may include elements of (stylized) improvisation, bantering dialogue, role-playing or the enacting of a play within a play. While the impact of an ancient drama in performance can no longer be recovered completely, a performance approach recognizes such characteristics in the scripts, identifies them as features of performance and thus can add a particular dimension to interpretation.

One aspect of performance about which information can be gained from scripts is 'metatheatre', i.e. indications of the awareness of producing a dramatic performance in the theatre on the part of poets and actors.[50]

---

[49] For calls to pay attention to performance see N. W. Slater 1985; Bond 1999 (with reference to Plautus); Gilula 1989b (with reference to Terence's prologues).

[50] For a definition of the term see N. W. Slater 1990: 103: 'I define metatheatre as theatrically self-conscious theatre, theatre which is aware of its own nature as a medium and capable of exploiting its own conventions and devices for comic and occasionally pathetic effect.'; Frangoulidis 1997: 2: 'Pioneering is the work of Niall W. Slater, who has revolutionized our approach to Roman comedy, directing our attention to those elements of the plays' comic structure that show an awareness of their dimension as performances. In his use of the term metatheatre as "theatre that demonstrates an awareness of its own theatricality," Slater differs from M. Barchiesi who defines metatheatre as *play within a play*. Bruno Gentili, on the other hand, employs the term metatheatre but uses it as a synonym for metatext, since Roman plays, as adaptations of Greek ones, are based on previously existing (written) texts.' Anderson (1993: 139) calls for a cautious use of the term 'metatheatre' with reference to Plautus, since he 'is not provoking or exploring large existential questions about the nature of reality and the relativism of illusion' as some modern poets do. This

'Metatheatrical' elements (being on a meta-level) imply views on 'theatre' and 'drama' that can be reflected upon. The opinions of Republican dramatists on 'theatre' and 'drama', however, can only be inferred from their 'metatheatrical' remarks, with the possible exception of the views of the last tragic poet, Accius, who wrote treatises on dramatic questions.[51] Although, strictly speaking, these comments are nothing but the utterances of specific characters in plays, they are indicative of the concerns of the respective playwrights. The mere fact that Republican playwrights included meta-remarks in their plays demonstrates that they were aware of the basis of their work.[52] As they confronted spectators with such issues, engagement with those must have extended to audiences. The poets' techniques reveal a high level of generic and theatrical self-consciousness; perhaps because Roman drama was established on the basis of a fully fledged set-up in Greece, playwrights immediately dealt with a highly developed form in 'theory' and 'practice'.

Probably in order to offset the generic set and the lack of scenery, there are descriptions of the setting or narratives of the background to the plot (as well as statements that could be taken out of context as general sayings) in all dramatic genres; yet these can be regarded as elements required by the early Roman settings and not actually metatheatrical in an obvious sense. Beyond such descriptions there is a noticeable generic distinction: in the preserved fragments of tragedy or praetexta there are no explicit references to their being performances or dramatic re-enactments.[53] Tragedies may include intertextual references to earlier works or an implicit awareness

---

is true, but not a problem with the appropriate definition: in Plautus' case 'metatheatre' means calling attention to stage fiction and breaking the dramatic illusion. In order to be exact one would probably have to distinguish between 'metatheatre' and 'metadrama', the difference between the two terms being, like that between 'theatre' and 'drama' (see Introduction above), that they refer to productions/performances in the theatre and texts written for the theatre and techniques associated therewith respectively. Since, however, the term 'metatheatre' has generally been adopted and precise distinctions cannot always be made, 'metatheatre' will be used here for meta-remarks on dramas and performances (in N. W. Slater's sense).

[51] Metatheatre is mostly studied with respect to Plautus' comedies (see M. Barchiesi 1969, who applied the term to Plautus, and the fundamental study of N. W. Slater 1985; González Vásquez 2001b, with definitions and an overview of scholarship on pp. 102–5; on metatheatre in connection with the element of disguise in Plautus see Muecke 1986), but it applies to other dramatic poets and genres as well (on metatheatrical humour in Terence see Knorr 2007). González Vásquez (2001b: esp. 101) distinguishes between two types of Plautine comedies: those in which metatheatre is just present and those in which it is used with full awareness as a constituent element. While there are certainly different degrees of 'metatheatre' in individual comedies, clear-cut distinctions are difficult. She also defines 'three levels of metatheatre' in Plautus (2001b: 104).

[52] For an overview of the use of terms referring to literary genres and theatre business in Plautus and Terence see Knapp 1919.

[53] See N. W. Slater 1992a: 98; also Taplin 1986: esp. 164, 172.

of their status as poetry, but they do not have references to their being performed in the theatre or disruptions of the dramatic illusion.[54]

This contrasts with the light dramatic genres: they include comments on the respective dramatic genre and on other poets and their plays, references to the status of the characters as actors and to the fact that what is going on is a performance, allusions to standard comic elements and to the poet's own principles as well as addresses to the audience. However, this distinction seems not to be a characteristic exclusive to Roman drama. Metatheatrical references are also features of Aristophanes' parabaseis, where the dramatic illusion is interrupted. In these passages, which, apart from their position, are structurally similar to prologues, the audience may be addressed and their fairness, discernment and approval appealed to; besides, these pieces provide a forum for the discussion of metaliterary issues, such as the principles, aims and standing of the playwright, the refutation of accusations against the poet, standard comic features or the practices of other poets, and thereby allow the poet to distinguish himself from others.[55] Even after the loss of the parabasis there are ruptures of the dramatic illusion and metatheatrical comments elsewhere in Aristophanes.[56] Nothing comparable is found in classical Greek tragedy or in the more 'realistic' comedy of Menander, although he has occasional addresses to audiences (e.g. Men. *Dys.* 657–9; *Epit.* 878–905).

For most Republican playwrights the material is too scattered to allow the establishment of a pattern. The most extended metatheatrical comments in Roman dramas are found in comic prologues.[57] Yet between the two comic playwrights of whom complete plays are extant there is a noticeable difference in the distribution of metatheatrical material: Plautus may have metatheatrical remarks in prologues, and he may also break the dramatic illusion in the course of the drama.[58] By contrast, Terence confines explicit

---

[54] For instance, Pacuvius' tragic fragments include a remark about *poetae* (Pac. *Trag.* 337–9 R.³ = 366–7 W.), but it is unclear to what kind of poets it refers.

[55] Cf. e.g. Ar. *Ach.* 626–64; *Eq.* 507–50; *Nub.* 518–62; *Pax* 729–44; *Vesp.* 1015–59. For a discussion of Aristophanes' parabaseis in relation to the prologues of Plautus or Terence see e.g. Hubbard 1991: 1–2 and n. 1, highlighting the formal difference that a prologue is a separate entity standing outside the dramatic action, whereas a parabasis is inserted into it. For a comparison between parabaseis and Terentian prologues cf. Ehrman 1985, though this typological parallelism does not imply other similarities in comic technique.

[56] See Hubbard 1991: 246–51.

[57] There are a few indications for comments on dramatic technique in togata (Afr. *Tog.* 25–8; 29 R.³). The Atellana writer Pomponius talks about 'slaves in comedy' (Pomp. *Atell.* 138 R.³: *servi comici*). The mime writer Laberius seems to have discussed principles of versification (Lab. *Mim.* 55 R.³).

[58] On dramatic illusion in ancient comedy see Görler 1973.

metatheatrical remarks to prologues, which he uses for literary discussions, and has subtle play with dramatic conventions in the body of the dramas.

Identifiable metatheatrical comments concern various areas: one type consists of comments on dramatic genres, almost discussions about questions of literary criticism. Such references are discernible in the light dramatic genres virtually from the beginning. Both Plautus and Terence use some of their prologues to talk about the characteristics of comedy. They define their own plays against the stock characteristics of their dramatic genre (Plaut. *Amph.*, *Capt.*, *Poen.*; Ter. *Haut.*, *Eun.*) or make fun of these conventions (e.g. Plaut. *Capt.* 778–9; *Merc.* 1–8; *Mil.* 213).

These prologues are presented by special prologue speakers or gods; the former at least may have worn a 'neutral' costume that was not specifically associated with a particular dramatic genre or character. Indeed, the prologue speaker in Plautus' *Poenulus* leaves the stage, announcing that he will get dressed and become someone else, i.e. he will put on a comic costume so as to represent a character within the comic plot (Plaut. *Poen.* 123; 126).[59] Since the appearance of prologue speakers is undetermined, they might tease audiences about their expectations until they reveal that the audience will indeed see a comedy, even if it may have unusual features.[60] Plautus exploited the relationship between tragedy and comedy more than any other Republican dramatist, both explicitly and implicitly (at least on the basis of the available evidence). Apart from special effects by means of particular combinations (see ch. 5.4), he used the connection for generic distinctions, when the social status of characters is given as a criterion for defining the dramatic genres of comedy and tragedy in the prologue to *Amphitruo* (Plaut. *Amph.* 50–63).

In his prologues Terence rather focused on compositional issues, such as the choice of Greek plays, the relationship to earlier Roman versions, translation methods or the use of stock characters.[61] These prologues are used in their entirety to discuss the dramatist's 'poetics' and his position in contemporary theatre business. In Plautus there is only one comparable statement, towards the end of *Mostellaria*. Tranio, one of Plautus' scheming slaves, says to his master: 'If you are a friend of Diphilus or Philemon, tell them how your slave has tricked you: you will have provided the

---

[59] See also N. W. Slater 1992b: 137.
[60] N. W. Slater (1992b: 137) assumes that there were no designated days for tragedies or comedies in Rome and audiences therefore could indeed be made to believe for a moment that a tragedy was to follow until the truth was revealed.
[61] See also Dumont 1992: 42.

best deceits in comedies.'[62] Earlier the slave had defined his intrigue as a 'story/drama' (*fabula*: Plaut. *Mostell.* 510). Hence the poet (who has given Tranio these words) apparently considered the Greek comic poets Diphilus and Philemon as paradigms of comedy, while he was proudly sure of having surpassed them in the creation of this slave intrigue, a widespread comedy structure. This also indicates that the poet regarded his own activity not as mere translation, but as the creation of something original (see ch. 4.6).

Another group of metatheatrical references consists of those that remind audiences that they are watching a play performed by actors, thus disrupting the dramatic illusion (cf. Euanth. *Fab.* 3.8).[63] That a dramatic performance is essentially a fictional story for audiences, though it can be hard work for performers, is memorably and wittily expressed in Plautus' *Captivi*, where the prologue speaker says: 'This matter will be acted out by us; but for you it is a story/play.'[64] At the same time such a remark reminds audiences of how the action on stage is created. Typical disruptions of the dramatic illusion occur when actors talk of the thrashing they might receive if they have performed badly (e.g. Plaut. *Cas.* 784–5), when they reflect on audiences' possible reactions, when they mention props or costumes they need to get or have got (e.g. Plaut. *Pers.* 159–60; *Trin.* 858) or their artificiality (e.g. Plaut. *Poen.* 597–9), or when prologue speakers refer to details of the physical set-up or earlier performances (e.g. Plaut. *Amph.* 89–93; *Poen.* 1–45; Ter. *Hec.* 1–57; *Phorm.* 30–4).

A remarkable instance of this type of metatheatre occurs in Plautus' *Curculio* (see ch. 2.6), when the supplier of props (*choragus*) appears on stage in the middle of the play and delivers a monologue, starting from his role in the performance and moving on to a description of the actual situation in Rome, namely the presence of various vicious people around the Roman Forum (Plaut. *Curc.* 462–86).[65] This speech is metatheatrical in the double sense of disrupting the illusion of the plot and of alluding to the practical organization of the performance, although there is not a complete break with the dramatic setting. Since the *choragus* is allegedly a 'real Roman' gentleman and not a character in the play, he is well positioned to describe actual Roman conditions and thus voice social comment; at

---

[62] Cf. Plaut. *Mostell.* 1149–51: *si amicus Diphilo aut Philemoni es, / dicito eis, quo pacto tuos te servos / ludificaverit:/optumas frustrationes dederis in comoediis.*

[63] See e.g. Duckworth 1952: 132–6. Frangoulidis (1997: 4) has coined the term 'counter-theatricalization' 'in order to describe the interruption of the dramatic illusion within the play', but it does not seem to have gained wider currency so far.

[64] Cf. Plaut. *Capt.* 52: *haec res agetur nobis, vobis fabula.*   [65] On this speech see Moore 1991.

the same time he is close enough to the performance to have the authority and freedom to make such comments.

A further important aspect of metatheatre consists in what might be called improvisation in performance: characters, typically scheming slaves, consider their situation in front of the audience, acquaint the spectators with their problems in finding solutions and announce further actions. Such addresses to the audience are mostly found in Plautus. Some later critics regarded them as faults, since they disrupt the illusion (cf. Euanth. *Fab.* 3.8), but they constitute essential elements of the plot structure. This feature becomes particularly significant, for instance, in Plautus' *Pseudolus*: the play's eponymous slave compares the pressure on him to find a solution within the intrigue with the situation of a poet who is forced to invent something out of nowhere and always succeeds; in the same way he is confident that he will find a solution. He later confirms that he is sure that something will happen and that a person on stage must provide something new (Plaut. *Pseud.* 394–414; 562–74; also Plaut. *Mostell.* 510; *Cas.* 860–1). Similarly, the slave Palaestrio in Plautus' *Miles gloriosus* is described in a pensive pose and later develops an intrigue, instructing his fellow players (Plaut. *Mil.* 196–215; 246–8; 596–610; 770–811; 874–935). This makes it appear as if the actors or the main actor improvise the next steps on the spot, depending on how the plot proceeds, and order other characters around as it suits their step-by-step decisions. This is perhaps a residue of improvisation found in basic, unscripted drama carried over into scripted drama with a plot (rather than actual 'improvisation'), with the poet taking over the part of the original improvising actor and creating the appearance of spontaneous improvisation.[66]

At any rate, comic characters developing intrigues will shape the action and are therefore important for the plot.[67] In order to carry out intrigues, scheming slaves depend on the participation of other actors/characters. This is perhaps the reason why the slave in Plautus' *Trinummus* congratulates one of the young men, saying: 'You easily take the prize. He has been

---

[66] On improvisation in Plautus' *Pseudolus* see Barsby 1995; in Roman drama see Marshall 2006: 245–79. Marshall states: 'Improvisation is a process of composition in which the moment of composition coincides with the moment of performance. Improvisation is not a genre of theatre, but a process for generating theatre in any of a number of genres.' (245), and elsewhere: 'Improvisation is not a theatrical genre but is a means of producing a dramatic text.' (265). Barsby (1995: 65, 70) rightly stresses that a piece like *Pseudolus* is not an improvised play but deliberately written so that it appears to be one.

[67] Frangoulidis (1997) proposes a construction according to which these characters develop 'subplots' (regarded as implicit statements of poetics) within the main plot, which are either complementary or contrary to the main plot. This is perhaps unnecessarily complex and schematic.

defeated; your play has won.' and adds, addressing the other one: 'He acts more in line with the plot and makes better verses.',[68] while fining the 'loser' for his failure. The 'winner' has acted more in line with the plot the slave had devised and has produced appropriate verses.

Although it is not clear how much room for improvisation actors had when a play from a written script was performed for the first time, a certain level of freedom seems to have applied to revival performances (see ch. 2.9). This is indicated on the one hand by the so-called actors' interpolations, which have entered the transmitted text of palliatae, and on the other hand by the political actualization of performances in the late Republic (which might even include the insertion of verses from other plays or of lines invented by actors).

The special position of actors as characters in a play can be highlighted when characters align themselves with audiences and create the impression that they are 'real' individuals watching performances in theatres, just like the audiences, as they refer to 'what actors say in the theatre' (e.g. Plaut. *Rud.* 1249–53; *Truc.* 931–2). Similarly, characters can enter a conversation with audiences on an equal footing, as it were, when characters address the audience, for instance seeking confirmation, sharing secrets or appealing to their own experiences.[69] If such addresses occur in prologues, they are less remarkable, since prologues are detached sections and not part of the plot. If, however, they happen in the body of the plays, they initiate a dialogue between audiences and characters. Finally, characters may talk about the audience as if they were not present or could not hear them, thereby making good-humoured fun of both themselves and the audience (e.g. Plaut. *Merc.* 160).

All these varieties of metatheatre seem to have been frequently used by early palliata poets: they disrupted the dramatic illusion, engaged with the audience and commented on the process of performing the play and its practical realization. They also alluded to their own poetic activity and their place in the comic tradition. This latter aspect seems to have become dominant in later poets; they referred to the comic tradition and conventions or discussed and defended their own poetic techniques. Terence avoided openly breaking the dramatic illusion in the body of the dramas and rather played with comic conventions in an indirect way. For instance, he has

---

[68] Cf. Plaut. *Trin.* 706–7: *facile palmam habes: hic victust, vicit tua comoedia. / hic agit magis ex argumento et vorsus meliores facit.*

[69] Cf. e.g. Plaut. *Men.* 50–6; *Merc.* 1–8; 313–15; *Mostell.* 280–1; 708–9; *Pseud.* 584–5; *Stich.* 446–9; *Truc.* 105; 482–3. For a collection of passages and some discussion see e.g. Kraus 1934; González Vázquez 2000.

characters invent stories for others, which then match the typical comic set-up (e.g. Ter. *An.* 1 3; *Phorm.* III 2), or he slightly diverges from typical comedy conventions while pointing to them (e.g. Ter. *An.* 794–5; *Hec.* 866–8). Metatheatrical reflections in Roman comedy obviously developed over the centuries.

5.4 DRAMATIC GENRES AND INTERTEXTUALITY

Each dramatic genre in Republican Rome (i.e. each form of serious or light drama) was defined by its own set of characteristics, for instance the social status of characters, the setting or common topics and plot structures. Besides, there was a basic distinction between serious and light drama (cf. Cic. *Opt. gen.* 1–3); differences include the degree of explicit self-consciousness and the amount of allusion to other dramatic poets and genres (see ch. 5.3). Yet tragedy and comedy on the basis of Greek precedents emerged in Rome at about the same time, and the first Roman playwrights are well known to have been active in both serious and light dramatic genres. They are therefore likely to have worked along the same lines in both varieties, and formal elements such as metrical patterns or use of musical accompaniment seem to have been shared among the two. Therefore comedy and tragedy in Rome are generally thought to have been closer to each other in formal and structural terms than they had been in Greece.

Obviously, there were generic distinctions that were not to be transgressed, while the individual dramatic genres were not so different that they could not share or adopt elements from each other. Thus it is not inappropriate to ask what range of options each dramatic genre offered, what connections and intertextual relationships between the different dramatic genres (beyond the more technical level) might have existed and what the poets' views on the generic attribution of their plays might have been.

Although there are few 'theoretical' remarks revealing the views of Roman playwrights on their position in a generic tradition, it is almost certain that they were clear about the dramatic genre of their plays and about the relationship of their own pieces to earlier and contemporary works of the same or other dramatic genres. Playwrights primarily refer to predecessors in the same dramatic genre or allude to their writings in metaliterary statements: comic poets mention other poets or distinctive features of their dramatic genre in prologues, whereas tragic poets allude to lines of predecessors.

Comic playwrights occasionally refer to poets and texts of other dramatic genres, but such remarks typically have a parodying or illustrative effect and are marked as having an external point of reference. For instance, the comparison of a storm with Euripides' *Alcumena* in Plautus (Plaut. *Rud.* 86) seems to make use of a well-known scene from a tragedy (perhaps in Latin adaptation) to illustrate the force of a storm experienced by the comic characters just prior to the start of the action, while Terence uses an Ennian line (according to Donatus) in a description of Jupiter (Ter. *Eun.* 590, with Donat. on Ter. *Eun.* 590[2]–[3]: Enn. *Trag.* 372 R.³ = 386 W.). Tragic language and situations in comedy can exaggerate scenes or cause comic effects by means of contexts that contrast with those of similar scenes in tragedy (e.g. Plaut. *Amph.* 633–53; *Merc.* 195–7; *Mostell.* 496b–504; see below).

Roman playwrights looked not only to Greek plays as paradigms, but also to the emerging Roman tradition in all dramatic genres. In both cases the Roman poets' 'originality' and 'creativity' consist in the particular selection of elements provided by the tradition and the way in which they adopt them or comment on them in their own plays.[70] References to earlier Roman dramatic poets, either explicitly or implicitly by intertextual allusions to lines in their plays or negatively by avoiding overlap, only became possible after a Roman tradition had established itself and was recognized as such. It is not surprising therefore that intertextual references (of which only a limited number can be identified, because of the scattered evidence) are found in greater numbers in the works of playwrights active later in the Republican period.[71]

As regards the poets' views on intertextual relationships to predecessors, there is an interesting difference between the comic poets Terence and Afranius, who are chronologically close to each other.[72] While Terence refers to the techniques of predecessors in his dramatic genre in order to describe and justify his own principles, he is at pains to stress that he did not know of earlier Latin plays treating the same characters as his drama and has not copied from them (Ter. *An.* 18–21; *Haut.* 16–21; *Eun.* 19b–41). Slightly later, Afranius seems almost proud of stating that he feels free to borrow from any earlier poet, be they Greek or even Latin, including

---

[70] See also Goldberg 1981: 108. On 'originality in generic composition' see Cairns 2007: 99.

[71] Cf. e.g. Liv. Andr. *Trag.* 5–6 R.³ = 5–6 W.: Pac. *Trag.* 408 R.³ = 352 W.; Enn. *Trag.* 234 R.³ = 287 W.: Acc. *Trag.* 581–4 R.³ = 585–8 W. vs. e.g. Enn. *Medea*; Pac. *Medus*; Acc. *Medea sive Argonautae*. Boyle (2006: 61) states intertextual references for Ennius, but does not give examples. In his epic Ennius certainly showed himself aware of predecessors. For examples of Accius' relationship to Roman predecessors see Casaceli 1976: 99–110.

[72] On differences between the two poets see Degl'Innocenti Pierini 1991: 245–6.

Menander and Terence (whom he admires), and apparently thinks that the association with these predecessors ennobles his own work (Afr. *Tog.* 25–8; 29 R.³). There is of course a difference in that the writers mentioned by name are representatives of another light dramatic genre different from Afranius' own, which might have facilitated borrowing and admitting it, but Afranius' statement is general and does not exclude predecessors in his own dramatic genre.

Since Afranius obviously felt that he could state these views and principles without compromising his success, it is possible that in his time, in the second half of the second century BCE, when Roman scholars started to analyse Roman drama as a literary genre (see ch. 2.10), a change in its appreciation occurred, which made obvious connections with Greek and Roman 'classics' desirable. For Afranius also 'quotes' explicitly from Pacuvius (Afr. *Tog.* 7 R.³: Pac. *Trag. inc.* LIV R.³ = 35 W.).[73] In this context it is remarkable that Afranius stresses that he is ready to borrow 'even from a Latin' poet (Afr. *Tog.* 25–8 R.³). This also indicates that a Latin tradition was seen as established to such a degree that Latin writers (just like Greek ones) could be exploited by other Latin poets. Afranius' technique foreshadows what Ovid allegedly did with respect to Vergil: borrowing verses, not in order to steal them unnoticed, but for recipients to recognize the connection (cf. Sen. *Suas.* 3.7).

Whatever claims Terence has his prologue speakers make, he knew at least some older plays: he mentions a comedy by Plautus, which omitted a scene from a Greek model that Terence is now going to use (Ter. *Ad.* 6–11). And in addition to the reference to a line by Ennius, later ancient writers noted an allusion to Livius Andronicus (Ter. *Eun.* 426, with SHA 30, *Car.* 13.5: Liv. Andr. *Pall.* 8 R.³ = *Inc.* 6 W.). It is even reported in the same context that comic poets often had their soldiers use 'old words' (*vetera dicta*) by Livius Andronicus, Plautus or Caecilius. If this was true, it would point to noticeable interactions within Roman comedy after a Roman dramatic tradition had emerged.

Intertextual relationships among the different types of light drama (and occasionally beyond those) are observable from the second generation of Roman literary poets onwards and could take various forms: for instance, titles were shared between palliatae, togatae, Atellanae or mimes (e.g. *Compitalia, Fullones, Gemini*), and there were similarities in plots that centre on love affairs. The slight distinctions between the various light genres in some

---

[73] See Zorzetti 1973.

areas might lead to a partial blurring of generic boundaries, which came to be noted and criticized by later writers: Gellius finds fault with Caecilius for bypassing Menander's elegant diction and putting in elements of mime (Gell. *NA* 2.23.12: *alia nescio quae mimica inculcavit*); Horace seems to feel that Plautine parasites are too close to a Dossennus, the parasite figure in Atellana (Hor. *Epist.* 2.1.173; see ch. 3.5, 4.6).

In the area of serious drama, praetexta presented a world different from that in tragedy, but both dramatic genres are likely to have had the same dramatic structure, and there are examples of later Republican praetextae alluding to verses from earlier tragedies.[74] In some aspects, therefore, there were apparently no generic distinctions between the subtypes of serious drama. Tragedies and praetextae continued to be written by the same poets until imperial times (cf. Tac. *Dial.* 3.3–4).

Despite the various intertextual connections between the subtypes of serious and light drama as well as occasional crossovers, basic generic distinctions were apparently to be observed.[75] Later Roman writers insisted on the existence of generic distinctions and the need to maintain those, particularly between tragedy and comedy, so that a mixture of tragic subject matter and comic diction was avoided (cf. Cic. *Opt. gen.* 1; Hor. *Ars P.* 89–93; Quint. *Inst.* 10.2.21–2). The late-antique commentator Euanthius regarded it as one of Terence's virtues that he stuck to a true comic style and did not include elements reminiscent of tragedy or of mime in his comedies as other comic poets did (Euanth. *Fab.* 3.5; cf. also Gell. *NA* 2.23.12; 2.23.21). As for the distribution of dramatic genres, after playwrights had started to specialize in specific dramatic genres, the same poets might write both tragedies and praetextae, but there was no overlap between serious and light drama.

Metatheatrical discussions by comic poets and the terminology used (see ch. 3, 5.3) indicate that not only were dramatic poets conscious of the standard features of comic plots, but they also assumed audiences to be familiar with them. At the same time they played with generic distinctions and almost reached the point of blurring them. Perhaps because they had noticed the essential sameness of comic plots (and a consequent possible limit of their attractiveness), they did not always stick to them, but tried

---

[74] Cf. e.g. Acc. *Praet.* 2 R.³ = 13 W.: Enn. *Trag.* 163 R.³ = 203 W.; Pac. *Trag.* 223 R.³ = 264 W. – Acc. *Praet.* 34 R.³ = 34 W.: Pac. *Trag.* 55 R.³ = 70 W.

[75] On distinctions between tragedy and comedy as well as mixed forms (with references to ancient theory) see Seidensticker 1982: esp. 14–45, 249–60; for an overview over research on this issue see Taplin 1986: 163; on the relationship between tragedy and comedy with reference to Aristophanes see Silk 2000: 42–97.

variations up to the boundaries of the generic framework: for instance, they introduced standard characters, but gave them slightly unusual character- istics, they left out characters who might be expected, or they modified standard plots in novel ways. When the extent of such variations might jeopardize the generic identity of a play, they justified or explained them (Plaut. *Amph.* 50–63; *Capt.* 55–62; 1029–36).[76] Later commentators noted deviations of different degrees from the generic standard (Euanth. *Fab.* 3.4; Donat. on Ter. *Hec., praef.* 1.9).

That comedy engaged with tragedy as a major generic intertext and as one of its main points of reference was not new for Rome, but was also the case for Athenian comedy, both Old and New. Aristophanes is well known for his parodies of tragedy and particularly for bringing tragic poets onto the stage, most famously in the contest between Aeschylus and Euripides in *Frogs*. Menander did not discuss or mock tragedy as Aristophanes did, though tragedy remained a point of reference; he did not engage with contemporary tragic poets, but rather looked back to the 'classics' and appropriated the techniques of tragedy, particularly of late Euripidean tragedy.[77] Quintilian noted that Menander admired and followed Euripides across genres (Quint. *Inst.* 10.1.69: *quamquam in opere diverso*).

Similar techniques are frequently used in both Plautus and Terence, who might have adopted them from Menander or fused them independently; anyway Menander's precedent may have motivated Roman poets to look to 'classic' tragic techniques. Due to the simultaneous evolution and formal similarities of comedy and tragedy in Rome, there were more possibilities of interaction, and it was easier to amalgamate elements from both dramatic genres. The use in comedy of techniques and structures first developed for tragedy might enhance a drama's impact or add another, more 'serious' dimension.

For togatae Seneca claims that they were midway between tragoedia and comoedia and contained serious statements; he implies that they talked

---

[76] Segal (1987: 191–214) warns against interpreting the prologue to *Captivi* over-literally, since Plautus played with generic conventions, and there was no lack of trickery, farce, word play and comic structure in this play despite protestations to the contrary at the start and the end. However, Segal admits that the drama contains a moving scene of loyalty. And although it is true that such descriptions by comic poets should be taken with a pinch of salt, it is clear that *Captivi* exhibits features that are typically less common in Roman comedy.

[77] On the relationship between Old Comedy and tragedy see N. J. Lowe 2008: 23–9; between New Comedy and tragedy see Hunter 1985: 114–36. On tragedy and comedy in Aristophanes' *Frogs* see Heiden 1991; on 'tragic' techniques in Menander and his relationship to tragedy see Katsouris 1975; Cusset 2003; N. J. Lowe 2008: 65, 66–7.

about philosophical questions (Sen. *Ep.* 8.8; 89.7). In the text of Fronto's letters *sententiae* in togatae are described as *urbanae*, in contrast to those in other light dramatic genres (Fronto, *Ep. ad Ant.* 4.2, *m² in margine^d*) [p. 106 v.d.H.]).

The most interesting Roman dramatist in the context of cross-generic features (at least on the basis of the available evidence) is Plautus. He was the first Roman playwright to concentrate on one dramatic genre only, *fabula palliata*; at the same time he included numerous comments on and elements of tragedy in his plays and even wrote one piece that he described as 'tragicomedy' (*Amphitruo*).[78] The prologue to Plautus' *Poenulus* starts by implying that a tragedy is about to be performed and reveals only at the end of the fourth line that it is a joke and the play is going to be a comedy (Plaut. *Poen.* 1–4).[79] In *Captivi* Plautus assures the audience that, although the plot and the setting are slightly unusual for New Comedy, battles, which are appropriate for tragedy, will not feature in this play (Plaut. *Capt.* 55–62; 1029–36).

The most celebrated case of Plautus engaging creatively with various dramatic genres is his *Amphitruo*.[80] Here the poet has developed the mixture of generic elements to such a level and made it so immediately obvious by the fusion of different types of characters that assigning the whole play to the dramatic genre of comedy no longer works. He therefore comes up with a new term for this specific dramatic form: it is not pure tragedy either, but a mixture of comedy and tragedy (on the basis of the social status of the characters according to the prologue, but also including structural elements of tragedy and a corresponding tone and outlook in places), which he calls 'tragicomedy', in an expression that seems to have been coined on this occasion (Plaut. *Amph.* 50–63).[81]

---

[78] See also Boyle 2006: 57.   [79] On the prologue to Plautus' *Poenulus* see N. W. Slater 1992b.

[80] On 'tragicomedy' in *Amphitruo* and possible models (comedy or tragedy) see Stewart 1958; N. W. Slater 1990; Moore 1995; Bond 1999; E. A. Schmidt 2003.

[81] The compound appears twice (Plaut. *Amph.* 59; 63) and is transmitted as *tragicocomoedia* in both instances. As this gives an unmetrical line in the second case, the term is generally emended to *tragicomoedia* there. Because of the poet's explicit emphasis on repetition (Plaut. *Amph.* 63), the first occurrence is also widely emended to *tragicomoedia* (as in the OCT). It has been suggested, however, that initially the form is still *tragico-comoedia*, illustrating the mix, and that only on the second occurrence is the newly formed actual compound used (see Schwering 1916/17; Seidensticker 1982: 21–2). This would illustrate the emergence of the term, but goes against the argumentative structure of the passage. In antiquity the term *tragicomoedia* is attested only in this prologue and later in Lactantius Placidus referring back to it (Lactant. on Stat. *Theb.* 4.146–7). By inverting the order of the two parts of the compound in comparison with possible Greek forerunners such as *hilarotragoidia*, Plautus makes it clear that his play is mainly a 'comedy', including 'tragic' elements.

Plautus' *Rudens* could be regarded as at least equally 'tragic'; yet in this case there are no explicit comments on the dramatic genre. A possible reason might be that *Rudens* does not present such a big generic problem as it fulfils some of the criteria for comedy mentioned elsewhere by both Plautus and Terence in terms of cast and plot (see ch. 3.3). Also, it defies clear definition on formal grounds since it contains elements that seem to be more frequent in contemporary tragedy than in comedy, but none that can occur only in tragedy or that Plautus seems to have regarded as specific to tragedy.

The prologue of *Rudens* is spoken by the god Arcturus (Plaut. *Rud.* 1–82), and he not only gives his name and his practical function in the plot, but also adds ethical considerations, which he immediately applies. Therefore his appearance goes beyond the standard function of prologue speakers and sketches a moral framework for the play. The necessity of morally correct, honest and just behaviour, the punishment of those who violate the ethical code, attempts at satisfying the rights of all parties concerned and an acknowledgement of beneficial guidance by supernatural powers remain constant themes throughout the play, sometimes brought to the fore by explicit reflections. Particular problems discussed by the play are the justification of slavery and the request for proper conditions for slaves. That the characters do not merely satisfy their desire for fulfilling their wishes and taking revenge is shown by the unusual ending: the pimp is not punished; by contrast, he is paid and invited to dinner by the father of the girl whom he had kept in his possession. When neither the proposed marriage nor this feast is shown on stage, the most likely reason is that their realization in entertaining scenes would have violated the atmosphere of the play, which aims at showing decisions important for human society and the motives provoking them.

In such cases there is a smooth and seamless integration of 'tragic' themes and structures, which may enhance the comic genre. The 'choruses' in two comedies of Plautus (*Poenulus, Rudens*) might have been influenced by contemporary Roman tragedy rather than by New Comedy (see ch. 4.6); this would show paradigmatically how comedy might make use of individual elements of tragedy. At the same time Plautus has parody of tragedy.[82] For

---

[82] For allusions to tragedy cf. e.g. Plaut. *Cas.* 759–62; *Pers.* 11–12; 712–13; *Pseud.* 771–2: Pac. *Trag.* 20[a–b] R.³ = 13–14 W.; Plaut. *Amph.* 232–3: Pac. *Trag.* 223 R.³ = 264 W.; Plaut. *Amph.* 1062: Pac. *Trag.* 336 R.³ = 365 W. On paratragedy, parody and the use of elements from tragedy in Plautus see also Arnott 1972 (on *Stichus*); Blänsdorf 1993 (on *Rudens* and *Amphitruo*), 1996; Petrone and Bianco 2006; Bianco 2007; Sharrock 2009: 204–19. Goldberg (1993: 55) has observed that the metrical and technical closeness of tragedy and comedy in Rome made parody of tragedy easy, but subtler

instance, a topic presented in Republican tragedies is comically referred to in *Bacchides*, when Plautus has the scheming slave deliver a long speech in which he compares his attack on his master with the attack of the Greeks on Troy by means of the Trojan Horse (Plaut. *Bacch.* 925–78). This is not parody due to a tragic situation incongruously applied to comedy; it is a self-contained comparison between an action within the comedy and an event typically narrated in other literary genres, enhanced by the use of tragic language, which gains its comic effect from the incompatibility of the two items.

Plautus' inclusion of 'tragic' elements thus covers the whole range from parody and pastiche via imitation for comic effect to using tragic elements for the purposes of giving his plot another dimension.[83] The playwright not only commented on the fusion of 'comic' and 'tragic' elements in *Amphitruo*, but he seems also to have noticed that the imitation of tragic characteristics in an inappropriate environment results in parody or comic imitation of tragedy. In *Pseudolus* another character comments upon a remark by the eponymous slave (Plaut. *Pseud.* 703–6): 'how the rascal para-tragedizes!' (Plaut. *Pseud.* 707: *ut paratragoedat carnufex!*). The words of the slave had imitated tragic language in an exaggerated and highly stylized fashion, without a wider-ranging function in the context. Use of tragic diction in inappropriate contexts may lead to a comic discrepancy between elevated language on the one hand and down-to-earth incidents on the other.

In Terence the synthesis of comic and tragic material is different, as he gives his comic plots a more serious outlook. The topics he presents and the ways in which he discusses them bring his plays close to tragedy in some respects. The most 'serious' of Terence's comedies is perhaps *Adelphoe*, which presents different forms of education; at the same time Terence adds an entertaining scene (by the practice known as 'contamination'), which provides comic relief after long discussions (Ter. *Ad.* 6–11; 155–96a). *Andria* is described by Donatus as having an 'almost tragic catastrophe' (Donat. on Ter. *An.*, *praef.* 1.5), while he notes for *Phormio* that Terence kept the appropriate comic framework throughout, for instance by balancing the intensity of sad events with comic serenity (e.g. Donat. on Ter. *Phorm.*, *praef.* 1.5; cf. also Euanth. *Fab.* 3.5). Terence's mock battle in *Eunuchus*

---

allusions difficult. However, structural similarities do not present an obstacle to merging elements of the two dramatic genres smoothly.

[83] Horace allows both comedy and tragedy to use the style of the other dramatic genre in appropriate situations (Hor. *Ars P.* 93–8). According to Donatus comedy can be given a serious gravity without implying a switch of dramatic genre (Donat. on Ter. *Ad.*, *praef.* 1.6).

(IV 7) could be interpreted as one instance where he left comedy proper and included parody of tragedy, since, according to Plautus, battles were rather a feature of tragedy (Plaut. *Cas.* 58b–62), which is supported by the style of a battle narrative in *Amphitruo* (Plaut. *Amph.* 186–262). Yet the section in Terence is a purely comic scene, which gains its effect from the discrepancy between the cause, the inappropriate manner and the ridiculous equipment of the fighting on the one hand and the attitude and language of the people involved on the other.

The myths chosen for tragedies, some longer fragments and later writers' reactions allow the inference that Roman tragic poets created dramatic and vivid actions and inserted stunning scenes and sensational stage effects to attract audience attention. Additionally, they seem to have used language full of rhetoric and pathos, rich in sound effects and high-flown compounds. Furthermore, tragedy adopted features of comedy, for instance personnel of low social status, plots with intrigues and happy endings, emphasis on the role of Tyche or solutions remaining within a human sphere without the involvement of *dei ex machina*, developments already foreshadowed in the late Euripides.[84] Over time, tragedy thereby became more down to earth and presumably more entertaining by making use of comedy's dramatic potential.

One aspect that illustrates tragedy's incorporation of comedy features is that scenes of everyday life and the experiences of ordinary characters became more prominent in tragedy, even though such figures remained closely connected to mythical plots, since the social status of characters was a distinctive criterion for dramatic genres, as confirmed by later theorists. Accius' *Medea sive Argonautae*, for instance, features a shepherd, who describes the *Argo* from the perspective of a person who has never seen a ship before (Acc. *Trag.* 391–402 R.³ = 381–92 W.), and the same poet's *Deiphobus* includes a fisherman (Acc. *Trag.* 128–9 R.³ = 248–9 W.), a character type that also appears in Plautus' *Rudens* (Plaut. *Rud.* 290–324a).

Despite such features Roman tragedy did not become 'comic' in character; it merely developed into a perhaps less austere and more entertaining type of tragedy. The rhetorician Demetrius describes a tragedy that includes laughter as something impossible and the resulting product as a satyr-play

---

[84] Arcellaschi (1990: 129–131) notes the mixture of 'comic' and 'tragic' for Pacuvius' *Medus*. There is no evidence, however, for his hypothesis that this should be connected with the influence of Rhinthon's dramas (on those see ch. 1.4).

(Demetr. *Eloc.* 169). Interestingly, he does not envisage tragedy developing straight into comedy, but rather into satyr-play, probably caused by the fact that satyr-play in Greece is close to tragedy in terms of authorship, place of performance at the festivals and mythical subject matter, though its tone and plot structure are different and resemble comedy. The equivalent in Rome might be mythical Atellana, but this remained a dramatic genre distinct from tragedy. Only some topics (though presented differently) and a few elements common among all light dramatic genres might be shared by tragedies and Atellanae in the late Republic.

When tragedy and comedy were adapting elements from each other over the course of the Republican period, they may have continued a process that started in late classical Greece and went on during the Hellenistic period; but the almost complete lack of evidence on Hellenistic Greek drama precludes further assumptions on a continuous development.[85] Still, some late Euripidean tragedies are not 'tragic' in the strict sense and share features with Republican tragedies when they include happy endings, ordinary characters and stunning effects (e.g. Eur. *El.*, *Hel.*, *IT*, *Or.*); Menander's comedy is more serious and less directly topical than that of Aristophanes. Besides, Plato had his Socrates insist that the same person could write both tragedy and comedy (Pl. *Symp.* 223d3–6), a statement that may have been triggered by the contemporary dramatic situation, but it is not elaborated on or seen as realized at present.[86]

In sum, in Rome each dramatic genre retained its distinctive character during the Republican period, while they all shared characteristics and adopted elements from each other, despite poets' increasing specialization. In the final analysis plays brought onto the stage in Rome, irrespective of their dramatic genres, consisted of sensational show effects and the presentation of topics relevant to Roman society, while the respective proportions of these elements differed according to dramatic genres and periods. Thus plays discussed problems of human life in an entertaining way and offered examples of behaviour. They thereby anticipated Horace's 'to offer something of use' and 'to provide pleasure' (*prodesse* and *delectare* or *utile* and

---

[85] Taplin (1986: 174) points out that the distinctions between tragedy and comedy observable in the fifth century collapse for the New Comedy of Menander. Tarrant (1978; see sceptical remarks in Dingel 1985: 1053–4) puts forward the theory 'that the synthesis of fifth-century subject matter, post-Euripidean form and technique, stylistic and metrical refinement, sporadic archaism of language, and abstraction from the physical realities of the stage which is generally associated with Seneca was in fact an Augustan achievement' (261) and developed from the convergence of tragic and comic techniques in Republican drama.

[86] See N. J. Lowe 2008: 24.

dulce: Hor. *Ars P.* 333–4; 343–4); and this is what Roman audiences seem to have asked for (cf. also Donat. on Ter. *Hec.*, *praef.* 1.3).

In addition to the multi-faceted relationships among the different dramatic genres, there were connections to other literary genres, particularly since many of these emerged in Rome at about the same time as the dramatic genres. That the first dramatic poets were versatile and wrote epic poetry besides dramas might be seen to point to a closeness of epic and drama. However, while there were formal similarities between different dramatic genres, there was a basic formal distinction between epic and drama from the start, indicated for instance by the different types of metres used. At the same time there may have been an overlap in topics and focus: Naevius, for example, turned from the transposition of Greek models to producing genuine works on Roman history in both epic and drama. The presentation of heroes and the conveying of moral messages is true of both tragedy and epic. Equally on the level of content, plays about the early history of Rome (praetextae) will have shared topics and the focus on paradigmatic figures with early historiography in Latin and may have overlapped with some sections in historical epic.

A major stylistic paradigm for drama seems to have been early Roman oratory.[87] From the late second century BCE onwards there were people such as C. Titius (*fl.* probably *c.* 130 BCE; cf. Macrob. *Sat.* 3.16.14; Fronto, *Ep. ad Caes. et inv.* 1.7.4 [p. 15 v.d.H.]) who were both orators and tragic playwrights and whose rhetorical training could be noticed in their plays (cf. Cic. *Brut.* 167), and also playwrights such as Afranius who imitated orators and could be described as 'eloquent in plays' (*in fabulis... disertus*: Cic. *Brut.* 167). Accius was reportedly asked why he did not plead in the Forum since his characters did this so well in his tragedies (cf. Quint. *Inst.* 5.13.43).[88]

Such pieces of external evidence are confirmed by the plays themselves, particularly by those from the later Republican period; they demonstrate that poets made use of rhetorical techniques and oratorical structures. For instance, some of Terence's prologue speakers state that they have the function of orators defending the poet: 'He wanted me to be an orator, not a prologue speaker.' (Ter. *Haut.* 11: *oratorem esse voluit me, non prologum*) or 'I come to you as an orator in the costume of a prologue speaker.' (Ter. *Hec.* 9:

---

[87] On drama's relationship to contemporary oratory see esp. Goldberg 1983. Quintilian noted the similarity of Euripides' and Menander's dramas to oratory (Quint. *Inst.* 10.1.68; 10.1.70).

[88] See also Degl'Innocenti Pierini 1991: 243–4 n. 10.

orator ad vos venio ornatu prologi). Also, plays such as *Armorum iudicium* (by Pacuvius and by Accius) or others that include speaking contests between two or more characters must have had several set speeches, which aimed at influencing the opponent as well as internal and external audiences. One fragment of Pacuvius describes eloquence as 'mind-bending and queen of all things' (Pac. *Trag.* 177 R.³ = 187 W.: *o flexanima atque omnium regina rerum oratio*); that such a thought was voiced by one of the characters points to an awareness of the impact of rhetoric on the part of the poet.

Drama seems to have adopted techniques developed for the literary genre of oratory and used them for its own purposes. Since both orators and characters in plays make arguments to influence others and put views across in speeches, there is a structural similarity between oratory and drama, which perhaps made it possible for drama to adopt elements beyond its generic framework.

5.5 DRAMATURGY AND DRAMATIC STRUCTURE

Roman dramatists apparently aimed at providing an exciting dramatic experience. From the outset, Roman dramas tended to include more stage-action and spectacle than Greek dramas, and this element increased over the course of time.[89] This agrees with Horace's view that what is seen has a greater impact on audiences than what is heard (Hor. *Ars P.* 180–2a). Dramatic 'effects' already formed part of Greek drama; yet they appear to have multiplied in Rome. Initially there seems to have been a balanced mixture of meaningful content and exciting effects, while at the end of the Republic impressive presentation gained greater prominence, as is also indicated by the emergence of new dramatic genres privileging this aspect.

The element of dramatization in Republican drama manifests itself in various significant features: the physical layout of the stage area in Roman theatres and the lack of a restriction on the number of actors (see ch. 2.4, 2.6) facilitated the presentation of large groups and the procession of pageants across the stage. This is obvious in the great number of slaves that can accompany characters in comedy, for example the young ladies Bacchis and Antiphila entering with maids and lots of baggage in Terence's *Heautontimorumenus* (Ter. *Haut.* II 3–4). It may also apply to choruses

---

[89] See Grimal 1975: 265–6. This feature has been connected with the fact that Romans valued action and characters more highly than speech (see Goldberg 1993: 59–60).

who take part in the action in tragedies such as Ennius' *Iphigenia*, Ennius' *Medea* or Pacuvius' *Niptra*.

As regards the arrangement of dramatic performances, there is a preference for actual depictions of events on stage rather than descriptions, although limits to what can be shown on stage remain (e.g. Enn. / Acc. *Andromeda*). Effects within the stage-action can be achieved by a variety of elements: for instance, one-off exciting incidents, such as Medea appearing on her winged chariot (Pac. *Medus*), the shade of a dead person rising from below (Pac. *Iliona*) or noble characters appearing in rags (esp. Pac.; Acc.); colourful descriptions, such as Medea being given a kind of tour of Athens (Enn. *Medea*) or a shepherd who had never seen a ship before reporting the approach of the *Argo* (Acc. *Medea sive Argonautae*); emotional scenes, when e.g. family members almost kill each other and recognize each other just in time; recognition scenes more generally; friends ready to die for each other (Pac. *Chryses*); characters having been exiled or having lost everything; the introduction of sub-plots and second plots (esp. Ter.); elaborate speeches, such as Andromacha's lament after the fall of Troy (Enn. *Andromacha*) or the contest between Ajax and Ulixes over Achilles' arms (Pac. / Acc. *Armorum iudicium*); natural disasters and their consequences, such as storm or shipwreck (various tragedies; Plaut. *Rud.*); supernatural and irrational elements such as augury, dreams, portents, frenzy and madness; various types of joke, farce and slapstick in light dramatic genres; entertaining effects due to stupid and simple stock figures in Atellana or female actresses appearing naked on stage in mime; continuous actions accompanied by music throughout the play.

Some of these elements, such as tangled prologues, supernatural appearances, characters in reduced circumstances or lack of realism, were ridiculed by the satirist Lucilius in the second century BCE, particularly with regard to tragedy.[90] Frequent references to a few scenes in later writers invite the conclusion that these were particularly memorable; they were criticized by people who had different expectations of drama, but may have been enjoyed by others.[91] During the last century of the Republic such dramatic effects developed into actual pageants, which intellectuals such as Cicero and Horace disapproved of (Cic. *Fam.* 7.1.2; Hor. *Epist.* 2.1.187–207). Nevertheless, meaningful elements even in the 'late' dramatic genres show that

---

[90] Cf. e.g. Lucil. 587; 597–8; 599–600; 653; 875; 876 M. = 723; 729–30; 727–8; 665; 879; 880 W.

[91] Cf. e.g. Plaut. *Cas.* 759–62; *Pers.* 11–12; 712–13; *Pseud.* 771–2; Pers. 1.76–8; Cic. *Inv.* 1.27; Mar. Victor. *Expl. in rhet. Cic.*, p. 202.18–21 Halm; August. *Soliloq.* 2.29.

this aspect was not lost and that all genres of Republican drama were characterized by a mixture of messages and impressive presentation.[92]

As palliatae constitute the only dramatic genre in Republican Rome of which examples have been preserved in their entirety, it is impossible to give a precise description of the dramatic structure of Republican drama in general or to distinguish between structural features characteristic of individual dramatic genres.[93] So one can only analyse the structure of palliatae and draw inferences for other dramatic genres on the basis of significant fragments, *testimonia* and comparisons with Greek plays, later Roman plays and Republican palliatae.

Palliata, togata, tragedy and literary mime could have introductory prologues, which might be technical and expository, giving information about the play (its playwright, title, Greek model and plot), or might be used for discussions of other issues such as literary questions. Prologues are attested for Plautus and Terence and can be inferred for Naevius, Ennius, Pacuvius, Accius, Afranius and Laberius. These prologues normally opened the plays, but, as ancient commentators noted (cf. Donat. on Ter. *Phorm.*, *praef.* 1.11), they might be postponed (e.g. Plaut. *Mil.* 79–155).

Terence in particular, but perhaps also Naevius, Caecilius and Afranius, used prologues not for narrating the argument, but rather for discussing literary and metatheatrical questions (cf. Ter. *An.* 5–7; *Ad.* 22–4a), although Plautus' prologues too may include comments on the play and the performative situation. Prologues seem to have been spoken by unspecific prologue speakers (apparently often younger actors), impresarios (cf. Ter. *Haut.* 1–2) or concrete personalities such as gods (cf. Plaut. *Aul.* 1–3).[94] The fact that both Plautus and Terence mention the audience's possible confusion about the identity of a prologue speaker if there is anything unusual, or have him identify himself, indicates that conventions were established and familiar to audiences, so that deviations would be noted and had to be commented on.

Since prologues could be delivered by characters not directly involved in the plot, a brief hiatus is likely to have occurred between the

---

[92] Grimal (1975: 294), however, calls Roman comedy 'a total comedy', since in comparison with Greek New Comedy the stunning presentation 'transforms entirely the nature of the spectacle and reduces obviously the importance of the word'.

[93] On dramatic conventions in Roman comedy see Duckworth 1952: 102–36.

[94] For Terence Gilula (1989b) distinguishes two types of prologues and two sorts of actors who delivered them (prologues of the impresario on himself and the poet and prologues of young actors referring to incidents affecting the entire troupe). Eugraphius seems to imply that Terence's use of prologues differed from that of all other dramatists (Eugr. on Ter. *Phorm. prol.*; *An. prol.*).

prologue and the play proper in those cases (cf. esp. Plaut. *Poen.* 123; 126). When special prologue speakers presented the prologues, the discussion of metatheatrical questions is not a disruption of the dramatic illusion, since this section is clearly separated from the dramatic action. There is, however, an interesting mixture of conveying technical information about the plot (and its background) and setting the action in motion at the beginning of Plautus' *Mercator*, when the young man opens the play by announcing that he will explain both the plot and his love affair and distinguishes his practice from that of other people in comedy (Plaut. *Merc.* 1–8); the poet thereby mocks the convention of separating an overview of the plot from characters introducing themselves and manages to create an interesting and immediate start. In his plays Terence maintains the dramatic illusion by limiting metaliterary discussions to prologues; he has actors or impresarios deliver the prologues and talk about the poet in the third person, while Afranius uses the first person, perhaps imitating orators (cf. Cic. *Brut.* 167).[95]

If the argument or the background to the action is not given in the prologue, sufficient information must be provided in the body of the play, particularly in its initial scenes. For this purpose, as ancient commentators on comedy have remarked, so-called 'characters for the beginning' (*prosopa protatika*) could be introduced.[96] These individuals have no function in the action and typically appear only in a single scene; they provide another person who has all the information with an interlocutor to whom they can communicate this information (and thereby also to the audience) in a dialogue rather than in a monologue.

The end of a play was marked by a brief address to the audience from one of the actors or the group of actors, asking for the spectators' applause, as palliatae demonstrate (cf. also Hor. *Ars P.* 155). Throughout the performance it was important to retain the audience's attention and make them watch the play until the very end (cf. also Hor. *Ars P.* 153–5). Features of Republican drama such as the abolition of choral interludes and the increase in stage-action have been connected by ancient scholars with the aim of maintaining suspense (Donat. on Ter. *Ad.*, *praef.* 1.4*; *Eun.*, *praef.* 1.5*; Euanth. *Fab.* 3.1).

---

[95] See Degl'Innocenti Pierini 1991: 243. A late sequel is perhaps the exchange between Seneca and Pomponius Secundus, tragic poets of the first century CE, about the appropriate diction for tragedy in 'prefaces' (*praefationes*), which might refer to prologues, but could also denote introductions to written texts (cf. Quint. *Inst.* 8.3.31).

[96] Cf. Euanth. *Fab.* 3.2; Donat. on Ter. *An.*, *praef.* 1.8; *Ad.*, *praef.* 1.8; *Hec.*, *praef.* 1.8; *Phorm.*, *praef.* 1.8.

Extant palliatae show that there were no act-divisions marked by choral interludes; and there is no reason to assume that this was different for other dramatic genres, particularly in view of the formal similarities between tragedy and comedy in Rome. Tragedy and praetexta had choruses, whereas light dramas seem not to have used them; only in two plays by Plautus do groups of people make a brief appearance who could be seen as assuming the functions of a 'chorus' (Plaut. *Poen.*, *Rud.*). Existing fragments and *testimonia* indicate that the chorus, where it was used, was involved in the action almost like an actor, and all utterances that can be attributed to choruses make sense as part of the dramatic action (cf. also ch. 3.1).

Divisions between scenes (in palliatae) are marked by characters' entrances and/or exits or by an alternation of dialogues and monologues.[97] Even so, later grammarians and commentators tried to identify basic five-act structures as in corresponding Greek dramas (cf. also Hor. *Ars P*. 189–90); yet they realized that act-divisions were hard to pin down in Roman comedy, since there were no breaks in the action marked by choral interludes, and the movements of individual characters were sometimes hard to follow (Donat. on Ter. *An.*, *praef.* 2.3; *Ad.*, *praef.* 1.4*; *Eun.*, *praef.* 1.5*), just as they were aware of the fact that 'acts' could be of different length depending on their function (Donat. on Ter. *Ad.*, *praef.* 3.7; *Hec.*, *praef.* 3.6).

Since the Greek rule of a limit to three speaking actors was not valid for Rome, livelier scenes with four speaking actors involved were possible (in contrast to Horace's doctrine: *Ars P*. 192). This includes scenes featuring eavesdropping and asides, which allows several conversations or at least trains of thought to run simultaneously. Other features such as the 'running slave' (*servus currens*) helped to increase the dramatic momentum. On the other hand monologues, often spoken between scenes, provided further information, looked forward to the continuation of the plot or revealed a character's thoughts and feelings.[98]

Although Roman drama had a greater tendency for dramatization and bringing actions onto the stage, some scenes still could not or should not be presented on stage. For according to convention, the stage featured an open street in front of a row of houses (or other open spaces), and scenes happening indoors or in another location could not be shown, but had to be reported (see ch. 2.4). Those scenes, along with those not

---

[97] Terence's *primo actu placeo* ('The first act went well.') (Ter. *Hec.* 39) therefore refers to the beginning of the play in more general terms and not to the 'first act' in a technical sense (see Blänsdorf in Suerbaum 2002: 176). The music requested in Plautus' *Pseudolus* to pass the time between scenes constitutes an exception, which is signalled by the explicit reference (Plaut. *Pseud.* 573a).

[98] On monologues in Roman comedy see e.g. Duckworth 1952: 102–9.

suitable for presentation on stage (cf. Hor. *Ars P.* 182b–8), were conveyed by 'messengers', characters who had witnessed the incident taking place elsewhere and had come to narrate what they had seen.

Generally, the dramatic set-up of plays (at least in palliata) was designed to assist the audience in gaining a clear grasp of the plot: for instance, there are usually entrance and exit announcements, and characters reappearing explain what they have done in the meantime, especially when they return by an entrance different from the exit through which they had left.

5.6 LANGUAGE, STYLE, METRE, MUSIC

Since in Rome a single language variety, Latin, became the idiom for all kinds of literature, there are no specific dialects for drama or particular dramatic forms as there were in Greece; instead, in this respect drama does not differ from other forms of speech in Rome. Presumably, the language of Roman drama was originally not too artificial: in serious drama it was not too far removed from what contemporary Romans might use on formal occasions, or in light drama it was not too different from what educated Romans might use in everyday life (cf. also Hor. *Sat.* 1.4.45–62).[99]

Yet, obviously, the metrical structure of all Roman drama led to some linguistic constraints. More importantly, since almost all surviving texts and fragments of Republican drama date to the period before Cicero, they use a variety of Latin that can be called 'pre-classical' and differs from the more regular classical Latin in several aspects of phonology, morphology and syntax. The language of early Republican poets was therefore liable to be condemned by later critics. Naturally, however, throughout the period of Republican drama itself the Latin language developed, both enriched by neologisms and moving towards a less experimental form, so that Terence was later praised for his 'pure' language (see below). Also, there were differences in register and level between the various dramatic genres.

Nevertheless, a certain formal unity across all genres of Republican drama can be observed as they employ stylistic elements that seem to be typical of early Latin poetry more generally: these include sound effects (e.g. alliteration, assonance, anaphora, paronomasia), stylistic figures based on choice and arrangement of words (e.g. anadiplosis, tricolon, climax,

---

[99] See e.g. Jocelyn 1967: 38–40, 1972: 1002. For some cautious remarks on methodological problems in assessing the poetic language of early drama cf. Jocelyn 1986. On features of the language and style of early Roman poetry see Haffter 1934; Blänsdorf 1967.

polysyndeton, other types of artificial word order) or play with meaning and
sense (e.g. antithesis, zeugma, metonymy, literal interpretation of common
phrases, pun, etymological jingles). Such stylistic features are more frequent
in serious dramatic genres and in elevated sections in light dramatic genres,
i.e. when characters make passionate speeches or when issues of a more
general nature are being discussed. Passages in iambic senarii, which are
spoken and often provide factual information, tend to be simpler in style
and language than those in other metres.

In palliata, the only dramatic genre for which there is a sufficient number
of lines clearly attributed to individual speakers, basic linguistic differenti-
ations can be observed, for instance differences between male and female
speakers.[100] This accords with the views of later writers on the language of
individuals: these authors demanded that the words and style of the utterances of figures on stage must agree with their character and emotional
state and that poets and actors must actually experience the emotions they
express (cf. Cic. *De or.* 2.193; Hor. *Ars P.* 101–18).

Beyond that, Cicero records that recipients recognized the individual
styles of playwrights of a single dramatic genre and that different people
preferred different styles (Cic. *Orat.* 36). Extant lines and plays corroborate
the distinctive styles of individual poets: for instance, Terence's language is
more restrained than that of his predecessors in palliata (e.g. less alliteration
and assonance, fewer bold similes and allusions, digressions, neologisms
and comic long words) and was therefore praised as 'pure'.[101] The tragic
genre as a whole saw a development towards increasing sophistication, elaboration, rhetorical style and use of neologisms; some of Ennius' creations
entered Latin poetic language, while Pacuvius and Accius were criticized
for their artificial language, starting with their contemporary Lucilius.[102]
Horace remarks (for the purposes of his argument) that Republican dramatists such as Caecilius, Plautus and Ennius coined new words without being
criticized for this in their time (Hor. *Ars P.* 46–72). Hence the playwrights'
linguistic creativity and the public's reactions to their poetry will have made
an important contribution to shaping a Latin poetic idiom.

'Lyric poetry' or 'music' (*melopoiia*) already belonged to the constituent
elements of drama for Aristotle (Arist. *Poet.* 6: 1449b28–36; 1450a10). In

---

[100] See e.g. Barsby 1999: 19–27; Dutsch 2008.
[101] Cf. Suet./Donat. *Vita Ter.* 7 = Cic. fr. 2 *FPL³* / Caes. fr. 1 *FPL³*.
[102] Cf. e.g. Lucil. 587 M. = 723 W.; Cic. *Brut.* 258 (but cf. *Orat.* 36); Pers. 1.76–8; Sen. *Ep.* 58.5;
      Mart. 11.90.5–6; Tac. *Dial.* 20.5; 21.7. On Lucilius' criticism of tragedy, including its language, see
      Manuwald 2001c.

Roman Republican drama, music functioned as an important element in creating the appropriate atmosphere and thus supporting the emotional impact on audiences (cf. e.g. Cic. *Tusc.* 1.106–7). Particularly by restricting the role of the chorus and having actors sing more monodies instead, Roman playwrights departed from Greek custom and increased the musical element.[103] It is generally acknowledged that Republican tragedy and comedy were metrically and rhythmically closer together than their Greek counterparts,[104] probably a consequence of their being established in Rome as (formally) fully fledged dramatic genres by the same poets at about the same time. The origin of the metrical structure of Republican drama is still a matter of dispute, but it seems to have been created from a mixture of elements adopted from dramas of the Greek classical and Hellenistic periods and from native Italic traditions.

The main indication of the musical quality of Republican drama today is its metrical shape: the iambic senarius is the metre used for spoken parts (cf. also Arist. *Poet.* 4: 1449a19–28; Hor. *Ars P.* 79–82), differing from the corresponding Greek trimeter by the fact that it consists of six individual feet, where resolution is possible for every metrical position except the penultimate (cf. also Hor. *Ars P.* 251–62). In metre and rhythm it is closest to normal speech; Cicero even claimed that because of this similarity it was hard to detect the verse structure of senarii in comedy (Cic. *Orat.* 184), while Quintilian described their position as situated between everyday speech and artificial language (Quint. *Inst.* 2.10.13; cf. also Hor. *Sat.* 1.4.45–62). 'Sung' parts can consist of longer iambic or trochaic verses, such as trochaic septenarius (*versus quadratus*), iambic septenarius (*comicus quadratus*), trochaic octonarius or iambic octonarius, as well as various other metres, including lyric ones, such as anapaest, cretic or bacchiac.[105]

---

[103] Cf. Diom. *Ars* 3, *Gramm. Lat.* 1, p. 490.22–3: *in Latinis enim fabulis plura sunt cantica quae canuntur* ('for in Latin plays there are more "arias", which are sung'). The origin of the so-called *cantica* has been much debated since Fraenkel's ([1922/1960] 2007: 219–51) seminal study: the respective influences of Hellenistic theatrical activity and of Greek/Roman tragedy remain controversial (see more recently Wille 1967: 165; Gentili 1979: 35–41; Dumont 1997; Blänsdorf in Suerbaum 2002: 219–20; N. J. Lowe 2008: 92; on the development of *cantica* in Roman tragedy see Hurka 2008).

[104] On the similarity of style, metre, technical devices and dramatic set-up see e.g. Jocelyn 1967: 24, 31–8; La Penna (1977) 1979: 53–4; Gratwick 1982a: 82; Hunter 1985: 15–16; Goldberg 1993: 55. On music and metre in Roman Republican drama see e.g. Beare 1964: 219–32; Wille 1967: 158–87; Grimal 1975: 263–5; Blänsdorf 1978: 202–6; Moore 1998b, 1999, 2007, 2008; Marshall 2006: 203–44, 280–4.

[105] On the metre in Plautus and Terence see Questa 2007 (based on numerous earlier studies); on the development of Latin metre see Rix 1989.

The most important effect of metrical choices consists of differences in tone and delivery. Primarily there is a distinction between 'unaccompanied' and 'accompanied', i.e. whether lines were spoken or recited to music by the piper (*tibicen*).[106] In the terminology of later scholars and also in manuscripts of Plautus and Terence there is a distinction between 'spoken/unaccompanied part' (DV: *deverbium*) and 'sung/accompanied part' (C: *canticum*), while *cantica* employing various types of melody and rhythm might be marked as 'arias with changing rhythm/polymetric songs' (MMC: *mutatis modis cantata*).[107] Passages in iambic senarius are almost always unaccompanied, whereas passages in all other metres are almost always accompanied. The 'sung' or accompanied parts can be either stichic or polymetric, the latter generally being musically more complex.

Despite the musical accompaniment, verses could be seen as remaining close to spoken speech so that they almost seemed to lose their poetic character when the accompanying music was removed (cf. Cic. *Orat.* 183–4). As time went on, the amount of spoken verse increased, the greatest percentage being found in Accius and Terence.[108] Plautus, who was famous for his 'countless rhythms' (*numeri innumeri*: Gell. *NA* 1.24.3), employed the widest variety of metres among those poets from whom a sizeable number of verses remain.

On the basis of the distribution of metres, patterns for the use of accompanied and unaccompanied sections can be observed in Plautus and Terence: accompanied and unaccompanied passages alternate; plays always end accompanied; efforts are made so that audiences get all important information in that essential details are conveyed in spoken metre (e.g. narrative prologues or documents read out); the music can stop right before the climax of a play, which ensures that the major scene is understood, but also increases its impact.

The selection of metres (and consequently music) can be used for characterization when figures or actions are associated with particular metrical shapes; it may help to structure a drama when units are set off from each other by changes from accompanied to unaccompanied or vice versa. However, not all changes mark the beginning or end of units of action; they can also indicate shifts in the tone of speeches and conversations; and they

---

[106] On the *tibicen* and his instrument see ch. 2.6.

[107] Cf. e.g. Diom. *Ars* 3, *Gramm. Lat.* 1, pp. 490.22–3; 491.20–30; Donat. *Com.* 8.9; on Ter. *Ad., praef.* 1.7. On these terms, their meanings and use see Moore 2008: 20–38.

[108] See e.g. Jocelyn 1967: 30; Cancik 1978: 316–17. Isidorus describes the activity of tragic and comic actors as 'singing' (Isid. *Etym.* 18.43–6).

may call attention to similar or contrasting moments in the plot through musical parallels.[109]

Cicero attests to the musical and rhythmical sensibility of average audiences, who, albeit without any technical knowledge, were quick to notice when actors got the rhythm wrong and reacted with loud criticism, shouting and hissing (Cic. *De or.* 3.196; *Parad.* 26; *Orat.* 173). Besides, in a discussion on the power of the senses, Cicero has a reference to 'experts' (*in eo genere* [i.e. *cantu*] *exercitati*; *periti*) who are so sensitive to music that, as soon as a musician strikes up the first bars, they recognize the 'song/play' (*carmen*) and they know whether it is Antiopa or Andromacha (Cic. *Acad.* 2.20; 2.86; cf. also Donat. *Com.* 8.11). Since there is no more context, it is uncertain what is being described: perhaps revivals of tragedies of these titles (Pacuvius' *Antiopa* and Ennius' *Andromacha*) are envisaged, when at the beginning of the plays or at the first sound of a tune that functioned as leitmotif,[110] these 'experts' would not only recognize that the play was a tragedy, but in particular which drama and which character was to come onto the stage; or this might be a reference to individual virtuoso performances of well-known 'arias'.[111]

One can infer that at least in Cicero's time there were melodies that could be clearly assigned to particular plays in the repertoire (or extracts from them). However, it remains uncertain whether these tunes were the 'original' ones composed for the first performances of those plays or later reworkings in a similar style, and also how these 'experts' would have got to know the music. They could have become familiar with the tunes via earlier performances of the same plays, or the music might have been written down[112] and become available to the public just as texts of plays did in Cicero's time (Cic. *Rab. Post.* 29; *Opt. gen.* 18). At any rate, if specific plays were associated with recognizable music, this must have been handed down among impresarios and troupes of actors.

At least some music, then, seems to have been kept for dramatic performances until the end of the Republic; at the same time Cicero and Horace noted critically that musical styles and forms of musical performance had

---

[109] See Moore, esp. 1998b, 1999.

[110] The view that theatrical performances in Rome began with musical overtures (so Wille 1967: 169) has been inferred from the Cicero passages under discussion and cannot be corroborated by other evidence. The fact that some Plautine prologue speakers apparently had to make an effort to make themselves heard (e.g. Plaut. *Poen.* 1–15) might indicate that performances did not have musical preludes.

[111] So Jory 1988: 79.

[112] Musical notation is first attested securely in Quintilian (Quint. *Inst.* 1.12.14; 9.4.51), but is thought to have been common in Rome earlier (see Wille 1967: 489).

changed since the times of Livius Andronicus and Naevius, and regarded them as degenerate in comparison with traditional forms (Cic. *Leg.* 2.39; Hor. *Ars P.* 202–19). If their descriptions are reliable, they show a tendency towards more elaborate and impressive musical display, which agrees with the general development of performances and spectacle over the course of the Republican period.

Overview and conclusions: Republican drama

Although it has been claimed that it is impossible to produce a 'history of Roman drama',[1] this study has tried to collect and discuss all the material that could form the basis of such an attempt. Whether one believes that a coherent narrative against this background is sensible or can be successful presumably depends on the definition of '(literary) history' and the assessment of the surviving evidence. Because of these problems, the following outline, though based on the available data and the arguments presented in the body of this study (not repeated here), should be seen as tentative. Nevertheless, it seems worthwhile to draw together information and insights that are distributed over the preceding chapters. Preliminary conclusions have been presented in individual sections; the purpose of this final chapter is to combine the results, achieved by looking at the material from a variety of angles, into a coherent presentation. It might sound too coherent and slightly simplified in places, but this is an unavoidable consequence of a narrative exposition and necessary for a comprehensible presentation of possible developments and connections.

When Roman literary drama came into being in the mid-third century BCE, Greek drama had already existed for centuries, gone through several stages and spread from Athens to other parts of the Mediterranean. Besides, various indigenous forms of 'pre-literary' dramatic performances were in existence all over Italy. By the time they started to have literary drama themselves, Romans had had close cultural, economic and political links with a number of peoples, including Etruscans and Oscans in Italy, Greeks in mainland Greece, Greek colonists in Magna Graecia and Carthaginians, for many centuries. All these elements combined to form the background to the birth of Roman literary drama; but there was apparently a need for one decisive event and public backing to get it started.

---

[1] See Cancik 1978: 321–2; Dupont 1985: 311. See also Introduction.

According to later scholars (esp. Liv. 7.2), scenic games were introduced to Rome in 364 BCE as a result of a pestilence, when, in order to appease the gods, Etruscan performers were brought to Rome, who danced to musical accompaniment. The move to 'scripted' or 'literary' drama followed in 240 BCE, according to the prevailing Roman chronology, when, one year after the conclusion of the First Punic War (264–241 BCE), Roman magistrates commissioned Livius Andronicus, who had probably just shown his poetic credentials in his epic *Odusia* (a Latin version of Homer's *Odyssey*), to produce a play or plays for the public festival in that year. As the Romans were beginning to assert their position as a major power in the Mediterranean at this time, they were apparently eager to shape their cultural sophistication and national identity and to demonstrate it to their own people as well as to other nations. Since Greece seems to have been perceived as the dominant culture and as representing the level of civilization other societies aspired to, it was natural to look to Greek drama as the main model for more elaborate dramatic forms.

Roman drama as a literary genre and a public institution with a wide audience appeal therefore came suddenly into being at one particular time. Accordingly, the eventual literary product is not the direct result of a long and smooth preceding development, but rather the consequence of a conscious decision by the authorities to introduce this literary form (though pre-literary performances will have prepared this decision). On a literary level such a step was possible because a variety of dramatic forms had already been developed elsewhere, particularly in Greece. Romans had become familiar with these and could adopt and adapt convenient dramatic structures and elements, making them relevant to their own lives. They did not take over the existing forms of Greek literary drama unchanged; instead, on the basis of this material they developed something new and tailored to their own situation. This testifies to their high receptiveness and flexibility in appropriating whatever suited them, which can also be observed in other contexts and distinguishes the Romans from other peoples in the Mediterranean.

Due to its genesis, Roman drama was a public and official event from its inception; a connection between public festivals organized by the authorities and dramatic performances remained throughout the Republican period. All regular festivals were organized by public officials, who bought the plays to be performed (either directly from poets or with the assistance of impresarios). Even if it seems unlikely that prior to the first century BCE, when magistrates spent more and more money on festival entertainment, extravagant games were a direct means of ensuring a political career, magistrates would be keen to see the spectacle they presented to the populace well received. Soon, as early as during the productive years of the first playwrights, both the number of festivals and the number of days for dramatic performances at each festival began to increase. Eventually there were numerous opportunities throughout the year for magistrates and poets to present plays as well as for audiences to watch them.

In addition to their official and political character, Roman festivals had a religious element, since all regular public festivals were held in honour of a god or goddess and included religious rituals. Originally dramatic performances were often closely linked to the place of worship for the festival's patron god or goddess. Early performances took place on temporary stages, which could be erected in front of the temple of the deity honoured by the respective festival (cf. esp. Cic. *Har. resp.* 24). The stage apparently was the essential element of a Roman theatre while an auditorium could be improvised and provisional. For some later structures the Romans adopted the 'theatre temple', which had been developed in Italy outside Rome: a temple towered above the auditorium, and the steps in the auditorium did double duty as a monumental staircase ascending to the temple and as access to the rows of seats for spectators.

The first permanent stone theatre in Rome, the Theatre of Pompey, which was inaugurated in 55 BCE, realized such a set-up. Up to this time there had been only temporary wooden stages in the city of Rome, even though other towns in Italy had had stone theatres much earlier and Greece had had them for centuries. Rome had seen attempts at erecting a stone theatre by several officials from the early second century BCE, but they all failed because of opposition from other magistrates, while temporary stage buildings became more and more lavish within an expanding festival culture. Various explanations for this peculiar situation have been put forward; in addition to possible political reasons it seems most likely that a fixed structure would have interfered with Roman religious customs. Objections of this sort were forestalled by the layout of Pompey's theatre temple. At the same time such a permanent demonstration of one person's wealth and power became possible only in the middle of the first century BCE, when, in anticipation of the Principate, individuals were able to gain prominence in society.

The shape of a Roman theatre in its eventual form differed from that of a Greek one in a number of ways: in Greek theatres the auditorium, for instance, was typically more than a half-circle, enclosing the stage, around a round orchestra. In Roman theatres the auditorium was only about a half-circle, which was placed opposite the stage and divided from it by monumental entrances, and there was no real orchestra. Although in early palliatae the audience is frequently addressed and thus drawn into the play, in a fully established Roman theatre the audience watched an action that took place in a separate world. In the remaining texts there are hardly any direct addresses to audiences (apart from prologues) for playwrights after Plautus. The architectural structure, along with the professionalism of the theatre business, facilitated presenting Greek or other foreign settings and hence unusual customs (in plays based on Greek models) to Roman audiences. In the most developed theatres the back of the stage (which was longer and thinner than in Greece) was marked by the high and ornamented façade of the stage building: this turned the whole theatre into an enclosed space and one continuous, solid structure.

Even before the erection of the first permanent theatre in Rome, the theatrical set-up had become both more formal and more sumptuous. Over the course of time laws were introduced that made seating stratified, giving first senators (in 194 BCE) and then equestrians (in 67 BCE) special seating areas in prominent positions close to the stage. On the one hand these rules demonstrate that the authorities had recognized dramatic performances as a vital part of public life, and on the other hand theatre audiences were turned into comprehensive and structured representations of Roman society and could be referred to accordingly. In line with the increasing importance of theatrical performances in Rome's political and social life and with a general tendency towards display, temporary stage buildings became increasingly luxurious and sophisticated towards the end of the Republican period. Changes to the physical setting of performances, including the use of machinery or elaborate designs and (stone) structures, necessarily affected the performance style of dramas, which tended to include more and more spectacular effects and parading of equipment.

For all venues and performances, set and scenery were broadly similar, which could function as a fixed starting point for both playwrights and audiences: the stage in front of the back wall represented an open area, frequently a street, with doors indicating several buildings behind it; on the two sides of the stage there were exits to the further distance (often the countryside and the harbour) and to the nearer distance (often the city centre). Additional stage equipment was scarce. The performance relied mainly on the imagination of audiences, to whom the particular meaning of buildings and locations in each play would have been made clear by information given in the plays, typically in the prologue or the initial scenes. Players would have worn conventional costumes and masks (according to the dramatic genre). Clarity was increased by the announcement of characters' entrances and exits, the use of gestures and stage-action underlining what was being said.

The first performers to appear on stage in Rome came from Etruria in 364 BCE, according to Livy (Liv. 7.2), and actors continued to be mainly foreigners and/or of low social status (presumably with the exception of Atellana players). After theatrical performances had established themselves, actors seem to have been organized in troupes led by a chief actor or impresario. Thus, when a play had been composed by a playwright and sold to the magistrates organizing the games, an impresario seems to have taken charge of the production and arranged for a troupe of actors (including a musician) to perform and to obtain costumes from a supplier of props.

Although the number of players engaged in a performance as well as that of speaking actors simultaneously present on stage was not limited to three as it had been in classical Greece, actors' troupes in Rome still seem to have been rather small. Dramatic performances were a 'business' run by a particular group of people specialized in the theatre and paid for by the authorities: therefore audiences enjoyed performances as entertainment provided by professionals. Due to their low social and/or foreign status, actors were generally denied basic citizen rights. In the first century BCE, however, when individuals' achievements were admired in sophisticated performances based on qualities of display, talented actors could win high recognition as 'stars' and reach higher levels of society, as did Aesopus and Roscius in Cicero's time.

Since dramatic performances in Rome were public events, they were potentially open to the whole populace. However, it seems that at least some early venues could seat only a few thousand spectators at a time. Still, these spectators might consist of people with a wide and diverse range of backgrounds. Some comic prologues, just like comments by late Republican and early Augustan writers, indicate that Roman audiences could relish the spectacle as a whole and that therefore actors had to make an effort to secure a hearing at the start; at the same time dramatic scripts tend to presuppose a certain familiarity with both Roman conventions and Greek customs, language, history, literature and culture. Hence Roman audiences are likely not to have been entirely unruly or uneducated; the circumstantial details attested are rather common consequences of open-air performances in a festival environment. The holiday atmosphere, however, did not mean that plays provided merely escapist fare; they also conveyed meaningful messages.

Another remarkable fact concerning the constituent elements of the Roman theatre is that it is not only the institution, the practitioners and some of the subject matter that the Romans adopted from elsewhere, but even the dramatic poets. For all early 'Roman' poets were not Romans by birth; they had arrived in Rome from other parts of Italy or from outside Italy. Several came from southern Italy, where Greek culture flourished and indigenous traditions were strong. Despite their obvious familiarity with Greek and local conventions, these poets did not decide on developing a literature in their own languages, but rather turned their creative energy to appropriating Greek (as well as Etruscan and Oscan) elements to create plays in Latin for Roman audiences. Though foreigners strictly speaking, they were apparently ready and able to engage with Roman issues; thus they helped the Romans to develop their own literary language as well as a sense of national identity and self-confidence by producing new literary genres with wide public appeal.

These poets thus became the first to transfer sophisticated literary forms successfully from one European culture to another, adapt those to the conditions and requirements of the receiving people and thereby create something specific that developed into a constituent element of the national context in which they worked. Although some Romans apparently felt that poetry was something foreign that came to Rome rather late, generally Romans seem to have had no problems with foreigners creating a literary idiom for them. Indeed, they accepted these poets and their works as vital parts of their literary and political history, making their literature commence with Livius Andronicus and regarding Ennius (from Rudiae) as 'father Ennius' (*pater Ennius*: Hor. *Epist.* 1.19.7). Later literary critics, however, judging from an aesthetic point of view, could not but note that the beginnings were rather primitive and that literature properly speaking started only with Ennius (e.g. Cic. *Brut.* 71).

Although Republican dramatic poets typically came from outside Rome, often started off in a relatively low social position and relied on public commissions, they are unlikely to have been 'clients' who were entirely dependent on particular 'patrons'. Individual noblemen might have commissioned plays from them for special occasions; yet the poets worked for various members of the elite, and they ultimately produced plays for festivals open to the public. Since, however, poets will have had connections with members of the highest classes of society, they will have been aware of the state of public affairs and especially of the concerns of this group, in addition to the views of the general populace. Thus they will have been able to present plays with potential relevance to the whole Roman people, which also ensured their success.

Although all that remains of Roman drama is texts (many of them in fragmentary state), dramatic scripts were only one aspect of the entire theatre event: this was a comprehensive performance including all sorts of visual, acoustic and situational effects, while the stage-action may have been influenced by the possibilities offered by the layout of the respective venues.

Even the surviving texts and fragments do not always provide sufficient information. The lack of complete scripts for dramatic genres other than comedy in Greek style is felt most noticeably in the area of dramatic structure. Nevertheless it can be inferred tentatively that dramatic structures were broadly similar across all Roman serious and light dramatic genres with a proper plot: they consisted of a prologue (not obligatory) and a subsequent series of monologues and dialogues. In contrast to Greek drama, Roman palliatae of the Republican period did not have choral interludes between scenes, and the same was presumably true for other dramatic genres; instead, the dramatic action formed one continuous story. There was, however, a strong musical element, extended (in comparison with Greece) and transferred to individual actors: as extant scripts show, only a limited number of lines were in spoken metre (iambic senarius); a large proportion of verses was accompanied by the flute player (in longer iambic or trochaic metres or lyric metres). Serious dramatic genres retained choruses, where they were integrated into the action, just as another actor, while almost all plays of the light dramatic genres seem to have done without a chorus.

Descriptions of the full range of dramatic genres known for Rome are found in late-antique grammarians and commentators, who also give explanations of the generic names (which have often been derived from particular types of clothing). Although the works of these scholars date to a time well after the creative period of Republican drama and are the result of later, organizing approaches, they provide useful starting points; what they say, though selective, is basically confirmed by earlier evidence. Some of the terms conventionally applied to Roman drama go back to these late-antique scholars or rather their predecessors in the late Republican and Augustan periods.

The first 'literary' dramatic genres to be introduced to Rome were Greek-style tragedy (*fabula crepidata/tragoedia*) and Greek-style comedy (*fabula palliata/comoedia*). Plays of these types are set in a fictional Greek environment; their plots tend to be based on specific Greek dramas or on Greek stories narrated elsewhere, which have been adapted for Roman audiences.

Roman poets apparently did not translate or transpose Greek dramas word for word, but rather used a method often called 'free translation': they transferred Greek stories and plays according to the conventions of the Latin language and Roman thinking, transposing the main ideas of the Greek models, replacing and altering, adding and combining in points of detail. Even if Roman poets thus started off by using existing Greek dramas as their basis and therefore might display little 'originality' in the modern sense, the poets' choices of what to transpose and how to do it are signs of their poetic individuality. This is also proved by the so-called technique of 'contamination', when Roman playwrights combined parts from different Greek dramas into one new play.

The first playwrights in Rome did not limit themselves to the literary genre of drama in their poetic activity. From the start, however, the literary genres of drama and epic differed in their specific styles (e.g. in the areas of language and metre). For tragedy and comedy, by contrast, there was a greater similarity in formal terms: there is little distinction in metre and dramatic technique between the serious and the light forms of drama in Rome; instead there are noticeable mutual influences. Over the course of time dramatic poets started to specialize in particular dramatic genres, either in one of the light genres or in the two forms of serious drama, tragedy and praetexta. Plautus is the first known playwright to have concentrated on one dramatic genre only (palliata). Such focusing became common practice from the time of the two successors of the versatile Ennius in the late second century BCE, when his nephew Pacuvius concentrated on serious drama and his house-mate Caecilius on palliata.

The gradual increase in differentiation between dramatic genres went hand in hand with the development of further dramatic genres. These new forms were more 'Roman' or 'Italic' in terms of topics and atmosphere; they therefore mark a further development of drama in Rome, while they still remained under the influence of the Greek precedent, at least in structure and dramatic technique. The first step in this direction was made by Naevius: he not only turned the emerging genre of epic more 'Roman' in that he wrote a poem about the First Punic War (*Bellum Poenicum*) rather than transposing a Greek story, as his predecessor Livius Andronicus had done, but also introduced the genre of serious drama on events from Roman history, *fabula praetexta*, at the end of the third century BCE. From that time onwards all major playwrights of serious drama wrote both tragedies and praetextae. Not much later (though the precise dating is uncertain) something similar happened on the comic side: a light drama set in Rome or Italy, featuring Roman characters and Roman conventions, *fabula togata*, was born.

This completes the Roman set-up that is canonical in the descriptions of later grammarians and commentators: four major dramatic genres, two 'Greek' ones and two 'Roman' ones or two serious ones and two light ones. In their fully established systems these scholars account for more dramatic genres on each side, even though the status of the other dramatic genres is slightly different from a generic point of view: while these four dramatic genres in Rome can be seen to have been developed from Greek models (in different ways) without direct indigenous precedents, other dramatic genres were linked to native customs and therefore had pre-literary precursors before they became literary and entered the framework of Roman dramatic genres. These genres are Atellana, mime and pantomime.

Atellana, originating from the Oscans, had been present in Rome in pre-literary form from an early period. It apparently became literary at the turn of the second to the first centuries BCE. This move seems already to have been noticed as a decisive step in antiquity, since the Atellana writer Pomponius was regarded as the inventor of this dramatic genre despite a (non-literary) tradition before him (cf. Vell. Pat. 2.9.6). This process again shows the openness of the Romans and their readiness to adopt and develop material from other cultures. Although some titles, characters and plot elements of Atellana plays recall other light dramatic genres in Rome, Atellanae are distinguished by their plots' being based on the experiences of fixed stock characters and by the prominence of particular figures such as fullers. Literary Atellanae could be given as 'after-pieces' after performances of plays of other dramatic genres.

In the first century BCE mime and pantomime completed the repertoire. Mime, light drama in a simple Roman environment, was particularly associated with the festival of *Ludi Florales*, which had become annual in 173 BCE. Mimes turned literary only in the final decades of the Republican period and gradually replaced Atellanae as 'after-pieces'. Even though later writers commented on mime mainly critically, since they regarded it as low, crude and vulgar, mime was not necessarily merely superficial entertainment: mimes could present well-phrased serious content and also include aspects of political relevance.

The last dramatic genre that made its appearance in Rome and might still be called a dramatic form of the 'Republican' period is pantomime. Roman pantomime consists of a silent (sometimes elaborately equipped) solo dancer who, by his movement and gestures, interprets a libretto sung by a choir, accompanied by a variety of musical instruments. Although, therefore, pantomime could be seen as a form of dance, the fact that the dance illustrates a story makes pantomime comparable with other dramatic genres in Rome. While the 'official recognition' of pantomime in Rome probably dates to the 20s BCE, it is likely to have become prominent by the 40s BCE. Emergence at this time would make pantomime a dramatic genre with roots in the Republican period. The final decades of the Republic saw the flourishing of mime, the rise of individual star actors in all dramatic genres, and performances of proper dramas developing into pageants of the sort condemned by Cicero and Horace (Cic. *Fam.* 7.1.2; Hor. *Epist.* 2.1.187–207). Hence pantomime's emphasis on individuals and on 'realistic' display as well as its derivative relationship to tragedy and comedy would be in line with developments in the middle of the first century BCE. Pantomime became a dominant dramatic form in the imperial period.

The gradual emergence of the various dramatic genres and their prominence at different phases within the Republican period correspond with the number of famous poets known for each dramatic genre and their dates. Writers of tragedies and comedies cover the period from the beginnings of dramatic poetry in Rome to the early first century BCE; for tragedy five well-known poets are attested (Livius Andronicus, Naevius, Ennius, Pacuvius, Accius), for comedy there are at least eight major poets (Livius Andronicus, Naevius, Ennius, Plautus, Caecilius Statius, Luscius Lanuvinus, Terence, Turpilius). The series for praetexta and togata have fewer representatives, but end about the same time; the known poets for praetextae are Naevius, Ennius, Pacuvius, Accius, while for togatae there are Titinius, Afranius, Atta. For literary Atellana, literary mime and pantomime, which flourished throughout much shorter periods, fewer poets are attested, and their dates are closer together: for literary Atellana there are Pomponius and Novius in the early first century; literary mimes were written by Decimus Laberius and Publilius Syrus in the mid-first century; and for pantomime Pylades from Cilicia and Bathyllus from Alexandria are credited with 'having developed the Italian style of dance' in the mid- to late first century BCE.

The proliferation of dramatic genres and the lack of new poets writing works of the established dramatic genres for the stage after a certain point in time did not mean an immediate, complete change of the dramatic landscape: although dramas in Rome were originally composed for performance at a single festival, revival performances of successful plays became established from the mid-second century BCE onwards (similar to developments in classical Greece much earlier). Consequently, even when the constant supply of new plays for a given dramatic genre dried up, it did not suddenly disappear from the public conscience, though only selected pieces (or extracts of them) would continue to be performed and these might be altered for re-performances in line with changing tastes. Revival performances seem to have taken off at a time when the first scholarly activities devoted to Roman drama are discernible, which suggests that 'old' plays started to acquire the status of 'classics'; revivals then continued throughout the Republican period (and beyond).

Each dramatic genre and each playwright as well as original performances and revivals have their own individual characteristics, as was already recognized in antiquity (e.g. Cic. *De or.* 3.27). Within the framework of their chosen dramatic genre, Roman dramatic poets could give their pieces a distinctive shape by choosing and emphasizing particular stories, themes and styles of presentation. Despite the fragmentary state of the evidence, it is therefore possible to some extent to establish the specific characteristics of individual playwrights.

Equally, one can identify certain features that Republican playwrights seem to have had in common and hence can be seen as typical of (early) Roman drama: when Roman poets took over Greek plays with the corresponding stories in their characteristic settings, this fact contributed to creating a distance between the immediate, everyday experiences of audiences and the world presented on stage; consequently audiences will have felt less directly involved and could thus both be entertained and be encouraged to reflect on the issues presented; owing to the human problems addressed, even dramas based on Greek stories could be of interest and relevance to Roman audiences.

This impact was heightened by dramatists since Roman adaptations of Greek drama privileged topics that were particularly important to Roman society (by means of choices and modifications), such as adequate moral conduct, social behaviour, the relationship between family members, the role of a major power, dealing with other nations and conquered people, the treatment of foreigners, the influx of Greek customs or incoming new religious and philosophical ideas. Similar emphases can be observed in dramatic genres that are not directly based on Greek models. Therefore, dramatic forms relying on Greek precedents as well as other dramatic genres later developed in Rome played a role in confirming Roman self-understanding and confidence against the background of political and social changes.

At the same time plays were not too obviously educational or topical. So, while praetextae naturally referred to specific events in Roman history, which might be recent incidents, in other dramatic genres poets typically avoided explicit allusions to topical issues of contemporary politics. Additionally, plays were prevented from being too serious due to the issues touched upon by combining those with entertaining features. This is obvious for light dramatic genres, which contained various forms of jokes, slapstick, ridiculous characters and bizarre actions, although the Roman dramatic genre of togata remained more sober and did not go as far in this direction as the Greek-based palliata. Over the course of time tragedy too increasingly included spectacular scenic effects, sudden reversals, the prominence of ordinary figures and their experiences or noble characters in reduced circumstances (found similarly in the late Euripides). The only dramatic genre somewhat immune to these developments was perhaps praetexta, since events from Roman history could hardly be mixed with entertaining elements; they might just have been given spectacular battle scenes.

What characterizes Roman drama overall, therefore, is the mixture of two aspects: presentation of themes that concern the life of individuals or the community in Rome on the one hand and provision of enjoyable entertainment and spectacle on the other hand; in other words Horace's 'to offer something of use' and 'to provide pleasure' (*prodesse* and *delectare* or *utile* and *dulce*: Hor. *Ars P.* 333–4; 343–4).[2] These two poles are already present in the work of Rome's first poet, Livius Andronicus, as he seems to have chosen Greek plays for adaptation that included discussions of moral, social or political questions that could be or could be made relevant for Roman audiences and facilitated impressive plots. Livius Andronicus thereby showed successful ways to transpose Greek works for Roman audiences and laid the groundwork for further development.

Livius Andronicus' successor and near-contemporary Naevius made drama (as well as epic, also transferred to Rome from Greece by Livius Andronicus) more 'Roman' and thus more relevant to local audiences: he introduced the genre of Roman historical drama (praetexta) and included allusions to Roman and Italic reality in his comedies. Naevius' successor Ennius continued to 'Romanize' emerging Roman literature, by more frequent and more dominant references to Roman values and Roman terminology, such as fighting prowess and working for the benefit of the community. Ennius' activity in a variety of literary genres indicates that the number of literary genres present in Rome increased in this period, as did their cross-fertilization; from Ennius onwards the influence of other

---

[2] For Roman tragedy see also Aricò 1997: 74.

literary genres, particularly oratory (as speeches started to be published in this period), on dramatic forms is noticeable.

In a later generation, the dramas of Pacuvius (tragedies and praetextae) took up some of the new ideas, such as philosophy, coming in from Greece. He altered the ethical and political topics addressed in accordance with the concerns of the period, by presenting, for instance, questions of legitimate rule in an era of expansion. Thus Pacuvius might have met the interests of the contemporary intellectual elite, but he also catered for the needs of the audience as a whole as he made more difficult topics acceptable by an emphasis on stage business, stunning stage effects and spectacular plots. His successor Accius continued the approaches of both Ennius and Pacuvius.

After the time of Accius the production of serious drama as proper and regular stage drama virtually ceased, which may be due to a combination of factors. Perhaps poets like Accius were too learned and did not make enough concessions to public taste. Moreover, the general preferences of average audiences are likely to have changed further, and a desire for entertainment had become dominant. Besides, by this time principles of ethical and political behaviour had come to be debated in other, specifically developed literary genres (e.g. philosophical treatises); therefore there was less need or incentive to engage with them in drama in order to cater for people interested in such issues. Therefore the combination of serious thoughts and entertainment, which had characterized tragedy from the start, seems no longer to have met with the same appreciation by the general public (hence the two issues were continued in separate forms).

A similar development can be observed in comedy, though with emphases reversed. Plautus followed Naevius' approach of inserting Roman allusions; he also enlarged the element of entertainment by means of turbulent and burlesque stage-action. His form of comedy might have provided comic relief in times of war and thus have been a reaction to the contemporary situation. In a later generation Caecilius and Terence gave more room to the presentation of social and moral topics (just as their contemporary Pacuvius did in the area of tragedy), presumably in response to the changing interests of the period. At the same time they still catered for the provision of entertainment by means of effective drama.

Over the course of the Republican period, tragedy and comedy gradually adopted elements from each other, since they exploited similar dramatic features and motifs: tragedy increasingly employed effective elements, some of which have comic potential, such as mistaken identity, deception, misapprehension, the experiences of ordinary characters and solutions of problems on the human level without divine intervention; comedy increasingly addressed issues confronting contemporary society. Both dramatic genres thus yielded the characteristic mixture of good entertainment and weighty content. At some point at the end of the Republican period tragedy and comedy had developed so far that they almost converged; hence this process could not continue beyond a certain level.[3]

As the traditional forms of tragedy and comedy were no longer able to adapt to changes in demand, the momentum shifted to other dramatic genres that appeared in literary form from the late second century onwards and throughout the first century BCE (Atellana, mime, pantomime). These dramatic genres developed the current tendencies in their own ways, since all new forms of performances continued characteristics observable in the latest comedies and tragedies: they presented the experiences of ordinary, rather simple characters, impressive scenic effects, elaborate stage business and a large amount of pageantry on stage, while also conveying moral messages (perhaps often in simplified form, as the number of attested isolated *sententiae* suggests) and, eventually, topical comment.

In spite of this development 'old' plays continued to be valued as 'classics': revivals of 'old' plays, which seem to have started a generation after Plautus and became a major feature in the first century BCE, complemented the range of performances on offer in the late Republic. In revivals individual lines might be given a new meaning, when they were taken out of the original context and interpreted as references to the contemporary situation; this could be done by actors (by means of emphasis or gestures, or even by altering and adding phrases) or by audiences. The political relevance of an existing play could thereby be revived or modified at a revival performance. Such a use of drama is in line with new plays produced in this period: some lines surviving from first-century literary Atellanae and mimes can only be understood as comments on the current political situation (most obvious at the contest of mime writers before the dictator Caesar). References included in these simpler and more recent dramatic genres were perhaps more direct than those in the traditional ones. Revivals of Atellanae continued into imperial times; in this period they were exploited politically in the same way as revivals of tragedies and comedies could be in the first century BCE.

The developments in preferred dramatic genres and changes in performance style affected the composition of the body of playwrights: poets writing professionally for the stage in the late Republic turned to new

---

[3] See also Fantham 1977: 49; Goldberg 1996: 219–20.

dramatic genres, while writers who stuck to traditional dramatic genres such as tragedy and praetexta were increasingly of higher social classes and composed poetry as a spare-time activity (mainly to be read or recited) rather than for a living and for full-scale representation on stage.

In the late Republic the politicization of drama not only influenced dramatic scripts, but was also observable on an institutional level, along with an increase of pageant: the emergence of successful individuals in theatre business was supported by promotion from men such as Sulla and Caesar, at about the time when Pompey built the first permanent stone theatre in Rome, inaugurated in 55 BCE. Just like the larger and larger sums of money spent on temporary stage buildings, this engagement shows that the theatre had become a factor in the policies of individuals. Powerful figures apparently regarded it as useful and could expect it to be effective when they exploited the theatre to impress and satisfy the populace; this situation foreshadowed the Principate with its predominance of individual men, just as did the admiration individual actors might win in the late Republic. The political exploitation of the theatre and audience expectations caused more spectacular productions, which went hand in hand with more lavish settings and an emphasis on impressive acting.[4]

Roman drama had had an element of pageant from the beginning, which was criticized by intellectuals such as the satirist Lucilius from the second half of the second century BCE onwards, but this element apparently became more prominent over time, until men like Cicero and Horace were disgusted by it (Cic. *Fam.* 7.1.2; Hor. *Epist.* 2.1.187–207). In the early imperial period it had apparently reached such an extent that serious content of equal value could no longer be accommodated; this is when the stories of burlesque entertaining performances and of plot-based drama started to diverge.[5] This process may have been supported by the expansion of the Empire over numerous peoples with different languages and traditions, where performances that did not require a high level of linguistic competence in Latin could easily spread and function as a unifying factor.[6] Hardly any genuine full-length performances of traditional dramas of the serious or light dramatic genres are known for the imperial period; performances seem to have consisted mainly of mimes

---

[4] Developments in the popularity of particular dramatic genres and in the choice of themes should be seen as connected with political changes (see Flower 2010: 164–8).

[5] See also Goldberg 1996: esp. 272–3; Beacham 1999: 44. A separation between popular culture and elite culture, including performances in the theatre, has also been suggested for fourth-century Athens (see Wallace 1997: 110).

[6] An anecdote from the time of Nero demonstrates that pantomime performances could be understood by anyone, even those without any linguistic competence (cf. Lucian, *Salt.* 64).

and pantomimes, dances, musicals or individual celebrated pieces from 'old' plays.

What continued into the imperial period was the other aspect of Roman drama: plays used as vehicles for conveying thought-provoking messages. Yet these plays were no longer intended to reach as wide an audience as they had in the Republic; they were mainly designed to be read or recited (in a variety of venues) and were stripped of most elements that create impressive effects on a full-scale stage. This reduction of features in comparison with Republican drama presumably meant that dramatic genres that had always been more sober and relied less on effective stage business had a higher chance of being taken up under the changed circumstances. This could explain why a number of tragedies by Seneca and one praetexta (transmitted under Seneca's name) are extant from early imperial times, and more examples of these two dramatic genres are attested or preserved in fragments for this period (e.g. plays by Pomponius Secundus and Curiatius Maternus), while there is less evidence for light dramatic genres: Juvenal seems to mention recitations of togatae (Juv. 1.3) and Pliny those of palliatae by a contemporary poet. The comedies referred to by Pliny include some of the 'old' type containing allusions to contemporary issues and individuals as well as criticism of vices (Plin. *Ep.* 6.21), although it may be questioned how direct these remarks could have been in the imperial period. Dramas were obviously intended to be stylistically polished and relevant to current debates. A writer of comedies based on Menander is attested by inscriptional evidence and was probably active in approximately Pliny's time (*CIL* 9.1164: M. Pomponius Bassulus).

Those dramatic genres that were taken up in the imperial period seamlessly continued developments observable at the end of the Republic, even though plays no longer had a necessary connection with full-scale performances in the theatre: just like revivals or plays of new dramatic genres in late Republican times, dramas composed in the early imperial period can be understood to have a topical political aspect. However, in the imperial period this political emphasis is no longer supportive as it was in the early days of Roman drama, but critical instead. One may conclude that even in the imperial period Roman drama remained a literary genre that was rooted in Roman society and engaged with issues concerning it, while the forms of production and reception had changed.[7]

---

[7] The development from politically affirmative to critical messages between the Republican and the imperial periods had already been noted for tragedy by Stärk (2000) and for praetexta by Manuwald (2001a: 342–3).

Some of the characteristics of Roman Republican drama have parallels in Greek drama; still, what developed in Rome long after the time of classical Greek drama cannot be described as a smooth, continuous development from classical or Hellenistic Greek drama, even though firm conclusions are hampered by insufficient knowledge about Greek drama in the Hellenistic period.

For instance, a chorus integrated into the action, which can be found in Republican tragedy and some comedies, resembles Aeschylus' practice more closely than that of Euripides or Hellenistic poets, in whose plays choral songs famously were 'interludes' (*embolima*). Political topical references and metatheatrical sections (as employed in Republican comedy) recall Aristophanes' parabaseis, while the plots of Republican comedy follow the New Comedy of Menander and his contemporaries (which, however, had choral songs between acts). Motifs in Republican tragedy, such as recognition, the involvement of ordinary characters, the presentation of noble figures in rags, and satisfactory solutions on the human level, are reminiscent of Euripides, who had already influenced Greek New Comedy. The models of Roman tragic playwrights might have included fourth-century Greek tragedy, which is thought to have developed features of the late Euripides.

Generally, for plot construction and subject matter Republican playwrights seem to have looked back to the 'classics': writers of tragedy to the classical Greek tragic poets, Euripides in particular, and writers of comedy to the poets of Hellenistic New Comedy, who were already 'classics' of a past age by the time comedy took off in Rome. Both of these main groups of models had a potential for transferability, which, for instance, Aristophanes' comedies (just like Roman praetextae) did not have to the same extent, because of clear references to particular events in a specific people's history. Contemporary Hellenistic drama is more likely to have been one of the vehicles by which Roman poets got to know the Greek 'classics' and to have demonstrated aspects of dramatic technique and methods of presentation that Roman poets could adopt.[8] That there is no smooth, continuous development from Greece to Rome is probably a consequence of the fact that the introduction of Greek-style drama to Rome was not initiated by writers and actors in search of literary expansion, but was rather the result of a decision by Roman authorities.

Supplementary to the history of the production of Roman drama (along with immediate audience reactions) is the history of its reception in literary

[8] See also Jocelyn 1967: 17; Aricò 1997: 63–4.

circles, which includes the reactions of playwrights to other practitioners of the dramatic genre as well as comments by scholars. Perhaps the fact that what Roman poets could build on from the start included a fully developed literature in Greek, complete with literary criticism and early commentaries, is one of the reasons why Roman poets seem to have been aware of literary techniques and literary history from the outset. This is obvious in numerous explicit metatheatrical references in light dramatic genres: these comment on the fact that what is going on is a performance in which actors take part, play with the characteristics of the respective dramatic genre, allude to other dramatic genres or even discuss other poets. Playwrights also take the work of predecessors into account in that they refer to it (seriously or parodically) or avoid overlap. The same is true for writers of serious dramatic genres, who, as they tend to limit direct metatheatrical references, might allude to lines by earlier playwrights, pass over topics and plots already dramatized by predecessors or prefer to present those in different ways.

This awareness, along with specialization and differentiation among dramatic genres, means that a genuine Roman literary tradition began to take shape from a relatively early stage in the development of drama at Rome. This led to intertextual relationships among Roman representatives of the dramatic genres (in addition to similar connections to Greek texts). At the same time the proliferation of poets and their restrictions to specific dramatic genres may have been one of the reasons for rivalry between poets, as demonstrated by Terence's prologues, since competition to be the foremost poet in any one dramatic genre and arguments about keeping to the rules of dramatic composition arose.

The emergence of a Roman literary tradition and the establishment of drama as a proper literary genre were obviously recognized by recipients; scholarly work was prompted on the characteristics of drama, often against the background of its Greek counterpart. Dramatic poets themselves were the first to discuss the literary issues of their dramatic genres, mainly within the plays themselves and later also in separate works: at the end of the Republican period Accius was the first dramatic poet also to compose treatises on drama (*Didascalica, Pragmatica*). Moreover, a number of parameters and categories either observed explicitly or applied implicitly by Republican playwrights correspond to criteria outlined in Aristotle's *Poetics* or in works by his pupil Theophrastus. While this could be a typological overlap, it is not impossible that Roman playwrights, who are known to have been widely read in Roman and Greek literature including scholiasts, were familiar with these doctrines.

From the second half of the second century BCE onwards, scholars who did not produce dramas themselves started to discuss issues of the chronology or ranking of dramatic poets; 'old' plays apparently came to be regarded as 'classics', and their scripts must have become available outside the theatre. Dramatic genres eventually turned 'literary' (in a narrow sense) when dramatic scripts were no longer seen as manuals for performances, but acquired an existence and value in their own right as they were read, edited and commented on by scholars. This started in a period when performances of dramas were still regularly taking place.

Scholarly activity increased towards the first century BCE, where it is best known from the works of Cicero. He not only discussed technical questions such as the chronology of dramatic poets, but also engaged with the content of dramas by analysing characters' remarks in terms of meaning and argumentative structure. Cicero's works thus demonstrate that engagement with drama was not restricted to scholarly activity: he used the views, sentiments and actions of dramatic figures as positive or negative examples for the life of ordinary Roman citizens, or quoted them as proverbial maxims, not only in his philosophical treatises, but also in his speeches and letters. Such references to dramatic speeches and actions and their underlying principles must mean that these plays were well known and appreciated by Cicero's audience, so that he could expect their familiarity with the plays alluded to. Hence issues presented in drama are likely to have been taken seriously and to have continued to be regarded as relevant to Roman society.

Cicero's remarks on Roman drama, however, also include criticism of some characteristic aspects: he disapproves of pageants and elaborate stage business that suppress meaningful dialogue and messages. Besides, he prefers to quote from poets in whose works the latter element was more noticeable, such as Caecilius and Terence (rather than Naevius and Plautus) or Afranius or Ennius, Pacuvius and Accius. This attitude seems to have strengthened over the course of Cicero's career; such a development is in line with the growing proliferation of entertainments such as mime and pantomime in his time, the dearth of playwrights for traditional dramatic genres and the focus of intellectuals on the meaning of texts rather than on spectacular performances. Nevertheless, in his time performances of all dramatic genres were still taking place and were an important factor in public life. Therefore Cicero the politician looked down upon mime as crude and vulgar while he simultaneously feared its political potential due to topical references; on the one hand he despised elaborate stage business displacing a proper plot, on the other hand he realized the political importance of performances, and he enjoyed being celebrated himself by modifications of old plays at revivals.

The particular poets and plays quoted or mentioned by Cicero largely overlap with those for which revivals are attested in the first century (for which Cicero again is the most important source). This suggests that a 'canon' was being created; presumably, the preferences of audiences and the dramatic poets themselves as well as scholars contributed to its formation: Ennius, for instance, distinguished himself from his predecessors by calling them 'Fauns and seers' (*Fauni vatesque*) in his epic *Annales* (Enn. *Ann.* 232 W. = 207 Sk.), and Terence used his prologues to ridicule the works of his opponent Luscius Lanuvinus. Cicero later speaks of a tragic triad of Ennius, Pacuvius, Accius, comparing them to the three classical Greek tragic poets (Cic. *De or.* 3.27); at the same time he criticizes the primitive quality of the early poets Livius Andronicus and Naevius (Cic. *Brut.* 71; 75–6). Such ancient assessments of Roman poets and scholars have obviously influenced transmission, as the surviving amount of information, testimonies and fragments for each poet varies.

Due to their 'archaic' language, Republican poets were looked down upon by Augustan and early imperial writers, but they found favour again with 'archaists' such as Fronto or Gellius in the second century CE. Since there were hardly any performances of full dramas from the beginning of the imperial period, it was the scripts that were read, mainly for scholarly purposes. Even later, in about the fourth century CE, lexicographers, grammarians, scholiasts and commentators dealt with Republican dramas; they quoted sample lines for linguistic purposes, while they might not always have had access to the plays in their entirety or have been concerned about their content. Christian writers condemned the theatre as a pagan institution, but the fact that those late writers engaged with drama indicates that it was still regarded as an issue worth addressing. They thereby contributed to preserving at least fragments of the works of those playwrights who did not have the good fortune to become school authors and have their works (or some of their works) preserved in their entirety.

In conclusion, one might try to distinguish certain phases or generations within the development of Republican drama, although neat distinctions are well known to be impossible in literary history and 'poets of different periods' overlap.[9]

---

[9] For other proposals cf. Suerbaum 2002 (see also Lefèvre 1978b: 8), who distinguishes between the pioneers Livius Andronicus, Naevius and Ennius, on the one hand, and drama, encompassing all

Roman drama started with the 'pioneers' Livius Andronicus and Naevius in the second half of the third century BCE: commissioned by the authorities at a favourable point in time, they introduced drama to Rome. They were the first to transpose and adapt Greek literary genres for Roman audiences, taking the specific social and political situation in Rome into account. This pair of playwrights was followed by another group of early poets in the late third and early second centuries BCE, who helped to develop the various dramatic genres and to distinguish between them: Plautus, Ennius and Titinius. Since their works already came closer to what was to become the canonical dramatic form, they are often no longer regarded as pioneers, but as actual founders or even representatives of the 'classic' form of a particular dramatic genre. Their dramas are marked by the promotion of traditional Roman values in a time of major wars for Rome. From this period onwards there was a Roman dramatic tradition for Roman playwrights to engage with.

The next phase is represented by poets of the early second century: Pacuvius and Caecilius, who mark a transitional period from early to late Republican drama. In this time the emerging dramatic genres developed to comply with changing audience expectations; for instance, dramas now included more references to Greek philosophy, but also placed more emphasis on impressive performance. The dramatists of the mid-second century, Terence and Afranius (still overlapping with the long-lived Pacuvius), then constituted a period of rather intellectual drama, which seems to have been received favourably. The subsequent group of playwrights in the late second and early first centuries, Turpilius, Accius, Atta, tried to retain a place for proper drama under circumstances changing once again; for instance, they made plays more 'realistic' by giving prominence to everyday characters and also discussed more scholarly topics such as genealogies or Roman festivals. The poets of further dramatic genres that emerged in the later first century, Pomponius, Novius, Decimus Laberius and Publilius Syrus, introduced new dramatic genres, which included a significant component of spectacle and topical allusion, while not forsaking the presentation of

---

the later poets, on the other (see Goldberg 2007b: 575); Dupont 1985: 313–14, who has two periods, the first one from Livius Andronicus to Ennius and the second one from Ennius to Varius Rufus; Boyle 2006, who divides into 'founding fathers: the appropriation of Greece' (Livius Andronicus, Naevius), 'the second wave: generic confidence' (Ennius, Pacuvius) and 'tragic apex: poetic form and political crisis' (Accius); N. J. Lowe 2008: 86, who defines 'an early phase of translated Greek plays by versatile multi-specialist poets in the Hellenistic mould', 'a . . . phase of specialist translations by poets such as Plautus, Caecilius, Terence, and the tragedian Pacuvius, who work in one genre exclusively' and 'the disengagement of new tragedy and comedy from actual performance to become a vehicle for original poetic compositions on the Greek formal model but never intended to be staged'.

messages. This again seems to have corresponded to changes in society and the expectations of contemporary audiences.[10]

These developments did not occur as a result of exclusively literary processes, but can rather be explained as adaptations to audience expectations, which altered over the course of time: the rise of Rome to being a major power, intensified contacts with other cultures, and developments in political structures and social circumstances triggered changes in the interests of audiences. While at the beginning dramas addressing issues concerning the entire community, combined with entertaining features, seem to have appealed to a broad range of spectators, there was a split between works catering for different tastes at the end of the Republic. However, the popularity of 'classical' pieces and their revivals shows that the established dramas continued to hold their place.

It seems, therefore, that Republican drama – despite its emergence from and dependence on Greek models – had a genuine and independent Roman development, during which it was susceptible to all sorts of movements and became a self-conscious literary genre; it even functioned as a form and instrument of voicing and influencing public opinion, firmly rooted in Rome's politics, society and culture.

---

[10] Interestingly, changes in taste and artistic expression at certain points in time can also be observed in Roman architecture during the Republican period (see von Hesberg 2005: 49). Developments in the theatre roughly correspond to the sequence of 'republics' during the Republican period (300–180 BCE: republic of the *nobiles* 1; 180–139: republic of the *nobiles* 2; 139–88: republic of the *nobiles* 3; 88–81: transitional period; 81–60: republic of Sulla) recently suggested by Flower (2010: esp. 33).

Bibliography

1 EDITIONS AND COMMENTARIES

Artigas, E. (1990) *Pacuviana. Marco Pacuvio en Cicerón*. Barcelona (Aurea Saecula 3).

(ed.) (2009) *Marc Pacuvi. Tragèdies. Fragments*. Barcelona (*Collecció de clàssics grecs i llatins 376*).

Barsby, J. (ed.) (1986) *Plautus. Bacchides. Edited with Translation and Commentary*. Warminster.

(ed.) (1999) *Terence. Eunuchus. Edited*. Cambridge (Cambridge Greek and Latin Classics).

Bonaria, M. (ed.) [B.] (1965) *Romani Mimi*. Rome (Poetarum Latinorum reliquiae: Aetas rei publicae VI 2); orig.: M. Bonaria, *Mimorum Romanorum fragmenta*. Collegit, disposuit, recensuit. 2 vols. Genoa 1955/6 (Università di Genova, Facoltà di Lettere, Pubblicazioni dell'Istituto di Filologia Classica 5/9).

Brink, C. O. (1982) *Horace on Poetry. Epistles Book II: The Letters to Augustus and Florus*. Cambridge, London, New York, New Rochelle, Melbourne and Sydney.

Christenson, D. M. (ed.) (2000) *Plautus. Amphitruo. Edited*. Cambridge (Cambridge Greek and Latin Classics).

Courtney, E. (1980) *A Commentary on the Satires of Juvenal*. London.

Cupaiuolo, G. (ed.) (1992a) *Evanzio. De Fabula. Introduzione, testo critico, traduzione e note di commento*. Nuova edizione. Naples (1st edn: 1979).

Dangel, J. (ed.) [D.] (1995) *Accius. Œuvres (Fragments)*. Paris (CUF lat.).

D'Anna, G. (ed.) (1967) *M. Pacuvii fragmenta*. Rome (Poetarum Latinorum reliquiae: Aetas rei publicae III 1).

D'Antò, V. (ed.) (1980) *L. Accio. I frammenti delle tragedie*. Lecce.

Daviault, A. (ed.) [Dav.] (1981) *Comoedia Togata. Fragments. Texte établi, traduit et annoté*. Paris (CUF lat.).

Douglas, A. E. (ed.) (1966) *M. Tulli Ciceronis Brutus*. Oxford.

de Durante, G. (ed.) (1966) *Le fabulae praetextae*. Rome (Testi e studi per la scuola universitaria. Testi 1).

Fortenbaugh, W. W. (2005) *Theophrastus of Eresus. Sources for his Life, Writings, Thought and Influence. Commentary Vol. 8. Sources on Rhetoric and Poetics (Texts 666–713)*. Leiden and Boston (Philosophia Antiqua XCVII).

Fortenbaugh, W. W. *et al.* (eds.) (1992) *Theophrastus of Eresus. Sources for his Life, Writings, Thought and Influence.* Ed. and trans. W. W. Fortenbaugh, P. M. Huby, R. W. Sharples (Greek and Latin) and D. Gutas (Arabic). Together with A. D. Barker, J. J. Keaney, D. G. Mirhady, D. Sedley and M. G. Sollenberger. *Part Two. Psychology, Human Physiology, Living Creatures, Botany, Ethics, Religion, Politics, Rhetoric and Poetics, Music, Miscellanea.* Leiden, New York and Cologne (Philosophia Antiqua LIV, 2).

FPL³: Blänsdorf, J. (ed.) (1995) *Fragmenta poetarum Latinorum epicorum et lyricorum praeter Ennium et Lucilium, post W. Morel novis curis adhibitis ed. C. Büchner.* Editionem tertiam auctam curavit J. Blänsdorf. Stuttgart.

Frassinetti, P. (ed.) [F.] (1967) *Atellanae fabulae.* Rome (Poetarum Latinorum reliquiae: Aetas rei publicae, vol. vi 1); orig.: P. Frassinetti (ed.), *Fabularum Atellanarum fragmenta.* Turin, Milan, Padua, Florence, Pescara, Rome, Naples, Catania and Palermo 1955 (Corpus scriptorum Latinorum Patavianum) [without translation and separate commentary].

Garbarino, G. (1973) *Roma e la filosofia greca dalle origini alla fine del secolo II a.C. Raccolta di testi con introduzione e commento, Vol. I – Introduzione e testi, Vol. II – Commento e indici.* Turin, Milan, Genoa, Padua, Bologna, Florence, Pescara, Rome, Naples, Bari and Palermo (Historia, Politica, Philosophica. Il pensiero antico – Studi e testi 6).

Guardì, T. (ed.) [G.] (1974) *Cecilio Stazio. I frammenti.* Palermo (Hermes 9).

(ed.) (1985) *Titinio e Atta. Fabula togata. I frammenti. Introduzione, testo, traduzione e commento.* Milan (Líthoi 2; Le Edizioni Universitarie Jaca 6).

Hordern, J. H. (2004) *Sophron's Mimes. Text, Translation, and Commentary.* Oxford.

Jacobson, H. (1983) *The Exagoge of Ezekiel.* Cambridge, London, New York, New Rochelle, Melbourne and Sydney.

Jocelyn, H. D. (ed.) [J.] (1967) *The Tragedies of Ennius. The Fragments edited with an Introduction and Commentary.* Cambridge (repr. with corr. 1969) (Cambridge Classical Texts and Commentaries 10).

Kaibel, G. (ed.) (1899) *Comicorum Graecorum fragmenta. Voluminis I fasciculus prior. Doriensium comoedia mimi phlyaces.* Berlin [Diomedea et duplicem de comoedia tractatum recensuit F. Leo; see p. 53].

Kaster, R. A. (ed.) (1995) *C. Suetonius Tranquillus. De Grammaticis et Rhetoribus. Edited with a Translation, Introduction, and Commentary.* Oxford.

(2006) *Marcus Tullius Cicero. Speech on Behalf of Publius Sestius. Translated with Introduction and Commentary.* Oxford (Clarendon Ancient History Series).

Kauer, R. and Lindsay, W. M. (eds.) (1958) *P. Terenti Afri comoediae,* recognoverunt brevique adnotatione critica instruxerunt R. K. et W. M. L. Supplementa apparatus curavit O. Skutsch. Oxford.

Keil, H. (ed.) (1855–70) *Grammatici Latini.* 8 vols. Leipzig (repr. Hildesheim 1961).

Klotz, A. (ed.) (1953) *Scaenicorum Romanorum fragmenta volumen prius. Tragicorum fragmenta, adiuvantibus O. Seel et L. Voit ed.* Munich.

Krumeich, R., Pechstein, N. and Seidensticker, B. (eds.) (1999) *Das griechische Satyrspiel.* Darmstadt (Texte zur Forschung 72).

Lanfranchi, P. (ed.) (2006) *L'Exagoge d'Ezéchiel le Tragique. Introduction, texte, traduction et commentaire.* Leiden and Boston (Studia in Veteris Testamenti pseudepigrapha 21).

Lindsay, W. M. (ed.) (1904/5) *T. Macci Plauti comoediae*, recognovit brevique adnotatione critica instruxit, 2 vols. Oxford (repr.).

López López, A. (ed.) (1983) *Fabularum togatarum fragmenta (edicion critica).* Salamanca (Acta Salmanticensia 141).

Marmorale, E. V. (ed.) (1950) *Naevius poeta. Introduzione biobibliografica, testo dei frammenti e commento.* 2nd edn. Florence (seconda tiratura 1953) (Biblioteca di studi superiori VIII).

Marx, F. (ed.) [M.] (1904/5) *C. Lucilii carminum reliquiae*, 2 vols. Leipzig (repr. Amsterdam 1963).

Maurach, G. (1975) *Plauti Poenulus. Einleitung, Textherstellung und Kommentar.* Heidelberg.

Neukirch, I. H. (ed.) (1833) *De fabula togata Romanorum. Accedunt fabularum togatarum reliquiae.* Scripsit et edidit. Leipzig.

Oakley, S. P. (1998) *A Commentary on Livy Books VI–X. Vol. II. Books VII–VIII.* Oxford.

Panayotakis, C. (ed.) [P.] (2010) *Decimus Laberius. The Fragments.* Cambridge (Cambridge Classical Texts and Commentaries 46).

Pedroli, L. (ed.) (1954) *Fabularum praetextarum quae extant. Introduzione – Testi – Commenti.* Genoa (Università di Genova, Facoltà di Lettere, Pubblicazioni dell'Istituto di Filologia Classica).

Ribbeck, O. (ed.) [R.²] (1871) *Scaenicae Romanorum poesis fragmenta. Vol. I. Tragicorum Romanorum fragmenta*, secundis curis rec. Leipzig (repr. Hildesheim 1962).

(ed.) [R.²] (1873) *Scaenicae Romanorum poesis fragmenta. Vol. II. Comicorum Romanorum praeter Plautum et Terentium fragmenta*, secundis curis rec. Leipzig.

(ed.) [R.³] (1897) *Scaenicae Romanorum poesis fragmenta. Vol. I. Tragicorum Romanorum fragmenta*, tertiis curis rec. Leipzig.

(ed.) [R.³] (1898) *Scaenicae Romanorum poesis fragmenta. Vol. II. Comicorum Romanorum praeter Plautum et Syri quae feruntur sententias fragmenta*, tertiis curis rec. Leipzig.

Romano, D. (ed.) (1953) *Atellana fabula.* Palermo (Testi antichi e medievali per esercitazioni universitarie 7).

Rostagni, A. (1956) *Suetonio, De Poetis e biografi minori. Restituzione e commento.* Turin (Biblioteca di filologia classica).

Rychlewska, L. (ed.) [Ry.] (1971) *Turpilii comici fragmenta.* Leipzig.

Schierl, P. (2006) [S.] *Die Tragödien des Pacuvius. Ein Kommentar zu den Fragmenten mit Einleitung, Text und Übersetzung.* Berlin and New York (TuK 28).

Skutsch, O. (ed.) [Sk.] (1985) *The Annals of Q. Ennius, ed. with Introduction and Commentary.* Oxford.

Spaltenstein, F. (2008) *Commentaire des fragments dramatiques de Livius Andronicus.* Brussels (Collection Latomus 318).

Tragicorum Graecorum Fragmenta (TrGF) (1977–2004), 5 vols. Göttingen.

Traglia, A. (ed.) (1986) *Poeti latini arcaici. Volume primo. Livio Andronico, Nevio, Ennio.* Turin (Classici Latini).

Traina, A. (ed.) ([1960] 2000) *Comoedia. Antologia della palliata. In appendice: Elogia e tabulae triumphales.* Padua 1960; 5a ed. aggiornata, Padua 2000.

Vahlen, I. (ed.) [V.²] (1903) *Ennianae poesis reliquiae*, iteratis curis rec. Leipzig (= Leipzig ³1928, Amsterdam 1963, 1967).

Warmington, E. H. (ed.) [W.] (1935) *Remains of Old Latin. Newly ed. and transl. Vol. I. Ennius and Caecilius.* London and Cambridge, Mass. (rev. and repr. 1967; several repr.) (LCL 294).

(ed.) [W.] (1936) *Remains of Old Latin. Newly ed. and transl. Vol. II. Livius Andronicus, Naevius, Pacuvius and Accius.* London and Cambridge, Mass. (repr. 1957, with minor bibliographical additions; several repr.) (LCL 314).

(ed.) [W.] (1938) *Remains of Old Latin. Newly ed. and transl. Vol. III. Lucilius, The Twelve Tables.* London and Cambridge, Mass. (rev. and repr. 1979) (LCL 329).

Wessner, P. (ed.) (1902/5) *Aeli Donati quod fertur commentum Terenti, accedunt Eugraphi commentum et scholia Bembina*, rec. 2 vols. Leipzig.

Willcock, M. M. (ed.) (1987) *Plautus. Pseudolus.* Bristol.

Wünsch, R. (ed.) (1903) *Ioannis Lydi de magistratibus populi Romani libri tres.* Leipzig.

Zwierlein, O. (ed.) (1986) *L. Annaei Senecae Tragoediae, incertorum auctorum Hercules [Oetaeus] Octavia*, recogn. brevique adn. crit. instr. Oxford (repr. with corr.).

2 SECONDARY LITERATURE

Abbot, F. F. (1907) 'The theatre as a factor in Roman politics under the Republic', *TAPhA* 38: 49–56.

Adams, J. N. (2003) *Bilingualism and the Latin Language.* Cambridge.

von Albrecht, M. (1997) *A History of Roman Literature. From Livius Andronicus to Boethius. With Special Regard to its Influence on World Literature.* Rev. G. Schmeling and the author, 2 vols, vol. 1 trans. with the assistance of F. and K. Newman, vol. 2 trans. with the assistance of R. R. Caston and F. R. Schwartz. Leiden, New York and Cologne (Mnemosyne Suppl. 165); German original: 1994.

Anderson, W. S. (1993) *Barbarian Play: Plautus' Roman Comedy.* Toronto, Buffalo and London (The Robson Classical Lectures).

Arcellaschi, A. (1990) *Médée dans le théâtre latin d'Ennius à Sénèque*, Rome (Collection de l'École française de Rome 132).

Aricò, G. (1997) 'La tragedia romana arcaica', *Lexis* 15: 59–78.

Arnott, W. G. (1972) 'Targets, techniques, and tradition in Plautus' *Stichus*', *BICS* 19: 54–79.

(1975) *Menander, Plautus, Terence.* Oxford (New Surveys in the Classics 9).

(1977) 'Plautus, the entertainer', *Lampas* 10: 306–15.

Bain, D. (1977) *Actors and Audience. A Study of Asides and Related Conventions in Greek Drama*. Oxford.

(1979) '*Plautus vortit barbare*: Plautus, *Bacchides* 526–61 and Menander, *Dis exapaton* 102–12', in *Creative Imitation and Latin Literature*, eds. D. West and T. Woodman. Cambridge, London, New York and Melbourne: 17–34.

Baldarelli, B. (2004) *Accius und die vortrojanische Pelopidensage*. Paderborn, Munich, Vienna and Zurich (Studien zur Kultur und Geschichte des Altertums, Neue Folge, 1. Reihe: Monographien, 24. Band).

Balsdon, J. P. V. D. (1969) *Life and Leisure in Ancient Rome*. New York, St. Louis and San Francisco.

Barchiesi, A. (2002) review of '*Von Göttern und Menschen erzählen. Formkonstanzen und Funktionswandel vormoderner Epik*, ed. J. Rüpke. Stuttgart 2001', *BMCR* 2002.06.26.

Barchiesi, M. (1969) 'Plauto e il "metateatro" antico', *Il Verri* 31: 113–30.

Barsby, J. (1995) 'Plautus' *Pseudolus* as improvisatory drama', in *Plautus und die Tradition des Stegreifspiels. Festgabe für Eckard Lefèvre zum 60. Geburtstag*, eds. L. Benz, E. Stärk and G. Vogt-Spira. Tübingen (ScriptOralia 75, Reihe A: Altertumswiss. Reihe, Bd. 19): 55–70.

(2002) 'Terence and his Greek models', in *Due seminari plautini. La tradizione del testo – I modelli*, eds. C. Questa and R. Raffaelli. Urbino (Ludus philologiae 11): 251–77.

Bartsch, S. (1994) *Actors in the Audience. Theatricality and Doublespeak from Nero to Hadrian*. Cambridge, Mass. and London.

Batstone, W. W. (2006) 'Literature', in *A Companion to the Roman Republic*, eds. N. Rosenstein and R. Morstein-Marx. Oxford (Blackwell Companions to the Ancient World): 543–63.

Beacham, R. C. (1980) 'The development of the Roman stage: a missing link restored', *Theatre Research International* 5: 37–45.

(1991) *The Roman Theatre and its Audience*. London.

(1999) *Spectacle Entertainments of Early Imperial Rome*. New Haven, Conn. and London.

(2007) 'Playing places: the temporary and the permanent', in *The Cambridge Companion to Greek and Roman Theatre*, eds. M. McDonald and J. M. Walton. Cambridge: 202–26.

Beard, M. (2003) 'The triumph of the absurd: Roman street theatre', in *Rome the Cosmopolis*, eds. C. Edwards and G. Woolf. Cambridge: 21–43.

(2007) *The Roman Triumph*. Cambridge, Mass. and London.

Beare, W. (1964) *The Roman Stage. A Short History of Latin Drama in the Time of the Republic*. 3rd edn. London (1st edn: 1950).

Beaujeu, J. (1988) 'Jeux latins et jeux grecs (à propos de Cic., *Fam.*, VII, 1 et *Att.*, XVI, 5)', in *Hommages à H. Le Bonniec. Res sacrae*. Publ. par D. Porte et J.-P. Néraudau, Brussels (Collection Latomus 201): 10–18.

Bell, A. (2004) *Spectacular Power in the Greek and Roman City*. Oxford.

Bennett, S. (1997) *Theatre Audiences. A Theory of Production and Reception*. 2nd edn. London and New York.

Benz, L. (1995) 'Die römisch-italische Stegreifspieltradition zur Zeit der Palliata', in
    *Plautus und die Tradition des Stegreifspiels. Festgabe für Eckard Lefèvre zum 60.
    Geburtstag*, eds. L. Benz, E. Stärk and G. Vogt-Spira. Tübingen (ScriptOralia
    75, Reihe A: Altertumswiss. Reihe, Bd. 19): 139–54.
Bernstein, F. (1998) *Ludi publici. Untersuchungen zur Entstehung und Entwick-
    lung der öffentlichen Spiele im republikanischen Rom.* Stuttgart (Historia,
    Einzelschriften 119).
Berry, D. H. (1996) 'The value of prose rhythm in questions of authenticity: the
    case of *De optimo Genere Oratorum* attributed to Cicero', in *Papers of the
    Leeds International Latin Seminar. Ninth Volume 1996. Roman Poetry and
    Prose, Greek Poetry, Etymology, Historiography*, eds. F. Cairns and M. Heath.
    Leeds (ARCA 34): 47–74.
Bianco, M. M. (2007) *Interdum vocem comoedia tollit. Paratragedia 'al femminile'
    nella commedia plautina.* Bologna (Testi e manuali per l'insegnamento uni-
    versitario del latino 93).
Bieber, M. (1961) *The History of the Greek and Roman Theater.* 2nd edn, rev. and
    enl. Princeton, N.J. (4th print.: 1971; 1st edn: 1939).
Biliński, B. (1962) *Contrastanti ideali di cultura sulla scena di Pacuvio.* Rome
    (Accademia Polacca di Scienze e Lettere, Biblioteca di Roma, Conferenze,
    Fascicolo 16).
Blänsdorf, J. (1967) *Archaische Gedankengänge in den Komödien des Plautus.* Wies-
    baden (Hermes, Einzelschriften 20).
    (1974) 'Das Bild der Komödie in der späten Republik', in *Musa Iocosa. Arbeiten
        über Humor und Witz, Komik und Komödie in der Antike. Andreas Thierfelder
        zum siebzigsten Geburtstag am 15. Juni 1973*, eds. U. Reinhardt, K. Sallmann
        and H. Chelius. Hildesheim and New York: 141–57.
    (1978) 'Voraussetzungen und Entstehung der römischen Komödie' / 'Plau-
        tus', in *Das römische Drama*, ed. E. Lefèvre. Darmstadt (Grundriß der Lite-
        raturgeschichten nach Gattungen): 91–134 / 135–222.
    (1983) 'Die *Palliata* als Spiegel des Lebens?', in *Hommages à Robert Schilling*,
        eds. H. Zehnacker and G. Hentz. Paris (Collection d'études latines, Série
        scientifique XXXVII): 233–48.
    (1987) 'Antike Theaterbauten und ihre Funktion', in *Theaterwesen und drama-
        tische Literatur. Beiträge zur Geschichte des Theaters*, ed. G. Holtus. Tübingen
        (Mainzer Forschungen zu Drama und Theater 1): 75–107.
    (1993) 'Plautus, Amphitruo und Rudens – oder wieviel literarische Parodie
        verträgt eine populäre Komödie?', in *Literaturparodie in Antike und Mittelal-
        ter*, eds. W. Ax and R. F. Glei. Trier (BAC 15): 57–74.
    (1996) 'Un trait original de la comédie de Plaute: le goût de la parodie', in
        Panorama du théâtre antique. D'Eschyle aux dramaturges d'Amérique latine,
        ed. A. Moreau, *CGITA* 9: 133–51.
    (2000) 'Loin – passé – présent. L'apport des dimensions du temps et du lieu à
        la structure de la comédie de Plaute', *Pallas* 54: 249–57.
Blume, H.-D. (1991) *Einführung in das antike Theaterwesen.* 3rd edn. Darmstadt.
    (1998) *Menander.* Darmstadt (Erträge der Forschung 293).

Bollinger, T. (1969) *Theatralis Licentia. Die Publikumsdemonstrationen an den öffentlichen Spielen im Rom der früheren Kaiserzeit und ihre Bedeutung im politischen Leben*. Winterthur.

Bond, R. P. (1999) 'Plautus' *Amphitryo* as tragi-comedy', *G&R* 46: 203–20.

Bonfante, G. and Bonfante, L. (1983) *The Etruscan Language. An Introduction*. Manchester.

Bonfante, L. and Swaddling, J. (eds.) (2006) *Etruscan Myths*. London (The Legendary Past).

Boyle, A. J. (ed.) (1983) *Seneca Tragicus. Ramus Essays on Senecan Drama*. Bendigo.
(1997) *Tragic Seneca. An Essay in the Theatrical Tradition*. London.
(2006) *An Introduction to Roman Tragedy*. London and New York.

Breyer, G. (1993) *Etruskisches Sprachgut im Lateinischen unter Ausschluss des spezifisch onomastischen Bereiches*. Leuven (Orientalia Lovaniensia Analecta 53).

Brothers, A. J. (1989) 'Buildings for entertainment', in *Roman Public Buildings*, ed. I. M. Barton. Exeter (Exeter Studies in History 20): 97–125.

Brown, P. G. McC. (2002) 'Actors and actor-managers at Rome in the time of Plautus and Terence', in *Greek and Roman Actors: Aspects of an Ancient Profession*, eds. P. Easterling and E. Hall. Cambridge: 225–37.

Bubel, F. (1992) *Bibliographie zu Plautus 1976–1989*. Bonn.

Büchner, K. (1974) *Das Theater des Terenz*. Heidelberg (Bibliothek der klassischen Altertumswissenschaften, Neue Folge, 1. Reihe, Bd. 4).

Buck, C. H. (1940) 'A chronology of the plays of Plautus', dissertation, University of Baltimore.

Butler, J. H. (1972) *The Theatre and Drama of Greece and Rome*. San Francisco, Scranton, London and Toronto (Chandler Publications in *History of Theatre*).

Cacciaglia, M. (1972) 'Ricerche sulla fabula togata', *RCCM* 14: 207–45.

Cairns, F. (2007) *Generic composition in Greek and Roman Poetry*. Edinburgh 1972; rev. edn, Ann Arbor, Mich. 2007.

Cancik, H. (1978) 'Die republikanische Tragödie', in *Das römische Drama*, ed. E. Lefèvre. Darmstadt (Grundriß der Literaturgeschichten nach Gattungen): 308–47.

Carlson, M. (1989) *Places of Performance. The Semiotics of Theatre Architecture*. Ithaca, N.Y. and London.

Cartledge, P. (1997) '"Deep plays": theatre as process in Greek civic life', in *The Cambridge Companion to Greek Tragedy*, ed. P. E. Easterling. Cambridge: 3–35.

Casaceli, F. (1976) *Lingua e stile in Accio*. Palermo.

Castagna, L. (1990) 'Pacuvio *doctus poeta*: esempi dall'*Antiopa*', *QCTC* 8: 33–45 (discussion: 45–6).

Cèbe, J.-P. (1960) 'Le niveau culturel du public plautinien', *REL* 38: 101–6.
(1966) *La caricature et la parodie, dans le monde romain antique des origines à Juvénal*. Paris.

Chalmers, W. R. (1965) 'Plautus and his audience', in *Roman Drama*, eds. T. A. Dorey and D. R. Dudley. London (Studies in Latin Literature and its Influence): 21–50.

Chiarini, G. (1979) *La recita. Plauto, la farsa, la festa*. Bologna (Edizioni e saggi universitari di filologia classica 25).

Cicu, L. (1988) *Problemi e strutture del mimo a Roma*. Sassari (Pubblicazioni di 'Sandalion' 3).

Classen, C. J. ([1992] 1993) 'Ennius: ein Fremder in Rom', *Gymnasium* 99: 121–45; repr. in: C. J. Classen, *Die Welt der Römer. Studien zu ihrer Literatur, Geschichte und Religion*. Unter Mitwirkung v. H. Bernsdorff hg. v. M. Vielberg. Berlin and New York 1993 (UaLG 41): 62–83 [quoted from the reprint].

Clavel-Lévèque, M. (1984) *L'Empire en jeux. Espace symbolique et pratique sociale dans le monde romain*. Paris.

(1986) 'L'espace des jeux dans le monde romain: hégémonie, symbolique et pratique sociale', *ANRW* ii.16.3. Berlin and New York: 2405–563.

Coarelli, F. (1987) *I santuari del Lazio in età repubblicana*. Rome (Studi NIS Archeologia 7).

Cole, T. (1990/1) 'Comment on Zorzetti 1990/1', *CJ* 86: 377–82.

Conte, G. B. (1994) *Latin Literature. A History*. Trans. J. B. Solodow. Rev. D. Fowler and G. W. Most. Baltimore and London.

Coppola, G. (1940) 'Il teatro tragico in Roma repubblicana', *Rendiconto delle sessioni della R. Accademia delle scienze dell'Istituto di Bologna, Classe di scienze morali, Serie iv, Vol. iii (1939–40)*. Bologna: 11–84.

Cornell, T. J. (1995) *The Beginnings of Rome. Italy and Rome from the Bronze Age to the Punic Wars (c. 1000–264 BC)*. London and New York (Routledge History of the Ancient World).

Courbaud, E. (1899) 'De comoedia togata', dissertation, University of Paris.

Courtois, C. (1989) *Le bâtiment de scène des théâtres d'Italie et de Sicile. Étude chronologique et typologique*. Providence, R.I. and Louvain-la-Neuve (Archaeologica Transatlantica viii, Publications d'histoire de l'art et d'archéologie de l'Université Catholique de Louvain lxv).

(1992) 'Evolution architecturale au bâtiment de scène des théâtres antiques d'Italie et de Sicile', in *Spectacula – ii. Le théâtre antique et ses spectacles. Actes du colloque tenu au Musée Archéologique Henri Prades de Lattes les 27, 28, 29 et 30 avril 1989*, eds. C. Landes and de V. Kramérovskis. Lattes: 171–8.

Crawford, M. (1993) *The Roman Republic*. 2nd edn. Cambridge, Mass.

Crowther, N. B. (1973) 'The *collegium poetarum* at Rome: fact and conjecture', *Latomus* 32: 575–80.

Csapo, E. G. (1993) 'A case study in the use of theatre iconography as evidence for ancient acting', *AK* 36: 41–58.

(2000) 'From Aristophanes to Menander? Genre transformation in Greek comedy', in *Matrices of Genre. Authors, Canons, and Society*, eds. M. Depew and D. Obbink. Cambridge, Mass. and London: 115–33.

Csapo, E. and Slater, W. J. (1995) *The Context of Ancient Drama*. Ann Arbor, Mich.

Cupaiuolo, G. (1984) *Bibliografia terenziana (1470–1983)*. Naples.

(1991) *Terenzio. Teatro e società*. Naples (Studi Latini 5).

(1992) 'Supplementum Terentianum', *BStudLat* 22: 32–57.

Cusset, C. (2003) *Ménandre ou la comédie tragique.* Paris (CNRS littérature).

Danese, R. M. (2002) 'Modelli letterari e modelli culturali del teatro Plautino. Qualche problema di metodo', in *Due seminari plautini. La tradizione del testo – I modelli*, eds. C. Questa and R. Raffelli. Urbino (Ludus philologiae 11): 133–53.

Dangel, J. (1990) 'Les généalogies d'Accius', *Euphrosyne* 18: 53–72.

D'Anna, G. (1955) 'Contributo alla cronologia dei poeti latini arcaici. iii. Quando esordì Cn. Nevio?', *RIL* 88: 301–10.

———(1965) '*Fabellae Latinae ad verbum e Graecis expressae*', *RCCM* 7 (Studi in onore di Alfredo Schiaffini): 364–83.

———(1976) 'La dottrina di Marco Pacuvio', in: G. D'Anna, *Problemi di letteratura latina arcaica.* Rome: 173–97.

Daviault, A. (1979) '*Togata et Palliata*', *BAGB*: 422–30.

Degl'Innocenti Pierini, R. (1980) *Studi su Accio.* Florence (Quaderni dell'Istituto di Filologia Classica 'Giorgio Pasquali' dell'Università degli Studi di Firenze 1).

———(1991) 'Un prologo polemico di Afranio: *Compitalia* 25–28 R.³', *Prometheus* 17: 242–6.

Denard, H. (2007) 'Lost theatre and performance traditions in Greece and Italy', in *The Cambridge Companion to Greek and Roman Theatre*, eds. M. McDonald and J. M. Walton. Cambridge: 139–60.

Dench, E. (1995) *From Barbarians to New Men. Greek, Roman, and Modern Perceptions of Peoples from the Central Apennines.* Oxford (Oxford Classical Monographs).

Dénes, T. (1973) 'Quelques problèmes de la "Fabula togata"', *BAGB*: 187–201.

Dér, K. (1989) 'Terence and Luscius Lanuvinus', *AAntHung* 32: 283–97.

De Rosalia, A. (1989) 'Rassegna degli studi sulla tragedia latina arcaica (1965–1986)', *BStudLat* 19: 76–144.

Deufert, M. (2002) *Textgeschichte und Rezeption der plautinischen Komödien im Altertum.* Berlin and New York (UaLG 62).

Dieterich, A. (1897) *Pulcinella. Pompejanische Wandbilder and römische Satyrspiele.* Leipzig.

Di Gregorio, L. (1988) 'Gellio e il teatro', *Aevum(ant)* 1: 95–147.

Dihle, A. (1955) 'Ein Spurium unter den rhetorischen Werken Ciceros', *Hermes* 83: 303–14.

Dingel, J. (1985) 'Senecas Tragödien: Vorbilder und poetische Aspekte', *ANRW* ii.32.2. Berlin and New York: 1052–99.

Dodge, H. (1999) 'Amusing the masses: buildings for entertainment and leisure in the Roman world', in *Life, Death, and Entertainment in the Roman Empire*, eds. D. S. Potter and D. J. Mattingly. Ann Arbor, Mich.: 205–55.

Dolç, M. (1971) 'El *collegium poetarum*: discrepancias y tensiones en la poesia latina', *Emerita* 39: 265–92.

Dorey, T. A. and Dudley, D. R. (eds.) (1965) *Roman Drama.* New York (Studies in Latin Literature and its Influence).

Dox, D. (2004) *The Idea of the Theater in Latin Christian Thought. Augustine to the Fourteenth Century.* Ann Arbor, Mich.

Drury, M. (1982) 'Appendix of authors and works', in *The Cambridge History of Classical Literature. II: Latin Literature*, eds. E. J. Kenney and W. V. Clausen. Cambridge, London, New York, New Rochelle, Melbourne and Sydney: 799–935.

Duckworth, G. E. (1952/1994) *The Nature of Roman Comedy. A Study in Popular Entertainment.* Princeton, N.J. 1952; *Second Edition. With a Foreword and Bibliographical Appendix by R. Hunter.* Norman, Okla. and Bristol 1994.

Ducos, M. (1990) 'La condition des acteurs à Rome. Données juridiques et sociales', in *Theater und Gesellschaft im Imperium Romanum / Théâtre et société dans l'empire romain*, eds. J. Blänsdorf, J.-M. André and N. Fick. Tübingen (Mainzer Forschungen zu Drama und Theater 4): 19–33.

Dumont, J.-C. (1975) 'Cicéron et le théatre', in *Association Guillaume Budé. Actes du ixe Congrès (Rome, 13–18 avril 1973). Tome 1.* Paris: 424–30.

(1982) '*Cogi in scaena ponere personam*', *REL* 60: 123–7.

(1983) 'Les gens de théâtre originaires des municipes', in *Les 'bourgeoisies' municipales italiennes aux IIe et Ier siècles av. J.-C. Centre Jean Bérard. Institut Français de Naples, 7–10 décembre 1981.* Paris and Naples (Colloques internationaux du Centre national de la recherche scientifique N. 609 sciences humaines): 333–45.

(1984) 'La comédie phlyaque et les origines du théâtre romain', in *Texte et image. Actes du Colloque Chantilly (13 au 15 octobre 1982)*, ed. F. Vian. Paris: 135–50.

(1987) *Servus. Rome et l'esclavage sous la république.* Paris and Rome (Collection de l'École française de Rome 103).

(1992) '*Ludi scaenici* et comédie romaine', *Ktèma* 17: 39–45.

(1997) '*Cantica* et espace de représentation dans le théâtre latin', in *De la scène aux gradins. Théâtre et représentations dramatiques après Alexandre le grand*, ed. B. Le Guen, *Pallas* 47: 41–50.

(2000) 'L'espace plautinien: de la place publique à la ville', *Pallas* 54: 103–12.

Dunbabin, K. (2004) 'Problems in the iconography of Roman mime', in *Le statut de l'acteur dans l'Antiquité grecque et romaine (Actes du colloque qui s'est tenu à Tours les 3 et 4 mai 2002)*, eds. C. Hugoniot, F. Hurlet and S. Milanezi. Tours (Collection Perspectives Historiques 9): 161–81.

Duncan, A. (2006) *Performance and Identity in the Classical World.* Cambridge.

Dupont, F. (1985) *L'acteur-roi ou le théâtre dans la Rome antique.* Paris (Realia).

(1988/99) *Le Théâtre latin.* Paris 1988 (Cursus); Nouvelle édition revue et corrigée. Paris 1999 (Collection Cursus, Lettres, Série Littéraire).

Dutsch, D. M. (2008) *Feminine Discourse in Roman Comedy. On Echoes and Voices.* Oxford (Oxford Studies in Classical Literature and Gender Theory).

Earl, D. C. (1960) 'Political terminology in Plautus', *Historia* 9: 235–43.

Edwards, C. (1993) *The Politics of Immorality in Ancient Rome.* Cambridge.

Ehrman, R. K. (1985) 'Terentian prologues and the parabases of Old Comedy', *Latomus* 44: 370–6.

Elam, K. (2002) *The Semiotics of Theatre and Drama*. 2nd edn. London and New York (New Accents) (1st edn: 1980).

Erasmo, M. (2004) *Roman Tragedy: Theatre to Theatricality*. Austin, Tex.

Erskine, A. (1998) 'Trojan horseplay in Rome', *Dialogos* 5: 131–8.

Fabia, P. (1888) *Les prologues de Térence*. Paris and Avignon.

Falchetti, F. and Romualdi, A. (2001) *Die Etrusker. Aus dem Italienischen von Helmut Schareika*. Darmstadt.

Faller, S. (2000) 'Romanisierungstendenzen in der *Iphigenia* des Ennius', in *Identität und Alterität in der frührömischen Tragödie*, ed. G. Manuwald. Würzburg (Identitäten und Alteritäten, Bd. 3, Altertumswiss. Reihe, Bd. 1): 211–29.

Fantham, E. (1977) 'Adaptation and survival: a genre study of Roman comedy in relation to its Greek sources', in *Versions of Medieval Comedy. Edited and with an Introduction*, ed. P. G. Ruggiers. Norman, Okla.: 19–49.

(1984) 'Roman experience of Menander in the late Republic and early Empire', *TAPhA* 114: 299–310.

(1989a) 'The earliest comic theatre at Rome: Atellan farce, comedy and mime as antecedents of the *commedia dell'arte*', in *The Science of Buffoonery. Theory and History of the Commedia dell'Arte*, ed. D. Pietropaolo. Ottawa (University of Toronto Italian Studies 3): 23–32.

(1989b) 'Mime: the missing link in Roman literary history', *CW* 82: 153–63.

(1989c) 'The growth of literature and criticism at Rome', in *The Cambridge History of Literary Criticism. Vol. 1: Classical Criticism*, ed. G. A. Kennedy. Cambridge, New York, Port Chester, Melbourne and Sydney: 220–44.

(2002) 'Orator and / et actor', in *Greek and Roman Actors: Aspects of an Ancient Profession*, eds. P. Easterling and E. Hall. Cambridge: 362–76.

(2003) 'Pacuvius: melodrama, reversals and recognitions', in *Myth, History and Culture in Republican Rome. Studies in Honour of T. P. Wiseman*, eds. D. Braund and C. Gill. Exeter: 98–118.

(2004) 'Terence and the familiarisation of comedy', in *Rethinking Terence*, ed. A. J. Boyle, *Ramus* 33.1–2: 20–34.

(2005) 'Roman tragedy', in *A Companion to Latin Literature*, ed. S. Harrison. Oxford (Blackwell Companions to the Ancient World): 116–29.

Farrell, J. (2005) 'The origins and essence of Roman epic', in *A Companion to Ancient Epic*, ed. J. M. Foley. Oxford (Blackwell Companions to the Ancient World): 417–28.

Feeney, D. (1998) *Literature and Religion at Rome. Cultures, Contexts, and Beliefs*. Cambridge (Roman Literature and its Contexts).

(2002) '*Vna cum scriptore meo*. Poetry, principate and the tradition of literary history in the Epistle to Augustus', in *Traditions and Contexts in the Poetry of Horace*, eds. T. Woodman and D. Feeney. Cambridge: 172–87.

(2005) 'The beginnings of a literature in Latin [review article on Suerbaum 2002]', *JRS* 95: 226–40.

(2006) 'review of Goldberg 2005', *BMCR* 2006.08.45.

Feldherr, A. (1998) *Spectacle and Society in Livy's History*. Berkeley, Los Angeles and London.

Fensterbusch, C. (1934) 'Theatron (1)', *RE* v A 2: 1384–422.

Fertl, E. (2005) *Von Musen, Miminnen und leichten Mädchen.... Die Schauspielerin in der römischen Antike.* Vienna (Blickpunkte IX).

Fischer-Lichte, E. (2003) '151. Semiotische Aspekte der Theaterwissenschaft: Theatersemiotik', in *Semiotik / Semiotics. Ein Handbuch zu den zeichentheoretischen Grundlagen von Natur und Kultur / A Handbook on the Sign-Theoretic Foundations of Nature and Culture. 3. Teilband / Vol. 3*, eds. R. Posner, K. Robering and T. A. Sebeok. Berlin and New York (Handbücher zur Sprach- und Kommunikationswissenschaft / Handbooks of Linguistics and Communication Science 13.3): 3103–19.

Fitzgerald, W. and Gowers, E. (eds.) (2007) *Ennius perennis. The Annals and Beyond.* Oxford (Cambridge Classical Journal, Proceedings of the Cambridge Philological Society, Suppl. Vol. 31).

Flaig, E. (1995) 'Entscheidung und Konsens. Zu den Feldern der politischen Kommunikation zwischen Aristokratie und Plebs', in *Demokratie in Rom? Die Rolle des Volkes in der Politik der römischen Republik*, ed. M. Jehne. Stuttgart (Historia, Einzelschriften 96): 77–127.

(2003) *Ritualisierte Politik. Zeichen, Gesten und Herrschaft im Alten Rom.* Göttingen (Historische Semantik 1).

Fless, F. (2004) 'Römische Prozessionen', in *Thesaurus Cultus et Rituum Antiquorum (ThesCRA)* 1. Los Angeles: 33–58.

Flintoff, E. (1990) 'The *Satires* of Marcus Pacuvius', *Latomus* 49: 575–90.

Flower, H. I. (1995) '*Fabulae praetextae* in context: when were plays on contemporary subjects performed in Republican Rome?', *CQ* 45: 170–90.

(2000) '*Fabula de Bacchanalibus*: the Bacchanalian cult of the second century BC and Roman drama', in *Identität und Alterität in der frührömischen Tragödie*, ed. G. Manuwald. Würzburg (Identitäten und Alteritäten, Bd. 3, Altertumswiss. Reihe, Bd. 1): 23–35.

(2004) 'Spectacle and political culture in the Roman Republic', in *The Cambridge Companion to the Roman Republic*, ed. H. I. Flower. Cambridge: 322–43.

(2010) *Roman Republics.* Princeton, N.J. and Oxford.

Fogazza, D. (1976 [1978]) 'Plauto 1935–1975', *Lustrum* 19: 79–296.

Forehand, W. E. (1985) *Terence.* Boston (Twayne's World Authors Series 745, Latin Literature).

Fraenkel, E. (2007) *Plautine Elements in Plautus (Plautinisches im Plautus).* Trans. T. Drevikovsky and F. Muecke. Oxford; German original: *Plautinisches im Plautus.* Berlin 1922 (Philologische Untersuchungen 28); Italian translation (by F. Munari; with *Addenda* by the author): *Elementi Plautini in Plauto (Plautinisches im Plautus).* Florence 1960 (Il pensiero storico 41).

Frangoulidis, S. A. (1997) *Handlung und Nebenhandlung. Theater, Metatheater und Gattungsbewußtsein in der römischen Komödie.* Stuttgart (Drama Beiheft 6) [in English].

Frank, T. (1931) 'The status of actors at Rome', *CPh* 26: 11–20.

Franko, G. F. (2001) 'Plautus and Roman New Comedy', in *Greek and Roman Comedy. Translations and Interpretations of Four Representative Plays*, ed. S. O'Bryhim. Austin, Tex.: 147–88.

Frassinetti, P. (1953) *Fabula Atellana. Saggio sul teatro popolare latino.* Pavia (Università di Genova, Pubblicazioni dell'Istituto di Filologia Classica 4).

Frézouls, E. (1974) 'L'architecture du théâtre romain en Italie', *Bollettino di Centro Internazionale di Studi di Architettura Andrea Palladio* 16: 35–71.

(1982) 'Aspects de l'histoire architecturale du théâtre romain', *ANRW* II.12.1. Berlin and New York: 343–441.

(1983) 'La construction du *theatrum lapideum* et son contexte politique', in *Théâtre et spectacles dans l'antiquité. Actes du Colloque de Strasbourg, 5–7 novembre 1981*, ed. H. Zehnacker. Leiden (Université des Sciences Humaines de Strasbourg, Travaux du Centre de Recherches sur le Proche-Orient et la Grèce Antiques 7): 193–214.

(1989) 'Architecture théâtrale et mise en scène', *Dioniso* 59: 313–44.

Fuchs, M. (1987) *Untersuchugen zur Ausstattung römischer Theater in Italien und den Westprovinzen des Imperium Romanum.* Mainz.

Gagliardo, M. C. and Packer, J. E. (2006) 'A new look at Pompey's Theater: history, documentation, and recent excavation', *AJA* 110: 93–122.

Gaiser, K. (1972) 'Zur Eigenart der römischen Komödie: Plautus und Terenz gegenüber ihren griechischen Vorbildern', *ANRW* I.2. Berlin and New York: 1027–113.

Garton, C. (1972) *Personal Aspects of the Roman Theatre.* Toronto.

Geffcken, K. A. (1973) *Comedy in the Pro Caelio. With an Appendix on the In Clodium et Curionem.* Leiden (Mnemosyne Suppl. 30).

Gentili, B. (1979) *Theatrical Performances in the Ancient World. Hellenistic and Early Roman Theatre.* Amsterdam and Uithoorn (London Studies in Classical Philology 2); rev. and corr. version of the Italian edition: *Lo spettacolo nel mondo classico. Teatro ellenistico e teatro romano arcaico.* Rome and Bari 1977 (Universale Laterza 379).

Giancotti, F. (1967) *Mimo e Gnome. Studio su Decimo Laberio e Publilio Siro.* Messina and Florence (Biblioteca di cultura contemporanea XCVIII).

Gianotti, G. F. (1993) '*Histriones, mimi et saltatores*: per una storia degli spettacoli "leggeri" d'età imperiale', in *Incontri del Dipartimento* VI. *Vitae mimus. Forme e funzione del teatro comico greco e latino. Pavia, 18 marzo 1993.* Como: 45–77.

(1996) 'Forme di consumo teatrale: mimo e spettacoli affini', in *La letteratura di consumo nel mondo greco-latino. Atti del convegno internazionale. Cassino, 14–17 settembre 1994*, eds. O. Pecere and A. Stramaglia. Cassino: 265–92.

Gigante, M. (1967/8) 'Teatro greco in Magna Grecia', *Annali dell'Istituto Italiano per gli Studi Storici* 1: 35–87.

(1971) *Rintone e il teatro in Magna Grecia.* Naples.

Gildenhard, I. (2003) 'review of Suerbaum 2002', *BMCR* 2003.09.39.

Gilula, D. (1978) 'Where did the audience go?', *SCI* 4: 45–9.

(1981) 'Who's afraid of rope-walkers and gladiators? (Ter. Hec. 1–57)', *Athenaeum* 59: 29–37.

(1985/8) 'How rich was Terence?', *SCI* 8–9: 74–8.

(1989a) 'Greek drama in Rome: some aspects of cultural transposition', in *The Play out of Context. Transferring Plays from Culture to Culture*, eds. H. Scolnicov and P. Holland. Cambridge, New York, New Rochelle, Melbourne and Sydney: 99–109.

(1989b) 'The first realistic roles in European theatre: Terence's prologues', *QUCC* 62 (n.s. 33): 95–106.

(1991) 'Plots are not stories: the so-called "duality method" of Terence', in *Reading Plays. Interpretation and Reception*, eds. H. Scolnicov and P. Holland. Cambridge, New York, Port Chester, Melbourne and Sydney: 81–93.

Gold, B. K. (1987) *Literary Patronage in Greece and Rome*. Chapel Hill, N.C. and London.

Goldberg, S. M. (1981) 'Scholarship on Terence and the fragments of Roman comedy (1959–1980)', *CW* 75: 77–115.

(1983) 'Terence, Cato, and the rhetorical prologue', *CPh* 78: 198–211.

(1986) *Understanding Terence*. Princeton, N.J.

(1993) 'Terence and the death of comedy', in *Drama and the Classical Heritage. Comparative and Critical Essays*, eds. C. Davidson, R. Johnson and J. H. Stroupe. New York (AMS Ancient and Classical Studies 1): 52–64.

(1995) *Epic in Republican Rome*. New York and Oxford.

(1996) 'The fall and rise of Roman tragedy', *TAPhA* 126: 265–86.

(1998) 'Plautus on the Palatine', *JRS* 88: 1–20.

(2005a) 'The early Republic: the beginnings to 90 BC', in *A Companion to Latin Literature*, ed. S. Harrison. Oxford (Blackwell Companions to the Ancient World): 15–30.

(2005b) *Constructing Literature in the Roman Republic. Poetry and its Reception*. Cambridge.

(2006) 'Ennius after the banquet', *Arethusa* 39.3: 429–47.

(2007a) 'Antiquity's antiquity', in *Latinitas Perennis. Vol. 1: The Continuity of Latin Literature*, eds. W. Verbaal, Y. Maes and J. Papy. Leiden and Boston (Brill's Studies in Intellectual History 144): 17–29.

(2007b) 'Research report: reading Roman tragedy', *IJCT* 13: 571–84.

Goldhill, S. (1999) 'Literary history without literature: reading practices in the ancient world', *SubStance* 28.88: 57–89.

González Vázquez, C. (2000) 'La escena imaginaria del espectador plautino', *Pallas* 54: 239–47.

(2001a) 'La organización de la cartelera en el teatro romano', *Latomus* 60: 890–9.

(2001b) 'La comédie «métathéâtrale» chez Plaute', in *D'un «genre» à l'autre*, eds. M.-H. Garelli-François, P. Sauzeaz and M.-P. Noël, *CGITA* 14: 101–14.

(2004) *Diccionario del teatro latino. Léxico, dramaturgia, escenografía*. Madrid.

Görler, W. (1973) 'Über die Illusion in der antiken Komödie', *A&A* 18: 41–57.

Gowers, E. (2004) 'The plot thickens: hidden outlines in Terence's prologues', in *Rethinking Terence*, ed. A. J. Boyle, *Ramus* 33.1–2: 150–66.

Gratwick, A. S. (1982a) '5. Drama', in *The Cambridge History of Classical Literature. II: Latin Literature*, eds. E. J. Kenney and W. V. Clausen. Cambridge, London, New York, New Rochelle, Melbourne and Sydney: 77–137.

(1982b) 'review of Daviault 1981', *Gnomon* 54: 725–33.

(2000) 'review of Dangel 1995', *CR* 50: 598–9.

Green, J. R. (1991) 'Notes on phlyax vases', *NAC* 20: 49–56.

Green, W. M. (1933) 'The status of actors at Rome', *CPh* 28: 301–4.

Grimal, P. (1975) 'Le théâtre à Rome', in *Association Guillaume Budé. Actes du IXe Congrès (Rome, 13–18 avril 1973). Tome 1*. Paris: 249–305.

Gruen, E. S. (1990) *Studies in Greek Culture and Roman Policy*. Leiden, New York, Copenhagen and Cologne (Cincinnati Classical Studies. New Series. Vol. VII) (paperback edn: Berkeley and London 1996).

(1991) 'The exercise of power in the Roman Republic', in *City States in Classical Antiquity and Medieval Italy*, eds. A. Molho, K. Raaflaub and L. Emlen. Ann Arbor, Mich.: 251–67.

(1992) *Culture and National Identity in Republican Rome*. Ithaca, N.Y. (Cornell Studies in Classical Philology LII).

Guardì, T. (1978) 'I *fullones* e la commedia romana', *Pan* 6: 37–45.

(1981) 'Note sulla lingua di Titinio', *Pan* 7: 145–65.

(1991) 'La togata', *Dioniso* 61: 209–20.

(1993) 'La *fabula togata*: moduli formali ed evoluzione del genere', in *Cultura e lingue classiche. 3° Convegno di aggiornamento e di didattica. Palermo, 29 ottobre – 1 novembre 1989*, ed. B. Amata. Rome: 271–7.

Guillemin, A. (1934) 'Le public et la vie littéraire à Rome au temps de la République', *REL* 12: 52–71, 329–43.

Habinek, T. (1998) *The Politics of Latin Literature. Writing, Identity, and Empire in Ancient Rome*. Princeton, N.J.

Haffter, H. (1934) *Untersuchungen zur altlateinischen Dichtersprache*. Berlin (Problemata 10).

Hall, E. and Wyles, R. (eds.) (2008) *New Directions in Ancient Pantomime*. Oxford.

Halporn, J. (1993) 'Roman comedy and Greek models', in *Theater and Society in the Classical World*, ed. R. Scodel. Ann Arbor, Mich.: 191–213.

Handley, E. W. (1975) 'Plautus and his public: some thoughts on New Comedy in Latin', *Dioniso* 46: 117–32.

Hanson, J. A. (1959) 'Roman Theater-Temples', dissertation, Princeton University.

(1965/6) 'Scholarship on Plautus since 1950', *CW* 59: 103–7, 126–9, 141–8.

Harries, B. (2007) 'Acting the part: techniques of the comic stage in Cicero's early speeches', in *Cicero on the Attack. Invective and Subversion in the Orations and Beyond*, ed. J. Booth. Swansea: 129–47.

Harris, W. V. (1971) *Rome in Etruria and Umbria*. Oxford.

Harrison, S. (ed.) (2005) *A Companion to Latin Literature*. Oxford (Blackwell Companions to the Ancient World).

Häußler, R. (1987/8) 'Grundzüge der *fabula praetexta*', *AFLN* 30 (n.s. 18): 297–319.

(1990/2) 'Zur Terminologie des römischen Dramas', *AAntHung* 33: 55–62.

Heiden, B. (1991) 'Tragedy and comedy in the *Frogs* of Aristophanes', *Ramus* 20: 95–111.

Heldmann, G. (2000) 'Die griechische und lateinische Tragödie und Komödie in der Kaiserzeit', *WJA* 24: 185–205.

von Hesberg, H. (2005) *Römische Baukunst*. Munich (Beck's Archäologische Bibliothek).

Hiltbrunner, O. (1985) 'Seneca als Tragödiendichter in der Forschung von 1965–1975', *ANRW* 11.32.2. Berlin and New York: 969–1051.

Hinds, S. (1998) *Allusion and Intertext. Dynamics of Appropriation in Roman Poetry*. Cambridge (Roman Literature and its Contexts).

Honzl, J. (1976) 'Dynamics of the sign in the theater', in *Semiotics of Art. Prague School Contributions*, eds. L. Matejka and I. R. Titunik. Cambridge, Mass. and London: 74–93; Czech original: 1940; trans. I. R. Titunik.

Horsfall, N. (1976) 'The collegium poetarum', *BICS* 23: 79–95.

(1993) 'Roma', in *Lo spazio letterario della Grecia antica. Volume 1: La produzione e la circolazione del testo. Tomo 11: L'Ellenismo*, eds. G. Cambiano, L. Canfora and D. Lanza. Rome: 791–822.

(1994) 'The prehistory of Latin poetry. Some problems of method', *RFIC* 122: 50–75.

Hose, M. (1999) 'Anmerkungen zur Verwendung des Chores in der römischen Tragödie der Republik', in *Drama 7. Der Chor im antiken und modernen Drama*, eds. P. Riemer and B. Zimmermann. Stuttgart and Weimar: 113–38.

Höttemann, B. (1993) 'Phlyakenposse und Atellane', in *Beiträge zur mündlichen Kultur der Römer*, ed. G. Vogt-Spira. Tübingen (ScriptOralia 47; Reihe A: Altertumswiss. Reihe, Bd. 11): 89–112.

Hubbard, T. K. (1991) *The Mask of Comedy. Aristophanes and the Intertextual Parabasis*. Ithaca, N.Y. and London.

Hughes, J. D. (1975) *A Bibliography of Scholarship on Plautus*. Amsterdam.

Hugoniot, C., Hurlet, F. and Milanezi, S. (eds.) (2004) *Le statut de l'acteur dans l'Antiquité grecque et romaine (Actes du colloque qui s'est tenu à Tours les 3 et 4 mai 2002)*. Tours (Collection Perspectives Historiques 9).

Hülsemann, M. (1987) *Theater, Kult und bürgerlicher Widerstand im antiken Rom. Die Entstehung der architektonischen Struktur des römischen Theaters im Rahmen der gesellschaftlichen Auseinandersetzung zur Zeit der Republik*. Frankfurt, Bern and New York (European University Studies, Series 111: History and Allied Studies, Vol. 307).

Humphrey, J. H. (1986) *Roman Circuses. Arenas for Chariot Racing*. London.

Hunter, R. L. (1979) 'The comic chorus in the fourth century', *ZPE* 36: 23–38.

(1985) *The New Comedy of Greece and Rome*. Cambridge, London, New York, New Rochelle, Melbourne and Sydney.

(1987) 'Middle Comedy and the *Amphitruo* of Plautus', *Dioniso* 57: 281–98.

Hupperth, W. (1961) 'Horaz über die *scaenicae origines* der Römer (epist. 2,1,139ff)', dissertation, University of Cologne.

Hurka, F. (2008) 'Entwicklungslinien in der Liedkomposition der republikanischen Tragödie', in *Amicitiae templa serena. Studi in onore di Giuseppe Aricò*, eds. L. Castagna and C. Riboldi. Milan: 789–811.

Jannot, J.-R. (1993) 'Phersu, phersuna, persona. A propos du masque étrusque', in *Spectacles sportifs et scéniques dans le monde étrusco-italique. Actes de la table ronde organisée par l'Équipe de recherches étrusco-italiques de l'UMR 126 (CNRS, Paris) et l'École française de Rome, Rome, 3–4 1991*, ed. J.-P. Thuillier. Rome and Paris (CEFR 172): 281–320.

Jauß, H. R. (1967) *Literaturgeschichte als Provokation der Literaturwissenschaft.* Konstanz; 2nd edn, 1969 (Konstanzer Universitätsreden 3); repr. in: H. R. Jauß, *Literaturgeschichte als Provokation*. Frankfurt 1970 [10th edn: 1992] (Edition Suhrkamp 418): 144–207.

Jiménez Gazapo, J. (1978) 'El teatro latino', *EClás* 22: 323–40.

Jocelyn, H. D. (1969) 'The poet Cn. Naevius, P. Cornelius Scipio and Q. Caecilius Metellus', *Antichthon* 3: 32–47.

(1972) 'The poems of Quintus Ennius', *ANRW* I.2. Berlin and New York: 987–1026.

(1982) 'review of Daviault 1981', *CR* 32: 154–7.

(1986) 'review of Guardì 1985', *Gnomon* 58: 608–11.

(1991) 'The status of the "fabula togata" in the Roman theatre and the fortune of the scripts', *Dioniso* 61: 277–81.

(1995) 'Horace and the reputation of Plautus in the late first century BC', in *Homage to Horace. A Bimillenary Celebration*, ed. S. J. Harrison. Oxford: 228–47.

(2001) 'review of Dangel 1995', *Gnomon* 73: 116–22.

Jolivet, V. (1983) 'Aspects du théâtre comique en Étrurie préromaine et romaine. A propos d'un vase étrusque à figures rouges du Musée du Louvre', *RA*: 13–50.

(1993) 'Les jeux scéniques en Étrurie. Premiers témoignages (vie–ive siècle av. J.-C.)', in *Spectacles sportifs et scéniques dans le monde étrusco-italique. Actes de la table ronde organisée par l'Équipe de recherches étrusco-italiques de l'UMR 126 (CNRS, Paris) et l'École française de Rome, Rome, 3–4 1991*, ed. J.-P. Thuillier. Rome and Paris (CEFR 172): 349–77.

Jory, E. J. (1966) '*Dominus gregis?*', *CPh* 61: 102–4.

(1970) 'Associations of actors at Rome', *Hermes* 98: 224–53.

(1981) 'The literary evidence for the beginnings of imperial pantomime', *BICS* 28: 147–61.

(1986a) 'Continuity and change in the Roman theatre', in *Studies in Honour of T. B. L. Webster. Vol. 1*, eds. J. H. Betts, J. T. Hooker and J. R. Green. Bristol: 143–52.

(1986b) 'Gladiators in the theatre', *CQ* 36: 537–9.

(1988) 'Publilius Syrus and the element of competition in the theatre of the Republic', in *Vir Bonus Discendi Peritus. Studies in Celebration of Otto Skutsch's Eightieth Birthday*, ed. N. Horsfall. London (BICS Suppl. 51): 73–81.

(1995) '*Ars ludicra* and the *ludus talarius*', in *Stage Directions. Essays in Ancient Drama in Honour of E. W. Handley*, ed. A. Griffiths. London (BICS Suppl. 66): 139–52.

(1996) 'The drama of the dance: prolegomena to an iconography of imperial pantomime', in *Roman Theater and Society*, ed. W. J. Slater. Ann Arbor, Mich. (E. Togo Salmon Papers 1): 1–27.

(2008) 'The pantomime dancer and his libretto', in *New Directions in Ancient Pantomime*, eds. E. Hall and R. Wyles. Oxford: 159–68.

Juhnke, H. (1978) 'Terenz', in *Das römische Drama*, ed. E. Lefèvre. Darmstadt (Grundriß der Literaturgeschichten nach Gattungen): 223–307.

Karakasis, E. (2005) *Terence and the Language of Roman Comedy*. Cambridge (Cambridge Classical Studies).

Katsouris, A. G. (1975) *Tragic Patterns in Menander*. Athens (Hellenic Society for Humanistic Studies, International Centre for Classical Research, Second Series: Studies and Researches 28).

Kenney, E. J. and Clausen, W. V. (eds.) (1982) *The Cambridge History of Classical Literature. II: Latin Literature*. Cambridge, London, New York, New Rochelle, Melbourne and Sydney.

Kerkhof, R. (2001) *Dorische Posse, Epicharm und attische Komödie*. Munich and Leipzig (BzA 147).

Kindermann, H. (1979) *Das Theaterpublikum der Antike*. Salzburg.

Kleve, K. (1996) 'How to read an illegible papyrus. Towards an edition of *PHerc.* 78, Caecilius Statius, *Obolostates sive Faenerator*', *CronHerc* 26: 5–14.

(2001) 'Caecilius Statius, the money-lender (PHerc. 78)', in *Atti del XXII Congresso Internazionale di Papirologia. Firenze, 23–29 agosto 1998*, 2 vols, eds. I. Andorlini, G. Bastianini, M. Manfredi and G. Menci. Florence: 2.725.

Klose, D. (1966) 'Die Didaskalien und Prologe des Terenz', dissertation, University of Freiburg.

Knapp, C. (1919) 'References in Plautus and Terence to plays, players, and playwrights', *CPh* 14: 35–55.

Knorr, O. (2007) 'Metatheatrical humor in the comedies of Terence', in *Terentius Poeta*, eds. P. Kruschwitz, W.-W. Ehlers and F. Felgentreu. Munich (Zetemata 127): 167–74.

Konstan, D. (1983) *Roman Comedy*. Ithaca, N.Y. and London.

Kragelund, P. (2002) '*SO* debate: historical drama in ancient Rome: Republican flourishing and imperial decline?', *SO* 77: 5–105.

Kraus, W. (1934) '"*Ad spectatores*" in der römischen Komödie', *WS* 52: 66–83.

Kruschwitz, P. (2004) *Terenz*. Hildesheim, Zurich and New York (Studienbücher Antike 12).

Kruschwitz, P., Ehlers, W.-W. and Felgentreu, F. (eds.) (2007) *Terentius Poeta*. Munich (Zetemata 127).

Kunkel, W. and Wittmann, R. (1995) *Staatsordnung und Staatspraxis der römischen Republik. Zweiter Abschnitt. Die Magistratur*. Munich (HbdA III.2.2).

La Conte, M. G. (2008) 'Per una rivisitazione della "praetexta" repubblicana', *ACD* 44: 35–54.

Lada-Richards, I. (2004) 'Authorial voice and theatrical self-definition in Terence and beyond: the *Hecyra* prologues in ancient and modern contexts', *G&R* 51: 55–82.

Laidlaw, W. A. (1960) 'Cicero and the stage', *Hermathena* 94: 56–66.

Lana, I. (1947) 'Terenzio e il movimento filellenico in Roma', *RFIC* 75: 44–80, 155–75.

La Penna, A. ([1977] 1979) 'Funzione e interpretazioni del mito nella tragedia arcaica latina', in *Caratteri dell'ellenismo nelle urne etrusche. Atti dell'incontro di Studi (Siena, 28–30 aprile 1976)*. Florence 1977 (supplemento di *Prospettiva. Rivista di storia dell'arte antica e moderna*): 10–27; repr. in: A. La Penna, *Fra teatro, poesia e politica romana. Con due scritti sulla cultura classica di oggi*. Turin 1979 (Politica e cultura in Roma antica e nella tradizione classica moderna, Serie Seconda. Piccola Biblioteca Einaudi. Filologia. Linguistica. Critica letteraria 381): 49–104 [quoted from the reprint].

(1979) 'Aspetti e momenti della cultura letteraria in Magna Grecia nell'età romana', in: A. La Penna, *Fra teatro, poesia e politica romana. Con due scritti sulla cultura classica di oggi*. Turin (Politica e cultura in Roma antica e nella tradizione classica moderna, Serie Seconda. Piccola Biblioteca Einaudi. Filologia. Linguistica. Critica letteraria 381): 5–47.

Lauter, H. (1976) 'Die hellenistischen Theater der Samniten und Latiner in ihrer Beziehung zur Theaterarchitektur der Griechen', in *Hellenismus in Mittelitalien. Kolloquium in Göttingen vom 5. bis 9. Juni 1974*, ed. P. Zanker. Göttingen (Abhandlungen der Akademie der Wissenschaften in Göttingen, Philologisch-historische Klasse, Dritte Folge, N. 97): 413–22 (discussion: 422–5).

Leach, E. W. (2004) *The Social Life of Painting in Ancient Rome and on the Bay of Naples*. Cambridge.

Lebek, W. D. (1996) 'Moneymaking on the Roman stage', in *Roman Theater and Society*, ed. W. J. Slater. Ann Arbor, Mich. (E. Togo Salmon Papers I): 29–48.

Lefèvre, E. (ed.) (1972) *Senecas Tragödien*. Darmstadt (WdF cccx).

(ed.) (1973) *Die römische Komödie: Plautus und Terenz*. Darmstadt (WdF ccxxxvi).

(ed.) (1978a) *Das römische Drama*. Darmstadt (Grundriß der Literaturgeschichten nach Gattungen).

(1978b) 'Versuch einer Typologie des römischen Dramas', in *Das römische Drama*, ed. E. Lefèvre. Darmstadt (Grundriß der Literaturgeschichten nach Gattungen): 1–90.

(1988) 'Saturnalien und Palliata', *Poetica* 20: 32–46.

(1990) 'Die politisch-aitiologische Ideologie der Tragödien des Livius Andronicus', *QCTC* 8: 9–19 (discussion: 19–20).

(2000) 'Aitiologisch-politische Implikationen in Naevius' *Danae*', in *Identität und Alterität in der frührömischen Tragödie*, ed. G. Manuwald. Würzburg (Identitäten und Alteritäten, Bd. 3, Altertumswiss. Reihe, Bd. 1): 175–84.

Lefèvre, E., Stärk, E. and Vogt-Spira, G. (1991) *Plautus barbarus. Sechs Kapitel zur Originalität des Plautus*. Tübingen (ScriptOralia 25, Reihe A: Altertumswiss. Reihe, Bd. 8).

Leigh, M. (2004a) *Comedy and the Rise of Rome*. Oxford.

(2004b) 'The *Pro Caelio* and comedy', *CPh* 99: 300–35.

Lennartz, K. (1994) *Non verba sed vim. Kritisch-exegetische Untersuchungen zu den Fragmenten archaischer römischer Tragiker.* Stuttgart and Leipzig (BzA 54).

Lentano, M. (1997) 'Quindici anni di studi terenziani. Parte prima: studi sulle commedie (1979–1993)', *BStudLat* 27: 497–564.

(1998) 'Quindici anni di studi terenziani. Parte seconda: tradizione manoscritta ed esegesi antica (1979–1993)', *BStudLat* 28: 78–104.

Leo, F. (1912) *Plautinische Forschungen. Zur Kritik und Geschichte der Komödie.* 2nd edn. Berlin.

(1913) *Geschichte der römischen Literatur. Erster Band. Die archaische Literatur.* Berlin.

Leppin, H. (1992) *Histrionen. Untersuchungen zur sozialen Stellung von Bühnenkünstlern im Westen des Römischen Reiches zur Zeit der Republik und des Principats.* Bonn (Antiquitas, Reihe 1, Bd. 41).

Lilja, S. (1985) 'Seating problems in Roman theatre and circus', *Arctos* 19: 67–73.

Little, A. McN. G. (1938) 'Plautus and popular drama', *HSPh* 49: 205–28.

López, A. (1977) 'El adjetivo "togatus" y la comedia "togata"', *Helmantica* 28: 331–42; repr. in *Estudios sobre comedia romana*, eds. A. López and A. Pociña. Frankfurt, Berlin, Bern, Brussels, New York and Vienna 2000 (Studien zur klassischen Philologie 119): 341–53.

(1982) 'Los estudios sobre fabula togata en el decenio 1970–80', in *Actas del I Congreso Andaluz de Estudios Clásicos.* Jaén: 255–9; repr. in *Estudios sobre comedia romana*, eds. A. López and A. Pociña. Frankfurt, Berlin, Bern, Brussels, New York and Vienna 2000 (Studien zur klassischen Philologie 119): 377–83.

(1994) 'Los estudios sobre fabula togata en el decenio 1980–90', in *Actas del VIII Congreso Español de Estudios Clásicos.* Madrid: vol. II, 719–24; repr. in *Estudios sobre comedia romana*, eds. A. López and A. Pociña. Frankfurt, Berlin, Bern, Brussels, New York and Vienna 2000 (Studien zur klassischen Philologie 119): 385–93.

Lowe, J. C. B. (1989) 'Plautus' parasites and the Atellana', in *Studien zur vorliterarischen Periode im frühen Rom*, ed. G. Vogt-Spira. Tübingen (ScriptOralia 12, Reihe A: Altertumswiss. Reihe, Bd. 2): 161–9.

(1990) 'Plautus' choruses', *RhM* 130: 274–97.

Lowe, N. J. (2008) *Comedy.* Cambridge (Greece and Rome, New Surveys in the Classics 37, 2007).

Lowenstam, S. (2008) *As Witnessed by Images. The Trojan War Tradition in Greek and Etruscan Art.* Baltimore.

MacMullen, R. (1991) 'Hellenizing the Romans (2nd century B.C.)', *Historia* 40: 419–38.

Maltby, R. (1991) *A Lexicon of Ancient Latin Etymologies.* Leeds (ARCA 25).

Manuwald, G. (2001a) *Fabulae praetextae. Spuren einer literarischen Gattung der Römer.* Munich (Zetemata 108).

(2001b) 'Accius' *Phoenissae.* Zur Arbeitsweise eines römischen Tragikers', in *Studien zu antiken Identitäten*, ed. S. Faller. Würzburg (Identitäten und Alteritäten, Bd. 9, Altertumswiss. Reihe, Bd. 2): 59–80.

(2001c) 'Lucilius und die Tragödie', in *Der Satiriker Lucilius und seine Zeit*, ed. G. Manuwald. Munich (Zetemata 110): 150–65.

(2001 [2004]) 'Römische Tragödien und Praetexten republikanischer Zeit: 1964–2002', *Lustrum* 43: 11–237.

(2003) *Pacuvius – summus tragicus poeta. Zum dramatischen Profil seiner Tragödien*. Munich and Leipzig (BzA 191).

(2007) 'Vaterfiguren der Palliata als paradigmatische "Bilder" für die römische Lebenswirklichkeit', in *Generationenkonflikte auf der Bühne. Perspektiven im antiken und mittelalterlichen Drama*, ed. T. Baier. Tübingen (Drama n.s. 3): 127–45.

(2010) *Roman Drama. A Reader*. London.

Marconi, G. (1967) 'Attilio Regolo tra Andronico ed Orazio', *RCCM* 9: 15–47.

Marshall, C. W. (2006) *The Stagecraft and Performance of Roman Comedy*. Cambridge.

Martina, M. (1978) 'Sulla cronologia di Titinio', *QFC* 1: 5–25.

(1979) 'Ennio "poeta cliens"', *QFC* 2: 13–74.

Marzullo, A. (1956) 'Le origini italiche e lo sviluppo letterario delle Atellane: Nuove richerche su Novio', *Atti e Memorie, Accademia di Scienze, Lettere e Arti di Modena*, Serie v, vol. xiv. Modena: 160–84.

(1973) *Dalla satira al teatro popolare latino. Richerche varie*. Milan.

Mattingly, H. B. (1957) 'The Plautine "Didascaliae"', *Athenaeum* 35: 78–88.

(1960) 'The first period of Plautine revival', *Latomus* 19: 230–52.

Maurach, G. (2005) *Kleine Geschichte der antiken Komödie*. Darmstadt.

Maxwell, R. L. (1996) '*Quia ister Tusco verbo ludio vocabatur*: the Etruscan contribution to the development of Roman theater', in *Etruscan Italy: Etruscan Influences on the Civilizations of Italy from Antiquity to the Modern Era*, ed. J. F. Hall. Provo, UT (Museum of Art, Brigham Young University, M. Seth and Maurine D. Horne Center for the Study of Art, Scholarly Series): 267–85.

Mayer, R. G. (1995) '*Graecia capta*: the Roman reception of Greek literature', in *Papers of the Leeds International Seminar. Eighth Volume 1995. Roman Comedy, Augustan Poetry, Historigraphy*, eds. R. Brock and A. J. Woodman. Leeds (ARCA 33): 289–307.

Mazzoli, G. (1998) 'La tragedia latina', in *Géneros literarios poéticos grecolatinos*, eds. D. Estefanía, M. Domínguez and M. T. Amado. Madrid and Santiago de Compostela (Cuadernos de literatura griega y latina 11): 167–81.

McCarthy, K. (2000) *Slaves, Masters, and the Art of Authority in Plautine Comedy*. Princeton, N.J. and Oxford (repr. 2004).

McDonald, M. and Walton, J. M. (eds.) (2007) *The Cambridge Companion to Greek and Roman Theatre*. Cambridge.

McElduff, S. (2004) 'More than Menander's acolyte: Terence on translation', in *Rethinking Terence*, ed. A. J. Boyle, *Ramus* 33.1–2: 120–9.

Mette, H. J. (1964 [1965]) 'Die römische Tragödie und die Neufunde zur griechischen Tragödie (insbesondere für die Jahre 1945–1964)', *Lustrum* 9: 5–211.

Michels, A. K. (1967) *The Calendar of the Roman Republic*. Princeton, N.J.

Minarini, A (1997) 'Il linguaggio della *togata* fra innovazione e tradizione: consi-derazioni sullo stile', *BStudLat* 27: 34–55.

Mitens, K. (1988) *Teatri greci e teatri ispirati all'architettura greca in Sicilia e nell'Italia meridionale c. 350–50 a.C., Un catalogo.* Rome (Analecta Romana Instituti Danici Suppl. XIII).

(1993) 'Theatre architecture in central Italy: reception and resistance', in *Aspects of Hellenism in Italy: Towards a Cultural Unity?*, eds. P. G. Bilde, I. Nielsen and M. Nielsen, *ActaHyp* 5: 91–106.

Mommsen, T. (1850) *Die unteritalischen Dialekte.* Leipzig.

(1889) *Römische Geschichte.* Dritter Band. 8th edn. Berlin.

Moore, T. J. (1991) '*Palliata togata*: Plautus, *Curculio* 462–86', *AJPh* 112: 343–62.

(1994) 'Seats and social status in the Plautine theatre', *CJ* 90: 113–23.

(1995) 'How is it played? Tragicomedy as a running joke: Plautus' Amphitruo in performance', *Didaskalia* Suppl. 1 (www.didaskalia.net/issues/supplement1/moore.html).

(1998a) *The Theater of Plautus. Playing to the Audience.* Austin, Tex.

(1998b) 'Music and structure in Roman comedy', *AJPh* 119: 245–73.

(1999) 'Facing the music: character and musical accompaniment in Roman comedy', in *Crossing the Stages: The Production, Performance and Reception of Ancient Theater. Selected Papers Presented at a Conference Held in Saskatoon, Saskatchewan, on 22–25 October, 1997*, eds. J. Porter, E. Csapo, C. W. Marshall and R. C. Ketterer, *SyllClass* 10: 130–53.

(2001) 'Terence and Roman New Comedy', in *Greek and Roman Comedy. Translations and Interpretations of Four Representative Plays*, ed. S. O'Bryhim. Austin, Tex.: 241–65.

(2007) 'Terence as musical innovator', in *Terentius Poeta*, eds. P. Kruschwitz, W.-W. Ehlers and F. Felgentreu. Munich (Zetemata 127): 93–109.

(2008) 'When did the *tibicen* play? Meter and musical accompaniment in Roman comedy', *TAPhA* 138: 3–46.

Morel, J.-P. (1969) 'La *iuventus* et les origines du théâtre romain (Tite-Live, VII, 2; Valère Maxime, II, 4, 4.)', *REL* 47: 208–52.

Moretti Sgubini, A. M. (ed.) (2004) *Eroi etruschi e miti greci. Gli affreschi della Tomba François tornano a Vulci.* Florence.

Morgan, M. G. (1990) 'Politics, religion and the games in Rome, 200–150 B.C.', *Philologus* 134: 14–36.

Motto, A. L. and Clark, R. J. (1989) *Seneca. A Critical Bibliography 1900–1980. Scholarship on His Life, Thought, Prose, and Influence.* Amsterdam.

Muecke, F. (1986) 'Plautus and the Theater of disguise', *ClAnt* 5: 216–29.

Munk, E. (1840) *De fabulis Atellanis scripsit fragmentaque Atellanarum poetarum adiecit.* Leipzig.

Neiiendam, K. (1992) *The Art of Acting in Antiquity. Iconographical Studies in Classical, Hellenistic and Byzantine Theatre.* Copenhagen.

Nesselrath, H.-G. (1990) *Die attische Mittlere Komödie. Ihre Stellung in der antiken Literaturkritik und Literaturgeschichte.* Berlin and New York (UaLG 36).

Nicolet, C. (1980) *The World of the Citizen in Republican Rome*. Trans. P. S. Falla. Berkeley and Los Angeles; French original: *Le métier de citoyen dans la Rome républicaine*. Paris 1976.

Nicoll, A. (1931) *Masks, Mimes and Miracles. Studies in the Popular Theatre*. London (repr. New York 1963).

North, J. A. (1992) 'Deconstructing stone theatres', in *Apodosis. Essays Presented to Dr W. W. Cruikshank to Mark His Eightieth Birthday*. London: 75–83.

Oppermann, H. (1939a) 'Caecilius und die Entwicklung der römischen Komödie', *Forschungen und Fortschritte* 15: 196–7.

(1939b) 'Zur Entwicklung der fabula palliata', *Hermes* 74: 113–29.

Owens, W. M. (2000) 'Plautus' *Stichus* and the political crisis of 200 B.C.', *AJPh* 121: 385–407.

Palmer, R. E. A. (1997) *Rome and Carthage at Peace*. Stuttgart (Historia, Einzelschriften 113).

Panayotakis, C. (2005a) 'Comedy, Atellane farce and mime', in *A Companion to Latin Literature*, ed. S. Harrison. Oxford (Blackwell Companions to the Ancient World): 130–47.

(2005b) 'Nonverbal behaviour on the Roman comic stage', in *Body Language in the Greek and Roman Worlds*, ed. D. Cairns. Swansea: 175–93.

Paratore, E. (1957/2005) *Storia del teatro latino*. Milan 1957 (Estratto dalla 'Storia del teatro' diretta da M. Praz); repr. in: E. Paratore, *Storia del teatro latino, con un'Appendice di scritti sul teatro latino arcaico e un inedito autobiografico*, a cura di L. Gamberale and A. Marchetta. Venosa 2005 [quoted from the reprint].

Parker, H. N. (1996) 'Plautus v. Terence: audience and popularity re-examined', *AJPh* 117: 585–617.

(1999) 'The observed of all observers: spectacle, applause, and cultural poetics in the Roman theater audience', in *The Art of Ancient Spectacle*, eds. B. Bergmann and C. Kondoleon. New Haven, Conn. and London (Studies in the History of Art 56, Center for Advanced Study in the Visual Arts, Symposium Papers XXXIV): 163–79.

Pasquazi Bagnolini, A. (1974) 'Sulla *fabula togata*', *C&S* 52: 70–9.

(1975) 'Sulla *fabula togata*. II', *C&S* 56: 39–47.

(1977) *Note sulla lingua di Afranio*. Florence (Bibliotechina del Saggiatore 41).

Perelli, L. (1973) *Il teatro rivoluzionario di Terenzio*. Florence (Biblioteca di cultura 112) (repr. 1976).

Perkins, D. (1992) *Is Literary History Possible?* Baltimore and London.

Petersmann, H. (1974) 'Die altitalische Volksposse', *WHB* 16: 13–29.

(1989) 'Mündlichkeit und Schriftlichkeit in der Atellane', in *Studien zur vorliterarischen Periode im frühen Rom*, ed. G. Vogt-Spira. Tübingen (ScriptOralia 12, Reihe A: Altertumswiss. Reihe, Bd. 2): 135–59.

Petrone, G. (1983) *Teatro antico e inganno: Finzioni plautine*. Palermo.

(1992) 'I Romani', in U. Albini and G. Petrone, *Storia del teatro. I Greci – I Romani*. Milan: 339–684.

(1996) *Metafora e tragedia. Immagini culturali e modelli tragici nel mondo romano.* Palermo (Nuovo Prisma 4).

(2001) 'La praetexta repubblicana e la fondazione della memoria', in *D'un «genre» à l'autre*, eds. M.-H. Garelli-François, P. Sauzeaz and M.-P. Noël, *CGITA* 14: 167–75.

Petrone, G. and Bianco, M. M. (eds.) (2006) *La commedia di Plauto e la parodia. Il lato comico dei paradigmi tragici.* Palermo (Leuconoe: L'invenzione dei classici 9).

Phillips, III, C. R. (1990/1) 'Comment on Zorzetti 1990/1', *CJ* 86: 382–9.

Pickard-Cambridge, A. W. (1946) *The Theatre of Dionysus at Athens.* Oxford.

(1988) *The Dramatic Festivals of Athens. Second Edition.* Rev. J. Gould and D. M. Lewis. Oxford 1968 (reissued with suppl. and corr. 1988).

Piganiol, A. (1923) *Recherches sur les jeux romains. Notes d'archéologie et d'histoire religieuse.* Strasbourg (Publications de la Faculté des Lettres de l'Université de Strasbourg, Fascicule 13).

Pighi, G. B. (1952) 'Le origini del teatro latino', *Dioniso* 15: 274–81.

Pociña, A. and López, A. (2001) 'Pour une vision globale de la comédie *togata*', in *D'un «genre» à l'autre*, eds. M.-H. Garelli-François, P. Sauzeaz and M.-P. Noël, *CGITA* 14: 177–99.

Pociña Pérez, A. (1975a) 'Naissance et originalité de la comédie "*togata*"', *AC* 44: 79–88; repr. in Spanish as 'Nacimiento y originalidad de la comedia *togata*' in *Estudios sobre comedia romana*, eds. A. López and A. Pociña. Frankfurt, Berlin, Bern, Brussels, New York and Vienna 2000 (Studien zur klassischen Philologie 119): 355–65 [quoted from the original].

(1975b) 'Lucio Afranio y la evolución de la *fabula togata*', *Habis* 6: 99–107; repr. in *Estudios sobre comedia romana*, eds. A. López and A. Pociña. Frankfurt, Berlin, Bern, Brussels, New York and Vienna 2000 (Studien zur klassischen Philologie 119): 367–76 [quoted from the reprint].

(1976) 'Los espectadores, la *Lex Roscia Theatralis* y la organización de la *cavea* en los teatros romanos', *Zephyrus* 26–7: 435–42.

(1980) 'El comediógrafo Cecilio Estacio', *Sodalitas* 1: 211–31 = *EClás* 25, 1981–3, 64–78; repr. in *Estudios sobre comedia romana*, eds. A. López and A. Pociña. Frankfurt, Berlin, Bern, Brussels, New York and Vienna 2000 (Studien zur klassischen Philologie 119): 289–99.

(1984) *El tragediógrafo Lucio Accio.* Granada.

(1991) 'Popularidad de la comedia latina en los siglos iii–ii a.C.' in *Excerpta Philologica Antonio Holgado Redondo sacra.* Cádiz: 637–48; repr. in *Estudios sobre comedia romana*, eds. A. López and A. Pociña. Frankfurt, Berlin, Bern, Brussels, New York and Vienna 2000 (Studien zur klassischen Philologie 119): 97–113.

(1996a) 'La comedia latina: definición, clases, nacimiento', in *Géneros literarios romanos (Aproximación a su estudio)*, eds. D. Estefanía and A. Pociña. Madrid: 1–26.

(1996b) 'L'évolution vers le ménandrisme. De la perte progressive d'originalité dans la comédie latine', in *Panorama du théâtre antique. D'Eschyle aux dramaturges d'Amérique latine*, ed. A. Moreau, *CGITA* 9: 119–31.

(1998) 'La comedia latina: notas definidoras de la *palliata*', in *Géneros literarios poéticos grecolatinos*, eds. D. Estefanía, M. Domínguez and M. T. Amado. Madrid and Santiago de Compostela (Cuadernos de literatura griega y latina 11): 209–19.

Pöhlmann, E. (1997) 'La scène ambulante des Technites', in *De la scène aux gradins. Théâtre et représentations dramatiques après Alexandre le grand*, ed. B. Le Guen, *Pallas* 47: 3–12.

Pratt, M. L. (1992) *Imperial Eyes. Travel Writing and Transculturation*. London and New York.

Préaux, J.-G. (1962) 'Manducus', in *Hommages à Albert Grenier*, ed. M. Renard. Brussels (Collection Latomus LVIII): vol. 3, 1282–91.

(1963) 'Ars ludicra. Aux origines du théâtre latin', *AC* 32: 63–77.

Prinzen, H. (1998) *Ennius im Urteil der Antike*. Stuttgart and Weimar (Drama Beiheft 8).

Przychocki, G. (1922) 'De Titinii aetate', in *Charisteria Casimiro de Morawski septuagenario oblata ab amicis, collegis, discipulis*. Krakow: 180–8.

Questa, C. (2007) *La metrica di Plauto e di Terenzio*. Urbino (Ludus philologiae 16).

Quinn, K. (1982) 'The poet and his audience in the Augustan age', *ANRW* 11.30.1. Berlin and New York: 75–180.

Raffaelli, R. (1987) 'Pomponio e l'Atellana (spunti di analisi stilistiche e tematiche)', in *Cispadana e letteratura antica*, ed. Dipartimento di Storia antica dell'Università di Bologna. *Atti del Convegno di studi tenuto ad Imola nel maggio 1986, con il concorso della Provincia di Bologna e del Comune di Imola*. Bologna: 115–33.

Rambo, E. F. (1915) 'The significance of the wing-entrances in Roman comedy', *CPh* 10: 411–31.

Rawson, E. ([1985] 1991) 'Theatrical life in Republican Rome and Italy', *PBSR* 53, 1985: 97–113; repr. in: E. Rawson, *Roman Culture and Society. Collected Papers*. Oxford: 468–87 [quoted from the reprint].

([1987] 1991) '*Discrimina ordinum*: the *Lex Julia Theatralis*', *PBSR* 55, 1987: 83–114; repr. in: E. Rawson, *Roman Culture and Society. Collected Papers*. Oxford: 508–45 [quoted from the reprint].

Reeve, M. D. (1983) 'Terence', in *Texts and Transmission. A Survey of the Latin Classics*, ed. L. D. Reynolds. Oxford (repr. with corr. 1986, repr. 1990): 412–20.

Reich, H. (1903) *Der Mimus. Ein litterar-entwickelungsgeschichtlicher Versuch*. Berlin (repr. Hildesheim 1974, 2005).

Ribbeck, O. (1875) *Die römische Tragödie im Zeitalter der Republik*. Leipzig (repr. Hildesheim 1968, Mit einem Vorwort v. W.-H. Friedrich).

Richardson, L., Jr. (1987) 'A note on the architecture of the *Theatrum Pompei* in Rome', *AJA* 91: 123–6.

Riedweg, C. (1993) 'Menander in Rom – Beobachtungen zu Caecilius Statius *Plocium* fr. I (136–53 Guardì)', *Drama* 2: 133–59.

Rieks, R. (1978) 'Mimus und Atellane', in *Das römische Drama*, ed. E. Lefèvre. Darmstadt (Grundriß der Literaturgeschichten nach Gattungen): 348–77.

Rix, H. (1989) 'Dichtersprachliche Traditionen aus vorliterarischer Zeit?', in *Studien zur vorliterarischen Periode im frühen Rom*, ed. G. Vogt-Spira. Tübingen (ScriptOralia 12; Altertumswiss. Reihe, Bd. 2): 29–39.

Romano, A. (1990) *Il 'collegium scribarum'. Aspetti sociali e giuridici della produzione letteraria tra III e II secolo a.C.* Naples (Pubblicazioni del Dipartimento di diritto romano e storia della scienza romanistica dell'Università degli Studi di Napoli 'Federico II' III).

Rosenstein, N. and Morstein-Marx, R. (eds.) (2006) *A Companion to the Roman Republic.* Oxford (Blackwell Companions to the Ancient World).

Rossi, A. and Breed, B. W. (2006) 'Introduction: Ennius and the traditions of epic', *Arethusa* 39.3: 397–425.

Rotolo, V. (1957) *Il pantomimo. Studi e testi.* Palermo (Quaderni dello Istituto di Filologia Greca della Università di Palermo 1).

Rumpf, A. (1950) 'Die Entstehung des römischen Theaters', *MDAI* 3: 40–50.

Rüpke, J. (2001) 'Kulturtransfer als Rekodierung: Zum literaturgeschichtlichen und sozialen Ort der frühen römischen Epik', in *Von Göttern und Menschen erzählen. Formkonstanzen und Funktionswandel vormoderner Epik*, ed. J. Rüpke. Stuttgart (PAwB 4): 42–64.

Sandbach, F. H. (1977) *The Comic Theatre of Greece and Rome.* London (Ancient Culture and Society).

(1982) 'How Terence's *Hecyra* failed', *CQ* 32: 134–5.

Sander-Pieper, G. (2007) *Das Komische bei Plautus. Eine Analyse zur plautinischen Poetik.* Berlin and New York (BzA 244).

Santorelli, P. (1980) 'Accio: un emarginato consapevole?', *Vichiana* 9: 46–60.

Saunders, C. (1909) *Costume in Roman Comedy.* New York (repr. 1966).

(1913) 'The site of dramatic performances at Rome in the times of Plautus and Terence', *TAPhA* 44: 87–97.

Scafoglio, G. (2005) 'Plautus and Ennius: a note on Plautus, *Bacchides* 962–5', *CQ* 55: 632–8.

Scamuzzi, U. (1969–70) 'Studio sulla Lex Roscia Theatralis (con una Breve Appendice sulla Gens Roscia)', *RSC* 17, 1969, 133–65, 259–319; 18, 1970, 5–57, 374–447.

Schickert, K. (2005) *Der Schutz literarischer Urheberschaft im Rom der klassischen Antike.* Tübingen.

Schiesaro, A. (2005) 'Republican tragedy', in *A Companion to Tragedy*, ed. R. Bushnell. Oxford: 269–86.

Schlesinger, B. (1910) 'Über philosophische Einflüsse bei den römischen Dramen-Dichtern der republikanischen Zeit', dissertation, University of Bonn.

Schmidt, E. A. (2003) 'Die Tragikomödie *Amphitruo* des Plautus als Komödie und Tragödie', *MH* 60: 80–104.

Schmidt, P. L. (1989) 'Postquam ludus in artem paulatim verterat. Varro und die Frühgeschichte des römischen Theaters', in *Studien zur vorliterarischen Periode im frühen Rom*, ed. G. Vogt-Spira. Tübingen (ScriptOralia 12, Reihe A: Altertumswiss. Reihe, Bd. 2): 77–134.

Schnurr, C. (1992) 'The *Lex Julia Theatralis* of Augustus: some remarks on seating problems in theatre, amphitheatre and circus', *LCM* 17: 147–60.

Schweitzer, E. (1968) 'Studien zu Publilius Syrus' , dissertation, University of Vienna.

Schwering, W. (1916/17) 'Die Entstehung des Wortes *tragicomoedia*', *IF* 37: 139–41.

Sciarrino, E. (2006) 'The introduction of epic in Rome: cultural thefts and social contests', *Arethusa* 39.3: 449–69.

Scullard, H. H. (1981) *Festivals and Ceremonies of the Roman Republic*. London (Aspects of Greek and Roman Life).

Sear, F. (2006) *Roman Theatres. An Architectural Study*. Oxford (Oxford Monographs on Classical Archaeology).

Séchan, L. (1926) *Études sur la tragédie grecque dans ses rapports avec la céramique*. Paris.

Segal, E. (1981) 'Scholarship on Plautus 1965–1976', *CW* 74: 353–433.

(1987) *Roman Laughter. The Comedy of Plautus*. 2nd edn. Oxford [1st edn: Cambridge, Mass. 1968; chapter 'Is the *Captivi* Plautine?', pp. 191–214, also in *Studi di filologia classica in onore di Giusto Monaco*. Palermo 1991: 2.553–68].

Seidensticker, B. (1982) *Palintonos Harmonia. Studien zu komischen Elementen in der griechischen Tragödie*. Göttingen (Hypomnemata 72).

(2010) *Das antike Theater*. Munich (C. H. Beck Wissen).

Seidensticker, B. and Armstrong, D. (1985) 'Seneca tragicus 1878–1978 (with Addenda 1979ff.)', *ANRW* II.32.2. Berlin and New York: 916–68.

Serbat, G. (1975) 'Théâtre et société au second siècle avant J.-C.', in *Association Guillaume Budé. Actes du IXe Congrès (Rome, 13–18 avril 1973). Tome I*. Paris: 394–403.

Sharrock, A. (2009) *Reading Roman Comedy. Poetics and Playfulness in Plautus and Terence*. Cambridge (The W. B. Stanford Memorial Lectures).

Sidwell, K. (2000) 'From Old to Middle to New? Aristotle's *Poetics* and the history of Athenian comedy', in *The Rivals of Aristophanes. Studies in Athenian Old Comedy. With a Foreword by Kenneth Dover*, eds. D. Harvey and J. Wilkins. London and Swansea: 247–58.

Sifakis, G. M. (1967) *Studies in the History of Hellenistic Drama*. London (University of London Classical Studies IV).

Silk, M. S. (2000) *Aristophanes and the Definition of Comedy*. Oxford.

Simon, M. (1961) '"Contaminatio" und "furtum" bei Terenz. Verhältnis zu Vorbildern und Vorgängern', *Helikon* 1: 487–92.

Skutsch, O. (1954) 'review of Klotz 1953', *Gnomon* 26: 465–70.

Slater, N. W. (1985/2000) *Plautus in Performance. The Theatre of the Mind*. Princeton, N.J. 1985; 2nd edn, Amsterdam 2000 (Greek and Roman Theatre Archive 2) [page numbers refer to the original edition].

(1990) '*Amphitruo, Bacchae*, and metatheatre', *Lexis* 5–6: 101–25; repr. in: N. W. Slater, *Plautus in Performance. The Theatre of the Mind*. 2nd edn, Amsterdam 2000 (Greek and Roman Theatre Archive 2): 181–202 [quoted from the original].

(1992a) 'Two Republican poets on drama: Terence and Accius', in *Antike Dramentheorien und ihre Rezeption*, ed. B. Zimmermann. Stuttgart (Drama 1): 85–103.

(1992b) 'Plautine negotiations: the *Poenulus* prologue unpacked', *YClS* 29: 131–46; repr. in: N. W. Slater, *Plautus in Performance. The Theatre of the Mind*. 2nd edn, Amsterdam 2000 (Greek and Roman Theatre Archive 2): 149–162 [quoted from the original].

Slater, W. (2004) 'Where are the actors?', in *Le statut de l'acteur dans l'Antiquité grecque et romaine (Actes du colloque qui s'est tenu à Tours les 3 et 4 mai 2002)*, eds. C. Hugoniot, F. Hurlet and S. Milanezi. Tours (Collection Perspectives Historiques 9): 143–60.

Smith, M. F. (1940) *The Technique of Solution in Roman Comedy*. Chicago.

Sordi, M. (1988) 'La decadenza della repubblica e il teatro del 154 a.C.', *InvLuc* 10: 327–41.

Spruit, J. E. (1966) 'De juridische en sociale positie van de romeinse acteurs' ['La condition juridique et sociale des acteurs romains, suivi d'un résumé en français'], dissertation, University of Utrecht.

Staccioli, R. A. (1961) 'Spettacoli antichi e moderni al Foro Romano', *Capitolium* 36: 18–22.

Stamper, J. W. (2005) *The Architecture of Roman Temples. The Republic to the Middle Empire*. Cambridge.

Stankiewicz, L. (1984) 'Źródła antyczne o Titiniuszu – przyczynek do chronologii togaty' (= 'De tempore quo Titinius togatarum scriptor vixerit'), *Meander* 39: 207–12.

Stärk, E. (2000) 'Politische Anspielungen in der römischen Tragödie und der Einfluß der Schauspieler', in *Identität und Alterität in der frührömischen Tragödie*, ed. G. Manuwald. Würzburg (Identitäten und Alteritäten, Bd. 3, Altertumswiss. Reihe, Bd. 1): 123–33.

Stein, M. (2003) 'Der Dichter und sein Kritiker: Interpretationsprobleme im Prolog des Terenzischen Eunuchus', *RhM* 146: 184–217.

Steuernagel, D. (1998) *Menschenopfer und Mord am Altar. Griechische Mythen in etruskischen Gräbern*. Wiesbaden (Palilia 3).

Stewart, Z. (1958) 'The *Amphitruo* of Plautus and Euripides' *Bacchae*', *TAPhA* 89: 348–73.

Suerbaum, W. (1968) *Untersuchungen zur Selbstdarstellung älterer römischer Dichter. Livius Andronicus, Naevius, Ennius*. Hildesheim (Spudasmata 19).

(2000a) 'Naevius comicus. Der Komödiendichter Naevius in der neueren Forschung', in *Dramatische Wäldchen. Festschrift für Eckard Lefèvre zum 65. Geburtstag*, eds. E. Stärk and G. Vogt-Spira. Hildesheim, Zurich and New York (Spudasmata 80): 301–20.

(2000b) 'Religiöse Identitäts- und Alteritätsangebote im *Equos Troianus* und im *Lycurgus* des Naevius', in *Identität und Alterität in der frührömischen Tragödie*, ed. G. Manuwald. Würzburg (Identitäten und Alteritäten, Bd. 3, Altertumswiss. Reihe, Bd. 1): 185–98.

(ed.) (2002) *Handbuch der Lateinischen Literatur der Antike. Erster Band. Die archaische Literatur. Von den Anfängen bis Sullas Tod. Die vorliterarische Periode und die Zeit von 240 bis 78 v. Chr. (HLL 1)*. Munich (HbdA VIII.1).

(2003) *Ennius in der Forschung des 20. Jahrhunderts. Eine kommentierte Bibliographie für 1900–1999 mit systematischen Hinweisen nebst einer Kurzdarstellung des Q. Ennius (239–169 v. Chr.)*. Hildesheim, Zurich and New York (Bibliographien zur Klassischen Philologie 1).

Szemerényi, O. (1975) 'The origins of Roman drama and Greek tragedy', *Hermes* 103: 300–32.

Szilágyi, J. G. (1941) *Atellana. Tanulmányok az antik színjatszásról – Studi sull'arte scenica antica*. Budapest [summary in Italian].

(1981) 'Impletae modis saturae', *Prospettiva* 24: 2–23.

Tabacco, R. (1975) 'Il problema della togata nella critica moderna', *BStudLat* 5: 33–57.

Tanner, R. G. (1969) 'Problems in Plautus', *PCPhS* 195 (n.s. 15): 95–105.

Tansey, P. (2001) 'New light on the Roman stage. A revival of Terence's *Phormio* rediscovered', *RhM* 144: 22–43.

Taplin, O. (1986) 'Fifth-century tragedy and comedy: a *synkrisis*', *JHS* 106: 163–74.

(1993) *Comic Angels and Other Approaches to Greek Drama through Vase-Paintings*. Oxford.

(1997) 'The pictorial record', in *The Cambridge Companion to Greek Tragedy*, ed. P. E. Easterling. Cambridge: 69–90.

(2007) *Pots and Plays. Interactions between Tragedy and Greek Vase-Painting of the Fourth Century B.C.* Los Angeles.

Tarrant, R. J. (1978) 'Senecan drama and its antecedents', *HSPh* 82: 213–63.

(1983) 'Plautus', in *Texts and Transmission. A Survey of the Latin Classics*, ed. L. D. Reynolds. Oxford (repr. with corr. 1986, repr. 1990): 302–7.

Tatum, W. J. (1990) 'Another look at the spectators at the Roman games', *AHB* 4.5: 104–7.

Taylor, L. R. (1935) 'The *sellisternium* and the theatrical *pompa*', *CPh* 30: 122–30.

(1937) 'The opportunities for dramatic performances in the time of Plautus and Terence', *TAPhA* 68: 284–304.

Thierfelder, A. (1936) 'Die Motive der griechischen Komödie im Bewußtsein ihrer Dichter', *Hermes* 71: 320–37.

Thuillier, J.-P. (1992) 'Sur les origines étrusques du théâtre romain', in *Spectacula – II. Le théâtre antique et ses spectacles. Actes du colloque tenu au Musée Archéologique Henri Prades de Lattes les 27, 28, 29 et 30 avril 1989*, eds. C. Landes and V. Kramérovskis. Lattes: 201–8.

Till, R. (1975) 'Laberius und Caesar', *Historia* 24: 260–86.

Traina, A. (1974) *Vortit barbare. Le traduzioni poetiche da Livio Andronico a Cicerone.* Seconda edizione riveduta e aggiornata. Rome (Ricerche di storia della lingua latina 7) (1st edn: Rome 1970).

Trendall, A. D. (1967) *Phlyax Vases.* 2nd edn, rev. and enl. London (BICS Suppl. 19) (1st edn: London 1959 [BICS Suppl. 8]).

(1989) *Red Figure Vases of South Italy and Sicily. A Handbook.* London.

(1991) 'Farce and tragedy in South Italian vase-painting', in *Looking at Greek Vases*, eds. T. Rasmussen and N. Spivey. Cambridge, New York, Port Chester, Melbourne and Sydney: 151–82.

von Ungern-Sternberg, J. (1975) 'Die Einführung spezieller Sitze für die Senatoren bei den Spielen (194 v. Chr.)', *Chiron* 5: 157–63.

Ussani, V., Jr. (1967/8) *Lezioni di lingua e letteratura latina. Problemi del teatro arcaico latino.* Rome.

(1969) 'Per la storia del teatro latino. II. Seneca e la commedia togata', *GIF* 21: 375–410.

(1981) 'Per la storia del teatro latino. III. Ancora su Varrone e le *Togatae*', in *Letterature comparate. Problemi e metodo. Studi in onore di E. Paratore.* Bologna: vol. 1, 337–45.

Vanderbroeck, P. J. J. (1987) *Popular Leadership and Collective Behavior in the Late Roman Republic (ca. 80–50 B.C.).* Amsterdam (Dutch Monographs on Ancient History and Archaeology III).

Van Der Meer, L. B. (1993) 'Tragédie et réalité. Programmes iconographiques des sarcophages étrusques', in *Spectacles sportifs et scéniques dans le monde étrusco-italique. Actes de la table ronde organisée par l'Équipe de recherches étrusco-italiques de l'UMR 126 (CNRS, Paris) et l'École française de Rome, Rome, 3–4 1991*, ed. J.-P. Thuillier. Rome and Paris (CEFR 172): 379–93.

Vereecke, E. (1968) 'Titinius, témoin de son époque', *Recherches de Philologie et de Linguistique*, 2e série. Louvain (Travaux de la Faculté de philosophie et lettres de l'Université catholique de Louvain – III, Section de philologie classique – II): 63–92.

(1971) 'Titinius, Plaute et les origines de la "fabula togata"', *AC* 40: 156–85.

Vogt-Spira, G. (1996) 'Die Kulturbegegnung Roms mit den Griechen', in *Die Begegnung mit dem Fremden. Wertungen und Wirkungen in Hochkulturen vom Altertum bis zur Gegenwart*, ed. M. Schuster. Stuttgart and Leipzig (Colloquium Rauricum 4): 11–33.

Walde, A. and Hofmann, J. B. (1982) *Lateinisches etymologisches Wörterbuch.* Fünfte, unveränderte Auflage. 2 vols. Heidelberg (Indogermanistische Bibliothek, Zweite Reihe: Wörterbücher).

Wallace, R. W. (1997) 'Poet, public, and "theatrocracy": audience performance in classical Athens', in *Poet, Public, and Performance in Ancient Greece*, eds. L. Edmunds and R. W. Wallace. Baltimore and London: 97–111.

Wallace-Hadrill, A. (1988) 'Greek knowledge, Roman power', *CPh* 83: 224–33.

Waszink, J. H. (1948) 'Varro, Livy and Tertullian on the history of Roman dramatic art', *Vigiliae Christianae* 2: 224–42.

(1972) 'Zum Anfangsstadium der römischen Literatur', *ANRW* i.2. Berlin and New York: 869–927.

Webster, T. B. L. (1970) *Studies in Later Greek Comedy.* 2nd edn. Manchester (1st edn: 1953).

Welch, K. E. (2007) *The Roman Amphitheatre. From its Origins to the Colosseum.* Cambridge.

Wiemken, H. (1972) *Der griechische Mimus. Dokumente zur Geschichte des antiken Volkstheaters.* Bremen.

(1979) 'Der Mimus', in *Das griechische Drama,* ed. G. A. Seeck. Darmstadt (Grundriß der Literaturgeschichten nach Gattungen): 401–33.

Wiles, D. (1988) 'Taking farce seriously: recent critical approaches to Plautus', in *Farce,* ed. J. Redmond. Cambridge, New York, New Rochelle, Melbourne and Sydney (Themes in Drama 10): 261–71.

(1991) *The Masks of Menander: Sign and Meaning in Greek and Roman Performance.* Cambridge, New York, Port Chester, Melbourne and Sydney.

Wille, G. (1967) *Musica Romana. Die Bedeutung der Musik im Leben der Römer.* Amsterdam.

Williams, G. (1968) *Tradition and Originality in Latin Poetry.* Oxford.

(1972) 'Roman drama', in *Literature and Western Civilization. Vol. 1: The Classical World,* eds. D. Daiches and A. Thorlby. London: 213–32.

(1982) 'Phases in political patronage of literature in Rome', in *Literary and Artistic Patronage in Ancient Rome,* ed. B. K. Gold. Austin, Tex.: 3–27.

Williams, G. J. (ed.) (2010) *Theatre Histories: An Introduction. Second Edition.* New York and London.

Wilson, P. (2002) 'The musicians among the actors', in *Greek and Roman Actors: Aspects of an Ancient Profession,* eds. P. Easterling and E. Hall. Cambridge: 39–68.

Wiseman, T. P. (1971) *New Men in the Roman Senate 139* b.c. – a.d. *14.* Oxford.

([1973] 1987) 'review of E. Badian, *Publicans and Sinners', Phoenix* 27, 1973: 189–98; repr. in: T. P. Wiseman, *Roman Studies. Literary and Historical.* Liverpool (Collected Classical Papers, 1): 74–82 [quoted from the reprint].

(1994) *Historiography and Imagination. Eight Essays on Roman Culture.* Exeter (Exeter Studies in History 33).

(1998) *Roman Drama and Roman History.* Exeter (Exeter Studies in History).

(1999) 'The games of Flora', in *The Art of Ancient Spectacle,* eds. B. Bergmann and C. Kondoleon. New Haven, Conn. and London (Studies in the History of Art 56, Center for Advanced Study in the Visual Arts, Symposium Papers xxxiv): 195–203.

(2000) 'Liber: myth, drama and ideology in Republican Rome', in *The Roman Middle Republic. Politics, Religion, and Historiography c. 400–133* b.c. *(Papers from a Conference at the Institutum Romanum Finlandiae, September 11–12, 1998),* ed. C. Bruun. Rome (Acta Instituti Romani Finlandiae Vol. 23): 265–99; repr. in: T. P. Wiseman, *Unwritten Rome.* Exeter 2008: 84–139 [quoted from the original].

(2004) *The Myths of Rome.* Exeter.

Wissowa, G. (1912) *Religion und Kultus der Römer.* 2nd edn. Munich (HbdA IV.5).

Wright, F. W. (1931) *Cicero and the Theater.* Northampton, Mass. (Smith College Classical Studies II).

Wright, J. (1972) 'Naevius, Tarentilla Fr. I (72–74 R³)', *RhM* 115: 239–42.

(1974) *Dancing in Chains: The Stylistic Unity of the Comoedia Palliata.* Rome (Papers and Monographs of the American Academy in Rome XXV).

Xanthakis-Karamanos, G. (1980) *Studies in Fourth-Century Tragedy.* Athens.

Zagagi, N. (1980) *Tradition and Originality in Plautus. Studies of the Amatory Motifs in Plautine Comedy.* Göttingen (Hypomnemata 62).

Zehnacker, H. (1983) 'Tragédie prétexte et spectacle romain', in *Théâtre et spectacles dans l'antiquité. Actes du colloque de Strasbourg, 5–7 novembre 1981,* ed. H. Zehnacker. Leiden (Université des Sciences Humaines de Strasbourg. Travaux du Centre de Recherche sur le Proche-Orient et la Grèce antiques 7): 31–48.

Zetzel, J. G. (2007) 'The influence of Cicero on Ennius', in *Ennius Perennis. The Annals and Beyond,* eds. W. Fitzgerald and E. Gowers. Oxford (Cambridge Classical Journal, Proceedings of the Cambridge Philological Society, Suppl. Vol. 31): 1–16.

Zillinger, W. (1911) 'Cicero und die altrömischen Dichter', dissertation, University of Erlangen.

Zimmermann, B. (2004) '*Graecia capta ferum victorem cepit.* Überlegungen zum Verhältnis der römischen republikanischen zur griechischen Tragödie', in *Theater, Theaterpraxis, Theaterkritik im kaiserzeitlichen Rom* (Kolloquium anlässlich des 70. Geburtstages von Prof. Dr. Peter Lebrecht Schmidt, 24./25. Juli 2003, Universität Konstanz), eds. J. Fugmann, M. Janka, U. Schmitzer and H. Seng. Munich and Leipzig: 13–24.

Zorzetti, N. (1973) 'Una citazione di Pacuvio in Afranio', *QTTA* 3: 71–5.

(1980) *La pretesta e il teatro latino arcaico.* Naples (Forme materiali e ideologie del mondo antico 14).

(1990) 'The *carmina convivalia*', in *Sympotica. A Symposium on the Symposion,* ed. O. Murray. Oxford: 289–307.

(1990/1) 'Poetry and ancient city: the case of Rome', *CJ* 86: 311–29.

Zwierlein, O. (1990–2) *Zur Kritik und Exegese des Plautus,* 4 vols. Stuttgart (AAWM 4, 1990 / 3, 1991 / 14, 1991 / 4, 1992).

Index

This index lists the major topics discussed in this study, some of which can also be located by means of the detailed table of contents. The selective inclusion of passages from ancient texts covers pieces that are analysed in the main text, but excludes those that are merely quoted as evidence for particular issues that are found as items in this index. Ancient authors are given under the name that is most commonly used in English (e.g. Cicero, Terence). Unless otherwise indicated, dramatic fragments are numbered according to Ribbeck's third editions (for details and abbreviations used see Bibliography and 'Technical notes and abbreviations').

Lightning Source UK Ltd.
Milton Keynes UK
UKOW05n2134220117
292627UK00003B/113/P